A STUDY OF WOMEN DELINQUENTS IN NEW YORK STATE

Publications of the Bureau of Social Hygiene

A Study of Women Delinquents in New York State

BY

MABEL RUTH FERNALD
Assistant Professor of Psychology, University of Minnesota;
Formerly Director, Laboratory of Social Hygiene

MARY HOLMES STEVENS HAYES
Member of The Scott Company; Formerly Psychologist,
Laboratory of Social Hygiene

ALMENA DAWLEY
Supervisor, Department of Social Investigation, Pennsylvania School for
Social Service; Formerly Sociologist, Laboratory of Social Hygiene

With Statistical Chapter by
BEARDSLEY RUML
Assistant to the President, Carnegie Corporation;
Secretary, The Scott Company

Preface by
KATHARINE BEMENT DAVIS
General Secretary, Bureau of Social Hygiene

NEW YORK
THE CENTURY CO.
1920

AUTHORS' NOTE

To a peculiar degree the investigation of which this book is the report was a composite piece of work, the difficulties and problems of which were shared by all the individuals of the group concerned in its accomplishment. It would be impossible to acknowledge with any adequacy the special contribution which each person made. We may, however, indicate the general lines along which the work was divided. The following members of the staff were responsible for the psychological examinations: Mary H. S. Hayes, Mabel R. Fernald, Jessie J. Taft, Buford J. Johnson, Margaret V. Cobb. The task of social investigation was carried through by the following: Almena Dawley (in charge of investigations for Bedford and Auburn), Virginia P. Robinson (in charge of investigations for the city institutions), Veda Elvin, Marie Lawrence, Mabel C. Huschka, Grace Massonneau, Maude W. Moore. The general plan of statistical treatment was mapped out by Beardsley Ruml, who acted as consultant on statistical problems arising throughout the study. The detailed work of statistical analysis and computation was under the supervision of Mary A. Clark. The following members of the staff assisted in this phase of the work: Agnes Crowley, Christine Brigham, Helen Towey, Marjorie Taft, Louise Russell.

For the statements as actually formulated in this book, the three authors assume entire responsibility. While there has been necessarily much overlapping of work in the compilation of the book, Miss Dawley was mainly responsible for the sociological portions, Mrs. Hayes and Miss Fernald for the psychological.

We have noted in Chapter II our indebtedness to the authorities in the various institutions who made possible this investigation through their interest and coöperation.

PREFACE

So long as prisons were used merely for the purpose of punishment or for holding in safety those who were dangerous to society, the behavior of prisoners was a matter of relatively small importance. They could be kept in subjection by force if necessary and tractability on their part was desirable chiefly because it made life easier for those in charge.

With the coming of the reformatory and the adoption of the principle of indeterminate sentence and release on parole behavior within the institution assumed supreme importance. This could not be otherwise for there were no other criteria in the hands of prison authorities. If a prisoner were obedient, observed all rules cheerfully, was respectful to his superiors, in the institutional school showed himself willing to learn, in the shop or at other tasks worked faithfully and more or less well, if he expressed to his spiritual adviser contrition for his wrong doing and his resolve to amend his ways, he was a "good prisoner." Another prisoner "kicked against the pricks" from the moment of entrance; he was moody or sullen, or quick tempered, or stupid, or resentful, disrespectful to his keepers, quarrelsome among his mates. He was unwilling to take advantage of any opportunities for self-improvement, possibly he exhibited not only no inclination to learn but showed absolute incapacity for so doing. He was a malingerer or he did his work so poorly that no one wanted him in the gang. He was a "bad prisoner." The former received privileges within the institution and an early parole. The latter was held and daily became a worse prisoner until the time came when under the law he had to be released. Sometimes, not infrequently, the "good prisoner" failed to make good outside. Sometimes to the surprise of the authorities the "bad prisoner" made good. Such disappointments and surprises could have but one effect. Slowly but surely there dawned the recognition of the need of an intensive study of the individual, not only of his behavior in the institution but why his behavior was what it was. What were the causes of which his behavior was the symptom?

When the first reformatories for adults opened their doors we had no such thing as applied psychology. Psychology did not concern itself with practical problems of behavior but restricted itself to theoretic discussions on mental processes and the like. To be sure we had alienists, but there was little recognition of those peculiar mental conditions which do not amount to insanity, but which if not treated make their victims unfit for society outside or inside the prison. There was no such thing as a science of sociology, nor any hint of the need of careful study of the pre-institutional life of the prisoner with a view to understanding him.

In a number of states we had schools and asylums for the feeble-minded but much more was expected from education of these persons than has been shown by experience to be possible. That the feeble-minded were not suitable inmates of a reformatory was recognized as early as the First Annual Report of the Reformatory Prison for Women at Sherborn, Mass.,[1] when the managers recommended "changes in existing laws" authorizing the transfer of certain unsuitable persons committed for minor offenses, who among other things were "weak minded."

New York State in establishing its reformatory institutions for women sought to profit by the experience of the two other institutions for women by providing in the State Charities Law that Boards of Managers might return to committing judges any person who "is insane or mentally incapable of being materially benefited by the discipline of the institution." The difficulties of securing her admission to crowded custodial institutions and the undesirability of turning her back into a community in which she had already proved herself a social menace, together with differences of opinion as to whether in a given case a woman was so far incapacitated as to be "mentally incapable of being materially benefited" have worked together to prevent in our own state the relief which was intended for the reformatories. In other types of institutions and in many other states there is not even this possibility of transfer.

The Laboratory of Social Hygiene maintained for six years by the Bureau of Social Hygiene in coöperation with the State Reformatory for Women at Bedford Hills, grew out of the recognition of a

[1] First Annual Report of the Commissioners and Advisory Board of the Reformatory Prison for Women at Sherborn, Mass., Oct., 1878. The Woman's Prison at Sherborn, Mass., was the second prison exclusively for the care of women in the United States. The Indiana Reformatory for Women and Girls opened in 1873.

practical need in the actual handling of delinquent women if a maximum number were to be returned to society prepared to lead a self-supporting, law-abiding life. As a result of experience it was believed that before one could apply methods of treatment with any certainty it was necessary to have an accurate diagnosis of the individual case, taking into consideration social, physical and mental factors. Such case studies of the social and mental aspects begun with the women committed to the State Reformatory at Bedford Hills and extended to other groups of delinquent women in New York State forms the basis of the work presented in this volume. These case studies have a threefold value. First as pointed out above, their immediate practical importance is in indicating the actual treatment of the case within the institution. If it were possible to put in use a careful clearing house method for treating the wards of the state in accordance with their own needs and the best interests of society such case histories would be the proper basis of scientific classification. Pending this their use is limited to the special institution in which the case is studied and to the existing possibilities of transfer. The value of the publication of case histories is discussed in the first chapter of this book. The use of the material determined upon for this study does not preclude a later publication of these histories.

Second, the value of standards of comparison is clearly pointed out in chapter one. Although without more extended studies of the general population we cannot make accurate comparisons with the delinquent groups, it is of great importance to have a standard by which we can measure the inmates within a given institution or compare the inmate population of one institution with another. Even though this study fails to show a distinct criminal type it seems to clearly indicate that the average woman prisoner of New York State falls somewhat below the average individual in society in mentality and economic efficiency.

Unfortunately no comparable data of the physical states of the groups studied were available, nor are there comparable studies of the health and physical condition of the general population. A detailed study of 200 non-selected individuals at the State Reformatory for Women at Bedford Hills[1] made prior to the studies presented in this

[1] Physical States of Criminal Women. A study made at the Laboratory of Social Hygiene, Bedford Hills, by Alberta S. Guibord, M.D., Journal of Criminal Law and Criminology, May 1, 1917.

volume showed a very high degree of physical deficiencies "primarily to a large extent preventable in that they are the result of faulty nutrition, bad hygiene, bacterial infection and other concomitants of unintelligence and poverty."

Even if it were conceivably possible to select and study an absolutely representative group of non-delinquent women and the results showed the same, or practically the same, averages and the same dispersion of the particular factors, the standard would still be necessary for purposes of classification and discussion.

A third use to which it was hoped our studies could be put was the pointing out with greater definiteness the causes of delinquency. If any deductions can be made, our studies would seem to indicate the great complexity of causal factors in individual cases as well as in the various groups.

It is not possible, as yet at least, to single out a *few* factors to which we can point as predominantly causative, whether these lie in the social and economic conditions which govern environment, public health, education and recreation, or in the constitutional factors which are the most obvious in individual cases; but in a study carefully made we believe it is not without significance that no one or two outstanding environmental or constitutional causes were discoverable.

KATHARINE BEMENT DAVIS,
General Secretary, Bureau of Social Hygiene.

CONTENTS

CHAPTER I

CHAPTER II

CHAPTER III

CHAPTER IV

CHAPTER V

CHAPTER VI

CHAPTER VII

CHAPTER VIII

CHAPTER IX

CHAPTER X

CHAPTER XI

CHAPTER XII

CHAPTER XIII

CHAPTER XIV

CHAPTER XV

CHAPTER XVI

A STUDY OF WOMEN DELINQUENTS IN NEW YORK STATE

STUDY OF WOMEN DELINQUENTS IN NEW YORK STATE

CHAPTER I

INTRODUCTION: GENERAL ORIENTATION WITH REFERENCE TO PROBLEMS AND METHODS OF TREATMENT

SOME knowledge of the characteristics of those who make up the criminal and delinquent population of any country seems a slight thing to demand as a prerequisite for the development of adequate methods of handling the problem which this group represents. The recognition of this demand as elementary may account for the fact that ready generalizations regarding the criminal have been so abundant. The work of Lombroso introduced certain tendencies which had, at least, not been clearly defined, in connection with earlier expressions of opinion. In the first place, these earlier statements made no pretense of being scientific in the sense of being based on investigation, an *ipse dixit* being considered quite sufficient to establish their claims. Lombroso introduced at least the appearance of investigation, puerile though it was for the most part. In the second place, these accounts were offered, in the main, merely as descriptive literature of some interest to the general population, but not as the basis on which the treatment of the criminal should be determined. The insistence upon the fact that the understanding of the criminal should play a larger part in determining his treatment than should the facts concerning his crime, constitutes Lombroso's great achievement; an achievement which stands even after it has become clear that the majority of the conclusions which he proffered are unsound.

NECESSITY OF MORE ADEQUATE DEFINITION OF CONCEPTIONS REGARDING WOMEN DELINQUENTS

There is at present abundant literature regarding the criminal group, much of which is not even worth citing because it rests, at its best, upon the most casual and superficial observation and at its worst upon what the writer thinks he would find on observation. Possibly no great harm was done by reliance upon such generalizations, when little attention was paid to the treatment of either men or women offenders, the problem of their incarceration being considered as solved if two demands were met, *viz.:* the demand of *punishment* for the crime and the demand of *protection* of the state from further crimes. With the development within recent years, first, of an insistence on humanitarian treatment of the criminal merely on the ground that he is a "human being" [1] and, more recently, of a tendency to insist that the penal institutions must be thought of as places for readjustment of individuals to society, it becomes of primary importance to know of what nature this human material is. The system of penal institutions of any state and the plan of administration of each given institution are determined, in part at least, by certain conceptions regarding the persons who are to be handled. These conceptions may be vague and unformulated, or they may be definite and dogmatically propounded. In either case they form one important element in the determination of procedure and so become of practical importance.

The acceptance of this point of view has become almost universal among those who interest themselves in modern penology from either its theoretical or its more practical aspects. As has been indicated in the preface, the Laboratory of Social Hygiene was a direct outgrowth of Dr. Davis' conviction regarding the importance of a more intelligent study of delinquent women,[2] a conviction, it should be noted, which represented a plea for more information from one who was daily in personal contact with such women and constantly facing the practical problems of their management. More recently we find Osborne, who likewise approached the problem from the practical side, making the following statement:

> "To lay the foundation of a new and genuinely scientific penology, we must make absolutely clear to ourselves the real nature and character of the men who populate our prisons; there must be no uncertainty in the minds of any of us as to what is meant when we refer to 'criminals,' 'convicts,' or 'prisoners.' " [3]

[1] The work of Elizabeth Frye in England represented the most significant development of the humanitarian trend as applied to women delinquents.

[2] See Davis, Katharine Bement. "The Rational Treatment of Women Convicted of Crime in the Courts of New York City."

[3] Osborne, Thomas Mott. "Society and Prisons," p. 15, Yale University Press, 1916.

Instances indicative of the same point of view could be multiplied by reference to the discussions of any of the many conferences called for the consideration of penal problems. It has shown itself in most important fashion, also, by the actual introduction into prisons, reformatories, juvenile institutions, and courts of experts capable of carrying out investigations designed to throw more light on the character of the individuals under observation.

The purpose of the present study may be stated as an attempt to furnish a scientific basis for the conceptions regarding woman offenders, through an investigation concerning the distinguishing characteristics of women convicted of either serious crimes or minor offenses in New York State. It has not been our object either to defend any specific thesis or to combat established ideas regarding the characteristics of these woman. We have merely aimed to determine, so far as possible, the facts.

INADEQUACY OF MATERIAL FROM OTHER SOURCES AND LIMITATIONS ON COMPLETION OF DESIRED COMPARISONS WITH OTHER GROUPS

Our efforts were directed first toward making a survey of the group of women delinquents under consideration, with a view to securing as much information as possible with regard to their mental capacities and the main facts of their personal and environmental histories. With that material at hand we have attempted to make such comparisons as might be enlightening on the basis of our own data, and also such other comparisons as were made possible by the data available as the result of other investigations. In this study, physical and medical facts have been almost entirely disregarded since the conditions of our inquiry have been such as to make impossible the securing of adequate medical data for most of the groups studied. Though we recognize this omission as unfortunate, it has seemed to us preferable to have our study incomplete in this direction rather than to use information so inadequate that misleading conclusions might be drawn.

The first comparison which seems called for is that between our group of women delinquents and women in general, to determine whether the group of delinquent women represents in any of its aspects, a special selection out of the general female population, or whether we may think of them as a mere random sample from the total, differentiated at present by their criminal careers but not otherwise. Specifically, we wish to know, for example, whether the delinquent group is markedly different in respect to mentality or whether it merely shows distribution of high and low mentality around a central tendency with no significant difference from the distribution of the general population. Similarly, we wish to know whether those who break the law have differed markedly from the sum total of women in their general environmental background as represented by their early home conditions, their educational opportunities, the economic stress to which they have been subjected, and numerous other conditions which have acted upon them. Again, they should be compared with the whole female population with reference to physical condition and the presence or absence of disturbing hereditary factors. Such a comparison of the delinquent group with the whole population of women is obviously of first importance for the determination of the significance to be attached to these various conditions as causative factors in connection with criminality. In fact, one of the great sources of fallacy in the literature concerning pathological conditions of all kinds, whether medical or social, has been the tendency to study only the deviating group and to assume that conditions present here in large numbers have been factors occasioning the abnormality of the group, without first determining whether they may not be present in equal measure in an unselected sample of the general population.

A mere recital of some of the factors which it is important to study should be sufficient to suggest that, unfortunately, one side of the comparison, that represented by the non-delinquent population, will be lacking for the great majority of points on which we wish enlightenment. Such information as is given in the United States Census reports is the most comprehensive material available, but this is presented under such general headings that its usefulness for our purpose is limited. Other less extensive sources of information give a certain amount of scattering data regarding special groups of women, but none of these can be taken as adequately representative of women as a whole. The fact is, therefore, that at present the comparison suggested as of prime importance, namely, that between the general female population and our special group of offenders, cannot be carried through in any satisfactory fashion.

As approximations to that result, two makeshifts are possible. The first of these is the one just mentioned, namely, a comparison of this group with such general data as are available on the whole female population through the census reports. For all such information, however, not only are we restricted to the most general data, but we must refer back to the 13th census which represents facts which were true of the population in 1910. We cannot be certain that relationships held the same for the years covered by our study, 1915-7, especially in the light of the war conditions of this period. The second possibility is a comparison with data on separate groups of women for such information as may be available. Such comparisons may be suggestive, though not final, and we shall not hesitate to make use of these sources whenever possible.

Even in the face of these limitations on the satisfactory rounding out of our comparisons, it has appeared desirable to present, in considerable detail, the phase of the comparison which we are able to furnish as the result of our investigations, in order that this may be accessible at such time in the future as more complete data concerning the non-delinquent female population may have been secured.

The second comparison which naturally suggests itself is almost as much out of the question in any complete form at present as is the preceding, namely, the comparison of women offenders with similar groups of men offenders. It is true that most of the work which has been done on the subject of crime and criminals has been the result of the study of men criminals. Goring's important work on the English convict [4] is concerned entirely with men. Dr. Glueck's report on a year's admissions to Sing Sing prison [5] gives comparative data of special interest to us since it is concerned with men convicted in this state. Dr. Heacox has put at our disposal certain unpublished results of his study of men at Auburn prison which also furnish valuable material for comparison. These and other studies of men offenders will be made use of for purposes of comparison, but it should be noted that they are confined almost entirely to the study of men convicted of relatively serious offenses and committed to state prisons. We lack similar extensive studies of adult men convicted of minor offenses and committed to work-houses, county penitentiaries and reformatories. It will be apparent from our account of the character of the offenses which the women under consideration have committed that these fall in the latter class of relatively minor offenses. The group of women that is in any way comparable with the type of men offenders who have been most extensively studied is so small as seriously to hamper the working out of any extensive comparison. We note, for example, that while the total number of men committed to the

[4] Goring, Charles. "The English Convict. A Statistical Study." T. Fisher Unwin, London, W.C., 1913.

[5] Glueck, Bernard. "A Study of 608 Admissions to Sing Sing Prison." *Mental Hygiene,* Vol. 2, No. 1, Jan., 1918.

state prisons of New York during the fiscal year ending July 1, 1917, is 1403[6] the total number of women received in Auburn prison, the only prison of the state which receives women, during the same period of time is 27.[7] A fuller discussion of this phase of the comparison will be offered in detail under our account of the nature of offenses committed by women. For any close comparisons between our group and the men convicted of crime, studied in the investigations mentioned above, we feel it necessary to restrict ourselves to those women who have been convicted of felonies, of whom we have 126 cases. These are not entirely comparable with the men sentenced to state prisons, since they include, in addition to Auburn commitments, cases committed for felonies to the State Reformatory at Bedford Hills, the New York County Penitentiary, and the Magdalen Home. They do represent, however, cases all of whom might have been sentenced to state prisons, so that comparison seems reasonably justifiable. The number of commitments of women to the State Prison is so small that it would be necessary either to spread the study over the whole country or to extend it over a long period of time. To have secured 500 cases of women given State Prison terms in New York State would have required an investigation covering the commitments during a period of twelve years, whereas this number of cases can be secured in less than six months from the men's prisons of the state.

With reference to this comparison, therefore, of women delinquents as a whole with men delinquents as a whole, we are in practically the same position as for the first comparison suggested; that is, we must offer data on one side of the comparison without being able to secure the complementary information on the group to be compared. Since we feel certain that studies of male misdemeanants and of male felons not committed to State Prisons will be completed before many more years, we have no hesitation in offering our data as useful for this comparison at some future time.

[6] "Report of the Superintendent of State Prisons." New York, 1917, p. 20, table 5; p. 116, statement 1; p. 232, table 8. The total number given above is obtained by combining the figures given in the tables specified as the number of cases *received in each prison from the district assigned to that prison.* A combination of the total number *received* during the year in all the prisons of the state would be misleading since a given individual might thus appear several times, being recorded, for example, as received at Sing Sing from Sing Sing district and received at Auburn later from Sing Sing prison, and possibly again received at Clinton or at Great Meadow prison from Auburn prison.

[7] *Ibid.*, p. 198, table 1 (number received exclusive of those returned for violation of parole).

The third type of comparison which requires consideration is more directly possible from our own data. We refer to the study of the inter-relations observed within the group of delinquent women themselves. The total group may be divided into numerous subdivisions selected now on one basis of classification, now on another, in accordance with the special interest of the moment. For example, there is first the division with which we began; namely, of groups in terms of the institution to which the women have been sentenced. It seems desirable to determine what general principles of selection, if any, have been operative to determine commitment to one institution rather than to another. Cutting across this classification is that in terms of nature of offense committed, since we are equally concerned to know whether individuals committing one type of offense are distinguished in any important ways from those committing other offenses. Similarly we may reclassify our whole number for special consideration into groups according to nationality and color, or according to criminal record, or sex history, or record of juvenile offenses. These and numerous other groupings which suggest themselves offer fields wherein inquiries regarding the characteristic marks of the special group as distinguished from the whole group of delinquent women are pertinent.

It is important to bear in mind, with reference to all discussion of such inter-relationships, that we offer our data as applying only to relationships within the group of women delinquents under consideration. We make no claims to their extension to other groups, as for example to men criminals who may differ in many respects from women criminals, or to juvenile delinquents, who constitute another quite distinct problem.

USE OF MASS METHODS OF TREATMENT RATHER THAN CASE HISTORY METHODS IN PRESENT STUDY

The methods of approach to these problems naturally divide themselves into methods of investigation and methods of analysis of results. These are described in detail in Chapters III, IV and V. A few points of general significance may, however, be noted here.

First of these is the fact that the methods of investigation have consisted of careful individual studies, while the methods of analysis have treated the results as mass data and handled these statistically.

From the standpoint of the present study the main object in the detailed individual studies was the increased accuracy of the information secured.[8] The fact that our numbers are not large made us feel the necessity of making our data as reliable as possible. The more thoroughly an investigator comes to know a given woman, the more likely is she to acquire the main facts of importance concerning her and to pass judgment satisfactorily on the trustworthiness of the facts. Moreover, the mere knowledge on the part of the inmate that facts are to be verified tends of itself to reduce the amount of false statement. And, in addition to these aids to accuracy, there is always the possibility that a thorough investigation will unearth clues which will lead to clearing up the case and giving an entirely different picture of significant factors from that offered by the inmate herself.

In our account of the sociological methods (Chapter IV) the fact is emphasized that there was much difference in the completeness of this investigation in the various groups studied: that it was most satisfactory for the Bedford group and least so for the Workhouse. We feel, however, that even for the latter group our data are considerably more reliable than any information based on an inmate's statement alone.

Having accumulated the material by individual methods the question may arise regarding the reasons for applying mass methods of treatment to them. These methods were chosen consciously and in spite of full recognition of the importance of careful study of the individual for understanding of that individual. Wherever practical direction of the treatment of the individual case has been an issue we have acted on this principle. At the same time we are not in sympathy with the attitude of distrust toward all methods approaching the statistical, as we find this manifested by many modern leaders in the field of criminology, especially those of the medical profession.

In the first place, we believe that some background of knowledge regarding many individuals is essential even for the adequate understanding of a given individual. For example, if we leave the field of criminology for the moment and turn to the province of medicine which has been particularly wary of mass methods, it will probably be admitted that a patient suffering with a given combination of symptoms at a given time will feel more confidence in a physician who not only studies the individual case before him "as an individual" with thoroughness, but who brings to such study a background of knowledge

[8] It should be remembered that there was another entirely different reason for prosecuting the individual studies with thoroughness. This was the fact that, in the case of the Bedford women especially, this information was relied upon in the institution as a basis for treatment of the case.

of some cases other than the present one. Some such background may be acquired through the physician's own experiences and the anecdotal material which he may acquire from professional friends. Such information, not organized nor tabulated in any way, may contribute materially to his skilful handling of the given patient at the given time. However, there are few of us who would elect to trust ourselves to the physician with only that background. Some contact with the generalized experience of others is the least that we can accept from our physician.

The method of case histories has been the favorite medical device for securing this background, and it has unquestionably its uses. In our opinion it has also its dangers, in its very lack of objectivity. It is too susceptible to the whim or prejudice of the person who selects the cases to be used and compiles their histories. It is not possible, through case histories, to prove or disprove any facts, but it is possible to convey impressions and establish convictions. Whether or not these are trustworthy depends entirely on the background, the insight and the intellectual honesty of the person who presents them. It would be quite possible so to select cases that they would convey, more or less convincingly, the impression that women convicted of larceny are blue-eyed. It would be only necessary that we cite only blue-eyed women, and that we always mention this characteristic and that we happen to mention other characteristics with less regularity. Lombroso's work exemplifies this treatment, carried almost to the degree of absurdity suggested above, in the attempt to establish the physical stigmata of the criminal.

It has seemed to us that the dangers involved in mere individual treatment, or mere series of case studies, were so great that the more organized mass presentation must precede any special studies of individuals. Without the background of such a study there is the risk of making much of facts which are in no sense unusual and at the same time disregarding facts of importance which genuinely distinguish this individual from his fellows.

We would not urge that it is possible to say which are the more important,—the common, characteristic facts or the unusual distinguishing traits. The essential thing is that the correct poin of view be associated with each. The traits which occur infrequently in a delinquent group are especially important to note as a basis for differentiating the treatment of the individual or the small group of individuals in whom this trait occurs from the whole group.

On the other hand it is important for the treatment of delinquent groups as a whole both that common characteristics be noted and that they be recognized as common. As we have already stated, methods of treatment are inevitably affected by the preconceptions of the governing bodies concerning the characteristics of the group with which they deal. Obviously the plan of organization of the penal system will be influenced by the existence of any of the following assumptions: that all criminals are congenitally degenerate; that they are predominantly feeble-minded; that they are abnormally clever; that they are victims of early environmental conditions; that they are produced by economic necessity; that they are predominantly uneducated, and that this lack of education has been a factor in their criminal career; that they have more than the average education for their social or racial group and that this fact has affected them adversely. These, and many other generalizations have figured in the minds of persons dealing with delinquents and have contributed toward the penal systems which have been inaugurated. Many of them are open to scientific study, as Goring has so conclusively demonstrated with reference to Lombroso's theories of the physical degeneracy of criminals. Presumably the problem of the delinquent will not prove so simple as to be summarized in any of the above general formulæ, but, if we can avoid being misled into assuming that a condition which exists commonly must be a cause, the discovery that a state of affairs is to be expected with frequency in any delinquent group should have at least some bearing on their treatment.

The great advantage of the case history method is the fact that it presents a picture of the whole personality, which the present type of study fails to show. In our opinion both types of study should be used since each can throw light on the other. We have chosen the mass method as particularly applicable to our data and as meeting, in our opinion, a definite need in the study of criminology.

CHAPTER II

GENERAL ACCOUNT OF DELINQUENT GROUPS STUDIED

THE total group under consideration is made up of women convicted of offenses against the law in the courts of New York State. We shall refer to this constantly as an adult group, since all cases have a legal age [1] of sixteen years or over. There is no upper age limit for the individuals included although there is a tendency toward such an upper limit for certain of the groups.

Though any offense against the law is technically a crime, and any person committing a crime may be called a criminal, we have preferred to refer to these women as "delinquents," or, using a most general term, as "offenders." The term "criminal" connotes to most persons an individual guilty of one of the more serious offenses and is approximately synonymous with the term "felon." Since the major part of the group of women whom we are studying is not of this type, we have preferred to avoid the term "criminal." It seems a far cry to designate as "criminal" the girl of sixteen or seventeen who may be convicted of "associating with vicious and dissolute persons and being in danger of becoming morally depraved," or the woman who is convicted, even for the twentieth time, of intoxication, or, in fact, even the common prostitute whose offense against the law is made possible only by the participation of men, who are not even considered accomplices in a criminal act in the eyes of the law. The very fact that there is such extreme lack of uniformity between this and other countries, and even between different sections of this country, as to whether these acts constitute even legal offenses, furnishes another reason for hesitating to brand those committing them by the term "criminal."

GENERAL MAKE-UP OF GROUPS, WITH A VIEW TO SECURING REPRESENTATIVES OF ALL TYPES

In planning the make-up of the total number to be studied our main desire was to secure, as our composite group, one which should con-

[1] We distinguish between "legal" age and "actual" age, the former being the age which the court accepts at the time of conviction. There are a few cases, in our total number, where the actual age was under sixteen.

tain representatives of all types and degrees of delinquency ordinarily found among women offenders. It seemed hopeless to plan to obtain these in the actual proportions in which they occur, but we hoped, by proper weighting of the groups, to be able to offer eventually a satisfactory picture of the sum total of the women offenders of the state. We realized that any particular institutional group could not be considered representative, since numerous factors, many of which would be impossible of evaluation, enter into the selection of cases to be sent to any given institution. This was, in fact, the main consideration which led us to the extension of our study beyond the scope of the Reformatory at Bedford Hills, where the work was initiated.

The first problem was to determine how we could best secure the representative total desired. The two possibilities which suggested themselves were the following: (1) to secure the women at the time of conviction as they came through the various courts of the state; or (2) to take them after commitment as they were to be found in the various institutions. The former method, had it been feasible, would have had many advantages over the latter, since it would have made possible the elimination of the factors of selection represented by the sentence to one institution or another. However, it appeared utterly impracticable to approach our problem from the avenue of the court, under present conditions. If a clearing house or a series of clearing houses were in existence, this method of approach would be possible, but in the absence of some such plan, whereby the women could be held, subject to study, for a short time at least, conditions are too variable and not adapted to the successful carrying out of any plan of investigation. Women would be shifted from one place to another while their investigation was in progress, which would mean endless waste of time in the mere attempt to keep track of their location. Moreover, the majority of city and county jails offer no places which would be even reasonably satisfactory for interviews and mental examinations. The approach by way of the institutions to which the cases had been committed seemed therefore the only practicable method. This line of approach we have accordingly followed.

Within the several institutions we have made it our practice to take consecutive commitments, in order that the individuals used might be representative of the group, with no further selection than that which was made by the court when the commitment was determined upon. In our account of the various groups we shall indicate to what extent we have been able to follow this plan absolutely, and where we have had to make adjustments to meet special conditions. We feel justified in saying that tendencies toward special selection have been reduced to a minimum within our groups. In one case only, that of the New York City Workhouse, have these tendencies proved very serious. In that case, as we shall see, we have found it necessary to eliminate a part of the very large group under consideration and to treat our cases as typical of a specially defined portion of the Workhouse rather than of the whole.

Since it was not feasible to make a survey of all the institutions of the state it became necessary to make a selection from among the available institutions and delinquent groups. In the effort to include all types and degrees of offenders the following groups were chosen: (1) The New York State Reformatory for Women at Bedford Hills; (2) The State Prison for Women at Auburn; (3) The New York Magdalen Home (Inwood House); (4) The New York County Penitentiary; (5) The New York City Workhouse; (6) A group of women placed on probation through the Night Court for women for the boroughs of Manhattan and the Bronx (Ninth District Court). A brief description of the general characteristics of these groups may serve to make clear the reasons for their selection. Detailed analysis of the personnel of the various institutions will constitute one of the problems to be discussed later in the text.

DESCRIPTIVE ACCOUNT OF GROUPS

(a) *The New York State Reformatory for Women, Bedford Hills, N. Y.*

The State Reformatory for women at Bedford Hills receives women from the eastern part of the state.[2] The Western House of Refuge at Albion is the reformatory for the rest of the state and receives women under exactly the same conditions as does the reformatory at Bedford Hills. The institution at Bedford Hills was chosen as representative of both reformatories of the state and no study was made of the institution at Albion.

These institutions receive women convicted of a wide range of offenses, including both felonies and misdemeanors. Of the felonies,

[2] Commitments to the New York State Reformatory for Women at Bedford Hills are from the first, second, third and ninth judicial districts. This includes 19 counties: the five counties within Greater New York, the counties on Long Island, and the counties bordering the Hudson River as far north as Rensselaer County.

murder in the first or the second degree is the only offense for which one cannot be committed, except that a woman cannot be sentenced to the reformatory for a felony after having had any previous conviction for a felony. Of the misdemeanors and other minor offenses there are very few for which one cannot be committed to a reformatory, except in case of offenses for which no institutional commitment is provided. Accordingly the Bedford group has the possibility of including almost the whole range of offenses for which women are imprisoned. All cases committed to these reformatories are given an indeterminate sentence not to exceed three years, power being vested in the Board of Managers to parole or discharge at any time before the expiration of the three years. No cases are received under sixteen years of age, and it was formerly true that none were received over thirty. There is at present legal provision for the commitment to the reformatory of individuals over thirty, convicted of specified offenses in certain parts of the district covered. There is, however, a tendency to think of thirty as an upper age limit for the reformatory groups.

From many points of view our study of the Bedford women is more satisfactory and complete than is our study of any of the other groups. For the understanding of this group we had more background than for any of the others included because of the fact that the work of the Laboratory had been centered here from its beginning. In fact this type of study had been inaugurated by Dr. Davis in her "Study of Prostitutes at Bedford" published in 1913.[3] The investigation made by Dr. Weidensall, reported in "The Mentality of the Criminal Woman,"[4] dealt also with this group. In addition to this general background of understanding there was the fact that all the conditions made possible here a particularly thorough and reliable investigation. The physical conditions surrounding the work, which are important for their influence on the success of both interviewing and examining, are much better than in any of the other institutions. Moreover, the work was so well established that it was accepted as a regular part of the routine of admission to the institution. In addition to these factors, there is the fact that the organization of the Laboratory made possible a greater thoroughness of investigation here than for any of the other institutions. For all these reasons we shall tend to consider

[3] Kneeland, George J. "Commercialized Prostitution in New York City." Chapter VIII by Katharine Bement Davis. "A Study of Prostitutes Committed to the State Reformatory for Women at Bedford Hills."

[4] Weidensall, Jean. "The Mentality of the Criminal Woman," 1916.

the Bedford group as of rather central interest; and shall use it frequently as a point of reference for other groups.

The Bedford commitments under consideration for the main part of the present inquiry consist of 102 consecutive cases committed between September 1, 1916, and August 9, 1917. In addition to these, whom we have designated the "Contemporary Group," we have used for much of the material on the psychological tests other cases examined prior to the study of this group. These have been used for the greater certainty which they offered that the Bedford group is actually a fair sample of commitments to Bedford in general. The details as to numbers used will be given at a later point. We have not used the earlier groups on the social data, since the methods used for securing such data were not entirely the same during the early part of the Laboratory work and the forms for recording data were very different. This latter difference made the work of including the early Bedford groups so great as to be prohibitive within the time limits of the present investigation.

(*b*) *The State Prison for Women, Auburn, N. Y.*

The state prison for women at Auburn represents for women offenders of this state the same type of institution as is furnished in Sing Sing, Auburn, Clinton, and Great Meadow prisons for men felons. We have already commented on the great discrepancy between the number of men and the number of women committed to institutions of this type. Any woman convicted of a felony may be sentenced to Auburn prison. No cases other than felonies are legally committable there. It is to be expected that in the case of offenses for which there is a range of choice regarding the institution to which they shall be sent, commitment to state prison will be used where the offense is especially grave or where the offender appears to be a particularly dangerous member of the community. Sentence to state prison is commonly thought of as—by its very nature—the most severe sentence which can be given, although it is possible for one to receive a shorter term in state prison than that made possible by the indeterminate reformatory sentence with its three-year maximum. No person under sixteen years of age can be committed to state prison, but there is no upper age limit.

We have already commented on the slow rate of admission of women to Auburn prison. For this reason it was necessary to begin our study with cases whose admission antedated by a considerable period of time the actual beginning of our investigation. In doing this we lost entirely from our series eight cases, five of whom had served their time and left the institution before we began our work, one of whom had died, and two of whom refused to talk about their cases or take any examinations.[5] The first case of our regular Auburn series was committed February 4, 1915, and the last case, June 27, 1917, making the range of time covered by the commitments of this group more than two years. The total number of cases received during this time was 88. These numbers were supplemented, for certain of the tests where we were particularly desirous to increase our numbers, by additional cases preceding and following this regular group.

There were many difficulties inherent in carrying on such an investigation with this group. In fact without the cordial coöperation which we received from the authorities of the prison it would have been entirely impracticable to attempt this study.[6] Those women especially whose commitments dated back one or two years before the beginning of our study, were naturally inclined to resent going over the facts of their cases again. Moreover, on general principles they were inclined to object to the inauguration of any such a careful study of them as individuals. It required much tact and ingenuity to meet this attitude of mind. We were fortunate in finding an opportunity to be of some real value to certain of the women in the course of our investigations, by clearing up misunderstandings with members of their family and establishing more friendly relations between them. This helped toward the creation of a more friendly feeling toward our work.

(c) *The New York Magdalen Home*[7]

The New York Magdalen Home is one of several institutions under private management which receive women committed through the courts. The main other institutions of the state coming under this

[5] The commitment data were available on these cases and they are accordingly included in the tables which give information concerning the offenses for which committed.

[6] We cannot express too warmly our appreciation of the coöperation which we received. Dr. Frank L. Heacox, physician of the Prison, aided us at every turn. Not only did he permit us the use of his offices in the women's prison for our work, but his friendly attitude of coöperation helped much to overcome the antagonism which the inmates felt toward any strange innovation. He also permitted us the use of his records. For all the medical data which we offer on this group of women we are directly indebted to Dr. Heacox. To Mrs. Margaret E. Daly, matron of the women's prison, Miss Curtis, first assistant, and Mrs. Stone, head of the school, we are also indebted for constant coöperation and assistance.

[7] This institution is now known as Inwood House.

classification are the following: the House of the Good Shepherd (New York City), the House of the Good Shepherd in the City of Brooklyn, the House of Mercy (New York City), the Wayside Home of the City of Brooklyn (now at Valley Stream, Long Island), the Asylum of Our Lady of Refuge (Buffalo), the Mount Magdalen School of Industry and Reformatory of the Good Shepherd (Troy), St. Anne's School of Industry and Reformatory of the Good Shepherd (Albany), the Shelter for Unprotected Girls (Syracuse).

Since it was obviously not feasible to obtain representatives from all of the above institutions, we hoped to secure a fairly adequate representation through one group of 100 cases, including 50 cases from the New York Magdalen Home and 50 cases from the New York House of the Good Shepherd. The latter institution, however, refused our request for permission to undertake the study, stating that it was contrary to their method of government "to subject our inmates to scrutiny relative to their past." Accordingly it was decided to accept the group from the Magdalen Home as typical of commitments to the private institutions. Observation of the women as they pass through the courts has convinced us that this is not entirely true, and that the House of the Good Shepherd, at least, has probably a somewhat distinctive group. Specifically it appears to receive more cases of older women, and of women convicted of offenses of the intoxication type, than does the Magdalen Home. We regret that it was impossible to include these in our study. The fact remains, however, that it would be difficult to designate with certainty any one or two of these institutions as characteristic of the group, since, by their very nature, there is much scope for individuality in their organization. Accordingly, while we have chosen the Magdalen Home as the representative of this group of institutions, we do not claim that its cases are necessarily characteristic of commitments to private institutions as a whole.

The Magdalen Home receives women between 16 and 35 years of age from New York City and from a few of the neighboring counties. The range of misdemeanors for which one may be committed is very similar to that for the State Reformatories. The law does not provide for conviction to this institution for felonies, though occasional cases so convicted have been sent here, when the individual seemed especially likely to profit by the lighter sentence. In such cases the procedure has amounted practically to suspension of sentence by the judge under the condition that the woman voluntarily commit herself to the institution. One important characteristic of the private institutions is their privilege of returning to the court, for recommitment elsewhere, cases who prove to be undesirable members of their community. This introduces a tendency toward selection which, although exercised after commitment in particular cases, may well react upon the judges, leading them to refrain from committing cases who are likely to be misfits in these institutions.

Cases are committed for three different kinds of terms: (1) for definite periods not exceeding one year; (2) for the period of their minority; (3) for an indeterminate period not to exceed three years, power of discharge at any time prior to this being vested in the Board of Managers. The last-mentioned type of commitment is the most frequent, but as a rule women are discharged or paroled after a shorter period of time than is commonly required at the Reformatory at Bedford Hills. This fact operates in the same direction as the principle just mentioned: *viz.*, toward the selection of more promising and less confirmed offenders, in so far as it affects the judges making the commitments.

We include in our study 76 consecutive cases received at the Magdalen Home between September 29, 1916, and June 15, 1917. It was not necessary to omit completely any case from this series, though several cases were omitted from a part of the study. These will be discussed later.[8]

(*d*) *The New York County Penitentiary*

The New York County Penitentiary is one of the five penitentiaries [9] of the state which receive women. Commitments are made for specified offenses through City Magistrates Court and for felonies and misdemeanors through courts of Special Sessions, General Sessions, Supreme Court or County Court. At present as a result of the parole law, all commitments from New York County are given an indeterminate sentence not to exceed three years, although other neighboring counties may commit women for definite terms. There is no age limit other than the lower limit of sixteen years.

[8] We are greatly indebted to the management of the Magdalen Home for the cordiality with which they granted us permission to carry out this investigation. We are especially grateful to Mrs. Mary E. Paddon, Executive Secretary, and to Miss Janet Macchonachie, Superintendent, for their assistance and cooperation.

[9] Since the completion of our study the Westchester County Penitentiary has been opened, but this receives only commitments of men at present.

This institution is characterized by an inability to offer anything in the way of constructive training during the period of imprisonment. Formerly there was no provision for employment other than the ordinary work of the place. That need was met at the time of this study by a sewing room which accommodates about thirty women at a time. Beyond this there was no organized training or occupation. We might expect therefore that there would be a tendency to commit to the Penitentiary unpromising cases who could profit little by the opportunities offered in an institution of the Reformatory type, or older cases whose habits and characters were so "set" that there was little prospect of altering this. This tendency is even more to be expected here than in the case of the Workhouse, since there are no short term sentences to take care of the more trivial offenders.

Though our investigation was not started until August, 1916, it was made retroactive beginning with the first case committed under the Parole Law. No definite sentence cases were included. Our study covered a total of 110 cases committed consecutively between January 12, 1916, and May 14, 1917. Four cases were lost from this total because they had already been paroled at the time that we began our study. The commitment data concerning the present offenses of these four cases, being available and trustworthy, were used, however.

(*e*) *The New York City Workhouse*

The New York City Workhouse receives only misdemeanants, but can receive almost all varieties of these. The terms for which they may be committed vary from definite sentences of from one day to six months duration to the indeterminate sentence, for which the maximum is two years. By observation we are convinced that the Workhouse receives individuals of a wide variety of types. As is to be expected from the fact that it is primarily simply a place for holding persons in confinement to serve their time, and that opportunities for constructive individual readjustment along educational, vocational and medical lines are conspicuously lacking, it is preëminently the place for "old rounders" of all sorts, for cases who have been given opportunities and have failed and whose prognosis is considered most unfavorable. Under the Parole Law it is made imperative that persons having as many as two previous convictions within two years or three at any time shall be sentenced for the indeterminate term, if sentenced to the Workhouse at all. This law of itself tends to divert the stream of old offenders among the misdemeanants to the Workhouse.

But there is an entirely different principle operative also in determining Workhouse commitments, since the Workhouse offers a short sentence of a few days or weeks which is, from point of view of punishment, the most lenient penalty, except probation, suspended sentence or fines, that can be offered to a trivial offender.[10] Accordingly a short Workhouse term is very frequently given a first offender with the idea that her offense is not serious enough to justify a longer sentence. This leads to the inclusion within the total Workhouse commitments of at least two quite disparate groups: *viz.* (1) the old offenders who are given for the most part terms of more than ten days, and (2) fairly new offenders who are frequently given the shortest sentences possible for their offenses.

There is, however, still another element in the Workhouse to complicate the situation, *viz.:* the group of old intoxication cases. The majority of cases convicted of intoxication in the New York City Courts are given one of the following three penalties: (1) they may be fined not more than $10 with the alternative of serving time, a day for a dollar, in the city prison; (2) they may be given suspended sentence[11] especially used with first offenders, and (3) they may be sentenced to the Workhouse for periods of one day to six months. Of the above mentioned three possibilities the Workhouse term is given least frequently to first offenders, being used for such cases as a rule only when it is evident that they cannot take care of themselves, and that they have no one else to take care of them if turned loose.

Of the first two groups—those fined and those given suspended sentence—we have no direct knowledge. With the intoxication group committed to the Workhouse we had some experience, enough to convince us that they were in many respects different from the rest of the Workhouse population. Most notably did they differ in degree of recidivism. All the longest records of previous convictions were found among this group and the mean number of previous convictions was larger than for any other group. In addition to this it is an older group than the Workhouse group as a whole, the range of nationalities included is very different and the mentality as measured at the present time at least, is lower than that of the rest of the group.

[10] By many of the women themselves a short workhouse sentence appears definitely preferable to even a chance on probation. The custom of imposing fines is now discontinued for all offenses involving prostitution, though they are still imposed for intoxication and disorderly conduct.

[11] A small number are given probation, but this is infrequent. Suspended sentence is more commonly used for intoxication cases.

The Workhouse then may be thought of as made up of at least three quite distinct portions: (1) General misdemeanants, exclusive of cases of intoxication, who give the impression of being hardened and unpromising or who have failed on previous opportunities; (2) new and relatively hopeful cases who are let off with a few days at the Workhouse, and (3) the intoxication cases who are given Workhouse terms. Of these three groups we confined our study almost entirely to the first.

The exclusion of the other two groups was brought about by two quite distinct conditions. The second group, made up of the new and more hopeful offenders, had been given for the most part terms of ten days or less. The present policy of the Department of Correction is not to transfer such cases to the Workhouse on Blackwell's Island at all but to allow them to serve their terms in the various city prisons. The physical impracticability of their locations together with the temporal difficulties introduced by the shortness of their terms and the consequent difficulty in completing their study before they went out made it out of the question to include them in our investigation.

The intoxication group introduced a different complication. Though all cases committed for a term longer than ten days were actually in the Workhouse they made, of all our groups, the most difficult cases to examine or interview. In the first place, when they had been coming to the "Island" for almost as long as they could remember, they resented the innovation of such a study, just as one might resent a change in his favorite hotel. In the second place, they frequently appeared to be still suffering more or less from the effects of their latest debauch, during the major part of their term. Where this was not the case they often showed so much evidence of senility and possible deterioration resultant upon their alcoholism that it was impossible to estimate what their original mental ability might have been. Their interviews showed either marked lack of veracity or a slurring of the accuracy of their memory for facts which made their accounts both incomplete and unreliable. The fact that they probably represent the most drifting elements of the population adds to the difficulty of securing even reasonably satisfactory information concerning them. Since this group of alcoholic cases constituted at this time over fifty per cent of the cases committed to the Workhouse for periods of over ten days it became apparent to us that our study of the Workhouse, which as we shall see later was the least satisfactory of all our groups even without this handicap, would be made almost entirely valueless by the erratic qualities of this group. The desirable solution of the problem would have been to make separate studies of these two Workhouse groups, including 100 in each. That was not feasible and accordingly when nineteen intoxication cases had been studied it was decided to restrict our studies for the remaining cases to individuals whose present conviction did not involve intoxication in any form.[12]

Owing to the great rapidity with which cases are received at the Workhouse it seemed impracticable to attempt to cover 100 *consecutive* cases, especially if both intoxication and other cases were included. Our first plan, therefore, was to take them in four groups of 25 each. We started our first group in accordance with this plan in December, 1916, and covered 27 cases within seven days. By this time we had come to appreciate the special difficulties incidental to work with the group of intoxication cases and had decided to discontinue testing them. Eliminating these left thirteen cases received consecutively at the Workhouse during this period. After excluding the intoxication cases we found it possible to cover the remaining number of cases as one group of consecutive admissions. During the latter period 96 cases were received, making the total number received at the Workhouse and available for study under the conditions as defined above, 109 cases. Of these it was necessary to omit entirely, except for commitment data, seven cases,[13] making a total of 102 cases studied more or less completely.

The special group of women committed for intoxication included twenty-one cases, one of whom was committed to Matteawan and one died before there was opportunity to give mental tests. These twenty-one cases include ten committed for public intoxication, seven for disorderly conduct, and four for vagrancy, the latter two charges both signifying intoxication in these cases. This small group of cases studied will be mentioned at various points in our study for the light which they may throw on the characteristics of cases of this type. The numbers are, however, too small to justify the same sort of statistical

[12] In addition to the cases specified as public intoxication we have eliminated cases committed for disorderly conduct or vagrancy where the account of the offense makes clear that it was primarily a case of intoxication.

[13] The reasons for omission of these seven cases were as follows: One was transferred to Matteawan, two were transferred to other city jails as workers, one was in the hospital during the whole of her term, two were taken out on bail pending the results of an appeal and did not return during the period of investigation, one though received at the Workhouse was a ten-day commitment and was therefore not included.

treatment as the rest of the material. Whenever mentioned they will be clearly referred to as "Workhouse Intoxication Group." In consulting the tables it is important to remember that the so-called "Workhouse Group" does not include any representatives of the large portion of the Workhouse population who have been committed for intoxication.

(*f*) *Probation cases from the Women's Night Court of Manhattan and the Bronx*

Our probation group is made up of women placed on probation through the Women's Night Court of Manhattan and the Bronx. The original plan was to secure a total of 100 probation cases made up of women sentenced through the three types of courts in New York City: *viz.*, the City Magistrates' Courts, the Courts of Special Sessions and the Courts of General Sessions. Since the probation cases from the Night Court are the largest and most important group placed on probation through the City Magistrates' Courts, it was decided to consider these representative of the whole group of women probationers from the Magistrates' Courts.

We chose this as the probation group with which to begin our study, considering it entirely problematical whether such an investigation was practicable under the conditions of probation. After we had established the fact that such a study could be made to advantage from our point of view and yet without disturbing the friendly relations existing between the probationer and her probation officer, we asked permission to begin a study of a smaller group from the Court of Special Sessions. This request was not granted. Accordingly it was decided to restrict our study to the group of probationers from the Night Court with whom its practicability had been demonstrated. We regretted the necessity of omitting the other two probation groups, since it prevented our total probation group from including all types of offenders who are put on probation.[14]

[14] We wish to express our gratitude to Mr. Edwin J. Cooley, Chief Probation Officer, City Magistrates' Courts, for his ready interest in the carrying out of this study and his willingness that it be undertaken. To Miss Alice Smith, Probation Officer of the Night Court, we are indebted for constant and detailed coöperation which was mainly responsible for making the work practicable. She devised an arrangement which operated, we feel sure, to the advantage of the probation officer and the woman under consideration as well as to that of the Laboratory study. According to this plan women who seemed likely to be selected for probation were assigned to members of the Laboratory staff for investigation, just as, at other times, they are assigned to various volunteer organizations who assist the probation officer. In this way we had a perfectly natural avenue of approach to the women, friendly relations were established, and it was easy to keep in touch with them and complete our in-

The women placed on probation through the Night Court may be of any age over sixteen years, though the opportunity for probation is naturally given more frequently to the younger women. By virtue of the selection which the court itself exercises, they fall into the general groups of offenders against chastity, intoxication cases, and various forms of disorderly conduct and of incorrigibility. All are misdemeanants, but the group does not include all types of misdemeanants, since there are certain of these, such as offenders against property, drug users, etc., who cannot be convicted through the Magistrates' Courts. The group tends to be made up of first offenders or of cases who offer special promise of making good, either because of their own personal qualities or because of unusually satisfactory conditions in which they can be placed. There is a general tendency, quite definitely stated as such, to give all first offenders an opportunity on probation, unless there are very clear reasons why they need the supervision and protection of an institution.

Cases were taken in consecutive order as they were placed on probation by the court, our actual procedure being to have at least one member of the Laboratory staff in court each night, ready to interview each woman referred by the judge to the probation officer as a probable case for probation. There were 102 cases admitted to probation between the beginning of the study in March and its close in July, 1917. Of these, eleven were omitted almost completely from our study, only the information which we received through the probation officers' record, covering the woman's present offense, her criminal record, and a few other scattering bits of information being available. These omissions were due to a variety of reasons, such that we feel satisfied that no single type of cases was being selected out.[15] The only exception to this is the omission of the

vestigations after they had been placed on probation. Report of our preliminary investigations in each case was made to Miss Smith, making it unnecessary that this work be duplicated. In many cases it was possible for us to make a more complete investigation than would have been possible for the probation officer with the many demands upon her time for supervision of probationers as well as for investigation.

[15] The reasons for these omissions were as follows: Four were sent out of the city to relatives, either the same night that they were placed on probation or so shortly after this that no investigation was practicable; four were older women whom we omitted intentionally since we felt that we should have too great difficulty in securing their coöperation; one case was committed to Bellevue for observation the day after her admission to probation, and was later committed to a hospital for the insane; two were omitted because it happened that their initial interview was taken entirely by the probation officer and it seemed unwise in their cases to transfer any of the work of investigation to another person.

four older women. Because of this omission our figures fail to show this small, but possibly fairly constant, proportion of more mature women in this group. We should add that, in addition to these eleven complete omissions, there are a considerable number of cases on whom our study is incomplete in some direction. Several of the cases, in order to be included in the series at all, had to have all the work that was to be done, including the testing, completed within one or two days, since they were being sent to parts of the country too far away for visits to be practicable.

GROUPS OF WOMEN OF THIS STATE WHO ARE NOT INCLUDED IN PRESENT STUDY

In the foregoing statement we have shown what groups of delinquent women were included in our study. It is doubtless important to indicate also what groups were entirely omitted. We have already mentioned the groups, closely similar to those selected for our study, which were omitted to prevent duplication. These omissions were the following: Of the two reformatories, the Western House of Refuge at Albion; of the private institutions, eight or more institutions of the state listed on page 19; of the County Penitentiaries, those for Albany, Erie, Monroe and Onondaga Counties. There were no omissions of Workhouses so-called, though we did omit two portions of the Workhouse total, *viz.*, the very short term commitments and the intoxication cases. For the rest of the state, outside of New York City, county jails doubtless come nearer than anything else to serving the function of the Workhouse. These it was necessary to omit entirely. They probably add no cases different in type from those committed to the Workhouse, though they might materially alter the proportions of different types. The other important omission from the institutional groups is that of the State Farm for Women at Valatie.[16] This institution receives women over 30 years of age who have had at least five previous convictions within two years. The commitments are largely for intoxication, so that this group corresponds closely with that of the alcoholics omitted from the Workhouse study.

In addition to these omissions from the institutional groups there are certain obvious omissions from the total number of delinquents, from among those who are not institutional cases. These are: (1) The cases fined. The numbers of these are large and cover a great

[16] This institution has been closed since the above account was written.

variety of offenses, though fines cannot be imposed for the most grave offenses, and are not given at present in New York City for offenses involving prostitution. Fines may be given to first offenders or, for certain offenses, notably intoxication and disorderly conduct, to very old offenders. (2) Cases given suspended sentence. This form of treatment also is very common and is applied to a wide range of offenses. It is given mainly in the case of either first or nearly first offenders. In the various court reports these cases are not always clearly distinguished from the group of those placed on probation. (3) Cases placed on probation through Courts of General and Special Sessions, through the Supreme Court and County Courts, and through local police courts. The one group of probation cases which we secured from the Women's Night Court of New York City cannot be considered as representative of all groups.

It should be noted that when we speak of these various omissions we are speaking of present convictions only. If we consider the total range of sentences which our women have had in the course of their careers it is probable that all types mentioned above have some representative in our total.

From a consideration of all our groups and from a certain amount of observation of courts and of other groups we feel that we have, among our selected total, representatives of all important types of women delinquents of this state, with the single exception of those cases committed for intoxication, of whom we have an inadequate representation. Aside from this, we have women committed for all types of offenses, through all types of courts, given sentences varying from probation to a term of twenty years or life. There are first offenders and recidivists. There are women committed for prostitution in some form, women who are prostitutes but who are committed for some other offense, and women who have, so far as we can learn, never been sexually irregular. There are women whose court careers began in childhood and women whose first offense came late in life. There are women of widely different ages and from many social classes. We feel convinced, therefore, that all the usual types of women delinquents are included in our study, although we cannot claim that the several types are present in correct proportions.

We may note further, among the omissions from this study, the women offenders, who are known to exist in appreciable numbers, who escape conviction altogether. How large their numbers may be and what their dominant characteristics we have no means of determining. That they represent, on the whole, the more efficient members of the delinquent group seems self-evident, since they manage to pursue their chosen careers without interruption at the hands of the law. This may be due to the fact that they evade detection more cleverly, or that they secure protection more effectively, or that, even if arrested, they marshal their forces more skilfully to escape conviction.

REASONS FOR PRESENTING DATA CLASSIFIED BY INSTITUTIONAL GROUPS

The question may be raised, on considering the data offered in the chapters which follow, as to why prominence is given to the classification by institutional groups, when these may be largely arbitrarily determined and are local in their interest. Two reasons may be offered, of which the first is the more important.

(1) The separate institutional groups are the actual concrete units with which we started. Selection within any given group is as nearly random as it could possibly be, whereas the make-up of the total was necessarily determined by the relative numbers in the various sub-groups, as well as by the choice of sub-groups. With the material presented in this way it is possible for other investigators to re-group the data in other ways in accordance with their special interests. For example, probation cases might be disregarded and only institutional commitments considered, institutions of the reformatory type might be thrown together, or still other special combinations made.

(2) Some interest attaches, locally at least, to the attempt to discover what principles of selection were effective in determining commitments at the time when this investigation was made. The answer to this question may well contribute to the solution of the further question as to whether the present system of commitment is adequate, or whether there is need for some additional device, such as that offered by a clearing-house, for more careful study of women offenders before commitment.

The interest, from this point of view, need not be exclusively local, since other communities contain institutions corresponding in type with those here considered, though any one community may fail to contain all types. With this in mind we might well have listed the groups by type names, discarding the more specific designations, using some such terms as these: (a) State Reformatory, (b)

State Prison, (c) Private Reformatory Institution, (d) County Penitentiary, (e) City Workhouse, (f) Probation Group (Sex Offenders). Additional data from similar groups in other parts of the country should make it possible eventually to determine whether any uniform tendencies are operative affecting the selection of cases for particular types of institutions, or whether selection is entirely determined by changing local conditions. If the latter should prove to be the case no permanent significance can be attached to the comparison of the local groups.

CHAPTER III

STATISTICAL METHODS

THIS investigation attempts to discover the extent to which certain social, economic and psychological factors are associated in a delinquent group. If relationships are to be found whose significance is *general,* it is clear that a *general* group must be studied. Particular cases, dramatic though they may be, cannot give justification in themselves for action affecting the group as a whole. General relationships can be established only through the study of a sample selected at random from the continual flow of women into the prisons and reformatories.

Such a truly representative group of delinquent women can only be approximated. We have selected our cases by studying consecutive commitments to a number of typical institutions. Using consecutive commitments seemed the surest way to obtain a sampling of the general group of delinquent women that would be free from the influence of arbitrary selection whether conscious or unconscious. The presence of an individual in our group is due to no other fact than that she entered an institution during the period of investigation.

The concepts underlying a study of the facts and relationships characteristic of such a representative group are fairly simple. In the first place, the various qualities of the group observed must be *described.* We want to know something of the intelligence of the group, the amount of recidivism, the economic condition prior to conviction. In the second place, *relationships* must be pointed out where they exist. We are interested both in comparisons between groups of individuals, as for example in the intelligence of delinquent women as compared with the general population, and in relationships between the factors we are studying, as between intelligence and number of commitments or between age at first conviction and type of offense. In the third place, there must be some statement of what *reservations* must be made in extending generalizations valid for the particular group under observation to the larger group of which the cases studied are only a chance sample.

These three concepts include all that is involved in the statistical treatment of our material. The concepts themselves are not statistical. They are too matter of fact for that. The statistics are merely a method of realizing as far as possible the scientific ideal embodied in the concepts.

THE DESCRIPTION OF THE QUALITIES OF A GROUP

In describing a quality or factor, intelligence for example, as it occurs in the group of women which we have studied, we shall ordinarily state two things about it. First, we shall give a figure which indicates a center about which the measurements tend to cluster, an average of the group in the quality. In some cases we shall give the arithmetic mean, in other cases the median, sometimes perhaps the mode. Each of these statistical terms has a special meaning of its own; but the function of all is to indicate a somewhat central point of reference for the group. Second, we shall give a figure which indicates the amount the individual cases are scattered about the average or central tendency. The scatter or dispersion is a most important consideration, since this shows the diversity or variability of the group. Sometimes groups that are of the same average intelligence differ greatly in variability, and, of course, when the variability is high, extreme cases are much more likely to be found. Variability or the dispersion of a group is indicated by statistical constants, sometimes by the average deviation, more frequently by the standard deviation (σ). These two constants have each a special significance, but for most purposes of interpretation, they may be thought of as meaning the same thing. Roughly, about two-thirds of the cases measured will be found within the distance of the standard deviation from the central tendency. Thus, if the average intelligence of the Bedford women is 80 points and the standard deviation is 6 points, about two-thirds of them will normally fall between 74 and 86, that is within 6 points on either side of 80. Cases as far removed from the average as two times the standard deviation rarely occur, and cases at a distance of three times this constant are most exceptional. In the illustration just imagined, very few women indeed would be found to score as low as 62 or as high as 98.

Thus the average or *central tendency* and the standard deviation or *index of variability* are the statistical constants we shall most need to *describe* a quality or trait of our groups. Both are important in judging the nature of any quality.

COMPARISONS AND RELATIONSHIPS

After a quality of one group of individuals has been described, it is often desirable to compare it with the same quality of another group. In this way, we may discover that the average intelligence of women sent to Bedford is lower than that of the general population. When we compare standard deviations, we may find that the variability of the Bedford group in intelligence is not so great as that of the general population.

These comparisons are easily made, the one precaution necessary being to make certain that the quality or trait is being observed under like circumstances for the two groups.

Relationships are only more extended comparisons. We may find by comparison that the Workhouse women are lower in intelligence than Bedford women; and again that Bedford women are lower than Penitentiary; and Penitentiary lower than Magdalen. If we put all three comparisons together, we have clearly a relationship between type of institution and intelligence.

The interpretation of relationships is a practical matter. It is through relationships that the many tangled threads of social causes can be partially straightened out. Relationships can be made the basis of prediction and of action; and the closer the relationship, the more definite the prediction and the surer the action. For this reason, we require a method of expressing closeness of relation.

The common ways of stating degree of relationship are the correlation coefficient, the correlation ratio and the contingency coefficient. All are misleading in that they give an unwarranted impression of the possibility of accurate prediction. These coefficients vary from 0 to 1, 0 for a relation such as would occur in the long run by chance, 1 for a perfect agreement. The coefficients are usually expressed as decimals, as .18, .37, .53. The reader should be warned that a coefficient of .50 by no means indicates that 50 per cent of the error of prediction has been removed.

The correlation coefficient and correlation ratio refer to different types of mathematical relationships between the variables related. If there is a large difference between these constants, it means that the methods of prediction must be studied mathematically with great care if the best is to be found. For interpretative purposes in this investigation, it is usually not necessary to distinguish between the correlation ratio and correlation coefficient. Usually both are relatively low, the number of cases is not large, and under these circumstances the differences between these two measures of relationship are less significant.

The partial correlation coefficient is occasionally used in this investigation. This coefficient varies from 0 to 1 as does the correlation coefficient proper. It is used to express the relation between two variables for constant values of a third (or more) which cannot be experimentally controlled. Care should be taken to ascertain exactly what this third variable is in every case, and to appreciate just what it would mean to have all individuals equal in this variable. The meaning of the partial relationship of the two variables in question can be more easily understood in this way.

STATISTICAL RESERVATIONS

When we find the average intelligence of a group which we measure to be 80 points, we want to be able to make some statement about the intelligence of the larger group of which the individuals we actually did observe are only a small, chance sample. How accurate a measure of the total group's intelligence is 80? What reservations must be made?

The amount of reservation is stated as plus or minus a certain amount. That is, the true value may be more or less than that observed. Thus, the average intelligence of the total group might be stated as 80 ± 2. The 2 is really an index of reservation,—it is a sort of standard deviation of the average.

The ± 2 is computed mathematically,—its purpose is to give us a definite point to start from. The amount of reservation we make depends on how cautious we must be. With intelligence stated as 80 ± 2, the chances are somewhat better than 2 to 1 that the average of the whole group, judging from the measurements on our sampling of individuals, is not less than 78 nor more than 82. The chances are about 20 to 1 that it lies between 76 and 84; they are more than 300 to 1 that it lies between 74 and 86. Thus it is fairly unlikely that the true constant lies outside a range of twice the ± 2, and it is almost certain not to lie outside a range of three times this figure.

An observed difference between two averages also must be stated with reservations. The difference between Bedford women and women in general in intelligence might be 20 ± 4, in favor of the general group. ± 4 is our starting point, and we can qualify our statements as much as we like. We are reasonably sure in this example that women in general excel Bedford women by more than 12 points, and we are practically certain that the difference is more than 8, these figures 12 and 8 being respectively 2 and 3 times the $\pm$ 4 from 20 points—the difference observed. We are sure that the difference in intelligence is not 0, and that the Bedford women do not excel.

Correlations are also stated with reservations, as .32 $\pm$ .05. Is there any chance that if we had measured all possible cases instead of only our sample, we would have found a zero relationship? Practically none, for this correlation coefficient .32 is more than 6 times the index of reservation.

When we are studying the differences between averages or between standard deviations or between correlation coefficients, we always find out how many times larger the observed difference is than the index of reservation. We compute the ratio of the difference to this index. If the ratio is 2 we are fairly sure the difference is really in the direction we observed it, if it is 2.5 we are very confident, and if it is 3 we are practically certain. No arbitrary ratio can be set as indicating absolute certainty, for after all certainty is at best a matter of probabilities.

TECHNICAL NOTES

1. The σ of statistical constants is used throughout instead of the P. E. There appears no virtue in the further reduction to P. E. since σ tables are now available.

2. In the histograms, showing distribution of groups according to various categories, the mean and σ have been indicated, respectively, by a dot, whose location indicates the position of the mean, and arrows leading from the dot, thus $\longleftarrow \cdot \longrightarrow$. The distance from the dot to the tip of either arrow equals σ. The entire figure illustrated above, therefore, represents 2σ and indicates graphically the range of variation from the mean implied in the expression $\pm\sigma$.

3. The probabilities favoring the sign of an observed difference are twice as great as those favoring inclusion within $\pm\sigma$, due to the fact that only one-half the outlying probabilities are critical for the argument.

4. Testing by Blakeman's criterion was done extensively, but little light came from it. Where inexcusable non-linearity was found by test, the regression was frequently excessively irregular, with no indication of the form of the relation, while a few cases of appreciable non-linear form tested linear.

CHAPTER IV

METHODS OF PSYCHOLOGICAL EXAMINATION

METHOD OF ESTIMATION VERSUS METHOD OF EXAMINATION

IN studying the mental capacity of a given group there are two methods possible: the method of estimation and the method of examination.

The first method figures mainly where the groups studied are very large or so conditioned that individual examinations are not practicable. This is the method used by Goring[1] in his study of 3000 English convicts, by Lombroso and the older penologists, and in most of the "surveys" of large districts.

Its necessity is evident under certain conditions where the groups are too large or the time too short to make individual examining feasible—although the system of group testing employed in the Army has opened a way to the solution of many of these difficulties. There are certain other conditions which render examining impracticable, as for example, where one is dealing with a group over which one has no control, as in the house-to-house canvass method of many of the surveys, or the grading of large industrial groups where the novelty and seeming tendency of the examination method toward paternalism may, for a time yet, force us to have recourse to the older method of mere estimation. But on the whole this method is fast being supplanted by the more exact one.

The method of the intelligence examination is comparatively recent in development but not so recent but that one is surprised to find in so important a work as Goring's no mention made of it. He, in fact, specifically deplores the lack of instruments which would allow one to give to mental measurements the same degree of exactness that the tape and the callipers afford for physical, but does not even suggest that anything is being done toward the realization of such an object. More clearly, perhaps, than any one else, he recognizes the pitfalls of

[1] *Op. cit.*

the method which he is employing and makes every effort to safeguard himself. He says:

"Estimates of mental qualities can be made: and every day the world, colloquially, does make them, with a more or less broad degree of accuracy. Many judgments of the kind, truly, are quite valueless; for, in so many cases, distinctions of mental and moral characters are animated by personal feeling. Yet, because opinions, biassed by feelings of generosity or malice, must be ignored, that is no reason for disregarding the judgments of a just critic on the grounds that mental characters are beyond the range of legitimate observation. Personal estimations of both mental and physical attributes, if carefully made and recorded by an unbiassed and disinterested investigator, whose personal equation can be estimated and allowed for, represent evidence of substantially the same character, and of equal value scientifically, as that produced by measurement. And it is precisely for this reason—because, starting as they did from preconceived theories, we cannot be certain that criminological investigators in the past were not prejudiced, that their observations upon criminals were not warped by the desire to fit fact to theory—it is precisely for this reason, and not because we discredit the human power of estimating broad differences of degree or magnitude without the aid of callipers and tape, that we asserted at the commencement of the present work that criminal anthropology must be built upon measurements, and upon measurements only. Measurements are relatively free from the personal equation of the investigator; they record the actual dimensions of an object, and not its apparent size, as viewed by a biassed observer: and, consequently, the atmosphere of disquieting doubt is absent from generalization or theory based upon measurements. But coming now to mental characters, we do not say that, because non-measurable, these therefore cannot be observed; we do, however, contend that broad generalizations upon the mental characters of the criminal must leave the critical mind cold and unconvinced until they have been based upon facts, more unquestionably accurate, and more concise in statement, than those general impressions of the truth which have been presented in the past by the leading exponents of criminal anthropology."[2]

Turning now to the other method, that of examination, it seems inconsistent at the first glance to insist that the method of estimation is less satisfactory, since we are compelled to admit that the criterion of value for a mental test is in the last analysis its agreement with the judgments of competent observers. It may, therefore, seem illogical to argue for the supplanting of the method of estimation by the establishment of a system of mental examinations, but its justi-

[2] *Op. cit.*, page 237.

fication rests on two facts. First, it enables one to obtain in a brief period information which it would take many times as long to obtain by the other method; and, second, it possesses a quality of uniformity very difficult to obtain by estimates. Even if one could assume the judgment of the observer to be entirely intelligent and free from any emotional bias it would still happen, in all probability, that each observer would tend to make his judgment in terms of the persons with whom he has been in contact. That is, the college professor might judge as "stupid" such of his students as fell markedly below the others in ability, while the manager of a group of unskilled laborers might rank as "bright" individuals who excelled their fellows but who actually fell below the mental level of even the most stupid of the other group. Such a scale as that of Pearson, to be described later, aims to reduce such discrepancies by presenting an absolute scale on which judgments should be made. Adequate evidence has not been offered, however, to show that judgments based even on such a scale are free from the influence of personal bias of one sort or another.

The method of examination, therefore, while it calls for the services of a special examiner and the time necessary to make the examination, and requires as well a certain amount of coöperation from the individuals to be tested, outranks the older method in that it enables a judgment of mentality to be made within a few days which it would take weeks or months to reach by the judgment method, and in that it provides a uniform and impersonal grading extremely difficult and in many instances impossible to obtain in any other way. It thus makes possible comparison of groups of very different mental levels.

FACTORS AFFECTING CHOICE OF TESTS

The selection of a series of psychological tests which will satisfactorily diagnose the mentality of a particular group of individuals is, however, even at the present time, a condition which is still devoutly to be sought. The work that has been done toward establishing norms for one test or another has been carried on mostly on some specific group and is applicable mainly *to* that group. Due to the fact that this problem has been in the past mainly of interest to the schoolmen, we find that the "subjects" for their studies have been largely recruited from the ranks of college students, or grade school children. But with the recognition of the importance of such examinations there is fast piling up an accumulation of data in other fields, less scholastic, which will furnish a more nearly unselected group for comparison.

There are two important aspects of the field of mental testing: first, the diagnosing of the mentality of a developing child and determining his mental ability as proportionate to his physical age, and second, the estimating of the mental capacity of an individual from a particular group with reference to his rank in that group. This latter problem will, of course, remain unfinished until the time when each specific group can itself be compared with figures for the general population, since any individual may be thought of as belonging to an indefinite number of groups of which the most comprehensive is the whole population. As we have earlier stated, ours is a group which may fairly be assumed to be mentally adult so that the first problem is not properly applicable here. The "mental ages," used in expressing the results of the Stanford-Binet, we think of as merely a quantitative expression of the score.

Recognizing that ours is clearly an aberrant group, we have aimed, in so far as possible, to employ only tests which have been previously standardized with more nearly unselected subjects. It is because of their wide application to a relatively heterogeneous population that we have given so much weight to the tests of the Binet type and those of the Woolley series. In view of the eccentricity of our group and our lack of facilities for establishing norms we have ourselves devised no new tests.

ESTABLISHMENT OF METHODS ON BEDFORD GROUP

The data on which our establishment of measures of the mental status of these individuals was mainly based were obtained from a more intensive study on a large group of women committed to the Bedford Reformatory between March, 1915, and August, 1917. This group includes the 102 cases which we have called the "Contemporary Bedford Group" which were studied during the year 1916-1917 and used in comparison with our other prison groups. The number is raised to 343 by the addition of 241 cases which were committed to Bedford between the dates of March, 1915, and September, 1916. They represent a practically consecutive series of commitments between the dates mentioned. (The actual number of commitments during this time was 352.)

Conditions of Testing

The conditions for testing this group were exceptionally good. The women on their arrival at Bedford are taken directly to the Reception

Cottage where they are held in strict quarantine for a minimum of two weeks. During this time each woman is locked in a separate room, and is allowed no communication with the other inmates. This resulted very happily for our work, as it not only cut out the factor of one subject coaching another on the problems she was to be given, but also enabled us to deal with each individual alone, without the background of her position among her fellows. One is tempted to emphasize this point after working with a group where the subjects were taken directly from the general prison population. We have one case in mind which had to be dropped from our series because an initial "grouchiness" was augmented to such a degree by her desire to "save her face" before her mates that it developed into so determined an obstinacy as to make the results of our testing worthless.

The first contact between the Bedford girl and the Laboratory was made by the sociologist who established friendly relations by showing a sympathetic interest in her case and a willingness to do whatever she could to help her to adjust herself to the new conditions. After this, one of the psychologists brought the girl to the Laboratory for a series of testings. These series generally covered a period of five or ten days, depending on whether the longer or shorter series was used.

The physical conditions of testing were excellent. The Laboratory, being located in the country, is spared all the street noises ordinarily unavoidable. We have allowed no visitors to be present during the testing and have never attempted to use the examination as anything like a clinic.

The examiners always aimed to maintain a cordial and friendly attitude. Introducing the "play element" so much recommended in dealing with children is of course quite out of place here. We endeavored particularly to dispel the bugaboo of a "brain test," and of ourselves as "the doctors that send you to the crazy house."

We tried in general to get our subjects into an attitude that was friendly, responsive and eager, without being hampered by self-consciousness or the nervousness which results from an over-anxiety to do well. We benefited indirectly by the quarantine period in that by the time a girl had been alone in her room for a few days she quite enjoyed her visit to the Laboratory and welcomed the labor of working at tests for an hour in preference to the tedium of sitting idle in her room. If the examination was interrupted or any serious error in administering a test occurred the results were dropped from the series.

On the whole we feel satisfied that the showing which these women made on the tests given them represents pretty closely what they are capable of doing under optimal conditions. Attempts to malinger or try to appear stupid or erratic on the tests have not made any serious trouble for us. In the possible two instances where it was tried, it was very clearly an attempt to avoid taking the tests without openly refusing, rather than an overt effort to deceive. There is of course no real incentive to malingering in our problems. We encountered one psychopathic girl who was a "practical joker," to whom we doffed our hats. She impressed upon us the conviction that once a subject's sense of humor is allowed to run rampant, the end of the science of mental testing is in sight.

Standardization of Methods of Giving and of Scoring Tests

In the giving of tests throughout our work we aimed at a close uniformity of method. To this end the instructions for giving each test were written out in detail and committed to memory by each one of the examiners. In this way we endeavored to make certain that the personal equation which enters into every mental examination was reduced to a point where its effects were negligible.

The methods of scoring the results were likewise worked out in most complete detail and reduced to writing. Each examiner marked the results on this basis. During the examination the subject's response was taken down verbatim on blanks specially prepared for each test. This slowed down the progress of the examination somewhat, but we felt that the gain in accuracy obtained thereby justified it, since this enabled a second examiner to check from the actual data the marking of the first. We feel that this method gives results fully as uniform as Terman's method of having all the evaluating done by one person.

Preliminary Intensive Test Series

Recognizing that in selecting a series of tests for final use, it was an easier task to prune down from an over-extensive series than to build up from one too meager, we started our work with a very intensive study of 120 successive commitments. This study covered a period of at least ten days' individual testing—each day's period being an hour in length—and approximately three days of group testing. The limits of the present report force us merely to list here the tests used and reserve any description of them or of the results obtained thereon for later publication.

Wherever it was practicable to do so we attempted to gage the reliability of a test by giving two series of the same test, *e.g.*, two lists of opposites, two forms of canceling unfamiliar figures.

We made it a basic principle that in giving a test we should, as far as possible, make sure that the subject understands what she is expected to do. To this end we made extensive use of examples and sample sheets. It has been contended that this capacity to understand quickly is in itself a part of what is being tested, but such arguments seem to us to cloud the issue, because in that case one would be consistently overweighting this factor by complicating every test with its presence. It is quite true that in some tests, like the Capacity to Follow Directions, a stupid subject often loses track of what he is expected to do and finishes the test, so to speak, *ad lib.*, and that this is in itself an essential part of the test. But we feel that this is an entirely different performance from that of a subject who is entirely at sea from the start and who, in consequence, confuses his record by demanding more instructions, or, becoming discouraged at his inability to understand, gives up the test without a real effort.

To speak first of the tests of the Binet type—we had been quite puzzled at the conflicting figures obtained therewith by various examiners and on closer examination were equally appalled at the variations in the technique of giving and method of scoring them. We were finally driven to the necessity of reducing to tabular form the specific instructions for giving and evaluating these tests, as formulated by the principal exponents of the Binet system in this country. After we had finished this time-consuming task we became convinced that a problem of considerable interest would be a comparison of the same individuals when tested by the original Binet method and by the two chief modifications of this, *viz.*, the Yerkes-Bridges Point Scale and the Stanford-Binet. We accordingly drew up a series of instructions that enabled us to score an individual by each of the three methods without repeating separate tests where these were identical or nearly so. The process will be described in detail in a later paper.

Dr. Weidensall,[3] formerly psychologist at this Laboratory, has made an extensive study of the results of testing 88 Bedford women by the scale devised by Dr. Woolley[4] as compared with the results obtained by Dr. Woolley in her study of the working children of

[3] *Op. cit.*

[4] Woolley, Helen Thompson, and Fischer, Charlotte R., "Mental and Physical Measurements of Working Children." *Psychol. Monog.*, vol. 18, no. 1, 1914.

Cincinnati. We regard Dr. Woolley's norms as the best data available for comparison with our women, and we accordingly duplicated Dr. Weidensall's work, in that we used practically all of the tests reported by Dr. Woolley in her paper of 1914. It had been our intention to make a comparison of our results with those of Dr. Woolley by using the same method of treatment, *i.e.*, the method of percentile groupings, but since one such report has already come out from this Laboratory it seemed wiser to postpone such a study.

We list briefly the tests which were given in our intensive series:

I. *Test Series Used.*[5]

1. Binet-Simon Scale 1911 (both Binet (Town translation) and Goddard forms).
2. Yerkes-Bridges Point Scale.
3. Stanford-Binet Scale.
4. Woolley Series.
   a. Sentence completion.
   b. Association by opposites.
   c. Cancelation of a's.
   d. Memory for digits after the auditory-visual-articulatory method of presentation.
   e. Substitution or symbol digit test.
   f. Strength of grip.
   g. Steadiness of hand.
   h. Rapidity of hand movement.
   i. Card sorting.
   j. Visual and auditory acuity.

Height and weight records were taken from the measurements made by the Reformatory physician. Tests of vital capacity were not made.

II. *Individual Tests Used.*

The remaining tests have been drawn from many sources. Some are standard tests of very wide application and others are quite recent and have been in less general use.

[5] For account of the procedures used in these series see the following references:

Binet, A. and Simon, Th., "A Method of Measuring the Development of the Intelligence of Young Children." Translated by Town, C. H.

Goddard, H. H. "The Binet-Simon Measuring Scale for Intelligence." Revised. *The Training School,* Vol. VIII, No. 4, June, 1911.

Goddard, H. H. "Standard Method for Giving the Binet Test." *Training School,* Vol. X, No. 2, 1913.

Yerkes, R. M., Bridges, J. W., and Hardwick, R. "A Point Scale for Measuring Mental Ability." 1915.

Terman, L. M. "The Measurement of Intelligence." 1916.

Woolley, H. T. and Fischer, C. R. *Op. cit.*

1. Memory for digits after the visual method of presentation.

2. Memory for digits after the auditory method of presentation. Same type of number series used for 1 and 2 as for auditory-visual-articulatory presentation (Woolley series).

3. Memory for ideas of a logical passage visually presented (Healy).[6]

4. Memory for ideas of a logical passage auditorily presented (Healy).[6]

5. Memory for objects in a series (Ellis—unpublished data).

6. Knox cubes. Memory for movement in a serial order. Both the original Knox series and the series devised by Pintner were used.[7]

7. "Aussage" tests—suggestibility and fidelity of report. Two pictures used—"The Disputed Case" and "The Doctor."[8]

8. Free association test. Kent-Rosanoff list.[9]

9. Controlled association—action-agent. Two lists taken from Woodworth and Wells.[10]

10. Controlled association—mixed relations. Two lists taken from Woodworth and Wells.[10]

11. Cancelation of single digits.[10]

12. Cancelation of number groups containing a specified pair of digits.[10]

13. Cancelation of words containing a specified pair of letters.[11]

14. Cancelation of unfamiliar figures. Two sets designed by Franz.[12]

15. Trabue completion test. Both the preliminary set of 56 sentences and the later Language Scale A were used.[13]

16. Pictorial completion (Healy).[14]

17. Construction puzzles A and B (Healy and Fernald).[15]

18. Ellis Island construction puzzles: Knox's "Moron" and "Diamond Frame," and Kempf's "Diagonal."[16]

[6] Healy, W. and Fernald, G. M. "Tests for Practical Mental Classification," *Psychol. Monog.*, 1911, vol. 13 (no. 54), pp. 34-40.

[7] Knox, H. A. "A Scale Based on the Work at Ellis Island for Estimating Mental Defect." *J. of the Amer. Med. Assoc.*, vol. 62, 1914, p. 742. Pintner, R. and Paterson, D. G. "A Scale of Performance Tests," 1917, pp. 67-69.

[8] Whipple, G. M. "Manual of Mental and Physical Tests," 1915, Part II, pp. 17-42.

[9] Kent, G. H. and Rosanoff, A. J. "A Study of Association in Insanity." *Amer. J. of Insanity,* 1910, vol. 47, pp. 37-96, 317-390.

[10] Woodworth, R. S. and Wells, F. L. "Association Tests." *Psychol. Monog.*, vol. 13, whole no. 57, 1911, pp. 24-29, 32-41, 62-67.

[11] Norsworthy, N. "The Psychology of the Mentally Deficient."

[12] Franz, S. I. "Mental Examination Methods," 1912, pp. 130-132.

[13] Trabue, M. R. "Completion-Test Language Scales." *Teachers College, Columbia University, Contributions to Education,* no. 77. 1916

[14] Healy, W. "A Pictorial Completion Test." *Psychol. Rev.*, vol. 21, 1914, pp. 189-203.

Pintner, R. and Anderson, M. M. "The Picture Completion Test." *Educ. Psychol. Monog.* No. 20.

[15] *Op. cit.*, pp. 14-17.

[16] *Op. cit.*, pp. 743-4.

19. Sequin form-board by the tactual method.[17]
20. Mirror drawing test.[18]
21. Hard and easy directions test. (Woodworth and Wells.)[19]
22. Woolley ingenuity test.[20]
23. Test of mechanical construction. (Stenquist.)[21]
24. Test of selective judgment. (Bonser.)[22]
25. Steadiness of movement.[23]
26. Bogardus factory test.[24]

III. *Educational Tests.*

A series of educational tests were given with a view to determining the extent of formal education the subject had received and retained. These were given by Mary A. Clark of the Laboratory staff. The women came to the Laboratory after the period of quarantine was over and were tested in groups of from three to eight, the aim being to avoid having women of very varying ability in the same group. The tests extended generally over a period of four days. The tests given were as follows:

1. Arithmetic.

   Courtis Test Series A, forms 1 and 3, and Series B, form 1.[25]

2. Spelling.

   A combination made by Thorndike of some of the words standardized by Buckingham.[26]

[17] See Goddard, H. H. "The Form Board as a Measure of Intellectual Development in Children." *Training School,* 1912, vol. 9, pp. 49-52.
——Sylvester, R. H. "The Form Board Test." *Psychol. Monog.,* vol. 15, no. 65, 1913.

[18] Whipple, *op. cit.,* Part II, pp. 119-133.

[19] *Op. cit.,* pp. 68-72.

[20] Thompson, H. B. "Psychological Norms in Men and Women," 1903, pp. 110-113.

[21] Stenquist, J. L., Thorndike, E. L., and Trabue, M. R. "The Intellectual Status of Children Who Are Public Charges." *Arch. of Psychol.,* 1915, vol. 5, no. 33, pp. 1-9.

[22] Bonser, F. G. "The Reasoning Ability of Children of the Fourth, Fifth and Sixth School Grades." *Teachers College, Columbia University, Contributions to Education,* no. 37, 1910, pp. 5-6.

[23] Whipple, G. M. "Manual of Mental and Physical Tests," 1914, Part I, pp. 151-155.

[24] Bogardus, E. S. "The Relation of Fatigue to Industrial Accidents," *Amer. J. of Sociol.,* 1911-12, vol. 17, pp. 1-69.

[25] Courtis, S. A. "Manual of Instruction for Giving and Scoring the Courtis Standard tests."

[26] Buckingham, B. R. "Spelling Ability, Its Measurement and Distribution." *Teachers College, Columbia University, Contributions to Education,* No. 59. 1913.

3. Handwriting.

   A passage to be scored by both the Ayres and the Thorndike Scales.[27]

   A test of accurate copying.

   An original letter.

4. Reading.

   Thorndike's Scale A and early form of Scale Alpha.[28]

5. History.

   A list of questions compiled by Van Wagenen and not yet published.

6. Geography.

   A selection from a series of questions being standardized by the Boston Public Schools.

7. General information.

   A brief set of questions on general information, compiled by us.

8. Practical knowledge.

   Tests of ability to tell time, name money and make change, use of tape measure, etc.

SELECTION OF TESTS FOR PRESENT INVESTIGATION

In August of 1916 it was decided to undertake the study of other penal groups. For this, so extended a series of tests was impossible. After careful study we accordingly reduced our series to those included in the following sections. Our criteria for this reduction were four:

1. Some tests we had found of more intrinsic value than others. Our criteria of value will be discussed later.
2. Some tests were retained because they furnish a basis for comparison with the work of others.
3. Some tests were discarded because they were too cumbersome to be easily applied outside of a laboratory.
4. Some tests were omitted to avoid duplication.

The conditions of testing in the other institutions were less ideal than in our earlier work, but, for the most part, reasonably satisfactory. The testing of the Probation Group was done in part at the Florence

[27] Ayres, L. P. "A Scale for Measuring the Quality of Handwriting of School Children." *Russell Sage Foundation*, 1912.

Thorndike, E. L. "Handwriting." *Teachers College Record*, 1910, vol. 11, No. 2.

[28] Thorndike, E. L. "Reading Scale and Visual Vocabulary Scale A," and also the "Administration Scale A for Visual Vocabulary." *Teachers College Record*, September, 1914.

Crittenton Home where the women were sometimes held pending a decision on their cases. In other instances they came to the city office of the Laboratory.

The factor which caused the most trouble at the institutions other than Bedford was the necessity of making the tests after the women had already become an integral part of the prison population. The business of testing was something then which was suddenly introduced into their program, and was not an already established custom to which they were expected to conform. Taking as we did the commitments for the current year only, it left a goodly remainder of old inhabitants who never had been called upon to be tested, and these often formed a background of scoffers against which it was hard to contend. On the whole, however, we fared very well in this matter of recalcitration. One girl at the Magdalen Home refused to coöperate. Three of the older and more intelligent women at Auburn argued cannily that the less there was on record about them the better for them, and several cases of old rounders at the Workhouse declined to put up with such "new-fangled notions."

The matter of one inmate being coached by another was not so serious a matter as we feared it might be. The really intelligent women who might be the most effective teachers could generally be made to see our point of view on the matter of communication, and where the less intelligent attempted instruction it was often a case of the blind leading the blind. There were instances where we felt that the subjects had been tutored, but they were quite as likely to have misunderstood their instructions as to have profited by them, so that the total results were not materially affected. The testing covered generally a period of six days, of about an hour a day.

As in our earlier series, the instructions after being carefully worked over were reduced to writing and committed to memory. The methods of scoring were worked out in detail and each examiner was provided with a copy and marked the tests in accordance therewith. Where ambiguous answers occurred these were discussed in conference and marked on the basis of a joint decision. In every case the tests after being marked were checked by another examiner to catch up any errors.

Yerkes-Bridges Point Scale and Stanford-Binet Scale

Both the Yerkes-Bridges Point Scale and the Stanford-Binet were included, in spite of their similarity, because of the basis of comparison which these series afford with the work done by other investigators. Our methods for giving the two were changed from the original methods of the authors in question at the following points, all of which are minor ones, made to enable us to score the test for both series without being forced to repeat ourselves.

In fourteen of the tests on the Point Scale there is duplication which involves seventeen of the tests on the Stanford-Binet. In two of these, *viz.*, the defining of abstract words, and detecting absurdities, the two methods overlap in part and it is only necessary to ask the additional questions in order to score the test for both. In seven tests the variation in the method of giving seemed to us so slight as to be immaterial. These tests are comprehension of questions (easy and difficult), the comparison of two objects from memory, æsthetic comparison, comparison of two lines, sixty words, and the arranging of weights. In the tests of copying a square, and copying a diamond, the change in difficulty from drawing with a pencil (Yerkes-Bridges) to drawing with a pen as required in the Stanford-Binet seemed so great that, where either of these was included for the latter, we repeated the test, using pen and ink, and scored it on that showing.

In five tests, *viz.*, the comparison of two weights, omissions in pictures, counting backward, definition by use, and dissected sentences, we used the Yerkes-Bridges form. In drawing the design from memory we penalized the Yerkes-Bridges Scale somewhat in that we followed the Stanford directions of giving only 10″ exposure instead of 15″ as instructed by Yerkes.

Tests of the Woolley Series

We aimed to use as many as possible of the tests of the Woolley series because of its extensive use on non-delinquent groups otherwise comparable with ours. The tests of steadiness and rapidity of movement, involving as they do even a small amount of mechanical apparatus, we discarded as impractical, because it was necessary under the conditions of working away from the Laboratory to put all material out of the way after each day's testing and the labor involved in constantly re-setting was too time-consuming.

Throughout the giving of these tests we have used the material specified by Dr. Woolley[29] and followed carefully the instructions devised by her. We feel, therefore, that our findings are comparable with hers. The tests selected are as follows:

[29] *Op. cit.*

1. Sentence completion test. (Series beginning "If some child".)

Here the subject is required to complete the beginnings of thirteen sentences. These are exposed one at a time to the subject who writes an ending to each sentence. The test is scored on total time, individual reaction time, and the number of ideas expressed. Our instructions for giving are practically the same as those given by Dr. Woolley, and our method of scoring follows the same lines as hers but has been made a little more specific.

2. Association by opposites. (List 6, beginning "Inside".)

The responses are written by the subject and the test is scored both for accuracy and for total time of the performance.

3. Cancelation of a's. (Form beginning "hplg".)

Our directions for giving and evaluating are but little modified from Dr. Woolley's.

4. Memory for digits, by the visual-auditory-articulatory method.

The numbers, printed in heavy type, are read aloud by the subject and examiner together. Dr. Woolley used two series each of 7, 8, and 9 place numbers. We have added pairs of 10, 11, 12 and 6, 5, 4, and 3 place numbers where it was necessary to go in either direction in order to ascertain the memory span. We have used her method in giving and scoring this test.

5. Substitution or symbol digit test.

A series of nine geometrical figures are to be associated respectively with the nine digits. After the association has been established by means of three practice pages it is reproduced from memory on a fourth page. Time and accuracy are both scored here. Our directions for giving are practically identical with those of Dr. Woolley.

6. Card sorting test.

The Jastrow card sorting box with the colored cards described by Dr. Woolley was used. Our instructions for giving were essentially similar to hers but we varied her procedure in that we gave three trials. We found the best time of the three to be the most satisfactory measure.

Additional Tests

1. Action-agent association.

The list we used is selected from the two lists used in our earlier series. One of these was taken directly from the Woodworth and Wells monograph and the other we compiled ourselves. We print below the selected list:

1. gallops	11. scratches
2. bites	12. flies
3. cuts	13. ticks
4. rings	14. creeps
5. explodes	15. blows
6. stings	16. evaporates
7. crows	17. rolls
8. aches	18. burns
9. growls	19. pricks
10. cries	20. roars

The responses were given orally and the reaction time of each taken with a stop watch. The degree of accuracy was credited in whole and half credits.

2. Mixed relations association.

Here again we made a selection of twenty words from two lists used in our earlier work. Both of these are given by Woodworth and Wells in the paper just cited. We print below the composite form used:

1. Eye—see	Ear—
2. Monday—Tuesday	April—
3. Do—did	See—
4. Bird—sings	Dog—
5. Straw—hat	Leather—
6. Hammer—tool	Dictionary—
7. Dog—puppy	Cat—
8. House—room	Book—
9. Sky—blue	Grass—
10. Swim—water	Fly—
11. Once—one	Twice—
12. Cat—fur	Bird—
13. Pan—tin	Table—
14. Good—bad	Long—
15. Fruit—orange	Vegetable—
16. Sit—chair	Sleep—
17. Pen—write	Knife—
18. Nose—face	Toe—
19. Hungry—food	Thirsty—
20. Man—woman	Boy—

Our instructions for giving were but slightly modified from the directions of these authors. The accuracy here also was credited in whole and half credits.

3. Cancelation of unfamiliar figures.

One of the sets of unfamiliar figures described by Franz was used. This consists of eight uncommon but generally similar figures, each repeated twenty-five times in haphazard arrangement. We are indebted to Dr. Franz for the use of his plates. Time and accuracy were both recorded.

4. Directions test.

We used the form of hard directions devised by Woodworth and

Wells and their form of easy directions which begins: "Cross out the smallest dot." Time was recorded and the accuracy marked on a score of twenty credits.

5. Knox's cubes.

Our material is comparable with Pintner's rather than with Knox's, in that the blocks were uniform in color instead of being varied, and the series devised by Pintner and Anderson was used. The measure used in this study is the number of lines reproduced without error.

6. Rossolimo dissected pictures.[30]

This test is taken directly from Rossolimo's profile method and represents one of the tests of what he designates "capacity to combine." It consists of ten pictures, five in colors of familiar objects, and five of conventional designs in black on a white ground. They increase progressively in difficulty, depending, Rossolimo says, "on the increasing complexity of the pictures and the increasing complexity of the dissection." The pictures in order of increasing difficulty are presented one at a time with the direction: "See if you can put these pieces together to make a picture." The time for a successful completion is recorded. The time limit for each is three minutes.

7. Pictorial completion. (Healy.)

The blocks were always presented in a haphazard but definitely specified order. Our directions are varied from those given by Healy and by Pintner and Anderson chiefly by the addition of this definite arrangement of blocks. We have used the system of evaluation devised by Pintner and Anderson.

8. Trabue completion test. Scale A.

This test was given and scored in accordance with Trabue's directions.

9. Woody arithmetic test.

Form B of the Woody series[31] and all of the four fundamental operations were given. They were scored according to Woody's directions.

10. Courtis arithmetic test.

Form B of the Courtis Series was used. It was given and scored in exact accordance with Courtis' instructions. Since it had appeared

[30] Rossolimo, G. "Die Psychologische Profile zur Methodik der quantitativen Untersuchung der psychische Vorgänge in normale und pathologische Fällen." *Klinik d. psych. u. nerv. Krankh.*, 1911, vol. 6. We are indebted to Dr. Whipple for the loan of his materials, from which we had copies made.

[31] Woody, C. "Measurement of Some Achievements in Arithmetic." *Teachers College, Columbia University, Contributions to Education,* No. 80, 1916.

from our earlier use of the scale that the addition and the division tests were a fair index of one's capacity in all four processes, only these two were used in the present investigation.

11. Reading.

We used Thorndike's two reading scales, A and Alpha, employing his directions for giving and scoring.

12. Spelling.

For this test a list of sentences suggested by Dr. Thorndike was used. They contain twenty-seven of the words standardized by Buckingham for children ranging from third to super-eighth grade. Each word misspelled, omitted or illegible was counted as an error.

Tests 8, 9, 10, 11 and 12 were given as group tests when practicable, the number in the group varying from two to ten.

13. Handwriting.

This was meant to test both the speed and the quality of writing. It was possible to grade the copy by both the Thorndike and the Ayres scales. The speed was measured in terms of the number of letters per minute. The subject was instructed to write repeatedly the words *one, two, three,* up to *ten* over a period of one minute about as fast as he ordinarily wrote in writing a letter. He was first allowed to practise on a sample sheet to make sure he understood what was expected of him.

14. Practical information.

A series of tests of practical information was devised which consists of the following simple operations: naming money; making change, telling time; counting the value of stamps; repeating days of the week and months of the year; and measuring feet and inches with a tape measure.

USE OF PEARSON SCALE FOR JUDGING MENTAL ABILITY AS CRITERION OF RELIABILITY OF TESTS USED

As a criterion for measuring the reliability of a test we have made use of the judgment scale devised by Pearson.[32] His method of obtaining this scale may be briefly described as follows: He assumed the hypothesis that grades of intelligence for the general population distribute their frequencies in the form of the normal probability curve. He constructed a descriptive scale of intellectual levels, on the basis of which he secured judgments from the instructors of approximately

[32] Pearson, Karl. "On the Relationship of Intelligence to Size and Shape of Head, and to Other Physical and Mental Characters." *Biometrika,* vol. 5, p. 105.

1000 Cambridge students and 5000 unselected English school children. By this means he obtained the frequencies for each class and so determined the numerical equivalents for each interval on the scale. He was thus able to assign quantitative values to different intellectual classes obtained by judgmental methods, which made possible quantitative comparisons with other measurable factors. The form of the scale as we used it is as follows:

Class M. Especially able. A mind especially bright and quick, both in perception and in reasoning, not only about customary but about novel facts; able and accustomed to reason rightly about things on purely self-initiative.

Class N. Capable. A mind less likely than M to originate inquiry, but quick in perception and reasoning about the perceived.

Class O. Fair intelligence. A mind ready to grasp and capable of perceiving facts in most fields; capable of good reasoning with moderate effort. This group comprises, say, one-third of the population at large.

Class P. Slow intelligence. A mind slow generally, although possibly more rapid in certain fields, but quite sure of knowledge once acquired.

Class Q. Slow. A mind advancing in general but very slowly; with time and considerable effort not incapable of progress. Very slow in thought generally, but with time understanding is reached.

Class R. Slow, dull. A mind capable of perceiving relationships between facts in some few fields with long and continuous effort but not generally or without external assistance.

Class S. Very dull. A mind capable of holding only the simplest facts and incapable of reasoning or grasping the relationship between facts.

Class X. Judge a girl to be in Class X if you are not familiar enough with her ability to justify an estimation of her intelligence.

Class Y. Judge a girl to be in Class Y if you feel that you are prejudiced in favor of or against the girl, and are for that reason incapable of judging her mental ability fairly.

We ourselves added Classes X and Y to the scale, not because we intend to make statistical use of them but because we felt they would relieve the judges from being forced into making a judgment where they felt incapable of doing so. We have also adopted Ruml's[33] device of allowing the judges to add a plus or a minus sign to their decision, indicating that they consider a subject to belong in a given class but inclining toward a higher or lower interval.

[33] Ruml, Beardsley. "The Reliability of Mental Tests in the Division of an Academic Group." *Psychol. Monog.* vol. 24, no. 4, 1917.

The numerical equivalents, which Pearson calls "mentaces," for each class are given below:

M+	471 mentaces	O	322 mentaces	Q—	177 mentaces
M	451 "	O—	302 "	R+	157 "
M—	416 "	P+	282 "	R	130 "
N+	391 "	P	262 "	R—	116 "
N	371 "	P—	242 "	S+	96 "
N—	353 "	Q+	220 "	S	62 "
O+	337 "	Q	192 "		

We wish now to say something of the qualifications of the persons who made these judgments for us and to express our grateful appreciation of their service. Our method has been to use only those cases where we have been able to secure judgments from three observers. We have then taken the numerical equivalents of these and used their average as a measure to correlate with each test or series of tests.

At Bedford, which has served as the basis for most of this part of our work, the judgments were made by persons who had unusually good opportunity to size up the individuals under consideration. Miss Ida Murphy was superintendent of the school and had direction also of the assigning of the women to the various forms of employment in the institution. In this way she came to study very carefully the ability of each. Mrs. Louise Engle, the matron of the Reception Cottage where the women remained for a period of at least two months after their arrival, was in direct contact with them during this period and thus had ample opportunity to form an adequate opinion. Miss Dawley, the sociologist of the Laboratory, was the third of the main observers and she from her intensive study of each woman had occasion constantly to make such judgments. In the great majority of cases it is the average of these three judgments that we have used. To supplement these for certain groups we secured judgments from Miss Eleanor Miller, who had direction of all the agricultural work and supervision of the "Farm Group," from Miss Winspere and Miss Decker, two of the teachers in the institution, and from Mrs. Hoffman, who was in charge of the work in the laundry.

Our confidence in the reliability of this group of judges is such that we do not feel that the value of their estimates is seriously affected by the fact that they had some knowledge of the test results. That they should have this knowledge was unavoidable since each commitment was discussed at a staff meeting within a month or so of her arrival. It was impossible to secure judgments upon her prior to this discussion since she was not yet known by most of the persons mentioned above.

The influence of this previous knowledge was lessened by the fact that several months had elapsed between the staff meeting and the time that judgment was made, and that results of the tests were not actually before the judges as they made their estimates.

At Auburn the judgments were made by Dr. Frank Heacox, the prison physician; by Mrs. Margaret E. Daly, the superintendent of the women's prison; by her assistant, Miss Curtis; and by Mrs. Helen P. Stone, the school-teacher of the women. Except in occasional instances they had no knowledge of the outcome of the tests. We regret that the smallness of the group prevented our making any extended use of these figures.

At the Magdalen Home we were so fortunate as to obtain judgments from Miss Janet Macconachie, the superintendent; from Mrs. Mary E. Paddon, the executive secretary; from Mrs. Nellie R. Crane, the school-teacher; and from the field worker, Miss Esther Cook. Like the Auburn judgments, these were made without knowledge of the test results, but were less serviceable than the Bedford data because of the smallness of the group on which we were actually able to secure three judgments.

On the other groups we have been unable to obtain enough reliable judgments to make a satisfactory average. In the Workhouse, many cases are not even known by sight except by the matron having direct charge of them. Combining of results from the three institutions to obtain larger numbers proved not to be feasible since there was an evident tendency to use different standards of reference in the different institutions. In other words, the factor discussed on page 38 as limiting the application of the method of estimates from one group to another appeared here as a limitation on our comparisons.

SELECTION OF TESTS FOR SPECIAL CONSIDERATION IN PRESENT STUDY

With this scale as a criterion, we have selected from our data for use in the present study a group of tests which, taken singly, give a reasonably high correlation, as determined for the Bedford group, and which, thrown into combination, give a still higher correlation. This scheme is admittedly less satisfactory than the method of eliminating tests by multiple correlation, but in view of the small number of cases on which we were able to secure three reliable judgments we have felt that we have refined our method as far as our data warranted. We cannot say with certainty that, of the tests which we have given, we have selected that combination which would give the highest possible correlation with our criterion, but we *can* say that by this method we have been able to select a group of tests which give a correlation with the judgments of competent observers sufficiently high to make it certain that they furnish a reliable measure of intellectual capacity.

It is not possible within the limits of this book to describe in detail the results of the correlation of all of our individual tests with the judgmental scale. We hope at an early date to publish these data in one of the psychological periodicals, but for the present can only state the principle on which the tests were chosen and from there on restrict our discussion to these tests. We should state, however, that we have no intention of implying that the tests not included were found unsatisfactory. Their range of efficiency as measured by the judgment scale runs from zero to sixty odd. Some of them would thus seem to be quite useless as measures of intelligence and others might prove to be as useful as those we have chosen or even more so.

Considering first the correlations between the judgment scale and the two measures of the Binet type—the Yerkes-Bridges Point Scale and the Stanford Revision—we find the coefficients to be, in the case of the Bedford group, $.78 \pm .042$ and $.81 \pm .037$ respectively—figures sufficiently large to make our data another proof that these series furnish reliable measures of intellectual capacity.

From our data we next assembled the four individual tests from the psychological series whose correlation with the judgment scale was highest and combined these into a group to serve as another measure of intellectual capacity. These are: (1) accuracy of response in the opposites test, (2) accuracy of response in the mixed relations test, (3) the vocabulary score (Stanford-Binet), and (4) the score on Trabue's completion test. The coefficients of correlation of these with the judgment scale, for the Bedford group, are respectively:

	Opp. Acc.	Mixed Rel. Acc.	Vocab. Score	Trabue Com. Score
Judgments	.65	.69	.71	.69

The scores on these tests were combined by the method, suggested by Woodworth, of expressing each individual score as a deviation from the mean of the group as a whole and in terms of the standard deviation as a unit. $\left(\frac{d}{\sigma}\right)$ In this way one is able to combine measures regardless of whether they are expressed in terms of time, errors or any other form of measurement which may have been employed. We added these individual standings, $\left(\frac{d}{\sigma}\right)$, unweighted, and thus obtained a standing on the group of tests. The series of these combined standings gives a correlation of .81 with the judgment scale. We have accordingly regarded this group of tests also as a reliable measure of intellectual capacity.

In this combination we have consciously selected a group of tests where the language factor is especially starred, designating the series as the language group. Our justification for such a selection lies in their high correlation with the judgment scale. If, as seems not improbable, an individual's capacity to handle language is one of the important determinants of the judgment which is made on his intellectual capacity, then there would seem to be no impropriety in using such tests as a measure.

In an effort to counteract this emphasis on the language factor, we endeavored to evolve a series of performance tests, recognizing the importance of such tests where one is dealing with those whose knowledge of English is limited or whose emotional characteristics are such as to hamper them in an effort to express themselves verbally under conditions of examination. With a view to compiling such a series we picked from our data four tests where the factor of language is emphasized as little as possible and whose correlations with judgments are among the highest of such non-language tests. These are: (1) card sorting (Woolley), (2) memory for digits (Woolley, A. V. A. method), (3) Knox cubes, (4) cancellation of unfamiliar figures (Franz). Specifically, we used as a measure for the card sorting the time of the best of three trials; for the memory for digits the sum of the averages of the pairs of seven, eight and nine place numbers; for the Knox cubes the number of lines of the Pintner series correctly repeated; and for the cancellation of unfamiliar figures we used one-half of the sum of the standings of time and errors; that is to say, we obtained standings for time and for errors, added them, and, to avoid weighting this test too heavily in relation to the others, divided the sum by two.

We thus have four tests represented unweighted, although one of these is made up of two measures. We combined these four tests in the same way in which we combined the language group—by a simple sum of their standings.

The coefficients of correlation of each individual test with the judgment scale are respectively:

	Card sorting	AVA digits	Knox cubes	Cancel. time	Cancel. score
Judgments	.67	.61	.54	.40	.32

By combining them into a group the correlation was found to be .77 ± .053, a coefficient sufficiently large to indicate that we have here also a useful measure of intellectual capacity.

We have, now, four series which would seem to be reliable measures of intellectual ability in that they show high correlation with intelligence as estimated in terms of the Pearson scale by the judgments of three competent observers—the coefficients ranging from .77 to .81, with standard deviations in no case large enough to cast doubt on their significance. We figure below the table of inter-correlations of these four with each other and with the judgments.

INTER-CORRELATION OF TESTS

	Yerkes Points	Stanford-Binet	Language Tests	Performance Tests	Judgments
Yerkes Points	—	.87	.88	.63	.78
Stanford-Binet ...		—	.89	.66	.81
Language Tests ..			—	.68	.81
Performance Tests				—	.77
Judgments					—

As measures of mentality available for purposes of comparison with the work done by others, we have used chiefly the figures on the results obtained by the Yerkes and the Stanford scales. For purposes of inter-comparison on our own data, we combined the results on the several series just described into a single measure which we called "Test Aggregate." We obtained this by taking the average of all four standings, where all of the series were given, and of three where only three were available. For this we have used no records where the subject had not taken at least three of the test groups. This measure was correlated with the judgment scale and found to give a coefficient of .86. The inter-correlations of this measure with the others which are integral parts of the combination are as follows:

	Yerkes Point	Stanford-Binet	Language Group	Performance Group
Test Aggregate ..	.93	.94	.95	.82

This, then, is the measure which we shall figure for the most part as our means of comparison of one group of our subjects with another, whether the grouping be by institutions, by color, by crime committed or any other mode of separation. This series which we have called Test Aggregate, can, of course, only be used fairly with subjects who can understand spoken English. In order to call a case "English-speaking" in this work, we have arbitrarily ruled to limit the term to those born in this or any other English-speaking country or who have had at least two years' schooling in this country. This ruling we felt, from our personal knowledge of the subjects, served effectively to eliminate all those with serious language difficulty.[34] English-speaking illiterates were not eliminated. Only one of the four groups of test is appreciably affected by inability to read and write. An illiterate could therefore make his Test Aggregate score on the other three scales.

For those comparisons where we have sought to include the non-English-speaking women as well, we have used the records of our group of performance tests as a measure of mental capacity. The great majority of our comparisons have, however, been made with Test Aggregate, which means that we have been forced to omit from such comparisons the non-English-speaking women. We recognized that this limits the completeness of our comparisons, but purposely chose this horn of the dilemma since Test Aggregate appears to give a more satisfactory measure of intelligence than does our Performance Group. We should be penalizing the whole in our efforts to include a few, if we had carried through our comparisons on the basis of the Performance Group.

[34] In order to determine whether we had lowered the standing of our group by including, even where language tests were used, some individuals for whom English was an acquired tongue, we compared the total which we have called "English-speaking" with a group selected on a much more conservative basis, *namely,* individuals who were born in English-speaking countries themselves, as were both of their parents. There was no appreciable difference between the two groups as measured by Test Aggregate, but strangely enough, what shade of advantage there was was in favor of the former.

CHAPTER V

METHODS OF SOCIAL INVESTIGATION

IN discussing the method of social investigation of the six groups of delinquent women with which we are dealing, it is important at the outset to bear in mind that these women have committed offenses against the law and that with the exception of one group they were confined in institutions for varying lengths of time. Three hundred and twenty-eight women or 54.6 per cent of the 587 cases studied have had at least one previous conviction. Many of the women, especially the sex offenders, have been violators of the law many times when they were not arrested. This means that the majority of them have important episodes in their lives which it is to their advantage not to talk about to an investigator. The effort to keep back information concerning a previous delinquency often tends to make a suspicious woman untruthful about other events in her life which, however, may have no bearing on the thing she is trying to conceal.

Our case studies, therefore, differ to quite an extent in the method of approach and investigation from the case histories which most social organizations are able to make. Miss Mary Richmond's book on "Social Diagnosis," which is most comprehensive in outlining a plan for case workers, presupposes that "case work . . . has for its immediate aim the betterment of individuals or families, one by one, as distinguished from their betterment in the mass." [1] The initiative is taken, in many of these cases, by the individual or family who needs help. The women in this study, on the contrary, were questioned entirely without request on their part, and with the exception of the probation group, they could hope to gain very little by talking freely and frankly. To establish a friendly relationship and make it agreeable for these women to give the information necessary to conduct an investigation was one of our most difficult and time-consuming problems.

[1] Richmond, Mary E. "Social Diagnosis." Russell Sage Foundation, New York, 1917, page 25.

GENERAL PLAN OF STUDY

In general, the form of social investigation used was intensive, with an attempt to understand the individual thoroughly, not only through obtaining her own reactions, but by complete investigation of all outside sources which could help in making such an understanding possible. A study of our results and comparison of the woman's story alone with the full investigation would indicate that the facts are obscured by using either plan exclusively, and that the intensive method is essential in gaining a true insight into the individual and the factors related to her delinquency. This work differs, therefore, from most extensive studies of delinquency in that the subject's statement has been corrected and added to by as thorough an investigation as was possible.

The main trend of our sociological study was to obtain from each woman delinquent studied an oral statement giving the details of her personal history and her background, such as heredity and early environmental influences. From her initial statement a first-hand study of these factors was made, by visits to and correspondence with the various individuals or organizations which had come into contact with her at any time. In all of the groups information given by the subject was recorded separately from the verified data about her, in order that the two kinds of material might be used for comparison and to determine whether there was any consistent tendency on the part of the women studied to misrepresent or fail to give information concerning any important factors in their lives.

To accomplish this work there were six trained investigators, with occasional help from one other person. The general plan was followed of having the same worker take the bulk of the cases in one group. Such a plan is time saving and also is necessary in making the worker known among the inmates of an institution, and in having the investigation appear to be more nearly a routine of the institution. In each group, however, a number of the cases were worked on by individuals other than the one who was doing the main part of the work in that place. This was necessary at times when the work with one group would become particularly heavy. Such an arrangement was also felt to be of benefit in determining, by a liberal sampling of cases investigated by other workers, whether there was any personal bias entering into the work of the one who was mainly interested in any one institution.

In order to eliminate the personal equation as much as possible and have the work on all of the groups comparable, a uniform set of record blanks and the same general scheme of recording material was used by each worker. A particular effort was made to keep distinct and separate information obtained concerning the subject, and the worker's impression of the informant. Both of these are necessary information, but if carefully recorded as separate items, may be used in a much more uniform scheme by one or two persons, who may weigh the reliability of the information for all groups alike.

THE INITIAL INTERVIEW

Probably the most important part of any such investigation as this is the initial interview with the subject. There are two main reasons for the need of obtaining accurate information at this interview. The first and most important perhaps, because it applies to a larger number of cases is, that by obtaining reliable information to start with, the work of the investigator will be considerably lessened, and the final investigation will be more satisfactory. If a wrong address is given, or if a woman says that her parents are living in a city miles away, when they are, as a matter of fact, nearby, much of the worker's time is consumed in trying to trace them, and there is always a chance that they cannot be found. This involves either questioning the subject again, or losing much valuable information from outside sources. A second reason of importance for getting a true initial story is that this information may be all that can be obtained. There are cases where no investigation is possible, and where the subject's statement must be taken as the best information available. This is true of many foreign-born women whose families are not in this country, or of native-born who have no close friends. There is also much information which can be obtained in no other way than through the subject. This includes such subjective material as the attitude of the subject toward persons and environmental influences, her reasons for doing certain things, and the resulting reactions. Usually, no amount of investigation can discover these intimate personal facts which are often important elements in the delinquency, and so it is very necessary that these be obtained from the interviews with the women involved.

The possibility of obtaining reliable information from a woman when she is in prison and the investigator is a stranger to her is dependent largely upon the worker's ability to establish a personal relationship, and to win the subject's confidence. In some cases it was necessary to promise not to investigate certain things which the woman was willing to talk about because she trusted the worker's word. In such cases there was undoubtedly more value in getting the story directly from the woman, but with no investigation, than in failing to win her confidence sufficiently to get her story, and running the chance of getting part of the information from another source.

Needless to say, it is difficult to create a personal relationship in a brief interview under unfavorable surroundings. Wherever it was possible, therefore, particularly among the women in the Magdalen Home, the New York County Penitentiary, Auburn State Prison and the Reformatory at Bedford, the women were seen several times. If she was in an antagonistic mood the first day, usually no effort was made to continue the questioning at that time, but on another day she was approached again. With the more intelligent and older women, it was often necessary to explain the purpose of the questioning, and to say that an investigation was being made for research purposes, but that in each case the welfare and interest of the individual concerned were considered first.

Though it is preferable to have a complete statement from the woman before starting the investigation, this was not always possible, especially in the Probation and Workhouse groups. In the Probation group, where often the girl was seen for only a few minutes in the court room on the night of her conviction, and the investigation had to be made before the next night when she was to be sentenced, it was difficult to get from her more than a few important addresses and references. In such cases the fuller "Statement of Girl" had to come after the first investigation. The Workhouse group of women presented difficulties of a different nature. They are such a large, heterogeneous group, composed of women sentenced from one day to two years, that it is impossible for one or two workers to make any impression on them in a short time. The women who were there on a short term or who were about to be freed from the institution were particularly difficult to obtain satisfactory information from, because there was no incentive for them to tell about their past histories. If they expected to go back to their old life upon release, they did not want any worker to be able to trace them, and if they expected to go to work they did not care to have the employer know about their record, as he might if there was a chance of the worker's coming to visit. There are also a goodly number of older women among them, many of whom could not remember details of their early life. Typical among them is the old lady, who, when questioned about some detail of her childhood, replied—"God knows, dearie, I don't." Because of the inherent difficulties involved in this group, no effort was made, in most cases, to see a woman more than once, and at that time the best information possible was obtained. This information, we realize, is much less reliable than the statements obtained from any other groups.

In each case, after the first interview, the information obtained was recorded on the "Statement of Girl" folder. A copy of the folder is given here with the statement of a girl committed to the Reformatory at Bedford Hills. (See pages 65-8.)

Uniform methods of technique in questioning were used in all of the cases. With age, for instance, the woman was asked how old she was and was further asked if she was twenty-two or twenty-three, as the case might be, on her last birthday, or whether she was to be that age on her next birthday. Such further questioning we found was essential in getting the correct age, since many persons, particularly the foreign women, counted the age they were "going on" as their present age. Many of them were unable to figure out the year of birth, so we did not rely on their statement for that, but used only the statement of number of years old, and day and month of birth.

The section on residences and addresses was used primarily as a check on dove-tailing together the facts in the woman's history, and as an aid to the investigator in visiting old home addresses. Such a summary has been particularly helpful in working over the data because it gives in a condensed form the frame on which the other facts of the history may be based. Under this section each year of the woman's life was accounted for, and the information was grouped as follows:

Assuming that the subject was born in 1890,

1890-1902, lived with parents at — E. 10th St., New York City.
1902-1906, lived with parents at — E. 176th St., New York City.
1906-1910, lived with employer, Mrs. ——, at ——.
1910-1915, lived with husband at —— —— ——.
April-July, 1915, lived in furnished room at —— —— ——.
July, 1915—present conviction, lived with consort at —— —— ——.

All of the section on family history was obtained with great care from each woman. By so doing and by getting accurate addresses, much time of the worker was saved later. This section, perhaps more than any other, required tact and persistence in getting reliable information. If the woman did not want certain members of her family

Date of commitment 2/8/17 **No.**...1.................
Date of interview 2/14/17 **Field worker**.....A. B....

STATEMENT OF GIRL

NAME AND LAST ADDRESS Jane Dow, furnished rooms at 35 Pine St. and 64 Spruce St., B—, N. Y.
Alias Josette Raemaeker

AGE AND DATE OF BIRTH 19 years, 8 mos. Born 6/23/97 **RACE** American

PLACE OF BIRTH R——, N. Y. **COLOR** White

HOW LONG IN U. S. Always

RELIGION Methodist

MARITAL CONDITION Single **If married, when**....... **Where**......
Under what name.... **To whom**....

RESIDENCES AND ADDRESSES (In chronological order)

1897–1913, lived in R——, with her parents. Worked in several places but always came home at night.

1913– until 3 wks. before arrest, lived in N——, N. Y., with her parents except for short period of time in O—— and C—— where she was working.

3 weeks before arrest, lived in furnished rooms in B——, N. Y.

FAMILY HISTORY

	Name and address	Age	Birthplace	Time in U.S.	Occupation	Education
Father	Wm. Dow, 3 Center St., N——, N.Y.	40	N.Y.C.	Always	Fireman in boiler factory	Reads and writes
	Naturalized					
Mother	Carrie Black,—Mrs. Dow, 3 Center St., N——, N. Y.	38	"	"	......	Left in 8th grade
Sibs	1. Girl, died at 2 days					
	2. Subject					
	3. Charles, N——, N. Y.	13	R——, N.Y.	"	......	In 6th gr.
	4. John, died in 1907 at age of	2	"	"	......	......
	5. Marietta, N——, N. Y.	4	"	"	......	......

Husband None

Children None

Other relatives
Paternal uncle, R. M. Dow, F——, N. Y.
Maternal aunts: Mrs. J. Street, M——, N. Y.
Mrs. P. Gray, M——, N. Y.

Institutional record

Relative	Institution	Dates	Complaint
None			

HOME CONDITIONS

During Childhood and Adolescence Lived in R——, N. Y., with her people until 1913. Always had a good home there. At first her people lived near the creek, then on M. Ave. and later on S. St. In all of these places they had a separate house with quite a little ground so that they could have a garden. Each of these houses had at least 7 or 8 rooms.

Economic conditions Father used to earn $25 to $30 a week in a rubber factory in R——. With this income her mother was able to make a very comfortable home.

Moral standards Father has very strict standards. "Would never allow cider in the house even to make mince-meat because he was afraid that the boys would learn to drink." Both her mother and father are good church people.

Attitude toward family Seems to feel kindly toward her people but thinks that they should have come to B—— when she was arrested. Says that her father is so severe that he will never feel the same toward her again because she has disgraced his name.

During Recent Life

Total income of family (Specify items) Has worked a little during the last two years but has been at home most of the time. Her father is now earning $16 a week. They have vegetables which they raised on their farm last summer and they have cows and chickens so that there is little necessity for buying much food.

Expenses of family

Rent Lease house and 45 acres of ground for $15 month.
Insurance All of family are insured. Jane is insured in Prudential and Colonial for $500.
Benefit societies, etc. Father belongs to the Order of Foresters.
Miscellaneous "Mother has to squeeze every penny in order to get along. She will not run a grocery bill and insists upon paying for the lease as soon as the money is due. I did not think I could stay with them any longer unless I was working."

Character of locality (Factory, business, suburban, residence, etc.) Lives out in the country, some distance from a railroad station. Says that they have very good neighbors and that everybody around them is respectable.

Type of dwelling (Tenement, separate house, etc.) 8 room, wooden house, in good condition.

Number of rooms 8
Number of persons in household (Specify lodgers) 3 adults and 2 children.
Sleeping accommodations 4 bedrooms. Jane had a room to herself.

Moral standards See above.

Attitude toward family Feels very sorry for her mother who is pregnant again. Thinks that this trouble will make her very ill and worries a great deal for fear that her mother may not live through her confinement.

EDUCATION

English-speaking Yes **Read and write** English

School Address (Last school) Public school, R——, N. Y.

Age at starting school 5 yrs. **Attendance** Regular

Age at leaving school (If under 16, had she obtained an employment certificate) 12 yrs.

Grade at leaving school Lacked only 3 weeks of finishing grammar school.

Reason for leaving school A boy threw ink on the back of Jane's dress. She turned around and slapped his face, and because she did this her teacher shook her, pinched her arm so hard that the scar lasted for two years, and made her nose bleed. Jane was so upset over this occurrence that her doctor said she must not go back to school, and gave her a doctor's certificate stating that she was not able to attend school.

Later schooling None

Language spoken at home English

WORK HISTORY (Places of employment in chronological order and in each:)

	Kind of work	Employer and Address	Dates of employment	Weekly Wage	Reason for Leaving	Disposition of Money
1.	Operator	L—— Embroidery factory, R——, N. Y.	6 wks. 1909	$5 wk.	Work made her nervous	Mother
2.	Gen'l housework	Mrs. M——, R——, N. Y.	2½ mos. 1913	$3 wk.	Employer "queer"	"
3.	" "	Mrs. M——, Main St., R——, N. Y.	4 mos. 1913	$2½ wk.	Moved with parents	"
4.	" "	Mrs. M——, N——, N. Y.	2 wks. 1914	$6 wk.	Too nervous	"
5.	Waitress	H—— Sanitarium, O——, N. Y.	2 wks. 1915	$18 mo.	Employer too domineering	Self
6.	"	J—— Hospital, C——, N. Y.	2 wks. 1916	$20 mo.	Too many supervisors	"

INSTITUTIONAL HISTORY

Previous Court Record of Delinquency (Chronological order)

Date	Place	Complaint	Disposition
None			

Commitment to Non-Penal Institutions (Chronological order)

Institution (As Orphan Asylum, etc.)	Dates	Record of Conduct
None		

Hospitals	Dates	Diagnosis
None		

Attitude toward institutional experience Insists that she is innocent and that it is wrong for a girl of her refinement and sensibilities to be forced to associate with the "street-girls" in a reformatory.

SEX HISTORY

First sex instructions **When** 11 years old

From whom Mother. (Menstruation was established when 11 yrs. old)

Age at first sexual offense 17 yrs.

With whom Boy she knew in N——.

Rape or by consent Consent

Approximate age at entering prostitution Never. Has had sexual intercourse twice, the first time when she was 17 years, by consent, and the second time when she was in O——. She had a "lonesome road" to walk after she left the street car and one night a man who had noticed her on the car, followed her and forced her to have relations with him.

Only means of support

Practised continually since

Practised where (Hotels, furnished rooms, etc.) ......

Average weekly earnings from prostitution ......

HEALTH (Diseases, accidents, operations, etc.) Has always been very nervous and has had the tic of twitching her mouth since she was a little girl. As a child she had chicken-pox, measles, mumps and rheumatism. She also had an abscess on her neck which her mother "drew up" with a poultice, until it broke. Four years ago she had tubercular adenoids removed by Dr. B. in N——. She seems to be extremely nervous at present and is conscious all the time of the twitching of her face Is troubled with neuralgia a great deal. For several years has had spells when "everything goes black for 10 or 15 minutes."

Habits: **Alcohol** No **Drugs** No **Tobacco** No

RECREATION (Opportunities, favorite amusements, friends, etc.) Says she has never had an opportunity for much recreation. When she was a child in R—— she always went directly home from school and never knew other children very well. In N—— she became acquainted with some young people who were very kind to her. She went out to church with them every week and occasionally had supper with them at a small inn in N——. Says she does not care much for dancing and has never been to a theatre.

SUPPLEMENTARY FACTS AND EXPLANATION (Details of offense for which committed, etc.) Jane says that she left the Hospital where she was working three weeks before her arrest because there were too many supervisors. She went to B——, New York, where she rented a furnished room, and was living there on the money she had saved when she was arrested. She says that on the night of her arrest she had been to a dance, the third one she had ever attended. She went directly from the dance to a hotel, engaged a room, and had just entered it when a detective came in and said she was under arrest on a charge of vagrancy. She says she was going to work the next day, and had enough money to pay for her room that night.

interviewed, her tendency at first was to be suspicious and refuse to tell anything. Later when she felt she could rely upon the worker's word, she would give a correct statement concerning her family with the understanding that certain members were not to be seen.

The material on home conditions was intended to give a picture of each woman's reaction toward her childhood and later home. This was not usually obtained by direct questioning, but more often came out in her story as she told it, uninterrupted. The other details such as rent, income, kind of home, etc., were in response to direct questions. A particular effort was made to get the woman's attitude toward her family, her treatment by them, and to find out whether the conditions in her early home seemed in any way responsible for her delinquency.

On the whole, very little antagonism was met in asking for information concerning the school history. In a few cases the last school address was refused, but usually it was possible to obtain this, if the subject understood that in writing for the school record, no statement would be made that she had been arrested. The reliability of the information given by the women of the various groups concerning their school attainments seems to be, as would be expected, in direct proportion to the degree of personal relationship that could be established between worker and subject. Here, again, the Workhouse group has suffered most. Many of the first statements among them were so unreliable that repeated efforts to locate school records were unsuccessful. Many of the women professed to have forgotten the address of the last school, and knowing that the record could not be found without it, exaggerated the statement of their attainments. Among the younger women, and in the groups where several interviews were possible, there was rarely a case where information enabling us to verify the record was refused.

The work record was the most difficult information to obtain from all of the women. An attempt was made to find out about each job she had held and to get, especially, about each job, the kind of work done, the length of time employed, wage received, reason for leaving and the address of the employer so that the record could be verified. Absolute accuracy in obtaining such a record is probably impossible, especially with the older women who have worked during a number of years, and have had many jobs. For the most part, however, the material is quite satisfactory, and checked up by the verification not only of the work record itself, but by visits to members of the family and friends who have known intimately of the subject's life. It seems probable that records of most of the important jobs have been obtained. The very irregular work records have been the ones to suffer most because of the woman's inability to remember about each of fifteen or twenty jobs. But by persistent questioning as to the kind of work she was doing at given times, it has been possible in many of even these most irregular cases, to obtain from the women and to verify the bulk of the jobs during her work period. With a few exceptions, such questioning met little antagonism. It seemed a natural outgrowth of friendly questions about the kind of work she was doing in the institution, and the work she would like to know how to do, to her past work experience.

The record of previous convictions and arrests was not difficult to obtain from most of the women. The general feeling among them seemed to be that a record of their convictions was on file at the court, and that it was useless to contradict a finger-print record. In this connection again, the older women in the Workhouse were least able to give a satisfactory statement. Those who had had ten or twenty previous terms would say: "I've been coming here off and on for the last ten years—don't ask me how many times, because I can't remember."

Occasionally some woman refused to give the facts of her sex history, but as a rule no embarrassment seemed to be felt in talking of these details. The method of approach varied in this with the different groups. With the women at Bedford where the initial interview came the day after the first physical examination, the most satisfactory way of approaching the subject was by questioning first about previous health, the age menstruation was established, whether at that time sex instructions were given and from that to questions about the nature of the first sex offense and later sexual irregularities. The greatest difficulties in obtaining these facts came from the more intelligent women in Auburn Prison and the New York County Penitentiary—women who, possibly, had been sent to these institutions on larceny charges and who had not been sex offenders more than a few times. To many such a woman any implication that she was a prostitute was most distressing, and had to be handled carefully.

The section on supplementary facts was made to include a brief statement dove-tailing together the main facts otherwise indicated on the folder, and such additional factors as conduct, abnormal traits, attitude toward her delinquency, etc.

METHOD OF INVESTIGATION

With these data from the initial interview the field worker started the investigation. In all of the groups except Bedford, where it was necessary for one who had most intimate contact with the woman to be near the institution all of the time, the worker investigated the cases she had interviewed. This method of procedure is preferable where the investigation *per se* is the object of interest, not only because it is time-saving but also because the worker has a better knowledge of the case if she has had the first interview.

(a) *General Procedure of Investigation*

The general plan of investigation was aimed to cover by visits and letters verification of all points which are included on the "Statement of Girl" folder, with such additional data as could be given by friends or relatives on conduct, traits, etc.

A general order of investigation was followed in all cases where it was feasible. Many times it was impracticable to follow any given arrangement particularly when it happened that the worker had several calls to be made on different cases in the same locality.

Every case that had at any time lived in New York or Brooklyn, was first registered with the Social Service Exchange. In this way, information giving the social agencies interested in the family was obtained in many cases.

Wherever possible the court record, including the probation officer's report, was obtained early in the investigation. The probation officer was also interviewed, so that the worker might know what work had been done on the case before starting on her own investigation. If the finger-print record giving the number of previous convictions was not included in the probation officer's report, this record was obtained directly from the Finger-Print Bureau. With all of the Penitentiary women and with the women sentenced to the Workhouse on an indeterminate sentence, it was not necessary to get the court and probation officer's records since these were included in the report of the Parole Commission, through whose hands these women had passed. Our workers were given the benefit of all of the investigation done by the parole officers, and in this way were able to save much duplication of work.

With women who were convicted in districts outside of New York City, it was usually possible to interview the Chief of Police and the arresting officer who, in the smaller localities at least, had a fair knowledge of the extent of the woman's delinquencies, and of her family history. On the other hand, there is no probation officer in most of these smaller places, and no record of finger-prints to determine number of past convictions. This necessitates going through many volumes of inaccurately kept records, year by year, to get a woman's past record, and if she has used several aliases it is very difficult to obtain her complete record.

The difficulty in obtaining finger-print records for women committed to Auburn State Prison was particularly marked. The women convicted in New York City are not usually finger-printed after conviction until they are received in Auburn Prison. The Police Department of New York finger-prints only a few felony cases who permit this to be done before conviction. After conviction, the prisoner is out of the jurisdiction of the Police Department and need not go to the Police Headquarters. The finger-prints and Bertillon measurements are taken, however, in Auburn State Prison, and two copies are made. One is sent to the Bureau of Identification of the State Prison Department in Albany, and one is filed at the prison. The subject's statement of previous record is taken at the time of the finger print, and is transmitted with the copies of the finger-prints to the Bureau in Albany. This means that the Bureau of Identification has the actual finger-print, any previous record in a state prison, and the subject's statement except in occasional cases where the finger-print expert in the prison has written to other cities to find out whether the woman has a longer record than she is willing to admit. The Bureau of Identification in Albany does not as a matter of routine have a record of misdemeanors and other less serious offenses which could be obtained by sending a finger print to the Police Department in New York, so that previous convictions there could be traced.

Therefore, in order to get a complete verified criminal record of the women in Auburn Prison, it was necessary in each case to obtain the statement filed with the Bureau of Identification at Albany and to send for whatever record could be obtained from the Police Department in New York. If the woman had used many aliases unknown to our worker such a record could seldom be located in the index of names in New York. If the woman had had a previous conviction before being received at Auburn, however, and the exact date and name used were known, her record in New York previous to that conviction could be obtained through her finger-print taken at that time. In addition to applying to the two above-named bureaus, we wrote, in every case where a woman had a record in another city, to the chief of police in that city, to verify the woman's statement and to find out whether there was any further record.

After obtaining the data from the courts and those connected with the courts, the worker in most cases visited the social organizations which had come into contact with the subject or her family. From such organizations a full record was obtained. These data furnished a background for understanding the subject, and made the subsequent visits to the immediate family more valuable.

There seem to be many advantages in thus obtaining records of the court and social agencies before any members of the immediate family are seen. Such information often enables the worker to question the family about facts which she would know nothing of without first having seen the records. Again, many families are loath to tell that the woman under investigation has done certain reprehensible things and had many convictions if they feel that the worker knows nothing of these delinquencies, but if they understand that the worker has a knowledge of what has occurred, they often tell more than could possibly be obtained from any record.

After having seen members of the immediate family, the general trend of the investigation was to interview other relatives who might be able to throw light on either the subject or her family, and following that to see the subject's husband or consort if there were one, friends, landladies, and other persons who might be able to give anything concerning important events which stood out in the subject's life. On the whole, these latter informants are considered far less reliable than any of those first mentioned. A landlady, for instance, often gives inaccurate information concerning the number of men a girl takes to her room because she realizes that she herself could be prosecuted for maintaining a disorderly house, if she admitted that she allowed such things. In many cases, if the landlady felt the girl had given evidence which would incriminate her, she exaggerated the girl's untruthfulness and dishonesty.

(*b*) *Form of Report of Investigation*

The information incorporated in the field worker's report was divided throughout into three main parts:—

I. Information concerning the subject.
II. Information concerning the subject's family.
III. Correspondence relating to the subject and her family.

This material was written up in detail, in the order in which the visits were made, with all of the information received from each informant recorded separately. The first part of the report includes all of the information obtained by the field worker, relating to the history of the subject. Where an individual, not a member of the family, was interviewed, a brief description of the informant was given, with the field worker's impression of his reliability and accuracy. Aside from this, no other extraneous data were included in Section I. A summary of the order used in this section is as follows:—

I. Information Concerning the Subject.
   A. Information obtained from court records, probation officer, fingerprints.
   B. Information obtained from social organizations which have been interested in the subject.
   C. Information of some member of immediate family,—mother, father or older sister or brother as case may be. This information, wherever possible, was made to cover the following groups of facts. The grouping was very flexible, however, and in many cases certain sections were omitted where there was nothing of importance.
      1. *Infancy.* Includes date and place of birth, whether or not a full term child, health during infancy, age at beginning to walk, talk, etc.
      2. *Childhood.* Includes health, any abnormal traits, conduct, development.
      3. *School Period.* Age at starting and leaving school, the grade reached, conduct in school, health.
      4. *Adolescent Period.* Age menstruation was established, and general health and conduct at that time.
      5. *Work Period.* All jobs in chronological order, with kind of work done, length of employment, wage, ability, and disposition of wages for each job.
      6. *Adult Period.* This section applies particularly to the older women, and includes any important data on marital life, delinquency, institutional commitments, etc.
      7. *Health.* This section was used where it was desirable to have a summary of health, such as cases of certain epileptics in whom it was of interest to observe the development of

the disease. In many instances, where health was considered under the various periods, it was not repeated here.

8. *Conduct, Traits, Etc.* This section was used particularly where it seemed advisable to show development of traits and behavior, as in many psychopathic cases, or where there was a history of continued maladaptation.

D. Information of all other relatives. Facts from several informants were recorded separately in the order in which they were obtained.

E. Information of consort or pimp.

F. Information of landlady and friends. All information under this section and the following one was preceded by a statement as to general impression and probable reliability of the informant.

G. Information of certain employers. Includes information relative to kind of work done, ability, wage, conduct, etc.

II. Family History. All of the information under this section was grouped by separate interviews, so that the statement of any unreliable or prejudiced informant could be selected from the rest.

A. Home conditions.

1. Early home during childhood and adolescence, including description of economic and moral standards, parental supervision, income, spirit in the home, etc.
2. Later home life, with information similar to that given above, and in addition more detailed facts regarding rent, insurance, exact income, size of home, etc.

B. Information concerning the husband or consort.

1. Field worker's impression after interview.
2. Information of husband or consort, including statement as to age, birthplace, education, occupation, habits, health, wage, and personal history in brief.
3. Information of other informants, including court, institutional and employment records, statements of friends, relatives, etc. An effort was made to obtain information concerning his characteristics, traits, and treatment of the subject.

C. Information concerning the subject's children. The information in this and in the other three sections follows the order and general form used in Section B on Subject's Husband.

D. Information concerning the subject's father.

E. Information concerning the subject's mother.

F. Information concerning the subject's fraternity.

Wherever it was possible to do any more intensive work on

family history, the order used by Dr. Charles B. Davenport[2] at Cold Spring Harbor, was followed: *i.e.*

Father's fraternity.
Father's parents and their fraternities.
Mother's fraternity.
Mother's parents and their fraternities.

III. Correspondence. In general, letters were written to the following sources of information, asking for the main facts in which we were particularly interested. Many of these letters were written not only to obtain information about the subject, but also to obtain institutional records, school records, etc., concerning other members of the family.

A. *Schools.* Request was made for record card, or information giving years in school, grade reached, age and date at leaving, conduct.

B. *Institutions,* both Orphanages or Homes and Penal Institutions. Request was made for cause of commitment, dates of entrance and discharge, conduct.

C. *Hospitals.* A form letter was sent to hospitals asking for length of stay, diagnosis, and any personal or family history obtained.

D. *Employers.* Nearly all of the work records were verified by correspondence, though occasionally the worker visited where the subject had been employed for a long time in one place, or where it was felt that the employer could give valuable information bearing directly on the girl's delinquency.

E. *Bureau of Records.* An effort was made to verify each marriage, and in many cases where there was confusion as to age, to verify the date of birth.

SUMMARY OF STUDY

When the preceding information had been obtained, and the replies to the letters had come in, all of the data were summarized, and recorded in condensed form on the Verified History Blank which is given here. The case presented shows how the summarized verified data varies from the girl's own statement which has previously been given.

This blank, it will be noticed, is comparable in form to the "Statement of Girl" blank presented in preceding pages, except that it lacks certain sections on "Attitude" which were included to portray the subject's own feeling. This summary of the investigation was intended to

[2] Davenport, Charles B. "The Family History Book." *Bulletin No. 7,* Eugenics Record Office. Cold Spring Harbor, N. Y. September, 1912. Appendix 1, p. 95.

Date of commitment 2/ 8/17
Date of interview 2/14/17

No...1..................
Field worker..A. B......

VERIFIED HISTORY

NAME Jane Dow

OFFENSE Vagrant, having no visible means of support, living without employment and having contracted an infectious disease in practise of debauchery.

SENTENCE Indeterminate 3 years.

JUDGE Brown **COURT** Recorder's Court, B——, New York. X County

---

AGE AND DATE OF BIRTH 16 years, 7 months. Born June 23, 1900 [1]

PLACE OF BIRTH R——, New York [1] **RACE** American

HOW LONG IN U. S. Always [1] **COLOR** White

RELIGION Methodist [1]

MARITAL CONDITION Married [2] **If married, when** July 30, 1916 **Where** C——, New York
Under what name Jane Dow **To whom** John Gray

RESIDENCES AND ADDRESSES **(In chronological order)**

1900–1913, lived in R——, New York, with parents.

1913– three weeks before arrest, lived in N——, New York, with parents, except for short periods of time in O——, C——, S——, and M——, New York.[1]

Three weeks before arrest lived in furnished rooms in B——, New York.[4]

FAMILY HISTORY

	Name and address	Age	Birthplace	Time in U. S.	Occupation	Education
Father	William Dow, 3 Center St., N——, New York. Works steadily and is respectable.[1c,4] **Naturalized**	48	New York State	Always	In dye works	Reads and writes [1a]
Mother	Carrie Black, Mrs. Dow, 3 Center St., N——, New York. Seems fairly intelligent. Is quite nervous. Said to be unreliable.[4]	37	"	"	......	Left in 8th grade
Sibs [1]						
	1. Girl, died in infancy.					
	2. Subject.					
	3. Miscarriage at two months.					
	4. Charles, N——, New York. Was threatened with tuberculosis a few years ago. Is said to be troublesome and does petty thieving.	12	"	"	......	In 5th grade
	5. John, died in 1907 at the age of Had pneumonia and tubercular abscess in his neck.	2	"	"	......	......
	6. Marietta, N——, New York.	4	"	"	......	......
	7. Child, born April 1917.					
Husband	John Gray, address unknown.	26	Utah	"	Brakeman	? [1]

Children None [1]

Other relatives Paternal uncle, R. M. Dow, F——, New York.[1]

Institutional Record

Relative	Institution	Dates	Complaint
None [1]			

HOME CONDITIONS

During Childhood and Adolescence Has lived with her parents most of the time until 1916. At one time she went to her grandmother in Massachusetts where she remained for six months. It seems probable that she has always had a fairly good home and that the mother has tried to give Jane some training and supervision. The home spirit seems fairly good though the mother is sometimes sharp in speaking to the children. Father has always worked steadily and has earned a regular wage. Two years ago the family moved from R—— into the country where they had a house of eight rooms and paid $10 rent. They had a garden but did not raise much more than enough for their own use. Jane always had her own room when she was a child.[1] A school teacher who used to know the family says that the mother was quite slack and did not keep the home clean.[4]

Economic conditions Probably fair because father worked steadily. Usually earned from $25 to $30 a week.[1]

Moral standards Probably good. Parents have fairly good reputation and the father especially seems to have been very strict in his moral standards.[4]

During Marital or Recent Life Has worked a little during the last two years but has been at home the most of the time.[1] When away from home last summer was married and shortly after that was committed to an institution.[2] Has been at home off and on since her release from the institution.[1]

Total income of family (Specify items) Father earns $3 a day. Jane earned a small and irregular wage but spent it all for herself.[1a]

Expenses of family
Rent Parents pay $8 a month rent now.[1]
Insurance All of the family are insured, Jane in the Prudential & Colonial for $500.[A]
Benefit societies, etc. Father belongs to Order of Foresters.[A]
Miscellaneous ......

Character of locality (Factory, business, suburban, residence, etc.) Present home in unpretentious but respectable neighborhood, about twenty minutes' walk from the railroad station, in a country district.[2]

Type of dwelling (Tenement, separate house, etc.) Two story, frame house, rather attractive and in good repair.[2]
Number of rooms 7 [1]
Number of persons in household (Specify lodgers) 5, including patient.[1]
Sleeping accommodations Jane has always had a room to herself.[1]

Moral standards See above. While away from home probably got in with a fast crowd of people so that her moral standards became lowered.[4]

EDUCATION

English-speaking Yes **Read and write** English

School Address (Last school) Public school, R——, New York.[2]

Age at starting school 5 years [2] **Attendance** Very poor [2]

Age at leaving school (If under 16, had she obtained an employment certificate) 13 years. No employment certificate.[2]

Grade at leaving school 5B grade.[2]

Reason for leaving school Moved. Was in a very nervous condition and the doctor advised that she be taken out of school.[1]

Later schooling None [1]

Language spoken at home English [1]

WORK HISTORY (Places of employment in chronological order and in each:)

	Kind of work	Employer and Address	Dates of employment	Weekly Wage	Reason for Leaving	Ability
1.	Operator	Green's Embroidery Factory, R——, New York.	Several times. 6 or 7 weeks, 1913.	$5 wk.	Ill.	? [2]
2.	Gen'l housework	Mrs. M——, R——, New York.	2½ mos., 1913	$3 wk.	Employer "queer."	? [A, 1]
3.	" "	Mrs. M——, Main St., R——, New York.	4 mos., 1913.	$2.50 wk.	Moved from R——.	? [A, 1]
4.	Housework	Mrs. M——, N——, New York.	5 days, Nov., 1916.	$5 wk.	Discharged.	Very poor worker.[2]
5.	Waitress	H—— Sanitarium, O——, New York.	1 week, 1916.	$18 mo.	Discharged.	No training. Not clean. Immoral.
6.	Waitress	J—— Hospital, C——, New York.	2 weeks, Dec. 5-23, 1916.	$20 mo.	Discharged.	Unsatisfactory, rude, impertinent and indiscreet with men.[2]

Disposition of Money Spent money on self.[1]

INSTITUTIONAL HISTORY

Previous Court Record of Delinquency (Chronological order)

Date	Place	Complaint	Disposition
August 15, 1916	R——, New York.	Soliciting	St. Ann's School,[1] Albany.[2] Committed for 6 months but served only 1 month.

Commitment to Non-Penal Institutions (Chronological order)

Institution (As Orphan Asylum, etc.)	Dates	Record of Conduct
None [1]		

Hospitals	Dates	Diagnosis
None [1]		

SEX HISTORY

First sex instructions **When** 12 years. (Menstruation was established at 12 years.)[1]
From whom Mother.[1]

Age at first sexual offense 14 years.[A]
With whom Boy she knew in N——, New York.[A]
Rape or by consent Consent.[A]

Approximate age at entering prostitution Never. Has had sexual intercourse only twice.[A] Has reputation of having been immoral for at least two years.[4] Two weeks previous to last arrest was hanging around the docks at R—— and consorting with soldiers. Took men into empty freight cars. *Chief of Police*, [4].

Only means of support....

Practised continually since....

Practised where (Hotels, furnished rooms, etc.)....

Average weekly earnings from prostitution....

HEALTH (Diseases, accidents, operations, etc.) (5′ 7″ tall and weighs 141½ lbs. Has quite a high palate. Has two carious teeth. Heart shows slight systolic murmur. Vaginal examination showed hypertrophy of external genitals and considerable yellowish discharge. Wassermann and complement fixation test for gonorrhea, negative.)[2] Had painter's colic when a baby. Cried steadily for three days after birth. Has been troubled with constipation since she was a baby. Never had any diseases except measles and whooping cough. Began to be very nervous when 9 or 10 years old. Her face twitched and she gave a little kick with one foot when she walked. When 9 years old had her adenoids removed and examination of them showed presence of tuberculosis.[1]

Habits: **Alcohol** No[A, 1] **Drugs** No[A, 1] **Tobacco** No[A, 1]

RECREATION (Opportunities, favorite amusements, friends, etc.) See Statement of Girl.

SUPPLEMENTARY FACTS AND EXPLANATION (Details of offense for which committed, etc.)

When Jane was a very young child she was inclined to be disobedient. Frequently she did not come home from school promptly and would be whipped. Jane's aunt feels that because she was so nervous she should not have been whipped so much and that her treatment only exaggerated her nervous condition. She has always been quick-tempered and irritable.[1c] Since leaving home in 1916, Jane has undoubtedly been promiscuous sexually. One employer writes of her that "she is not personally physically clean and I am afraid that her morals are even worse." Another employer writes that she was very indiscreet in her attitude toward male employees.[2] She was married to a man she had known only a short time and he left the night after they were married to go to Texas with his regiment.[3b,1]

Jane's heredity is fairly good. Her father is quite intelligent and steady. The mother seems to be normal mentally and physically, though she may not have a very strict standard of truthfulness. The mother has had seven children, two of whom died during infancy and one was a miscarriage at two months. One of the children died of a tubercular abscess in his neck.

The details of Jane's life preceding her arrest are as follows: She did not tell her mother that she was discharged from the J—— Hospital in C——, New York, and after she had been home for a short time she told her mother that she was going back to the hospital. Instead, she went to B—— and had been there about a week before her arrest. She met some woman in the station and asked her about getting a room. The woman referred her to the Y.W.C.A., which gave her a list of boarding places. With this list, Jane went to one of the places and told the woman who was running the house that she was doing investigations for the National Board of the Y.W.C.A. She stayed with this woman for two nights. On the third night she did not come in. On the following night she went to one of the other places about twelve at night and told the same story and was let in. The night after that, she did not get in until three o'clock and the woman thought there was something queer about it and reported it to the Y.W.C.A., who put the matter into the hands of the police. She was found going into the D—— House, a poor hotel, about two o'clock at night and although they had no very definite charge against her the police arrested her. At that time, Jane told the Recorder that she had a venereal disease and so he committed her here on her own statement.[4]

present a digest of the various opinions on the case. It was planned primarily in an effort to get away from the usual form of having the worker make out an arbitrary statement of what she considered were probably the correct facts and interpretation of certain events in the subject's life. It seemed necessary, in order to minimize the personal equation as much as possible, to have all of these data in the form of a summary of the material obtained, rather than as a clear-cut, one-sided picture of the subject's life summarized by the worker. With the plan used, all of the cases were treated in the same way by a few persons who finally worked over the data, choosing in each instance where two contradictory statements were given, the one which seemed most consistent with the general plan used for all of the cases.

On the "Verified History" folders, each important fact recorded was followed by a small index number in red ink, which indicated by what source that information had been given. This was particularly useful in the data on sex history where there were often varying indefinite opinions. The following illustration will show how many opinions there may be on the same case:

Approximate Age at Entering Prostitution

Never (A). Eighteen years—one year ago when she ran away from home ([1]). Nineteen years—four weeks before arrest began to be wild, and stayed out late at night ([4]). Fifteen years—has been known on the street for four years, as a prostitute ([3]).

Here, the subject (A) denies prostitution, while her mother ([1]) admits that since the girl ran away a year before, she had prostituted. The mother seemed frank and truthful in giving information and told of places where the girl had worked steadily until a year before. These we were able to verify, and found that up to that time she had been doing good work, and there was no cause to suspect immoral conduct. The landlady ([4]) with whom the girl had lived during the preceding year, seemed evasive and suspicious. Not wishing to incriminate herself, she was unwilling to say that the girl had prostituted in her home, but had to admit that recently she had had reason to suspect she was not doing right. The chief of police ([3]), on the other hand, probably exaggerated greatly the information he gave. For a year he had heard of this girl, and perhaps before that he had noticed her, especially if she had made undesirable acquaintances. In giving his information, he unconsciously made her out to be much worse than she really was. This we were able to prove by verification of her work and school records, which gave her a good reputation during the period the chief of police in the small town had said she was prostituting. The best judgment on the case seems then to be that she began to prostitute at eighteen, after leaving home. By having all of these data recorded on the folder, similar information on a dozen cases would be decided alike by the one working over the data, whereas a dozen persons working independently might have decided differently on each case.

The following index numbers were used on the verified history to indicate sources of information:

A = Statement of girl.
1 = Information of mother.
  (1a) = Information of father.
  (1b) = Information of sibs. If necessary to differentiate between conflicting information of different sibs, the following distinction was used.
    (1b 1) = oldest sib.
    (1b 2) = next oldest sib, etc.
  (1c) = Information of other relatives. If necessary, we indicated in note which relative was informant: grandparent, aunt, etc.
  (1d) = Information of husband.
  (1e) = Information of children.
2 = Information received by directly writing to or visiting source indicated, as: "Reached 5B grade[2]", indicating that information is from the *school* record.
  "Worked Paper Box Factory, 6 mos. $10 a week[2]", indicating that we have *employer's* record.
  "Arrest 6/5/12. T. H. L. 5 days [2]", indicating that we have *finger-print record.*
  "Magdalen Home, 6/5/13—6/5/14. Good worker and behaved well[2]", indicating that we have *record from the Magdalen Home.*
3 = Information of probation officer, as "Worked Paper Box Factory, 6 mos. $10 a week[3]", showing probation officer has verified that fact, and we are taking her verification.
    (3a) Parole officer (Penitentiary records).
    (3b) Detective.
    (3c) Social agency.
4 = Information of landlady or persons who have lived in same house or near the girl.

After the completion of the investigations, and the making up of the "Verified History" folders, much of the material was reduced to code form for use on statistical cards. This was done by a few persons working together, so that the work was uniform. The general considerations as to the classifications used for certain groups of facts will be discussed later under the chapters dealing with such facts.

The sociological investigation, in brief, aimed to make an intensive study of the women delinquents considered, not only through knowing the woman herself, but by becoming informed about the environment in which she grew up and her manner of living outside the prison. A particular effort has been made to weigh carefully the information obtained concerning her, and to use similar methods of recording and summarizing data on all cases. This has been of great value in making the work in the various groups comparable so far as methods of obtaining and evaluating the material are concerned.

CHAPTER VI

NATURE AND EXTENT OF DELINQUENCY

THE study of the association of various environmental factors in the life of a criminal with the nature and extent of crime must necessarily be preceded by a clear understanding of the classification of crime, and the measure of degree of criminality to be used. Many criminal sociologists within the last thirty years have made studies of the environmental influences in the lives of criminals, but have treated their material in a descriptive manner, and have assumed that the frequency of an abnormal environmental condition among a group of criminals was proof that the condition was a cause of the delinquency. Often no attempt has been made to show how the relationship varied with any measure of the extent of delinquency, or with the frequency of this condition in the general population. One of the first difficulties, it must be granted, in treating in mass form the material in such a study as this, is the inability to obtain comparative figures for the general population. Until such figures can be obtained, however, it seems futile to assume that the repeated occurrence of a condition within a criminal group is a cause of criminality, when it may be a commonly occurring condition among the general population as well. Not having the figures for the larger group makes it all the more necessary that we show the relationships of observed factors to the *degree* of delinquency and treat such relationships as concomitant with, not necessarily causative of, delinquency.

In this study, a delinquent has been regarded as one who has been convicted of an offense against the law. The measurement of the extent of delinquency might be based on one or more of four factors, (1) the age at first conviction, (2) number of convictions, (3) number of terms served in penal institutions, or (4) length of time served in penal institutions. This chapter aims to give a picture of the criminal record of the women in the various groups studied, and will discuss the nature of the offense committed by the women at the time of the present study, the advantages or disadvantages in using one or more of the above-named measures of delinquency, and the factors connected with the first contact with the law. We shall attempt to show the relationships beween several of the elements entering into the criminal record, and shall use the material in this chapter as a basis for later showing the relationship between extent of delinquency and various environmental conditions.

CLASSIFICATION OF OFFENSES

The problem of classifying the offenses is no small one. As Miss Mary Conyngton[1] writes,—"the classification of offenses is a complex affair. Going from place to place, one finds identical terms used for different offenses and identical offenses described by different terms. Thus, in one locality if a woman is convicted of keeping a disorderly house it may mean only that a considerable amount of loud talking, singing, and quarreling goes on there which makes it a nuisance to the neighbors. In another it invariably means that she maintains a house of ill fame. 'Violation of city ordinance' is a comprehensive term, covering offenses which may range from a serious infraction of public order to shaking a rug from a front window. Obviously any attempt to classify according to the charges under which the prisoners are committed would lead to grouping together widely varying offenses." Though our study did not cover convictions outside of New York State, it was found that within one state alone the classification of offenses varied considerably in different localities, and sometimes within the same city. In particular, the use of "Disorderly Conduct" is striking, as meaning, even in New York City, drunkenness, soliciting, attracting a crowd on the street, soliciting alms, etc. In all cases where "Disorderly Conduct" unqualified was given as the offense, therefore, it was necessary to find out from the arresting officer what specific violation of the law had taken place. There are many other instances of vague and indefinite returns of offense committed, which necessitated careful investigation of the details of the affair, so that the classification might be as definite as possible.

The New York City Police Department classification of crime[2] was chosen as being the best adapted to show the general relationships in our groups of delinquent women. This system of classification was made up on the basis of crimes which had passed through the New York City Police Department, and, therefore, took account of the local

[1] "Report on Condition of Woman and Child Wage-earners in the United States." Vol. XV. "Relation between Occupation and Criminality of Women." By Miss Mary Conyngton. Washington Gov't. Printing Office, 1911, p. 16.
[2] Police Department, City of New York, *Annual Report,* 1916, pp. 30-64.

idiosyncrasies in many laws, such as the specific sections of a general law which might be lost sight of in a more universal classification. An instance of this occurs in what is commonly known as the "Vagrancy Law." Under a more general application, undoubtedly many of the persons convicted under the general heading entitled "Vagrants" would be so classified under a somewhat miscellaneous grouping. To one who knows this particular law in New York State, however, it is evident that very specific charges can be made in each of the ten sections of the law. The New York City Police Department classification has taken cognizance of the fact that section 1 defines as vagrants those who "living without employment, have not visible means to maintain themselves;" that section 2 defines habitual drunkards; that section 3 refers to those who have contracted an infectious disease in the practice of debauchery, etc.; and that section 4 defines those who are guilty of prostitution and soliciting.[3] Recognizing the sections of the law which are given in the record of conviction, the Vagrancy heading has been regrouped into "Vagrancy intoxication," "Vagrancy prostitution," etc., so that each falls into the large group where it would properly belong.

TABLE 1

COUNTIES IN WHICH DELINQUENT WOMEN WERE CONVICTED

County	Institutional Groups						Total	
	Bedford	Auburn	Magdalen	Penitentiary	Workhouse	Probation	Number	Per cent
Counties included in Greater New York....	67	57	74	110	107	102	517	88.1
Counties outside of Greater New York....	35	31	2	...	2	...	70	11.9
Total.............	102	88	76	110	109	102	587	100.0

Of the group of delinquent women under consideration, Table 1 shows that 517 or 88.1 per cent were convicted in the five counties included in Greater New York. The Police Department has prisoners from each of these counties, thereby making it possible to fit the ma-

[3] "Code of Criminal Procedure, State of New York." Title VI, § 887, sections 1, 2, 3, 4.

jority of our cases into the details of a scheme which was worked out from returns of convictions in the counties which represented our group most largely.

TABLE 2

KIND OF COURT

Number of Delinquent Women in Institutional Groups and Number and Per Cent Distribution for Total, Classified by Kind of Court in Which Convicted

Kind of Court	Institutional Groups						Total	
	Bedford	Auburn	Magdalen	Penitentiary	Workhouse	Probation	Number	Per cent
1. Children's Court...	...	...	1	...	...	...	1	.2
2. City Court........	3	...	1	...	...	...	4	.7
3. City Magistrates' Court	47	...	66	2	97	102	314	53.6
4. County Court.....	7	33	...	12	...	...	52	8.9
5. General Sessions Court...........	5	31	2	32	...	...	70	11.9
6. Justice of the Peace Court...........	7	...	...	...	...	...	7	1.2
7. Police Court.......	9	...	...	...	...	...	9	1.5
8. Recorder's Court...	9	...	...	...	...	...	9	1.5
9. Special Sessions Court	13	...	6	63	12	...	94	16.0
10. Supreme Court....	2	23	...	1	...	...	26	4.4
Total...........	102	87	76	110	109	102	586	100.0

Table 2 shows the distribution of the women in our group by the courts in which they were convicted. The City Magistrates' Courts, it will be seen, have the largest number of cases, with Special Sessions, General Sessions and County Court following. The one case convicted in Children's Court was very nearly sixteen years old, and needed continued institutional supervision, so the judge committed her to the Magdalen.

NATURE OF PRESENT OFFENSE

(a) *Classified by New York City Police Department Classification*

Table 3 shows for each of the institutional groups studied, the nature of the present offense, classified by the New York City Police Department classification. The classification is flexible enough so that various offenses may be included under either of two or more general headings as necessity arises for doing this. Assault, for instance, is ordinarily classified as an offense against the person. When the assault, however, is with intent to commit rape, it becomes an offense against chastity. In classifying our offenses, not only the offense of which the delinquent was convicted was taken into consideration, but also the actual nature of the crime, about which we were able to learn by investigation. There is, therefore, no need of falling into the difficulty cited by Dr. Glueck[4] when he says,—"there seems to be no valid reason for following the legal classification. This classification is frequently not in accord with the actual nature of the crime, as is the case, for example, when a man who has committed rape is permitted to plead to assault. Furthermore, the legal classification, already extensive, is growing constantly with the addition of new legislation, so that data obtained to-day may lose in value by to-morrow. It has been found, on the other hand, that as a result of the examination carried out in these cases, a classification on the basis of motive was possible in practically all instances, and the inception of the motive could be traced to one of the several fundamental human, instinctive attitudes."

With the group of delinquent women studied, it was found to be impossible in many cases to attempt a classification of offenses on the basis of motive. Whether or not the girl who solicits a man and takes him to a "creep house" where he is robbed, is guilty of a crime having its impulse in the instinct of acquisitiveness or of sex is very often hard to determine. Another type of case difficult to decide upon is found in the history of a Polish peasant woman sent to Auburn for twenty years for murder in the second degree. Her husband was a drunkard and would not support her. Neither would he allow her to work and send money to her four children in Russian Poland. After he had threatened to kill her one night, and had scoffed at her for worrying over her children, whom she had heard were starving, she

[4] *Mental Hygiene*, January, 1918, vol. II, no. 1. "A Study of 608 Admissions to Sing Sing Prison," by Bernard Glueck, p. 92.

killed him in a most brutal manner. The next day, before the murder had been discovered, she tried to find work so she could get money for her children. The instinct that prompted the killing was difficult to determine, since, viewed from various viewpoints, it may have been self-protection, protection of children, or possibly a "crime which had its impulse in the instinct of pugnacity." There are other numerous examples among the offenses committed by the Auburn women, particularly, which were not easy to attribute to any one motive, so that a plan such as that used by Dr. Glueck did not seem feasible.

In order to show the relative seriousness of the offenses committed, a further classification into felonies and misdemeanors was used. Many of the petty offenses, such as violations of city ordinances, which are not, in a strictly legal sense, misdemeanors, were, however, classed as such, since we wanted to show by felonies the type of crime which may be punishable by a state prison term or death, and by misdemeanors the less serious offenses which call for sentences in private institutions, reformatories, probation, etc., but which can not be sentenced to a state prison. Often the distinction is only a question of degree, as, for instance, if a man steals goods valued at $25 from a store during the day time he is guilty of petit larceny, a misdemeanor for which he can not be sent to a state prison. If, however, he takes one cent more, making the amount over $25, from the home of the owner of the store, at night time, he is guilty of grand larceny, first degree, and may be punished by a term not exceeding ten years in state prison. Obviously, the distinction between the two is absurd, so far as motive, intent and real seriousness of offense are concerned. With the cases which fall near the dividing line of felony and misdemeanor, it is true that any attempt at classification into these two large groups is worth little, except in a legal sense. It seemed advisable, however, to use such a classification because the cases near the border-line of such a distinction are comparatively few, and because by distinguishing the felony cases, we have material comparable to the studies of men in state prisons, as Sing Sing and Auburn, which include only felons.

Both the New York City Police Department classification of offenses and the grouping into felonies and misdemeanors have been used in considering the nature of the present offense and the first offense. Table 3 indicates in detail the nature of the present offense for the 587 women in our study, and shows what types of crimes are included under the general headings.

Under "Offenses against the Person," Auburn Prison has delin-

TABLE 3

NATURE OF PRESENT OFFENSE

Number of Delinquent Women in Institutional Groups, Classified by New York City Police Department Classification

Nature of Offense	Institutional Groups						Total
	Bedford	Auburn	Magdalen	Penitentiary	Workhouse	Probation	
Offenses against the Person	1	22	...	8	...	...	31
Abortion	...	2	...	2	...	...	4
Assault	...	6	...	6	...	...	12
Manslaughter	1	8	...	...	...	...	9
Murder	...	5	...	...	...	...	5
Suicide, attempted	...	1	...	...	...	...	1
Offenses against Chastity	64	6	59	7	91	89	316
Abduction	...	2	...	...	...	...	2
Adultery	...	...	...	1	...	...	1
Associating with vicious and dissolute persons	5	...	18	1	...	7	31
Committing lewd and indecent acts	...	...	1	...	...	...	1
Compulsory prostitution	...	1	...	...	...	...	1
Disorderly house, keeping	1	...	...	4	2	...	7
Exposure of person	1	...	...	...	...	...	1
Incest	...	1	...	...	...	...	1
Loitering	11	...	1	...	...	1	13
Prostitution, general	1	...	...	...	...	...	1
Prostitution in tenement house	8	...	17	...	63	...	88
Rape, 2nd degree	...	1	...	...	...	...	1
Sodomy	...	1	...	...	...	...	1
Soliciting	29	...	22	1	26	81	159
Vagrancy: contracting infectious disease in practice of debauchery	8	...	...	...	...	...	8
Offenses against Family and Children	6	4	1	1	...	...	12
Abandonment of child under fourteen	1	1	...	...	...	...	2
Bigamy	1	3	...	...	...	...	4
Endangering health and morals of children	4	...	1	1	...	...	6

TABLE 3—Continued

Nature of Offense	Institutional Groups: Bedford	Auburn	Magdalen	Penitentiary	Workhouse	Probation	Total
Offenses against Regulations for Public Health and Safety..	6	1	9	30	3	7	56
Habitual drunkard..........	...	...	1	...	...	...	1
Intoxication...............	...	...	4	...	...	7	11
Possessing drugs............	4	...	4	27	3	...	38
Possessing and selling drugs..	...	1	...	3	...	...	4
Violating liquor tax law.....	1	...	...	...	...	...	1
Yelling and disturbing public peace..................	1	...	...	...	...	...	1
Offenses against Administration of Government.......	2	1	...	...	...	...	3
Bribery....................	...	1	...	...	...	...	1
Perjury....................	2	...	...	...	...	...	2
Offenses against Property Rights..................	17	54	4	62	5	...	142
Arson......................	...	2	...	2	...	...	4
Breaking window while intoxicated................	...	...	...	1	...	...	1
Bringing stolen property into state.....................	...	...	...	1	...	...	1
Burglary...................	...	...	...	2	...	...	2
Extortion..................	...	1	...	...	...	...	1
Forgery	...	1	1	...	...	...	2
Grand larceny..............	3	40	1	13	...	...	57
Petit larceny...............	14	1	2	41	5	...	63
Receiving stolen property....	...	3	...	1	...	...	4
Robbery....................	...	6	...	...	...	...	6
Throwing stones at street car	...	...	...	1	...	...	1
General Criminality...........	6	...	3	2	10	6	27
Disorderly conduct, unqualified.....................	...	...	...	...	5	...	5
Disorderly conduct, soliciting alms.....................	...	...	...	...	2	...	2
Possessing pistol............	...	...	...	2	...	...	2
Ungovernable child..........	3	...	...	...	...	6	9
Vagrancy, unqualified.......	3	...	3	...	3	...	9
Total.................	102	88	76	110	109	102	587

quents under each one of the sub-headings listed, and contains the more serious offenses such as murder and manslaughter, which do not appear in other groups.[5]

Under "Offenses against Chastity," the distribution through all the groups is more general. But for a few exceptions, the Penitentiary and Auburn Prison have the more serious offenses of abduction, adultery, compulsory prostitution, incest, sodomy and rape. The offenses in the other four institutions fall largely into the prostitution offenses, including soliciting, loitering, and violating the Tenement House Law.

Among "Offenses against the Family and Children," three types of offenses occurred among our cases. Under the "Abandonment of a child under fourteen" there were only two cases, one in Bedford and one in Auburn. The Bedford girl was twenty years old, Polish, and spoke very little English. She was of imbecile grade mentally, and showed her lack of intelligence in the act which led to her arrest. Her consort, the child's father, refused to work, and she thought that she had to support him. She knew she would be able to do more work if she did not have the care of the child, and so she took it to a vacant lot near her home, when it was four weeks old, and buried it under a pile of ashes. When the child was found several hours later, the mother showed no feeling and was willing to tell just what she had done. The Auburn case was that of a woman twenty-eight years old, who with her husband abandoned their four children because they thought they were not able to support them. Two of the babies were left in a hallway and one of them died because it was exposed to the rain and cold. The other two were abandoned in a store and taken charge of by the Children's Society. The Polish girl might have been sent to Auburn, but probably because of her youth, her foreignness and stupidity, which to a casual observer made her appear innocent and frightened, the judge sentenced her to Bedford. Ruling out the intelligence factor, her motive, however, was as reprehensible, since she intended to kill her child, while the Auburn woman wanted to shift the responsibility for the care of her child to some other person.

The bigamy case in Bedford differed in no radical way from the three who were sentenced to Auburn, except that she was pretty, attractive, and was clever enough to make her plea of her own good

[5] The one manslaughter case which appears in Bedford was first sentenced to Auburn Prison. The two women against whom she had turned state's evidence threatened to kill her while she was in the prison, and so she was brought back to court for resentence and committed to Bedford.

motives, but her great gullibility, carry weight with the probation officer and judge.

"Endangering the Health and Morals of Children" included in the Bedford group two women who had been prostitutes and heavy drinkers for a long time, but who could not be caught by the police until one day when they were found drinking and entertaining several women of bad character, in the presence of three small children. One other Bedford case was an Austrian woman who persisted in locking her two small children in her apartment for the day while she went out to work, and neglecting them in other ways. The fourth Bedford case was that of a girl sixteen years old who had sexual relations with a strange man in the presence of her fourteen year old sister. The Magdalen and Penitentiary cases are similar to the two Bedford cases first noted.

"Offenses against Regulations for Public Health and Safety" are supposed to include mainly the intoxication and drug cases. Since the using of alcohol or drugs is never a felony, we should not expect to find any of these cases in Auburn Prison. Selling drugs, however, is a felony and we find one such case in Auburn. There are, it will be noticed, no convictions for drug using in the Probation group. This was determined by the court in which the Probation cases were studied, since the Women's Night Court does not have jurisdiction over drug charges.[6]

"Offenses against the Administration of Government" are represented by only two sub-heads in our group. The two perjury cases in Bedford were both young girls who had perjured themselves in court but who had been given a chance on probation. The perjury charges were brought against them in the first place, largely because there was no other charge on which to hold them, and it was felt that they needed supervision. When they violated their probation rules they were brought back to court and were resentenced to Bedford. The perjury involved was no more serious than is committed many times a day by cases against whom no perjury charge is lodged. Accordingly these offenses should not be thought of as being so unusual and important as they might seem from their title and the smallness of the

[6] It is important to remember that the great bulk of intoxication cases who would come under the head of "Offenses against Regulations for Public Health and Safety" were omitted from our group. Had these been included we should have a second large sub-division in our Workhouse group. In Chart I the bar representing these offenses would at least equal in length that indicating offenses against chastity, these two types of offenses making up the great body of the Workhouse population.

numbers. The bribery case in Auburn was that of an old woman who gave an officer forty dollars with intent to influence him to release her from custody. Her case was probably no more serious than either of the two Bedford perjury cases, but the age factor made it obligatory on the judge to send her either to the Penitentiary or to Auburn.

The group of "Offenses against Property Rights," we may note at the outset, is not represented in the Probation group since the Women's Night Court has no jurisdiction over such cases. The Workhouse has only five cases and those all of petit larceny. In the Bedford group, both grand and petit larceny cases are found. One of these grand larceny cases was first sentenced to Auburn but the sentence was changed later to a Reformatory term. The Auburn group of cases includes various types of offense, such as arson, extortion, forgery, receiving stolen property, and robbery, in addition to grand and petit larceny.[7] The range of offenses against property rights in the Magdalen is very small, covering only the three offenses of forgery, grand and petit larceny. In the Penitentiary, the range covers all of the offenses included in any other group, except extortion, forgery and robbery.

The last group, called "General Criminality" in the New York City Police Department classification, includes offenses difficult to place in any scheme of classification. Such general terms as disorderly conduct and vagrancy, with no qualifying statements, in cases on which we were unable to get further information, could not be put in any logical grouping. "Ungovernable child" should rightly fall in more closely with a group of juvenile offenses, but since the women under consideration are adults we have put the few semi-juvenile offenses into the miscellaneous group. Possessing a pistol and disorderly conduct, each represented by only two cases, also seem to fit into none of the other divisions, and following the New York City Police Department classification are treated as "General Criminality."

Table 3 shows, then, that the specific offenses under the seven main divisions are divided unevenly among the six institutional groups. We should expect this, since the institutional groups we have selected differ in the kind of commitments permitted them by law. That is, Auburn may receive only felonies, the Workhouse and Probation only

[7] The one petit larceny case in Auburn was an illegal commitment, since a person convicted of a misdemeanor may not be sent to state prison. This woman was indicted on a charge of grand larceny, first degree, but pled guilty to and was convicted of petit larceny.

misdemeanors, and the other three institutions both felonies and misdemeanors, though the Penitentiary has a much larger percentage of its cases felonies than have Bedford or the Magdalen.

In order to give in large the main divisions of the New York City Police Department classification, Table 4 has been made on a percentage basis giving only the totals of each division, in per cent, for each institutional group and for the total group.

TABLE 4

NATURE OF PRESENT OFFENSE

Per Cent Distribution of Delinquent Women in Institutional Groups, Classified by Main Divisions of New York City Police Department Classification

Nature of Offense	Institutional Groups						Total
	Bedford	Auburn	Magdalen	Penitentiary	Workhouse	Probation	
Offenses against the Person....	1.0	25.0	...	7.3	...	...	5.3
Offenses against Chastity......	62.7	6.8	77.6	6.4	83.5	87.2	53.8
Offenses against Family and Children..................	5.9	4.6	1.3	.9	...	...	2.0
Offenses against Regulations for Public Health, Safety and Policy..............	5.9	1.1	11.8	27.3	2.7	6.9	9.5
Offenses against Administration of Government...........	2.0	1.1	...	...	...	...	.5
Offenses against Property Rights..................	16.7	61.4	5.3	56.4	4.6	...	24.2
General Criminality...........	5.9	...	3.9	1.8	9.2	5.9	4.6
Total................	100.0	100.0	100.0	100.0	100.0	100.0	100.0

Chart 1 shows in graphic form the percentage figures which are given in Table 4. The most striking thing in the chart is, first of all, the great irregularity within each group, and between any two of the institutional groups which may be used for comparison. As has been stated, this is due largely to the unevenness of distribution of felonies and misdemeanors among the main divisions of the New York City Police Department classification (See Chart 3), and the

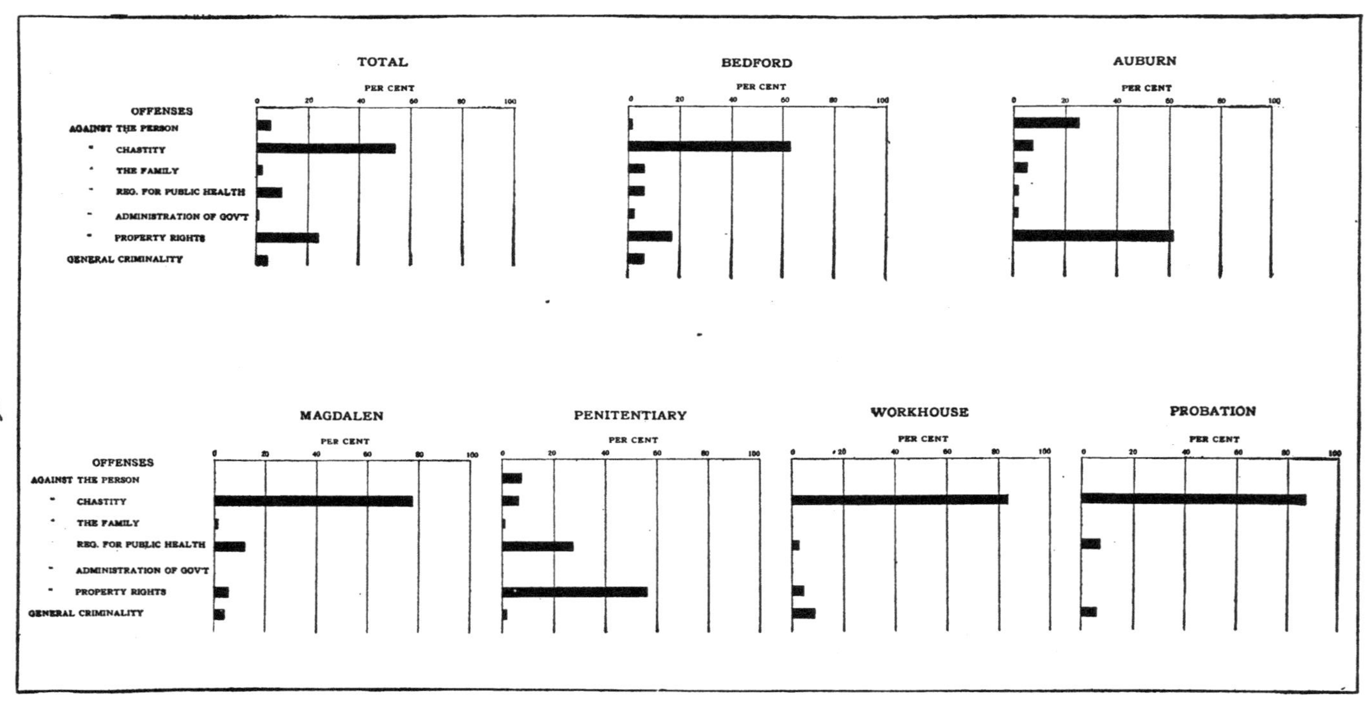

Chart I

Nature of Present Offense

Per cent distribution of offenses in New York City Police Department classification, by institutional groups.

distribution of felonies and misdemeanors among our institutional groups. It will be seen at a glance that the offenses against chastity constitute the largest percentage of offenses of any one group, except in Auburn and the Penitentiary which have the highest percentage of felony cases. In these two groups, again, the offenses against property rights constitute the largest percentage. The second largest percentage of offenses in Auburn is offenses against the person, made up of 93.5 per cent felonies. In the Penitentiary, offenses against regulations for public health, etc., have second place, and they are made up of only 7.1 per cent felonies. This high percentage in the Penitentiary may be partly explained by the fact that though possessing drugs, which is the largest factor in the offenses against regulations for public health, is legally a misdemeanor, it is considered one of the more serious misdemeanors and is therefore punished by one of the more serious and longer sentences, *i.e.*, the indeterminate sentence at the Penitentiary. The Bedford group of cases which is third highest in percentage of felons, has, as might be expected, a representation in each division of offenses of the New York City Police Department classification. The three groups of delinquents having the highest percentage of misdemeanors, the Magdalen Home, the Workhouse and the Probation group, have, naturally, few or no cases in the divisions of the New York City Police Department classification largely made up of felons. That is, in none of these three groups are there any cases among the offenses against the person or against the administration of government, and only in the Magdalen group are there a small percentage of offenders against property rights.

(*b*) *Classified by Felonies and Misdemeanors*

Table 5 in connection with Chart 2 will indicate how the institutional groups are divided into felonies and misdemeanors.

As stated in a footnote on page 94, the only misdemeanor case in Auburn was not a legal commitment. This one petit larceny case, therefore, gives a slightly erroneous impression in the graph, since one would naturally expect to see the entire Auburn bar marked as felony. Bedford includes only seven felony cases, or 6.9 per cent of her total number.[8] The Magdalen with two women, or 2.6 per

[8] The decrease in percentage of felons in the Reformatory at Bedford during the last few years is very marked. There have been as high as 32.2 per cent of the Bedford women, felons, but since 1907 there has been a steady and consistent decrease.

TABLE 5

NATURE OF PRESENT OFFENSE

Number and Per Cent of Delinquent Women in Institutional Groups, Classified by Felonies and Misdemeanors

Nature of Offense	Institutional Groups												Total	
	Bedford		Auburn		Magdalen		Penitentiary		Workhouse		Probation			
	Number	Per cent	Number	Per cent	Number	Per cent	Number	Per cent	Number	Per cent	Number	Per cent	Number	Per cent
Felonies	7	6.9	87	98.9	2	2.6	30	27.3	....	....	....	....	126	21.5
Misdemeanors	95	93.1	1	1.1	74	97.4	80	72.7	109	100.0	102	100.0	461	78.5
Total	102	100.0	88	100.0	76	100.0	110	100.0	109	100.0	102	100.0	587	100.0

cent of her total cases, felons, indicates that there is much less of a tendency to send the more serious offenders to an institution which is designed primarily for the younger and more hopeful girls. The Penitentiary with thirty felons, or 27.3 per cent of its total, ranks next

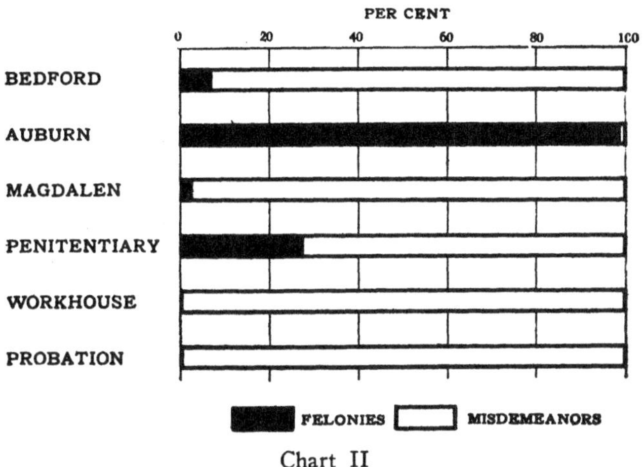

Chart II
Nature of Present Offense
Per cent distribution of felonies and misdemeanors by institutional groups.

to Auburn in having the largest number of serious offenders. The Workhouse and Probation groups are entirely made up of misdemeanants.

(c) *Felonies and Misdemeanors in New York City Police Department Classification*

Table 6, presented graphically in Chart 3, indicates what percentage of each of the divisions of the New York City Police Department classification are felons and misdemeanants.

As discussed on page 97, we may note that the offenses against the person, a total of only 31 cases, have only two misdemeanants or 6.5 per cent of its total number. The offenses against chastity, however, with a liberal sample of 316 cases, contain 310 misdemeanants or 98.1 per cent of its total. The group of offenders against the family and children, as well as the offenders against the administration of government, have very few cases on which to base any percentages, but as the figures stand, the percentage of misdemeanants is 50 per cent in the one, and 33.3 per cent in the other. Out of 56 cases,

TABLE 6

NATURE OF PRESENT OFFENSE

Number and Per Cent of Felons and Misdemeanants Classified by New York City Police Department Classification

Nature of Offense	Felons		Misdemeanants		Total	
	Number	Per cent	Number	Per cent	Number	Per cent
Offenses against the Person	29	93.5	2	6.5	31	100.0
Offenses against Chastity	6	1.9	310	98.1	316	100.0
Offenses against Family and Children	6	50.0	6	50.0	12	100.0
Offenses against Regulations for Public Health, Safety and Policy	4	7.1	52	92.9	56	100.0
Offenses against Administration of Government	2	66.7	1	33.3	3	100.0
Offenses against Property Rights	78	54.9	64	45.1	142	100.0
General Criminality	1	3.7	26	96.3	27	100.0
Total	126	21.5	461	78.5	587	100.0

52 or 92.9 per cent of the offenses against regulations for public health, safety and policy are misdemeanants. Next to the offenders against chastity, in size of group, are the offenders against property rights, a total of 142 cases, 45.1 per cent of which are misdemeanants. The last group of cases, the general criminality group, has out of 27 cases all but one, that is 96.3 per cent of the total, misdemeanants. Of our total group of cases, 461 or 78.5 per cent are misdemeanants.

(*d*) *Comparison of Nature of Offense of Female Felons, and Male Felons in Sing Sing and the New York State Reformatory at Elmira*

Before discussing the extent of delinquency found in the various institutional groups, it may be of interest to note the comparison of nature of offense of the 126 felons in our group with the felons as found in two of the institutions for male criminals in New York State. For this comparison we have chosen Sing Sing Prison, which may receive male felons of any adult age for any offense, and the New York State Reformatory at Elmira, which receives only felons sixteen to thirty years of age who have never before been convicted of a felony. The figures chosen for this comparison are the latest figures obtainable in the annual reports of these two institutions and include in each case, the consecutive commitments during the nine months ending June 30, 1916.[9] In the first comparison (Chart 4), the most marked observation is that there is no striking difference in the distribution of offenses in the two groups selected. It is particularly interesting, however, to note that the female felons have a smaller

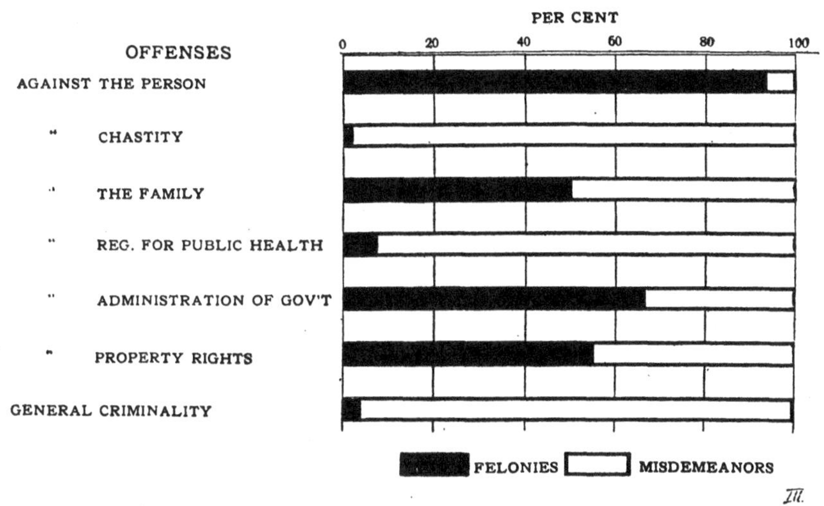

Chart III

Felonies and Misdemeanors

Per cent distribution among offenses classified by New York City Police Department classification.

percentage, 4.8 per cent, of offenses against chastity than the male felons with 8.0 per cent of their offenses in this group. In view of the fact that of the total group of 587 women, 53.8 per cent are offenders against chastity, it is important to observe the difference between the female felons and either the total or the misdemeanant group of females. The female felons have a slightly higher percentage than the male felons in the offenses against the person, the family, regulations for public health, and administration of government, but

[9] "Twenty-second Annual Report of the State Commission of Prisons." 1916, pp. 413-415 and 446-447. The offenses as given in the report are listed in alphabetical order with no attempt at classification. We have used the N. Y. C. Classification in classifying these offenses, as we did for our group of delinquent women.

fall slightly below in the offenses against property rights and general criminality.

In comparing the female felons with the male felons in the Reformatory at Elmira (Chart 5), the same trend is shown as in Chart 4, except that there are slightly more marked differences, especially in offenses against the person, where there is a difference of 10.4 per cent between the two groups, and offenses against property rights where the male felons exceed the female by 16.7 per cent. The

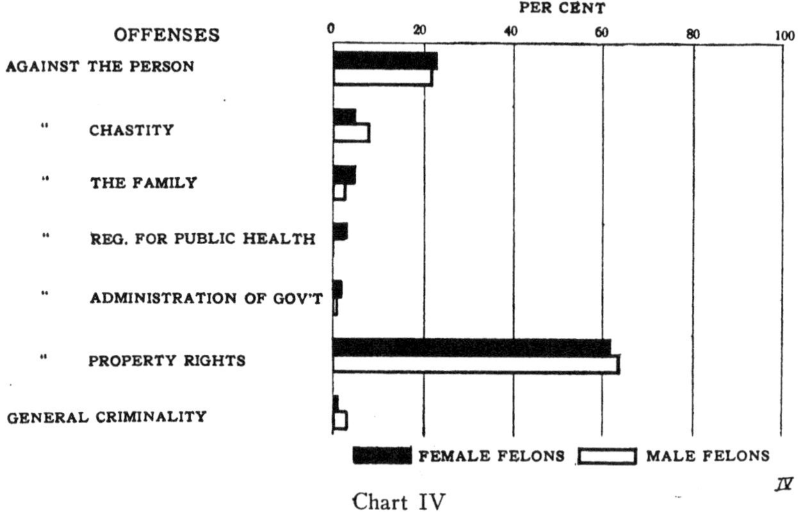

Chart IV

Percentage Comparison Showing: 1. Nature of Offense of 126 Female Felons in this Study; 2. Nature of Offense of 839 Male Felons Committed to Sing Sing during the Nine Months ending June 30, 1916.

difference between the two groups in offenses against chastity is very slight, only one-tenth of a per cent, which again is of interest since the statement is often made that the percentage of offenders against chastity is much higher among women in state prisons than among men.

EXTENT OF DELINQUENCY

In considering the extent of the delinquency of the women in this study, the measurement used has been for the most part the age at first conviction and the number of previous convictions, keeping in mind, wherever possible, the factor of present age, which determines to some degree, the number of convictions. That is, a girl of sixteen has had less opportunity to be convicted many times than has a woman of sixty. The number of months and the number of terms served have also been used, but are felt to be of far less value than the number of convictions, since the sentences in similar cases may vary radically, depending upon the impression the woman makes on the judge, while the conviction is usually a matter of law, likely to be settled for all cases alike. The colored women, especially, would have an unfair showing if any measure of term or length of time

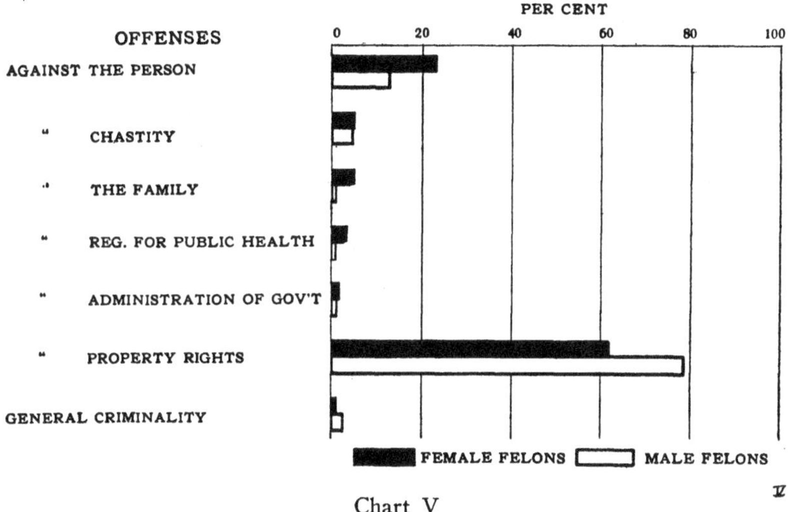

Chart V

Percentage Comparison Showing: 1. Nature of Offense of 126 Female Felons in this Study; 2. Nature of Offense of 760 Male Felons Committed to the New York State Reformatory at Elmira during the Nine Months ending June 30, 1916.

served were used, since the facilities for probation of colored women in New York City are so poor that in most cases they are sentenced to an institution for the same offense that would mean probation to a white first offender.

In this study, a conviction has been interpreted as including those who, in court, are convicted of the violation of any law. If, after conviction, a woman was put on probation but violated her probation within a week, was brought back to court on a bench warrant, and resentenced to an institution, only one conviction would be counted, since the probation was theoretically only a suspension of sentence for a definite period of time. If, however, she had been put on probation for soliciting and while on probation stole, was brought back to court and convicted again on the petit larceny charge, this would be counted as a second conviction. Also, when returned to court from an institution to which previously sentenced, and resentenced on the same charge, only one conviction would be counted, though in number of months the first institutional experience would count. If, however, she was returned to court from an institution for being incorrigible, etc., and sentenced to another institution on a new charge, this would be counted as a second conviction, and the first institutional experience would count as a term served, and number of months served. Time spent in a jail, hospital or Home preceding any conviction, no matter how long the time, was never counted as a term served. Juvenile convictions have been counted as convictions, but juvenile commitments to penal institutions as dependent children have not been so counted. To those who may object to including juvenile with adult convictions, it will be of interest to note the discussion at the end of this chapter, showing that only 6.8 per cent of our cases were convicted before the age of sixteen.

In this connection we might note the method used by Goring in his study of the English convict,[10] in "gauging a man's degree of criminal tendency." He used the three standards of: (1) age at first conviction, (2) frequency of conviction per year of freedom, and (3) the fraction of each year of life hitherto passed in confinement. The second and third standards were obtained by noting the first and last conviction of each convict, and taking the period of time between the two as the length of his criminal career. "Next, the frequency of his convictions to, and the length of time spent in, prison, during this period between his first and last conviction, is noted—the fraction of this period passed in freedom being obtained by subtracting from it the length of time in prison. Finally, the number of convictions, including the first but excluding the present, divided by the years of freedom, gives the frequency of convictions per year of freedom; and the years in prison, divided by the total years of his criminal career, give the fraction of each year spent in prison."

This method excludes all convicts who are at the time of the study first offenders. Since 259 or 45.4 per cent of the women in this study were first offenders, it seemed inadvisable to use a measure of extent of delinquency which would at the outset eliminate nearly

[10] Goring, Charles. "The English Convict. A Statistical Study." T. Fisher Unwin, London, 1913, p. 269.

half of the group. There are also certain difficulties in applying such a scheme to a group which contains as many kinds of sentences as does the group under consideration. Goring did not have to meet the problem of an offender who, though he may have had three previous convictions, had been placed on probation each time and had, therefore, never served any time in prison. Again, his scheme makes no allowance for cases of offenders who may be convicted of larceny, sentenced to an institution and while there become so troublesome that they are returned to court, reconvicted as incorrigible and sentenced to another institution. Here there are no years in freedom, though there have been two previous convictions. The great differences in sentences for relatively petty offenses may not have had great weight in a study of English men prisoners twelve years ago. In this study, however, there are numerous cases of women who have been convicted of soliciting at some time and have received either probation, five days in the Workhouse, an indefinite reformatory sentence of three years, or in some cases, a sentence in a Home for the period of minority which may be as much as five years. Such varying sentences for the same offense obviously distort the value of a scheme which is based on number of convictions per year of freedom, or fraction of year passed in prison, since the individual who shows up worst by the use of such a measure may be one whom the judge felt could be benefited by a reformatory sentence. The more hopeless case, on the other hand, who was given a short Workhouse term, would figure as less criminal by this scheme, because of the short term.

(*a*) *Number of Previous Convictions*

(1) *Relationship Between Number of Previous Convictions and Age.*—It is true that the criminal records of these women are in different stages of completion because of their differences in age, and that in order to make valid comparisons, some account must be taken of the age factor. The correlation between number of previous convictions and present age is therefore of importance, both as an indication of the extent of the direct relationship between these two factors, and as furnishing a measure to be used in making allowance for age in connection with other comparisons. Table 7 presents the data regarding this relationship. The coefficient of correlation is found to be .23 with a standard deviation of .040. This is sufficient to indicate the existence of a genuine, though small, relationship. The correlation ratios are not appreciably larger than

TABLE 7

Correlation between Number of Previous Convictions and Age

Age	Number of Previous Convictions																						Totals	Means (Number of Previous Convictions)
	0	1	2	3	4	5	6	7	8	9	10	11	12	13	14	15	16	17	18	19	20	31		
72 to 75 years			1																				1	
68 " 72 "																								
65 " 68 "	1																						1	
62 " 65 "		1				1																	2	
59 " 62 "	2				1																		3	2.7
56 " 59 "	4											1										1	6	
53 " 56 "	4		1																				5	
50 " 53 "	4	2	2			1				1													10	
47 " 50 "	6	2		1	2			2						1									14	2.7
44 " 47 "	2	2	3	3			2																12	
41 " 44 "	8	5	2	1	1	1	1			1											1		21	2.3
38 " 41 "	10	5	1	5	1	1	2					1											26	
35 " 38 "	10	7	2	3	3	3			1		2		1						1				33	2.6
32 " 35 "	15	11	7		2	2		1			1				2								41	
29 " 32 "	23	12	7	8	3		1	1	2	1									1				59	1.9
26 " 29 "	25	12	9	5	2	4	1	2		1			1										62	
23 " 26 "	44	19	8	7	4	3	1	1	1														88	1.0
20 " 23 "	41	20	12	2	2			1															78	
17 " 20 "	43	26	6	4	2	1																	82	0.8
14 " 17 "	8	6			1																		15	
Totals	250	130	61	39	24	17	8	8	4	4	3	2	2	1	2				2		1	1	559	1.66
Means (Age)	27.9	27.6		30.6		34.1		33.5				39.6											28.79	

Number of previous convictions: Mean = 1.66 σ = 2.887
Age........................... Mean = 28.79 σ = 10.13

Coefficient of correlation: r = .23 ± .040

Correlation ratios: Number of previous convictions on age: η = .25 ± .040. Blakeman's Criterion = 1.7
Age on number of previous convictions: η = .23 ± .040. Blakeman's Criterion = .23

the above coefficient, being .23 ± .040 for age on number of previous convictions and .25 ± .040 for number of previous convictions on age. Reference to the mean number of convictions for the various age groups shows that there is a clear tendency to increase in number of convictions with age up to about thirty-three years of age, and that after this there seems no consistent tendency toward increase, though results are somewhat erratic because of the small numbers in the higher age groups. In any case, the relationship between age and number of convictions is low enough to show that age is not the sole nor even the main determinant of the number of convictions.

It is of interest to note that Goring found a somewhat lower correlation between age and number of convictions for his 2,225 men convicts: $r = .1240$.[11] This correlation coefficient is, however, not entirely comparable with ours, since he has not included first offenders in his table. While we admit that first offenders introduce a considerable source of difficulty, since these individuals represent all degrees of criminal tendency, from those who will never offend again to those who are to be the most confirmed criminals, we have not felt that our problem would be clarified by rejecting from consideration nearly half of our group, especially since it appears to us that the above-mentioned difficulty is found in only slightly lesser measure for second and third offenders, and so on down the line. Just as the first offender may either remain all his life a first offender, or may go on to accumulate a large number of convictions, so the second offender may remain only a second offender or may be merely at the beginning of a long career of crime.

(2) *Institutional Differences in Number of Previous Convictions.* —The distribution of the number of previous convictions, showing the irregularity among the various institutional groups, is indicated in actual percentages in Table 8 and graphically in Chart 6.

Those who have never had any previous convictions vary considerably between the groups. The Probation group has the largest number of first offenders, as would be expected, while in the order of next highest percentage follow Auburn, the Magdalen, Bedford, the Penitentiary, and last, the Workhouse with only 23.5 per cent first offenders. The range of number of convictions is also of interest among the various groups. Probation has the shortest range, and is followed by Bedford, the Magdalen, Auburn, the Penitentiary

[11] *Op. cit.*, p. 425.

TABLE 8

NUMBER OF PREVIOUS CONVICTIONS

Per Cent Distribution of Delinquent Women in Institutional Groups, with Constants for Each Group

Number of Previous Convictions	Institutional Groups						Total
	Bedford	Auburn	Magdalen	Penitentiary	Workhouse	Probation	
0	38.6	51.3	44.7	32.7	23.5	83.3	45.4
1	31.7	16.3	35.5	22.7	19.7	13.7	22.9
2	10.0	8.8	11.8	15.6	17.7	2.0	11.0
3	11.9	6.3	2.6	9.2	9.8	....	6.8
4	3.0	3.8	2.6	3.6	10.8	1.0	4.2
5	3.0	2.5	....	3.6	7.8	....	3.0
6	1.0	1.3	....	2.7	2.9	....	1.4
7	1.0	2.5	....	1.8	2.9	....	1.4
8	....	2.5	....	1.8	....	....	.7
9	....	1.3	1.3	.9	1.0	....	.7
10	....	2.5	1.3	....	....	....	.5
11	....	....	....	.9	1.0	....	.4
12	....	1.3	....	.9	....	....	.4
13	....	....	....	.9	....	....	.2
14	....	....	....	....	2.0	....	.4
18	....	....	....	1.8	....	....	.4
20	....	....	....	.9	....	....	.2
31	....	....	....	....	1.0	....	.2
Total	100.0	100.0	100.0	100.0	100.0	100.0	100.0
Number of cases	101	80	76	110	102	102	571
Mean	1.27	1.76	1.03	2.49	2.82	.216	1.63
σ_m	±.149	±.312	±.193	±.359	±.387	±.0565	±.120
σ	1.50	2.79	1.68	3.77	3.90	.571	2.864
σ_σ	±.105	±.221	±.136	±.254	±.273	±.0400	±.0848

and Workhouse. The fact that Auburn changes place with Bedford in the latter consideration would indicate that while there were more first offenders among the Auburn women, the recidivists showed a greater variability in the number of convictions. The Workhouse in both considerations comes out at the worst end.[12] It is interesting to observe that each of the eleven women in the total group who

[12] The Workhouse group, as used in these comparisons, does not include the intoxication cases, which will be considered in the next chapter. If these were added in the present comparison, the preponderance of recidivists with many convictions in the Workhouse would be greatly increased.

have had more than ten convictions have their cases complicated by the factor of excessive alcoholism and previous convictions for intoxication, though the present offense does not involve intoxication. The woman in the Workhouse, for example, who has had 31 previous convictions had eighteen convictions for intoxication, seven convictions for disorderly conduct, and six convictions for vagrancy.

Table 8 gives also, for each institutional group, the mean number of convictions and the standard deviation which are represented graphically in Chart 6. This affords a basis for comparison of the institu-

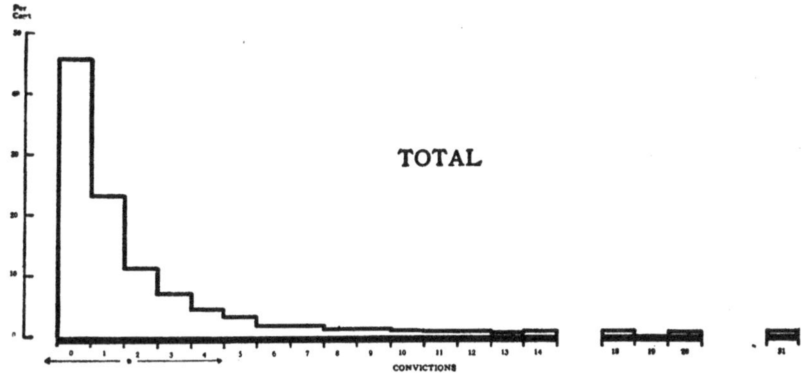

Chart VI
Number of Previous Convictions
Per cent distribution by institutional groups.

tional groups in terms of both their central tendencies and the amount of dispersion within the groups. These figures are, however, insufficient, since we are not able to say, by mere inspection of the table, whether a difference, which may be observed between two groups, is large enough to be considered probably valid or not. A certain amount of difference in constants is to be expected even if two samples are taken entirely at random from the same total. Our first problem is, therefore, to determine whether the differences observed are large enough to justify us in considering the groups distinguished from one another in respect to this factor, *viz.*, number of previous convictions.

The statistical basis for this comparison is explained in Chapter III. In general the method consists in finding the actual difference between the constants of any two groups under consideration and determining the ratio of this difference to the standard deviation of

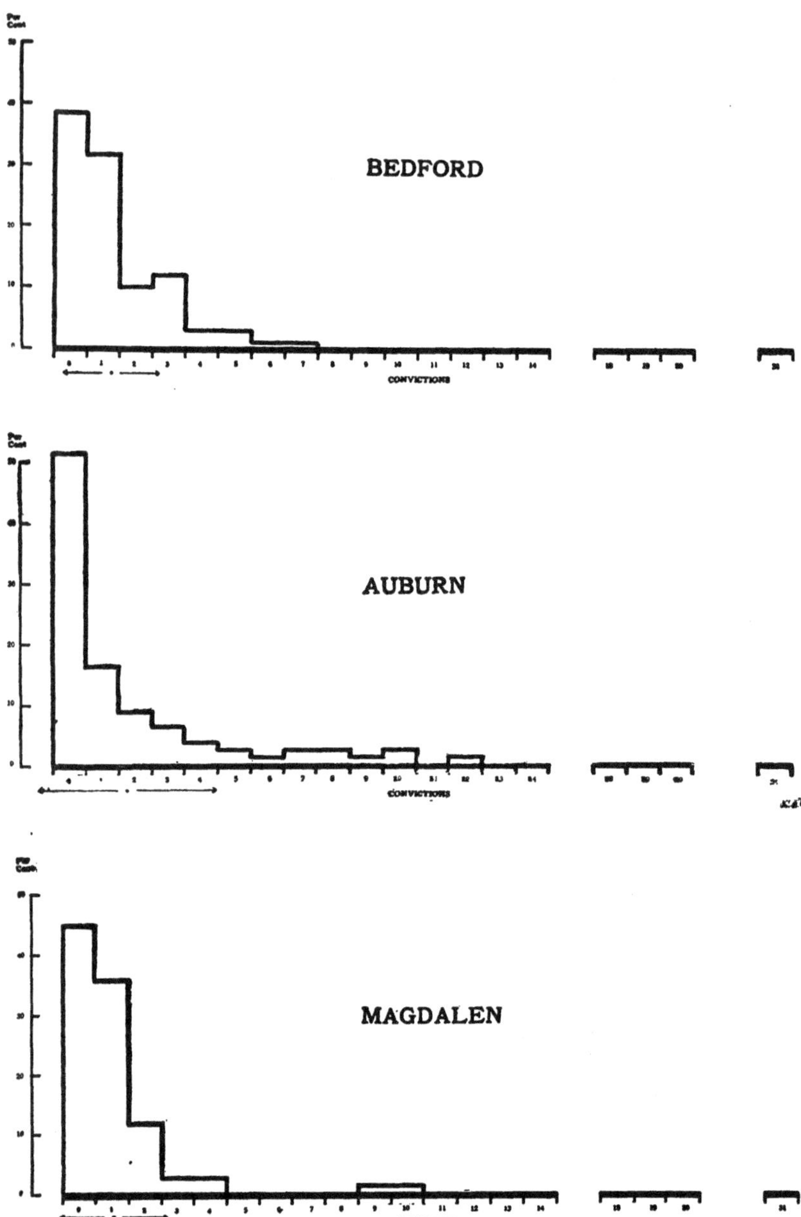

Chart VI—(Continued)
Number of Previous Convictions
Per cent distribution by institutional groups.

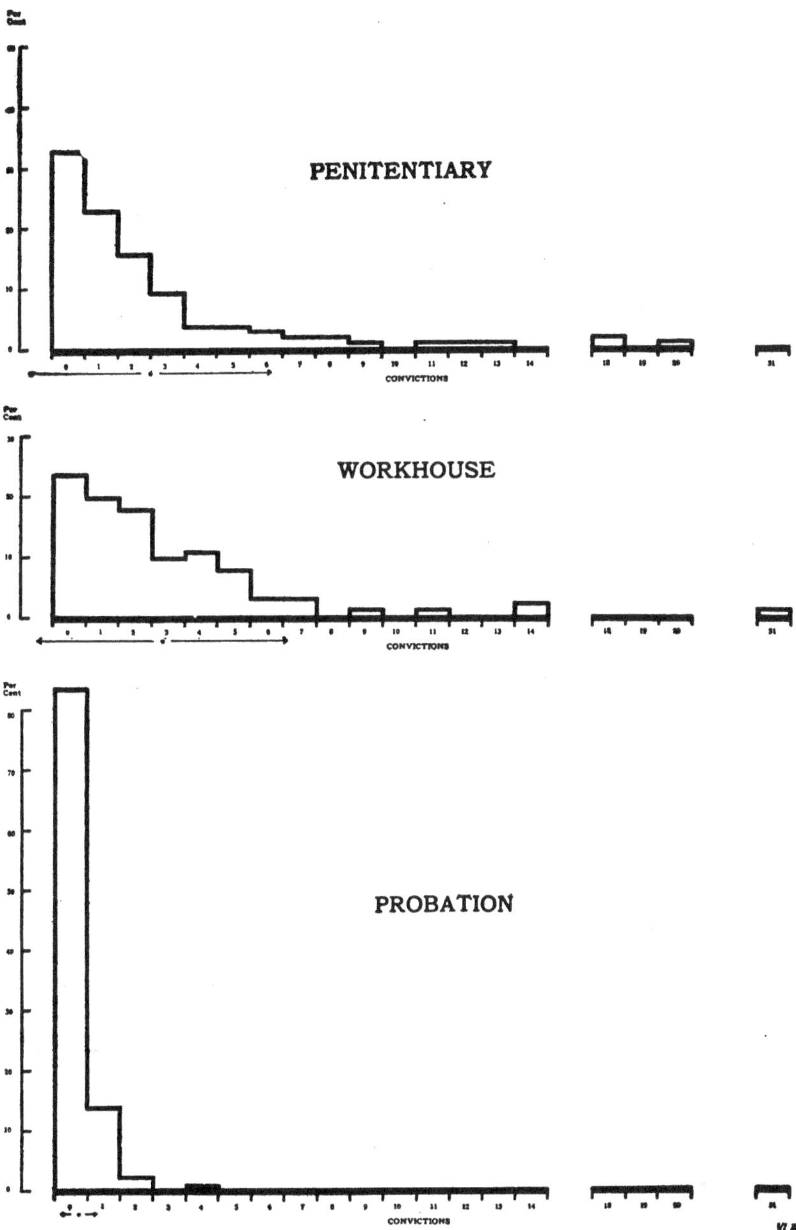

Chart VI—(Continued)
Number of Previous Convictions
Per cent distribution by institutional groups.

the difference.[13] Although no arbitrary dividing line can be laid down, on one side of which there is certainty that a difference exists and on the other side of which there is uncertainty, we shall accept a ratio of 2 as critical for practical purposes. When the ratio is 2 or more we shall feel a fair degree of confidence in the existence of a difference between the two groups. A ratio of 3 we shall accept as justifying practical certainty of the difference. When the ratio is less than 2 the inference is, not that there is no difference between the groups, but that our data fail to present convincing evidence of their difference. The more closely the ratio approaches 2 the greater the probability that the observed difference represents a genuine difference between the groups, even though the ratio fails to measure up to the standard of probability which we have accepted as critical.

In Table 9 we present the necessary data to supplement Table 8 and make possible comparison of groups with reference to their average number of convictions. This table gives, for all the different pairs of institutions, the ratio of the difference, between any two given means, to the standard deviation of the difference.

From these tables it appears that the Probation group, with a mean number of convictions of .216, holds the lowest place. Comparison with each other group in turn, moreover, makes it clear that the difference in favor of the Probation group is to be considered valid, since $\frac{d}{\sigma d}$ is decidedly over 3, which is sufficient for confident prediction. The mean of the Magdalen is next in absolute size, and is found to differ from each of the other groups except Bedford by an amount large enough to justify confidence in the genuineness of the difference. The difference between the Magdalen and Bedford groups, however, being only .991 times the standard deviation of the difference, does not justify more than the assertion that there is a possibility that there may be a real difference between the two groups. Bedford comes next with a mean number of convictions of 1.27. The differences between this value and the means for the Penitentiary and the Workhouse are such as to justify assertion of a difference. The difference between Bedford and Auburn, however, can not be stressed, since $\frac{d}{\sigma d}$ is only 1.44. Though Auburn and the Workhouse differ from one another, by what appears to

[13] This ratio appears in the tables as $\frac{d}{\sigma d}$, where d = the observed difference between the measures and σd = the standard deviation of the difference.

TABLE 9

NUMBER OF PREVIOUS CONVICTIONS

Inter-comparison of Means of Institutional Groups in Terms of the Ratio of the Difference Between the Means to the Standard Deviation of the Difference

	Auburn	Magdalen	Penitentiary	Workhouse	Probation
Bedford	−1.4	.99	−3.15	−3.76	6.60
Auburn		2.01	−1.53	−2.13	4.88
Magdalen			−3.60	−4.16	4.04
Penitentiary				− .63	6.26
Workhouse					6.67

Explanation of table: The number in each space gives the value for $\frac{d}{\sigma_d}$ for the two institutional groups designated at the head of the column and to the left of the row, respectively. A minus sign indicates that the mean of the institutional group at the left is smaller than the mean of the group heading the column.

be a valid degree, in the direction of a smaller average number of convictions for Auburn, neither of these groups can be distinguished with a high degree of certainty from the Penitentiary, whose mean falls between that for Auburn and that for the Workhouse.

Summarizing, the facts which seem at least reasonably well established with regard to the differences between the separate groups in the matter of the criminal record as measured by average number of convictions are as follows:

(1) The Probation group may be considered clearly differentiated from all the other groups by its small mean number of convictions, a conclusion which was to be expected, since one of the prime grounds for selection of a case for probation is the lack of a criminal record.

(2) The Magdalen group, while having a significantly larger mean number of convictions than the Probation group, has a definitely smaller mean number than Auburn, the Penitentiary or the Workhouse, but fails to be clearly distinguished from Bedford.

(3) The Bedford total is clearly distinguished, on the one hand, from the Probation group, and, on the other hand, from the Penitentiary and the Workhouse, but is not clearly distinguished from either the Magdalen or Auburn.

(4) Auburn shows a clear difference, on the one hand, from the Probation and Magdalen groups, and on the other hand, from

the Workhouse, but is not certainly distinguished from either Bedford or the Penitentiary.

(5) The Penitentiary is clearly distinguished, by its larger mean number of convictions, from all the groups except Bedford and Auburn, in which cases the difference can not be considered established as valid.

(6) The Workhouse is clearly differentiated, by its larger mean number of convictions, from all groups except the Penitentiary. Between the Workhouse and the Penitentiary the existence of a real difference can not be proved. In this connection it is important to remember again that our Workhouse group does not include the cases committed for intoxication, the average number of convictions for which is very large.

The comparison of the mean number of convictions in the various institutional groups may be summarized in another way by comparing the mean of each group with the mean for the total of all groups.[14] The results of this comparison are given in Table 10 supplementing Table 8. From this it appears that Bedford, the Magdalen and Probation are clearly distinguished from the total by a smaller mean number of convictions, whereas the Penitentiary and the Workhouse show a definitely larger mean number of convictions. The mean for Auburn is so close to the mean for the whole group that the difference might easily be accounted for by chance. These results are entirely in accord with those obtained by the more detailed comparison, and have the advantage of presenting the situation more concisely.

We may compare, also, the amount of dispersion in the various institutional groups, to discover, in the same way as in the case of the comparison of the means, whether the apparent difference constitutes a probably real difference.[15] Table 11 gives for the various institutions, by pairs, the ratio of the difference between any two given standard deviations to the standard deviation of the difference. The results of this comparison may be summarized

[14] The formula for the standard deviation of the difference between the mean of a sub-group and the mean of the total of which it is a part is given by Pearson ("Biometrika," vol. V, p. 182) as $\sqrt{\frac{\Sigma^2}{N}+\frac{\sigma^2}{n}\left(1-\frac{2n}{N}\right)-\frac{n(M-m)^2}{N(N-n)}}$ where Σ is the standard deviation of the total and N the number of cases in the total, σ the standard deviation of the sub-group and n the number of cases in the sub-group, M the mean of the total and m the mean of the sub-group.

[15] The formula for the standard deviation of the difference between the standard deviations is as follows: $\sigma_d=\sqrt{\sigma^2_{\sigma_{(1)}} + \sigma^2_{\sigma_{(2)}}}$

TABLE 10

NUMBER OF PREVIOUS CONVICTIONS

Comparison of Means of Institutional Groups with Mean of Total, in Terms of the Ratios of the Difference Between the Means to the Standard Deviation of the Difference

Institutional Group	Difference between mean of sub-group and mean of total	$\frac{d}{\sigma}$	Chances that real difference does not exist are 1 in:
Bedford	− .39	2.29	91
Auburn	.11	.37	3
Magdalen	− .63	3.09	1000
Penitentiary	.83	2.74	323
Workhouse	1.17	3.53	500
Probation	−1.44	11.33	∞

briefly as showing that the differences in the amount of dispersion in the various groups may be considered valid, except in the case of the comparison of Magdalen with Bedford, and that of the Penitentiary with the Workhouse. In all the other cases the ratio of the difference to the standard deviation of the difference is well over 2. Probation shows the least variability within the group, and the Workhouse the greatest, the order of variability being Probation,

TABLE 11

NUMBER OF PREVIOUS CONVICTIONS

Inter-comparison of Standard Deviations of Institutional Groups in Terms of the Ratio of the Difference Between the Standard Deviations to the Standard Deviation of the Difference

	Auburn	Magdalen	Penitentiary	Workhouse	Probation
Bedford	−5.30	−1.06	−8.27	−8.22	8.21
Auburn		4.29	−2.91	−3.17	9.90
Magdalen			−7.25	−7.29	7.80
Penitentiary				− .36	12.43
Workhouse					12.06

Explanation of table: The number in each space gives the value for $\frac{d}{\sigma d}$ for the two institutional groups designated at the head of the column and to the left of the row, respectively. A minus sign indicates that the mean of the institutional group at the left is smaller than the mean of the group heading the column.

Bedford, Magdalen, Auburn, Penitentiary, and Workhouse. It appears, thus, that the groups having the smallest mean number of convictions have also the lowest variability, a fact which is easily understood, since the mean values of these groups approach the lower limiting value of *no* previous convictions.

The above comparison of the groups, with reference to their mean number of convictions, is likely to be somewhat misleading, since no account is taken of the wide differences in actual ages of the groups, with the consequent differences in opportunity for accumulation of numerous convictions. From the point of view of a simple description of the groups as they stand, such crude comparison is not only justifiable but useful, since we have a certain interest in knowing how the groups compare with respect to the extent of criminal record of their women, whatever the reasons for this difference may be. For example, it is important to realize the marked tendency of the Workhouse and the Penitentiary to include considerable numbers of old offenders, because of the bearing which this fact would have on the sending of young and impressionable first offenders into these groups. On the other hand, the fact that Magdalen and Bedford tend to receive the less extensive recidivists should be a reason for considering well before sending into this group individuals with frequent experience of conflict with the law. Comparison of norms and of distributions of number of convictions is, therefore, of direct importance for descriptive purposes.

When, however, we endeavor to make use of the number of convictions as at least an approximate measure of criminal tendency, it becomes of great importance that we make allowance for the factor of age. In connection with the present inter-comparison of institutional groups the fact that the three institutions having the smallest mean numbers of convictions have also the lowest mean ages[16] may well raise a doubt as to whether there is any real difference between the groups with respect to criminal tendency, or whether there may not have been a selection primarily in terms of age which has naturally resulted in a difference in the extensiveness of the criminal records.

(3) *Number of Previous Convictions Among Felons and Misdemeanants.*—It will be of interest here to make the comparison between number of previous convictions among those convicted of felonies and

[16] For the necessary data regarding ages of groups, see Chapter VII, p. 148.

TABLE 12

Number and Per Cent of Previous Convictions Among Delinquent Women Classified as Felons and Misdemeanants

Number of Convictions	Nature of Offense				Total	
	Felonies		Misdemeanors			
	Number	Per Cent	Number	Per Cent	Number	Per Cent
0	61	51.7	198	43.7	259	45.4
1	23	19.4	108	23.8	131	22.9
2	11	9.2	52	11.5	63	11.0
3	6	5.1	33	7.3	39	6.8
4	3	2.5	21	4.6	24	4.2
5	2	1.7	15	3.3	17	3.0
6	2	1.7	6	1.3	8	1.4
7	3	2.5	5	1.1	8	1.4
8	2	1.7	2	.4	4	.7
9	1	.8	3	.7	4	.7
10	2	1.7	1	.2	3	.5
11	....	....	2	.4	2	.4
12	1	.8	1	.2	2	.4
13	....	....	1	.2	1	.2
14	....	....	2	.4	2	.4
18	....	....	2	.4	2	.4
20	1	.8	....	....	1	.2
31	....	....	1	.2	1	.2
Total	118	100.00	453	100.00	571	100.00

of misdemeanors, as well as to observe the difference among institutional groups.

Table 12 shows that a slightly larger percentage of the felons than of the misdemeanants are first offenders and that the range is slightly shorter in the felony group. The histogram which follows shows graphically the number of previous convictions among the two groups, and would seem to indicate that the seriousness of offense committed does not have an important relationship in our total group to the number of previous convictions.

Table 13, supplementing Table 12, makes possible a comparison between felons and misdemeanants in terms of the mean number of convictions and the amount of variations about these means in the two groups. While a comparison of the means alone would suggest that the felons as a group tend to have been convicted somewhat more often than the misdemeanants, since their central tendency is slightly larger, this point can not be safely maintained until we discover whether this difference can be considered valid or whether it might have occurred by chance. Since the ratio of the actual difference between the means

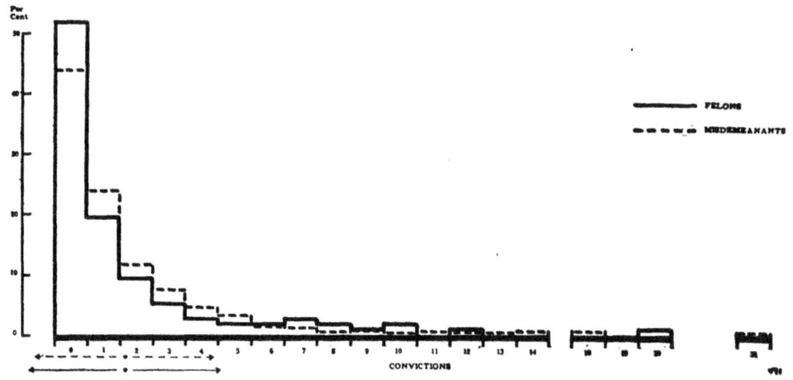

Chart VII
Number of Previous Convictions
Percentage comparison between felons and misdemeanants

to the standard deviation of the differences is only .09, the chances are even that the observed difference might have occurred by chance. Accordingly, we are justified in saying that there is no demonstrable difference between the felons and the misdemeanants with reference to

TABLE 13

FELONS AND MISDEMEANANTS

Comparison of the Means and Standard Deviations of Number of Previous Convictions Among Felons and Misdemeanants of Total Group

	Felons	Misdemeanants	Difference	$\frac{d}{\sigma_d}$	Chances that real difference does not exist are 1 in:
Mean	1.65	1.63	.03	.09	2
σ_m	±.277	±.133			
σ	3.01	2.825	.19	.85	5
σ_σ	±.196	±.0939			
Cases	118	453			

their mean number of convictions.[17] A comparison of the standard deviations, or the measures of dispersion, of the two groups, indicates a slightly wider scattering of cases in the felon group than in the misdemeanor. There is only a possible difference in the dispersion of these two groups.[18]

(4) *Number of Previous Convictions Among Offenders Against Chastity and Offenders Against Property.*—As previously noted, the two subdivisions of the New York City Police Department classification which are represented by the greatest number of cases from our group are the offenses against chastity and offenses against property.

TABLE 14

Number and Per Cent of Previous Convictions Among Delinquent Women Convicted of Offenses Against Chastity and Offenses Against Property Rights

Number of Convictions	Offenses Against:				Total	
	Chastity		Property Rights			
	Number	Per Cent	Number	Per Cent	Number	Per Cent
0	155	49.7	49	36.0	204	45.5
1	71	22.8	37	27.2	108	24.1
2	31	9.9	17	12.5	48	10.7
3	16	5.1	14	10.3	30	6.7
4	17	5.5	4	2.9	21	4.7
5	10	3.2	2	1.5	12	2.7
6	3	1.0	2	1.5	5	1.1
7	3	1.0	2	1.5	5	1.1
8	....	....	2	1.5	2	.5
9	2	.6	1	.7	3	.7
10	....	....	2	1.5	2	.5
11	1	.3	1	.7	2	.5
12	1	.3	....	....	1	.2
13	....	....	1	.7	1	.2
14	2	.6	....	....	2	.5
18	....	....	1	.7	1	.2
20	....	....	1	.7	1	.2
31	....	....	....	....	....	....
Total	312	100.00	136	100.00	448	100.0

[17] It is important to remember again, in connection with this comparison of felons and misdemeanants with regard to their mean number of convictions, that the intoxication commitments are omitted from the misdemeanant group. We are convinced that if these had been included, the misdemeanants would have shown a conclusively larger mean number of convictions. (See Chapter VII, p. 154.)

[18] See Chapter III.

These two divisions which comprise 78 per cent of our total group seem of sufficient importance to use for purposes of comparison. Accordingly, we shall proceed to Table 14, which shows the percentage of offenders against chastity and offenders against property rights who have had the number of previous convictions specified in the table. It would appear that among the first offenders there is considerable difference between the percentage of chastity and property offenders, 49.7 per cent as against 36.0 per cent. The range of number of convictions for the offenders against property rights is also wider.

Turning from the frequency table above to Table 15, we may consider whether or not the difference seemingly indicated in Table 14 is of any real significance. We may note, first of all, by comparing the means, that there is a tendency for the offenders against property rights to have a larger mean number of convictions than the offenders against chastity. There is almost certainly a real difference between the mean number of convictions of the two groups of offenders, with a tendency, as stated above, for the offenders against property rights to have more convictions. The difference between the standard deviations of the two groups is even more marked, showing that there is more variability in the number of convictions among the offenders against property rights than among the offenders against chastity.

TABLE 15

OFFENDERS AGAINST PROPERTY RIGHTS AND OFFENDERS AGAINST CHASTITY

Comparison of the Means and Standard Deviations of Number of Previous Convictions Among Offenders Against Property Rights and Offenders Against Chastity of Total Group

	Offenders against Property Rights	Offenders against Chastity	Difference	$\frac{d}{\sigma_d}$	Chances that real difference does not exist are 1 in:
Mean	2.00	1.30	.70	2.32	98
σ_m	±.275	±.120			
σ	3.20	2.121	1.08	5.10	∞
σ_σ	±.194	±.0849			
Cases	136	312			

(b) *Number of Previous Terms Served*

In addition to the consideration of the number of previous convictions as an indication of the extent of delinquency, we may note briefly the distribution among the various groups of the number of previous terms served. Table 16 will show this distribution. A term, as we have used it, may be defined as a sentence of any length of time to any Home or institution, as a delinquent. In comparison with Table 8, showing the number of previous convictions, it becomes evident, as would be expected, that the number who have never served any previous term is always slightly larger than those who have never had any previous convictions, since in each group there are a certain number who have been given a chance on probation or suspended sentence. The difference is fairly large in the Bedford group, *i.e.*, 12.9 per cent.

TABLE 16

Per Cent Distribution of Number of Previous Terms Served in Penal Institutions by Delinquent Women in Institutional Groups

Number of Terms	Institutional Groups						Total
	Bedford	Auburn	Magdalen	Penitentiary	Workhouse	Probation	
0	51.5	57.5	63.2	38.2	24.8	92.1	53.8
1	31.7	12.5	25.0	21.8	19.8	5.9	19.5
2	8.9	7.5	5.3	14.5	16.8	1.0	9.3
3	4.0	6.3	3.9	6.4	12.9	....	5.6
4	2.0	2.5	....	4.5	7.9	1.0	3.2
5	....	5.0	....	2.7	6.9	....	2.5
6	2.0	2.5	...	3.6	3.0	....	1.9
7	....	1.3	....	.9	3.0	....	.9
8	....	2.5	1.3	.9	....	....	.7
9	....	....	....	.9	1.0	....	.4
10	....	2.5	1.3	....	....	....	.5
11	....	....	....	.9	1.0	....	.4
12	....	....	....	.9	....	....	.2
13	....	....	....	.9	....	....	.2
14	....	....	....	....	2.0	....	.4
15	....	....	....	....	....	....	....
16	....	....	....	....	....	....	....
17	....	....	....	.9	....	....	.2
18	....	....	....	.9	....	....	.2
20	....	....	....	.9	....	....	.2
31	....	....	....	....	1.0	....	.2
Total	100.0	100.0	100.0	100.0	100.0	100.0	100.0
Number of cases	101	80	76	110	101	101	569

In the Auburn group we find a difference of 6.2 per cent, in the Magdalen 18.5 per cent, in the Penitentiary 5.5 per cent, in the Workhouse 1.3 per cent, and in the Probation group 8.8 per cent. The Workhouse has the smallest percentage, therefore, who have never served a previous term, and shows a smaller difference than any other group between the number of previous convictions and the number of previous terms served, indicating, as will later be shown in a table giving the number of times on probation, that the Workhouse women have been given sentences to institutions more than have the women in any other group. The range of number of previous terms served is very much like the range of number of previous convictions.

(*c*) *Length of Time Served in Penal Institutions*

If we turn to the length of time served in penal institutions,[19] the most striking thing in the distribution, as in Table 16, is the small percentage in the Workhouse who have never served time previous to the present conviction, and the comparatively high percentage of those who have served time amounting to less than a year altogether. This is accounted for by the fact that at their first sentence, 91.2 per cent of the women in the Workhouse were sentenced to the Workhouse, Penitentiary, or an institution like County Jails, in each of which, in the past, a short term was possible. Since the Workhouse has many commitments of five, ten, fifteen or twenty days, etc., it has been possible for many of the women in our group to serve a large number of terms, and still serve altogether a comparatively short time, less than one year. It will be noted from Table 17 that while only 17.8 per cent of the women in the Workhouse had served more than one year, though the mean number of convictions was 2.82, just the same percentage, 17.8, of the Bedford women had served more than one year, and the mean number of convictions was only 1.27. The Penitentiary women, also, with a mean number of convictions of 2.49, only slightly less than the mean for the Workhouse group, have 29.0 per cent of their total number who have served more than one year in penal institutions. The Probation group has only two cases, or 2.0 per cent of its total, who have served more than one year.

[19] We should expect the same percentage for those who had never served a previous term, and those who had never served any time, since, of course, one who has served even a few days has served a term, and conversely. The difference in percentages for those never serving time (Table 17) or a previous term (Table 16) comes from the difference in the total number of cases on which we were able to obtain data for both items.

TABLE 17

LENGTH OF TIME SERVED IN PENAL INSTITUTIONS PREVIOUS TO PRESENT CONVICTION

Per Cent Distribution of Delinquent Women in Institutional Groups

Length of Time Served	Institutional Groups						Total
	Bedford	Auburn	Magdalen	Penitentiary	Workhouse	Probation	
None	51.5	59.0	63.2	39.1	24.5	93.0	54.1
Less than 1 yr.	30.7	20.5	25.0	31.8	57.8	5.0	29.1
1 yr. to 2 yrs.	7.9	7.7	7.9	12.7	12.8	...	8.3
2 yrs. " 3 "	5.9	9.0	2.6	9.1	2.0	1.0	4.9
3 " " 4 "	3.0	1.3	1.3	4.5	2.0	...	2.1
4 " " 5 "	1.0	1.3	...	...	...	...	.4
5 " " 6 "	...	1.3	...	...	...	...	.2
6 " " 7 "	...	...	...	.9	...	...	.2
7 " " 8 "	...	...	...	1.8	...	1.0	.5
8 " " 9 "	...	...	...	...	...	...	...
9 " " 10 "	...	...	...	...	1.0	...	.2
Total	100.0	100.0	100.0	100.0	100.0	100.0	100.0
Number of cases	101	78	76	110	102	100	567

The comparisons between the three sets of tables of number of previous convictions, number of terms served, and length of time served in penal institutions, demonstrate that there is a very considerable difference in the results, according to whether one or another scheme of measurement of delinquency was used. In using number of terms the factor of length of term must be considered. A woman may have served twenty terms but each may have been for ten days, while another woman with one previous term may have served ten years. Again, the number of terms alone does not take cognizance of the factor of probation and suspended sentence, which are as important from the standpoint of a study in delinquency as is any other sentence. The length of time in penal institutions, in the same way, does not give a clear idea of one's record of delinquency, since the committing judge and the kind of institution to which he is able to send her are so variable in different communities. If a girl appears hardened and brazen, the judge may commit her to the Workhouse for ten days for soliciting, but if she seems young and repentant he may commit her to Bedford for an indefinite term of a possible three years. Obviously, the measure of extent of delinquency should not operate to make the one appear more and the other less criminal, as it would if the measure of length of time served were used.

(*d*) *Number of Times on Probation*

To show how much and how variable a factor probation or suspended sentence has been in the several institutional groups, Table 18 is given. By the nature of the group, all the Probation cases have been given at least one chance on probation if the present sentence is counted as one. Among the other groups, since the present sentence is to an institution, only past sentences will be considered in finding the number of times placed on probation. It is evident that there is great variability in this, and that the percentage who have never been given a chance on probation or suspended sentence ranges from 63.2 per cent in the Magdalen to 95.1 per cent in the Workhouse. In no institution, except Bedford, has any woman been given more than two chances in having her sentence suspended. This table becomes more significant if taken in connection with Table 8, which shows the percentage of each institutional group which has never had a previous conviction. The Workhouse has the smallest percentage, 23.5 per cent, of first offenders; it has the highest mean number of convictions, and the smallest percentage who have been given a suspended sentence of any kind. This would indicate that there is probably a process

TABLE 18

NUMBER OF TIMES PLACED ON PROBATION OR SUSPENDED SENTENCE

Per Cent Distribution of Delinquent Women in Institutional Groups

Number of Times on Probation	Institutional Groups						Total
	Bedford	Auburn	Magdalen	Penitentiary	Workhouse	Probation*	
0	69.3	89.9	63.2	84.5	95.1	....	66.6
1	20.8	6.3	32.9	13.6	3.9	90.1	28.3
2	5.9	3.8	3.9	1.8	1.0	9.9	4.4
3	3.0	....	....	....	....	....	.5
4	1.0	....	....	....	....	....	.2
Total	100.0	100.0	100.0	100.0	100.0	100.0	100.0
Number of cases	101	79	76	110	102	101	569

*Present probation is counted as one time on probation.

TABLE 19

RECIDIVISTS AND FIRST OFFENDERS

Number and Per Cent Among Institutional Groups

	Institutional Groups												Total	
	Bedford		Auburn		Magdalen		Penitentiary		Workhouse		Probation			
	Number	Per cent	Number	Per cent	Number	Per cent	Number	Per cent	Number	Per cent	Number	Per cent	Number	Per cent
Recidivists	62	61.4	39	48.8	42	55.3	73	67.6	77	77.0	15	16.3	308	55.3
First Offenders	39	38.6	41	51.3	34	44.7	35	32.4	23	23.0	77	83.7	249	44.7
Total	101	100.0	80	100.0	76	100.0	108	100.0	100	100.0	92	100.0	557	100.0

of selection in the courts which sends these women to institutions rather than giving them another form of sentence. One of the most striking things in the table is the fact that so few of the women in each group have, as the women express it, "been given a chance." This is probably due to the fact that the adult probation system is a comparatively new thing, and that it has not been extended to any degree to the higher courts which deal with the more serious offenders.

(*e*) *Recidivists and First Offenders*

(1) *Recidivists and First Offenders Among Institutional Groups.*—To show briefly the trend of extent of delinquency among the institutional groups, it may be well to divide the offenders into recidivists and first offenders. We have used the term "recidivist" to mean an individual who has been convicted of an offense against the law more than once. The kind of sentence after conviction has not been taken into account, since with the development of probation systems, it seems unfair to call a woman a recidivist if she was sentenced to prison by one judge, while another woman with the same charge might be given probation by a more lenient judge.[20] Table 19 shows that the percentage of recidivists is highest among the Workhouse women, and in decreasing order follow the Penitentiary, Bedford, Magdalen, Auburn, and the Probation group.

(2) *Recidivists and First Offenders Among Felons and Misdemeanants.*—If we turn to the number of recidivists among felons and misdemeanants (Table 20), we find that the percentage of recidivists among the felons is considerably smaller than among the misdemeanants. It would seem from this that there is a tendency for a larger number of those who commit the more serious offenses not to commit further offenses. If we turn back to Table 13, however, we find that there is no very significant difference, apparently, between the mean number of convictions among felons and misdemeanants. From this, it would seem that the recidivists among the felons tend to have a larger percentage of convictions than the recidivists among the misdemeanants.

[20] It is obvious, of course, that there are marked limitations to the use of "recidivist" as one who has been previously convicted by law. We might note here the case of one Bedford woman 32 years old who had been a prostitute in Chinatown for years and had smoked opium for some time. She had violated the law, undoubtedly, nearly every day during this time. She was not arrested, however, because of her own cleverness and the protection of her pimp, until she was sentenced to Bedford. Legally, she is a first offender, but in every other sense of the word she has violated the law for years.

TABLE 20

RECIDIVISTS AND FIRST OFFENDERS

Number and Per Cent Among Felons and Misdemeanants

	Felons		Misdemeanants		Total	
	Number	Per Cent	Number	Per Cent	Number	Per Cent
Recidivists	57	48.7	251	57.0	308	55.3
First Offenders	60	51.3	189	43.0	249	44.7
Total	117	100.0	440	100.0	557	100.0

(3) *Recidivists and First Offenders Among Female Felons and Male Felons.*—It may be of interest to compare with the felons in our group the percentage of recidivists which Dr. Glueck found in a study of 608 male felons in Sing Sing Prison.[21] Among his total group, he finds 66.8 per cent recidivists in comparison with the 48.7 per cent of the female felons of our study. Dr. Glueck has defined a recidivist as "an individual who in addition to his present term of imprisonment, has served one or more previous sentences in penal or reformatory institutions." Since he has not based recidivism on number of previous convictions, as we have, it is probably true that he has not counted as recidivists many who would be so counted in our classification and, therefore, that the difference between the percentage of recidivists in the two groups is larger than would appear. Even as the two stand, the difference is rather striking, that there should be 18.1 per cent more recidivists among the male than among the female felon group.

A further comparison of the recidivists and first offenders in our felony group with 200 consecutive admissions of male felons to Auburn Prison[22] shows that the recidivists among these male felons are 67.5 per cent of the total group, and the first offenders 32.5 per cent. These percentages approximate those among the male felons in Sing Sing Prison and show, again, a much larger percentage of recidivists than we find among the female felons in our group.

[21] *Op. cit.*, p. 140.

[22] These unpublished figures were obtained through the courtesy of Dr. Heacox, physician in Auburn Prison.

FIRST CONTACTS WITH THE LAW

Equally as important as a study of the extent of delinquency is a knowledge of the circumstances which attended the first contacts with the law. We have three groups of facts which serve in a general way to supply this information,—namely, the age at first conviction, the nature of the offense at the first conviction, and the first sentence.

(*a*) *Age at First Conviction*

(1) *Age at First Conviction Among Institutional Groups.*—Table 21 shows the per cent distribution of delinquent women in the various groups by the age at first conviction. Where there has been no previous conviction, present age is used. Each age, given in round numbers in years, includes the time between 6 months previous to and 6 months following that birthday. That is, 21 years as given in this study, includes offenders who at the time of the present conviction were of any age between 20 years, 6 months, and 21 years, 6 months. The range of years in the total group runs from 8 to 72. There was only one woman, in the Probation group, who was convicted at 8 years, and she as an incorrigible child. The only case at 72 years was a woman in the Workhouse. The range varies in the institutional groups, having a wide range in the Workhouse, Auburn, and the Penitentiary, and a progressively narrower range in the Probation, Magdalen, and Bedford groups. The latter two, by the laws regulating the ages of the inmates, could not take the very old cases which we find in the Workhouse, for instance. We may note that the lowest mean and standard deviation, for the age at first conviction, occurs in Bedford, and becomes increasingly larger in the Magdalen, Probation and the Penitentiary. Auburn follows next in the mean age and the Workhouse has the highest mean age. The standard deviations of these two groups is reversed, however, the Workhouse showing a less wide dispersion of ages than which will be used for several correlations, we find the mean age at wide range of ages, such as the Workhouse, Penitentiary, and Auburn, we should expect a large standard deviation. In the total group, which will be used for several correlations, we find the mean age at first conviction 27.51 ± .453, and the standard deviation 10.68 ± .321.

TABLE 21

AGE AT FIRST CONVICTION

Per Cent Distribution of Delinquent Women in Institutional Groups, with Constants for Each Group

Age at First Conviction	Institutional Groups						Total
	Bedford	Auburn	Magdalen	Peniten-tiary	Work-house	Probation	
8 to 12 years	1.0	1.3	1.3	....	....	1.1	0.7
12 " 16 "	8.9	1.3	4.0	4.6	2.0	2.2	4.0
16 " 20 "	47.5	14.1	39.5	3.7	8.2	20.7	21.7
20 " 24 "	23.8	12.8	27.6	19.3	13.3	28.3	20.8
24 " 28 "	11.9	15.4	15.8	18.4	16.3	25.0	17.2
28 " 32 "	4.0	9.0	6.6	18.4	9.2	15.2	10.7
32 " 36 "	3.0	12.8	4.0	8.3	19.4	2.2	8.3
36 " 40 "	....	9.0	1.3	11.0	8.2	1.1	5.2
40 " 44 "	....	12.8	....	6.4	9.2	2.2	5.1
44 " 48 "	....	2.6	....	1.8	5.1	2.2	2.0
48 " 52 "	....	1.3	....	3.7	4.1	....	1.6
52 " 56 "	....	5.1	....	....	2.0	....	1.1
56 " 60 "	....	....	....	3.7	1.0	....	.9
60 " 64 "	....	1.3	....	.9	1.0	....	.5
64 " 68 "	....	1.3	....	....	....	....	.2
68 " 72 "	....	....	....	....	1.0	....	.2
Total....	100.0	100.0	100.0	100.0	100.0	100.0	100.0
Number of cases	101	78	76	109	98	92	554
Mean.........	19.58	31.1	21.25	30.41	32.1	23.96	27.51
σ_m...........	±.450	±1.29	±.569	±.971	±1.10	±.657	±.453
σ............	4.52	11.41	4.96	10.13	10.84	6.30	10.68
σ_σ...........	±.318	±.914	±.402	±.686	±.775	±.464	±.321

(2) *Comparison with English Male Convicts.*—It is of some interest to compare the figures for our group of delinquent women with Goring's data for English men convicts, although his carry more weight because of the greater numbers. He gives[23] the means and standard deviations of the age at first conviction, for 2,225 men, first offenders being omitted from the numbers. From these data we computed the standard deviation of the mean. His constants are as follows:

Mean age at first conviction = 22.39 ± .194.
Standard deviation of age at first conviction = 9.172.

[23] *Op. cit.* Table 285, p. 424.

Our data, as given in Table 21, are not comparable with Goring's, since we have included first offenders. Dropping these cases we find the following constants for 304 cases, all of whom have been convicted at least once before the present conviction.

Mean age at first conviction = 25.41 ± .540.
Standard deviation of age at first conviction = 9.420.

Between the mean age at first conviction of Goring's group of men and that of our group of women there is a difference of 3.02 years—more than five times the standard deviation of the difference—which is sufficient to remove any uncertainty as to the genuineness of the difference. It is evident, therefore, that the men studied by Goring tended to have been convicted for the first time earlier than were our women. Whether this indicates a tendency common to men criminals as contrasted with women; whether it is due to differences in conditions between England and this country; or whether it is due to some peculiarity in the selection of the groups, we can not say. It is evidently not due simply to the fact that his group consists entirely of felons, while ours includes both felons

TABLE 22

AGE AT FIRST CONVICTION

Per Cent Distribution of Felons and Misdemeanants

Age at First Conviction	Felons	Misdemeanants	Total
8 to 12 years	.9	.7	.7
12 " 16 "	2.6	4.3	4.0
16 " 20 "	12.2	24.1	21.6
20 " 24 "	16.5	21.8	20.7
24 " 28 "	17.4	17.3	17.3
28 " 32 "	11.3	10.5	10.6
32 " 36 "	10.4	7.7	8.3
36 " 40 "	7.8	4.6	5.2
40 " 44 "	9.6	3.9	5.0
44 " 48 "	1.7	2.1	2.0
48 " 52 "	1.7	1.6	1.6
52 " 56 "	3.5	.5	1.1
56 " 60 "	1.7	.7	.9
60 " 64 "	1.7	.2	.5
64 " 68 "	.9	.....	.2
68 " 72 "	.....	.2	.2
Total	100.0	100.0	100.0
Number of cases	115	440	555

and misdemeanants, since the mean age of first conviction of the women felons (see Table 23) is higher than that of the women misdemeanants. The discrepancy between our group and Goring's would thus be increased rather than diminished if comparison were made with the women felons alone.

(3) *Age at First Conviction Among Felons and Misdemeanants.* —If we proceed to the consideration of age at first conviction as found among the felon and misdemeanant groups, we note that the range of ages is about the same in each group.

Table 23, however, which compares the means and standard deviations of the age at first conviction in the two groups, shows that there is a real difference between the central tendency of the two groups in favor of the felons being first convicted at an older age. There is also in all probability a valid difference between the dispersion in the two groups, with a tendency toward a wider scattering among the felons in the age at first conviction.

TABLE 23

FELONS AND MISDEMEANANTS

Comparison of the Means and Standard Deviations of Age at First Conviction of Felons and Misdemeanants of Total Group

	Felons	Misdemeanants	Difference	$\frac{d}{\sigma_d}$	Chances that real difference does not exist are 1 in:
Mean σ_m	30.3 ±1.07	25.51 ±.438	4.84	4.19	71,943
σ σ_σ	11.45 ±.755	9.20 ±.310	2.25	2.76	345
Cases	115	440			

(4) *Age at First Conviction Among Offenders Against Chastity and Offenders Against Property Rights.*—The two largest groups of delinquents in the New York City Police Department classification of offenders,—the offenders against chastity and the offenders against property rights,—are of interest also in a consideration of the age at first conviction. The frequency distribution in Table 24 indicates that the range is somewhat shorter for both groups, than in the total group,

since the two last age groups are lost, and only three cases fall in the first age group.

Table 25 gives the comparison of the means and standard deviations of the above table, and shows that there is a valid difference between the means,—that is, that there is a tendency for the women convicted of offenses against chastity to be first convicted younger than the women convicted of offenses against property rights. There is much less of a difference in the dispersion of the cases among these two groups of offenders, but the ratio of 1.96 would indicate that there might be a difference. It is of interest here to turn back to Table 15, and note the tendency for women convicted of offenses against property rights to have a greater number of convictions than women convicted of offenses against chastity. Table 14 shows that there is a larger percentage of recidivists also among those who are convicted of offenses against property rights. All of these facts together would make it seem probable that the offenders against property rights, though first convicted at a later age, are convicted more often after that time than are the offenders against chastity.

TABLE 24

AGE AT FIRST CONVICTION

Per Cent Distribution of Offenders Against Chastity and Offenders Against Property Rights

Age at First Conviction	Offenders against Chastity	Offenders against Property	Total
8 to 12 years	1.0	.....	.7
12 " 16 "	3.0	6.7	4.1
16 " 20 "	28.6	11.2	23.2
20 " 24 "	21.6	20.9	21.4
24 " 28 "	18.9	15.7	17.9
28 " 32 "	8.6	14.9	10.6
32 " 36 "	7.3	8.2	7.6
36 " 40 "	3.3	7.5	4.6
40 " 44 "	3.3	7.5	4.6
44 " 48 "	1.3	1.5	1.4
48 " 52 "	1.3	2.2	1.6
52 " 56 "	.7	1.5	.9
56 " 60 "	.7	1.5	.9
60 " 64 "	.3	.8	.5
Total	100.0	100.0	100.0
Number of cases	301	134	435

TABLE 25

OFFENDERS AGAINST PROPERTY RIGHTS AND OFFENDERS AGAINST CHASTITY

Comparison of the Means and Standard Deviations of Age at First Conviction Among Offenders Against Property Rights and Offenders Against Chastity of Total Group

	Offenders against Property Rights	Offenders against Chastity	Difference	$\frac{d}{\sigma_d}$	Chances that real difference does not exist are 1 in:
Mean	28.31	24.70	3.62	3.60	5,000
σ_m	±.871	±.501			
σ	10.09	8.70	1.39	1.96	40
σ_σ	±.616	±.354			
Cases	134	301			

(5) *Relation Between Age at First Conviction and Number of Convictions.*—In order to determine whether among our total group of delinquent women there is any relationship between age at first conviction and the total number of convictions,[24] the following correlation table (Table 26) is presented. We find that the coefficient of correlation, +.02 gives no evidence of any significant relationship. Correlation ratios were also determined which indicated the presence of a slight degree of relationship, but which are rendered of dubious significance by the irregularity in the lines of means. (See table, noting the means given in the right-hand column and the bottom row of the table.) This can not be considered an adequate indication of the amount of correlation without a correction for the influence of present age. While we should expect a tendency for individuals who were first convicted when very young to acquire a larger number of convictions than those first convicted late in life,[25] it is evident that, if any large number of those who had their first convictions at an early age are still relatively young, this tendency will not have an opportunity to show itself to its full degree.

[24] Our heading "Number of *previous* convictions" tends to be misleading in this connection, the term "previous" signifying "previous to the present," obviously not "previous to the first."

[25] Our expectation is based obviously on the assumption that the treatment given at the time of the first conviction is not likely to cut short the career of delinquency.

TABLE 26

Correlation between Number of Previous Convictions and Age at First Conviction

Total Group

Age at First Conviction	Number of Previous Convictions																							Totals	Means (Number of Previous Convictions)
	0	1	2	3	4	5	6	7	8	9	10	11	12	13	14	15	16	17	18	19	20		31		
69 to 72 years			1																					1	
66 " 69 "	1																							1	
63 " 66 "																									
60 " 63 "	1	1				1																		3	
57 " 60 "	4																							4	0.5
54 " 57 "	4																							4	
51 " 54 "	3		1																					4	
48 " 51 "	6	1	1																					8	
45 " 48 "	4	3	1																					8	
42 " 45 "	4	2	1	1	2			1						1									1	13	
39 " 42 "	11	4	3	3		1	1					1												24	2.9
36 " 39 "	8	6	2	3	1		1	1		1														23	
33 " 36 "	13	6	2	3	3	3	3					1												34	2.1
30 " 33 "	19	8	5	1		1		1	1	1	1										1			39	
27 " 30 "	25	9	4	4	3	3	1				1		1		1									52	2.0
24 " 27 "	41	17	7	4	2	1	1	1		1														75	
21 " 24 "	46	14	10	8		1		1	2	1	1								2					86	1.4
18 " 21 "	39	22	10	4	5	4	2		1						1									88	
15 " 18 "	21	29	11	6	2	1		2																72	1.4
12 " 15 "		6	2	1	1								1											11	
9 " 12 "		1			2																			3	2.8
6 " 9 "					1																			1	
Totals.....	250	129	61	38	22	16	9	7	4	4	3	2	2	1	2				2		1		1	554	1.64
Means..... (Age at First Conviction)	27.9	24.2	25.8	25.8	25.9		27.6			28.6														26.51	

Number of previous convictions: Mean = 1.64 σ = 2.89
Age at first conviction: Mean = 26.51 σ = 9.91

Coefficient of correlation: r = .02 ± .042

Correlation ratios: Age at first conviction on number of previous convictions: η = .15 ± .041. Blakeman's Criterion = 2.7
Number of previous convictions on age at first conviction: η = .19 ± .041. Blakeman's Criterion = 3.3

Partial correlation coefficient: Number of previous convictions with age at first conviction, for constant present age, $r_{NA_2.A}$ = —.619

To show the relationship between age at first conviction and total number of convictions cleared of the influence of age, we have determined the partial correlation coefficient of age at first conviction and number of "previous" convictions for constant age[26] which is as follows: $r_{1N.A} = -.619 \pm .072$. Although the size of the partial coefficient is affected by the smallness of r, which can not be considered a wholly reliable value in view of the non-linearity of the relationship, it remains true that, even were r as large as either of the η's, the partial would still be large enough to be significant and would be negative in sign. In other words, data on the group under consideration indicate clearly that the earlier the first conviction the greater the likelihood of many convictions.

It is easier, however, to determine the fact of the relationship than to account for it. There are several fairly obvious explanations. The first is the simple fact that one convicted early has a longer period of time ahead of him in which to accumulate a criminal record. Less superficial is the assumption that an early conviction is symptomatic of a marked criminal tendency, or, if one objects to the implications of this term, at least of a combination of characteristics which makes the individual particularly susceptible to pernicious influences. Still another explanation might be offered on the assumption that the influences of the courts and the penal institutions may be so unfortunate in their effect upon the young delinquent that they exaggerate, rather than diminish, his criminal susceptibility. We do not pretend to decide as to which of the above explanations is the more probable. Very possibly each factor suggested is operative to some degree.

(b) *Nature of First Offense*

The nature of the first offense committed has been classified, as was the present offense, by the New York City Police Department classification, and by felonies and misdemeanors. The first classification as given in Table 27 may be best interpreted in connection with Table 4, giving the nature of the present offense. It will be noted that the first offense still has its highest percentage in the group of offenders

[26] The data required for the above partial correlation are as follows:
Correlation coefficient of age at first conviction and number of "previous" convictions: $r_{1N} = .02$.
Correlation coefficient of age at first conviction and present age: $r_{1A} = .942$.
Correlation coefficient of number of "previous" convictions and present age: $r_{NA} = .23$.

The formula for the partial is $r_{N1.A} = \dfrac{r_{N1} - r_{NA}r}{\sqrt{1-r^2_{NA}}\sqrt{1-r^2_{1A}}}$.

TABLE 27

NATURE OF FIRST OFFENSE

Per Cent Distribution of Delinquent Women in Institutional Groups, Classified by Main Divisions of New York City Police Department Classification

Nature of Offense	Institutional Groups						Total
	Bed-ford	Auburn	Mag-dalen	Peni-tentiary	Work-house	Proba-tion	
Offenses against the Person....	1.0	17.9	...	5.6	...	...	3.8
Offenses against Chastity......	49.5	20.5	63.2	13.1	42.4	81.5	44.3
Offenses against Family and Children..................	5.0	5.1	...	.9	...	...	1.8
Offenses against Regulations for Public Health, Safety and Policy..................	6.9	5.1	9.2	12.1	9.1	6.5	8.3
Offenses against Administration of Government...........	1.0	1.3	...	...	...	...	.4
Offenses against Property Rights..................	11.0	42.3	7.9	47.7	2.0	1.1	18.8
General Criminality...........	25.7	7.7	19.7	20.6	46.5	10.9	22.6
Total.................	100.0	100.0	100.0	100.0	100.0	100.0	100.0
Number of cases..............	101	78	76	107	99	92	553

against chastity, but that the general criminality group takes second place. This is undoubtedly due to the fact that the charges of incorrigible and ungovernable child, and the semi-juvenile offenses come in this general group. Offenses against property rights have third highest place instead of second place as among the present offenses. Among the other four divisions of offenses there are slight but not noticeably large differences from the nature of the present offense.

The nature of the first offense as classified by felonies and misdemeanors is also only very slightly different from the percentage of felonies and misdemeanors at the time of the present offense. The only group which changes more than one per cent is Auburn which has 29 women or 37.2 per cent who were misdemeanants at the time of the

TABLE 28

NATURE OF FIRST OFFENSE

Number and Per Cent of Delinquent Women in Institutional Groups Classified by Felonies and Misdemeanors

Nature of Offense	Institutional Groups												Total	
	Bedford		Auburn		Magdalen		Penitentiary		Workhouse		Probation			
	Number	Per cent	Number	Per cent	Number	Per cent	Number	Per cent	Number	Per cent	Number	Per cent	Number	Per cent
Felonies	6	5.9	49	62.8	2	2.6	30	27.5	....	....	....	....	87	15.3
Misdemeanors	95	94.1	29	37.2	74	97.4	79	72.5	101	100.0	102	100.0	480	84.7
Total	101	100.0	78	100.0	76	100.0	109	100.0	101	100.0	102	100.0	567	100.0

TABLE 29

Correlation between Age at First Conviction and Nature of First Offense

Nature of First Offense	Age at First Conviction (Years)																						Totals	Means (Age at First Conviction)
	6–9	9–12	12–15	15–18	18–21	21–24	24–27	27–30	30–33	33–36	36–39	39–42	42 45	45–48	48–51	51–54	54–57	57–60	60–63	63–66	66–69	69–72		
Offenses against the Person			1		1	2	3	1	1	3	2	1	1	2	1		2		1				22	35.5
Offenses against Chastity				27	58	52	39	25	15	5	6	6		2	3	2	1	2					243	24.5
Offenses against the Family					1	1	1		2	2	1		2										10	31.8
Offenses against Reg. for Public Health, etc.				1		4	10	6	4	4	3	4	6	2	1								45	32.2
Offenses against Administration of Government						1															1		2	43.5
Offenses against Property Rights			2	6	9	16	16	12	9	8	7	8	1	1	3	1	1	2	1				103	29.4
General Criminality	1	3	7	38	18	10	6	8	7	12	4	5	3	1		1			1			1	126	23.8
Totals	1	3	10	72	87	86	75	52	38	34	23	24	13	8	8	4	4	4	3	·	1	1	551	26.54

Age at first conviction: Mean = 26.54 σ = 9.92
Correlation ratio: η = .35 ± .037

first conviction, and only one misdemeanant at the latest conviction. It is also of interest to note that in neither the Probation nor the Workhouse group, which are limited to misdemeanants, is there any woman who was convicted of a felony as the first offense.

One might expect, from a study of the differences between the first and latest offense of the women in this study that there would be a relationship between the age at first conviction and the nature of the first offense. This we find to be true in Table 29 where the correlation ratio between age at first conviction and nature of first offense has been calculated. The ratio of .35 ± .037 would indicate that there is a genuine relationship between these two factors. Reference to the mean values given in the extreme right-hand column shows that the order of arrangement of kinds of offenses in accordance with increasing age at first conviction is as follows: (1) General criminality, (2) Offenses against chastity, (3) Offenses against property rights, (4) Offenses against the family, (5) Offenses against regulations for public health, (6) Offenses against the person, (7) Offenses against the administration of government.

(*c*) *First Sentence*

After observing the similarity between the first and latest offenses, we might expect to see a similarity in the sentences imposed for them. This we find to be the case in Table 30. In each institutional group studied it is evident that the largest proportion of cases were sent to an institution of that type at the time of the first sentence. We must remember that a fairly large percentage in each group are first offenders and so in those cases the first sentence will apply to the present sentence. The similarity in type of sentence is especially striking in the Workhouse and Probation groups, one of which has 91.2 per cent first sentenced to institutions such as the Workhouse, the Penitentiary or County Jails, and the other with 92.1 per cent first put on probation. It would seem, particularly in the Workhouse group, that if one were once sentenced to the Workhouse, she would continue to be sent there after subsequent convictions, and that possibly there is some process of selection in the courts which makes women of a certain type more likely to be sentenced there.

TABLE 30

FIRST SENTENCE

Per Cent Distribution of Delinquent Women in Institutional Groups

First Sentence	Institutional Groups						Total
	Bedford	Auburn	Magdalen	Penitentiary	Workhouse	Probation	
Probation or Suspended Sentence	22.8	7.5	26.3	10.9	2.0	92.1	27.5
Fine	5.0	7.5	1.3	2.7	1.0	2.0	3.2
Juvenile Institution	5.0	1.3	...	1.8	1.0	1.0	1.8
Reformatory Institution	58.4	5.0	65.8	10.9	4.9	2.9	23.3
Penitentiary, Workhouse or County Jail	8.9	23.8	6.6	70.9	91.2	2.0	36.1
State Prison	...	55.0	...	2.7	...	...	8.2
Total	100.0	100.0	100.0	100.0	100.0	100.0	100.0
Number of cases	101	80	76	110	102	102	571

(*d*) *Juvenile Delinquents*

While we are discussing the first offense, it may be well to note the number of our cases who have been juvenile delinquents, in the sense of being convicted in a court of law before 16 years of age. In Table 21, where 16 years has been interpreted as being any age between 15 years, 6 months, and 16 years, 6 months, we find 26 cases or 4.4 per cent of our total group who appear as juvenile delinquents, though all were actually convicted before the age of 15 years, 6 months. If we select, however, cases of all those who were convicted before they had reached their 16th birthday, the upper limit of the Juvenile Court age, we find 40 women or 6.8 per cent of our total group.

This small percentage of women who have been convicted as juvenile delinquents is striking in view of the general belief that, as Dr. Healy states:[27]

[27] Healy, William. "The Individual Delinquent." Boston. Little, Brown & Co., 1915, p. 10.

"*Practically all confirmed criminals begin their careers in childhood or early youth.* The fact of this remarkable early development of a definite tendency towards criminality was soon clear to us, both through observable trends in young offenders, and through the life histories of older delinquents. . . . Another writer, cited by Morrison, states, 'It is an ascertained fact that there is scarcely an habitual criminal in the county of Staffordshire who has not been imprisoned as a child.' Even more important is the thorough research of Matz, who investigated the prison population of the province of Pommern. He found that in 70 per cent the first imprisonment had been inflicted before the 21st year, and that of the repeated offenders by far the greater number had received their first punishment before the 17th year. It must be remembered that here Matz is speaking not of the commission of the first offense, but of receiving the first punishment."

Lombroso writes, "All great criminals have given proof of perversity in their youth, especially at the age of puberty and sometimes even before."[28] He goes on to cite instances of numerous French-Italian penologists who have found many criminals with the "tendency to theft," "little pilferings," etc., when they were very young. He does not mean that these early delinquencies were necessarily brought into court, but that the individual had a "tendency" toward criminality and showed it in early youth by various forms of "perversity."

At present the chief criterion of assuming that a person is criminal is the fact of his conviction in a court of law. To argue that all great criminals, though not convicted when children, began their criminal careers in childhood, would be to assume that it was not common for those who grow to adult life without contact with the courts also to perform the acts which the criminal may have done when he was a child. Of this we have no proof. Normal children undoubtedly do a certain amount of pilfering and commit other anti-social acts. Until we have some way of measuring the extent of "perversity" in the normal youth who does not become a confirmed criminal, we are not in a position to state that the criminal who was not convicted during his childhood but who did show a "definite tendency towards criminality" necessarily began his "criminal career in early youth." To hold that view carried to the extreme would be to agree with Lombroso that "Precocity in crime points to the fact that criminality, much more than insanity, is an inherited characteristic. This reminds us

[28] Lombroso, Cæsare. "Crime: Its Causes and Remedies." Translated by Henry P. Horton. Boston. Little, Brown & Co., 1911, p. 178.

that precocity is one of the distinguishing features of savage peoples,—a new proof of the atavistic origin of crime." [29]

We might cite here cases of several of the women in Auburn Prison who were convicted of serious offenses in the eyes of the law, and who were recidivists. Yet in the group of eighty women, whose records were carefully investigated, there were only two cases where there had been convictions under sixteen years of age. One of the women was feeble-minded, epileptic and consequently very unstable. Her crimes seemed more a matter of her instability than of any criminal intent. The other juvenile delinquent in the Auburn group was a woman who would, without doubt, fit in with Dr. Healy's idea of a confirmed criminal beginning his career in childhood or early youth. Her first conviction occurred when she was ten years and eight months of age. At that time she ran away from home, and when found was so troublesome that she was committed to the Catholic Protectory as an ungovernable child. When fourteen, she was arrested as a common prostitute and sent to the New York State Training School at Hudson. In this institution she was so troublesome that she was thought to be insane and was transferred to Matteawan, where she remained seven months and was discharged as not insane. The report from Matteawan showed at that time a history of prostitution, stealing and drug habit. Since then she has been arrested many times for soliciting and loitering, but has served only two terms, one for running a disorderly house and one for assault. Her present conviction was for murder in the second degree. For $500 she had made the arrangement for two men, belonging to a Black Hand gang, to kill an Italian whose wife wanted him out of the way so she could marry another man. This one case is practically alone, out of the group of the most serious offenders we have, in showing marked criminal traits during childhood and adolescence. Since the group of women studied in Auburn Prison covered the commitments for two consecutive years, it would seem that the sample of offenders is representative enough for us to state that among the most serious women offenders in New York State during the years 1915-16, there was no proof that their criminal careers, in the sense of being convicted in court, began in childhood or early youth.

Some may object that the juvenile court age limit is set too low and that the convictions which take place within the next few years are as significant as those which may occur earlier. Out of 587 cases, however, we find that only 47.2 per cent were convicted under 24 years of

[29] *Op. cit.*, p. 177.

age; that is, that over half of our cases did not reach the courts until they were well into the adult period. From this observation, it would be difficult to state that the determinants of delinquent careers are necessarily the conditions of youth, since the first of the career in the courts comes at a period widely separated from the conditions of youth.

The forty women who had been juvenile delinquents are found in the institutional groups in the following numbers:

Bedford	18	cases
Auburn	2	"
Magdalen	8	"
Probation	5	"
Penitentiary	5	"
Workhouse	2	"

Two of the Bedford and one of the Magdalen cases came into this study at the time of their first conviction when they were nearly but not quite sixteen years of age, though their legal age was sixteen.[30]

The numbers are too small to make any comparison with other groups, but the main factors in the criminal record of the juvenile delinquents are given to show that there is no strikingly marked difference from the rest of our cases. The present offenses of this group are distributed as follows:

Offenses against the Person	2
Offenses against Chastity (all soliciting or loitering)	22
Offenses against the Family, etc.	1
Offenses against Regulations for Public Health	1
Offenses against Administration of Government	1
Offenses against Property Rights	10
General Criminality	3

Only five of the forty cases were felons at the time of this study.

The first offenses of the women in this delinquent group were as follows:

Offenses against Chastity	6	cases	or	15.0%
Offenses against Property Rights	3	"	"	7.5%
General Criminality	30	"	"	75.0%
Unknown	1	"	"	2.5%

All of the first offenses were misdemeanors with the exception of one case.

The number of previous convictions of this group who were juvenile delinquents does not show that they have been recidivists to as great an extent as have the women in some of our institutional groups. The mean number of convictions is 1.82, which is less than the mean number for either the Penitentiary or Workhouse groups.

[30] Legal age is the age given by the delinquent in court at the time of her conviction.

No previous convictions	....	3 cases
1 " conviction	....	22 "
2 " convictions	....	7 "
3 " "	....	3 "
4 " "	....	4 "
12 " "	....	1 case

The number of months served, as would be expected, is somewhat higher than for the institutional groups or the total group of cases, since juvenile delinquents usually receive an institutional commitment which in many cases involves a long and indefinite stay in a reformatory institution. The sentence for a similar offense among older persons would be much shorter in most cases. The distribution of time served in penal institutions follows:

Never served time	....	14 cases, or	34.8%
Served less than 1 year	....	6 " "	15.0%
" 1 to 2 years	....	7 " "	17.5%
" 2 " 3 "	....	4 " "	10.0%
" 3 " 4 "	....	6 " "	15.0%
" 4 " 5 "	....	1 case, "	2.5%
" 5 " 6 "	....	1 " "	2.5%
" 7 " 8 "	....	1 " "	2.5%

As a group, it may be said that the juvenile delinquents do not show up as noticeably different in any way from the rest of the cases. The numbers are too small for statistical comparisons, but the smallness is significant as showing that among the sample of women covered in our study, the problem of juvenile delinquency has been a minor one, and for the most part, there is no proof that the most serious female delinquents have begun their criminal careers in childhood or early youth.

It should be noted that the chief insistence on the extensiveness and importance of juvenile convictions in connection with the problem of recidivism has come from persons concerned primarily with men delinquents or with boy offenders. It is entirely possible that the situation is quite different as it affects women delinquents. Unfortunately, adequate data for comparison are not available. Goring's figures are the most valuable for this purpose.[31] We have already called attention to the fact that the mean age of first conviction is lower for his group than for ours. (See page 130). The difference in numbers of very youthful offenders is also striking.

Referring to Goring's table (Table 285) we find that 337 (or 15.1 per cent) out of a total of 2,225 men, none of whom were first offenders, had been convicted before they were fifteen years old. On the

[31] *Op. cit.* Table 285, p. 424.

other hand, out of a total of 304 women who had had one or more previous convictions, only fifteen cases (or 4.9 per cent) had been convicted prior to their fifteenth year.[32]

SUMMARY

In conclusion, we shall summarize the most important factors which arise in considering the delinquency among the women in our study. First, it is well to keep in mind that the New York City Police Department classification of offenses which we have used throughout is composed of seven main divisions, each of which is unevenly divided as to felonies and misdemeanors. Since two of our groups, the Workhouse and the Probation groups, are made up entirely of misdemeanants and Auburn entirely of felons, while both the more and less serious offenses are found in the other three groups, it is natural that we should find great irregularities in the distribution of the various divisions of the New York City Police Department classification among our several groups of delinquent women. While in the total group the largest percentage of women fall among the offenders against chastity, with offenders against property rights having the next largest percentage, this ratio holds true in no institution except Bedford, though the offenders against chastity have the highest percentage in each group except Auburn and the Penitentiary.

In showing the extent of delinquency, our best measure seems to be the number of previous convictions, since the number of terms and length of time served are both open to serious criticisms. They both disregard the possibility of the suspended sentence or probation, and in addition to this the sentences for the same offense vary so between institutions of a reformatory type and the Workhouse, for instance, that a term cannot mean the same in both cases, and the different length of time is no criterion. The distribution of number of convictions among the institutional groups shows that the Workhouse and Penitentiary have the largest mean number of convictions, and the Probation group the smallest, while the other three groups stand fairly close together on intermediate ground. Between felons and misdemeanants there appears to be no demonstrable difference in the mean number of convictions, but among the offenders against property rights and the offenders against chastity there seems to be a valid dif-

[32] The above data are easily obtained from Table 30 by subtracting from the total number of 554 the 250 cases of first offenders. The number convicted before 15 years of age can be counted up from the table directly.

ference both in the tendency of the offenders against property rights to have a larger number of convictions and in the variation of the distribution of convictions, the offenders against property rights having a wider scattering.

In the total group, the percentage of recidivists is 55.3. This percentage varies, however, in the institutional groups from 16.3 in the Probation to 77.0 in the Workhouse. Among the felons, the percentage of recidivists is 48.7, considerably lower than the percentage of male felon recidivists, in studies both of Sing Sing Prison and Auburn Prison.

The age at first conviction varies among the institutional groups, from 19.58 years in Bedford to 32.1 years in the Workhouse. Among the felons and misdemeanants it is interesting to note that there is apparently a real difference between the age at first conviction with a tendency for the felons to be convicted at a later age. There seems to be a somewhat like difference between the age at first conviction of the offenders against property rights and offenders against chastity, with a tendency for the offenders against property rights to be convicted at a later age.

In considering the nature of the first offense, we find that the offenders against chastity still have the largest percentage of cases in all institutions except Auburn and the Penitentiary, where the offenders against property rights have the highest percentage of cases. There is a large increase in the general criminality offenses due to the fact that in this group the semi-juvenile delinquencies occur which we should expect in many of the younger cases to be the first offense.

One of the most important things found in the study of the first contacts with the law, is the surprisingly small number of women who have been convicted as juvenile delinquents, and within this small group the lack of marked dissimilarity to the total number of cases studied.

The basic elements of the criminal record as given in this chapter will be used in the later chapters as showing the relationship between the nature and extent of delinquency, the various environmental factors and mentality. These relationships, as previously stated, will be treated as associated with the delinquency, but not necessarily as causative factors, since there are no figures for the general population to prove that such factors are not there also a commonly occurring condition.

CHAPTER VII

MISCELLANEOUS CONSIDERATIONS

THOUGH the problems in which we are primarily interested in this study are the larger ones of school, work, home, family background, and sex life in their relation to delinquency, there are various more general elements to be considered which affect these more important problems in numerous ways. The factor of age, for instance, may be very necessary in determining whether there is any significant difference in the number of convictions between two groups. It may also be the basic element in the difference between prevailing wages of any two groups to be compared, or in the length of time prostitution has been carried on, since in the one case we might expect those who are still very young to have a lower prevailing wage, and in the other, a shorter time in prostitution. There are various other miscellaneous points to be noted, relating to the social status of the women, and these will be presented briefly so that they may be used for reference in later chapters. Among these, we shall consider the record of previous commitments to hospitals for the insane, habits as shown by the amount of alcoholism, drug addiction, and use of tobacco among the different institutional groups, and a very brief summary of the criminal records of the twenty-one women in the special Intoxication Group of the Workhouse. Civil condition, age at marriage, and religion will also be shown in their distribution among the institutional groups. Though these quite unrelated factors do not add appreciably to the understanding of any one problem, they serve as a background to the later discussion of comparisons of institutional groups.

AGE

Probably one of the most significant factors in a study of a somewhat heterogeneous group of individuals is the element of age. Age may help to account for a very high or a very low number of convictions, for a long or short history of prostitution, for a high or a low prevailing wage. Accordingly, it is necessary to define clearly what unit is taken for measuring age, and to keep the factor of age in mind in connection with each important subject. Throughout this study, age is given in years, in round numbers. Each age in years includes the time between six months previous to and six months following that birthday. That is, sixteen years, as given in Table 31, includes offenders who at the time of the present conviction were of any age between fifteen years, six months, and sixteen years, six months.[1]

TABLE 31

AGE AT PRESENT CONVICTION

Per Cent Distribution of Delinquent Women in Institutional Groups

Age	Institutional Groups						Total
	Bedford	Auburn	Magdalen	Penitentiary	Workhouse	Probation	
14 to 18 yrs...	22.8	....	14.5	.9	2.0	5.5	7.5
18 " 22 " ..	37.6	8.9	32.9	4.6	4.0	35.9	20.1
22 " 26 " ..	19.9	18.8	25.0	16.6	14.9	24.0	19.6
26 " 30 " ..	11.9	13.9	15.7	17.4	16.8	17.4	15.7
30 " 34 " ..	6.0	11.3	3.9	18.4	14.9	12.1	11.5
34 " 38 " ..	1.0	16.3	6.6	13.8	9.9	....	7.9
38 " 42 " ..	1.0	10.1	1.3	8.3	14.9	3.3	6.7
42 " 46 " ..	....	7.6	....	4.6	5.9	....	3.0
46 " 50 " ..	....	3.9	....	8.3	5.0	2.2	3.5
50 " 54 " ..	....	5.1	....	1.8	5.0	....	2.1
54 " 58 " ..	....	2.5	....	1.8	3.0	....	1.3
58 " 62 " ..	....	1.3	....	2.8	2.0	....	1.1
62 " 66 " ..	....	....	....	.9	1.0	....	.4
66 " 70 " ..	....	1.3	....	....	....	....	.2
70 " 74 " ..	....	....	....	....	1.0	....	.2
Total...	100.0	100.0	100.0	100.0	100.0	100.0	100.0
Number of cases	101	80	76	109	101	92	559
Mean..........	21.67	33.8	22.97	33.67	34.9	24.47	28.79
σ_m..........	±.480	±1.17	±.603	±.950	±1.09	±.647	±.429
σ............	4.82	10.42	5.26	9.92	10.97	6.21	10.13
σ_σ..........	±.339	±.824	±.427	±.672	±.772	±.458	±.303

[1] The data on age which we have used in this study, is based on verified data where this could be obtained, but where we did not have any verification, the subject's statement has been used. For 88 Bedford cases, on which both the subject's statement of age and the verified age were available, we find, by calculating the correlation between these two factors, that the coefficient of correlation is .958, indicating that there is a very high relationship between the age which the subject gives as her age at time of the present conviction, and the actual age determined by verification.

Table 31, followed by Chart 8, shows the distribution by four-year intervals of the ages of delinquent women in the various institutional groups with the mean age and standard deviation for each group. The lower age limit of fourteen was found in only one case, that of a colored girl committed to the Workhouse.[2] This is the only case in which the age is below sixteen years. The chart indicates what has been stated previously concerning the range of ages within the institutional groups.[3] Bedford has only eight cases over the thirty-year age limit, while a high percentage of 22.8 falls in the lowest age group—from fourteen to eighteen years. The range of ages is comparatively short, running from 15 to 38 years. Auburn, on the other hand, starts with the later age group of 18 to 22, and has a long range up to 70 years. Here the mean, as we should expect, is much higher. The Magdalen group is more like the Bedford, with a fairly high percentage of cases in the first age group, and a range up to forty-two years, though there is somewhat more of a massing of cases toward the upper end of the scale, resulting in a larger mean age. The Penitentiary shows a range more like that in Auburn and very different from the Magdalen and Bedford. The mean age in the Penitentiary is also very close to that

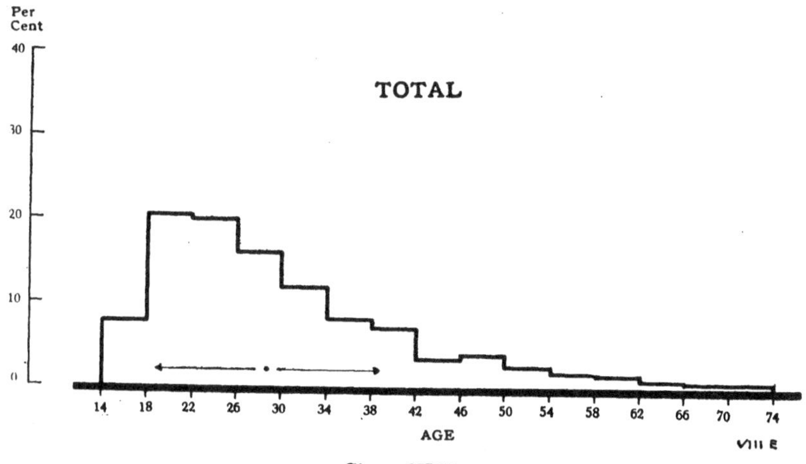

Chart VIII
Age at Present Conviction
Per cent distribution by institutional groups

[2] The girl had given her age to the judge as sixteen years when as a matter of fact she was only fourteen years, four months, of age. In addition to this, she had been convicted as an adult criminal four months earlier, when she was only fourteen, and had been sentenced to the Workhouse for thirty days.
[3] See Chapter II for accounts of institutional groups.

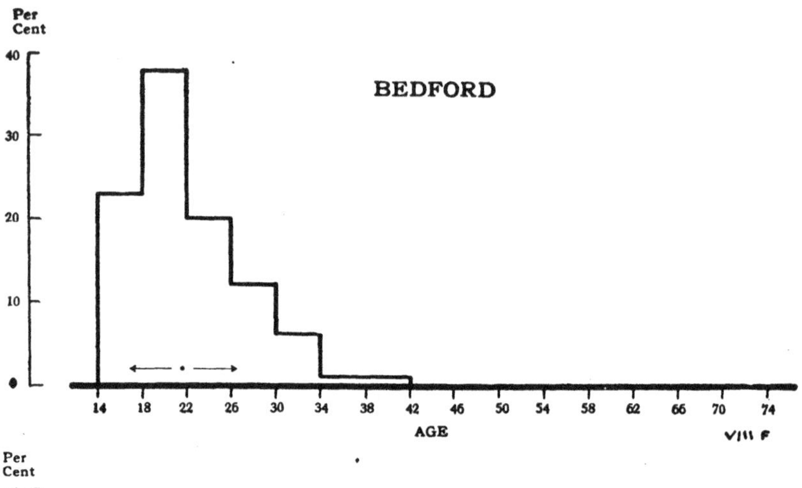

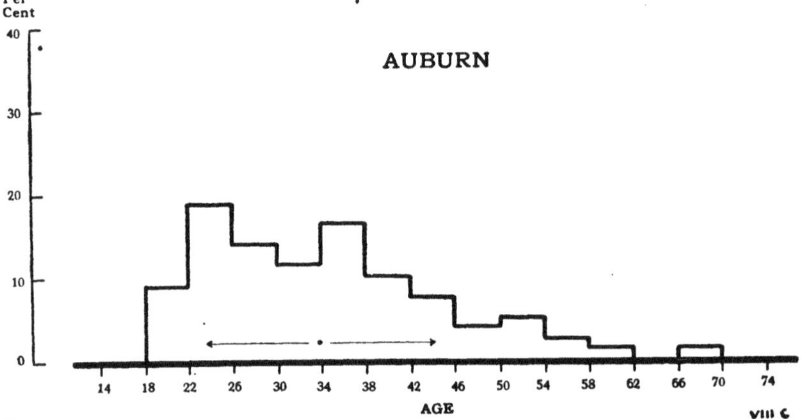

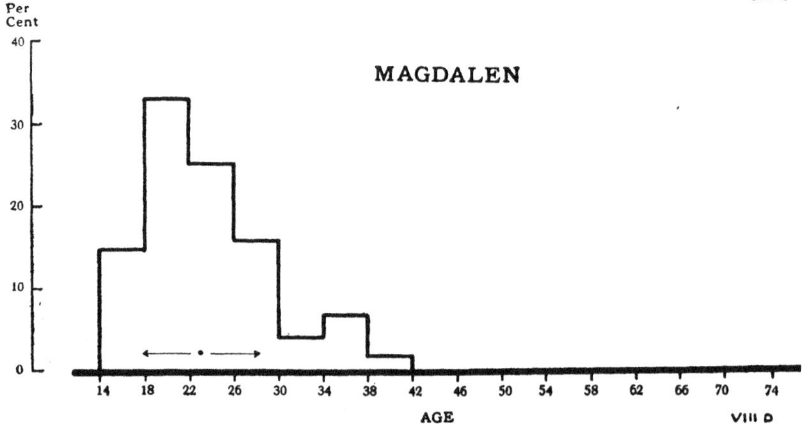

Chart VIII (Continued)
Age at Present Conviction
Per cent distribution by institutional groups

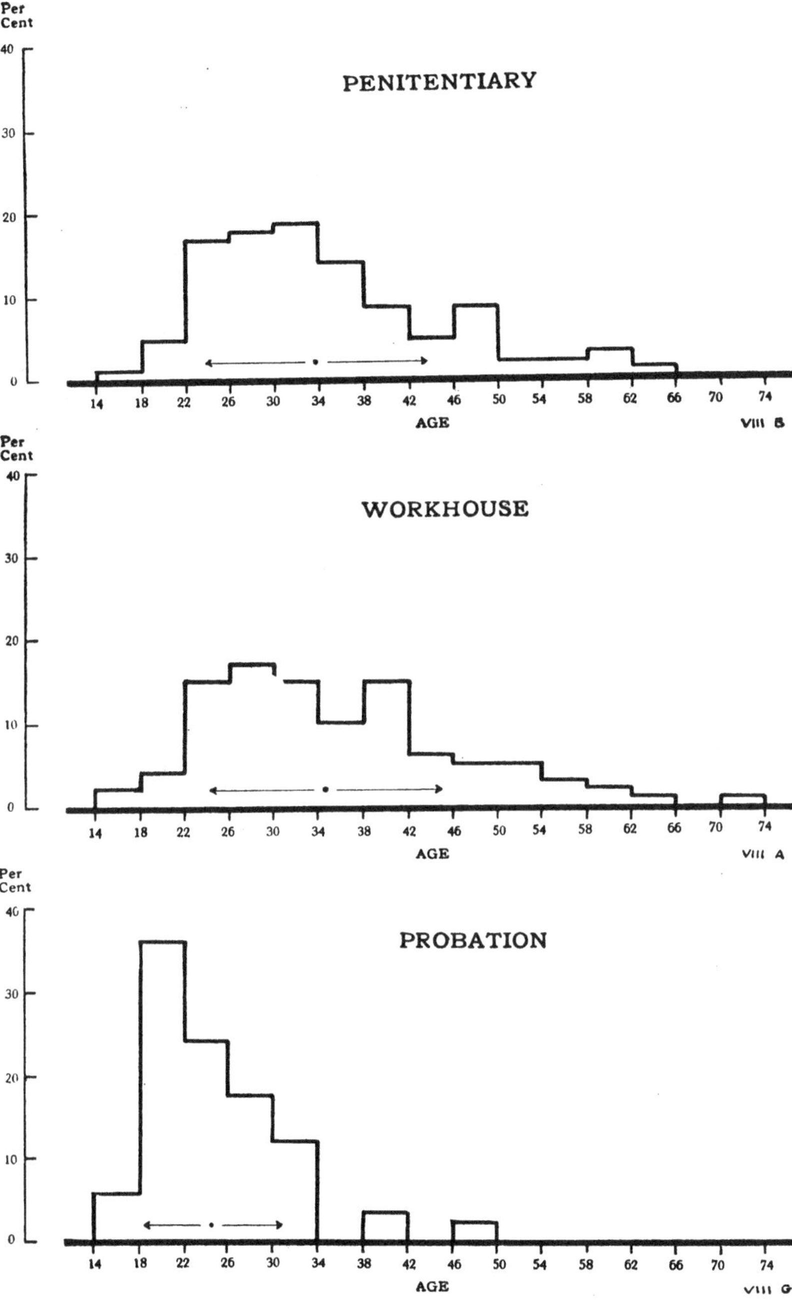

Chart VIII (Continued)
Age at Present Conviction
Per cent distribution by institutional groups

of Auburn. The Workhouse, as well as having the youngest case, also has the oldest case in the entire group, a woman of seventy-two years, and therefore has the longest range of years of any of the institutions. The mean age is slightly older than for any other group, though there is a large standard deviation. The Probation women with a comparatively short range of cases have a smaller percentage in the lowest age group, than have Bedford and the Magdalen, and a slightly higher percentage in the higher age groups so that we should expect the mean age to be higher than the average ages in the other two groups. The total group, which will be used in many of the correlations to follow, is based on 559 cases, and has a mean age of $28.79 \pm .429$ years, with a fairly large standard deviation of $10.13 \pm .303$ years. As a general basis of comparison, it is of interest to note that the institutions under consideration divide quite sharply into classes with respect to age. Bedford, the Magdalen, and the Probation group differ only slightly from one another in mean age, showing a marked selection of younger women. Auburn, the Penitentiary, and the Workhouse, on the other hand, while likewise differing only slightly from one another, are made up of considerably older groups, as shown by their mean ages given above. Wherever it has been felt that the factor of age was important to consider in the relation between any other two observed factors, the partial correlation coefficient between the two traits for constant age has been used.[4]

As stated in the introduction, it was found to be impossible to obtain a physical and medical history of the women in all of the institutional groups. Two of the institutions, the Workhouse and the Penitentiary, kept very meager records; the Probation group had no physical examination for the most part, and the physical records in the Magdalen, Auburn, and Bedford groups differed so substantially in the type of record kept that it seemed impracticable to try to use the medical data available, except for several unconnected items. A few of the general factors relating to the physical status of the women in this study will be considered in other chapters. Venereal disease, for instance, will be included in the chapter relating to sex history. The number of full-term children or miscarriages will be considered in connection with other family relationships and hereditary influences in Chapter IX.

[4] See Chapter III.

HABITS

There is, however, the consideration of certain habits relating to physical status which we will present here, as a means of helping to define the total group. These habits are the use of alcohol, drugs and tobacco. The material on which these figures are based is not only the statement of the subject but the corroboration of other informants interviewed by the field worker. We have not included as excessive alcoholics or drug addicts any women concerning whom there was reasonable doubt as to whether or not alcohol or drugs were used to excess.

TABLE 32

USE OF ALCOHOL

Per Cent Distribution Among Delinquent Women in Institutional Groups

Use of Alcohol	Institutional Groups						Total
	Bedford	Auburn	Magdalen	Penitentiary	Workhouse	Probation	
Never........	65.3	35.9	79.5	55.6	35.6	50.0	53.2
Moderate......	16.8	33.3	11.0	26.9	33.7	34.2	26.2
Excessive......	17.8	30.8	9.6	17.6	30.7	15.9	20.6
Total....	100.0	100.0	100.0	100.0	100.0	100.0	100.0
Number of cases	101	78	73	108	101	82	543

From Table 32 it is seen that the Magdalen and Bedford have the largest percentages of women who have never used alcohol, while the Penitentiary, Probation, Auburn, and Workhouse follow in order of decreasing percentages. It is of interest to note that Bedford and the Magdalen which have the lowest average ages also have the largest percentage of non-alcoholics.

The largest percentage of excessive drinkers, on the other hand, is found in the Auburn group, and is followed by the Workhouse, Bedford, Penitentiary, Probation, and the Magdalen. It is interesting to note that the degree of alcoholism is much alike in the Auburn and

Workhouse groups where one might expect to find wide discrepancies. The fact that from this group of Workhouse women all those convicted of intoxication are omitted, serves to change the general trend of Workhouse commitments. In this particular comparison, therefore, we must remember that only a part of the Workhouse is represented, and that if the total intoxication cases were included the comparison would be quite different.

The Special Intoxication group in the Workhouse which has been described in Chapter I [5] is composed of twenty-one cases. It may be well here to give some of the more important data on this small number of cases which, though not consecutive in admission to the Workhouse, were chosen from the total group of Workhouse women observed, with no conscious bias. The number is too small to use for any extensive comparison, but a few facts may serve to show how the group is different from the Workhouse group which we have used in this study. Though we hesitate to draw conclusions from results with so few cases, we believe, on the basis of rather extensive observation, that the discrepancy indicated above is genuine.

It is probably worthy of note that there are no colored women in this group of intoxication cases. Twelve of the women are native white, while of the nine foreign born, seven come from Ireland, one from England, and one from Finland.

As stated, the nature of the present offense in each of these cases is for intoxication and falls in the general classification of offenses against regulations for public health, safety and policy, and also in the misdemeanor group.

The extent of delinquency among the women of this group is of particular interest in that the mean number of convictions is 11.0 in comparison with 2.82 for the non-intoxication cases studied in the Workhouse and with 1.63 for the total of the six institutional groups. It is also probable that this mean number is based on only a part of the convictions for many of the older women in the intoxication group. Since they have been coming into the courts for years and before the finger-print system was established, it is likely that many of the written records for constant repeaters were not found by the field worker. The range of convictions is from no previous convictions in 2 cases to 35 in one case. The first offenders were only 2, or 9.5 per cent of the total, in comparison with 23.0 per cent for the rest of the Workhouse group, and with 44.7 per cent first offenders for the total group. The

[5] See Chapter II, p. 24.

length of time served runs from no time served to 94 months and 6 days. The mean number of months served is 20.42.

If we turn to the first offenses of the women in this intoxication group we find that the age at the first conviction has a range of from 25 to 71 years, with a mean age of 40.7 years. This is considerably older than the average age at first conviction of the larger Workhouse group, 32.1 years, but very likely does not represent the actual age at first conviction for several of the older women who say they have "been coming to the Island ever since I can remember." The nature of the first offense in ten cases or practically half of the total was in the same group of offenses against regulations for public health, and nearly all were intoxication cases. Nine women, or 47.4 per cent, were first convicted of general criminality offenses. If we add all of the convictions of each of the twenty-one cases, we have 212 previous convictions. Of this number, only four convictions were for offenses involving prostitution, all the others being for intoxication or disorderly conduct.[6]

[6] To show the impossibility of having reliable information if the statement of the woman is used when she has had a record like the following, both the woman's statement and the verified record of convictions are given for two of the intoxication cases in the Workhouse.

Woman's Statement		*Verified Record*		
1. "At first insisted that her first conviction was two years ago. Later stated that she 'stayed out of prison for three years at a time, two years ago.' Then said she had had 5 and 10 day sentences and 6 months the last time. No further information could be obtained from the woman, who seemed confused and said she 'never could remember dates'."	1.	1/14/03,	Disorderly conduct,	Workhouse, 5 days.
	2.	3/29/04,	Intoxication,	" 20 days.
	3.	4/30/04,	Disorderly conduct,	" 6 mos., or $500 fine.
	4.	8/12/04,	" "	Workhouse, 1 mo., or $500 fine.
	5.	9/14/05,	Intoxication,	Workhouse, 160 days.
	6.	4/ 3/05,	Disorderly conduct,	" 1 mo., or $300 fine.
	7.	5/ 7/05,	" "	Workhouse, 6 mos., or $500 fine.
	8.	9/ 1/05,	Intoxication,	Workhouse, 5 days.
	9.	11/18/05,	Disorderly conduct,	" 6 mos.
	10.	6/20/06,	Intoxication,	" 6 mos.
	11.	10/ 7/07,	"	" 6 mos.
	12.	5/16/08,	Disorderly conduct,	" 6 mos.
	13.	11/ 2/08,	" "	" 6 mos.
	14.	6/ 3/09,	" "	" 6 mos.
	15.	1/24/10,	" "	" 6 mos.
	16.	8/23/11,	Intoxication,	" 10 days
	17.	10/20/11,	Disorderly conduct,	" 10 days.
	18.	11/24/11,	" "	" 180 days.
	19.	7/ 9/12,	" "	" 5 days.
	20.	7/25/12,	" "	" 30 days.
	21.	10/14/12,	Intoxication,	" 60 days.
	22.	6/ 7/13,	Disorderly conduct,	" 10 days.
	23.	8/ 1/14,	" "	" 30 days.

By the nature of the group, all of the special intoxication cases have used alcohol to excess. None of the women in the group denied this. All denied use of drugs in any form and there was no outside evidence obtained to contradict their statements. It was found that three of the group used tobacco to excess.

While we are considering the question of alcoholism, it will be advisable to show the relation of the alcoholic and non-alcoholic groups to the number of convictions. For this comparison, alcoholic has been used to include both the excessive drinkers in the regular group of 587 cases, and the special intoxication cases in the Workhouse. The non-alcoholic includes those who never use alcohol and the moderate

Woman's Statement		*Verified Record*		
	24.	9/ 2/14,	Intoxication,	Workhouse, 5 days, or $5.00 fine.
	25.	9/29/14,	"	House of Good Shepherd, 9/29/14-4/5/15.
	26.	6/11/15,	Disorderly conduct,	Workhouse, 10 days.
	27.	6/23/15,	Intoxication,	" 15 days.
	28.	7/16/15,	"	" 30 days.
	29.	9/16/15,	"	" 30 days.
	30.	10/24/15,	Disorderly conduct,	" 5 days, or $5.00 fine.
	31.	10/31/15,	Intoxication,	Workhouse, 10 days.
	32.	11/10/15,	"	" 30 days.
	33.	12/20/15,	"	" 3 mos.
	34.	3/27/16,	Disorderly conduct,	" 30 days.
	35.	5/22/16,	Intoxication,	" 6 mos.
2. "Been coming here again and again for years. Came out of jail six months ago. Was arrested the next day and got six months."	1.	9/ 5/11,	Intoxication,	" 30 days.
	2.	11/22/11,	Disorderly conduct,	" 1 mo.
	3.	12/27/11,	" "	" 6 mos.
	4.	8/19/13,	" "	" 30 days.
	5.	12/30/13,	" "	" 30 days.
	6.	3/14/14,	" "	" 1 mo., or $500 fine.
	7.	8/ 4/14,	" "	Workhouse, 6 mos.
	8.	2/ 5/15,	Intoxication,	" 10 days, or $10 fine.
	9.	2/15/15,	Disorderly conduct,	Workhouse, 3 mos., or $100 fine.
	10.	7/22/15,	" "	Workhouse, 10 days.
	11.	9/15/15,	Intoxication and disorderly conduct.	" 60 days.
	12.	11/14/15,	Disorderly conduct,	" 20 days.
	13.	12/ 4/15,	" "	" 10 days, or $10 fine.
	14.	12/14/15,	Vagrancy, violation of Tenement House Law,	Workhouse, 5 days.
	15.	12/19/15,	Disorderly conduct,	" 30 days.
	16.	5/16/16,	Intoxication,	" 30 days.
	17.	6/23/16,	"	" 4 mos.
	18.	10/24/16,	"	" 6 mos.

drinkers, A comparison of the average number of previous convictions for the alcoholic and non-alcoholic groups showed that the average for the alcoholic group is 5.35 convictions, while the average for the non-alcoholic group is only 2.285 convictions. That this is a valid difference is shown by the ratio 5.83. A comparison of the dispersions of number of convictions among the two groups indicates that there is a valid difference in the dispersion of the two groups, with a wider scattering among the alcoholic group.

TABLE 33

ALCOHOLIC* AND NON-ALCOHOLIC

Comparison of the Means and Standard Deviations of the Number of Previous Convictions Among Alcoholic and Non-Alcoholic Women of Total Group

	Alcoholic	Non-Alcoholic	Difference	$\frac{d}{\sigma_d}$	Chances that real difference does not exist are 1 in:
Mean................	5.35	2.285	3.07	5.83	∞
σ_m................	±.517	±.0984			
σ...................	5.96	2.044	3.92	10.53	∞
σ_σ...................	±.365	±.0696			
Cases...............	133	431			

*Those who use alcohol to excess. Includes 21 cases from Special Intoxication Group in Workhouse.

In determining what percentage of the cases are drug-addicts, no measure of "moderate" has been used, and none have been counted as drug-users who did not have a habit at the time of the present conviction or shortly before. The following table shows that the percentage of drug-users varies from 6.2 per cent in the Probation group to 33.7 per cent in the Penitentiary, where a large percentage of the women convicted of possessing or selling drugs are sentenced. The five women drug-users in the Probation group were not convicted of using drugs and the fact of their being drug-addicts was not discovered until after the probation sentence was given.

The use of tobacco also varies considerably among the institutional groups. The Workhouse has the lowest percentage who never use tobacco and is followed by the Penitentiary, Auburn, Probation. Bedford, and Magdalen in order of increasing percentages. Of those

TABLE 34

USE OF DRUGS

Per Cent Distribution Among Delinquent Women in Institutional Groups

Use of Drugs	Institutional Groups						Total
	Bedford	Auburn	Magdalen	Peni-tentiary	Work-house	Probation	
Drug-Users....	14.9	13.0	13.7	33.7	22.8	6.2	18.3
Non-Drug-Users	85.1	87.0	86.3	66.4	77.2	93.8	81.7
Totals....	100.0	100.0	100.0	100.0	100.0	100.0	100.0
Number of cases	101	77	73	107	101	81	540

who use tobacco to excess, however, the order is changed from Probation with the smallest percentage to the Magdalen, Bedford, Penitentiary, Auburn, and Workhouse in increasing order.

TABLE 35

USE OF TOBACCO

Per Cent Distribution Among Delinquent Women in Institutional Groups

Use of Tobacco	Institutional Groups						Total
	Bedford	Auburn	Magdalen	Peni-tentiary	Work-house	Probation	
Never.........	82.2	79.2	84.7	72.0	59.0	81.3	75.6
Moderate......	2.0	....	2.8	9.4	8.0	10.7	5.6
Excessive......	15.8	20.8	12.5	18.7	33.0	8.0	18.8
Total....	100.0	100.0	100.0	100.0	100.0	100.0	100.0
Number of cases	101	77	72	107	100	75	532

There are many possibilities of comparison of habits with other studies of delinquents. Of these only two will be noted as directly comparable with certain of our institutional groups. First of all, a comparison of Dr. Guibord's study of 200 Bedford cases in 1914 may be of interest in showing whether there seems to be any marked change in the make-up of this group in a few years.[7]

	Habits of 200 Bedford Women in 1914.		Habits of Women in Present Study for:	
	Group A.	Group B.	Bedford	Total Group
Excessive or frequent use of alcohol	35.0%	27.0%	34.6%	46.8%
Drug-addicts	21.0%	7.0%	14.9%	18.3%
Excessive use of tobacco	20.0%	17.0%	15.8%	18.8%

The most noteworthy discrepancy is that between the percentages of drug-users in the three Bedford groups. This amount of variation would indicate that the proportion of drug-users in this institution varies from year to year to a considerable extent.

In a study of 200 male felons in Auburn Prison, Dr. Heacox finds results quite different from those for our group of women in Auburn Prison or for our total group. The latter, which includes a high percentage of misdemeanants, we should expect to differ from a group of male felons. The following percentages from the above groups are known to have used alcohol, drugs, or tobacco to either a moderate or an excessive degree.

	Auburn Men[8]	Auburn Women	Total Women
Alcohol	87.5%	64.1%	46.8%
Drugs	2.5%	13.0%	18.3%
Tobacco	95.0%	20.8%	24.4%

It is surprising to find so much larger a percentage of drug-addicts in the group of Auburn women than among the Auburn men. There seems to be no clear reason for the difference, since in neither group are commitments possible for drug-using.

RECORD OF COMMITMENTS TO HOSPITALS FOR THE INSANE

We may note briefly, at this point, the number of women in the institutional groups who have at any time been patients in a hospital

[7] Guibord, Alberta S. B. "Physical States of Criminal Women." *Journal of the American Institute of Criminal Law and Criminology*, vol. VIII, no. 1, May 1, 1917.

[8] From unpublished figures on 200 consecutive admissions to Auburn Prison.

for the insane. We have not included here the cases of obviously psychopathic women who have not been in hospitals, since there was no routine psychiatric examination in any group except Bedford, and there was no equally reliable information for comparison on the other groups. The numbers and percentages of women who have at some time been in a hospital for the insane are as follows:

	Number	Per Cent
Bedford	6	5.9
Auburn	3	3.4
Magdalen	0	0.0
Penitentiary	5	4.5
Workhouse	8	7.1
Probation	2	2.0
Total	24	4.1

This small percentage of 4.1, it must be remembered, does not include all who might have been diagnosed as insane, had a proper examination been given, but merely those who had at some time during their lives been diagnosed as insane and committed to a hospital for the insane.

The diagnoses as we were able to obtain them from the hospitals on these 24 cases are as follows:

Constitutionally inferior	5
Manic Depressive	5
Manic Depressive with Alcoholism	3
Dementia Præcox	2
Alcoholic Psychosis, Korsakoff Type	1
Stuporous Melancholia	1
Involutional Melancholia	1
Infective Exhaustion	1
Mental Defective with Psychosis	1
Not Insane	1
Diagnosis unknown	3

In Dr. Katharine B. Davis' study of 647 prostitutes at Bedford,[9] twenty cases, or 3.1 per cent of the group, were transferred to hospitals for the insane while they were at Bedford. This does not include, however, women who had at any time in the past been in such a hospital, so that the percentage is probably lower than it should be for exact comparison with our data.

[9] Kneeland, George J.: "Commercialized Prostitution in New York City," Chapter VIII by Katharine Bement Davis. A Study of Prostitutes Committed to the State Reformatory for Women at Bedford Hills. The Century Company, 1916, p. 186.

CIVIL CONDITION

Turning to other general items indicating the social status of the women delinquents, we may first consider the question of civil condition. The following table shows that the percentage of single women varies between the institutional groups to a large extent. As would be expected, the highest percentages of single women are found in two groups, Bedford and Magdalen, where the average age is lowest. The total group shows 42.4 per cent of the women single. Among those who have been married the percentage who were widowed or divorced at the time of the present conviction varies between the groups somewhat as the percentage of those married varies. That is, those groups with the highest percentage married, namely, Auburn, Penitentiary and Workhouse, have the highest percentage who are divorced or widowed. If we compare the total delinquent group with the general female population fifteen years of age and over in New York State, we see that the delinquent group has an appreciably smaller percentage of women who are married. This varies, however, in a comparison with the institutional groups, those groups with the highest average ages, Auburn, Penitentiary, and Workhouse, having a higher percentage of married women than the general population.

TABLE 36

CIVIL CONDITION

Per Cent Distribution of Delinquent Women in Institutional Groups and of General Female Population 15 Years of Age and Over in New York State, in 1910

Civil Condition	Institutional Groups						Total	General Female Population
	Bed-ford	Auburn	Mag-dalen	Peni-tentiary	Work-house	Proba-tion		
Single	63.4	16.3	69.7	29.6	27.7	50.5	42.4	33.8
Married	36.6	83.8	30.3	70.4	72.3	49.5	57.6	66.2
Widowed	2.0	3.8	1.3	2.8	4.9	2.2	2.9	11.3
Divorced	2.0	17.5	4.0	15.7	14.9	4.3	9.8	.3
Total	100.0	100.0	100.0	100.0	100 0	100.0	100.0	100.0
Number of cases	101	80	76	108	101	93	559	3,291,714

The age at first marriage is presented by institutional groups to show the range of ages and where the greatest massing occurs. The mean age at first marriage for the total group is 20.5 years±.268. The standard deviation of 4.68±.189 years indicates that there is not a particularly wide scattering of ages. There are 92 cases or 30.0 per cent of the total group who were married under 18 years, which is the legal age of consent in New York State. There were 30 cases or 9.8 per cent married under 16 years, the limit of the Juvenile Court age.

TABLE 37

AGE AT FIRST MARRIAGE

Per Cent Distribution of Delinquent Women in Institutional Groups

Age	Institutional Groups						Total
	Bedford	Auburn	Magdalen	Peni-tentiary	Work-house	Probation	
13 to 16 yrs...	8.3	10.8	4.4	9.2	11.9	10.3	9.8
16 " 19 " ..	44.4	30.8	13.1	27.6	22.4	43.6	30.1
19 " 22 " ..	25.0	29.2	30.5	22.4	23.9	23.1	25.2
22 " 25 " ..	13.9	15.4	34.8	17.1	26.9	7.7	18.6
25 " 28 " ..	5.6	9.2	13.1	9.2	7.5	7.7	8.5
28 " 31 " ..	2 8	3.1	4.4	7.9	4.5	5.1	4.9
31 " 34 " ..	....	1.5	....	1.3	1.5	....	1.0
34 " 37 " ..	....	....	....	2.6	....	....	.7
37 " 40 " ..	....	....	....	....	1.5	2.6	.7
40 " 43 " ..	....	....	....	1.3	....	....	.3
43 " 46 " ..	....	....	....	1.3	....	....	.3
Total....	100.0	100.0	100.0	100.0	100.0	100.0	100.0
Number of cases	36	65	23	76	67	39	306

Mean Age at First Marriage (Total Group)...20.50 ± .268 years.
σ (Total Group).......................... 4.68 ± .189 years.

If we compare the age of the husband at this first marriage, we see from Table 38 that the distribution begins at a later age and runs to a later age. Only eleven men or five per cent were married before they were eighteen years of age to the women in this study, and only two men or .9 per cent were married before they were sixteen. The average age of the first husband at marriage is 25.27±.475 years, with a standard deviation of 7.056±.336 years. This shows that the men were of a considerably older average age than the women whom they married.

TABLE 38

AGE OF FIRST HUSBAND AT MARRIAGE

Per Cent Distribution of Delinquent Women in Institutional Groups

Age	Institutional Groups						Total
	Bedford	Auburn	Magdalen	Peni-tentiary	Work-house	Probation	
13 to 16 yrs...	....	2.0	....	....	....	3.5	.9
16 " 19 " ..	2.8	13.7	6.3	7.0	13.0	6.9	9.1
19 " 22 " ..	22.2	19.6	18.8	20.9	10.9	34.5	20.4
22 " 25 " ..	27.8	15.7	37.5	27.9	30.4	31.0	26.7
25 " 28 " ..	19.4	17.7	12.5	20.9	19.6	10.4	17.7
28 " 31 " ..	16.7	11.8	....	9.3	4.4	10.4	9.5
31 " 34 " ..	2.8	11.8	18.8	4.7	8.7	....	7.2
34 " 37 " ..	....	....	6.3	2.3	4.4	3.5	2.3
37 " 40 " ..	....	....	....	2.3	....	....	.5
40 " 43 " ..	....	2.0	....	....	4.4	....	1.4
43 " 46 " ..	2.8	3.9	....	2.3	....	....	1.8
46 " 49 " ..	2.8	2.0	....	2.3	....	....	1.4
52 " 55 " ..	2.8	....	....	....	2.2	....	.9
61 " 63 " ..	....	....	....	....	2.2	....	.5
Total....	100.0	100.0	100.0	100.0	100.0	100.0	100.0
Number of cases	36	51	16	43	46	29	221

Mean Age of First Husband at Marriage (Total Group)..25.27 ± .475 years
σ (Total Group)....................................7.056 ± .336 years

RELIGION

The religion of the women shows varying differences in the institutional groups. Before discussing these differences in detail it will be well to bear in mind the fact that we have no representation here of institutions such as the House of the Good Shepherd where the inmates are very largely Catholic. This particularly affects the percentages in Bedford, Magdalen, and the Workhouse, which receive much the same kind of cases that are sent to the House of the Good Shepherd. Table 39 shows that in these three groups there are, as we should expect, a smaller percentage of Catholic than of Protestant women, but to offset this we must remember that the House of the Good Shepherd is almost entirely Catholic and that the percentages of women in these three institutional groups classified by religion are not, therefore, representative of the religion of delinquent women as a whole. In general, the figures for Auburn and Probation ought not to be seriously affected by the existence of Catholic institutions, since these two groups tend to receive a distinct type of case, which in most instances, would not receive any other kind of sentence. The Penitentiary might have been affected, to a certain extent, particularly with such offenses as possessing drugs, which are punishable by commitment to a private institution like the House of the Good Shepherd. In these three groups, Auburn, Penitentiary, and Probation, we see that the percentages of Catholics are larger than those of Protestants, and that the difference is most marked in the Probation group with 55.1 per cent of its cases Catholics and 30.3 per cent Protestants. The percentages for our total group of delinquent women are of little value for anything except material descriptive of the group, because this total includes the three institutional groups which are largely Protestant because the Catholic women have been sent to a Catholic institution. From the three groups, therefore, which can give any accurate indication of the percentage of Catholics, Hebrews and Protestants, it is interesting to note that the Catholics in each case make up the highest percentage, the Protestants next highest, and the Hebrews a relatively small percentage. It is impossible to obtain any recent figures from the Census or from any other extensive studies to compare the percentages from the denominational groups among delinquent women with the same for the general population, and it is, therefore, difficult to state whether the percentages of Catholics, Protestants and Hebrews are in excess or below the percentages for these denominational groups in the general population.

TABLE 39

RELIGION

Per Cent Distribution of Delinquent Women in Institutional Groups

Religion	Institutional Groups						Total
	Bedford	Auburn	Magdalen	Penitentiary	Workhouse	Probation	
Catholic.......	36.6	46.3	22.7	43.0	35.0	55.1	40.0
Greek Cath..	1.0	3.8	....	....	....	....	.7
Roman Cath.	35.6	42.5	22.7	43.0	35.0	55.1	39.3
Hebrew........	8.9	11.3	41.3	15.0	10.0	14.6	15.9
Protestant.....	54.5	42.5	36.0	42.1	55.0	30.3	44.0
Total.....	100.0	100.0	100.0	100.0	100.0	100.0	100.0
Number of cases	101	80	75	107	100	89	552

SUMMARY

From this chapter of somewhat heterogeneous social factors in the lives of the delinquent women under consideration, we may note the following points.

The average age varies from 21.7 years in the Bedford group to 34.9 years in the Workhouse. The institutional groups divide themselves into two groups, those of appreciably younger average ages, Bedford, Magdalen and Probation, and those of an older average age, Auburn, Penitentiary and Workhouse. The average age of the total group which we shall use in later chapters is 28.8 years.

The habits of the women in institutional groups are of considerable importance, especially in reference to the use of alcohol, drugs and tobacco. From Table 39, we found that the percentage who used alcohol moderately or to excess, varied considerably between the institutional groups, with the Magdalen having the largest percentage of non-alcoholics and the Workhouse the smallest percentage. A brief survey of the 21 intoxication cases from the Workhouse shows that the average number of convictions among this group is 11.0, almost seven times as large as the average number of convictions for the total of the six institutional groups. If we compare the mean number of convictions for the non-alcoholic group, that is, those who never use alcohol or do so moderately, with those who use alcohol to excess, including the special intoxication group in the Workhouse, we find that the crude differences of the mean convictions are large and that these differences are significant. That is, the average number of convictions for the alcoholic group is much larger than for the non-alcoholic group.

The use of drugs also varies markedly in the institutional groups, with the lowest percentage of drug-addicts in the Probation group from a court which has no jurisdiction over charges of possessing or using drugs, and the largest percentage in the Penitentiary which receives the bulk of the women who are convicted of possessing drugs.

The use of tobacco, while not of so much importance as the drug-addiction and use of alcohol, is of some interest, especially in comparison with other groups of delinquents. A group of male felons in Auburn Prison, for instance, has 95.0 per cent of the group using tobacco to excess, while in our group of Auburn women the excessive tobacco users are only 20.8 per cent.

The record of commitments to hospitals for the insane shows that 4.1 per cent of our total group have at some time been patients in such hospitals. This does not include those who may be mentally diseased or deteriorated, but who have not been in a hospital for the insane.

If we proceed to the other social factors of civil condition, age at marriage, etc., we find that the groups with the youngest average age at present conviction have the largest percentage unmarried. The average age at first marriage for the total group of women is 20.5 years, while the average age of the first husband at the time of marriage to the women in this study is 25.3 years.

The distribution by religion is difficult to interpret since the number of Catholics in Bedford, Magdalen, and the Workhouse is affected by the fact that the House of the Good Shepherd, a Catholic institution, takes the cases which could be committed to these three institutions, and therefore unduly increases the percentages of Protestants and Hebrews in these institutions. In the three institutional groups which would be little affected by the House of the Good Shepherd, the Catholics have the highest percentage of cases, the Protestants the next highest and the Hebrews a relatively small percentage.

CHAPTER VIII

NATIVITY AND COLOR IN RELATION TO DELINQUENCY

THE report of the City Council Committee on Crime in Chicago states that:

"Statistics furnished in the police report show that the native Americans, white and colored both, have a percentage of arrests and convictions considerably greater than their percentage of population. On the other hand, the various foreign groups show a smaller per cent of convictions than their proportion of the population entitles them to have. It is, of course, popularly believed that immigration is a cause of crime. This belief has largely been due to a comfortable theory that we are superior to the people of Europe, and to a desire to shift the responsibility for our shortcomings on to other people. No facts have ever been found to support this belief. The Chicago statistics in this respect agree with the statistics furnished by the United States census and the Federal Commission on Immigration. The report of the commission states emphatically that 'no satisfactory evidence has yet been produced to show that immigration has resulted in an increase in crime disproportionate to the increase in adult population. Such comparable statistics of crime and population as it has been possible to obtain indicate that immigrants are less prone to commit crime than are native Americans.' The special census report on prisoners after analyzing the statistics of nativity for the whole country said that it was 'evident that the popular belief that the foreign born are filling the prisons has little foundation in fact.' Chicago statistics furnish further confirmation of this statement."[1]

Our study of 587 delinquent women, including the important types of women offenders throughout New York State, adds to the data already collected in the reports which have been mentioned, by showing that the native born white women offenders have a representation among the total group of female delinquents slightly greater than their percentage of the general population in the state, the native born colored a percentage considerably greater than their

[1] "Report of the City Council Committee on Crime of the City of Chicago," March 22, 1915, p. 59.

percentage of the general population, and the total foreign born, on the other hand, a percentage considerably less than their proportion of the general female population of the same ages. In addition to a comparison of the numbers of delinquent women within the nativity and color groups, with the general female population in New York City over fifteen years of age, several comparisons have been made of the degree of delinquency between the total foreign, total native, native white, and native colored. These comparisons have been worked out in the order followed in Chapter VI, considering first the nature of the present offense in its two classifications, the number of previous convictions followed by the percentage of recidivists and first offenders, and finally the age at first conviction, nature of first offense and first sentence.

BIRTHPLACE AND COLOR

It is very desirable, in any comprehensive survey of the relation of nativity and color to delinquency, to show comparisons between the various foreign countries and groups of countries from which the delinquents come. Unfortunately, the total number of foreign born women in our entire group is only 172, and the largest number from any one foreign country is twenty-four. Even by grouping together those born in western Europe (65 cases) or southern and eastern Europe (79 cases), the number is too small for statistical uses, and it would not be safe to draw even the most general conclusions from so few observations.

There is, however, a vast amount of material which has been written to show the comparisons between the total foreign and the total native born in their relation to criminality. To supplement that material, we have used our total foreign born group which we believe to be a true sample of the foreign born women delinquents in New York State, and have compared this group with both the native white and native colored found in the same institutions.

The following frequency table shows the distribution of the women studied, by the country of birth and by color. It will be noted that there are four colored foreign born cases, one in Auburn, two in the Penitentiary, and one in the Probation group. These four cases were counted among the total foreign born throughout, except for purposes of comparison with the Census figures where they were added to the total negro group, leaving the foreign white for comparison with the

TABLE 40

BIRTHPLACE

Per Cent Distribution of Delinquent Women in Institutional Groups by Birthplace

Birthplace	Institutional Groups						Total
	Bedford	Auburn	Magdalen	Penitentiary	Workhouse	Probation	
Total Native Born	88.1	51.3	68.4	57.4	70.0	77.2	69.1
Native White	68.3	35.0	68.4	38.0	34.0	68.5	51.5
Native Colored	19.8	16.3	....	19.4	36.0	8.7	17.6
Total Foreign Born	11.9	48.8	31.6	42.6	30.0	22.8	30.9
Austria	3.0	6.3	10.5	4.6	2.0	6.5	5.2
Belgium	....	....	....	....	....	1.1	.2
Bermuda Islands	1.0	....	....	....	....	....	.2
Canada	....	1.3	....	2.8	....	....	.7
Cuba	....	....	....	....	....	1.1*	.2*
Denmark	....	1.3	....	....	....	....	.2
England	....	2.5	....	.9	....	1.1	.7
Finland	....	....	1.3	1.9	....	....	.5
France	....	....	....	1.9	2.0	....	.7
Germany	....	3.8	4.0	5.6	4.0	1.1	3.1
Hungary	1.0	1.3	1.3	2.8	1.0	1.1	1.4
Ireland	1.0	5.0	4.0	5.6	7.0	1.1	4.0
Italy	2.0	11.3	....	1.9	1.0	1.1	2.7
New Zealand	....	....	....	....	1.0	....	.2
Norway	....	....	1.3	.9	....	....	.4
Nova Scotia	....	....	....	.9	....	....	.2
Austrian Poland	1.0	....	....	.9	....	....	.4
Russian Poland	1.0	2.5	2.6	2.8	1.0	1.1	1.8
Porto Rico	....	1.3*	....	.9*	....	....	.4*
Rumania	....	....	2.6	....	....	....	.4
Russia	1.0	8.8	1.3	7.4	5.0	2.2	4.3
Scotland	1.0	....	1.3	....	....	1.1	.5
Sicily	....	....	....	....	1.0	1.1	.4
Sweden	....	1.3	1.3	....	5.0	3.3	1.8
Switzerland	....	1.3	....	....	....	....	.2
Syria	....	1.3	....	....	....	....	.2
British W. Indies	....	....	....	.9*	....	....	.2*
Total	100.0	100.0	100.0	100.0	100.0	100.0	100.0
Number of cases	101	80	76	108	100	92	557

*Colored.

native white.[2] Since the number of cases is too small to regroup satisfactorily, even into English-speaking and non-English-speaking foreign born women, we have listed the countries of birth in alphabetical order, with no attempt to classify as to geographical or language distribution. It is obvious, first of all, from this table, that the percentages of native and foreign born women vary considerably between the institutional groups.

Bedford has the lowest percentage of foreign born women. This may be partly explained by the fact that Bedford receives commitments not only from New York City, but also from the counties along the Hudson River as far north as Rensselaer County, and that Bedford has the smallest percentage of commitments from New York City where there is a higher percentage of foreign born in the general population than in the rest of New York State. On the other hand, Auburn Prison has the highest percentage of foreign born though it takes prisoners from all over the State. A later table will partially explain this by showing that a larger percentage of felons is found among the foreign born than among the native white or native colored. Since Auburn is distinctly a felony group, we may, then, expect a large percentage of its women to be foreign born. In all the New York City groups, which are made up almost entirely from women convicted in New York City, we should expect to find a higher percentage of foreign born than in Bedford. It is of interest to note that the Penitentiary, which has the highest percentage of felony cases, next to Auburn, has the second highest percentage of foreign born women. The total group of foreign born, 30.9 per cent of all women delinquents, which we shall use for the comparative data to follow, is of course, midway between the extremes of the Bedford and Auburn groups, but gives a picture of the total foreign born in a sample drawn from the whole of New York State.

If we turn to the percentage of native colored within the various institutional groups, it is obvious that there are marked differences here. The Magdalen does not take colored women, so that they are

[2] For the most part, these four cases are not extreme enough in any way seriously to affect the central tendency of the foreign born in any particular group of facts used. The ages are as follows: 27, 28, 31 and 27. Nature of present offense: offense against chastity, 1; offenses against property rights, 3. Number of previous convictions: none in two cases; 1 in one case; 10 in one case. Age at first conviction: 27, 28, 28, 29. First offense: offense against chastity, 1; offenses against property rights, 3. First sentence: Probation, 1; Reformatory, 1; Penitentiary, 1; State Prison, 1.

straightway eliminated from the discussion. The probation group has a small percentage of colored because of the meager facilities for supervising colored girls on probation. Only the most promising colored girls are considered for probation instead of an institutional sentence because of the difficulty of looking after them without an adequate staff of probation officers. Within the three groups, Bedford, Auburn and the Penitentiary, the differences in the percentages of colored women are not marked. The very high percentage of colored women in the Workhouse is undoubtedly partly due to the practice of giving short Workhouse terms to first or second offenders who might, if they had been white, have been given a chance on probation; and partly due to the fact that several of the private institutions in the city refuse to take colored women, for whom, then, there is no alternative but a long Reformatory sentence or a Workhouse term. The total group of colored women, 17.6 per cent of all the women in the study, will be used in the comparisons to follow.

(*a*) *Comparison of Nativity and Color Between Delinquent Women and General Female Population in New York City*

In comparing the delinquent women with the general female population, with respect to nativity and color, we have chosen the population of New York City rather than New York State for the comparison, and have used only the delinquent women convicted in New York City. This plan seemed more advisable since the distribution of the nativity groups varies so markedly between New York City and New York State, and so few of our cases, only 11.9 per cent, were convicted in the counties outside of Greater New York. From the Census figures for New York City in 1910, we were able to get only the number of females in the general population over fifteen years of age. Since the members of this delinquent group are all supposedly sixteen years of age or over, there will be a slight but unavoidable difference in the basis of comparison.

From chart 9, made up on the basis of the total group of delinquent women convicted in New York City, it is evident that the native white have a slightly larger representation in the group of delinquents than they have in the general female population of the same ages. We might also compare here the percentage of native white in the general population with the percentages of native white delinquent women in the Magdalen, Penitentiary, Workhouse and Probation groups in Table 40.[3]

It will be seen that the percentage of native white in the Magdalen is 68.4, or 21.6 per cent larger than the percentage of native white in the general female population in New York City over fifteen years. In the Penitentiary and the Workhouse, the native white run 8.8 per cent and 12.8 per cent below their representation of the native white in the general population. In the Probation group the native white delinquents have 21.7 per cent more than their propor-

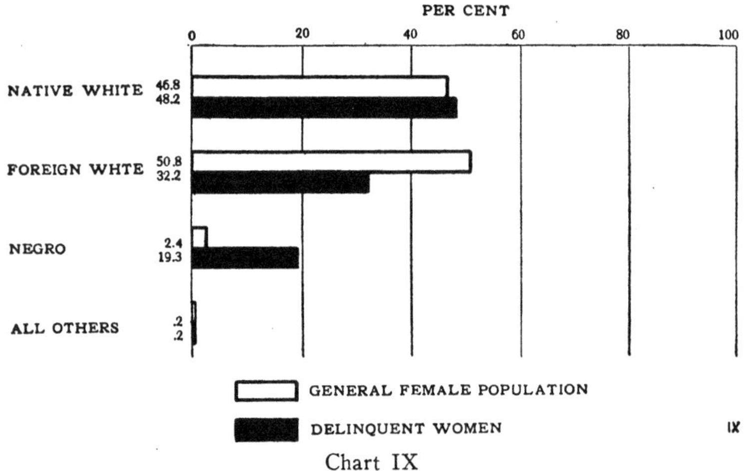

Chart IX

Percentage Comparison Showing Nativity and Color Among (1), General Female Population over 15 Years of Age in New York City in 1910, and (2), 481 Female Delinquents Convicted in New York City.

tionate representation among the general population. Our total delinquent group in New York City, then, while being only slightly higher in the percentage of native white than the same class in the population of New York City, varies within itself as to proportions, two of the institutional groups having less, and two of the groups more than their proportionate share of the native white.

If we turn to the group of negroes in Chart IX, we note that their proportion among the delinquent women is markedly higher than we should expect to find from the number of negro women over

[3] Since Bedford and Auburn each have a number of commitments from districts outside of New York City and Table 40 includes all the women studied, both from New York City and New York State, we shall not compare these two groups with the general female population in Chart 9.

fifteen years of age in New York City. While they are a small part, only 2.4 per cent of the population in question, they furnish 19.3 per cent of the delinquents. Within the New York City institutional groups in Table 40, it will not be possible to make many comparisons since the Magdalen takes no negro women. The Penitentiary, however, has 21.2 per cent of its group negroes,[4] the Workhouse 36.0 per cent and the Probation group 9.8 per cent. The Workhouse is particularly striking in having fifteen times as many negro women as one would expect from the female negro population over 15 years in New York City. As noted before, the very much larger proportion of colored in the Workhouse as compared with the Probation group is probably accounted for by the fact that many of these women are sent to the Workhouse on their first sentence instead of being given probation.

The foreign white delinquent women have a far smaller percentage in our total group than have the foreign white women in the female population over fifteen years of age in New York City. This is worthy of mention in view of the fact that many persons still believe that the amount of crime in this country, and especially in New York City, is greatly increased by immigration. New York City with a foreign born white population of females over fifteen years amounting to 50.8 per cent of its total female population offers a ready field for those of foreign birth who intend to violate the law. And yet they contribute only 32.2 per cent of our total delinquent group. In none of the institutional groups do the foreign born white contribute as high a percentage as they have in the general female population over fifteen years, and in most instances the difference is very marked.

The group of "All Others" shown on Chart 9 by the lowest bar is composed of 1 case only, in the delinquent group. It seems absurd to draw any comparison based on 1 case, but as the chart shows, the percentage of delinquent women and women in the general population included under "All Others" are the same.

It has been suggested that one reason why the foreign born ought to have a smaller percentage in the criminal class than in the general population in this country is because of the immigration law which excludes from admission into the United States "persons who have been convicted of or admit having committed a felony or other crime or misdemeanor involving moral turpitude," and "prostitutes, or women or girls coming into the United States for the purpose of pros-

[4] In the Penitentiary and Probation groups add percentage of foreign born colored, starred in Table 40, to native colored, to obtain total negro group.

titution or for any other immoral purpose."[5] Though this law is difficult for any Board of Review to enforce strictly since they have no knowledge of the past lives of the immigrants coming before them, it is probably true that the law does act as a deterrent on some criminals who would not risk being returned from the United States. The number of aliens who are actually debarred at the time of coming to this country or later deported as criminals, however, was only 912 or .8 per cent of the total aliens admitted to the United States from July 1, 1913, to June 30, 1914.[6] Though the number excluded as criminal aliens is small, this probably has a slight effect on the percentage of foreign born delinquents in New York City.

AGE CLASSIFIED BY NATIVITY AND COLOR

Before proceeding to the nature of delinquency among the nativity groups in our study, we shall consider the question of age at present conviction, since the age factor will to a certain extent affect the number of convictions to be discussed later. The following table (Table 41) gives the frequency distribution of age for all groups.[7] At first glance, it is obvious that the foreign born have the longest range of ages, the native white the next in order and the native colored the shortest in range. On the other hand, the massing of ages appears to be in the earlier age groups, particularly in the native white group.

In order to compare the central tendencies of the different nativity groups, the following three tables are presented.

Table 42 indicates that the mean age of the native white is 26.92 years, or slightly younger than the mean age of the native colored group, 27.00 years. Since the ratio of the actual difference between the means to the standard deviation of the differences is only .08, the chances are even that the observed differences might have occurred by chance. There is, therefore, no demonstrable difference between the mean age of the native colored and the native white. The comparison of the standard deviations of the two groups, however, indicates a wider scattering of ages in the native white than in the native colored group. The ratio of this difference to the standard deviation of the difference is 2.91, which indicates that there is with little doubt a

[5] Immigration Act of Feb. 20, 1907, as Amended by the Acts of March 26, 1910, and March 4, 1913. Section 2.

[6] "Annual Report of the Commissioner General of Immigration," pp. 104 and 108.

[7] All of the following discussion in this chapter is based on the total group of women delinquents committed from all of New York State.

TABLE 41

AGE AT PRESENT CONVICTION

Per Cent Distribution of Delinquent Women Classified by Nativity and Color

Total Group

Age	Nativity and Color				Total
	Total Foreign Born	Total Native Born	Native White	Native Colored	
14 to 18 years	1.2	10.1	11.2	7.1	7.4
18 " 22 "	12.9	23.1	25.8	15.3	20.0
22 " 26 "	15.8	21.3	18.5	29.6	19.6
26 " 30 "	14.6	15.8	15.7	16.3	15.5
30 " 34 "	16.4	9.4	9.1	10.2	11.5
34 " 38 "	11.1	6.5	5.2	10.2	7.9
38 " 42 "	7.6	6.2	5.6	8.2	6.7
42 " 46 "	5.9	1.8	2.1	1.0	3.1
46 " 50 "	4.1	3.1	3.8	1.0	3.4
50 " 54 "	4.1	1.4	1.1	1.0	2.0
54 " 58 "	2.3	.8	1.1	....	1.3
58 " 62 "	1.8	.8	1.1	....	1.1
62 " 66 "	1.2	....	....	....	.4
66 " 70 "	.6	....	....	....	.2
70 " 74 "	.6	....	....	....	.2
Total	100.0	100.0	100.0	100.0	100.0
Number of cases	171	385	287	98	556

TABLE 42

NATIVE WHITE AND NATIVE COLORED

Comparison of the Means and Standard Deviations of Age at Present Conviction for Native White and Native Colored

	Native White	Native Colored	Difference	$\frac{d}{\sigma_d}$	Chances that real difference does not exist are 1 in:
Mean	26.92	27.00	−.08	.08	2
σ_m	±.560	±.761			
σ	9.48	7.54	1.95	2.91	556
σ_σ	±.396	±.538			
Cases	287	98			

valid difference in the variability of the two groups, with the native white having a wider scattering.

Having indicated that there is no demonstrable difference between the mean ages of the native white and native colored, we should be justified in comparing the ages of the total native born and the total foreign born women. But, because of the apparently valid difference between the dispersion of ages in the native white and native colored groups, we have calculated the comparison of the differences between the mean ages of the native white and total foreign born—26.9 vs. 32.9. The ratio of the difference of the means to the standard deviation of the differences (5.92) indicates that there is undoubtedly a valid difference between the native white and total foreign born, with reference to their mean age, with a tendency for the foreign born delinquent women to be older than the native born. A difference, though less striking, in the dispersion of the ages of the two groups is also seen in the ratio of 1.89, with the foreign born having a wider scattering of ages.

TABLE 43

NATIVE WHITE AND TOTAL FOREIGN BORN

Comparison of the Means and Standard Deviations of Age at Present Conviction for Native White and Total Foreign Born

	Native White	Total Foreign Born	Difference	$\frac{d}{\sigma_d}$	Chances that real difference does not exist are 1 in:
Mean	26.92	32.85	−5.92	5.92	∞
σ_m	±.560	±.830			
σ	9.48	10.82	−1.34	1.89	34
σ_σ	±.396	±.587			
Cases	287	170			

Since there is a valid difference between the mean ages of the native white and total foreign born, and no demonstrable difference between the mean ages of native white and native colored, we should expect, as shown in Table 44, to find a real difference between the mean ages of the total native and the total foreign born. The ratio 6.22 indicates a valid difference between the mean ages of the two groups and the ratio 2.67 indicates that there is also a valid difference in the dispersion, the total foreign born group having a wider scattering. It will be well to keep this difference in mind for the later dis-

TABLE 44

TOTAL NATIVE BORN AND TOTAL FOREIGN BORN

Comparison of the Means and Standard Deviations of Age at Present Conviction for Total Native Born and Total Foreign Born

	Total Native Born	Total Foreign Born	Difference	$\frac{d}{\sigma_d}$	Chances that real difference does not exist are 1 in:
Mean............	26.94	32.85	−5.90	6.22	∞
σ_m..............	±.460	±.830			
σ................	9.03	10.82	−1.79	2.67	263
σ_σ...............	±.325	±.587			
Cases............	385	170			

cussion of the criminal record,—that the foreign born group show an older mean age than either the native white or total native born, and also a wider scattering than is found among the native white or total native born.

Very little has been done in gaging the nature and extent of criminality among the foreign born. Miss Grace Abbott writes:

"The United States Immigration Commission made 'the central feature' of its investigation the determination of how 'the criminality of the immigrant differs from that of the native born' (Vol. 36, p. 13). The material available or secured by the commission was, however, very meager and no attempt was made to discover to what extent apparent tendencies on the part of certain races to commit certain kinds of crime were the result of local conditions rather than race."[8]

As noted before, our numbers from individual foreign countries are too small for use, but with the total foreign born group we have been able to draw some conclusions as to the nature and extent of their delinquency.

NATURE OF PRESENT OFFENSE, CLASSIFIED BY NATIVITY GROUPS

(a) *New York City Police Department Classification*

Table 45, followed by Chart X, shows the nature of the present offense classified by the New York City Police Department classifica-

[8] Abbott, Grace. "Immigration and Crime." (Report of Committee "G" of the Institute.) *Journal of the American Institute of Criminal Law and Criminology.* Vol. VI, No. 4, Nov., 1915, p. 528.

TABLE 45

NATURE OF PRESENT OFFENSE

Per Cent Distribution of Delinquent Women in Nativity and Color Groups, Classified by New York City Police Department Classification

Nature of Offense	Nativity and Color				Total
	Total Foreign Born	Total Native Born	Native White	Native Colored	
Offenses against the Person	8.7	3.4	2.8	5.1	5.0
Offenses against Chastity	41.9	60.0	62.0	54.1	54.4
Offenses against Family and Children	1.7	2.3	3.1	....	2.2
Offenses against Regulations for Public Health, Safety and Policy	9.3	9.9	9.4	11.2	9.7
Offenses against Administration of Government	.6	.5	.7	....	.5
Offenses against Property Rights	34.3	19.7	17.4	26.5	24.2
General Criminality	3.5	4.2	4.5	3.1	4.0
Total	100.0	100.0	100.0	100.0	100.0
Number of cases	172	385	287	98	557

tion for the nativity and color groups. A first glance at the chart will show what was evident in a comparison of the institutional groups, that the offenses against chastity have the first place and offenses against property rights second, in each of the three nativity groups. The ratio between the two varies, however, in the groups, the foreign born having the smallest percentage of offenders against chastity, and the largest percentage of offenders against property rights, while the native white have the largest percentage of offenders against chastity and the smallest percentage of offenders against property rights. In each of these two large divisions of offenses, the native colored stand on middle ground. The other divisions of the classification show that the foreign born have a percentage of offenses against the person three times as large as that of the native white, but less than twice as large

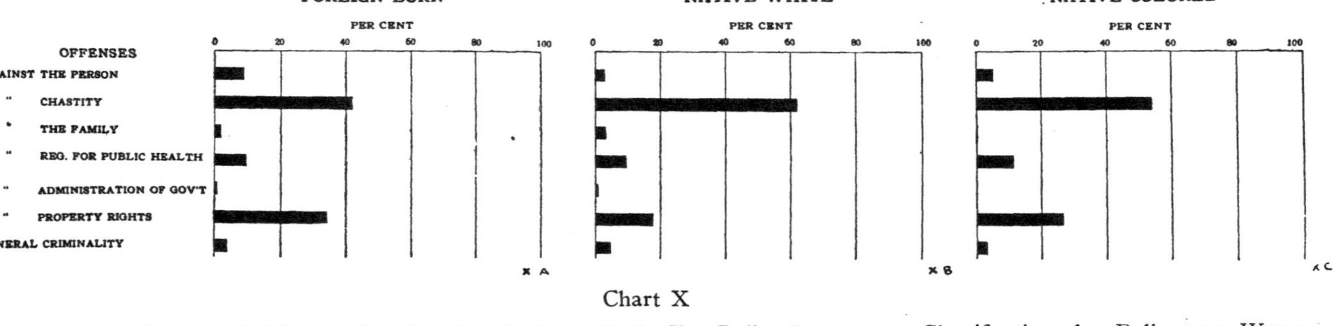

Chart X

Per cent Distribution of Offenses Classified by the New York City Police Department Classification, for Delinquent Women in Nativity and Color Groups.

as that of the native colored. The offenders against the family and children, and the offenders against administration of government are too few to use for comparison, since there are only a total of twelve cases in the one and three in the other. The offenders against regulations for public health have their largest percentage in the native colored group, all convicted of possessing or selling drugs. The general criminality group shows no marked differences in percentages between the nativity groups. Because the numbers are largest and because the difference is more marked, the most important conclusion we can draw from this table, is that the foreign born have a noticeably smaller percentage of offenders against chastity, and a noticeably larger percentage of offenders against property rights than have either the native white or native colored.

(*b*) *Felonies and Misdemeanors*

A natural deduction from the preceding table is that the foreign born probably have a higher percentage of felons than have the other groups. In Chart III, it appeared that the offenders against property rights are made up more largely of felons than is the group of offenders against chastity rights. Table 46 and Chart XI show that the foreign born have a percentage of felons considerably over twice that of the native white and nearly twice that of the native colored. In other words, about a third of the foreign born were convicted of felonies at the time we studied them, while approximately an eighth of the native white and a fifth of the native colored were convicted of felonies. Conversely, of course, the percentage of misdemeanants or minor offenders is much larger among the native white and native colored than among the foreign born.

The Special Report of the Census on Prisoners and Juvenile Delinquents in Institutions states that:

> "It is evident that the popular belief that the foreign born are filling the prisons has little foundation in fact. It would seem, however, that they are slightly more prone than the native whites to commit minor offenses." [9]

Our data would not bear out this observation, so far as women are concerned. On the contrary, we might say that within our group of delinquents there is a very considerable tendency for the foreign born women to commit more serious offenses than do the native born within the same group.

[9] "Special Report of the Census Office: Prisoners and Juvenile Delinquents in Institutions." 1904, pp. 18-19, 40-41.

EXTENT OF DELINQUENCY CLASSIFIED BY NATIVITY AND COLOR

We have seen so far that the foreign born group of women delinquents shows a smaller percentage among our total delinquent group than their proportion of the population entitles them to have, but that among the foreign born who are convicted there is a tendency for them to commit the more serious offenses. A natural sequence to this will be to measure the extent of delinquency among those of the foreign born who reach the courts, and compare this with the amount of de-

TABLE 46

NATURE OF PRESENT OFFENSE

Number and Per Cent of Delinquent Women Convicted of Felonies and Misdemeanors Classified by Nativity and Color

Nativity and Color	Nature of Present Offense				Total	
	Felonies		Misdemeanors			
	Number	Per Cent	Number	Per Cent	Number	Per Cent
Total Foreign Born	58	33.7	114	66.3	172	100.0
Total Native Born	59	15.3	326	84.7	385	100.0
Native White	40	13.9	247	86.1	287	100.0
Native Colored	19	19.4	79	80.6	98	100.0
Total	117	21.0	440	79.0	557	100.0

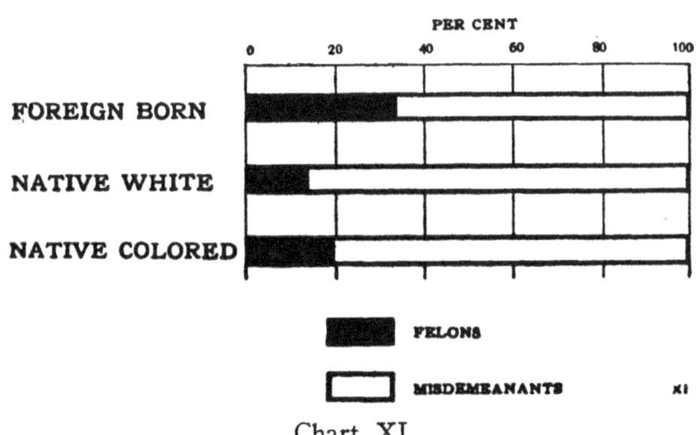

Chart XI

Per cent Distribution of Felons and Misdemeanants Classified by Nativity and Color.

linquency among the native born. The only measure of extent of delinquency which we shall use in this connection is the number of previous convictions.

(a) *Number of Previous Convictions*

(1) *Comparison of Differences Among Nativity Groups.*—Table 47 shows the range of number of previous convictions among the various nativity groups, and indicates that the range is longest in the native white group, and is of equal length among the foreign born and native colored. This table taken in connection with the three following tables is of value in enabling us to make comparisons between the mean number of convictions within the various groups.

TABLE 47

NUMBER OF PREVIOUS CONVICTIONS

Per Cent Distribution of Delinquent Women Classified by Nativity and Color

Number of Previous Convictions	Nativity and Color				Total
	Total Foreign Born	Total Native Born	Native White	Native Colored	
0	52.3	41.3	45.0	30.6	44.7
1	19.2	24.9	27.2	18.4	23.2
2	11.6	10.7	9.8	13.3	11.0
3	4.7	8.1	7.3	10.2	7.0
4	4.1	4.4	3.5	7.1	4.3
5	2.9	3.1	1.7	7.1	3.1
6	1.2	1.6	.7	4.1	1.4
7	....	2.1	1.4	4.1	1.4
8	.6	.8	.4	2.0	.7
9	.6	.8	.7	1.0	.7
10	.6	.5	.7	....	.5
11	.6	.3	.4	....	.4
12	....	.5	.4	1.0	.4
13	.6	....	....	....	.2
14	.6	.3	.4	....	.4
18	.6	.3	....	1.0	.4
20	....	.3	.4	....	.2
31	....	.3	.4	....	.2
Total	100.0	100.0	100.0	100.0	100.0
Number of cases	172	385	287	98	557

We shall first compare the mean number of convictions and the amount of variation about these means for the native white and native colored groups. Table 48 suggests that the native colored tend to have been convicted more often than the native white since the mean number of convictions in the one is 2.49 and in the other only 1.52. Since the ratio of the difference of the means to the standard deviation of the difference is 2.81, it would seem that this apparent difference is almost certainly valid. From a comparison of the standard deviations, however, it is clear that there is no demonstrable difference in the dispersion of the two groups.

Having shown that there is a significant tendency for the native colored to have a larger number of convictions than the native white, it is necessary for us to compare the total foreign born with the native white before extending this comparison to the total native born and total foreign born. A comparison of the means alone would suggest that the native white tend to have been convicted slightly more often than the foreign born, but since the difference between the means is only .36 times the standard deviation of the difference, we have no evidence that this is more than the chance variation which might occur through random sampling. (See Table 49.)

Since there is no demonstrable difference in number of convictions between the native white and the total foreign born, and since it has been shown (Table 48) that there is a tendency for the native colored to have a larger mean number of convictions than the native white, we are justified in stating that there must also be a valid difference in the

TABLE 48

NATIVE WHITE AND NATIVE COLORED

Comparison of the Means and Standard Deviations of Number of Previous Convictions for Native White and Native Colored

	Native White	Native Colored	Difference	$\frac{d}{\sigma_d}$	Chances that real difference does not exist are 1 in:
Mean	1.52	2.49	−.97	2.81	400
σ_m	±.175	±.299			
σ	2.96	2.96	.01	.02	2
σ_σ	±.124	±.211			
Cases	287	98			

TABLE 49

TOTAL FOREIGN BORN AND NATIVE WHITE

Comparison of the Means and Standard Deviations of Number of Previous Convictions for Total Foreign Born and Native White

	Total Foreign Born	Native White	Difference	$\frac{d}{\sigma_d}$	Chances that real difference does not exist are 1 in:
Mean	1.42	1.52	−.10	.36	3
σ_m	±.201	±.175			
σ	2.64	2.96	−.32	1.70	22
σ_σ	±.142	±.124			
Cases	172	287			

mean number of convictions of the native colored and the total foreign born, the native colored having a larger mean number of convictions.

For comparison with other groups of data, it may be well to combine the native white and native colored and compare the mean number of convictions and the standard deviation for the total native born with the same constants among the foreign born. Table 50 shows that in a comparison of the means, the total native born have a slightly larger mean number of convictions than the total foreign born. Since this difference is only 1.35 times the standard deviation of the difference, our figures fail to offer convincing evidence of a real

TABLE 50

TOTAL FOREIGN BORN AND TOTAL NATIVE BORN

Comparison of the Means and Standard Deviations of Number of Previous Convictions for Total Foreign Born and Total Native Born

	Total Foreign Born	Total Native Born	Difference	$\frac{d}{\sigma_d}$	Chances that real difference does not exist are 1 in:
Mean	1.42	1.77	−.34	1.35	11
σ_m	±.201	±.152			
σ	2.64	2.99	−.35	1.95	39
σ_σ	±.142	±.108			
Cases	172	385			

difference between the native and the foreign born with respect to this factor.

In interpreting the extent of delinquency of the groups distinguished by nativity and color, therefore, it will be well to bear in mind (1) that the native colored are distinguished from both the native white and the foreign born by having a larger mean number of convictions, and (2) that, although the foreign born show a slightly smaller mean number of convictions than do either the native white or the total native born, the evidence fails to justify our considering these differences demonstrably valid.

(2) *Comparison of Differences Between Felons and Misdemeanants in Nativity Groups.*—It will be of interest to turn from the total group of delinquent women classified by nativity and color to their classification into felons and misdemeanants, keeping in mind the fact that the foreign born have a larger percentage of their total group felons than have either the native white or native colored.

Table 51 shows the distribution of number of convictions for nativity groups among both the felons and misdemeanants. A hasty glance shows that the range of convictions for the foreign born felons is shorter than for any of the other groups of felons, and that it is slightly longer among the native white and total native born misdemeanants than among the foreign born or native colored misdemeanants.

In order to determine whether there is a valid difference in the number of previous convictions between the total foreign and the native born felons, the constants of the two groups have been compared. The total native born felons were used instead of the native white and native colored separately since the numbers were too small for this separate use. Table 52 shows that the native born felons have a larger mean number of convictions than have the total foreign born felons, and that this observed difference is more than three times the standard deviation of the difference.

From this we are entirely safe in saying that there appears to be a valid difference between the mean number of previous convictions of the total native born and total foreign born felons, with the native born felons having a considerably larger mean number of previous convictions. The difference in the dispersion of the groups also appears to be valid, with the native born felons having a much wider scattering.

TABLE 51

NUMBER OF PREVIOUS CONVICTIONS

Per Cent Distribution of Delinquent Women Convicted of Felonies and Misdemeanors Classified by Nativity and Color

Number of Previous Convictions	Felonies					Misdemeanors				
	Total Foreign Born	Total Native Born	Native White	Native Colored	Total	Total Foreign Born	Total Native Born	Native White	Native Colored	Total
0	60.3	42.4	50.0	26.3	51.0	48.3	41.1	44.1	31.7	43.0
1	24.1	15.3	15.0	15.8	19.6	16.7	26.7	29.2	19.0	24.1
2	8.6	10.1	10.0	10.5	9.4	13.2	10.7	9.7	13.9	11.4
3	1.7	8.5	7.5	10.5	5.1	6.1	8.0	7.3	10.1	7.5
4	1.7	3.4	2.5	5.3	2.6	5.3	4.6	3.6	7.6	4.8
5	1.7	1.7	......	5.3	1.7	3.5	3.4	2.0	7.6	3.4
6	......	3.4	......	10.5	1.7	1.8	1.2	.8	2.5	1.4
7	......	5.1	5.0	5.3	2.6	......	1.5	.8	3.8	1.1
8	......	3.4	......	10.5	1.7	.9	.3	.4	......	.5
9	......	1.7	2.5	......	.9	.9	.6	.4	1.3	.7
10	1.7	1.7	2.5	......	1.7	......	.3	.4	......	.2
11	......	......	......	......	....	.9	.3	.4	......	.5
12	......	1.7	2.5	......	.9	......	.3	......	1.3	.2
13	......	......	......	......	....	.9	......	......	......	.2
14	......	......	......	......	....	.9	.3	.4	......	.5
18	......	......	......	......	....	.9	.3	......	1.3	.5
20	......	1.7	2.5	......	.9	......	......	......	......	....
31	......	......	......	......	....	......	.3	.4	......	.2
Total	100.0	100.0	100.0	100.0	100.0	100.0	100.0	100.0	100.0	100.0
Number of cases	58	59	40	19	117	114	326	247	79	440

TABLE 52

TOTAL NATIVE BORN FELONS AND TOTAL FOREIGN BORN FELONS

Comparison of the Means and Standard Deviations of Number of Previous Convictions of Total Native Born Felons and Total Foreign Born Felons

	Total Native Born Felons	Total Foreign Born Felons	Difference	$\frac{d}{\sigma_d}$	Chances that real difference does not exist are 1 in:
Mean	2.53	.79	1.73	3.26	1667
σ_m	±.489	±.209			
σ	3.75	1.60	2.16	5.74	∞
σ_σ	±.345	±.148			
Cases	59	58			

Though it would be possible, so far as actual numbers are concerned, to make a comparison between the native white or colored and the total foreign born misdemeanants, we shall use only the total native born with the total foreign born (Table 53) so that this ratio will be comparable with that in Table 52. While a comparison of the means alone in Table 53 would suggest that the foreign born misdemeanants

TABLE 53

TOTAL NATIVE BORN MISDEMEANANTS AND TOTAL FOREIGN BORN MISDEMEANANTS

Comparison of the Means and Standard Deviations of Number of Previous Convictions of Total Native Born Misdemeanants and Total Foreign Born Misdemeanants

	Total Native Born Misdemeanants	Total Foreign Born Misdemeanants	Difference	$\frac{d}{\sigma_d}$	Chances that real difference does not exist are 1 in:
Mean	1.63	1.75	−.12	.37	3
σ_m	±.156	±.280			
σ	2.81	2.99	−.18	.79	5
σ_σ	±.110	±.198			
Cases	326	114			

have a slightly larger mean number of convictions, the ratio of the difference between the two to the standard deviation of the difference is only .37, indicating that there is no demonstrable difference between the central tendencies of the two groups of offenders. The difference between the standard deviations of the two groups is not demonstrably valid.

(b) *Recidivists and First Offenders Among Nativity and Color Groups*

If we turn to Table 54 showing the percentage of recidivists and first offenders among the felons and misdemeanants, as well as among the total group of delinquents classified by nativity and color, we note that within each of the groups the foreign born have a smaller percentage of recidivists than have either the native colored, native white or total native born. In each group the native colored have the highest percentage of recidivists, the native white and total native born the next highest, and the foreign born the smallest percentage. These groups differ from one another by more marked degrees, however, among the felons than among the misdemeanants. In the total group, including both felons and misdemeanants, 52.3 per cent of the foreign born have had no previous convictions, while only 44.9 per cent of the native white and 30.6 per cent of the native colored have had no previous convictions. Chart XII presents in graphic form the data regarding recidivism for the three nativity groups.

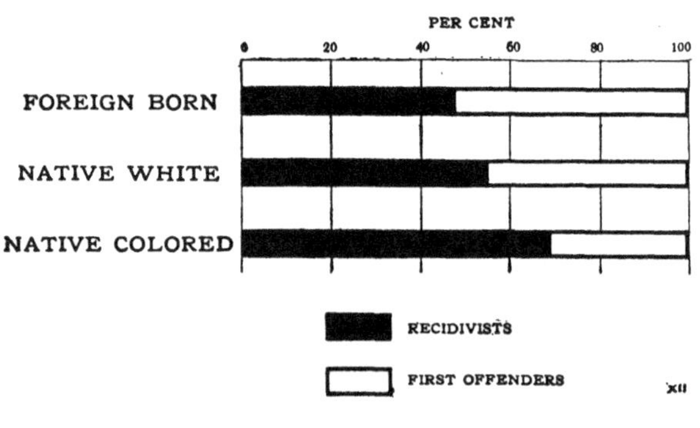

Chart XII

Per cent Distribution of Recidivists and First Offenders Classified by Nativity and Color.

TABLE 54

RECIDIVISTS AND FIRST OFFENDERS

Per Cent Distribution among Felons and Misdemeanants, Classified by Nativity and Color

	Felons					Misdemeanants					Total				
	Total Foreign Born	Total Native Born	Native White	Native Colored	Total	Total Foreign Born	Total Native Born	Native White	Native Colored	Total	Total Foreign Born	Total Native Born	Native White	Native Colored	Total
Recidivists	39.7	57.6	50.0	73.7	48.7	51.8	58.9	55.9	68.4	57.0	47.7	58.7	55.1	69.4	55.3
First Offenders	60.3	42.4	50.0	26.3	51.3	48.2	41.1	44.1	31.6	43.0	52.3	41.3	44.9	30.6	44.7
Total	100.0	100.0	100.0	100.0	100.0	100.0	100.0	100.0	100.0	100.0	100.0	100.0	100.0	100.0	100.0
Number of cases	58	59	40	19	117	114	326	247	79	440	172	385	287	98	557

(1) *Comparison With Male Felons in Sing Sing.*—If we use only the felons in Table 54, we have material comparable to the study made by Dr. Glueck at Sing Sing of 608 male felons.[11] This is illustrated in Chart XIII which makes four comparisons. The first of these, between the female foreign born felons and the male foreign born felons, shows that there is a much smaller percentage of recidivists among the female foreign born felons than among the males,

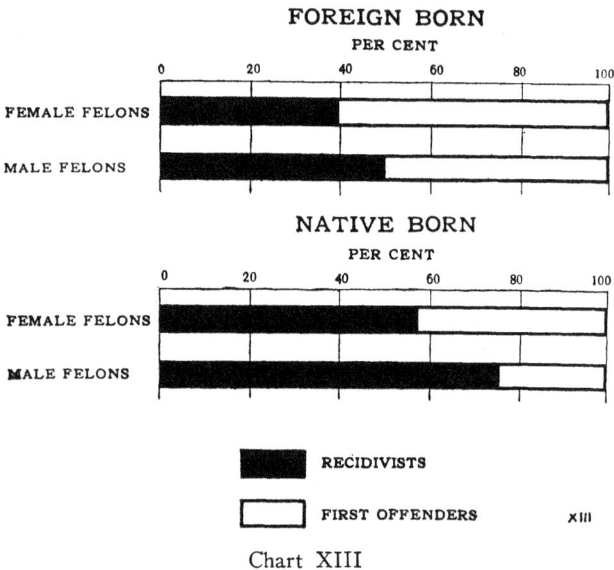

Chart XIII

Comparison of the Percentages of Recidivists and First Offenders Among the Foreign and Native-Born of 117 Female Felons and 608 Male Felons in Sing Sing Prison.

a difference between 39.7 per cent of recidivists in the one and 49.8 per cent in the other. A second comparison shows that the native born female felons have a smaller percentage of recidivists than the native born male felons, a difference between 57.6 per cent in the one case and 75.9 per cent in the other. The third comparison has been made in Table 54, showing that the foreign born female felons have a much smaller percentage of recidivists than the native born female felons. The fourth comparison between foreign born male felons and native born male felons shows that among the male felons also, the foreign born have a percentage of recidivists very much smaller than the per-

[11] *Op. cit.*, p. 140.

centage of recidivists among the native born. In a comparison between the nativity groups, then, in each case the foreign born show a smaller percentage of recidivists, and in a comparison between felons classified by sex, the foreign born female felons show the smaller percentage of recidivists.[12]

(c) *Relationship Between Length of Time in this Country and Number of Previous Convictions*

(1) *Number of Previous Convictions and Years in United States.*—Before concluding the discussion of the extent of criminality among the foreign and native born, we shall consider the objection that the foreign born delinquents are not represented in proportion to their quota in the general population and have a smaller percentage of the repeated offenders because they may have been in this country too short a time to have come into conflict with the law and to have had many convictions. In order to find out whether there seems to be any relation between the number of convictions of the foreign born and the length of time in the United States or the age at coming to the United States, the two following correlations are presented.

Table 55 shows that the range of number of years in the United States is from 1 to 46 years, with the mean number of years 14.04± 9.17. The coefficient of correlation (.33±.069) would indicate that there is a small, but significant, relationship between the length of time in this country and the number of convictions. The correlation ratios are slightly larger, .39±.065 and .36±.067. The tendency toward a higher record of convictions with a longer residence in this country is very evident from the table.

(2) *Number of Previous Convictions and Age at Coming to the United States.*—Table 56 correlates the number of previous convictions with the age at coming to the United States instead of with the number of years in the United States as in Table 55. The mean age at coming to this country is 18.88±9.29 years. The small negative coefficient of correlation, —.17, only slightly more than twice its standard deviation of .074, would indicate that the relationship is small, but that there is a slight tendency for the foreign born who come to the United States when young to have a larger number of convictions

[12] As stated in Chapter 6, p. 127, Dr. Glueck has used the term "recidivist" to mean an individual who has served a previous sentence in prison, while our use of recidivist includes all who have had a previous conviction. His percentage of recidivists would, therefore, be proportionately larger if put on a basis exactly comparable with ours.

TABLE 55

Correlation between Number of Previous Convictions and Number of Years in United States

Foreign Born Cases Only

Number of Years in United States	Number of Previous Convictions: 0	1	2	3	4	5	6	7	8	9	10	11	12	13	14	15	16	17	18	Totals	Means (Number of Previous Convictions)
41 to 46 years						1														1	3.5 (41 to 36 years)
36 " 41 "	1	1					1													3	
31 " 36 "	2		1												1					4	
26 " 31 "	6	2	3	2	1	1								1						16	2.3
21 " 26 "	4	2	1		2	1			1		1									12	2.9
16 " 21 "	9	7	4	2	1		1			1		1								26	2.0
11 " 16 "	17	8	8	1	2	2													1	39	1.6
6 " 11 "	23	7	2	1	1															34	0.5
1 " 6 "	28	6	1	1																36	0.3
Totals	90	33	20	7	7	5	2		1	1	1	1		1	1				1	171	1.42
Means (Number of Years in United States)	11.5	13.8	16.9	17.4 (3–4)		23.7 (5–18)														14.04	

Number of previous convictions: Mean = 1.42 σ = 2.65
Number of years in United States: Mean = 14.04 σ = 9.17
Coefficient of correlation: r = + .33 ± .068
Correlation ratios: Number of years in United States on number of previous convictions, . . η = .39 ± .065 Blakeman's Criterion = 2.1
Number of previous convictions on number of years in United States, . . η = .36 ± .067 Blakeman's Criterion = 1.4

TABLE 56

Correlation between Number of Previous Convictions and Age at Coming to United States

Foreign Born Cases Only

Age at Coming to United States	Number of Previous Convictions: 0	1	2	3	4	5	6	7	8	9	10	11	12	13	14	18	Totals	Means (Number of Previous Convictions)
51 to 56 years			1														1	0.9 (rows 51–56 to 31–36 together)
46 " 51 "	2																2	
41 " 46 "	2																2	
36 " 41 "	1	1	1	1		1											5	
31 " 36 "	6	1	1														8	
26 " 31 "	10	3	1				1										15	0.7
21 " 26 "	13	3	6									1					23	1.1
16 " 21 "	31	10	4	1	5	1								1		1	54	1.4
11 " 16 "	18	7	2	3	1	1				1	1						34	1.4
6 " 11 "	2	5	4	1	1	2											15	2.0
1 " 6 "	4	3		1			1		1						1		11	3.1
Totals	89	33	20	7	7	5	2	..	1	1	1	1	..	1	1	1	170	1.42
Means (Age at coming to United States)	20.5	16.5	20.7	16.1 (columns 3–4 together)		14.6 (columns 5–18 together)											18.88	

Number of previous convictions: Mean = 1.42 $\sigma = 2.65$

Age at coming to United States: Mean = 18.88 $\sigma = 9.29$

Coefficient of correlation: $r = -.17 \pm .074$

Correlation ratios: Number of previous convictions on age at coming to United States, $\eta = .20 \pm .074$ Blakeman's Criterion = 1.0

Age at coming to United States on number of previous convictions, $\eta = .24 \pm .072$ Blakeman's Criterion = 1.6

Partial correlation coefficient: Number of previous convictions with age at coming to the United States, for constant present age: $r_{NA_1 \cdot A} = -.377 \pm .066$

than those who come later in life. The correlation ratios are slightly larger, .20±.074 and .24 ± .072. Inspection of the table shows clearly that those having fewer convictions were older when they came to this country than those having many, and that the number of convictions decreases with increase in age of coming to this country.

Since, however, both the variables in the above correlation—number of previous convictions and age at coming to this country—are more or less closely related to the factor of present age, we have computed the partial correlation coefficient for the number of previous convictions with the age at coming to the United States, for constant present age.[13] This coefficient we find to be —.377±.066. In other words, when we eliminate the effect of actual age a higher degree of relationship is observed between frequency of conviction and an early age of immigration.

Accordingly, from both the correlation between number of convictions and years in the United States, and that between number of convictions and age at coming to this country, actual age being kept constant, it would seem that there is a certain amount of relationship between the length of time in this country or the age at coming to this country and the degree of recidivism, with a tendency for those who have been here longer or who came here younger to have more convictions.

Several explanations for this relationship might be sought. In the first place there is the very obvious possibility of inadequacy of information concerning convictions in other countries since these can not be verified as can those of this country. In the second place there is the probability that the same act might not constitute an offense against the law in another country. This is particularly true of the offense of prostitution which will not lead to arrest in most of the European countries if carried on under more or less exactly defined conditions. Of course, as has already been stated, a woman known to be a prostitute will not be admitted to this country, but there is no reason to believe that this law would ever be enforced with complete success.

Another way of stating the facts might be, that the longer the immigrant stays in this country, the more likely she becomes to be convicted of offenses against the law and the nearer the percentage of delinquents among the foreign born approaches the much higher per-

[13] The data required for this computation are the following:
r (number convictions with age coming U. S.) = —.173 (170 cases)
r (number convictions with age) = .197 (169 cases)
r (age at coming to this country with age) = .610 (170 cases)

centage of delinquents among the native born. It is true that the most of the foreign born delinquent women in this study have never lived outside of New York City and that the effect of the crowded urban conditions under which they are forced to live may serve to increase the number of their convictions the longer they live here.

Whatever the explanation of the relation may be, however, the fact of existence of correlations of this size between recidivism and time in this country would be sufficient to interfere with our stressing greatly the lesser degree of recidivism of the foreign group. The fact that they have not spent their whole lives in this country tends to counteract the allowance to be made for their higher mean age. Accordingly we are left uncertain as to whether there is any valid difference between the native born delinquents and the foreign born with respect to "criminalistic tendency" as indicated by number of convictions. The fact that there is a smaller percentage of the total foreign born population than of the native born who become delinquents at all, as indicated by our group, would not be affected by the above relationship between time in this country and number of convictions. Accordingly it seems possible to say that, while there are fewer, relatively, of the foreign born women than of the native born who become delinquents, the fact of a significantly lower degree of recidivism on the part of the foreign born delinquents can not be established by our data.

It is of interest to note that in the group of foreign born women studied, very few cases were found where the "crimes or misdemeanors were committed in entire ignorance of the law because of adherence to national customs which, innocent in a rural district, are dangerous in the city and have therefore been prohibited."[14] This may be because we have not included in our study the cases where fines were imposed, or the suspended sentences in the city magistrates' day courts for violation of city ordinances, etc.

A further opinion often voiced is that much of the crime among the foreign born is due to the different ethical standards in other countries which make it difficult for an immigrant with ideals unlike ours to adjust himself to our legal ways of thinking. In the group of 172 foreign born delinquents whose cases we studied there were very few where the ethical standards brought from another country seemed to

[14] Abbott, Grace. "Immigration and Crime" (Report of Committee "G" of the Institute). *Journal of the American Institute of Criminal Law and Criminology.* Vol. VI, No. 4. Nov., 1915, p. 529.

have any effect in the commission of the crimes for which the women were convicted at the time of our study. There are a few striking exceptions to this, particularly in the Auburn group, and therefore in connection with the most serious offenses.[15]

FIRST CONTACTS WITH THE LAW

The problem of the first contacts of the foreign born with the law is to many people of as much or more importance than the subsequent convictions. Some of the main factors of this first contact, the age at first conviction, nature and seriousness of first offense and first sentence will now be considered.

(*a*) *Age at First Conviction*

Table 57 shows that the range of age at first conviction is much longer among the foreign than among either of the native born groups. The percentage convicted under sixteen years of age is only 2.4 among the foreign born group, while it is 6.3 in the native white and 4.2 in the native colored. This smaller percentage of foreign born juvenile delinquents is undoubtedly affected by the fact that 64.7 per cent of the women did not come to this country until after they were over the juvenile court age, and the possibility of convictions at early ages in many foreign countries is not so great as in the United States, where the Juvenile Court has been more fully developed. The age at first conviction among the native groups will be more valuable if we compare the mean ages at first conviction. Table 58 indicates that there is very little difference between the means of the native white and native colored, 24.5 as against 24.4, a difference which does not appear demonstrably valid statistically. A comparison of the stand-

[15]A notable exception to this is the case of a Syrian girl, twenty-four years of age, who was seduced by her lover, M——, under promise of marriage. When she became pregnant he refused to marry her. The subject's brother-in-law, R——, with whom she was living, offered to give M—— the furniture of his own flat and help him financially in other ways if he would marry the girl, but he refused to do so. She became unable to stand the taunts and insults that M—— subjected her to and so one morning after she had met him to make a last appeal and he had refused her, she followed him into a restaurant and, according to her own statement, shot him. The story is complicated by the fact that the brother-in-law, R——, was supposed to have shot M——, was convicted of murder in the first degree and sentenced to the chair, while the girl was given a short term in Auburn. On account of her insistence, however, that she had committed the act, because M—— had "taken her honor," R——'s sentence was commuted to life imprisonment. Though the girl had lived in this country for eight years she followed the standard of the small Syrian community in which she had grown up, that if a man "takes a girl's honor" and refuses to "make it good" she may take his life.

TABLE 57

AGE AT FIRST CONVICTION

Per Cent Distribution of Delinquent Women Classified By Nativity and Color

Total Group

Age at First Conviction	Nativity and Color				Total
	Total Foreign Born	Total Native Born	Native White	Native Colored	
8 to 12 years	.6	.8	1.1	....	.7
12 " 16 "	1.8	5.0	5.2	4.2	4.0
16 " 20 "	8.9	27.0	28.0	24.0	21.4
20 " 24 "	16.6	22.8	22.0	25.0	20.9
24 " 28 "	16.0	17.5	16.4	20.8	17.1
28 " 32 "	14.2	9.2	10.1	6.3	10.7
32 " 36 "	14.8	5.5	3.9	10.4	8.4
36 " 40 "	8.3	3.9	3.5	5.2	5.3
40 " 44 "	5.9	4.7	5.2	3.1	5.1
44 " 48 "	3.0	1.6	1.8	1.0	2.0
48 " 52 "	2.4	1.3	1.8	....	1.6
52 " 56 "	2.4	.5	.7	....	1.1
56 " 60 "	2.4	.3	.4	....	.9
60 " 64 "	1.8	....	....	....	.5
64 " 68 "	.6	....	....	....	.2
68 " 72 "	.6	....	....	....	.2
Total	100.0	100.0	100.0	100.0	100.0
Number of cases	169	382	286	96	551

TABLE 58

NATIVE WHITE AND NATIVE COLORED

Comparison of the Means and Standard Deviations of Age at First Conviction For Native White and Native Colored

	Native White	Native Colored	Difference	$\frac{d}{\sigma_d}$	Chances that real difference does not exist are 1 in:
Mean	24.51	24.44	.08	.08	2
σ_m	±.523	±.727			
σ	8.84	7.12	1.72	2.72	303
σ_σ	±.370	±.514			
Cases	286	96			

ard deviations, however, indicates that there is probably a valid difference in the dispersion of these two groups, with the native white having a wider scattering.

Since there seems to be no valid difference in the central tendencies of the age at first conviction between the native white and native colored, we are justified in comparing the total native born and the total foreign born, instead of comparing the native white and native colored separately with the foreign born.

Table 59 shows that there is a valid difference in the mean age at first conviction between the total native and total foreign born, with a tendency for the foreign born to be convicted at a considerably later age. A comparison of the standard deviations shows that there is also a real difference between the dispersion of the two groups with a wider scattering of cases in the total foreign born group.

TABLE 59

TOTAL NATIVE BORN AND TOTAL FOREIGN BORN

Comparison of the Means and Standard Deviations of Age at First Conviction For Total Native Born and Total Foreign Born

	Total Native Born	Total Foreign Born	Difference	$\frac{d}{\sigma_d}$	Chances that real difference does not exist are 0 in:
Mean.............	24.50	31.18	−6.68	6.85	8
σ_m...............	±.432	±.874			
σ................	8.44	11.37	−2.93	4.24	89,286
σ_σ................	±.305	±.618			
Cases............	382	169			

(*b*) *Nature of First Offense*

The nature of the first offense will be considered as the offenses for the institutional groups were, in Chapter VI, first by the New York City Police Department classification, and second, by felonies and misdemeanors. We must bear in mind here that a considerable number of our group of delinquent women are first offenders and therefore that in those cases the first offense applies to the present offense.

Table 60 shows, as all the other classifications have, that within each group the highest percentage of first offenses are offenses against chastity. The foreign born, however, show a much smaller percentage

TABLE 60

NATURE OF FIRST OFFENSE

Per Cent Distribution of Delinquent Women in Nativity and Color Groups, Classified by New York City Police Department Classification

Nature of Offense	Nativity and Color				Total
	Total Foreign Born	Total Native Born	Native White	Native Colored	
Offenses against the Person	7.0	2.4	1.8	4.1	3.8
Offenses against Chastity	33.3	49.2	50.4	45.9	44.3
Offenses against Family and Children	2.3	1.6	2.1	....	1.8
Offenses against Regulations for Public Health, Safety and Policy	10.5	7.3	8.8	3.1	8.3
Offenses against Administration of Government	1.8	.3	.4	....	.7
Offenses against Property Rights	31.0	13.4	12.7	15.3	18.8
General Criminality	14.0	25.9	23.9	31.6	22.2
Total	100.0	100.0	100.0	100.0	100.0
Number of cases	171	382	284	98	553

of offenses against chastity than do either the native white or native colored. The second highest percentage of offenses falls in the offenses against property rights for the foreign born group and in the general criminality group for the native white and native colored. The other divisions of offenses show no particularly striking differences, except in offenses against the person where the foreign born have a slightly higher percentage of cases. The important thing shown in the table is that the foreign born tend to commit for their first offenses a much smaller percentage of offenses against chastity than do the other nativity groups, and that they have nearly as large a percentage of their first offenders committing offenses against property rights, while the native white and native colored have their second largest percentage of offenders in the general criminality group. This may partly be explained by the fact of the later age at first conviction among the foreign born. The general criminality offenses are very largely composed of semi-juvenile offenses such as ungovernable or incorrigible child, which apply only to those convicted at an early age. Since the difference in the age at first conviction between the total native and total foreign born seems to be valid, it is reasonable to suppose that the later age at first conviction of the foreign born is one reason for the few general criminality offenses within that group.

TABLE 61

NATURE OF FIRST OFFENSE

Per Cent Distribution of Delinquent Women in Nativity and Color Groups Classified as Felons and Misdemeanants for the First Offense

Nature of Offense	Nativity and Color				Total
	Total Foreign Born	Total Native Born	Native White	Native Colored	
Felons	28.1	10.0	9.5	11.2	15.6
Misdemeanants	71.9	90.1	90.5	88.8	84.5
Total	100.0	100.0	100.0	100.0	100.0
Number of cases	171	382	284	98	553

A further classification of the first offenses of the native and foreign born shows that the total foreign born have almost three times as high a percentage of felons as the native white and about two and a half times as many as the native colored. We should have expected this from the high percentage of offenders against property rights in Table 60, since this group of offenders has 54.9 per cent of its total, felons.[16]

Again, this is contrary to the report of the Census on Prisoners and Juvenile Delinquents in Institutions, that the foreign born "are slightly more prone than the native white to commit minor offenses."[17]

[16] See Chapter VI.
[17] *Op. cit.*, pp. 18-19, 40-41.

(c) *First Sentence*

Since the first offenses of the foreign born are in general more serious than the first offenses of the native white or colored, we might expect that the first sentence would be more severe. This we find to be the case.

TABLE 62

FIRST SENTENCE

Per Cent Distribution of Delinquent Women Classified by Nativity and Color

First Sentence	Nativity and Color				Total
	Total Foreign Born	Total Native Born	Native White	Native Colored	
Probation or Suspended Sentence	19.2	29.6	34.8	14.3	26.4
Fine	1.2	4.2	4.5	3.1	3.2
Juvenile Institution	1.7	1.8	2.1	1.0	1.8
Reformatory Institution	20.3	25.5	30.7	11.2	23.9
Penitentiary, Workhouse or County Jail	42.4	33.5	21.6	67.3	36.3
State Prison	15.1	5.5	6.3	3.1	8.4
Total	100.0	100.0	100.0	100.0	100.0
Number of cases	172	385	287	98	557

In a comparison between the groups it is obvious first of all that the foreign born have a much larger percentage of women whose first sentence was state prison than have either of the other groups. The total number of those committed to institutions for the first sentence is 79.5 per cent among the foreign born, while among the native white this number is 60.7 per cent, and among the native colored 82.6 per cent. The high percentage of colored committed to the Penitentiary, Workhouse group is, as has been explained previously, probably due to the fact that so few colored women are put on probation and instead are given a short Workhouse term. It seems obvious that the native white are more likely to be given a chance on probation or suspended sentence than the foreign born. Though 71.9 per cent of the foreign born were first convicted of misdemeanors, most of which might have been given a probation sentence, only 19.2 per cent were given such a sentence.

SUMMARY

In summarizing the relationship between nativity and delinquency, there are several points which stand out clearly. The first of these is that the foreign white group of delinquents studied from New York City is in much smaller proportion to the total group of delinquents than are the foreign white females over fifteen in New York City to the general female population over fifteen. That is, one might conclude, the foreign white in New York City are less likely to come into conflict with the law than either the native white or native colored.

Secondly, a consideration of present age shows that the foreign born are markedly older than the native white or native colored.

The nature of the present offense is more serious among the foreign born than among the native white or native colored, since the one has 33.7 per cent of its offenders felons, while the other two have 13.9 per cent and 19.4 per cent felons, respectively. Though the foreign born have their highest percentage in the offenses against chastity group, as have the native white and native colored, this percentage among the foreign born is considerably less than within the other groups. On the other hand, the offenders against property rights have their largest proportion in the foreign born group, though in each nativity group this class of delinquents has second place.

A comparison of the extent of delinquency among the three nativity groups shows that there is a tendency for the native colored to have more convictions than the native white, but that there is no demonstrable difference between the mean number of convictions for the native white and total foreign born groups. Due to the weight of the native colored in the total native born group, there is a possible slight tendency for the total native born to have a larger mean number of convictions than the total foreign born. When allowance is made for both present age and time in this country it seems clear that we can not consider that any significant difference in recidivism between these groups is established.

If we turn to the comparison of felons and misdemeanants within the nativity groups, we find that there seems to be a valid difference in the tendency for the total native born felons to have a larger mean number of convictions than the total foreign born felons. There seems to be no demonstrable difference in a like comparison between the misdemeanants in these two nativity groups.

Passing from the number of convictions to the more general view of the percentage of recidivists and first offenders, we find that only 47.7 per cent of the total foreign born are recidivists, while 55.1 per cent of the native white and 69.4 per cent of the native colored have had previous convictions. That is, in addition to being less likely to come into conflict with the law at all, there seems to be a slight tendency for the foreign born who get into the courts not to repeat their offenses, though lack of information concerning the early criminal record of the foreign group may operate in this connection also.

The partial correlation coefficient for the number of previous convictions with the age at coming to the United States, for constant present age shows that there is a certain amount of relationship between the age at coming to this country and the degree of recidivism, with a tendency for those who came here when younger to have more convictions. This must, of course, be given weight in any comparison of number of convictions among the native and foreign born, which shows that the foreign born have a smaller average number of convictions than the native born.

It is also of interest to note again that the foreign born show a valid difference in their tendency to be first convicted at a mean later age than the total native born group, and that there seems to be no demonstrable difference between the mean age at first conviction of the native white and native colored. While the foreign born are first convicted at a later age, they are also first convicted of more serious offenses than the native white or native colored. The sentences following these more serious first offenses are, as we should expect, more severe than in the groups of native white and native colored women where the percentage of misdemeanants is much higher. It seems true, however, even making allowance for the difference in seriousness of offense, that the native white are more likely to be given a chance on probation or suspended sentence than the foreign born. The figures would also indicate what is considered a well established fact in New York City, that the negroes are seldom considered for probation or suspended sentence because of the meager facilities in the probation system for supervising negro women.

The interest in the nativity and color groups in any such study as this is not, of course, confined solely to the consideration of the criminal record. The other factors of the educational background, economic efficiency, and history of sex irregularities of the foreign and native born will be considered in later chapters dealing especially with these subjects.

CHAPTER IX

SIGNIFICANT FACTORS IN EARLY HOME CONDITIONS AND FAMILY STATUS

IN attempting to understand any delinquent, and the possible factors which have been associated with her delinquency, one of the first queries is about the kind of home in which she has grown up, whether she has seen there such offenses as that which she has committed, or whether the lack of training in the home has permitted petty offenses to pass unnoticed which have finally culminated into contact with the law. Closely associated with the more external survey of the home conditions is the consideration of the woman's heredity, including the defective physical and mental strains and other defects, such as excessive alcoholism and criminal records of the parents. Other factors which determine to a certain extent the relative advantages or disadvantages of the early home surroundings are the number of children in the family, particularly in the poor family; the subject's order in her fraternity, that is, whether she was oldest or youngest in a large family; the parents' ages in relation to the ages of the women in whom we are interested; the parents' nativity; and the ages of the women at the time of either parent's death. These elements, of course, enter into the estimate of the home conditions, but are presented separately for comparison with similar data on delinquent groups. Since there are no figures comparable to ours on the home conditions of the general population, this most important comparison will have to be omitted for the most part.

METHOD OF ESTIMATING HOME CONDITIONS DURING CHILDHOOD AND ADOLESCENCE

In considering home conditions during childhood and adolescence, the factor of age again arises to make the situation difficult. In many of the younger cases, the home visited by the field worker was the home in which the woman had lived for years, and was with little change the home during childhood and adolescence. In these cases we have first-hand and reliable information concerning the home. When a woman is forty or fifty years old, however, it becomes much more difficult even to estimate what the earlier home conditions were. It has been necessary, therefore, in the cases of these older women, to obtain every possible record of social and charitable organizations, and to learn all that we could from older friends and relatives in order to have sufficient material on which to base an estimate. In many cases, however, we have had only the woman's statement to go by. We have thrown out of each group all of the subject's statements which we felt were too unreliable for use. In this respect, the Workhouse is, again, least satisfactory. The real data of interest concerning early background can not be obtained from a person unless there is a spirit of coöperation and friendliness. As previously stated, the heterogeneity of the group at the Workhouse, the hurry and confusion, made a satisfactory interview impossible in many cases, and the more personal details such as information regarding family and the status of the home suffered most as a result of this. The reasons for making this difficult are two. In the first place, many of the women felt that it was unnecessary for them to be accurate in giving information which they thought would be difficult to verify; also, many of the older women were too confused and their memories were too poor to give anything more than the most inaccurate and obviously incorrect statements. We have, therefore, omitted the estimate of home conditions for the Workhouse group, throughout, except in Table 67 which shows how much of this information was based on the subject's statement only and how marked the tendency is for the Workhouse women to place themselves in the higher estimates of the home conditions. We are convinced from our contact with the group of women in the Workhouse and from the material we have been able to verify, that such a percentage as 94.1 per cent in the three higher classes of home conditions is absurd, and that this high percentage is largely due to the tendency noted in other groups of facts about the Workhouse women—the tendency to make out their past as much better than it really was.

The material on home conditions, after the field worker's visits and interviews had been recorded and summarized, was carefully gone over by two persons, and with some of the institutional groups, a third person, each one making an estimate of the three factors considered under home conditions, and a total estimate of home conditions. The work was done by these persons independently of one another and finally re-checked by one person who treated in a uniform manner all of the cases in which a difference had been noted. We shall first take up the factors considered in making up the total estimate of the home during childhood and adolescence, namely, (1) the economic status, (2) the moral standards, (3) parental supervision. Throughout, if a child spent the most of her time until adolescence in a Home or Orphanage, the weight was given in making the estimate to the conditions in the Orphanage. If she spent the most of her life in her own home with a few years only in the Orphanage, the estimate was based on conditions in her own home.

(*a*) *Estimate of Economic Status in the Home*

The estimate of the economic status in the home is divided into five classes, which do not attempt to include all classes of society, but those from a very low economic status through those of considerable independent means. In general, the two lowest classes include those who are, for the most part, behind their income and unable to get along on what they earn. The third class which we have called mediocre or fair is made up of the poor, but the normally self-sustaining, while the two upper classes are those who are ahead of their income, and comfortably situated. In making this estimate, the following points were noted, not as arbitrary standards for determining the classification, but merely as suggestions:

1. *Very poor.* Includes families which are dependents all or a large part of the time and willing to accept aid repeatedly. May also include families which have accepted less financial aid, but have not had enough money to eke out a decent existence and have lived in primitive fashion.
2. *Poor.* Includes families able to get along with difficulty, but requiring only occasional financial aid; those with incomes obviously below a living wage, though some may have unusual ability in the management of the income.
3. *Mediocre or Fair.* Includes those who are normally self-supporting but without saving or surplus. An occasional free treatment in hospitals need not place a family in class 2, while an industrial insurance policy, for example, need not raise it to class 4.
4. *Good.* Includes those able to live comfortably on their incomes,—those who have money saved in the bank, or insurance. Those

who have property heavily mortgaged so that keeping up the interest is a great financial drain might lower the estimate to class 3 or 2, as the case might be.

5. *Very good.* Includes families of considerable means, so that luxuries are possible, such as extensive traveling, etc.

The distribution of these delinquent women by the estimate of the economic status is shown in Table 63. From this table it is clear that the same trend runs through each group, *i.e.,* a small percentage both in the very poor and the very good classes, and a concentration in the mediocre and poor classes. The largest percentage in each group, except Bedford, falls in the fair or mediocre class with the second largest percentage in the poor class. Bedford has the largest per cent of any of the groups in class 1, and the largest percentage of her total in class 2. This institution undoubtedly is affected by the element of having so many cases sent from the country districts. Out of the nine cases, for instance, classed as very poor in the economic status, seven cases or 77.7 per cent, were committed from country districts, while only 11.9 per cent of the total group were committed from courts outside of New York City. It is of interest to note that Bedford, in addition to having the largest percentage of women in the poorest classes, also has the only two cases where the early economic conditions were considered very good. In one of these cases, the girl was an only child. Her father, a wealthy man, was a member of a large publishing firm, a member of the Chamber of Commerce and a prominent man in the community. They lived in the most fashionable residence section in Brooklyn. The girl was given every opportunity, was sent to a private school, given music lessons, etc. The other case is that of a girl whose father was a foreign correspondent for a large newspaper, a mining expert, and a well-known politician. She and her sister traveled all over the world with the father, had private tutors for years, and finally went to an expensive finishing school. In both of these cases the economic standards were very good. The Magdalen has the largest percentage in the two best classes, while the Penitentiary comes second. The Penitentiary, on the other hand, has the smallest percentage in the two poorest classes, with the Probation group having the next smallest percentage in these two classes. For the total group, the table shows that 41.4 per cent of the cases come from homes where the economic status during childhood and adolescence was poor, and where the family was nearly always behind its income. Forty-five per cent of the cases were from families perhaps normally self-supporting but poor, while only 13.6 per cent come from comfortable homes. There are no figures which will make a comparison of our group with the total population possible, so that in our discussion of the home conditions of this group we can hope to give little more than a picture of the conditions as we found them.

TABLE 63

ESTIMATE OF ECONOMIC STATUS IN THE HOME DURING CHILDHOOD AND ADOLESCENCE

Per Cent Distribution of Delinquent Women in Institutional Groups (Workhouse Omitted)

Estimate of Economic Status	Institutional Groups					Total
	Bedford	Auburn	Magdalen	Penitentiary	Probation	
Very poor	9.8	9.0	5.7	2.2	2.3	5.7
Poor	50.1	38.4	32.9	22.7	34.5	35.7
Fair	31.6	43.5	42.9	57.2	49.5	45.0
Good	6.5	9.0	18.6	18.4	13.8	13.1
Very good	2.2	....	....	....	....	.5
Total	100.0	100.0	100.0	100.0	100.0	100.0
Number of cases	92	78	70	93	87	420

There are, however, certain comparisons from other studies of delinquency which may be of importance here. In the consideration of the economic status we may note particularly the study of children in the Juvenile Court in Chicago, made by Miss Breckinridge and Miss Abbott in 1912.[1] In discusing the "Poor Child" they have made four large economic groups indicating the status in the homes of the children. Their classes are:

Group I. Very poor families. Not normally self-sustaining.
Group II. Poor, but normally self-sustaining.
Group III. Fairly comfortable.
Group IV. Comfortable.

[1] Breckinridge, Sophonisba P., and Abbott, Edith. "The Delinquent Child and the Home." Russell Sage Foundation, 1912, p. 72.

Roughly, the cases they have included in Group I would correspond to those we have included in classes 1 and 2. Those in Group II would include our class 3, Group III would include class 4, and Group IV would include class 5. If we rearrange our classes in this way, we find that the rough percentage comparison is as follows:

	Children in Juvenile Court in Chicago		Our Delinquent Group
	Boys	Girls	
Group I	38.2	68.8	41.4
Group II	37.9	21.0	45.0
Group III	21.2	7.6	13.1
Group IV	1.7	1.3	.5
No Home	1.0	1.3	...

It is interesting to note that the boys in the Juvenile Court appear to come from better homes than the girls and that our group is between the two. Though no exact comparison is possible, we may observe that in each group the preponderance of cases is in the two lower groups of the very poor, and the poor but normally self-supporting. The study of the children in the Juvenile Court, of course, gave the worker an opportunity to visit the childhood home and make an estimate on what was actually observed at that time. Because our estimate necessarily had to be based on a matter of record and second-hand information for most of the older women, it is interesting to see that the same tendency is shown, for the delinquents in both groups to come from the poorer economic classes.

(*b*) *Estimate of Moral Standards in the Home*

A second general factor which was observed in a study of the home conditions was the moral standards in the home during childhood and adolescence. This again has been estimated, and is grouped into five classes, as follows:

1. *Very poor.* Here there were included the most flagrant cases of low moral standards, such as excessive alcoholism, sex offenses, criminal records, etc., in the immediate family in which the girl was brought up. Extreme overcrowding, with consequent lack of privacy, an extremely bad neighborhood and environment should be considered in connection with the standard of the immediate family.
2. *Poor.* Includes families with low moral standards but appreciably better than class 1. This class may include cases where there may not be definite active immorality of any kind in the immediate family, but where there is absence of standards in parents or where

parents have so little force that they are not able to establish decent standards. An example of this occurs in one of the Bedford cases where the parents did not themselves steal, drink or commit illegal acts, and yet they countenanced petty stealing in the girl, and were willing to accept the small things she had stolen and brought home.

3. *Fair or mediocre.* Includes cases where, for the most part, the members of the immediate family have a reputable standing in the community. A criminal record for one member of the family, if it does not directly affect the girl, or moderate alcoholism need not necessarily lower a case to class 2.
4. *Good.* Includes cases where all of family have good standards, and where there is every chance that the girl should have good moral standards, in so far as the character of her surroundings has affected her.
5. *Very Good.* Includes cases where there are unusually high standards in the parents and in the immediate environment.

With this classification, we see in Table 64 that the distribution of the estimate of moral standards is, in general, very like that of the previous estimate. In each institutional group there is a larger percentage of the cases in the lowest class than in the lowest economic class, but there are only two cases, and those in the Penitentiary, in the highest class. Bedford has the highest percentage in the poor class, while the other institutional groups have the highest percentage of their cases in the fair or mediocre group. The Penitentiary has the smallest percentage below mediocre, and is followed in order of increasing percentages for this group by Probation, Auburn, Magdalen and Bedford. The total group shows a larger percentage in the two highest classes of moral standards than is found in the two highest estimates of economic status. The factor of the number of country cases committed to Bedford for petty offenses undoubtedly helps, again, to swell the percentage of cases falling in the class of very low moral standards. Our observation has been that more flagrant offenses against moral standards will be tolerated in rural than in urban communities. Very likely several of the Bedford cases, which will be cited later, might have been spared contact with the law if they had been removed from the extremely immoral surroundings when they were young. Another factor which may account for Bedford's larger representation in these lower groups is that we know the women in Bedford much more thoroughly than the women in any other group, and it is true, we are convinced from observation, that the more

TABLE 64

ESTIMATE OF MORAL STANDARDS IN THE HOME DURING CHILDHOOD AND ADOLESCENCE

Per Cent Distribution of Delinquent Women in Institutional Groups (Workhouse Omitted)

Estimate of Moral Standards	Institutional Groups					Total
	Bedford	Auburn	Magdalen	Peni-tentiary	Probation	
Very poor	14.2	14.1	11.4	7.6	5.8	10.5
Poor	44.7	16.6	20.0	8.6	21.9	22.6
Fair	31.6	46.1	47.2	51.8	57.5	46.7
Good	9.8	23.0	21.5	30.1	15.0	20.0
Very good	....	....	....	2.2	....	.2
Total	100.0	100.0	100.0	100.0	100.0	100.0
Number of cases	92	78	70	93	87	420

thorough the investigation, the less advantageous to the subject is the trend away from the information which she has given.

(*c*) *Estimate of Parental Supervision in the Home*

The third factor, and one of the most important in making an estimate of the home conditions is the element of parental supervision in the home. A home may be economically very comfortable and the moral standards may be fair, yet the parents may be so harsh, or so lacking in force, understanding and sympathetic insight, that their effect on the children is very bad. We have not considered separately in this connection the markedly psychopathic and mentally abnormal girls who may have been brought up in a home where the parents had a fairly intelligent understanding, but were unable to manage the girl because she required the supervision of some one who had much more skill and experience in handling abnormal cases. In such a case, the parental supervision would be classed as fair, because our interest in this connection is in the status of the home, not in the idiosyncrasies of the individual. If the difficulty of adjustment lies in the individual herself, that will be considered in another connection. For determining this estimate which has been very carefully made, we have considered the following suggestions:

1. *Very poor.* Includes cases where one or both parents are dead, and the guardian makes no effort to look after the child. Extreme cases where one or both parents are living but do not attempt supervision of any kind fall here, and also cases where parents are very unintelligent in the control of the child.
2. *Poor.* Includes less extreme cases than 1. May include cases where the mother has to go out to work and no one is left at home to look after the girl, or where there may be very strict supervision, but so little understanding that the supervision does not count for anything.
3. *Fair.* Includes cases where the supervision and intelligent control in the home are sufficiently good that a normal child stands a fair chance of being guided by it. As noted before, parents who are fairly intelligent in their control of a normal child but who can not manage an abnormal child will be placed in this group, since we are desirous of showing in this place the kind of home from which the most of our delinquents come, and not the make-up of the child.
4. *Good.* Includes cases where children have been carefully and intelligently supervised, and ought certainly, if normal, to have been guided by their supervision.
5. *Very good.* Includes cases where supervision has been excellent and shows unusual insight into the nature of the child.

Table 65 shows how the women in institutional groups are distributed by this classification. Except for the Penitentiary, the percentage in the very poor class is considerably larger than in either the estimate of economic status or moral standards. In each institutional group the percentage in the poor class is also larger than this same class in any of the other estimates considered. Again, there are only 2 cases in the very good class, and those from the Penitentiary. These 2 cases which were also in the highest class of moral standards will be considered later. As a whole, it is interesting to note that in the bulk of the cases the estimate of parental supervision falls into much lower classes than either the moral or economic factors, and that only 3.1 per cent had good or unusually good supervision at home, while only 35.0 per cent were intelligently enough controlled so that they stood a fair chance of developing normally.

(*d*) *Total Estimate of the Home*

If we compare these three general factors which have gone into making an estimate of the home conditions, we may see that the element of very poor or poor parental supervision has affected the largest number of cases, while very poor or poor economic conditions have affected the next largest number. In considering the childhood home, as a whole, these three elements vary in weight in different cases. A child well supervised and living in a home with good moral standards may still be too poor economically to be thought of as growing up in a fair home, while a home with good moral standards and a fair amount of money, may be so lacking in control of the children as to lose all the effect of the other two elements.

In making up the total estimate of the home conditions during childhood and adolescence, the three estimates just discussed, the economic status, moral standards and parental supervision, were considered, and from a careful survey of these three factors and their

TABLE 65

ESTIMATE OF PARENTAL SUPERVISION IN THE HOME DURING CHILDHOOD AND ADOLESCENCE

Per Cent Distribution of Delinquent Women in Institutional Groups (Workhouse Omitted)

Estimate of Parental Supervision	Institutional Groups					Total
	Bedford	Auburn	Magdalen	Penitentiary	Probation	
Very poor	17.4	24.3	15.7	5.4	18.4	16.0
Poor	56.7	39.7	52.9	36.7	44.9	46.0
Fair	25.1	33.3	28.6	51.8	34.5	35.0
Good	1.1	2.6	2.9	4.3	2.3	2.9
Very good	....	....	....	2.2	....	.2
Total	100.0	100.0	100.0	100.0	100.0	100.0
Number of cases	92	78	70	93	87	420

relative weights in the home, a classification of 5 groups was made, which we have called:

1. *Very poor.* Includes cases where all of the elements entering into the home life are bad, and where there is every chance that the child has been subjected to surroundings too bad to make her a good citizen unless she is a very unusual child, and later able to get away from her early associations.
2. *Poor.* Includes homes which, in general, are better than those in the previous class. A home, fair in certain respects, may be so pulled down by one very bad element that the estimate falls here instead of in class 3.
3. *Fair.* Includes homes which are, for the most part, not markedly bad or markedly good in any one respect, though there may be cases here where the moral standards, for instance, are excellent, while the other factors are only mediocre and therefore keep the estimate in class 3.
4. *Good.* Includes homes which can offer good economic and moral standards, and where there is intelligent enough understanding of the child to make the other factors count for what they should.
5. *Very good.* Homes of unusual standards and offering excellent opportunities. It is not necessary that each of the previous 3 estimates should have been in the highest group in order to have a case fall here.

Table 66 shows the distribution of our cases by this method of estimation, and makes it clear, first of all, that the total estimate seems to approximate the estimate of economic status more than any other factor. From this it would seem that the economic factor determines to a very large extent whether or not the home seems a desirable place to bring up children. The table shows in each institutional group the concentration of cases in the poor and mediocre groups, with very few cases in the better classes. The Penitentiary group shows the smallest percentage falling in the two poorest classes while the Magdalen has the next larger, and is followed by Probation, Auburn and Bedford in order of increasing percentages. Of the total group of women, 8.3 per cent came from homes which were very bad in every way and which were not fit places for children to live, 38.1 per cent came from poor homes which had at least one and perhaps more bad elements, 47.1 per cent came from fair or mediocre homes, while only 6.5 per cent came from homes which were good or excellent.

Chart XIV shows graphically the figure given in Table 66, and indicates that the two upper classes contribute the smallest percentages

TABLE 66

ESTIMATE OF HOME CONDITIONS DURING CHILDHOOD AND ADOLESCENCE

Per Cent Distribution of Delinquent Women in Institutional Groups (Workhouse Omitted)

Estimate of Home Conditions	Institutional Groups					Total
	Bedford	Auburn	Magdalen	Peni-tentiary	Probation	
Very poor	10.9	12.8	10.0	5.4	3.4	8.3
Poor	51.1	42.3	38.5	22.6	36.8	38.1
Fair	31.5	37.2	47.1	63.4	55.2	47.1
Good	6.5	7.7	4.3	6.4	4.6	6.0
Very good	....	....	....	2.1	....	.5
Total	100.0	100.0	100.0	100.0	100.0	100.0
Number of cases	92	78	70	93	87	420

of delinquent women, while in each chart the second and third classes show the largest numbers.

(*e*) *Comparison Between Verified and Unverified Data on Home Conditions*

It may be advisable to give here the figures which show how the estimates were made up on the various groups, and how the subject's statement differs from the verified data. The estimates previously presented are on combined data; that is, in addition to all of the verified statements which enabled us to determine the kind of home, the subject's statement also was used where we felt such information was reliable. Table 67 shows that the percentage of verified material on home conditions varies in the different institutional groups. In Bedford none of the subject's statements alone have been used and in Auburn and the Magdalen the estimates were based on verified data in all but 15.4 per cent and 13.9 per cent of the cases, respectively. The Penitentiary estimate is based on the subject's statement only in 31.1 per cent of the cases, while the Probation group has 36.8 per

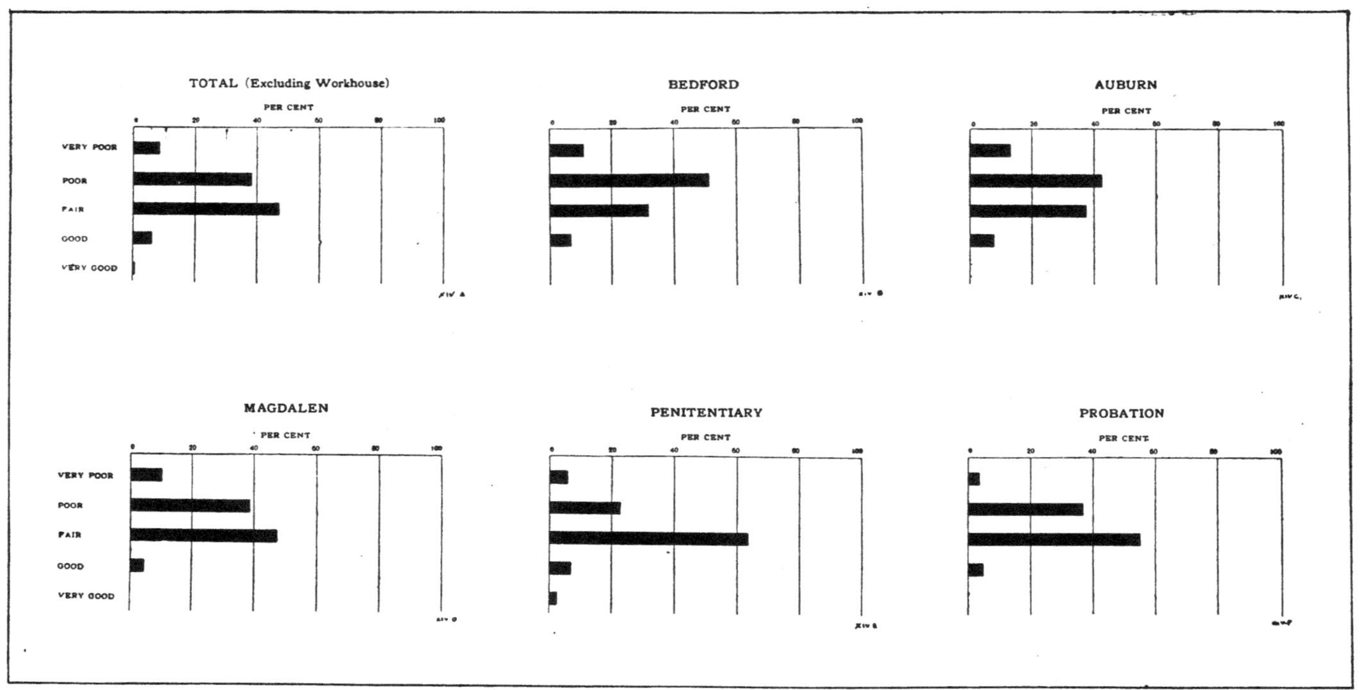

Chart XIV

Estimate of Home Conditions

Per cent distribution by institutional groups.

TABLE 67

ESTIMATE OF HOME CONDITIONS DURING CHILDHOOD AND ADOLESCENCE

Per Cent Distribution by Institutional Groups Showing Subject's Statement Only, Verified Data Only, and Combined Data

Estimate of Home Conditions	Institutional Group						Total
	Bedford	Auburn	Magdalen	Penitentiary	Workhouse	Probation	
Subject's Statement Only	....	100.0	100.0	100.0	100.0	100.0	100.0
Very poor and poor	....	50.0	30.0	17.2	5.9	25.0	17.2
Fair, good and very good	....	50.0	70.0	82.8	94.1	75.0	82.8
Number of cases	....	12	10	29	68	32	151
Verified Data Only	100.0	100.0	100.0	100.0	100.0	100.0	100.0
Very poor and poor	62.0	56.1	51.7	32.8	44.0	49.1	50.8
Fair, good and very good	38.0	43.9	48.3	67.2	56.0	50.9	49.2
Number of cases	92	66	60	64	25	55	362
Combined Data	100.0	100.0	100.0	100.0	100.0	100.0	100.0
Very poor and poor	62.0	55.1	48.6	28.0	16.1	40.2	40.9
Fair, good and very good	38.0	44.9	51.4	72.0	83.9	59.8	59.1
Number of cases	92	78	70	93	93	87	513

cent and the Workhouse 73.1 per cent of women whose statements of early home conditions could not be verified. To show how the percentages of cases in the two poorest classes and those in the three best classes vary between the subject's statement and the verified data, we may note in Table 67 that the two lowest classes have only 5.9 per cent in the Workhouse by the subject's statement alone, based on 68 cases, while there are 44.0 per cent in these two classes if we consider the 25 cases in the Workhouse group whose early home conditions we were able to verify. By combining the 68 statements and 25 verified cases, the percentage in the two lowest classes becomes 16.1 per cent, which is obviously much too low in comparison with the trend shown in the verified Workhouse data. For this reason the Workhouse group has been omitted in the discussion of home conditions. In each institutional group the percentage of the poorer classes is smaller when we take the subject's statement alone, than when we use the verified data alone, but in no group except the Workhouse is the difference between the combined data and the verified data so striking as to make the combined data of little value.

(f) *Presentation of Cases Representing Various Classes of Home Conditions*

Because the group of women in Bedford has been most carefully studied and because we have come to know these families most thoroughly, we shall present a number of the cases in this group and two cases in the Penitentiary, showing the various types of homes included in the five classes of home conditions.

The two cases we shall give, representing class 1, are in many ways alike, but show varying degrees of immorality, poor economic standards, and parental supervision. The method of treatment has also been different in these two cases.

1. Mary M——, 16 years and 2 months old at the time of her commitment to Bedford, was born in a small country town. Her father died one month before Mary was born; her mother, who had a questionable reputation, went to live with another man soon after the child's birth, and Mary and her sister were taken by the maternal grandmother, with whom Mary has lived nearly all of her life. The home conditions there have been very poor. The grandfather for years kept the "Penny Bridge" for which he received a very small pittance. Living in the same house were two of Mary's uncles, both of them shiftless, good-for-nothing and never contributing anything to the family support. As a result, the family often had to be aided by the town, in order to eke out the most miserable kind of an existence. The school record shows that Mary and her sister came to school very poorly clad and having had nothing to eat. Through the school, a complaint was made to a charitable organization who gave the family financial aid, but did not remove the children from the house. The house which the field worker visited was a small frame house consisting of 3 rooms with a rental of $3 a month. In this house, which was filthy and malodorous at the time of the visit, the grandmother and two uncles lived, but occasionally an aunt was there with one of her children. The grandmother said that there was a curtain in the upstairs room between the bed in which she and

Mary slept and her sons' bed. The moral standards have been, as the judge said, "as low as possible." The grandmother is notorious as an immoral woman, and at one time left home to live with a negro workman. Mary herself is supposed to have been immoral with her uncle who is undoubtedly mentally defective, and who has a long jail record for minor offenses. In this home, each of the three factors of economic status, moral standards and parental supervision was placed in the lowest class. These poor home conditions were known by the girl from shortly after her birth until the time of commitment to Bedford. She was convicted of prostitution but had, with little doubt, been promiscuous sexually long before, and is thought to have prostituted for money. This she had seen in her home, and in addition, the fact that no moral standards had been inculcated in her, her need of money and the willingness on the part of her family to have her prostitute, were all factors making this easy method of earning money the most desirable and profitable thing for her to do.

2. Another case which we grouped in the lowest class is that of Jane H——. At the time of her commitment to Bedford for "Exposure of person" she was twenty years and eight months of age. She was born in a small village in New York State and lived there with her people until she was about eight years old when she was placed in an Orphanage. Three years later she was returned to her people, but after a time was again brought back to the Orphanage where she remained until she was eighteen. Our information is obtained from the very complete records of the Orphanage, from the Humane Society which handled the case when the children were taken from the home, and from the older children in the family who were able to remember something of the early home conditions. There were eight children in the family and they all lived in the depths of the backwoods of R—— County, New York. Both the mother and father were very heavy drinkers and used to "carouse and act shameful." Three of the children in the family were illegitimate, and the father as well as the mother was known to be grossly immoral. When the children were brought to the Orphanage they seemed more like wild animals than human beings; they would run and hide when they saw any one coming. They had had no training of any kind. The house was "little better than a pig-pen"; the children were often left there at night with no fire, and even by huddling together they could not keep warm. There was never enough to eat—usually only dry bread in the house. The children were not sent to school and "ran wild the most of the time." In this family

the conditions of living were probably even lower than in the case just cited, but the children were found before they had spent their entire childhood in the home, and were given fair advantages during the time they were in the Orphanage. The effect on the girl under consideration, however, since she spent altogether over nine years with her parents, seemed important enough to estimate the home conditions as very poor.

For Class 2 we shall present two cases, one from New York and one from a small village. They both represent conditions appreciably better than those just given.

1. Alice B—— was committed to Bedford at the age of twenty years, seven months for contracting an infectious disease in the practise of debauchery. She was born in Brooklyn and lived there the most of her life. She lived with her parents until she was nine, when her mother died, and she was taken by her maternal grandmother. While the mother was living, the family had a hard time to get along because the father spent so much money for drink. He was not faithful to his wife and treated her very badly. The grandmother's home, to which Alice went when she was nine, is in a fairly good residential district and is a good house which the grandmother owns. The father gave no money for the children's support, however, and the grandmother would not spend her money in caring for them. Various complaints were made to the Children's Society concerning this home and alleging that the children did not have proper guardianship. The school reported that "the grandmother is a miser. She goes around picking up wood, etc. The children used to sleep on the floor, on piles of filthy rags infested with vermin with only newspapers over them in winter. Their clothing was filthy and ragged when they came to school, which was only irregularly." The Children's Society also had reports of Alice having to "get beer" for the grandmother, which necessitated her being on the streets entirely too much. Upon investigation by the Society, it seemed that these reports had been exaggerated but that there undoubtedly was some truth in them, and that there had not been proper supervision. These conditions were improved under the supervision of the Children's Society. In this home, the economic standards, except for the time before the intervention of the Children's Society, were not so low as in the other cases, and in the grandmother's home there was a certain amount of ready money which she later consented to use for the children. Under the supervision of the Children's Society, Alice and her sister were looked after more

carefully. The moral standards while low in the father's home were not so essentially a part of the home as in the cases of Mary M—— and Jane H——.

2. Jennie B——, committed to Bedford for violating the liquor tax law, was born in a small village 25 years and 6 months before her conviction. Her mother died when she was three years old and she went to live with her maternal grandparents where she remained for three years. She then went to live with her stepmother who did the best she could to provide for the family and was a very fine woman. The father was so alcoholic and abusive, however, that the stepmother left him when Jennie was eleven. After this, Jennie kept house for her grandfather, father, uncle and brother. The home conditions were bad for her during this period because she had little supervision and her father and uncle were drinking men. She used to go to the saloon for her father at that time, and the men who frequented this place would give her nickels to sit on the bar and sing for them. When she was fourteen she went out to do housework. This girl, aside from her father's drinking, had a decent home until she was 3 and from the time she was 6 until she was 11. After that, and at her most impressionable years, she was thrown on her own resources, had no one to look out for her, and there was no woman in the house. As a whole, we feel that each of the factors in the home,—the economic and moral standards, and the parental supervision belong in the poor class, and that the total estimate of the home would fall in this class.

For Class 3, which represents cases in appreciably better home surroundings, we shall give two cases.

1. Sarah S—— was committed to Bedford when seventeen years, six months of age for associating with dissolute persons and being in danger of becoming morally depraved. She was born in New York City and lived there all of her life. Her father has for years worked in a shoe factory and in the rush seasons earns from $14 to $18 a week though he only earns about $6 a week during the slack seasons. The oldest boy, who is not married, earns $14 a week and helps out with the family expenses. There are five children in the fraternity including Sarah. On the whole, because of the mother's good managing ability and the fact that the father has always worked steadily, though at times he earned little, the economic standards may be classed as mediocre. The family has never needed to accept charitable aid, and the father has

been able to keep up his membership in a Jewish benefit lodge. There seems to be a good family spirit and the family have good moral standards. Sarah is the only one in the family who has ever been in court. The parents are quite foreign and have not quickly adapted themselves to the customs in this country. As a result, a large part of the supervision has fallen on the oldest boy who has exerted his influence rather unpleasantly at times. On the whole, however, the home has been fair and the girl had a chance of making good so far as the influence of her home conditions was concerned. In our estimates of the factors in the home, we have classed the estimate of the moral standards as good and all of the other estimates as fair.

2. Kate M—— was sent to Bedford when eighteen years and five months old for prostitution. She was born in a village in Massachusetts and lived there and in a small city in New York state most of her life. Her father died shortly before her birth. He was an erratic, unstable sort of man, shiftless and quite lazy, so that there was no money left after his death, and his wife and children had to live with his father. A few years after his death, the mother remarried and took her children to New York state with her. The home with the stepfather was fairly good. He worked steadily and tried to provide well. When Kate was nine, however, her grandparents in Massachusetts offered to take care of her and so she went back to them, remaining until she was fourteen. The grandfather owned several houses and provided well for the child. She went to school regularly, finishing grammar school, and the grandfather was anxious to send her through college. They were very respectable old people and had a good standing in the community, but were undoubtedly too old to exert proper authority, so that Kate was allowed to have her own way in everything. When fourteen years old, she decided that she wanted to go back to her mother, and despite her grandparents' protestations, she did so. After reaching home, she found that she did not get on well with her mother, after having been away from home for five years. She resented her mother's affection for the children by the second husband and imagined that her mother slighted her in every possible way. Finally, she left home the day after Christmas because she thought her mother had not given her as many gifts as the other children had. Without any supervision on the outside, she steadily went from bad to worse and within a few months had been arrested and committed to Bedford. In estimating this girl's case, the economic status and moral standards were classed as good, parental supervision as poor, and the total estimate as

fair. It would seem that this girl with her good mentality, her responsiveness and desire to please, might have been managed so that she would not have come into contact with the law. She was always a difficult child, high-strung, nervous and irritable, but these qualities were only exaggerated by the lax supervision in her grandparents' home and the more strict and less sympathetic atmosphere in her mother's home when she was of the age where she needed very careful guidance.

Class 4, which includes good homes, comfortable economically, with good moral standards and parental supervision, comprises only 6.0 per cent of the cases in the total group. (Table 66.) The following case is typical of a large part of these cases.

1. Carrie C—— was committed to Bedford when 21 years, 5 months of age for petit larceny. She was born in a village on Long Island and lived there, always in the same house which her mother owned, until she was married at the age of twenty. The field worker in this case had an excellent opportunity to see for herself the house and neighborhood in which the girl had grown up. Carrie's father was a mason and earned from $30 to $40 a week. Since he worked steadily and had only three children to bring up, they were always comfortable economically. They bought a two-story and basement house in which Carrie was born, and when the father died in 1914 he left a $3,000 life insurance. Both the father and mother are well thought of in the community and are both spoken of as having good moral standards. The mother has meant to do well for her children, and since her husband's death has spent a great deal of money to make them comfortable. She is of a nagging, dictatorial disposition, however, and at times has undoubtedly been disagreeable. There was a certain amount of friction between Carrie and her mother, particularly over the man the girl wanted to marry. In her antagonism to him and her way of handling the situation, the mother showed poor judgment and little understanding. There does not seem to be evidence, here, of a very important connection between the girl's offense and her home conditions. Her family were honest and law-abiding and had taught her to be so. Her thefts from the department store in which she was working over the holidays seem to have been prompted by the suggestions of the floor-walker who wanted to share the proceeds with her and by her own economic need at that time, since her husband was ill and she was too proud to ask her mother for money.

2. A quite different case for this class is that of a colored girl, Sarah E——, 23 years, 9 months of age at the time of her commitment to Bedford for prostitution. She was an illegitimate child and was boarded by her mother with her foster mother from the time she was two weeks old until she was eighteen months old. Then, because her mother was not paying for the child's board, Mrs. E—— took Sarah to her mother and told her she could not keep her. The mother later abandoned Sarah and when Mrs. E—— heard of this she went to the Society which was caring for the child and took her home with her. Sarah has lived with her foster parents since then and has had a good home with them. They own their own home in Brooklyn, a two-story and basement frame house with a yard around it. The house is well furnished and in good condition. All of the family are insured and the foster father has earned good wages as a porter. The foster parents have good moral standards and are well spoken of by every one in the community. Undoubtedly, Sarah has been given excellent training. The only objection which could be raised in regard to the amount of supervision is that the foster mother left the home to work out quite often when Sarah was younger and this left her at home with no one to look out for her after school hours. On the whole, however, the home ranks high,—way above that for any other colored girl in our group. We have estimated the home as good in economic status and moral standards and as fair in parental supervision. The girl in question is very low grade mentally and probably no home training could have kept her from doing certain things if the temptation or opportunity to do so were put in her path. Certainly, in a survey of her actual home surroundings there is no obvious association with her delinquency.

The fifth class, those with excellent homes, has only two representatives in our total group, and they both come in the Penitentiary. In considering the estimates of certain factors in the home, only two other cases were found where any element in the home conditions came up to the highest class. These two cases, both in Bedford and previously mentioned in connection with the economic status, reached the highest class only in the economic status, however.

1. The first of the Penitentiary cases whose early home surroundings were very good is Nina R——, who at the time of her commitment to the Penitentiary for petit larceny was 49 years and 5 months of age. The field worker was able to visit the childhood home and obtain information both from members of the immediate family and

from friends, so that our information is probably reliable. Nina R—— was born in a small town in the East and lived there until she went to boarding school, when she was about fifteen. Her father, a wheelwright by trade, was a steady worker and "plain, simple and upright in every way." He owned his home and they were in comfortable circumstances, though never wealthy. The mother, also, was a woman of fine character. The grandfather was a Quaker preacher and all of his children were Quakers of strict standards. There were five children in Nina's fraternity. The oldest studied to be a doctor and one other child, after teaching school for fourteen years, took a nurse's training course. All who knew the parents felt that they were intelligent and made a very good home for their children. Nina herself was sent to boarding school from which she graduated and then taught school for twelve years. In moral standards and parental supervision, this family was rated as being very good, and the economic status was classed as good.

2. The other woman who came from a very good home is Hannah M—— who at 58 years, 4 months was committed to the Penitentiary for arson. She was born in Germany and lived there until she was nineteen years old, when she came to this country with her husband. We were able to interview the woman's older brother who seemed sincere and anxious to give any information which might be of benefit. He says that the family in Germany were comfortably well-to-do, very good people and well educated. The father was an interior decorator, not wealthy, but determined to give his children the best possible education. Hannah was educated for a teacher and was in school until she was nineteen, when she was married to a physician. So far as we know, this home offered very good advantages. We have estimated the economic status as good only, since there seemed to be no great surplus of money, but have considered the other factors as very good.

In neither of these two cases were the home conditions in any sense involved in the difficulty with the law which came much later in life.

As a whole, the home conditions of the bulk of our cases are represented by such homes as those of Alice B—— and Sarah S——, *i.e.*, (1) cases where the home has been poor, and where only a child of unusual initiative would reach out beyond what the home had offered her, and (2) cases where the home was sufficiently good so that there seemed a fair chance for the child to develop into a good instead of an anti-social person.

TABLE 68

Correlation between Age at First Conviction and Estimate of Home Conditions

Total Group. Workhouse Omitted

Estimate of Home Conditions	Age at First Conviction (Years)																					Totals	Means (Age at First Conviction)
	6–9	9–12	12–15	15–18	18–21	21–24	24–27	27–30	30–33	33–36	36–39	39–42	42–45	45–48	48–51	51–54	54–57	57–60	60–63	63–66	66–69		
Very good															1			1				2	53.5
Good				3	4	3	4		3	3		1		2	1		2					26	29.9
Fair	1		4	19	30	35	39	21	18	5	9	7	2	2	2	1			2			197	25.7
Poor		3	4	33	34	28	16	13	5	9	6	2	3		1						1	158	23.0
Very poor			2	10	8	8	1		1	1	1	2					1					35	22.1
Totals	1	3	10	65	76	74	60	34	27	18	16	12	5	4	5	1	3	1	2		1	418	24.77

Age at first conviction: Mean = 24.77 $\sigma = 8.93$
Correlation ratio: $\eta = .31 \pm .044$

(*g*) *Relationship Between Estimate of Home Conditions and Age at First Conviction*

In various later chapters we have considered the relationship of given social factors to the estimate of the home conditions. At this point we shall consider the relationship between the age at first conviction and the home conditions during childhood and adolescence. Table 68 presents these data in a correlation ratio. The ratio of .31 with a relatively small standard deviation of .044 would indicate that there is a significant relationship between the age at first conviction and the estimate of home conditions, with a tendency for those who come from the worst homes to be convicted earliest. This is shown by the mean age at first conviction for the various estimate groups, with the mean age at first conviction in the poorest class of home conditions at 22.1 years while there is a progression to a mean age at first conviction of 53.5 years for the two cases which fall in the best group of home conditions.

(*h*) *Relationship Between Estimate of Home Conditions and Number of Previous Convictions*

If we turn to Table 69, showing the correlation between the number of previous convictions and the estimate of home conditions, we find that the correlation ratio is .05 with a standard deviation of .049. This seems to indicate that there is no relationship between the kind of home in which a child grows up and the *extent* of criminality which develops later.

FAMILY STATUS

So closely associated with any survey of home conditions as to be almost inseparable from it are certain other factors, such as the nativity of the parents, their ages in relation to the age of the subject, the number of children in the family and the subject's order in the fraternity. Though these factors are taken into consideration, in general, in making the estimate of the home conditions, they seem important enough to repeat in detail at this point.

(*a*) *Nativity of Parents*

Table 70 gives the nativity of the parents by institutional groups, and shows that the percentage of women with both parents native born varies among the groups. Bedford has a high percentage, 57.3 with both parents native born, Auburn 30.7 per cent, Probation 28.4 per

TABLE 69

Correlation between Number of Previous Convictions and Estimate of Home Conditions

Total Group. Workhouse Omitted

Estimate of Home Conditions	Number of Previous Convictions																					Totals	Means (Number of Previous Convictions)
	0	1	2	3	4	5	6	7	8	9	10	11	12	13	14	15	16	17	18	19	20		
Very good	2																					2	0.0
Good	13	4	3	2	1	1		1														25	1.3
Fair	103	49	14	11	5	3	4	1		1	2	1	1						2		1	198	1.4
Poor	70	43	20	10	6	3	1	3	2	1	1											160	1.3
Very poor	21	6	4	2					1				1									35	1.1
Totals	209	102	41	25	12	7	5	5	3	2	3	1	2						2		1	420	1.36

Number of previous convictions: Mean = 1.36 $\sigma = 2.498$
Correlation ratio: $\eta = .05 \pm .049$

TABLE 70

NATIVITY OF PARENTS

Per Cent Distribution of Delinquent Women in Institutional Groups

Nativity	Institutional Groups						Total
	Bedford	Auburn	Magdalen	Penitentiary	Workhouse	Probation	
Both Native	57.3	30.7	18.8	26.9	40.5	28.4	34.8
White	40.6	17.3	18.8	12.9	14.6	27.2	22.3
Colored	16.7	13.3	....	14.0	25.8	1.2	12.5
Both Foreign	35.4	61.3	66.7	65.6	50.6	55.6	55.1
White	35.4	60.0	66.7	62.4	50.6	53.1	53.9
Colored	....	1.3	....	3.2	....	2.5	1.2
One Foreign: one Native	7.3	8.0	14.5	7.5	9.0	16.1	10.1
White	7.3	8.0	14.5	7.5	5.6	13.6	9.1
Colored	....	....	....	....	3.4	2.5	1.0
Total	100.0	100.0	100.0	100.0	100.0	100.0	100.0
Number of cases	96	75	69	93	89	81	503

cent, the Penitentiary 26.9 per cent and the Magdalen 18.8 per cent. In view of the fact that Auburn and the Penitentiary have the highest percentage of foreign born women, it is of interest to observe that the highest percentage of foreign or mixed parentage occurs in the Magdalen. The Probation group also has a higher percentage of women with foreign or mixed parentage than Auburn, though the percentage of foreign born women in the Probation group is smaller than that in Auburn.

If we compare the nativity and parentage of our total group with the nativity and parentage of the general female population in New York state in 1910[2] we find the following results:

Nativity and Parentage	General Female Population New York State	Delinquent Women in this Study
Native White	61.7	50.2
Native Parentage	34.1	20.4
Foreign or Mixed Parentage	27.6	29.8
Foreign White	36.5	30.9
Negro	1.7	18.8
All Others	.1	.2

[2] Thirteenth Census of the United States. 1910. Vol. III.

In view of the fact that the foreign born delinquent women in this study are represented in the total group of delinquents by much less than the representation we might expect from their numbers in the general population (See Chapter VIII), it is interesting to find that among the native white of foreign or mixed parentage the delinquent group has a larger percentage than the general female population. The native white of native parentage, on the other hand, are 34.1 per cent of the general population but only 20.4 per cent of the women in this study. It would seem from this, that the element of foreign parentage is significant as a factor in the home conditions which may be associated with delinquency. In many of the families studied the inability of the foreign parents to adjust themselves to American customs is striking, particularly when the children become quickly adapted to American customs and are ashamed of the parents because of their foreignness.

(*b*) *Age of Parents at Time of Subject's Birth*

A further factor of importance in the home is the relationship between the ages of the parents and the children. Table 71 shows the

TABLE 71

AGE OF MOTHER AT SUBJECT'S BIRTH

Per Cent Distribution of Delinquent Women in Institutional Groups

Age of Mother	Institutional Groups						Total
	Bedford	Auburn	Magdalen	Penitentiary	Workhouse	Probation	
11 to 16 years	....	3.2	1.8	1.9	4.3	4.8	2.4
16 " 21 "	22.2	17.5	10.7	13.5	27.7	11.3	17.3
21 " 26 "	33.3	22.2	26.8	19.2	19.2	27.4	25.7
26 " 31 "	17.8	23.7	23.2	34.6	14.9	24.2	22.7
31 " 36 "	18.9	11.1	14.3	11.5	19.2	21.0	16.2
36 " 41 "	3.3	14.3	16.1	11.5	4.3	4.8	8.7
41 " 46 "	2.2	4.8	5.4	3.9	8.5	4.8	4.6
46 " 51 "	2.2	3.2	1.8	1.9	2.1	1.6	2.2
51 " 56 "	....	....	....	1.9	....	....	.3
Total	100.0	100.0	100.0	100.0	100.0	100.0	100.0
Number of cases	90	63	56	52	47	62	370

Mean Age of Mother at Subject's Birth (Total Group)......27.66 ± .401 years
σ.................................. 7.71 ± .284

mother's age at the time of the subject's birth. The youngest mother was eleven years of age, and the oldest, 51 years of age when the subject was born. In the total group, 2.4 per cent of the cases or nine of the delinquent women were born while their mothers were between eleven and sixteen years of age. The largest number of cases occurs in the age group of 21 to 26 years. For the total group the mean age of the mother at time of the subject's birth was 27.66 years with a standard deviation of 7.71 years.

About the same trend as that noted above is shown with regard to the age of the father at the time of the subject's birth. Table 72 shows that the range of ages starts at 13 years and runs to 83 years. In this latter group there are only two cases and in both instances the father was 81 years old at the time the subject was born. The earlier age groups do not show as high a percentage for the father as they do for the mother. One woman in the Workhouse was born when her father was thirteen, and the four other women included in this group were born when their fathers were seventeen and eighteen years old. For the total group the average age of the father at the time of the subject's birth was 32.95 years with a standard deviation of 10.50 years. This average age, while somewhat higher than that of the mother at time of the subject's birth, is not so much higher as to make the extreme age of the father an important factor in the life of the delinquent.

(*c*) *Age of Subject at Time of Parent's Death*

Another factor often advanced as causative of delinquency, is the breaking up of the home, through death, divorce, etc., while the child is young. It is difficult for us to present in detail a table showing the exact status of homes regarding the parents who are separated, dead, imprisoned, etc., since our group of women is of varying ages, many of them so old that we should naturally expect their parents to be dead, and the fact of their being dead not significant as indicating any abnormal home condition. It seems of interest, however, to know what percentage of these women were very young when either parent died. Table 73 has been made to show the percentage of delinquent women who were under five, ten, fifteen and twenty years of age at the time of the father's and of the mother's death. The table shows that there are varying percentages of women in each of these age groups. The percentage of women who were under five at the time of the father's death runs from 8.3 per cent in Auburn and the Magdalen to 21.4 per

TABLE 72

AGE OF FATHER AT SUBJECT'S BIRTH

Per Cent Distribution of Delinquent Women in Institutional Groups

Age of Father	Institutional Groups						Total
	Bedford	Auburn	Magdalen	Penitentiary	Workhouse	Probation	
13 to 18 years	....	....	....	3.9	4.6	1.9	1.4
18 " 23 "	8.3	11.9	5.3	13.5	11.4	11.5	10.1
23 " 28 "	28.6	20.3	26.3	21.2	9.1	23.1	22.4
28 " 33 "	23.8	23.7	21.1	17.3	34.1	23.1	24.1
33 " 38 "	15.5	13.6	12.3	13.5	15.9	13.5	13.5
38 " 43 "	14.3	15.3	7.0	15.4	6.8	13.5	12.4
43 " 48 "	2.4	5.1	17.5	7.7	9.1	1.9	6.9
48 " 53 "	4.8	5.1	5.3	1.9	4.6	5.8	4.6
53 " 58 "	1.2	3.4	....	3.9	....	3.9	2.0
58 " 63 "	....	....	1.8	1.9	2.3	1.9	1.2
63 " 68 "	....	....	1.8	....	....	....	.3
68 " 73 "	1.2	....	....	....	....	....	.3
73 " 78 "	....	....	....	....	2.3	....	.3
78 " 83 "	....	1.7	1.8	....	....	....	.6
Total	100.0	100.0	100.0	100.0	100.0	100.0	100.0
Number of cases	84	59	57	52	44	52	348

Mean Age of Father at Subject's Birth (Total Group)......32.95 ± .562
σ......10.50 ± .397

cent in the Workhouse. The total group shows 11.8 per cent who were under five at the time of the father's death. Probably the next two age groups are of more importance, however, because they include not only those who were very young when the father died but also those who were of the ages where the absence of a father in the home would be of the greatest importance. For those children who were under ten at the time of the father's death there were 18.6 per cent for the total group, with varying percentages in the institutional groups. The percentage of children under fifteen at time of the father's death, 24.9 per cent for the total group, is probably large enough to indicate a serious lack of supervision in most of these childhood homes. The next age group, while of less importance, because many of the women affected had left home before their twentieth year, shows that 34.7 of the women were under twenty years at the time of the father's death. We have not presented any further figures since we are most interested in the home during childhood and adolescence.

TABLE 73

AGE AT TIME OF PARENTS' DEATH

Per Cent Distribution of Delinquent Women in Institutional Groups

Institutional Groups	Age at Time of Death of:							
	Father				Mother			
	Under 5 years	Under 10 years	Under 15 years	Under 20 years	Under 5 years	Under 10 years	Under 15 years	Under 20 years
Bedford	10.4	17.7	22.9	35.4	5.1	10.2	20.4	28.6
Auburn	8.3	15.3	20.8	26.4	10.4	14.3	20.8	23.4
Magdalen	8.3	15.3	20.8	26.4	10.8	16.2	23.0	28.4
Penitentiary	9.3	16.3	26.7	34.9	11.0	14.3	20.9	31.9
Workhouse	21.4	27.4	34.5	42.9	12.8	17.4	18.6	25.6
Probation	12.5	18.8	22.5	40.0	7.1	9.5	13.1	19.1
Total	11.8	18.6	24.9	34.7	9.4	13.5	19.4	26.3
Number of cases	58	91	122	170	48	69	99	134

If we turn to the child's age at time of the death of the mother we see that, for the most part, the percentages of delinquent women who were young at time of the mother's death are smaller than the percentages at the time of the father's death. There are 9.4 per cent of our total group of women who were under five at the time of the mother's death, 13.5 per cent who were under ten, 19.4 per cent under fifteen, and 26.3 per cent under twenty years of age.

At this point we may compare with our data Goring's [3] figures for the ages of male criminals at the time of the mother's death. The percentages are as follows:

	Goring's Study	Women in this Study
Under 5 years	7.7%	9.4%
" 10 "	15.4%	13.5%
" 15 "	25.2%	19.4%
" 20 "	35.5%	26.3%

This shows a smaller percentage of male criminals in the youngest age group, but a larger percentage in the other groups, than we find among the delinquent women of this study.

[3] *Op. cit.*, p. 422.

(*d*) *Number of Children in Fraternity*

Another element entering into the consideration of home and family conditions is the size of the family. Many contend that most criminals come from large families, especially those of poorer economic status where the large number of children makes decent living conditions impossible and leads to prostitution or stealing as a means of livelihood. Others feel that an only child is more likely to "go wrong" because she has had less training in the appreciation of property rights and in adapting herself to others. An instance of this occurs in the case we have mentioned previously in this chapter of the only child in a wealthy family. She was pampered and spoiled until she was eighteen when she insisted, despite her parents' protest, upon marrying a man who was of little account. Her life from that time on,—her unwillingness to take the responsibility of looking after her children, her selfishness at the time of her mother's illness and death, and her gradual drifting into prostitution—seems in part an outgrowth of her early training.

To show the range of number of children in the fraternities of the delinquents, we present Table 74. This indicates that the range is very long in Bedford, Auburn and the Penitentiary groups and progressively shorter in the Workhouse, Probation and Magdalen. The total group has a range of one to eighteen children in the family, with the greatest concentration between three and seven children. The mean number of children for the total group is 5.76±.148 with a standard deviation of 3.8±.105.

The Census figures for 1910 give the number of persons per family in New York State as 4.5.[4] The Census figures do not include the average number of children per family, but we are safe in saying that this number must be appreciably less than 4.5, the average number of persons per family. This would indicate that the women in our group come from families of appreciably larger average size than the families in the general population. We might also compare here the average number in the families of 647 prostitutes studied in Bedford and reported on by Dr. Katharine Bement Davis in Mr. Kneeland's book on "Commercialized Prostitution in New York City."[5] Dr. Davis found that the average number of children in the families was 3.99, a number somewhat less than the average number for our group.

[4] Thirteenth Census of the United States. 1910. Vol. III.
[5] *Op. cit.*, p. 170.

TABLE 74

NUMBER OF CHILDREN IN FRATERNITY

Per Cent Distribution by Institutional Groups

Number of Children in Fraternity	Institutional Groups						Total
	Bedford	Auburn	Magdalen	Penitentiary	Workhouse	Probation	
1	9.9	3.8	5.3	11.3	12.0	14.6	9.8
2	11.9	6.3	8.0	4.7	4.0	14.6	8.2
3	14.9	8.8	14.7	10.4	11.0	13.5	12.2
4	11.9	12.5	13.3	12.3	16.0	6.7	12.2
5	7.9	8.8	17.3	12.3	8.0	10.1	10.5
6	7.9	16.3	9.3	8.5	14.0	9.0	10.7
7	7.9	12.5	17.3	5.7	5.0	13.5	9.8
8	5.9	3.8	5.3	8.5	9.0	3.4	6.2
9	3.0	7.5	4.0	7.6	7.0	4.5	5.6
10	4.0	7.5	5.3	3.8	2.0	2.3	4.0
11	2.0	3.8	....	2.8	2.0	4.5	2.5
12	4.0	2.5	....	.9	4.0	2.3	2.4
13	5.9	2.5	....	7.6	3.0	1.1	3.6
14	1.0	2.5	....	2.8	3.0	....	1.6
17	2.0	....	....	.9	....	....	.5
18	....	1.3	....	....	....	....	.2
Total	100.0	100.0	100.0	100.0	100.0	100.0	100.0
Number of cases	101	80	75	106	100	89	551

Mean Number of Children in Fraternity (Total Group) . . . . 5.76 ± .148
σ . . . . 3.48 ± .105

This again we may compare with Goring's[6] figures for the families of male criminals. He finds that the mean number of children in the family is 6.89 with a standard deviation of 3.85. This would indicate that the men in his group came from slightly larger families than do the women in our group. He has computed from this the correlation ratio of nature of crime with the number of children in the family and finds that the ratio is .1±.04. From the values of his means, he finds that those convicted of fraud tend to be drawn from smaller families than those convicted of other offenses. He explains this by showing that the social class from which the fraudulent criminals are mainly drawn tends to be restricted in size of family.

[6] *Op. cit.*, p. 422.

(e) *Order in Fraternity, of Delinquent Women*

The order in the fraternity, which is closely connected with the number of children in the family, is of interest because of the belief that the oldest in a large family may have much of the responsibility of looking after the others and may be neglected if there are many others who are not able to look out for themselves. Table 75 shows that there is a large percentage in our group, 28.9 per cent, who were the oldest in the family. Since Table 74 shows that there are only 9.8 per cent of the cases where the subject was the only child, this leaves 19.1 per cent of the women who were not the only child and who were the oldest in the family. In the total group, and by comparison with Table 74, we find that the delinquent women, in large part, come from the older members in the fraternity.

(f) *Number of Full-term Children*

Though not logically related to the subject's home as a child or her own family conditions, we shall consider here, in connection with

TABLE 75

ORDER IN FRATERNITY

Per Cent Distribution by Institutional Groups

Order in Fraternity	Institutional Groups						Total
	Bedford	Auburn	Magdalen	Penitentiary	Workhouse	Probation	
1	29.7	22.8	23.3	28.6	29.8	37.5	28.9
2	20.8	15.2	20.6	26.4	10.6	17.1	18.4
3	16.8	10.1	11.0	16.5	19.2	18.2	15.6
4	15.8	17.7	9.6	14.3	13.8	8.0	13.3
5	6.9	8.9	12.3	5.5	8.5	3.4	7.4
6	5.0	7.6	15.1	4.4	8.5	5.7	7.4
7	2.0	3.8	4.1	....	6.4	6.8	3.8
8	1.0	2.5	1.4	1.1	....	1.2	1.1
9	....	5.1	2.7	....	1.1	1.2	1.5
10	1.0	1.3	....	2.2	....	....	.8
11	1.0	2.5	....	....	....	1.2	.8
12	....	1.3	....	1.1	1.1	....	.6
13	......	....	....	....	......	....	....
14	....	1.3	....	....	1.1	....	.4
Total	100.0	100.0	100.0	100.0	100.0	100.0	100.0
Number of cases	101	79	73	91	94	88	526

TABLE 76

NUMBER OF FULL-TERM CHILDREN

Per Cent Distribution by Institutional Groups

Number of Full-Term Children	Institutional Groups						Total
	Bedford	Auburn	Magdalen	Peni- tentiary	Work- house	Probation	
0	59.4	25.6	62.9	47.7	52.5	63.0	52.1
1	24.8	33.3	24.3	19.6	16.8	26.1	23.7
2	7.9	9.0	7.1	8.4	14.9	6.5	9.1
3	4.0	11.5	2.9	8.4	7.9	1.1	6.0
4	3.0	5.1	....	3.7	5.0	3.3	3.5
5	1.0	2.6	1.4	5.6	....	....	1.8
6	....	1.3	1.4	2.8	....	....	.9
7	....	5.1	....	....	1.0	....	.9
8	....	1.3	....	....	....	....	.2
9	....	2.6	....	1.9	....	....	.7
10	....	1.3	....	.9	....	....	.4
11	....	1.3	....	....	2.0	....	.6
18	....	....	......	.9	....	....	.2
Total	100.0	100.0	100.0	100.0	100.0	100.0	100.0
Number of cases	101	78	70	107	101	92	549

the size of her own fraternity, the number of full-term children, total number of pregnancies and number of illegitimate pregnancies she has had. The number of full-term children, which we shall present first, includes both legitimate and illegitimate children. Table 76 shows that the percentage of women who have had no children is 52.1 per cent for the total group, but that the percentage varies between institutional groups, the three groups where the average age is highest and where there are the highest percentages of married women, having the smallest percentage without children. The range of number of children is also longest in the three groups first mentioned, *i.e.*, Auburn, the Penitentiary and the Workhouse.

(*g*) *Number of Pregnancies*

If we compare with the number of full-term children the number of times the delinquent women in this study have been pregnant we find a somewhat different distribution. Table 77 shows that while the range for the total group remains the same as in the previous table (Table 76), the percentage who have never been pregnant is much smaller in each institutional group, indicating that there is, throughout, a considerable number of women who have had miscarriages or abortions. For the total group, there are 9.8 per cent of the women who have been pregnant but who have never had a full-term child.

The number of illegitimate pregnancies is difficult to obtain accurately, particularly when the subject herself is unwilling to talk freely about it. With the best data that could be obtained, however, we find as shown in Table 78 that a very high percentage in each institutional group have had no illegitimate children, the highest percentage being in the three groups where there are the largest numbers of married women and in the Probation group. Bedford and the Magdalen which have the largest number of illegitimate pregnancies have a range of none to six illegitimate pregnancies in the one case and none to three illegitimate pregnancies in the other. The Bedford woman who had six illegitimate pregnancies is an Austrian woman who has lived with

TABLE 77

NUMBER OF PREGNANCIES

Per Cent Distribution by Institutional Groups

Number of Pregnancies	Institutional Groups						Total
	Bedford	Auburn	Magdalen	Peni-tentiary	Work-house	Probation	
0	49.5	16.9	44.3	37.4	43.6	58.7	42.3
1	23.8	23.4	32.9	22.4	16.8	22.8	23.2
2	10.9	16.9	17.1	10.3	14.9	12.0	13.3
3	8.9	15.6	1.4	10.3	13.9	1.1	8.8
4	4.0	3.9	....	4.7	5.9	3.3	3.8
5	2.0	6.5	2.9	8.4	2.0	2.2	4.0
6	1.0	2.6	....	2.8	....	....	1.1
7	....	1.3	1.4	....	1.0	....	.6
8	....	1.3	....	....	....	....	.2
9	....	3.9	....	1.9	....	....	.9
10	....	2.6	....	.9	....	....	.6
11	....	1.3	....	....	1.0	....	.4
12	....	1.3	....	....	....	....	.2
13	....	1.3	....	....	....	....	.2
14	....	1.3	....	....	....	....	.2
17	....	....	....	....	1.0	....	.2
18	....	....	....	.9	....	....	.2
Total	100.0	100.0	100.0	100.0	100.0	100.0	100.0
Number of cases	101	77	70	107	101	92	548

TABLE 78

NUMBER OF ILLEGITIMATE PREGNANCIES

Per Cent Distribution by Institutional Groups

Number of Illegitimate Pregnancies	Institutional Groups						Total
	Bedford	Auburn	Magdalen	Penitentiary	Workhouse	Probation	
0	64.4	84.4	64.3	83.0	86.1	89.1	79.0
1	18.7	11.7	27.1	12.3	5.9	7.9	13.4
2	6.9	1.3	7.1	.9	3.0	3.3	3.7
3	6.9	....	1.4	.9	2.0	....	2.0
4	2.0	....	....	.9	1.0	....	.7
5	....	2.6	....	.9	2.0	....	.9
6	1.0	....	....	.9	....	....	.4
Total	100.0	100.0	100.0	100.0	100.0	100.0	100.0
Number of cases	101	77	70	106	101	92	547

two consorts. She was probably never sexually promiscuous and did not go with any other man while she was living steadily with one consort. In this total group there are 21 per cent of the women who have had one or more illegitimate pregnancies.

HEREDITARY FACTORS

The more important part of the family history which requires a much further study than we can give it at this point is the matter of the heredity and the details of certain defective strains in the family. Because this is such a large subject and needs careful presentation of family histories to make the material worth anything, we shall give here only the summarized data which we were able to obtain through the field workers' visits. This material shows the occurrence of certain specified defective strains in the mother, father, sisters or brothers of the women in this study. The distribution of delinquent women by institutional groups, for specified defects, gives in each case the number of women in whose immediate families (mother, father or sibs) the given defect occurs. We have selected for observation certain significant hereditary factors, particularly those stressed by modern criminologists.

"Alcoholic" as we have used it in this connection includes only those who are excessively alcoholic. "Criminal Record" includes those who have had a conviction in any court for any offense. "Epileptic" includes, wherever possible, those who have been so diagnosed by the family physician; where this diagnosis was not possible the statements of reliable informants have been used. "Feeble-minded" probably more than any other defect noted here has a much smaller percentage of cases than there should be because of the caution of the field workers in calling any one feeble-minded who was not obviously unable to look out for himself. "Insane" includes only those who have been confined in hospitals for the insane or who have been diagnosed as insane. "Neurotic" has been used to include persons of decidedly high-strung, irritable, unstable temperament, difficult to live with. "Sexually irregular" includes those concerning whom we have been able to get definite evidence of sexual promiscuity. "Suicide" and "Tubercular" are self-explanatory. "Venereal disease" is inclusive of both syphilis and gonorrhea; the information on this is probably very unreliable because of the difficulty of obtaining this information either from the subject or other members of the family, except in Bedford, where the immediate families of nearly all of the girls were very well known. "Wanderer," which is a term used in the eugenics studies made under Dr. Charles B. Davenport, includes those concerning whom we had definite evidence of marked nomadic tendencies.

Table 79 shows the frequency of occurrence of these defective strains in the immediate families of the women in this study.[7] There are, it is seen, 21.8 per cent of the women in whose families some member has been excessively alcoholic. This is a much higher percentage than Dr. Davis found in a study of prostitutes at Bedford,[8] where 35 girls or 5.4 per cent of her total group came from families in which there was alcoholism. However, as she states, her figures are largely based on the girls' own statements and are probably much lower than they should be.

The percentage of women in our group who come from homes in which some member of the family has had a conviction is 15.9. Though we have no way of measuring the percentage of families in the general population in which there has been a conviction, this percentage would seem to be so high as to be of great significance in

[7] The distribution does not show the amount of overlapping which occurs. There may be alcoholism, epilepsy and insanity all within the same family. In this event, each defective strain is counted separately so that the percentage of women having alcoholism in the family represents all cases where alcoholism occurs either as the only defective strain or in combination with others.

[8] *Op. cit.*, p. 172.

TABLE 79

DEFECTIVE STRAINS IN FATHER, MOTHER AND MEMBERS OF FRATERNITY

Distribution by Institutional Groups and Per Cent Distribution for Total Group of Delinquent Women in Whose Immediate Families Specified Defective Strains Occur

Defective Strains	Institutional Groups						Total	
	Bedford	Auburn	Magdalen	Penitentiary	Workhouse	Probation	Number	Per Cent
Alcoholic	32	21	18	12	12	19	114	21.8
Criminal Record	32	13	15	6	7	10	83	15.9
Epileptic	10	3	..	2	1	1	17	3.3
Feeble-minded	8	1	4	1	2	6	22	4.2
Insane	2	4	2	5	4	..	17	3.3
Neurotic	9	2	3	6	1	4	25	4.8
Sexually Irregular	32	8	13	7	8	11	79	15.1
Suicide	1	1	2	3	2	..	9	1.7
Tubercular	20	16	8	20	18	16	98	18.8
Venereal Disease	5	..	..	..	..	2	7	1.3
Wanderer	6	5	2	..	1	2	16	3.1
Number of Women with Specified Defective Strains in Family	67	38	35	39	35	42	256	49.0
Number of Women not Having Specified Defective Strains in Family	34	38	40	65	51	38	266	51.0
Total Number of Women	101	76	75	104	86	80	522	100.0

affecting home conditions. Closely associated with the criminal record is the amount of sexual irregularity. In our group we find that there was sexual irregularity in the homes of 15.1 per cent of the women.

Tuberculosis is found in the immediate families of 18.8 per cent of the cases. Each of the other defective strains noted occurs in less than 5 per cent of the families. We feel that the information concerning the defects which show the lower percentages is probably inadequate and that exact comparisons are not justified. As a whole, we find that 49.0 per cent of the women in our group had at least one of the defective strains we have observed, in one or more members of their families. Many of these families had several of the defects in both the mother and father, and the members of the fraternity.[9] Fifty-one per cent of the women in the group came from families in which we were unable to find any of the defects specified.

It is difficult to say whether any of these defects of poor heredity are directly responsible for the women getting into difficulties with the law, since we do not know whether such defects are present in the same proportion in the general population. The most we can say is that, from this brief survey of hereditary strains which are believed to be significant, the immediate families of at least 49.0 per cent of the women in our study are affected.

Dr. Davis found that 20.09 per cent of the prostitutes at Bedford had "degenerate strains"[10] very closely corresponding to the defective strains we have just discussed. As stated before, she felt that this did not include nearly all of the defects which should have been included had it been possible to make more thorough investigations. Dr. Glueck, in his study of men at Sing Sing,[11] found that "alcohol and tuberculosis seem to have been rather significant hereditary factors."

SUMMARY

In summarizing the more important factors which relate to the early home or the family status of the women whom we are studying, there stands out most clearly the fact that the large part of the women have come from poor homes, and that a large percentage come from families with defective strains. That we might treat the information on all of our cases alike, an estimate was made, uniformly for all cases, of the early home conditions and the three factors which we felt were most important in the home, *i.e.,* the economic status, moral standards and parental supervision. By each of these estimates, the majority of the cases fall in the very poor, poor or mediocre classes. In the total estimate of the home conditions during childhood and adolescence, 46.4 per cent of the cases fall in the two poorest groups,

[9] A girl of 17 committed to Bedford came from a family in which the father was excessively alcoholic, going off on "sprees" periodically; he was feeble-minded, and had never been able to learn to read or write; he was sexually promiscuous and syphilitic; he had had innumerable convictions for intoxication and stealing; and he was a "wanderer," leaving his family every few months and moving about from place to place, always thinking he could "do better" in another town. The mother of the girl was also feeble-minded, epileptic and sexually promiscuous. Two of the younger boys in the family, though under 16 years, had been brought into court several times for petty stealing, and were finally sentenced to a juvenile institution on larceny charges.

[10] *Op. cit.,* p. 173.

[11] *Op. cit.,* p. 107.

47.1 per cent in the mediocre class, and 6.5 per cent in the class of homes which are good or excellent.

How much of a factor the element of poor home conditions is, as causative of delinquency, it is difficult to judge, since we have no similar estimates for the general population. Within our own group, however, we are able to show that there is a significant relationship between the age at first conviction and the estimate of home conditions, with a tendency for those who were brought up in the poorest homes to be convicted at an earlier age than those who were brought up in better homes.

Certain of the details of family status have been separately considered, though to a certain extent they enter into the study of home conditions. Among these details we find that for the most part the age of the parents was not extreme in relation to the age of the subjects in this study. There is a fairly high percentage, 24.9 per cent, of these women who were under fifteen at the time of the father's death, and 19.4 per cent who were under fifteen at the time of the mother's death. A similar observation made by Goring shows that he found 25.2 per cent of male criminals under fifteen at the time of their mother's death. The number of children in the family shows that the general population for New York state has fewer children in the family than there are in the families of the delinquent women.

In any study of the conditions found in homes, we can not hope to do more than give a picture of the kind of homes from which the most of the persons in whom we are interested come. Very few attempts have been made to use uniform schemes for estimates or for grading homes, and up to this time the descriptive method has been felt to be of more value. Because of this trend, there is little available data for comparison, and we are able to say little more regarding the home conditions of our group than that these women come from the poorer classes, to a very large extent, and that, in addition to poor economic opportunities, there are low moral standards and poor supervision of the children.

CHAPTER X

EDUCATIONAL BACKGROUND

VIEWS REGARDING RELATION OF EDUCATION TO CRIME

THE significance of education as a factor in relation to crime has been an important moot point in criminology. There have been all varieties of contentions, including such diverse views as the assertion that education is a definitely harmful factor, increasing any latent tendency toward crime; the insistence that lack of education is an important cause of criminality; and the belief, at variance with both of the above, that education as such is not an important factor, but appears to figure merely because it is symptomatic of other genuinely significant influences, such as mentality and social background. Adequate data have not been offered as yet for establishing any of these views. Aschaffenburg[1] goes so far as to insist that it will inevitably remain lacking. He says:

"No statistical proof of the influence of education on criminality can ever be brought. . . . But—and this too, unfortunately, needs to be expressly mentioned—there can also be no proof to the contrary. The simple childlike view, that the degree of education obtained in the lower schools menaces the harmless, deeply moral, mode of thought of the people, this sentimental glorification of the people in their primitive state, is based on entirely vague and unfounded prejudices. It is not increasing education that causes the growth of crime, but the changes that have taken place in all external conditions in the course of the last centuries."

We are not willing to agree that it will be impossible ever to analyze the complex social situation sufficiently to reach any conclusions regarding the influence of the educational factor, since modern statistical methods can go far toward solving just such difficulties. Statistics, however, must have an adequate basis of facts on which to build, and that, we must admit, is not available at present. Such a

[1] Aschaffenburg, G. "Crime and Its Repression," p. 137. Trans. by A. Albrecht. Little, Brown & Co. 1913.

mode of approach as that of Lombroso,[2] in spite of its apparent foundation in fact, is worse than futile, since it may lead to the most erroneous conclusions. The general line of argument, with its almost inconceivable fallacies, is well illustrated by the following passage from Lombroso:

"Tocqueville shows that in Connecticut criminality has increased with the increase in instruction. In the United States the maximum figures for criminality . . . were noted in Wyoming, California, and Nevada, which gave the minimum number of illiterates . . .; and the minimum figures for criminality were found in New Mexico . . . South Carolina . . ., Alabama, Mississippi, Georgia, and Louisiana, which had the highest number of illiterates. Nebraska, Iowa, Maine, and Dakota were exceptional, having a small number of criminals and illiterates both, as a result of other causes which we shall see presently. In England the counties of Surrey, Kent, Gloucester, and Middlesex, where there is a higher degree of education, gave the maximum degree of criminality, while the minimum was shown by the more illiterate districts, North Wales, Essex, and Cornwall."[3]

It is obvious that no argument can carry weight if it is based simply on a crude comparison of different decades or different sections of the country with reference to the amount of illiteracy on the one hand and the amount of criminality on the other. The whole social situation underlying such differences in illiteracy may be responsible for the differences in criminality, the variations in illiteracy being merely side-products. Specifically, there are two conspicuous ways that this changing social situation might operate, both of which would tend to explain the apparent relationship mentioned above. In the first place, the same conditions which lead to better school opportunities are likely to involve a more complicated form of life, with more tensions, restrictions, and interferences of one individual with another, leading thus to a greater probability of at least the minor types of offenses. In the second place, the general social change is likely to be accompanied by the establishment of more rigid and more strictly enforced standards of conduct, so that what may be only deplored in one community may be a legal offense in another. These varying legal standards may well account for such differences in "criminality" as Lombroso cites between various sections of this

[2] See Lombroso, C. "Crime: Its Causes and Remedies." Chap. VIII. Trans. by H. P. Horton. Little, Brown & Co. 1911.
[3] *Op. cit.*, p. 106.

country, and which he naïvely accepts as proof that one section has more delinquency than another. The United States Census has pointed out very convincingly in such statements as the following that such an inference is untenable, and that the difference in apparent criminality must first be sought in a comparison of the laws and the provisions for law-enforcement of the several communities.

"In general it must be borne in mind that the number of commitments represents simply the number of violations of law which have been punished by imprisonment. A high ratio of commitments to population may, therefore, be indicative not so much of exceptional criminality and lawlessness as of exceptional efficiency on the part of the local authorities, the police, and the courts in following up infractions of the law, by detecting criminals and offenders and bringing them to trial. The ratio may thus reflect, in some degree, the public sentiment of the community as regards the punishment of crime and minor offenses."[4]

We may, therefore, disregard as quite unfounded Lombroso's fears regarding the dangers of education for criminals or prospective criminals—fears which he does not himself entirely dismiss with his "comforting assurance that education is not so fatal as it appears at first to be."[5] So foreign to the current acceptance in this country of the value of education is the point of view that is fearful of the influence of school training, that it seems a superfluity even to consider the proposition that education may tend to increase the amount of crime. We fear, however, that the present point of view on the matter is built on very little more adequate factual material than is its predecessor, but that this, like its predecessor, is mainly a matter of conviction. Reliance upon education as a deterrent from crime is in accord with the spirit of the times, and is doubtless the safest hypothesis to act upon, since, in the absence of evidence to the contrary, we believe that education is a desirable asset, whether it is a preventive of crime or not.

Goring's discussion of the problem,[6] though very cursory, has the merit of limiting itself to the actual data available. Considering first the relation to recidivism of what he designates as "formal" education, meaning thereby opportunity for instruction as represented by the kind of school attended and the age at leaving school, he reaches the following conclusions:

[4] United States Census, 1910, Volume on "Prisoners and Juvenile Delinquents," p. 19.
[5] *Op. cit.*, p. 108.
[6] *Op. cit.*, pp. 274-277.

"From the above differences of mean in relation to their probable errors, it would appear, firstly, that there is no significant relation between a convict's formal education, when a child, and the frequency of his subsequent convictions for crime, or that, if any relation there be, it is those who have received no school education who are the least frequently convicted; and, secondly, that convicts receiving the longest terms of imprisonment are those who have been industrial and reformatory school-boys, and that those receiving the shortest terms are those who have not been educated at any orthodox school. Our conclusion is that the kind of school-education they may have received has no traceable influence upon the subsequent careers of convicts; but that, since industrial and reformatory school-boys must be the pick of those with the greatest law-breaking proclivities, this accounts for the fact that convicts with the worst penal records consist of those who have passed through industrial and reformatory schools.

"With regard to age at leaving school, our conclusion is similar, and is based upon the partial correlation coefficients of age with penal record for constant intelligence. . . . This conclusion is that their age, on leaving school, has no appreciable influence upon the subsequent penal career of convicts."[7]

His conclusions regarding the significance of what he calls "effective" education are practically identical with the above. By effective education he means "the apparent profit derived from whatever formal education has been received," which he measures by "(1) the standard or form reached by the subjects on leaving school, and (2) the grade of education apportioned to each convict on his reception into prison by the school-master." With the second of these measures we shall not concern ourselves, since, as Goring points out, the effect of prison schools undoubtedly enters in here. Accordingly the prison experience itself is being measured to some extent. With regard to the relation of recidivism to the first-mentioned measure—grade attained on leaving school—he concludes, on the basis of his data (*op. cit.*, p. 276) that "with increasing number of convictions recorded against convicts, there is no significant change in the mean standard attained by them on leaving school." Before considering this point decisively established, however, he proceeds to eliminate the factor of intelligence, through the medium of partial correlations, making intelligence the constant factor. The partial correlation coefficient of school education with number of convictions per year, for constant

[7] *Op. cit.*, p. 275.

intelligence, is .0565±.0297; that of school education with fractions of year imprisoned, for constant intelligence, is .0632±.0297. It is evident that these small coefficients cannot be thought of as significant. Accordingly Goring concludes (*loc. cit.*, p. 276) "that the profit derived from school education exerts no influence upon the subsequent penal records of convicts."

LACK OF DATA ON EDUCATION FOR GENERAL POPULATION

The data offered by Goring are entirely convincing, as justifying such conclusions as he permits himself to draw. He leaves completely untouched, however, the question of how the "convict" group compares with the general adult population with regard to either "formal" or "effective" education. His reasons are doubtless the same as those that we shall have to offer: *viz.*, the lack of information regarding any random sample of the general population. Until we have such data regarding the educational background of adults, we shall not be able to make a pretense of answering the question as to whether the delinquent is differentiated from the average adult by either a deficit of schooling or an excess, or whether no difference at all can be demonstrated.

The fact remains, unfortunately, that for us, as for Goring and earlier investigators, the supplementary data are lacking which might make possible a solution of the problem. To any one familiar with the manifold recent studies of school systems and communities with special reference to problems of retardation and elimination, this may seem at first thought an unnecessarily pessimistic statement. Reference to such studies, however, will make clear the fact that they have been concerned entirely either with children actually in school, or with those leaving to go to work. These furnish no basis for estimating the educational status of the general adult population. Accordingly we shall be forced again into the position which we have had to take so frequently during the course of the present study, of finding it necessary to offer the facts regarding our group, without being able to draw any final conclusions because of the absence of the supplementary information about the total population. We shall follow our usual practice, however, of presenting the information which we have secured, in the hope that, at some future time, it may be of service in carrying through the necessary comparisons. Its present usefulness is largely confined to that of helping to describe our groups, and of furnishing a background for the interpretation of the educational status of an individual in the light of that of the whole delinquent group of which she is a part.

DISTINCTION BETWEEN EDUCATIONAL OPPORTUNITIES AND EDUCATIONAL ATTAINMENTS

We shall approach the educational problem from two quite different points of view, according as we think primarily of the educational *opportunities,* or of the educational *attainments* of these individuals. If we understand by educational opportunities genuine and not merely potential opportunities, it would appear that, if we could isolate this aspect of the total, we should have the best indication of the effect of "schooling" *per se.* This would be the angle of approach, for example, to the problem as to whether mere presence in school beyond the age of fourteen tends to be a deterrent of delinquency—a contention which may be urged entirely without reference to the question as to whether there is any important gain in educational *attainments* during these years. Any measure of educational achievement is complicated by the fact that achievement is to a marked degree a composite result of educational opportunity and the further factor of innate mental capacity. Accordingly, in measuring an individual's attainments, we may be measuring his mental capacity more than we are measuring the effect of general school training or the lack of it. In this chapter, therefore, we are quite certain to anticipate to some extent the discussion of the mental capacities of the women under consideration.

As we shall see, it will be impossible to distinguish satisfactorily between measures of opportunity and measures of attainment, and equally impossible to eliminate from either of these measures the effects of differences in mental capacity, in personality, and in emotional trends. We can, however, make a rough distinction on the basis of certain obvious implications of the data at hand.

Meaning by "opportunity" the amount and kind of schooling to which one was actually "exposed," and not simply the chance for such schooling, we should naturally consider under this head such facts as the kind of school attended, the regularity of attendance, the age at leaving school, and the total number of years in school. Only the first of the above factors, however,—kind of school attended—is in any thorough-going way independent of the characteristics of the person concerned. We should expect that the other three factors would be influenced by differences in mentality and in such traits as ambition, energy, and alertness, though probably not to the same degree that one's attainments are affected.

The best measure of school attainment for our purposes appears to be the school grade completed. Though comparisons with averages of the general community are out of the question, we can compare our data with the age-grade requirements set up by various school systems, taking into account the age of leaving school as the age which should determine the grade in the case of the delinquent women. We can also interpret the grade attainment with reference to the number of years actually spent in school, assuming that a year in school should net one grade completed.

Even without reference to these determining factors of age at leaving school, or of number of years in school, the grade attained has some descriptive value as an absolute measure of school accomplishment. In a general way, at least, the difference between having reached third grade, eighth grade, high school or college is significant of a difference in degree of academic education, entirely apart from the question as to whether the possibility of attaining one or another of these may not have been determined by the degree of mentality.

A still further means of measuring educational accomplishment is through a determination of the amount of the educational equipment which one has retained from her school experience. For this purpose we have made use of several varieties of educational tests which have recently been developed. The type of information furnished by these differs in two important ways from that afforded by school grade as an index of educational achievement. In the first place, it is more objective, since it is in no sense dependent on the subject's own statement of her attainment, as is the school grade for a large number of our cases where verification has proved impossible. In the second place, it affords an insight into the present educational working equipment of the individual, which may not be indicated adequately by the statement concerning the grade reached in school. Either of two influences may have been operative, tending in quite different directions. That is, the subject may have either dropped from the degree of ability represented by her last school grade, because of entire absence of practice, or she may have proceeded to reach a much higher level of accomplishment by virtue of her own initiative and ability stimulated by special demands of her environment. Whichever alteration occurs, the measure of present attainment is of considerable interest since it is the present individual that we are concerned with, at least in so far as we are planning for her institutional treatment or her later adjustments.

It is important, however, to recognize that the present status of educational attainments is likely to be even more closely associated with mental capacity than is the grade actually reached in school. The latter is subject to the various artificial factors operative to move all children through the schools at the same pace, provided differences in ability be not too striking. The amount retained from the school training and, still more, the additional amount built upon this should tend to differentiate more exactly the bright individual from the dull. In so far as this is true we are obviously measuring mentality by these educational tests, quite as much as we are measuring educational factors *per se*.

VERIFICATION OF SCHOOL RECORD

The general process of verification of records was explained in Chapter V. The most satisfactory means of verifying school records was by writing to the school and obtaining the individual's record card. To accomplish this necessitated, in the first place, having precise information regarding the school. It was not enough to know, for example, that the woman went to school in the Bronx or on the East Side, New York. The number and location of the school must also be obtained. In many cases, a woman was inaccurate in recalling these details, either purposely or because she had not thought of her school for many years. Accordingly it frequently required repeated efforts to obtain the desired information. In the second place, it was essential that the school in question should have the facts. In many smaller towns and country places there is no record-keeping system. Unless, then, the investigator could find some teacher who had known the woman when she was in school there was no way of verifying her statement. Even in New York City there was no systematic record-keeping until 1909. Accordingly, the record cards were usually incomplete for the earlier school years of our cases. With the women who had had their schooling in foreign countries there was practically no possibility of verification except through the statements of relatives.

With these conditions in mind, it is not surprising to find that verification was obtained for only about half of our total group. The wide differences in degree of verification of the various institutional groups may be indicated by the following figures showing percentages of verification:

Grade Finished: Percentage of Records Verified

Bedford	Auburn	Magdalen	Penitentiary	Workhouse	Probation	Total
77	38	72	27	14	42	46

It is evident that a particularly high degree of reliability attaches to the figures on Bedford and the Magdalen and that, on the other hand, the Workhouse figures amount to little more than the women's own unverified statements.

With a view to determining what difference, if any, was likely to exist between verified data and data based solely on the women's own statements, we computed the correlation of verified with unverified data on school grade for 207 cases and found the coefficient to be .85. The mean grade based on verified records was found to be 4.6, whereas the mean as given by the women's statements alone is 5.3. It is evident that the tendency is toward exaggeration, toward making a better impression. It must be remembered that the above figures are necessarily based simply on comparison of verified data with those original statements *on which additional information was later obtained.* Obviously, we can not compare the original statements with verified records where the latter were never obtained. It is, therefore, impossible to state whether the tendency to exaggerate holds to the same degree for the whole group. It might be assumed that those statements on the basis of which it was impossible ever to obtain a verified record would have shown an even greater discrepancy from the actual facts. Another factor, however, enters in since an appreciable portion of the unverifiable statements were those reporting little or no schooling, especially as given by the foreign group. To take this factor into account, we have compared the means, based on the original statements of all cases on whom we had *any* records, with the means, based on verified data of all cases on whom we had *verified* records, with the following results:

Mean School Grade Based on

Women's Statements	Verified Records
$4.88 \pm .135$	$4.63 \pm .178$
(437 cases)	(211 cases)

It is apparent, therefore, that the mean school grade as obtained from the women's statements alone is lower when we consider the entire group than when we consider that portion of the group whose records it was possible to verify (4.9 as against 5.3). In other words, the mean is actually lowered, as we assumed it might be, by the addition of the cases whose records were unverifiable. Even so, the mean based on women's statements alone is slightly higher than the mean based on verified records (4.9 as against 4.6).

By combining the verified data for all cases on whom this was available with the data based on original statements for the remainder of the group, we have the best available information on schooling for our group as a whole. This is the type of data used, therefore, throughout this chapter except in the few instances where we have confined the discussion to the verified data. From Table 87 we find that the mean grade based on the best available records for 447 cases is 4.58±.127, which is practically identical with the mean given by verified records alone on the 211 cases (4.63±.178). If we may assume that there was some degree of exaggeration in the additional 236 records which were based only on women's statements, it is evident that the true mean for the group would be slightly lower still. In other words, our data may be interpreted as probably giving, in all cases, a slightly higher mean value for school grade than the facts would warrant. On the other hand, they are lower by a slight but appreciable degree than data based on the women's statements alone. The latter point should be borne in mind when our data are compared with other data where there has been no verification.

EDUCATIONAL OPPORTUNITIES

(*a*) *Kind of School Attended*

Our first consideration under the head of educational opportunities is that of kind of school attended. (See Table 80.) While the various types of school doubtless represent, to some extent, differences in kind of opportunity, we have not attempted to evaluate these differences. The largest percentage in each group have had public school education. This is to be expected, since by far the largest portion of the *population* has been trained in the public schools. Bedford has the largest percentage of public school cases and Auburn the smallest, the other groups showing percentages almost identical with one another. The per cents from the parochial schools vary from 2.2 per cent in the Penitentiary to 16.2 per cent in Auburn. We see no explanation for so marked a variation of these two extremes, since both institutions are necessarily non-sectarian, both receive relatively older cases for the most part, and, moreover, in the two institutions the range of offenses is fairly similar. There is still more striking variation among the institutions regarding numbers educated entirely in foreign schools, Bedford having much the lowest per cent —3.1—and Auburn the largest—33.8. This difference appears mainly explicable in terms of the relative numbers of foreign cases in the various groups. (See Chapter VIII.) The data concerning foreign schools are of significance as showing that an appreciable number of women, in all groups except Bedford, have had all their schooling under markedly different social circumstances from those of the school systems of this country. Moreover, in the cases where attendance in foreign schools is reported, it is particularly likely to have been so brief and interrupted as to amount to little. The footnote to the table shows the numbers who have never attended school. It is noticeable that the institutions having the younger women have the fewest of such cases—Probation none, Magdalen 3, Bedford 4—indicating that, in this section of the country at least, complete absence of school training is not likely to be an important matter in the future.

TABLE 80

KIND OF SCHOOL ATTENDED*

Per Cent Distribution of Delinquent Women in Institutional Groups

Kind of School	Institutional Groups						Total
	Bedford	Auburn	Magdalen	Penitentiary	Workhouse	Probation	
Schools in U. S.							
Orphanage or Home	7.2	1.5	5.8	2.2	3.3	3.5	4.0
Parochial	6.2	16.2	4.3	2.2	8.7	11.8	8.0
Private	2.0	....	....	2.2	4.3	3.5	2.2
Public	77.3	47.1	63.8	64.0	62.0	62.4	63.6
Schools in Foreign Countries only	3.1	33.8	26.1	27.0	21.7	10.6	19.4
Schools in Foreign Countries and Public Schools in U.S.	4.1	1.5	....	2.2	....	8.2	2.8
Total	100.0	100.0	100.0	100.0	100.0	100.0	100.0
Number of cases	97	68	69	89	92	85	500

*The following numbers in the various groups never attended school: Bedford, 4; Auburn, 12; Magdalen, 3; Penitentiary, 15; Workhouse, 7; Total, 41.

(*b*) *Regularity of Attendance*

Of importance also in estimating the influence of schooling is information concerning regularity of attendance. Such information is peculiarly difficult to secure in the case of these older women, many of whom have only the vaguest of recollections as to their behavior with reference to the school situation. However, we have summarized in Table 81 the information available through school reports or parents' statements on this point. It is needless to point out that standards of judgment are far from uniform and that, accordingly, no careful comparisons can be made. We note that in each institutional group the largest percentage are described as having been "fair" in attendance, though a goodly number are referred to as "poor." The groups vary considerably in the per cents described as "very poor" but in general these numbers are low. Much lower still are the per cents to whom a record of "very good" attendance is attributed. It is of interest to note that the group is not so predominantly characterized by very poor school attendance as we might have anticipated. How they compare in this respect with an average group of adults we have no means of saying.

TABLE 81

ATTENDANCE IN SCHOOL

Per Cent Distribution of Delinquent Women in Institutional Groups

Attendance	Institutional Groups						Total
	Bedford	Auburn	Magdalen	Penitentiary	Workhouse	Probation	
Very poor	14.4	13.8	3.1	1.3	7.0	4.9	7.6
Poor	29.9	32.3	23.1	24.1	15.1	28.4	25.3
Fair	52.6	53.8	69.2	72.2	77.9	66.7	65.4
Very good	3.1	....	4.6	2.5	....	....	1.7
Total	100.0	100.0	100.0	100.0	100.0	100.0	100.0
Number of cases	97	65	65	79	86	81	473

(c) *Age at Leaving School*

We have indicated that both age at leaving school and number of years in school may be considered indices of amount of school opportunity. For comparisons of homogeneous communities, with definite and well-enforced standards regarding age at entering school and without influx of large numbers of children—especially foreign cases —who enter school late, the two measures may be used fairly interchangeably as measures of school contacts. The child who leaves school at fourteen years may *ipso facto* be thought of as having had less schooling than the one who leaves at sixteen, and more than the one who leaves at twelve. Where, however, the stationary conditions suggested above have not existed in a community the age of leaving school becomes a far more ambiguous measure of school opportunity than the figure which gives the actual time spent in school.

Nevertheless data on the age of leaving school can not be neglected, in the light of the importance attached to this factor in connection with the problems of compulsory education laws and of retardation. As a result of the interest in these directions during recent years we have before us numerous statements as to what should be the minimal standards of a modern community. These are higher than the actual records of even the more advanced communities, for the most part, and so can not be used as a means of comparing the delinquent group with the general population.

In the development of compulsory education and child labor laws there has been almost universal acceptance of the view that the age of fourteen is the lowest age at which dropping out of school should be tolerated. By most of those who deal directly with children leaving school to go to work this is considered too low a standard. We hear of the "wasted years" from fourteen to sixteen. In certain states the minimum age for leaving has been moved on to fifteen or sixteen, either absolutely or with some accompanying grade requirement. Thus in New York State, which concerns us most closely, the Compulsory Educational Law has required, since 1917, that in order to leave at fourteen years of age a child must have completed eighth grade; in order to leave at fifteen he must have completed sixth grade; if he has not completed sixth grade he may not leave school until he is sixteen.

(1) *Data on Institutional Groups and on Total.*—Table 82 shows the percentages leaving school at various ages, for the separate institutional groups and for the total. Women who never attended school are not included in this table, since it is obviously impossible to state their *age at leaving school.* The percentages of cases who never attended school may be obtained from Table 84. The age of leaving school as given is understood to be the nearest age. For example, any age falling between nine and a half and ten and a half is given as *ten.*

This custom has been followed at least where the age has been figured precisely from records. In cases where verbal statement has been relied upon, the informant may be assumed to have performed a rougher process of the same sort in turning the age into round numbers. In comparing the groups it is well to remember the discrepancies in chronological age between the Bedford, Magdalen and Probation groups on the one hand, and the Auburn, Penitentiary and Workhouse groups on the other. In each of the latter three there are considerable numbers of women who had their schooling at a time when compulsory education requirements concerning age at leaving school were less rigid than at present. (For the range of ages of the various groups see Table 31.)

TABLE 82*

AGE AT LEAVING SCHOOL

Per Cent Distribution of Delinquent Women in Institutional Groups

Age at Leaving School	Institutional Groups						Total
	Bedford	Auburn	Magdalen	Penitentiary	Workhouse	Probation	
7	....	3.1	....	....	....	....	0.4
8	....	....	1.5	....	....	....	0.2
9	1.0	3.1	2.9	1.2	1.2	....	1.5
10	....	9.4	2.9	3.7	2.4	....	2.7
11	2.1	7.8	4.4	3.7	3.5	2.4	3.8
12	7.3	10.9	7.3	8.7	17.6	2.4	9.0
13	7.3	18.8	11.6	18.5	11.8	18.1	14.0
14	27.1	20.3	30.4	25.9	15.3	35.0	25.7
15	29.2	10.9	24.6	16.1	28.2	26.5	23.2
16	20.8	7.8	13.0	11.1	8.2	7.2	11.7
17	2.1	4.7	....	6.2	5.9	6.0	4.2
18	2.1	1.6	1.5	....	3.5	2.4	1.9
19	1.0	1.6	....	4.9	1.2	....	1.5
20	....	....	....	....	1.2	....	0.2
Total	100.0	100.0	100.0	100.0	100.0	100.0	100.0
Number of cases	96	64	69	81	85	83	478
Mean	14.57	13.16	13.83	14.14	14.17	14.39	14.10
σ_m	±.158	±.304	±.224	±.226	±.223	±.148	±.088
σ	1.55	2.43	1.87	2.04	2.05	1.35	1.93
σ_σ	±.112	±.215	±.159	±.160	±.157	±.105	±.062

*This table includes only those cases who have attended school for at least a part of one year.

Referring to the table it may be noted that all the groups show an appreciable number who left school before they were fourteen; in other words, before the age which has now practically universal acceptance in this country as the minimum age at which dropping out of school should be allowed. For the total group the percentage who left before fourteen is 31.6, or approximately one-third of the group who actually attended school. (Reference to Table 84 shows that 8.8 per cent of the total group had never attended school at all.) For the three groups made up of younger women the percentages leaving school before fourteen are as follows: Bedford 17.7 per cent, Magdalen 30.6 per cent, and Probation 22.9 per cent. The relatively large percentage which appears for the Magdalen is shown by reference to the data to be due mainly to the large percentage of foreign cases in this group. The three groups which contain considerable numbers of older women give the following percentages: Auburn 53.1, Penitentiary 35.8, Workhouse 36.5. With reference to the very high percentage shown for Auburn it may be noted that there are not only many older women here but also large numbers of foreigners and a fair number of women from isolated country districts with poor school facilities. Table 82 shows the mean age at leaving school for the total group to be 14.1 years: for the various institutional groups the means range from 13.16 for Auburn to 14.57 years for Bedford.

(2) *Comparative Data on Non-Delinquent Groups.*—The foregoing figures are sufficient to show that the group of delinquent women fail to meet the demands of present-day public opinion regarding minimum age for leaving school. Whether they fall below the actual standards of the adult community, as represented by the facts of their school records, we have no means of knowing. The establishing of the facts regarding the ages of elimination of children dropping out of school within recent periods of time has not proved a simple problem. With the merits of the controversy centering about this point we can not here concern ourselves.[8] There has been agreement as to the fact that the source of the difficulty lies in the lack of facts regarding individual school histories and the necessity of making inferences from records of school attendance, after correcting for numerous changing conditions, such as death-rate and increase of population. No one has had the temerity, apparently, to

[8] See especially Thorndike, E. L. "The Elimination of Pupils from School." Bulletin No. 4, 1907. Whole No. 379. Department of the Interior, Bureau of Education.

Ayres, L. P. "Laggards in Our Schools," 1909.

attempt to estimate the ages of elimination for the general adult population. Accordingly our only available comparison is that with the disputed figures representing the estimates of the ages of elimination of children during fairly recent periods. It will be remembered that these figures vary not only with the method of estimating, but with the character of the communities considered as well.

We may consider the following figures representative of estimates which have received serious consideration:

(1) Thorndike's estimate of the numbers remaining in school at the various ages, for every hundred children who were in school at eight years of age, for cities of 25,000 or over in 1900. (*Op. cit.*, p. 23.)

Thorndike's figures, reversed to show percentages leaving at given ages, rather than those remaining,[9] are as follows:

Age at leaving school	8	9	10	11	12	13	14	15	16	17	18 or over.
Percentages leaving	0	0	2	1	9	18	23	17	13.5	7.9	8.6

(2) Ayres' figures on decline in attendance, summarized for 58 cities, assuming a stationary population. (*Op. cit.*, Table 11, p. 28 and Table 12, p. 30.)

Ayre's figures taken from Table 12 and expressed as percentages leaving school at given ages are as follows:

Age at leaving school	11	12	13	14	15	16 or over
Percentages leaving	.2	9.8	30	35	17	8

(3) Ayres' figures on the estimated ages of elimination for Cleveland, Ohio.[10] While these are more sectional in their interest than are the figures from the other groups, they have an advantage for that reason, in representing a definite community and not a composite of several. It should be remembered, however, that it represents a decidedly high-grade standard, as compared with the country as a whole, since the data are recent and should show the influence of the present compulsory education law of Ohio, which requires that boys remain in school until fifteen and girls until sixteen. (We are not concerned

[9] In reversing the figures, offered by Thorndike and by Ayres, our procedure has been as follows: If a given per cent. are indicated as remaining in school *till* a given age, it is assumed that the difference between this and 100 per cent had left *before* this age. For example, if 100 per cent were retained until ten years and 98 per cent until eleven, we infer that 2 per cent left school at ten years, *i. e.*, during the period that they were counted ten years old."

[10] Ayres, L. P. "Child Accounting in the Public Schools." *Cleveland Education Survey*, 1915, p. 28 and p. 34, table 4.

here with the evidence which the figures offer to the effect that the law is by no means adequately enforced.)

The figures for Cleveland as offered by Ayres are as follows:

Age at leaving school	12	13	14	15	16	17	18	19	20 or over.
Percentages leaving.......	3	14	30	20	12	9	8	3	1

The three estimates presented above evidently offer very different standards of comparison. Thus it appears by Thorndike's estimate that 30 per cent leave school before fourteen, by Ayres' estimate for fifty-eight cities that 40 per cent leave before this age, and by Ayres' estimate for Cleveland that 17 per cent drop out before fourteen. In the light of the discrepancies and disagreements we can not feel that the figures are very convincing. If we take them at their face value our delinquent groups, with the exception of Auburn, do not show up badly, except in comparison with the Cleveland data. Even in this comparison the Bedford group appears favorably, with only 17.7 per cent leaving before fourteen.

In the absence of more conclusive data we are forced to consider the relationship of the delinquent women to the remainder of the population, with respect to age at leaving school, an open question. The implications of the data before us are to the effect that, while the delinquent women have not met the standards of present opinion regarding the minimal age for leaving school, they are probably not seriously behind the population as a whole in this respect. All the arguments which apply to the population as a whole, to show the harmfulness and loss involved in a high rate of elimination in the earlier years, apply also to the delinquent group. But in the absence of a clear distinction between the delinquent women and the general population we lack evidence to show that an early age of leaving school is one of the determinants of delinquency.

(3) *Relationship Between Age at Leaving School and Age at First Conviction.*—Turning from comparison of the delinquent group with other groups to consideration of relationships within the delinquent group, special interest attaches to the relationship between age at leaving school and age of first conviction. It would appear quite possible that an early age of leaving school might be associated with an early age of first conviction. This comparison is shown in Table 83 for those of our total group who have actually attended school at some time. Inspection of the table fails to show any striking relationship. The coefficient of correlation is $-.03 \pm .046$, indicative of entire absence

of relationship. The correlation ratios were computed and found to be $.25 \pm .043$ and $.21 \pm .044$ respectively. Even this slight evidence of relationship can not, howeer, be taken at its face value because of the lack of consistent trend in the lines of means, at least in case of the ratio of age at leaving school on age of first conviction. In the case of the ratio of age at first conviction on age at leaving school, reference to the means given in the extreme right-hand column of the table shows the suggestion of a curious relationship, to the effect that those who left school at ages not far from the average—especially the ages from 13 to 16—tend to have been convicted at slightly earlier ages than either those who left school very young or who remained in school to ages considerably above the average. It is not surprising to find the tendency toward later first conviction with later age at leaving school. Aside from any question of increased advantage to the individual, accruing from longer school contacts, there is a tendency toward setting up a lower limit here. That is, except in case of the early juvenile convictions, a conviction is very likely to interrupt and thereby terminate the school career. Accordingly, the continuance in school beyond the age of sixteen or seventeen years is likely to be somewhat symptomatic of the fact that such interruption has not occurred. Examination of the table suggests the operation of this tendency. Reasons for the delayed age of first conviction of those who left school very early are not apparent from the table. Consideration of the facts regarding the foreign members of the group affords, however, a clue. It has been shown (see pp. 196-197) that these cases had a later average age of first conviction than the native-born. It is also known that their educational opportunities have been much slighter (see p. 265). Reference to our records shows that the foreign-born form the large majority of the group who left school earlier than thirteen. This factor, therefore, evidently accounts for the negative trend in the lower portion of the curve. In view of the slightness of the relationship indicated between age at leaving school and age at first conviction, and on consideration of the complication of the situation by other factors, it is apparent that we can offer no evidence to show that age at leaving school has operated, either positively or negatively, as a determinant of the age at first conviction.

We shall defer until our consideration of grade attainments the discussion of age at leaving school in relation to grade, which involves the problem of retardation.

TABLE 83 *

Correlation between Age at First Conviction and Age at Leaving School

Total Group

Age at Leaving School	Age at First Conviction: 6 to 9	9 to 12	12 to 15	15 to 18	18 to 21	21 to 24	24 to 27	27 to 30	30 to 33	33 to 36	36 to 39	39 to 42	42 to 45	45 to 48	48 to 51	51 to 54	54 to 57	57 to 60	60 to 63	Totals	Means (Age at First Conviction)
20									1											1	
19						2	2				1				1			1		7	30.9
18					1	2		2	2	1				1						9	
17				1	3	2	5	3	1	1	1	1	1						1	20	28.7
16			2	11	9	10	7	1	4	3	2	2	1	3		1				56	25.3
15			3	24	22	22	11	8	6	6	1	3	1		1	2	1			111	23.6
14	1		2	23	30	15	20	11	6	5	3	2	2		1		1	1		123	23.6
13		1	3	7	10	9	12	6	9	2	2	4	1		1					67	25.1
12		1		3	6	7	4	4	3	3	3	4	3	1				1		43	26.8
11		1			1	6	1	3	1	3	1	1								18	26.4
10			1			2	1	2		2	3	1	1							13	30.7
9						1	2	1	1	1	1									7	
8								1												1	27.5
7						1	1													2	
Totals	1	3	11	69	82	79	66	42	34	27	18	18	10	5	4	3	2	3	1	478	25.33
Means (Age at Leaving School)	13.6			14.4		14.1		13.9		13.4		13.5		15.3						14.096	

Age at first conviction: Mean = 25.33 σ = 8.90
Age at leaving school: Mean = 14.096 σ = 1.932

Coefficient of correlation: r = —.03 ± .046

Correlation ratios: Age at first conviction on age at leaving school, η = .25 ± .043 Blakeman's Criterion = 4.1

Age at leaving school on age at first conviction, η = .21 ± .044 Blakeman's Criterion = 3.4

* This table includes only those cases who have attended school for at least a part of one year.

(*d*) *Number of Years in School*

(1) *Data on Total Delinquent Group and on Institutional Sub-Groups.*—Table 84 presents data regarding number of years in school by institutional groups, the distribution of which are shown graphically in Chart XV. These distributions include, in all cases, those women who never attended school as well as those who were in school for varying periods.

TABLE 84

NUMBER OF YEARS IN SCHOOL

Per Cent Distribution of Delinquent Women in Institutional Groups

Number of Years	Institutional Groups						Total
	Bedford	Auburn	Magdalen	Penitentiary	Workhouse	Probation	
0	4.0	16.0	4.2	17.6	10.3	....	8.8
1	2.0	5.3	4.2	....	3.5	....	2.4
2	1.0	2.7	1.4	4.4	3.5	2.6	2.6
3	3.0	5.3	1.4	4.4.	2.3	2.6	3.2
4	3.0	8.0	2.8	5.5	5.8	5.1	5.0
5	5.1	4.0	9.9	3.3	6.9	5.1	5.6
6	7.1	10.7	11.3	11.0	13.8	12.8	11.0
7	16.2	26.7	16.9	13.2	12.6	25.6	18.2
8	28.3	5.3	25.4	16.5	14.9	24.4	19.4
9	15.2	5.3	12.7	11.0	13.8	11.5	11.8
10	9.1	6.7	4.2	5.5	5.8	3.9	6.0
11	2.0	2.7	5.6	4.4	3.5	6.4	4.0
12	3.0	1.3	....	2.2	3.5	....	1.8
13	1.0	....	....	....	....	....	.2
14	....	....	....	1.1	....	....	.2
Total	100.0	100.0	100.0	100.0	100.0	100.0	100.0
Number of cases	99	75	71	91	87	78	501
Mean	7.31	5.32	6.79	5.95	6.26	7.23	6.50
σ_m	±.267	±.384	±.312	±.377	±.348	±.223	±.136
σ	2.65	3.33	2.63	3.60	3.25	1.97	3.052
σ_σ	±.189	±.272	±.221	±.267	±.246	±.158	±.096

All groups show a wide range of years spent in school. In the total group this extends from no years to fourteen years. The dispersion as measured by the standard deviation is appreciably higher for the three groups containing older women. The average time spent in school for the total group is 6.5 years. The three groups containing on the whole younger women show higher average periods of attendance than do the other three, though the dividing lines are not sharp. Bedford and Probation show the highest average time spent in school (7.31 and 7.23 years respectively) and Auburn the lowest (5.32 years). The factors cited as explanatory of the low average age of leaving school of the Auburn women apply also here.

The numbers who have never been to school vary from 0 per cent for the Probation group to 17.6 per cent for the Penitentiary women. Of the total group 8.8 per cent had never attended school. Again the three groups of younger women make a much better showing than do the other three.

(2) *Data on Groups Classified by Nativity and Color.*—Comparison by nativity and color, rendered possible by Table 85, shows that the foreign born portion of the group contributes by far the largest number of those very deficient in school opportunity as measured by number of years in school. Practically one-fourth (24.5 per cent) have had no schooling, and the mean number of years in school is only 4.92. The group which falls next with respect to lack of schooling, the native colored, is separated from the foreign born by a wide gap. They show 4.7 per cent with no schooling, and a mean number of years in school of 6.42. When these two elements—the foreign-born and the negro—are eliminated from the total, we find

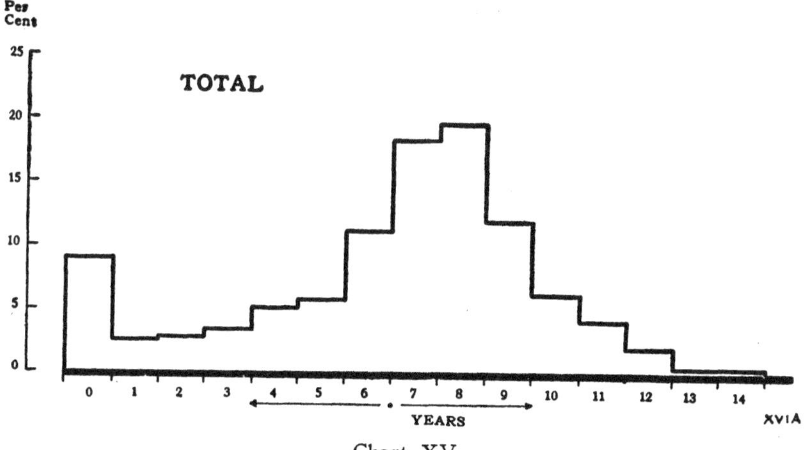

Chart XV
Number of Years in School
Per cent distribution by institutional groups.

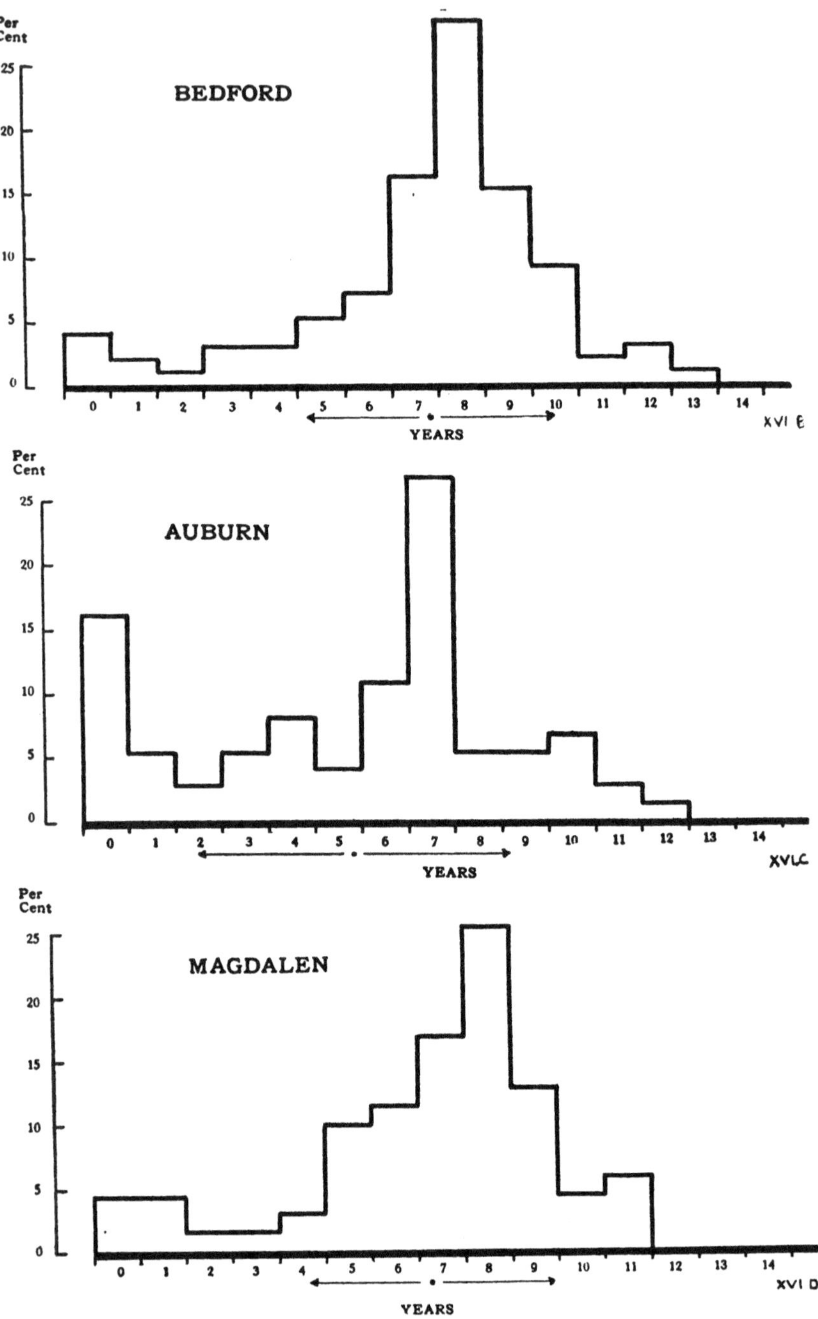

Chart XV (Continued)
Number of Years in School
Per cent distribution by institutional groups.

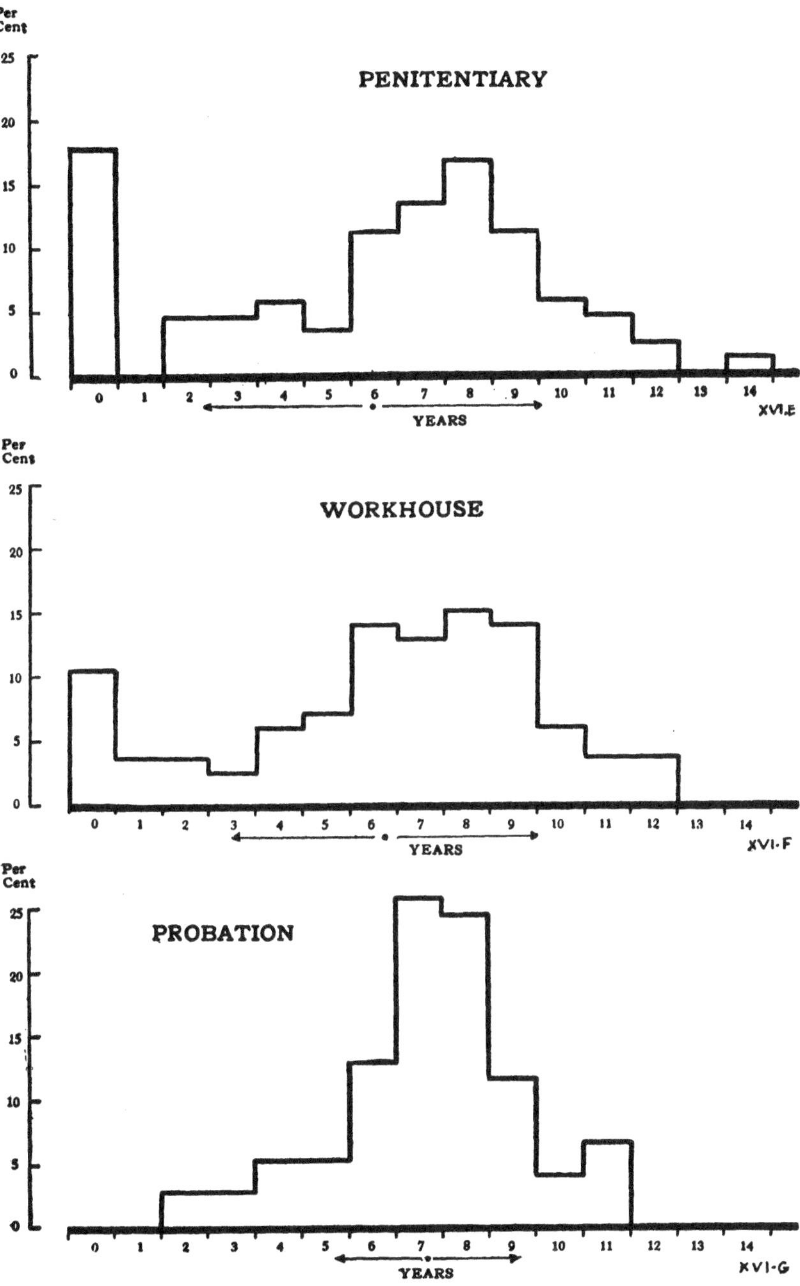

Chart XV (Continued)
Number of Years in School
Per cent distribution by institutional groups.

the native-white making a far more satisfactory showing. Only 0.8 per cent show no record of school attendance, and the mean number of years in school is 7.47—a mean which is almost high enough to permit of an average record of graduation from elementary school, assuming normal progress. We shall see however that the record falls decidedly short of this possibility.

TABLE 85

NUMBER OF YEARS IN SCHOOL

Per Cent Distribution of Delinquent Women Classified by Nativity and Color

Years in School	Nativity and Color				Total
	Total Foreign Born	Total Native Born	Native White	Native Colored	
0	24.5	1.7	.8	4.7	8.8
1	5.2	1.2	.4	3.5	2.4
2	1.9	2.9	.8	9.3	2.6
3	5.8	2.0	1.9	2.3	3.2
4	5.2	4.9	4.2	7.0	5.0
5	6.5	5.2	3.8	9.3	5.6
6	5.8	13.3	14.2	10.5	11.0
7	14.8	19.7	21.2	15.1	18.2
8	13.5	22.0	25.0	12.8	19.4
9	8.4	13.3	15.8	5.8	11.8
10	4.5	6.6	5.8	9.3	6.0
11	1.9	4.9	4.6	5.8	4.0
12	1.9	1.7	1.2	3.5	1.8
13	....	.3	.4	....	.2
14	....	.3	....	1.2	.2
Total	100.0	100.0	100.0	100.0	100.0
Number of cases	155	346	260	86	501
Mean	4.92	7.21	7.47	6.42	6.50
σ_m	±.294	±.130	±.125	±.351	±.136
σ	3.66	2.42	2.01	3.25	3.05
σ_σ	±.208	±.092	±.088	±.248	±.096

(3) *Impossibility of Comparison with General Population.*—In spite of the fact that we attach more importance to figures showing years in school than to those showing age at leaving, as measures of *amount* of schooling, the former are even less serviceable than the latter for purposes of comparison with other groups. Even estimates are lacking on this point. We are therefore forced to refrain from

TABLE 86

Correlation between Number of Previous Convictions and Number of Years in School

Total Group

Number of Years in School	Number of Previous Convictions: 0	1	2	3	4	5	6	7	8	9	10	11	12	13	14	15	16	17	18	19	20	21	22	23	Totals	Means (Number of Previous Convictions)
14			1																						1	
13		2																							2	1.3
12	3	3	1	1	1																				9	
11	9	5	1	1		2																			18	1.1
10	15	8	3	3			1																		30	1.0
9	24	17	5	4	2	2		2			1	1							1						59	1.9
8	41	25	8	7	3	3	2	4		1	1			1	1										97	1.8
7	42	20	12	4	5	2	1		1			1							1						89	1.5
6	26	13	7	3	1		2			2											1				55	1.6
5	10	8	5		2	1			1															1	28	2.2
4	9	7	4	3							1		1												25	1.8
3	9	2	1	2		1		1																	16	1.4
2	5	2	2	1		2	1																		13	1.9
1	4	1	3	3	1																				12	1.7
0	22	8	4	3		1			1	1					1										41	1.5
Totals	219	121	57	35	15	14	7	7	3	4	3	2	1	1	2	0	0	0	2	0	1	0	0	1	495	1.64
Means (Number of Years in School)	6.4	7.0	6.2	6.1	7.1	6.8			5.8																	6.53

Number of previous convictions: Mean = 1.64 σ = 2.94
Number of years in school: Mean = 6.53 σ = 3.03

Coefficient of correlation: r = .02 ± .045

Correlation ratios: Number of years in school on number of previous convictions, η = .11 ± .044 Blakeman's Criterion = 1.8
Number of previous convictions on number of years in school, η = .31 ± .041 Blakeman's Criterion = 5.1

any attempt to compare our groups with the general population with respect to this factor. We suspect that the general population would not show an appreciably better record in this respect.

Consideration of the relationship between years in school and grade attainment will be deferred until we have presented the data with regard to grade completed.

(4) *Relationship between Years in School and Number of Convictions.*—We are, however, interested to know whether we can discover any relationship between educational opportunity as indicated by years in school and extent of criminal record as shown by the number of convictions. Table 86 presents the data on this relationship. The coefficient of correlation is practically zero. The ratio of number of years in school on number of previous convictions (.11 ± .044) would indicate only the slightest of relationships at best. The ratio of number of previous convictions on years in school is, however, large enough (.31 ± .041) to call for careful inspection of the table to discover whether there is actually an observable tendency here. Referring to the values of the mean number of convictions for various periods of school attendance shown in the extreme right-hand column of the table, we note such oscillation of the various means about the mean of the whole group that it is impossible to discover the presence of any one tendency, other than an apparent trend toward a lower average number of convictions for those in the highest groups for length of schooling.

EDUCATIONAL ATTAINMENTS

(*a*) *Grade Finished*

In Tables 87 to 91 we present the main facts regarding grade attainment for the groups, classified by institution and by nativity and race. In considering these tables it is important to note that our figures refer always to grade *finished.* We have thus avoided the necessity of stating that one was in fifth grade, for example, merely because she had finished fourth, when possibly she had not returned the following year. Our usage, however, fails to take complete account of the facts, since in the reverse case we still refer to the woman as having completed only fourth grade, even though she may have spent part of the year in fifth. The distinction is not important and should be borne in mind merely to avoid misinterpretation in comparison of our data with other figures which are usually expressed as grade *reached.* For this comparison an additional year of credit

TABLE 87

GRADE FINISHED IN SCHOOL

Per Cent Distribution of Delinquent Women in Institutional Groups

Grade Finished	Institutional Groups						Total
	Bedford	Auburn	Magdalen	Penitentiary	Workhouse	Probation	
None*	9.2	25.0	6.7	15.1	12.7	....	11.4
1	4.1	5.9	1.7	3.5	....	....	2.7
2	12.2	10.3	6.7	2.3	11.1	5.6	8.1
3	19.4	8.8	3.3	14.0	7.9	9.7	11.4
4	14.3	8.8	23.3	17.4	14.3	9.7	14.5
5	15.3	13.2	18.3	9.3	11.1	18.1	14.1
6	10.2	5.9	18.3	12.8	7.9	23.6	13.0
7	2.0	8.8	8.3	3.5	22.2	18.1	9.6
8	11.2	8.8	10.0	14.0	12.7	9.7	11.2
1st Year High School	1.0	2.9	1.7	3.5	....	1.4	1.8
2nd " " "	....	....	....	1.2	....	2.8	.7
3rd " " "	....	....	....	....	....	....	....
4th " " "	1.0	1.5	1.7	3.5	....	1.4	1.6
Total	100.0	100.0	100.0	100.0	100.0	100.0	100.0
Number of cases	98	68	60	86	63	72	447
Mean	4.07	3.66	4.93	4.64	4.64	5.72	4.58
σ_m	±.247	±.367	±.300	±.328	±.324	±.233	±.127
σ	2.44	3.03	2.32	3.04	2.57	1.97	2.68
σ_σ	±.174	±.260	±.212	±.232	±.229	±.165	±.090

*Includes those who have never been in school and those who have attended but never finished first grade.

should be given to our groups. Thus, for example, a mean *grade finished* of 4.58 would signify a mean *grade reached* of 5.58.

(1) *Data on Institutional Groups and on Total.*—Chart XVI presents graphically the distributions shown in Table 87. Marked differences in distribution for the various groups appear, which it would be unprofitable to discuss in detail. Numerous factors such as the percentage of foreign cases, the range of age of the group, the mentality of the group and the operation of the compulsory education law, have doubtless operated together to produce certain curious irregularities in form.

The relatively high percentages, in Auburn, the Penitentiary, and the Workhouse, who never completed even the first grade reflect primarily the situation regarding time spent in school, thus becoming mainly measures of school opportunity. Such cases we note predominate in the groups having the largest proportion of foreign cases and of older women.

At the other extreme we find in all the groups an extremely small proportion who even entered high school and none who entered college. Occasionally a woman claimed to have been a college graduate but investigation never confirmed her statement on this point. The complete absence of women who had had college and professional training is at least interesting in view of the fact that our group includes all types of offenders—those guilty of such crimes as forgery, swindling and homicide, as well as of the minor social offenses. One wishing to hold a brief for the higher education of women might be inclined to point to these figures with some satisfaction as indicating that advanced education afforded a woman such resources in the way of training and personality that she was less subject to the allurements of a criminal career than her less educated sister, or that, at the very least, the figures should be interpreted as showing that the college and professional training fails to attract women of the delinquent or criminal "types." A more cynical view would represent the absence of college and professional women from our groups as indicative of nothing more than their probable greater skill in escaping detection when they have committed crimes or minor offenses. Obviously we lack the

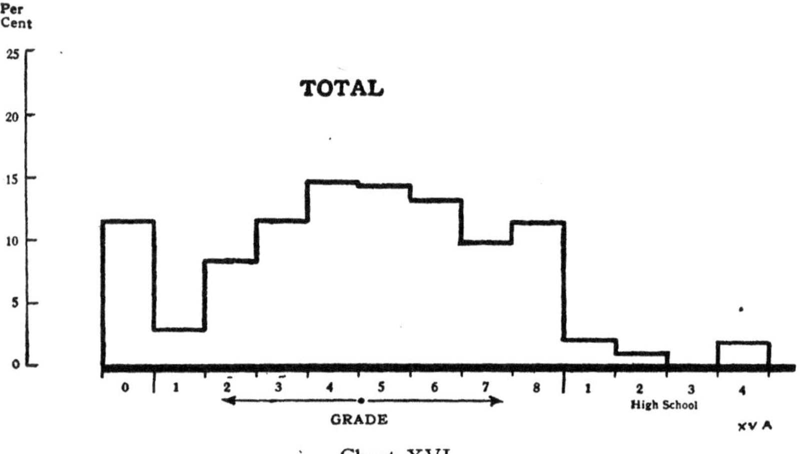

Chart XVI

Grade Finished

Per cent distribution by institutional groups.

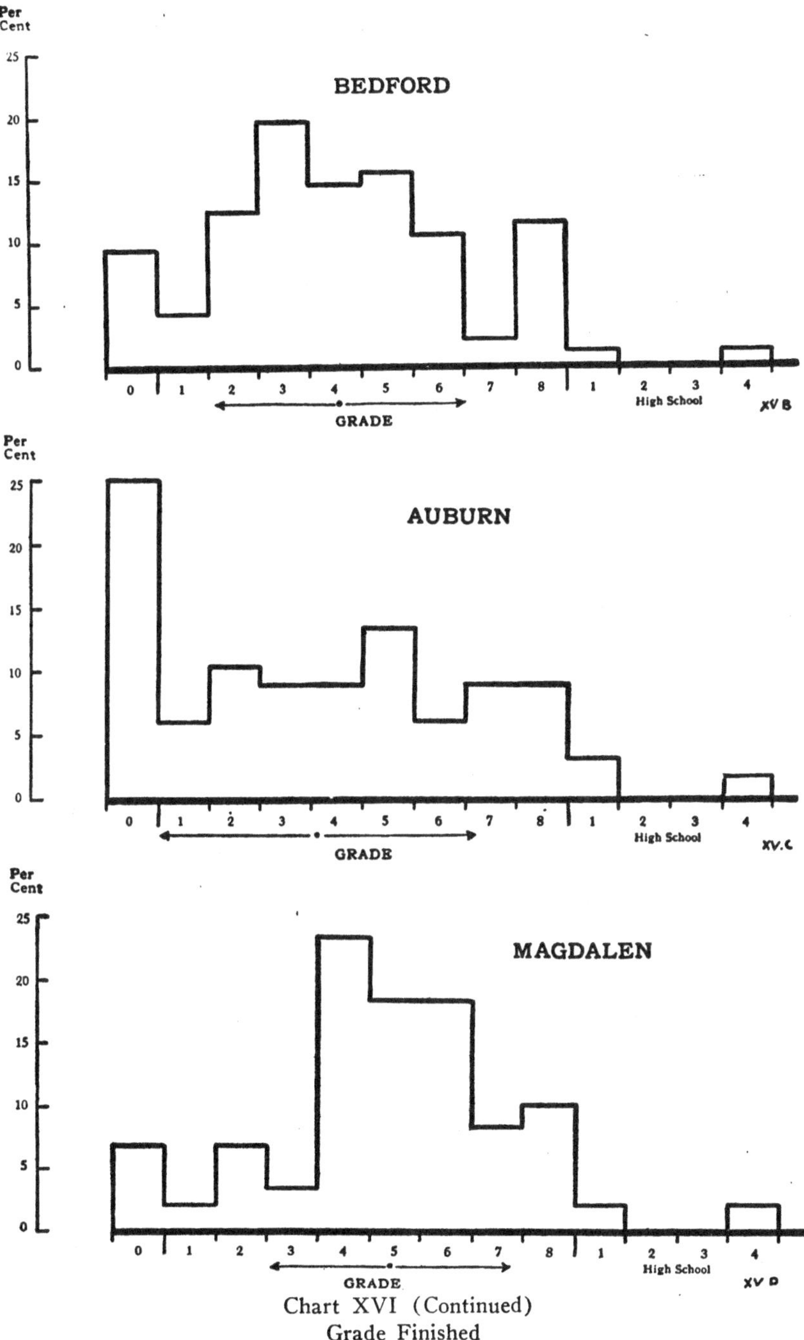

Chart XVI (Continued)
Grade Finished
Per cent distribution by institutional groups

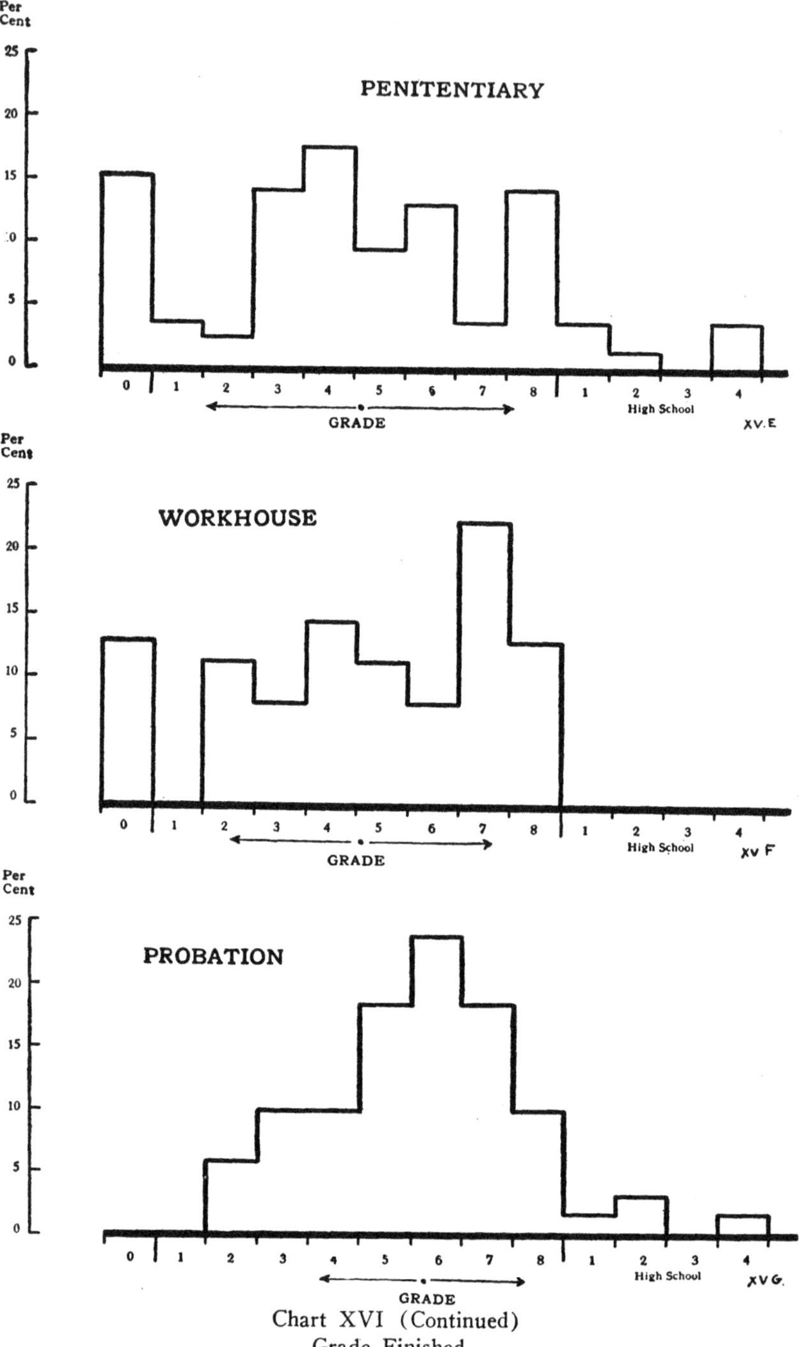

Chart XVI (Continued)
Grade Finished
Per cent distribution by institutional groups.

data which would enable us to pass judgment on the merits of these divergent interpretations.

In so far as comparison of institutional groups with respect to school grade is attempted it must be borne in mind that the reliability of the information on this point is particularly affected by the differences in completeness of verification among the various groups. We have seen that the percentage of cases on whom we have verified records regarding grade varies from 14 per cent for the Workhouse to 77 per cent for Bedford, and that the tendency of the women is, as one would expect, to better the record in their own accounts. With this qualification in mind it seems unsafe to give weight to the relatively slight differences in the constants for these groups as shown in Table 87. The Workhouse figures should undoubtedly be taken with several grains of salt. The relatively high rating for the Probation group, however, would seem sufficient to indicate a genuine superiority of this group. On the other hand, there seems no reason to question the significance of the low figure for Auburn as indicating an especially poor record of school attainment.

It is noteworthy that no group shows a record of an average attainment equal to completion of sixth grade, which we have seen is now the minimum attainment which permits a child to leave school before sixteen in New York State. The average attainment for the group as a whole is 4.6 grades.

(2) *Data on Groups Classified by Nativity and Color.*—The comparison of grade distributions for the different nativity and color groups has more reliability than the foregoing comparison by institutional groups, since any correction for lack of verification would tend to exaggerate rather than to reduce the difference. Referring to the means for these groups—Table 88—we note that the native born have a decidedly higher average than the foreign born and that among the native born the native white are appreciably higher than the colored. Tables 89 to 91 show that we are justified in considering all these differences valid. Even the native white group, however, shows only an average of 5.2 grades completed.

(3) *Relationship of Grade to Age Distinctions.*—We have seen that for both age at leaving school and number of years in school there was a sharp distinction between the three institutional groups having a higher average age and the three having a lower average, in favor of the latter. We should expect to find the same sort of thing with regard to grade. It does not appear, however, with any degree of definiteness.

TABLE 88

GRADE FINISHED

Per Cent Distribution of Delinquent Women Classified by Nativity and Color

Grade Finished	Nativity and Color				Total
	Total Foreign Born	Total Native Born	Native White	Native Colored	
None*	34.2	3.3	2.4	6.0	11.4
1	3.4	2.4	2.0	3.6	2.7
2	4.3	9.4	8.1	13.3	8.1
3	8.5	12.4	11.7	14.5	11.4
4	10.3	16.1	16.2	15.7	14.5
5	11.1	15.2	15.4	14.5	14.1
6	6.8	15.2	16.2	12.0	13.0
7	5.1	11.2	10.5	13.3	9.6
8	10.3	11.5	13.8	4.8	11.2
1st Year High School	3.4	1.2	.8	2.4	1.8
2nd " " "	....	.9	1.2	....	.7
4th " " "	2.6	1.2	1.6	....	1.6
Total	100.0	100.0	100.0	100.0	100.0
Number of cases	117	330	247	83	447
Mean	3.55	4.95	5.15	4.34	4.58
σ_m	±.304	±.128	±.147	±.247	±.127
σ	3.29	2.32	2.31	2.25	2.68
σ_σ	±.215	±.090	±.104	±.174	±.090

*Includes those who have never been in school and those who have attended but never finished first grade.

Bedford, in fact, shows a lower mean than the Penitentiary and the Workhouse, and the latter institutions are not greatly inferior to the Magdalen. Because of the differences in the extent of verification, as we have seen, these distinctions can not be stressed as important. We have, therefore, examined the relationship between grade and age directly. The correlation coefficient for age with grade for 449 cases was found to be —.124 ± .046, indicating a slight tendency toward lower school grade with increasing age. In order to discover whether there is a clear-cut tendency for the older women, for example, the women over 35, to have a poorer record of school attainment than the younger women, we have obtained the means for grade completed for the women over 35 and for the women under 35. Since the amount of verification is slight in the case of the older women, we have used the data based on the women's state-

TABLE 89

TOTAL FOREIGN BORN AND TOTAL NATIVE BORN

Comparison of the Means and Standard Deviations of the Grade Finished for Total Foreign Born and Total Native Born of Total Group

	Total Foreign Born	Total Native Born	Difference	$\frac{d}{\sigma_d}$	Chances that real difference does not exist are 1 in:
Mean	3.55	4.95	−1.40	4.24	89,286
σ_m	±.304	±.128			
σ	3.29	2.32	.97	4.16	62,893
σ_σ	±.215	±.090			
Cases	117	330			

ments entirely for this comparison. The mean grade for the women over 35 was found to be 5.11 ± .409 and that for the women under 35, 6.04 ± .137. There is, therefore, an obvious difference, amounting almost to one grade, between the averages for the older and the younger women. We are justified in assuming the validity of this difference since it amounts to more than twice the standard deviation of the difference.

Since so genuine a difference appears to exist between these groups distinguished in point of age, it has seemed desirable to

TABLE 90

NATIVE WHITE AND NATIVE COLORED

Comparison of the Means and Standard Deviations of the Grade Finished for Native White and Native Colored of Total Group

	Native White	Native Colored	Difference	$\frac{d}{\sigma_d}$	Chances that real difference does not exist are 1 in:
Mean	5.15	4.34	.81	2.83	435
σ_m	±.147	±.247			
σ	2.31	2.25	.06	.30	3
σ_σ	±.104	±.174			
Cases	247	83			

TABLE 91

TOTAL FOREIGN BORN AND NATIVE WHITE

Comparison of the Means and Standard Deviations of the Grade Finished for Total Foreign Born and Native White of Total Group

	Total Foreign Born	Native White	Difference	$\frac{d}{\sigma_d}$	Chances that real difference does not exist are 1 in:
Mean	3.55	5.15	−1.60	4.75	8
σ_m	±.304	±.147			
σ	3.29	2.31	.98	4.11	50,505
σ_σ	±.215	±.104			
Cases	117	247			

compute the constants for the group under 35 for use in comparison with any outside groups whose range of ages does not extend beyond this age. We have in mind, for example, especially the data which may be forthcoming regarding army recruits whose ages are predominantly lower than this. The figures for the delinquent women under 35 years of age are as follows:

	Grade Finished Based on Women's Statements	Verified Data
Mean	6.04 ± .137	5.59 ± .174
σ	2.60 ± .097	3.56 ± .289
Number of Cases	361	197

(4) *Relationship of Grade to Age at Leaving School.*—In view of the dearth of information regarding the educational status of the general adult population, it is particularly important to search our own data for internal evidences as to the normality of school progress. Two such lines of evidence are of particular interest, namely, the comparison of grade attainment with age at leaving school and with the number of years in school.

The former of these comparisons is closely related to the age-grade tables with which we have become so familiar in all recent discussions of retardation. Since, however, our women are all past the school period, it becomes necessary to substitute age at leaving school for actual age. Each school report in which such figures are discussed sets up some standard to be met and offers as statistics of retardation the percentages which fall behind this standard. That

TABLE 92

Correlation between Grade Finished and Age at Leaving School

Total Group

Age at Leaving School	Grade Finished 0*	1	2	3	4	5	6	7	8	†9	†10	†11	†12	Totals
19									1	1			1	3
18		1			1			2	1				1	6
17						6	3	3			1		1	14
16	1		1	4	6	9	5	3	7	3	1		1	41
15	1	1	4	9	12	19	16	12	12	1	1		1	89
14	1		8	13	19	15	20	13	9	1				99
13	2	1	5	8	8	5	6	5	6					46
12	2	2	6	8	6		1		1					26
11	1		3	1	5		1							11
10		1	1						1					3
9	1	1	1		1									4
8		1												1
7	1													1
Totals....	10	8	29	43	58	54	52	38	38	6	3	0	5	344

Grade finished: Mean = 5.01 ± 2.307
Age at leaving school: Mean = 14.221 ± 1.718
Coefficient of correlation: r = .44 ± .043

* Includes those who have attended, but never finished first grade, but not those who have never been in school.
† Grades 9 to 12 are the 1st to the 4th years of high school.

this standard represents an ideal, rather than an average, even for children who have all the advantages of present school opportunities, is evident from the fact that the proportion of "over-age" pupils is practically always considerably larger than the proportion of advanced, and that most school systems are struggling with a large problem of retardation.

We shall not attempt to consider the various age-grade standards which have been proposed, but shall consider especially interesting for our purposes the present New York City standards, the so-called "up-to-15" standard by which it is expected that a pupil will have graduated from elementary school by the time he is fifteen. The requirements as stated for each grade are as follows:[11]

	Grade Completed							
	1	2	3	4	5	6	7	8
Age	7-8	8-9	9-10	10-11	11-12	12-13	13-14	14-15

This means that one should have completed the first grade before his eighth birthday, the second grade before his ninth, etc.

Table 92 shows the age-grade relationships for our group. We have enclosed within heavy lines the spaces within which would fall those making normal progress in approximate accordance with the New York requirements.[12] Numbers in the columns above these lines represent "retarded" cases and numbers below represent "advanced." The enormous preponderance of retarded cases is evident to the most cursory inspection.

The correlation between grade finished and age at leaving school is found to be .44 ± .043. While this is sufficient to show that the grade attainment is related to the age at which one leaves school, it is far too low to suggest that the latter factor is mainly responsible for the amount of school progress.

(5) *Relationship of Grade to Number of Years in School.*—Of greater significance than the foregoing comparison, for determining whether normal progress has or has not been made, is a comparison of grade and number of years that the individual has actually been in school. Such a comparison is offered in Table 93. For this com-

[11] "Eighteenth Annual Report of the City Superintendent of Schools to the Board of Education of the City of New York for the Year Ending July, 1916." Appendix F, pp. 175 ff.

[12] A slight deviation, amounting to a half year's greater leniency, was made because of the fact that our round numbers made it impossible to follow the New York standards exactly. This is due to the fact that in our figures for age, 7 equals 6½ to 7½, 8 equals 7½ to 8½, etc.

TABLE 93

Correlation between Grade Finished in School and Number of Years in School

Includes women of total group who were 35 years of age or under at last convictio

Number of Years in School	Grade Finished 0*	1	2	3	4	5	6	7	8	9†	10†	11†	12†	Totals
14										1				1
13		1							1					2
12						2		2	2				1	7
11				1	2	3	1	2	2		2		1	14
10			1	2	2	5	6	3	3					22
9			1	5	3	12	6	7	7				1	42
8	1	1	3	8	16	13	17	10	11				1	81
7	1		5	7	15	6	16	7	8		1			66
6			7	8	10	7	3	3	1					39
5			5	7	7				1				1	21
4	3	3	1	3	1	2	1		1					15
3		1	3		1	1			1					7
2	2	1		2	1			1						7
1	4	1	1											6
0	21													21
Totals....	32	8	27	43	58	51	50	35	38	1	3	0	5	351

Grade finished in school: Mean = 4.63 $\sigma = 2.516$

Number of years in school: Mean = 6.91 $\sigma = 2.80$

Coefficient of correlation: r = .62 ± .033

* Includes those who have never been in school and those who have attended but never finished first grade.

† Grades 9 to 12 are the 1st to the 4th years of high school.

parison we have included only women now 35 years of age or less in order to reduce, to some extent, the heterogeneity of the group. The correlation coefficient of .62 ± .033 shows that there is an unquestionable relationship between school attainment, as indicated by grade completed, and school opportunity, as represented by the length of school attendance.

On first consideration the above figures would seem to indicate that grade is much more directly determined by the time spent in school than by the age at leaving, since the coefficient for the latter relationship is only .44. It must be remembered, however, that those who had never attended school were necessarily omitted from the figures on age at leaving school. Referring to Table 93 we note that there are 21 such cases and that they, naturally, show perfect correspondence between opportunity and accomplishment, both being nil. This would, of course, contribute materially to the size of the correlation. Accordingly, we have computed the correlation between grade and years in school, dropping out those cases who had had no schooling. This gives a coefficient of .48 ± .043, only slightly higher than the correlation between grade and age at leaving school.

Because of the importance of this relationship we have also computed the correlation using only those cases on whom we had verified data for both grade and years in school (159 cases). This gives a still lower correlation, .39 ± .067. We interpret this, not as meaning that the relationship is less when we have reliable data, but rather as due to the restriction of variability for the group whose records were verified and especially to the loss of those approaching the limiting value of no schooling. That these factors are operative is shown by the difference in the standard deviations for grade finished. For the total group under 35 years of age σ equals 2.5, whereas for the group on whom we have completely verified data for both grade and years in school σ is only 1.9.

We are interested further in considering whether the observed relationship between grade and years in school may be due mainly to a basic relationship of each of these factors with intelligence. Accordingly, we have figured the correlation of grade with years in school for constant intelligence, the latter being represented by the score on Test Aggregate.[13] The partial coefficient is found to

[13] The relationship of intelligence with schooling will be discussed in detail in Chapter XV, pp. 493-8. At this point we are merely interested in consid-

be .402. This indicates that the factor of intelligence has not contributed largely to produce the relationship noted between grade and years in school. On the other hand the closeness of this relationship is not raised when we control the factor of intelligence as in the above partial. It might have been expected that when the influence of intelligence was eliminated grade attainment would appear to be determined almost exclusively by the length of time in school.

In addition to the mere question of relationship between these factors we are also concerned to know whether the grade attainment approximates closely to that which should be expected in view of the number of years in school. That it fails to reach this level is apparent at once by comparison of the constants of Tables 84 and 85 with those of Tables 87 and 88, respectively. Discrepancies are striking whatever groups we compare. It is sufficient to note, for example, the figures on the Bedford group and on the total. The Bedford women show an average number of years in school of 7.3, whereas the average grade completed is only 4.1. The total group with an average number of years in school of 6.5 completed only 4.6 grades. The discrepancy between opportunity and accomplishment is also indicated graphically by Chart XVII, which shows the actual grade distribution for women under 35 in comparison with the distribution which would have been found had they progressed at the normal rate of one grade a year. The failure to accomplish anything approximating a reasonable rate of progress suggests at once the probability of a generally low level of intelligence in this group. That this factor is operative will be apparent from our discussion in Chapter XV. The evidence, therefore, tends to confirm the assumption made earlier in this chapter to the effect that the record of grade completion tends of itself to be at least a rough measure of mentality. In this connection, however, we should not overlook the probable influence of other environmental factors tending against normal progress at the rate of a grade a year. We have in mind especially poor home conditions, economic stress, etc., which are likely to produce irregularity of school attendance, so

ering the effect of this relationship on the correlation between the two measures of schooling under consideration. The correlation coefficients used in computing the partial are as follows:

$$r_{IG} = .596, \quad r_{IY} = .289, \quad r_{GY} = .481. \quad N = 383$$

(I equals intelligence as measured by Test Aggregate, G equals grade, Y equals years in school, and N equals the number of cases.)

that a year in school has not its full value as a measure of school opportunity.

(6) *Relationship of Grade to Nature of Present Offense.*—Turning to the question of the relation of grade attained to the various aspects of the criminal career of these women, we consider first its relationship to the nature of the present offense. This is shown in Table 94. By reference to this table we note the absence of any striking distinctions, although the presence of a slight

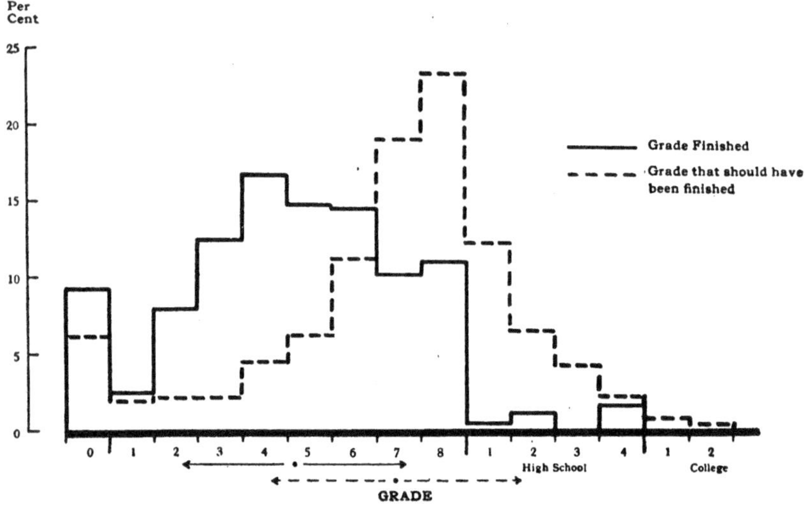

Chart XVII

Comparison of Grade Finished with Grade that Should Have Been Finished, Assuming One Grade Completed in Each Year in School. Based on 351 Delinquent Women under 35 Years of Age at Present Conviction.

degree of relationship is shown by the ratio of .23 ± .045. With the rough grouping here used, however, no single type of offense stands out as characteristic of the women of superior education. Two groups of offenses, those against the family and those against the administration of government, are conspicuous for the fact that they contain no women who had finished more than the fourth grade. In view of the extreme smallness of these groups no general significance can be attached to this point as characterizing these types of delinquencies. The fact merely serves to describe further the individuals of our group who fall in these two classes. We have noted previously that the instances with which we are dealing of

TABLE 94

Correlation between Grade Finished and Nature of Present Offense, Classified by New York City Police Department Classification

Nature of Present Offense	Grade Finished													Totals	Means (Grade Finished)
	0*	1	2	3	4	5	6	7	8	9†	10†	11†	12†		
Offenses against the Person......	9	1	3	1	4	2	2	1	1				1	25	3.0
Offenses against Chastity........	14	2	18	30	36	41	38	29	23		2		2	235	4.8
Offenses against the Family......	3		3	1	1									8	1.6
Offenses against Regulations for Public Health..............	6	4	2	4	6	5	5	3	6	2			1	44	4.5
Offenses against Administration of Government.............	1			2										3	2.0
Offenses against Property Rights..	17	5	9	9	14	12	11	7	16	5	1		3	109	4.6
General Criminality.............	3		2	2	2	2		2	2					15	3.9
Totals....................	53	12	37	49	63	62	56	42	48	7	3	0	7	439	4.52

Grade finished: Mean = 4.52 $\sigma = 2.70$
Correlation ratio: $\eta = .23 \pm .045$

* Includes those who have never been in school, and those who have attended but never finished first grade.
† Grades 9 to 12 are the 1st to the 4th years of high school.

offenses against the administration of government are not the impressive crimes that the name may suggest. Rather, they are examples of stupid attempts at evading the law through unskilful perjury or bribery. We are interested to note that there is no appreciable distinction in degree of education of those women guilty of offenses against chastity as compared with those guilty of offenses against property. This is of special interest since, as we shall see later, the latter group shows an appreciable superiority in general intelligence over the former.

(7) *Relationship of Grade to Number of Previous Convictions.* —Considering next the relationship between grade and the number of convictions, we obtain the correlation presented in Table 95. The coefficient, —.06 ± .047, is too small to have any significance. The ratios, though slightly larger, would indicate at most a barely appreciable relationship. Referring to the means, shown in the column at the extreme right and in the bottom row of the table, we find such irregularity that it is impossible to formulate the variations as indicative of any consistent trend. It appears, therefore, that the data of this table fail to provide any evidence to show that the amount of education of our delinquent women has influenced the extent of their criminal records to any degree or in any direction.

Since both the record of number of convictions and that of grade attended have shown appreciable, though slight, relationship with the factors of age and intelligence, it has seemed important to take account of these two factors, because of the possibility that their influence might have obscured whatever relationship between grade and number of convictions existed. Computing the correlation of grade with number of convictions for constant age, we obtain the coefficient —.027.[14] It is evident that allowance for age does not serve to show up a relationship which had been obscured by this factor.

The outcome is practically the same when we make allowance for the possible effect of intelligence in this connection. In order to utilize the whole group and not merely the English-speaking portion, we have used the score for the non-language tests as our measure of intelligence. The correlation coefficient of grade with

[14] The data from which this partial was computed are as follows:

$r_{GN} = -.055$, $r_{GA} = -.124$, $r_{NA} = .232$

(N equals number of convictions, G equals grade, A equals age.)

TABLE 95

Correlation between Number of Previous Convictions and Grade Finished in School

Total Group

Grade Finished	Number of Previous Convictions: 0	1	2	3	4	5	6	7	8	9	10	11	12	13	14	15	16	17	18	19	20	Totals	Means (Number of Previous Convictions)
4th Year High School..	3	2	2																			7	
3rd " " " ..																						0	0.9
2nd " " " ..	1	1	1																			3	
1st " " " ..	4	2	1		1																	8	
8..................	22	14	1	7	2	1	1	2			1											51	1.6
7..................	20	10	4	1	2		1	1	1	1	1								1			43	2.0
6..................	31	13	4	6	4			1														59	1.1
5..................	27	19	9	4		1		2		1		1										64	1.4
4..................	22	21	9	4	4	2		1	1			1										65	1.6
3..................	26	11	6	1		4	1			1											1	51	1.6
2..................	14	8	7	2	3		1						1									36	1.6
1..................	2	2	2	2		1	1	1			1											12	3.3
0*..................	26	10	5	3	3	3			1	1					1							53	0.6
Totals..............	198	113	51	30	19	12	5	8	3	4	3	2	1	0	1	0	0	0	1	0	1	452	1.56
Means (Grade Finished)	4.6	4.8	4.3	4.8	4.5	3.2		4.5														4.57	

Number of previous convictions: Mean = 1.56 σ = 2.49
Grade finished: Mean = 4.57 σ = 2.69

Coefficient of correlation: r —.06 ± .047

Correlation ratios: Grade finished on number of previous convictions, .11 ± .046 Blakeman's Criterion 1.6
Number of previous convictions on grade finished, .16 ± .046 Blakeman's Criterion 2.4

* Includes those who have never been in school and those who have attended but never finished first grade.

number of convictions, for constant intelligence, is found to be .053.[15] In view of the absence of correlation shown in these two partials we have not thought it necessary to compute the correlation of grade with number of convictions for both intelligence and age constant.

(8) *Relationship of Grade to Age at First Conviction.*—As indicative of any possible relationship between grade completed and the beginnings of the criminal career, we have computed the correlation between grade and age at first conviction, shown in Table 96. The coefficient is $-.08 \pm .047$ which fails obviously to afford evidence of the existence of any relationship. The ratio of grade on age at first conviction, $.17 \pm .046$, would show the presence of at most a very slight relationship. Since we are unable to discover any consistent trend in the variations in mean grade with changes in age at first conviction, we do not consider that the existence of even a slight relationship is established. The ratio of age at first conviction on grade is appreciably larger, $.35 \pm .041$. This is sufficient to call for a careful examination of the table to discover what trend of relationship is indicated by these figures. Reference to the means for age at first conviction in the extreme right-hand column shows a tendency toward earlier first conviction for those falling nearest to the average for grade finished. The tendency toward delayed age at first conviction for those who had no schooling and also for those who advanced beyond the elementary school is striking. It will be remembered that a similar tendency appeared for the relation between age at leaving school and age at first conviction. The factors, discussed in that connection as explanatory, doubtless apply also here.

(*b*) *Amount of Illiteracy*

As a further index of the school attainment of our group, from the negative side, we may consider the figures showing the extent of illiteracy. For comparison there are available certain figures on the general population, although it is quite certain that the standard of what constitutes illiteracy can not be considered entirely comparable with ours. We had very accurate knowledge with reference to the degree of literacy of each individual, so that we were not dependent on indirect information. The census figures, on the

[15] The data from which this partial was computed are as follows:

$$r_{GN} = -.055,\ r_{GI} = .543,\ r_{NI} = .127$$

(I equals intelligence, N and G have same significance as in Note 14.)

TABLE 96

Correlation between Age at First Conviction and Grade Finished in School

Total Group

Grade Finished	Age at First Conviction: 6–9	9–12	12–15	15–18	18–21	21–24	24–27	27–30	30–33	33–36	36–39	39–42	42–45	45–48	48–51	51–54	54–57	57–60	60–63	63–66	66–69	69–72	Totals	Means (Age at First Conviction)
4th Year H. S.							1	1	2	1				1	1								7	28.9
3rd " " "																							0	
2nd " " "						3																	3	
1st " " "				1	1	2	2					2											8	
8				3	10	8	8	1	7	3	5		3		1		1						50	24.5
7				7	5	8	9	7	3	2		1											42	24.0
6	1		3	13	12	6	10	4	3	1	2	1		1	1								58	22.6
5			2	15	14	9	7	4	2	2	2	4	1			1							63	23.5
4			1	15	8	11	12	4	4	4	1	2	1					1					64	24.0
3		1	3	7	13	10	5	3	5			1	1		1				1				51	23.1
2		1	1	6	6	2	3	8		4	2	1	1	1									36	25.3
1					4	3	1	3				1											12	24.8
0*				2	5	6	8	6	5	4	3	3	3	2	2	1	1		2		1	1	55	33.1
Totals	1	2	10	69	78	68	66	41	31	21	15	16	10	5	6	2	2	1	3	0	1	1	449	25.45
Means (Grade Finished)		4.2		4.6		4.9		4.4		4.4		4.0		4.5					2.0				4.53	

Age at first conviction: Mean = 25.45 $\sigma = 9.46$
Grade finished: Mean = 4.53 $\sigma = 2.704$
Coefficient of correlation: r = —.08 ± .047
Correlation ratios: Grade finished on age at first conviction, $\eta = .17 \pm .046$ Blakeman's Criterion = 2.4
Age at first conviction on grade finished, $\eta = .35 \pm .041$ Blakeman's Criterion = 5.4

* Includes those who have never been in school and those who have attended but never finished first grade.

other hand, are largely dependent on mere statement and on indirect statement at that—information given by one member of the family for the whole family. This is clearly pointed out in the discussion of this subject in the census reports. Such dependence on hearsay information for the general population is inevitable, but doubtless results in giving figures for illiteracy which are far too low. For this reason we cannot attach much importance to the comparison of our figures with those of the census report, but we offer this comparison as giving the best available clue to the facts.

We have used the figures for the general female population over ten years of age in New York State obtained in the census enumeration for 1910.[16] We have adopted the same definition of illiteracy, as signifying inability of a person ten years of age or over to write, regardless of whether he can read or not. For practical purposes this has meant that an individual must be able both to read and write, since we have found no cases who were able to write but not to read. Our standard of what constitutes reading and writing has been exceedingly rudimentary. Ability to get the sense of even the simplest sort of reading matter or to convey one's meaning by writing, even though the spelling be very grotesque, has been considered adequate.

Table 97 presents the data on the delinquent women classified both by institutions and by nativity and color, in comparison with the data on the general female population, as regards illiteracy in the sense of inability to read and write in any language. The chief interest attaches to the comparison of the delinquent group classified by nativity and color, with the figures for the general population by the same classification. We note that for each group thus classified the percentage of illiterates is appreciably higher among the delinquents than in the general population, according to these figures. In the delinquent group as in the general population the smallest percentage of illiteracy is found in the native whites (4.2), and the largest percentage among the foreign whites (24.0), the percentage among the negroes (10.6) falling between the other two figures. The intercomparison of these sub-groups among the delinquents—*i. e.*, of native-white with foreign-white, etc.—may be considered entirely trustworthy, since a uniform standard has been applied here. Some interest attaches also to consideration of the percentages of illiterates in the various institutional groups. Tak-

[16] Abstract "Thirteenth United States Census Report," 1910, pp. 237 ff.

TABLE 97

ILLITERACY *

Numbers and Percentages of Illiterates among Delinquent Women in Institutional Groups, Classified by Nativity and Color, in Comparison with Figures for the General Female Population Over 10 Years of Age in New York State. (1910)

Institutional Groups	Classification According to Nativity and Color											
	Total Group			Native White			Foreign White			Negro		
	Total Number	Number Illiterate	Percentage Illiterate	Total Number	Number Illiterate	Percentage Illiterate	Total Number	Number Illiterate	Percentage Illiterate	Total Number	Number Illiterate	Percentage Illiterate
Bedford	101	7	6.9	69	3	4.4	12	4	33.3	20	0	.0
Auburn	79	18	22.8	28	2	7.1	39	15	38.5	12	1	8.3
Magdalen	75	5	6.7	51	0	.0	24	5	20.8	0	..	....
Penitentiary	109	15	13.8	41	1	2.4	48	10	20.8	19	3	15.8
Workhouse	100	17	17.0	34	4	11.8	30	7	23.3	36	6	16.7
Probation	90	3	3.3	61	2	3.3	22	1	4.5	7	0	.0
Total	553	65	11.8	284	12	4.2	175	42	24.0	94	10	10.6
General female population†	3,683,601	218,913	5.9	2,370,708	16,266	.7	1,249,748	198,679	15.9	60,673	3,335	5.5

* Illiteracy signifies here inability to read and write in any language.

† The figures for the general population are to be found in the following volumes of the "Thirteenth Census of the United States taken in 1910". "Abstract of Thirteenth Census," Table 29, p. 244, and Table 31, p. 248; Vol. III, "Population, Report by States," Table 10, p. 215, and Table 7 p 214. In certain cases figures quoted have been obtained by subtracting number below ten years of age from total.

ing into account the total population of each institutional group, we note that the percentages vary from 3.3 per cent for the probation group to 22.8 per cent for Auburn, the latter group showing a decidedly larger percentage than any of the others. By reference to the comparisons by nativity and color, we note that this high percentage for Auburn is largely due to its foreign element.

In Table 98 we offer data showing the percentages in the various groups who were unable to read and write English. Although we have no comparable data for the general population, these figures have some importance as showing the percentages within the delinquent group, who are handicapped by inability to read and write the language of the country in which they live. As we should expect, the percentages of this table are identical with the preceding for the group of native white, but are many times larger for the foreign white. Half of the group of our foreign delinquents are unable to read even the simplest subject matter in English. The extent to which this fact keeps them from assimilating the standards of this country and from becoming informed regarding its laws is quite impossible to estimate. Its significance, however, should not be overlooked.

(*c*) *Results of Educational Tests*

We have already commented on the importance of the educational tests as furnishing another type of measure of educational attainment, the special advantage of which consists in the fact that it furnishes an objective measure and is thus free from the uncertainty which attaches to the women's own statements regarding educational progress. In the following section we offer data on certain of these tests. (For general account of the tests used see Chapter IV). Our selection of tests to report at this time has been determined, partly by the desire to have tests representative of a variety of educational processes, and partly by the desire to have tests which had been reasonably well standardized with school groups. With these objects in mind the following tests have been chosen: Trabue scale A for reading; Buckingham scale for spelling (Thorndike selection); Ayres scale for handwriting; Courtis—Series B—for arithmetic. Since we have no data on the general population based on these measures, we present our figures mainly for their value for later reference. We have indicated such standards as are available showing what

TABLE 98

INABILITY TO READ AND WRITE ENGLISH

Numbers and Percentages of Delinquent Women Illiterate in English in Institutional Groups, Classified by Nativity and Color

Institutional Groups	Classification According to Nativity and Color											
	Total Group			Native White			Foreign White			Negro		
	Total Number	Number Illiterate in English	Percentage Illiterate in English	Total Number	Number Illiterate in English	Percentage Illiterate in English	Total Number	Number Illiterate in English	Percentage Illiterate in English	Total Number	Number Illiterate in English	Percentage Illiterate in English
Bedford	101	8	7.9	69	3	4.4	12	5	41.7	20	0	.0
Auburn	79	30	38.0	28	2	7.1	39	27	69.2	12	1	8.3
Magdalen	75	11	14.7	51	0	.0	24	11	45.8	0	....	....
Penitentiary	109	28	25.9	41	1	2.4	48	23	47.9	19	4	21.1
Workhouse	100	26	26.0	34	4	11.8	30	16	53.3	36	6	16.7
Probation	90	7	7.8	61	2	3.3	22	5	22.7	7	0	.0
Total	553	110	19.9	284	12	4.2	175	87	49.7	94	11	11.7

score is to be expected from children now in school in any given grade. Formulation of the norms which we have used may be found in the appropriate references cited in Chapter IV.

(1) *Reading—Trabue Scale.*—Table 99 shows the numbers and percentages of the various institutional groups and of the total who reached the median score for each grade. It shows also the median for each group with the grade standard to which this corresponds. English-speaking cases only were considered. From inspection of the table it is apparent that all groups except the Magdalen show appreciable percentages who are unable to do better than children in the second grade.

The median score of the total group reaches the standard achieved by children in fifth grade. This is interesting in comparison with data regarding grade completed. We see by Table 88 that the native born women had completed, on the average, 5.0 grades. Their accomplishment along the lines of reading are obviously quite closely in accord with these figures on grade. Among the institutional groups the Magdalen, the Penitentiary and, strangely enough, Auburn, rank highest, rising to the standard for sixth grade. Bedford and Probation are, however, on approximately the same level as these, as shown by the median scores, even though they fall below the dividing line between the standard for sixth grade and that for fifth. The Workhouse is a distinct step lower, rising only to the level of fourth grade.

(2) *Spelling—Buckingham.*—Table 100 shows data in similar form to that given for the Trabue scale in Table 99. The grade standing for the group as a whole, as well as for most of the sub-groups, is higher by this measure than by the reading scale. The total reaches the 6th grade standard: the Magdalen group rises to the 8th grade, the Penitentiary and Probation to the 7th, Bedford and Auburn to the 6th, the Workhouse again drops as low as the 4th.

(3) *Handwriting—Ayres Scale.*—Handwriting has been measured from two points of view, quality and speed. To get the former measure, samples were compared with Ayres' samples of adult handwriting. The distributions of results are shown in Table 101. The lowness of the grade levels of our groups, measured by these standards, is very striking. In no case does the median of one of our groups exceed the median for the 2nd grade. For three of the groups, and for the total, the median falls below that for 2nd grade.

TABLE 99

READING (TRABUE SCALE A) 99

Distribution by Numbers and Per Cents with Median Scores and Corresponding Grade Norms

English-speaking Cases Only

	Bedford		Auburn		Magdalen		Penitentiary		Workhouse		Probation		Totals	
Grade Median Reached*	Number	Percentage	Number	Percentage	Number	Percentage	Number	Percentage	Number	Percentage	Number	Percentage	Number	Percentage
8th and above	52	22.1	4	10.5	12	23.1	23	30.7	8	10.8	10	18.9	109	20.7
7th	32	13.6	8	21.1	10	19.2	5	6.7	4	5.4	3	5.7	62	11.8
6th	25	10.6	7	18.4	6	11.5	10	13.3	8	10.8	10	18.9	66	12.5
5th	41	17.4	2	5.3	11	21.2	12	16.0	12	16.2	11	20.8	89	16.9
4th	34	14.5	5	13.2	8	15.4	9	12.0	18	24.3	9	17.0	83	15.7
3rd	20	8.5	5	13.2	5	9.6	4	5.3	9	12.2	6	11.3	49	9.3
2nd	13	5.5	2	5.3	..	....	1	1.3	6	8.1	2	3.8	24	4.6
Below 2nd	18	7.7	5	13.2	..	....	11	14.7	9	12.2	2	3.8	45	8.5
Totals	235	100.0	38	100.0	52	100.0	75	100.0	74	100.0	53	100.0	527	100.0
Median Score	21.2		22.2		23.3		22.3		17.0		20.9		20.8	
Grade Equivalent	5th		6th		6th		6th		4th		5th		5th	

*The figures of this table show the numbers and percentages of delinquent women reaching the medians of the various school grades as determined for school children.

TABLE 100

SPELLING (BUCKINGHAM)

Distribution by Numbers and Per Cents with Median Grades

English-speaking Cases Only

	Bedford		Auburn		Magdalen		Penitentiary		Workhouse		Probation		Totals	
Grade Median Reached*	Number	Percentage	Number	Percentage	Number	Percentage	Number	Percentage	Number	Percentage	Number	Percentage	Number	Percentage
Above 8th	40	16.1	5	13.5	15	30.0	17	22.7	8	10.8	13	25.5	98	18.3
8th	46	18.5	10	27.0	11	22.0	18	24.0	7	9.5	11	21.6	103	19.3
7th	24	9.7	2	5.4	6	12.0	4	5.3	2	2.7	2	3.9	40	7.5
6th	20	8.1	8	21.6	..	....	7	9.3	13	17.6	7	13.7	55	10.3
5th	26	10.5	1	2.7	8	16.0	5	6.7	6	8.1	5	9.8	51	9.5
4th	24	9.7	4	10.8	6	12.0	5	6.7	9	12.2	7	13.7	55	10.3
3rd	39	15.7	2	5.4	4	8.0	9	12.0	19	24.7	3	5.9	76	14.2
Below 3rd	29	11.7	5	13.5	..	....	10	13.3	10	13.5	3	5.9	57	10.7
Totals	248	100.0	37	100.0	50	100.0	75	100.0	74	100.0	51	100.0	535	100.0
Median Grade	6th		6th		8th		7th		4th		7th		6th	

* The figures of this table show the numbers and percentages of delinquent women reaching the medians of the various school grades as determined for school children.

TABLE 101

HANDWRITING — QUALITY (AYRES SCALE)

Distribution by Numbers and Per Cents with Median Scores and Corresponding Grade Norms

English-speaking Cases Only

Quality	Bedford		Auburn		Magdalen		Penitentiary		Workhouse		Probation		Totals	
	Number	Percentage	Number	Percentage	Number	Percentage	Number	Percentage	Number	Percentage	Number	Percentage	Number	Percentage
80	2	1.0	3	7.9	2	3.8	..	....	..	....	..	....	7	1.5
70	13	6.5	1	2.6	4	7.5	..	....	..	....	1	2.3	24	5.0
60	21	10.6	5	13.2	5	9.4	5	7.4	2	2.7	3	6.8	42	8.8
50	42	21.1	7	18.4	9	17.0	6	8.8	4	5.4	6	13.6	83	17.4
40	41	20.6	5	13.2	17	32.1	15	22.1	9	12.2	4	9.1	100	21.0
30	53	26.6	7	18.4	9	17.0	24	35.3	26	35.1	20	45.5	127	26.7
20	14	7.0	5	13.2	6	11.3	12	17.6	27	36.5	7	15.9	60	12.6
Below 20	13	6.5	5	13.2	1	1.9	6	8.8	6	8.1	3	6.8	33	6.9
Totals	199	100.0	38	100.0	53	100.0	68	100.0	74	100.0	44	100.0	476	100.0
Median Score	39.4		39.5		41.0		31.4		26.2		30.8		36.4	
Grade Equivalent	2nd		2nd		2nd		Below 2nd		Below 2nd		Below 2nd		Below 2nd	

When we turn to figures on rate of writing given in Table 102, we find a very different result. All of our groups but one—the Workhouse—achieve the level of 8th grade accomplishment. Even the Workhouse median is as high as that for 7th grade. It appears, therefore, that the members of our group have an admirable speed but a very inferior quality of penmanship.

(4) *Arithmetic—Courtis.*—As representative of accomplishment in arithmetic we offer data on the two fundamental processes of addition and division, as measured by the Courtis scale. In certain ways we preferred the Woody scale for our purposes since it does not exceed the limitations of the ability of our women so strikingly as does the Courtis scale. We have chosen to report on the latter, however, because of the importance of the grade norms established for this scale.

Table 103 shows the distribution of scores for the problems in addition. The superiority of the Magdalen is again apparent, both from inspection of the distribution and from consideration of the grade norm (5th) to which its median score corresponds. Bedford, the Workhouse and Probation reach only 4th grade standard, while Auburn and the Penitentiary fall below the 4th grade norm.

Table 104 shows the results obtained with the Courtis scale for division and makes apparent how markedly this scale overshot the ability of our group. Over half of the total group were unable to complete a single problem correctly. In the Workhouse as many as 86 per cent were unable to get a single problem, and even in the Magdalen 31 per cent failed entirely. Observation of the individuals at work indicated that a certain proportion of these failures were due to an inability to recall the method of long division, though this had at one time been learned. The attempt to recall this strange and never-used mechanism showed a marked similarity to the performance of the average college student when suddenly confronted with a problem in cube root. The level for the group as a whole was below the median for 4th grade. Only Bedford and the Magdalen rose above this, the former reaching the 4th grade standard and the latter the 5th grade.

It is apparent from the foregoing account that the educational tests do not offer a more favorable impression of the school attainments of these women than do the data regarding school grade. In only isolated instances do the groups rise above the level for 5th grade and in numerous instances they fall to 4th grade standards or below. The highest scores, from point of view of grade norms, were

TABLE 102

HANDWRITING — RATE (AYRES)

Distribution by Numbers and Per Cents with Median Scores and Corresponding Grade Norms

English-speaking Cases Only

	Bedford		Auburn		Magdalen		Penitentiary		Workhouse		Probation		Totals	
Grade Median Reached *	Number	Percentage	Number	Percentage	Number	Percentage	Number	Percentage	Number	Percentage	Number	Percentage	Number	Percentage
8th	142	71.4	22	57.9	43	81.1	43	63.2	29	39.7	32	72.7	311	65.5
7th	12	6.0	2	5.3	2	3.8	..	....	10	13.7	3	6.8	29	6.1
6th	10	5.0	2	5.3	3	5.7	4	5.9	4	5.5	1	2.3	24	5.1
5th	7	3.5	3	7.9	1	1.9	4	5.9	4	4.4	3	6.8	22	4.6
4th	11	5.5	..	....	1	1.9	5	7.4	7	9.6	1	2.3	25	5.3
3rd	3	1.5	4	10.5	1	1.9	2	2.9	5	6.8	1	2.3	16	3.4
2nd	5	2.5	..	....	2	3.8	3	4.4	5	6.8	1	2.3	16	3.4
Below 2nd	9	4.5	5	13.2	..	....	7	10.3	9	12.3	2	4.5	32	6.7
Totals	199	100.0	38	100.0	53	100.0	68	100.0	73	100.0	44	100.0	475	100.0
Median Score (Letters per minute).	Above 79		Above 79		Above 79		Above 79		76.9		Above 79		Above 79	
Grade Equivalent	8th		8th		8th		8th		7th		8th		8th	

* The figures of this table show the numbers and percentages of delinquent women reaching the medians of the various school grades as determined for school children.

TABLE 103

ARITHMETIC — ADDITION (COURTIS — SERIES B)

Distribution by Numbers and Per Cents, with Median Scores and Corresponding Grade Norms

English-speaking Cases Only

Number of problems correct	Bedford		Auburn		Magdalen		Penitentiary		Workhouse		Probation		Totals	
	Number	Percentage	Number	Percentage	Number	Percentage	Number	Percentage	Number	Percentage	Number	Percentage	Number	Percentage
22	..	..	..	....	1	2.2	1	1.4	..	....	..	....	2	.4
21	1	.4	..	....	..	....	..	....	..	....	..	....	1	.2
20	..	..	..	....	1	2.2	1	1.4	..	....	..	....	2	.4
19	..	..	..	....	1	2.2	..	....	..	....	..	....	1	.2
18	..	..	..	....	..	....	..	....	..	....	2	4.0	2	.4
17	..	..	..	....	..	....	..	....	..	....	..	....	0	.0
16	..	..	..	....	..	....	..	....	..	....	..	....	0	.0
15	2	.9	..	....	1	2.2	1	1.4	..	....	..	....	4	.8
14	1	.4	..	....	..	....	1	1.4	..	....	..	....	2	.4
13	2	.9	..	....	1	2.2	..	....	..	....	1	2.0	4	.8
12	1	.4	..	....	..	....	..	....	..	....	..	....	1	.2
11	1	.4	..	....	2	4.4	1	1.4	1	1.4	..	....	5	1.0
10	8	3.4	..	....	2	4.4	2	2.7	3	4.1	1	2.0	16	3.2
9	6	2.6	1	3.7	1	2.2	2	2.7	1	1.4	2	4.0	13	2.6
8	9	3.8	2	7.4	1	2.2	6	8.2	3	4.1	..	....	21	4.2
7	22	9.4	1	3.7	5	11.1	1	1.4	1	1.4	3	6.0	33	6.6
6	17	7.3	1	3.7	4	8.9	5	6.8	2	2.7	6	12.0	35	7.0
5	24	10.3	..	....	3	6.7	4	5.5	4	5.5	4	8.0	39	7.8
4	23	9.8	..	....	8	17.8	2	2.7	13	17.8	6	12.0	52	10.4
3	23	9.8	2	7.4	2	4.4	7	9.6	8	11.0	4	8.0	46	9.2
2	26	11.1	4	14.8	5	11.1	8	11.0	5	6.8	4	8.0	52	10.4
1	23	9.8	5	18.5	2	4.4	6	8.2	9	12.3	7	14.0	52	10.4
0	45	19.2	11	40.7	5	11.1	25	34.2	23	31.5	10	20.0	119	23.7
Totals	234	100.0	27	100.0	45	100.0	73	100.0	73	100.0	50	100.0	502	100.0
Median Score	4.0		1.6		5.3		2.8		3.0		4.1		3.6	
Grade Equivalent	4th		Below 4th		5th		Below 4th		4th		4th		4th	

TABLE 104

ARITHMETIC — LONG DIVISION (COURTIS — SERIES B)

Distribution by Numbers and Per Cents, with Median Scores and Corresponding Grade Norms

English-speaking Cases Only

Quality	Bedford		Auburn		Magdalen		Penitentiary		Workhouse		Probation		Totals	
	Number	Percentage	Number	Percentage	Number	Percentage	Number	Percentage	Number	Percentage	Number	Percentage	Number	Percentage
16	..	..	..	....	..	....	1	1.4	..	....	..	....	1	.2
15	..	..	..	....	..	....	..	....	..	....	..	....	..	..
14	1	.4	..	....	1	2.2	..	....	..	....	..	....	2	.4
13	2	.9	..	....	1	2.2	..	....	..	....	..	....	3	.6
12	2	.9	..	....	..	....	..	....	..	....	..	....	2	.4
11	4	1.7	..	....	..	....	1	1.4	..	....	..	....	5	1.0
10	2	.9	..	....	..	....	..	....	..	....	..	....	2	.4
9	2	.9	..	....	1	2.2	..	....	..	....	1	2.0	4	.8
8	6	2.6	..	....	4	8.9	1	1.4	..	....	..	....	11	2.2
7	3	1.3	..	....	4	8.9	2	2.7	..	....	2	4.0	11	2.2
6	10	4.3	..	....	3	6.7	1	1.4	..	....	2	4.0	16	3.2
5	18	7.7	1	3.7	2	4.4	4	5.5	1	1.4	6	12.0	32	6.4
4	8	3.4	..	....	3	6.7	6	8.2	1	1.4	3	6.0	21	4.2
3	12	5.1	4	14.8	7	15.6	2	2.7	3	4.1	3	6.0	31	6.2
2	27	11.5	..	....	3	6.7	5	6.8	..	....	5	10.0	40	8.0
1	14	6.0	3	11.1	2	4.4	4	5.5	5	6.8	3	6.0	31	6.2
0	123	52.6	19	70.4	14	31.1	46	63.0	63	86.3	25	50.0	290	57.8
Totals	234	100.0	27	100.0	45	100.0	73	100.0	73	100.0	50	100.0	502	100.0
Median Score	1.0		.7		3.6		.8		.6		1.2		.9	
Grade Equivalent	4th		Below 4th		5th		Below 4th		Below 4th		4th		Below 4th	

made on spelling and on rate of handwriting; the lowest on long division and on quality of handwriting.

The consistently low record of the Workhouse by these measures is of interest as tending to confirm our suspicion that they had overstated the facts regarding grade attainments.

SUMMARY

From the data presented in this chapter it appears:

1. That the delinquent women fall conspicuously below the standards of present-day opinion as to what should be expected regarding both the age at which one should be allowed to leave school and the minimum grade which he should have reached. Nevertheless we are unable to state whether our women fall below the level of the general public in these respects.

2. That their school attainment, as indicated by grade completed, has not kept pace with their opportunities as represented by the number of years in school.

3. That there is a distinct tendency toward poorer educational opportunity and attainments among the older women of our group as compared with the younger women.

4. That the native-white are superior to both the foreign born and the colored with respect to both school opportunity and school attainment: and that the foreign born are inferior to the colored in both respects.

5. That the more striking institutional differences appear to be due to one or the other of the two factors just mentioned—age and nativity differences—except in so far as they are occasioned by differences in degree of verification of facts.

6. That the amount of illiteracy among the delinquent groups is relatively high, varying from 4 per cent for the native white to 24 per cent for the foreign white: that these percentages are decidedly higher than those for similar groups in the general population, though the significance of this comparison is weakened by the fact that the two types of groups have not been measured by equally severe standards.

7. That the relationships between education and the various aspects of the delinquent career are at most slight.

Some tendency appeared for those with least schooling and those with most schooling to have been convicted first at a later age than those falling in the intermediate range regarding schooling. The influence of other factors than schooling was suspected as producing this relationship.

A slight relationship was found between grade and nature of offense, with those guilty of offenses against property, against chastity, and against regulations for public health having reached slightly higher grades than those guilty of other offenses.

Unambiguous evidence of relationship either between years in school and number of convictions, or between grade and number of convictions, was not found. Even allowance for the effect of age, and of intelligence, did not disclose the presence of such a relationship.

CHAPTER XI

OCCUPATIONAL HISTORY AND ECONOMIC EFFICIENCY

THE history of criminal science is rife with various contentions as to the essential factors most closely related to criminality. One of the most fruitful fields of discussion has been, and still is, the importance of stressing the economic system of recent years as entirely unassociated with, or, on the other hand, directly inherent in the etiology of crime. The two most divergent schools in this respect are probably the Italian School, fathered by Lombroso, and the Socialists, known as the "Third School." The doctrine of the Italian School, as has previously been stated, is based on the theory that there is a definite criminal type, distinguished from the non-criminal element of the population by physical and mental stigmata. Though these criminal anthropologists do not deny that adverse economic conditions may often be somewhat responsible for certain types of crime, they contend that the real cause of crime is innate. The Socialists, on the other hand, go to the extreme of emphasizing the economic factor over all others, and assuming that with a more socialistic régime of the economic system the amount of crime would gradually diminish. This theory was advanced by Karl Marx:

"In the social production which men carry on they enter into definite relations that are indispensable and independent of their will; these relations of production correspond to a definite stage of development of their material powers of production. The sum total of these relations of production constitutes the economic structure of society—the real foundation, on which rise legal and political superstructures and to which correspond definite forms of social consciousness. The mode of production in material life determines the general character of the social, political and spiritual processes of life. It is not the consciousness of men that determines their existence, but, on the contrary, their social existence determines their consciousness."[1]

[1] Marx, Karl. "A Contribution to the Critique of Political Economy," p. 11. Translated from the Second German Edition by N. I. Stone. New York: The International Library Publishing Co., 1904.

Many of the tenets of the criminal anthropologists have been proved unsound, particularly those relating to the presence of physical stigmata in the criminal. The work of the later criminologists has also discredited the extreme views of the Socialists, that all the relations of mankind, associated with criminality, are *exclusively* determined by economic relations.

Our study of 587 women, though comparatively small in numbers, includes women from all over New York state with the largest number from New York city. This city of infinite economic resources expending themselves in occupations of almost every description offers us an admirable opportunity for observation of the industrial situation as it has affected these women convicted of breaking the law. At the outset we must disagree with the extremists of the Socialist School in their lack of emphasis on the individual mental defect or abnormality which may be the determining factor in making one member of a family an offender against the law, while all the other members—under the same economic system—do not become anti-social in their actions. That the present economic system is undoubtedly responsible, to a certain extent, for many of the factors associated with delinquency, such as the economic status of home conditions discussed in Chapter IX, no one will deny. But that this alone is the prime cause of crime is as futile to assert as that the development of modern industry has had no effect on the complications which are associated with crime.

We have attempted in this study to give a bird's-eye survey of the work histories of these women from the time of starting work to the present conviction, and including not only the prevailing kind of work done, with the average wage for this work, but also the kind of work and the wage in the first job, at time of the first and present conviction and in the latest job.[2] An effort to summarize the various factors of the work record has been made in the estimate of regularity of the work, and the estimate of the entire work history.

It is not easy from such a summary to draw definite conclusions because of the fact that for the general population no adequate wage studies have recently been made for all occupations in a given community, and there are no other studies comparable to ours in the consideration of wage. Even studies of delinquency are notably lacking in more than brief statements of the average wage or the highest and

[2] Throughout, "work" has been used to signify work in which one was gainfully employed, and does not include the work of women who were doing their own housework.

lowest wage, with no effort to determine what kind of work was being done at any crucial time in the delinquent's life, how much of the time he had been idle, and what his earning capacity was at any given significant time. Wherever possible, comparisons will be made with isolated studies of wage and kind of work for the general population, but these are necessarily limited to few. That our group shows a low earning capacity and irregular work might not be significant if compared with equally reliable data for all women in New York state. But since the other part of the comparison is not available at this time, we shall present ours as indicative of the type of record that occurs among delinquent women, and leave the rest of the comparison to follow later.

AGE AT STARTING WORK

The Child Labor Law in New York State provides that no children may be legally employed under 14 years, and that children from 14 to 16 must secure certificates before they can be employed legally.[3] Although this law has been in effect for many years, it is interesting to note, from Table 105, that 80 women, or 14.8 per cent of the total group, began to work before they were fourteen years of age. Of this number, 21 women were foreign born so that this law would not apply to them, and 26, though native born, lived during their childhood in states other than New York, in most of which, however, there were restrictions against child labor under fourteen years. At the least consideration, there are between 7 and 13 per cent of the total group who began to work before the age at which they were legally allowed to, and which New York state has set as the minimum age possible for children to work and retain their good health. Each institutional group is represented among those who began to work before fourteen years, but Auburn has by far the largest percentage, probably due to the fact that there is in this institution a large percentage of foreign women and a preponderance of the older women who began to work years ago when the restrictions against child labor were few and not well enforced. If we compare the percentage of women starting to work between ten and fourteen years in our total group of delinquents, with the percentage of the general female population between ten and fourteen years of age in New York state who were working in 1910, we find that in the one case the percentage is 14.8, while in the other it is only .1 of a

[3] Consolidated Laws 1909, vol. 3, chapter 31, article 6, section 70, as amended by Chapter 529 of the laws of 1913.

per cent.[4] These figures are not exactly comparable since the age at starting work may extend over many different years while the census figures apply to those of given ages working during one specified year. They do, however, indicate a trend, which it is important to observe, for the delinquent women to go to work earlier than the women of the general population.

TABLE 105

AGE AT STARTING WORK

Per Cent Distribution of Delinquent Women in Institutional Groups

Age at Starting Work	Institutional Groups						Total
	Bedford	Auburn	Magdalen	Penitentiary	Workhouse	Probation	
6 to 10 years	4.1	5.3	1.4	....	1.4	....	1.9
10 " 14 "	14.3	24.6	14.9	15.0	20.0	2.7	14.8
14 " 18 "	69.4	45.6	56.8	34.0	32.9	65.8	51.1
18 " 22 "	10.2	5.3	21.6	21.0	18.6	17.8	16.1
22 " 26 "	....	10.5	2.7	8.0	10.0	6.9	5.9
26 " 30 "	2.0	1.8	2.7	8.0	2.9	5.5	4.2
30 " 34 "	....	....	....	7.0	2.9	1.4	2.1
34 " 38 "	....	1.8	....	1.0	4.3	....	1.1
38 " 42 "	....	1.8	....	3.0	1.4	....	1.1
42 " 46 "	....	1.8	....	1.0	2.9	....	.9
46 " 50 "	....	....	....	2.0	1.4	....	.6
50 " 54 "	....	1.8	....	....	....	....	.2
54 " 58 "	....	....	....	....	....	....	....
58 " 62 "	....	....	....	....	1.4	....	.2
Total	100.0	100.0	100.0	100.0	100.0	100.0	100.0
Number of cases	98	57	74	100	70	73	472

The range of age at starting work, it will be seen, divides itself into two distinct groups—those who have started work before 30 to 35 years, represented by the Bedford, Magdalen and Probation groups, in which the average age at present conviction is lowest, and those who have started work at a wide range of ages, represented by the Auburn, Penitentiary and Workhouse groups. In the latter three institutions it may be of interest to note briefly the women who were not gainfully employed until they were 42 years of age or over. The two Auburn women who fall in this group are both foreign, one born in Italy and

[4] Thirteenth Census of the United States, 1910. "Occupational Statistics," p. 46.

one in Russia. The Italian woman was married to a man who drank and finally began to go with other women. When she was 44 she left him, was forced to support her family and began to practise midwifery. She had done no work previous to this and was not trained to do anything. Her present conviction was for abortion performed on one of her patients. The Russian woman had never done any work outside of her home until six years before the present conviction when her husband died and she was obliged to support her children. At that time, at the age of 53, she bought a dry-goods store. The store did not prove to be very successful and she attempted to burn it. She was convicted of attempted arson and evidence was brought at the trial that she had made various previous attempts to dispose of the store in a like manner.

The three Penitentiary women represent somewhat different types than those just mentioned. One woman, now 47 years old, was married when 32. She never did any work before or after her marriage until three years before her conviction, when she was short of money. Previous to this her husband had left her because she was a drug user. He gave her a large sum of money, but she spent so much for drugs that it did not last long and she was forced to earn more. Another Penitentiary woman, now 63 years, born in Austria, was married when young and did no work except the housework and work on her father's and husband's farm. Years after, when she had been in this country for a short time, she worked three or four years as a coat finisher in a factory. This was only to tide over a critical period in the family finances. The third Penitentiary woman is 50 years old, colored, born in the South. She has probably worked very little, except for short and irregular times the year before the present conviction when her consort was in a hospital. She admitted that she had prostituted many years, had used heroin steadily, and that the work was only an incidental thing in her life.

The four Workhouse women who did no work outside of their homes until after they were 42 are all white, two native and two foreign. The first woman is now 43. She was born in Sweden and came to this country when 23. Two years later she married a man whom she later divorced, and after leaving him she worked for a short time at general housework. She has had a long record of prostitution and the only work she did was probably sporadic. Another woman, now 46 years old, did no work until the year before her present arrest, when she worked as waitress in a hotel. Her husband had died several years before. She was a most erratic, unstable person and had been in a hospital for the insane for some time after her husband's death. The third Workhouse case in question is a woman 51 years old who has been in this country for three years. Soon after arriving here she began to work as cook. Her husband had died fourteen years before her coming to this country and during that time she had a "lover," a prominent lawyer in Berlin, who supported her. The fourth Workhouse case is a woman who has been married twice, her second husband dying just one year previous to the time she began to work. She says that when she was a girl her family was in comfortable circumstances. "I never knew what it meant to soil my hands, we had so many Chinese servants." Her present conviction was for violation of the Tenement House Law, and it seems likely that she had been prostituting for some time. Her short work record was very irregular.

As a whole, the group of older women who did not begin to work until late in life is small and represents women who have not found it necessary to work before, either because they were married and being supported by their husbands or because they were obtaining money in an illegal manner. The work records of these women are, for the most part, very brief and the various jobs are so isolated that they are scarcely comparable to the records of most of the younger women.

A frequent contention is that starting to work at an early age is a common cause of getting into the courts through meeting bad acquaintances, losing respect for the head of the family through increased independence, as well as for other reasons intrinsic in the occupational situation, notably the tendency to get into "blind alley" jobs. Table 106 shows the relationship which exists for our group of women between age at first conviction and age at starting work. There is clear evidence of a relationship here as shown by the coefficient of correlation of $.51 \pm .034$. However, we can not accept these data as evidence that there is a real tendency for those who start work young to be convicted early in life and those who start work later not to be convicted until later years, until we have taken into account the effect of present age. This obviously affects both age at first conviction and age at starting work, since one who is now of a given age must both have been convicted before that age and have started work before then if at all. Accordingly, the correlation coefficient may measure simply the degree of dependence of each of these variables on the factor of age. We have, therefore, determined the partial correlation coefficient

TABLE 106

Correlation between Age at First Conviction and Age at Starting Work

Total Group

Age at Starting Work	Age at First Conviction (Years): 6 to 9	9 to 12	12 to 15	15 to 18	18 to 21	21 to 24	24 to 27	27 to 30	30 to 33	33 to 36	36 to 39	39 to 42	42 to 45	45 to 48	48 to 51	51 to 54	54 to 57	57 to 60	60 to 63	63 to 66	66 to 69	Totals	Means (Age at First Conviction)
58 to 62 Years																		1				1	
54 " 58 "																						0	
50 " 54 "																	1					1	
46 " 50 "											1					1			1			3	49.5
42 " 46 "												1	1	1					1			4	
38 " 42 "												1	1		2						1	5	
34 " 38 "									1	1	1	1		1								5	
30 " 34 "						1			2	1	1	1	2		1			1				10	38.1
26 " 30 "							1	3	7	3	2	1		1			1					19	33.9
22 " 26						6	7	5	4		2	1		1		1			1			28	30.3
18 " 22	1		1	2	16	14	17	6	4	6	4	2			2			1				76	25.9
14 " 18 "		1	9	53	56	41	29	23	10	7	4	4	2			1	1					241	22.2
10 " 14 "		1		11	7	11	10	7	4	7	2	6	3	1								70	26.4
6 " 10 "					1	2			2	2	1						1					9	31.4
Totals	1	2	10	66	80	75	64	44	34	27	18	18	9	5	5	3	4	3	3	0	1	472	25.88
Means (Age at Starting Work)	16.3			15.2		16.7		18.3		19.2		21.7		31.2								17.75	

Age at first conviction: Mean = 25.88 $\sigma = 9.54$
Age at starting work: Mean = 17.75 $\sigma = 6.82$
Coefficient of correlation: r = .51 ± .034
Correlation ratios: Age at first conviction on age at starting work, η = .60 ± .029 Blakeman's Criterion = 5.1
Age at starting work on age at first conviction, η = .52 ± .033 Blakeman's Criterion = 1.9
Partial correlation coefficient: Age at first conviction with age at starting work for constant age, r = .004 ± .046

for age at first conviction with age at starting work, making present age the constant factor.[5] The correlation coefficient, .004±.046, would indicate that the apparent relationship between age at first conviction and age at starting work is entirely due to the relationship of each of these to age. Accordingly, we find no confirmation for the view which regards an early age of starting work as one of the important determinants of early criminality.

KIND OF WORK DONE

(a) *Classification of Kind of Work*

Before discussing in detail the nature of work done at various times during the working careers of these women, the method of classifying kinds of work will be observed briefly. It is difficult to classify accurately kinds of work done by women of varying ages for different periods of time. To make this difficulty as slight as possible, therefore, questions relating to kind of work done were asked very carefully with a view to finding out what was meant by "factory work," "office girl," "nurse," etc., both from the woman and the employer. The results were codified by the main divisions of the Census Index to Occupations[6] and were later regrouped into eleven classes which seemed to fit the needs of a selected group of women better than did the entire census scheme which was made up from returns of occupations for all wage-earners in the country, both male and female. The eleven classes used were based on the conditions surrounding given kinds of work as well as on degree of skill involved in the work, and include the following occupations:

1. *Domestic Service* includes women working at general housework, nurse-girls, waitresses or cooks in private homes, lady's maids, and housekeepers. This group includes all cases where living is in addition to wage, and where the nature of the employment demands that the women live at the place where they work.
2. *Factory Work* includes women working in a factory where there is a group of people. Laundry workers in a laundry have been put in this group also, since the numbers seemed too small for a

[5] The necessary data for computing the partial are the following:
r (age at first conviction with age at starting work) = .508
r (age at first conviction with age) = .964
r (age at starting work with age) = .526

[6] Bureau of the Census: "Index to Occupations," 1915.

separate division, and the general conditions of work are similar to those in factories.

3. *Home Work* includes workers who are able to earn their living by remaining in their own homes and who work alone for the most part. This is a somewhat heterogeneous group of dressmakers at home, lodging-house-keepers, janitresses and those who bring work home from a factory. This class is intended to show especially the contrast in conditions of work from those of the previous group.
4. *Restaurant and Hotel Work* includes waitresses in restaurants and hotels, chambermaids in hotels, laundry workers in hotels, a very few restaurant keepers, and one manager of a small hotel.
5. *Work in Stores* includes clerks, salesladies, models, cash girls, messengers, errand girls, demonstrators, milliners, and five women who themselves kept small stores.
6. *Vaudeville Performers* include show girls, acrobats, one dancing teacher who occasionally gave exhibition performances in theaters, and one girl who sang in a cabaret in a saloon.
7. *Clerical Work* includes bookkeepers, two cashiers, stenographers and typewriters, shipping clerks and one office girl for a doctor.
8. *Professional Service* includes two school teachers, two authors, and one piano teacher.
9. *Personal Service* includes manicurists, hair-dressers, one masseuse, and ten practical nurses and midwives.
10. *Charwomen* include ten women who do cleaning by the day in office buildings, etc.
11. *Miscellaneous* includes seventeen occupations which fit into no general scheme and each of which is too small in number to be given a separate class. There are in this group two dog-fanciers, one fortune-teller, one peddler, one newspaper distributor, one helper in a greenhouse, one commission agent, six unskilled farm workers, two ushers in a theater and two telephone operators.

The discussion of kind of work done at various times in the work histories of these women will be based on comparisons of these eleven classes of work. We have selected as the most important specific jobs in a woman's work history the kind of work (1) in the first job, (2) in the latest job, (3) at the time of first conviction, (4) at the time of latest conviction, and (5) prevailing work. The method of determining the prevailing work will be discussed later. The kind of work at these given times will be considered separately by institutional groups, summarized for the total group and compared with percentages for the general female population when possible.

(*b*) *Kind of Work Done at Specified Times*

(1) *Kind of Work in First Job.*—The kind of work in the first employment is particularly important to consider in connection with prevailing work and the estimate of efficiency of a work record. It is difficult to draw any definite conclusions from the kind of work in the first job, *per se,* because of the fact that this first work represents in one case perhaps the beginning of a long and efficient work record while in another case it may be only the casual job performed in later life to tide over a financial embarrassment. As we have seen in Table 105, the age at starting work runs from the illegitimate employments under fourteen years up to the Workhouse woman who started to work at 58 years, after her husband's death. With these older women who have had no training and who take whatever work they can most easily get to tide them over any given financial stress, the first employment does not represent at it does with the younger women the beginning of a work history, but merely an isolated job. Since the number who started work late in life is comparatively small, however, we shall present Table 107, keeping in mind that there is this constant small element of women starting work late, and having no conscious selection of kind of work since the work itself is so casual.

From Table 107 it is observed, first of all, that the large bulk of cases in each institutional group, except Probation, falls in the domestic service class at the time of their first job. This varies, however, between the institutional groups, the Workhouse having the largest percentage of domestic service workers and Probation the smallest percentage. The factory workers who have the second highest percentage in all groups except Probation, where they have first place, do not vary markedly between the institutional groups except in the Workhouse which has a very much smaller percentage of factory workers than the other groups have. Home work is not of particular significance, apparently, in any of the groups, and is chiefly conspicuous because Bedford has no representative in this group. The restaurant and hotel workers vary to quite an extent and indicate that a larger percentage of women in the Workhouse than in any other group went first into this work. Workers in stores furnish 16.3 per cent of the Probation group, and are represented to a somewhat smaller degree in the other groups. Vaudeville performers have the highest percentages in the Probation and Workhouse groups, with no representative in Auburn. Clerical work, on the other hand, while it has a percentage of

TABLE 107

KIND OF WORK IN FIRST JOB

Per Cent Distribution of Delinquent Women by Institutional Groups

Kind of Work	Institutional Groups						Total
	Bedford	Auburn	Magdalen	Penitentiary	Workhouse	Probation	
Domestic Service	44.6	46.3	37.1	34.6	47.5	19.8	38.5
Factory Work	29.7	25.0	32.9	30.8	12.1	32.6	26.9
Home Work	....	6.3	4.3	.9	5.1	3.5	3.1
Restaurant and Hotel Work	5.0	2.5	2.9	4.7	10.1	7.0	5.5
Work in Stores	7.9	7.5	10.0	7.5	11.1	16.3	9.9
Vaudeville Performers	2.0	....	1.3	1.9	5.1	5.8	2.8
Clerical Work	4.0	....	4.3	5.6	2.0	5.8	3.7
Professional Service	1.0	1.3	1.3	2.8	....	....	1.1
Personal Service	1.0	3.8	4.3	2.8	1.0	3.5	2.6
Charwomen	....	....	....	1.9	....	....	.4
Miscellaneous	2.0	2.5	1.3	2.8	1.0	2.3	2.0
Never Worked	3.0	5.0	....	3.7	5.1	3.5	3.5
Total	100.0	100.0	100.0	100.0	100.0	100.0	100.0
Number of cases	101	80	70	107	99	86	543

5.8 in the Probation group, has only 2.0 per cent of the Workhouse women and none in Auburn. The Penitentiary, Magdalen and Bedford follow Probation in the percentage of clerical workers. Professional service workers are found only in Bedford, Auburn, the Magdalen and the Penitentiary, the first three being represented by one case and the fourth by two cases. It is of interest to note that these two classes of occupations which require most training, namely, clerical work and professional service, have the smallest percentage who first went into this work in Auburn, the next larger percentage in the Workhouse, the next in Bedford, the Magdalen, Probation, and the largest percentage in the Penitentiary. Personal service workers constitute only a small percentage of each institutional group and the variations between these are not large. In no group except the Penitentiary were there any women who first went to work as charwomen. The miscellaneous group contains cases from all institutions in not markedly varying percentages. It is particularly worthy of note that within each group the percentage who have never worked is very small. The Magdalen has no women who have never worked, while the other five groups have percentages ranging from 3.0 to 5.1 per cent. In our total group of cases, we may note that the largest percentage, 38.5, went first into housework, and that the next largest percentage was engaged first in factory work. The other occupations have very much smaller percentages.

(2) *Kind of Work in Latest Job.*—If we compare Table 108 with the foregoing table, we will note that in each of the institutional groups, except Probation, the percentage of domestic service workers is still highest, but that in all the groups except the Magdalen and Penitentiary there seems to be a slight decrease in the percentage of domestic service workers in the latest job. The factory workers have increased, on the other hand, in the percentage found in Bedford, Magdalen and the Workhouse, but have decreased rather noticeably in Auburn and the Penitentiary. These two latter institutions, however, have increased in the numbers found in the group of home workers, and this is probably due to the fact that a large percentage of these women are married and have a tendency, where it is necessary for them to help

TABLE 108

KIND OF WORK IN LATEST JOB

Per Cent Distribution of Delinquent Women in Institutional Groups (Includes only those who have had more than one job.)

Kind of Work	Institutional Groups						Total
	Bedford	Auburn	Magdalen	Penitentiary	Workhouse	Probation	
Domestic	35.5	43.8	38.7	39.4	37.4	15.7	34.9
Factory Work	36.6	9.6	40.3	16.0	17.2	28.9	24.2
Home Work	....	13.7	1.6	5.3	5.1	6.0	5.2
Restaurant and Hotel Work	6.5	12.3	9.7	8.5	20.2	8.4	11.1
Work in Stores	6.5	2.7	3.2	9.6	6.1	13.3	7.1
Vaudeville Performers	4.3	1.4	4.8	4.3	3.0	8.4	4.4
Clerical Work	1.1	2.7	1.6	3.2	1.0	9.6	3.2
Professional Service	1.1	1.4	....	....	....	....	.4
Personal Service	1.1	4.1	....	3.2	2.0	4.8	2.6
Charwomen	2.2	1.4	....	5.3	2.0	....	2.0
Miscellaneous	2.2	1.4	....	1.1	1.0	1.2	1.2
Never Worked	3.2	5.5	....	4.3	5.1	3.6	3.8
Total	100.0	100.0	100.0	100.0	100.0	100.0	100.0
Number of cases	93	73	62	94	99	83	504

piece out the family income, to do work which will not take them away from home. Restaurant and hotel workers, it will be noted, have increased in each institutional group, while workers in stores have decreased in each group except the Penitentiary. Vaudeville performers have increased in each group except the Workhouse. The clerical workers have decreased in percentage in each of the groups except Auburn and Probation, in each of which there is a slight increase. In the same way, the professional service workers entirely drop out of all groups except Bedford and Auburn, which have the same number of cases doing professional service in the latest job as in the first job. Personal service remains nearly unchanged and the number of charwomen increases only slightly in each group. The miscellaneous workers remain practically the same. In the total group it is of interest to note that there is not a striking change from the first to the latest jobs in the kind of work done. There is a slight decrease in the number of domestic service and factory workers and very slight increases in several of the other groups. The significant thing in the comparison seems to be that there is so little change and that there seems to be a marked tendency for these women to keep within somewhat the same kind of work so far as can be judged by the first and latest jobs.

(3) *Kind of Work at First Conviction.*—If we observe the kind of work done at time of the first conviction as given in Table 109, we may note first the very large percentages in each institutional group who were idle at the time of first conviction. "Idle" does not include those who were at home doing the work either in their own or their parents' homes. Such cases are included under "Own housework." Those who have never worked might, it is true, be added either to the "Idle" or "Own housework" group in this table, but have been kept separate so that they may show as a constant group in the later tables dealing with kind of work at specified times. Because such a large percentage were idle at this time, the numbers in many of the occupations are smaller than in the two previous tables. Domestic service still keeps first place in all except the Probation group. The factory workers have decreased in numbers perceptibly and are much smaller in proportion to the domestic service workers than in either the first or latest jobs, previously considered. Home work remains the same for the total group as in the first job, but in the institutional groups Auburn alone stands out as having a larger percentage of home workers than was found in a consideration of the first job. The restaurant and hotel workers, workers in stores, and vaudeville performers have de-

creased markedly from the first job. Only two women were doing clerical work at the time of first conviction, while there were twenty who had started their first work in a clerical job. The professional service workers, also, have a very small percentage, only two women at the time of first conviction. The number of women in each of the other three groups are also smaller at time of the first conviction than in the first job.

TABLE 109

KIND OF WORK AT TIME OF FIRST CONVICTION

Per Cent Distribution of Delinquent Women in Institutional Groups

Kind of Work	Institutional Groups						Total
	Bedford	Auburn	Magdalen	Penitentiary	Workhouse	Probation	
Domestic Service	18.8	20.8	8.8	10.0	4.8	2.3	11.2
Factory Work	12.9	1.4	5.9	2.2	1.6	5.7	5.4
Home Work	....	13.9	....	2.2	3.2	1.1	3.1
Restaurant and Hotel Work	3.0	1.4	1.5	1.1	3.2	....	1.7
Work in Stores	2.0	1.4	2.9	1.1	....	....	1.3
Vaudeville Performers	1.0	....	1.5	....	1.6	1.1	.8
Clerical Work	....	....	....	1.1	....	1.1	.4
Professional Service	....	1.4	....	1.1	....	....	.4
Personal Service	....	4.2	....	1.1	....	1.1	1.0
Charwomen	....	....	....	2.2	....	....	.4
Miscellaneous	....	....	....	1.1	1.6	....	.4
Own Housework	5.0	25.0	10.3	8.9	3.2	9.1	10.0
Idle	54.4	25.0	69.1	63.7	72.6	75.0	59.9
Never Worked	3.0	5.6	....	4.4	8.1	3.4	4.0
Total	100.0	100.0	100.0	100.0	100.0	100.0	100.0
Number of cases	101	72	68	90	62	88	481

(4) *Kind of Work at Present Conviction.*—The following table (Table 110) is of more interest if taken in connection with Table 109. Again, the percentage of idle persons is the most striking thing in the table; though when compared with the percentage of idle women at time of first conviction it is seen to be somewhat smaller. From these two tables it would seem obvious that the factor of unemployment has an important relation to the problem of delinquency. It is difficult even to estimate how much of this unemployment was unnecessary since there is no way of satisfactorily verifying attempts to obtain

work. It seems probable, however, from the statements of the women, and from a survey of industrial conditions in New York City during the time that the present convictions occurred, that there would have been no particular difficulty for many of the women who were idle to have obtained work.

TABLE 110

KIND OF WORK AT TIME OF PRESENT CONVICTION

Per Cent Distribution of Delinquent Women in Institutional Groups

Kind of Work	Institutional Groups						Total
	Bedford	Auburn	Magdalen	Penitentiary	Workhouse	Probation	
Domestic Service	14.9	19.5	10.7	17.5	11.2	4.5	13.1
Factory Work	10.9	1.3	6.7	1.0	4.1	3.4	4.6
Home Work	....	11.7	....	1.0	4.1	1.1	2.8
Restaurant and Hotel Work	2.0	2.6	1.3	1.9	4.1	....	2.0
Work in Stores	....	1.3	1.3	1.0	1.0	....	.7
Vaudeville Performers	2.0	....	....	....	2.0	1.1	.9
Clerical Work	....	....	....	1.0	....	1.1	.4
Professional Service	1.0	1.3	....	1.0	....	....	.4
Personal Service	....	3.9	....	1.9	1.0	1.1	1.3
Charwomen	....	....	....	1.9	....	....	.4
Miscellaneous	....	....	....	2.9	1.0	....	.7
Own housework	13.9	23.4	16.0	13.6	10.2	14.6	14.9
Idle	53.5	29.9	64.0	51.5	56.1	69.7	54.3
Never Worked	3.0	5.2	....	3.9	5.1	3.4	3.5
Total	100.0	100.0	100.0	100.0	100.0	100.0	100.0
Number of cases	101	77	75	103	98	89	543

(5) *Prevailing Work.*—The prevailing work of these women represents the occupations in which they have been engaged for the longest time. We have divided the work histories of the women in our group into three classes, (1) those who have done only one kind of work, (2) those who have done one kind of work almost entirely with perhaps one or two jobs in other occupations, and (3) those who have had variable records, now in one kind of work, now in another, but with one kind of work which might be called prevailing because the subject had worked longer in that occupation than in any other. By combining the first two classes we cover 71.3 per cent of our cases. The third group was also used in considering prevailing work so that

the total number of cases could be used. The prevailing work of this third group always represented the longest number of months of work.[7]

Table 111 shows that in each group, except Probation, the domestic service workers have the highest percentage. The other workers run in very much the same proportions as for the work in the first job. The comparison of these two tables indicates that, for the most part, there is little change in kind of work in the first job and kind of work done later. There is a slight tendency toward a smaller percentage of do-

[7] The few following examples from the Bedford group may serve to indicate how the work records vary in the kind of work done.

Class 1.—Those working in only one occupation.

a) Woman now 29 years, 10 months. Began work at 15. Singing and dancing in vaudeville performances from 1901-1912. Was forced to leave because she was using drugs. Has done no other work.

b) Woman now 26 years, 10 months. Began work at 15. She had 13 jobs, all housework, covering a work period of 6 years.

Class 2.—Almost entirely one kind of work, with a few exceptions.

a) Girl 16 years, 9 months. Began work at 15.
   1) Housework, 4 mos.
   2) Housework, 4 wks.
   3) Housework, 8 mos.
   4) Helper in hotel dining room, 7 wks.
   5) Housework, 2 wks.
   6) Cigar-making, 3 wks.
   7) Housework, 1 wk.

b) Colored woman 23 years, 8 months. Began work at 8 years.
   1) Nursegirl, 1 yr.
   2) Housework, 2½ yrs.
   3) Housework, 3 yrs.
   4) Housework, 2 yrs.
   5) Waitress, 3 mos.
   6) Housework, 1 yr.
   7) Housework, 1 yr.
   8) Housework, 1 yr.
   9) Waitress, 1 yr.

Class 3.—Those with variable records.

a) Woman 23 years, 2 months. Began work at 17 years. Prevailing work—saleslady in a store.
   1) Saleslady in store, 1 yr.
   2) Home work from embroidery factory, 6 mos.
   3) Served milk in milk station, 4 mos.
   4) Housework, 2 mos.
   5) Saleslady in store, 3 mos.

b) Girl, 18 years, 5 mos. Began work at 15. Prevailing work—sorting paper in paper mill.
   1) Housework—nursegirl, 2 wks.
   2) Sorting paper in paper mill, 1 yr.
   3) Banding cigars in cigar factory, 3 mos.
   4) Feeder on forming machine in hat factory, 3 mos.
   5) Banding cigars in cigar factory, 1 wk.

TABLE 111

PREVAILING KIND OF WORK

Per Cent Distribution of Delinquent Women in Institutional Groups

Kind of Work	Institutional Groups						Total
	Bedford	Auburn	Magdalen	Penitentiary	Workhouse	Probation	
Domestic Service	47.5	43.4	38.0	41.6	48.2	22.4	40.4
Factory Work	30.7	14.5	32.5	24.8	8.4	30.6	23.8
Home Work	....	13.2	2.8	2.0	7.2	3.5	4.5
Restaurant and Hotel Work	3.0	5.3	5.6	5.9	8.4	8.2	6.0
Work in Stores	8.9	4.0	11.3	5.9	10.8	11.8	8.7
Vaudeville Performers	3.0	1.3	2.8	4.0	4.8	7.1	3.9
Clerical Work	1.0	2.6	4.2	3.0	1.2	7.1	3.1
Professional Service	1.0	1.3	....	2.0	....	....	.8
Personal Service	1.0	5.3	2.8	3.0	2.4	4.7	3.1
Charwomen	....	1.3	....	2.0	....	....	.6
Miscellaneous	1.0	2.6	....	2.0	2.4	1.2	1.6
Never Worked	3.0	5.3	....	4.0	6.0	3.5	3.7
Total	100.0	100.0	100.0	100.0	100.0	100.0	100.0
Number of cases	101	76	71	101	83	85	517

mestic service workers in the first job than in the prevailing work, and there is a corresponding increase for factory workers.

(c) Comparison of Prevailing Work of Delinquents and General Population

A comparison at this point of the prevailing work of the delinquent women in this study with the kind of work done by females over 15 years of age in New York State as compiled in the 1910 census[8] shows that there are various differences in kind of occupations between the two groups (see Chart XVIII). The delinquent women have 42.0 per cent of their number domestic service workers, which is 18.3 per cent more than we find in the general population. There is also a larger percentage of factory workers, restaurant and hotel workers and vaudeville performers among the delinquents than among the general population. The vaudeville performers furnish to the whole group of delinquents eight times their proportional representation in the general population. It seems probable that with this group of women the

[8] *Op. cit.*, p. 574.

nature of the work is to a large extent an important factor in the delinquency. A traveling vaudeville company where the girl is thrown into contact with many people and many kinds of men, where there is little privacy and innumerable opportunities to earn money "on the side," affords ample chance for sexual irregularities. The occupations in which the delinquents have less than their expected percentages are among those doing home work, work in stores, and more especially among clerical workers and those in professional service. The clerical workers in this study furnish less than one-quarter of their quota in the general population, while the professional service workers furnish

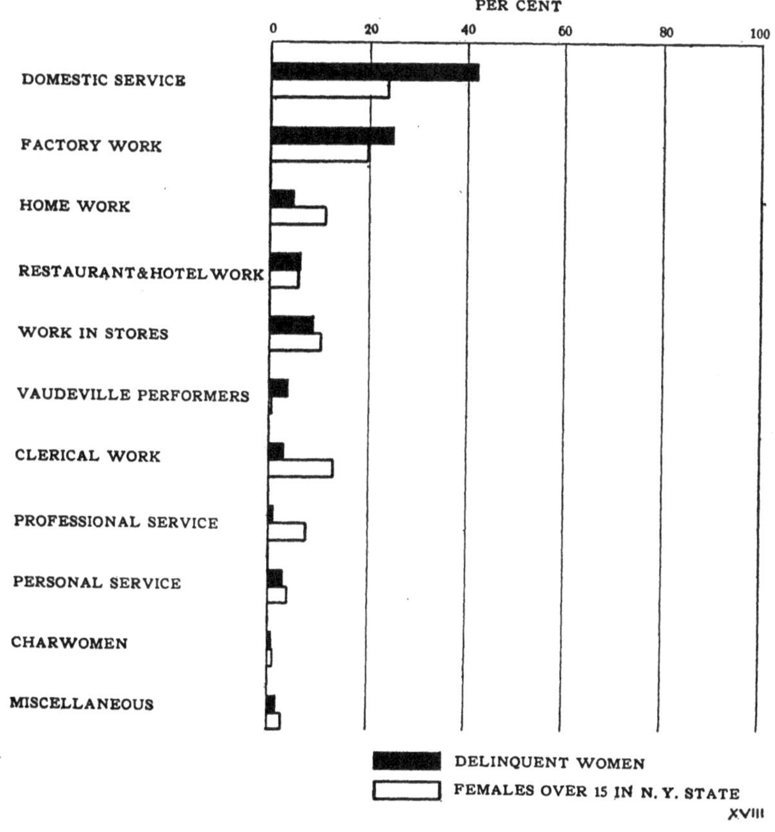

Chart XVIII

Percentage Comparison Showing Prevailing Kind of Work of 517 Women Delinquents in New York State, and Kind of Work Done by Females over 15 Years of Age in New York State, as Compiled in the 1910 Census.

less than one-ninth of what we might expect. The last three groups of personal service workers, charwomen and miscellaneous also have less than their expected representation. The largest differences, therefore, are as follows: with the exception of vaudeville performers who work under especially bad conditions, the delinquents have a larger representation than we should expect among the occupations which are comparatively unskilled, principally domestic service and, to a lesser degree, factory work, while they have a smaller percentage than the general population in occupations which require special training, such as clerical work and professional service.[9]

At this point we might observe the comparisons made between the occupations of a group of 3,229 women offenders in six states and the total female population sixteen years of age and over in the United States. In this study made by Miss Mary Conyngton in 1911 on the "Relations between Occupation and Criminality of Women"[10] she found in comparing the delinquents with the total female wage-earners sixteen years of age and over that "by far the largest proportion of offenders comes from the group engaged in domestic and personal service, and that the only subdivision under this general head furnishing more than its proportionate share of misdemeanants or criminals is that of servants and waiters. . . . These workers, constituting 24.1 per cent of the breadwinners, account for 70.3 per cent of the offenders, or very nearly three times their proportionate share. . . . With practically the same number in each group, the servants and waitresses furnish more than four times as many offenders as those engaged in manufacturing and mechanical pursuits." In referring to a group called "trade and transportation" in the Census classification, and including in Miss Conyngton's study cash girls, bookkeepers, clerks, saleswomen, stenographers, and telephone operators, she finds that this group of workers "furnish to the whole group of offenders studied only one-third of their proportionate representation. And this striking fact becomes even more striking when it is remembered that the investigation was carried on chiefly in industrial centers, where workers

[9] We recognize that the two groups of facts are not on exactly the same basis for comparison. That is, while the Census figures apply to women working in given occupations at a certain time, the prevailing work used here may apply to many work records of years past and, at best, it covers a period of time for each statement of prevailing work.

[10] "Report on Condition of Woman and Child Wage-earners in the United States," Vol. XV. "Relation between Occupation and Criminality of Women." By Mary Conyngton. Government Printing Office, Washington, 1911. p. 30.

of this kind are most numerous and where their temptations are greatest."

It is not easy to say whether this unduly large percentage of domestic service workers among the delinquent group is, in any sense, a result of the occupational influences, or whether those who go into domestic service represent the great mass of unskilled, untrained women, from which the most of our delinquents are drawn. It is true that the domestic service workers in our group have not gone so far in school as women in other occupations. This is indicated in Tables 131 and 132, which show that for the domestic service workers the average grade finished is 4.16 ± 2.48, while for those in occupations other than domestic service the average grade is 5.03 ± 2.56. A later chapter[11] shows that the domestic service workers are also of lower average mentality than the group of women in occupations other than domestic service. From our observation, we are inclined to think that the inherent conditions of work surrounding many of the young, inexperienced girls who go into housework may be responsible, to a small extent, for their delinquency, but that the occupational influences for the most part are secondary rather than direct causes of delinquency. It is true that in housework there is not the careful supervision which many factories, offices, shops and stores give, that there is opportunity for petty thieving with little danger of being caught, and in many instances the opportunity for meeting men, such as tradesmen, in an intimate way which may lead to sexual irregularities. Making allowances for these difficulties in domestic service work which, without doubt, affect a large number of the delinquent group, we believe that the more important phase of the question to be stressed is that a large proportion of those in our group going into domestic service are the untrained women of somewhat lower mentality, often impressionable and easily influenced.[12]

[11] See Chapter XV, p. 503.

[12] A case of interest at this point is that of a young Hungarian girl committed to Bedford for petit larceny. She was stupid, unattractive physically, and in addition had very poor eyesight which her brother told her would ultimately make her blind. She became infatuated with a negro man who was attentive to her, and who, it is thought, finally persuaded her to steal a diamond ring from her employer for whom she had been doing housework about three months. Her excuse was that the employer "had lots,—rings and jewels and things, and I had nothing." She wanted to make herself look beautiful, she wanted to please the negro, the only man who had ever paid any attention to her, and she was too stupid to realize that the theft as she committed it would surely lead to her being caught.

Dr. Davis in a study of prostitutes at Bedford writes:

"Almost all the studies of prostitution heretofore made have noted the high percentage of women who were engaged in domestic service previous to entering the life. So far as my observation goes, I do not believe that this indicates any greater danger from domestic service itself as an occupation than from any other in which unskilled girls engage. Domestic service for women under existing economic conditions corresponds to casual labor for men. It is the job where training and experience are unnecessary in order to find work. Such services would not be desired by families where efficiency is demanded and paid for. A very large proportion of our girls were not competent workers but were girls employed in the lowest stratum of families that employ domestic help at all and where standards of service do not exist. This group includes almost all the colored girls and a considerable number of the foreign-born white girls." [13]

While we are indicating the prevailing work among the institutional groups, it may also be advisable to show the prevailing work among nativity and color groups. Table 112 gives us this information and shows that the native colored have over 80.2 per cent of their number engaged in domestic service, while only 26.7 per cent of the native white were so engaged. The total foreign stand between these two groups with a percentage slightly higher than the percentage of domestic service workers for the total group. The percentage of factory workers, again, is less in the foreign born and native colored groups than among the native white, though very much less in the native colored. It seems very likely that the percentages in the Magdalen group in Table 111 have been affected by the fact that there are no colored women in the Magdalen and that there is, therefore, a tendency for the percentage of domestic service workers to be less and for the factory workers to have a slightly larger number than the same occupations in the other institutional groups. The Probation group which has a small percentage of colored is also undoubtedly affected in the same way. It will be noted that the colored have no representative in the professional service class and one only among the clerical workers. The foreign born also have only one professional woman and three clerical workers, while the native white have one professional woman and four clerical workers.

[13] *Op. cit.*, p. 175.

TABLE 112

PREVAILING KIND OF WORK

Per Cent Distribution of Delinquent Women Classified by Nativity and Color

Kind of Work	Nativity and Color				Total
	Total Foreign Born	Total Native Born	Native White	Native Colored	
Domestic Service	45.0	40.8	26.7	80.2	42.1
Factory Work	21.9	25.7	32.9	5.5	24.6
Home Work	6.6	3.8	4.7	1.1	4.6
Restaurant and Hotel Work	8.6	5.2	5.9	3.3	6.2
Work in Stores	6.6	10.1	12.9	2.2	9.1
Vaudeville Performers	1.3	5.2	5.9	3.3	4.0
Clerical Work	2.0	3.8	4.7	1.1	3.2
Professional Service	.7	.9	1.2	......	.8
Personal Service	4.6	2.6	3.1	1.1	3.2
Charwomen	.7	.6	.4	1.1	.6
Miscellaneous	2.0	1.5	1.6	1.1	1.6
Total	100.0	100.0	100.0	100.0	100.0
Number of cases	151	346	255	91	497

The trend of change of work at various times in the work histories may be shown by combining the preceding tables. Table 113 shows the predominance of domestic service workers at all times, and the small percentage throughout of workers in the more skilled occupations of clerical work and professional service. An increase in domestic service workers is shown between the first job and the prevailing work, while there is a decrease of factory workers. The markedly high percentage of idle women at the time of conviction, both first and present, is of greatest significance and would bear a much closer study of the causes of unemployment.

It is interesting to observe that a similar tendency was noted in a study of male felons made by Dr. Glueck in Sing Sing Prison.[14] In a discussion of the defective group, he notes that 57.1 per cent were unemployed at time of present conviction, 39.6 per cent of the psychopathic group were unemployed and 50 per cent of the Russian group were "unemployed at the time of the crime although 56.8 per cent were skilled mechanics." We do not find, however, with our group of de-

[14] *Op. cit.*, pp. 112, 123, 131 and 138.

linquent women as he did with male felons that "there seems to be a certain correlation between the degree of recidivism in a given group and the extent of unemployment at the time of the commission of the crime." From Tables 109 and 110, it is seen that the Probation group which has the smallest average number of convictions has in each case the highest percentage of idle women. Aside from this point, however, the fact of there being such a large percentage out of work at the time of conviction, among male criminals as well as among our delinquent groups, is of great importance.

Again, in Miss Conyngton's study,[15] she found that between the earliest occupation and the occupation at latest arrest:

> "The most significant changes are those which have taken place not between the great industrial groups, but from them into the non-gainful pursuits. . . . It will be noticed that each of the groups of gainful occupations diminishes, and that the increase is wholly among those who are either married and keeping house, or who have no lawful pursuit. It is rather curious to find these two groups at the time of the latest arrest so exactly the same in number, but the rate of increase has of course been enormously greater for those having no occupations than for those keeping house."

In our group of delinquent women we found 3.5 per cent who had never had a "lawful occupation" when we were considering the kind of work in first job (Table 113), while at time of the present conviction, corresponding to "latest arrest," there were 54.3 per cent of the women idle and 3.5 per cent who had never worked. This is a very much more striking increase in those without employment than Miss Conyngton finds in the percentages of 0.6 per cent who had no lawful employment when the earliest employment was being considered, and 17.5 per cent who had no lawful pursuit at the time of the latest arrest, but the trend is in the same direction in both groups. Also, the investigation mentioned was made from institutional records which are largely based on the subject's statement. The percentage of idle, we are convinced from our own investigations, is much larger than the women themselves are willing to admit.

(*d*) *Relationship Between Kind of Work and Grade Finished*

It may be of interest, since so large a percentage of the delinquent women are engaged in housework, to find the relationship between the kind of prevailing work and the grade finished in school in order to

[15] *Op. cit.*, pp. 46-47.

TABLE 113

KIND OF WORK DONE BY DELINQUENT WOMEN AT SPECIFIED TIMES DURING THEIR WORK HISTORIES

Per Cent Distribution for Total Group

Kind of Work	Specified Times				
	In First Job	In Latest Job*	At Time of First Conviction	At Time of Present Conviction	Prevailing Work
Domestic Service	38.5	34.9	11.2	13.1	40.4
Factory Work	26.9	24.2	5.4	4.6	23.8
Home Work	3.1	5.2	3.1	2.8	4.5
Restaurant and Hotel Work	5.5	11.1	1.7	2.0	6.0
Work in Stores	9.9	7.1	1.3	.7	8.7
Vaudeville Performers	2.8	4.4	.8	.9	3.9
Clerical Work	3.7	3.2	.4	.4	3.1
Professional Service	1.1	.4	.4	.4	.8
Personal Service	2.6	2.6	1.0	1.3	3.1
Charwomen	.4	2.0	.4	.4	.6
Miscellaneous	2.0	1.2	.4	.7	1.6
Own Housework	......	......	10.0	14.9	......
Idle	......	......	59.9	54.3	......
Never Worked	3.5	3.8	4.0	3.5	3.7
Total	100.0	100.0	100.0	100.0	100.0
Number of cases	543	504	481	543	517

* Includes only those who have had more than one job.

determine whether women in certain occupations tend to have had more or less education, and whether those in domestic service, particularly, are characterized as is often stated by reaching a much lower grade than those in other occupations. The correlation ratio, showing the differences in grade finished corresponding to differences in prevailing work (Table 114), is $.38 \pm .042$. This shows a fairly high relationship, indicating that the occupational groups differ in respect to school attainment. From the means for the grades we can roughly see what average attainment is characteristic of each occupation. Charwomen, miscellaneous and professional workers are too few in number to be of any value since so few cases might easily have occurred by chance. Bearing in mind the small numbers, we find that the order of grade reached by women in stated occupations, beginning with the lowest grade and running upwards, is as follows:

1. Charwomen
2. Miscellaneous
3. Domestic service
4. Home work
5. Factory work
6. Restaurant and hotel work
7. Personal service
8. Vaudeville performers
9. Work in stores
10. Clerical work
11. Professional service

From this it would seem, throwing out the first two, that the domestic service workers have finished the lowest mean grade, 4.1, the home and factory workers the next higher grade, and the clerical workers the highest mean grade of significance, 6.5. The bulk of our women, therefore, the domestic service and factory workers, fall in the two lower grade groups, indicating that the women who go into these occupations have not had the educational advantages that some of the other occupational groups have, such as workers in stores, clerical workers, etc. We are not justified, however, in assuming that the fact of more or less educational equipment is a determinant of the occupation chosen. The crude relationship, measured by the ratio of .38, may very probably be accounted for by a basic relationship between intelligence and kind of work. We shall see (p. 501) that the ratio of nature of prevailing work on intelligence (Test Aggregate) is .46±.043, and that the correlation coefficient of intelligence (Test Aggregate) with grade finished is .75±.034 (see p. 497). The statistical data give us no grounds for stating which is the primary factor, intelligence or education, but the logical presumption would be in favor of the former, as a constitutional factor which might well have affected both the degree of education and the choice of a job.

WAGE

The study of wage is in many ways the most difficult of all occupational data to work with, because of the difficulty in getting accurate wage information either from the subject or by verification, and in estimating what the living would be in all jobs such as domestic service, practical nursing, etc., where living is in addition to wage. Because the time represented by the first job varied in individual cases by many years, it seemed impossible to fix any arbitrary estimate of living which would be fair to all. A woman who did housework ten years ago for a poor family in the country for $3 a week would be receiving much less in monetary value than she would be earning today with the same wage, if she were working for a wealthy family in the city, since the estimate of cost of living would vary so between the two times and

TABLE 114

Correlation between Grade Finished in School and Nature of Prevailing Work

Total Group

Prevailing Work	Grade Finished												Totals	Means (Grade Finished)
	0*	1	2	3	4	5	6	7	8	1st Yr. H. S.	2nd Yr. H. S.	4th Yr. H. S.		
Domestic Service	17	6	18	25	31	26	11	12	10	6		1	163	4.1
Factory Work	13	4	9	15	13	20	20	6	9				109	4.2
Home Work	6		2	1	3	1	3	3	2			1	22	4.1
Restaurant and Hotel Work	2	1	1	1	3	3	3	2	5				21	5.0
Work in Stores	1			1	5	5	7	6	10	1	1	1	38	6.4
Vaudeville Performers				2	2	2	2	5	3			1	17	6.2
Clerical Work				1	1	3	2	2	5		1		15	6.5
Professional Service							1			1		1	3	8.7
Personal Service	2		2	1	1		5		2			2	15	5.3
Charwomen	2				1								3	1.3
Miscellaneous	3	1	1	1							1		7	2.3
Totals	46	12	33	48	60	60	54	36	46	8	3	7	413	4.56

Grade finished: Mean = 4.56 σ = 2.641

Correlation ratio: Grade finished on nature of prevailing work, η = .38 ± .042

* Includes those who have never been in school and those who have attended, but never finished first grade.

places. We have, therefore, throughout, kept separate the wages of those engaged in domestic service, including, in addition to those doing general housework, nursegirls, waitresses or cooks in private homes, lady's maids and housekeepers. There are also included here two practical nurses who, in addition to weekly wage, received living. All of the wages given for this group, therefore, are only the money received and do not include the allowance for maintenance which must be added in order to make these wages comparable with the non-housework group. We have presented percentage tables on the wage received by domestic service workers and those in occupations other than domestic service, by institutional groups, for the first and latest jobs, and at first and present conviction. Although the division of each group into two parts makes the number of cases very small, we have presented the frequency tables on wage in order to show the composition of the total groups, but have made few comments on the individual tables.

(*a*) *Wage Earned at Specified Times*

(1) *Wage in First Job.* If we turn to the weekly wage earned in the first job by women in domestic service, we will note that for the

TABLE 115

WEEKLY WAGE IN FIRST JOB

Per Cent Distribution by Institutional Groups of Women Employed at Domestic Service and Allied Occupations Where Living Was in Addition to Wage

Weekly Wage in First Job Plus Living	Institutional Groups						Total
	Bedford	Auburn	Magdalen	Peni-tentiary	Work-house	Probation	
Living only....	17.1	29.6	11.1	6.7	18.8	....	15.6
$1 to $2.....	19.5	7.4	5.6	13.3	9.4	....	11.3
2 " 3.....	26.8	18.5	27.8	40.0	12.5	25.0	25.0
3 " 4.....	12.2	25.9	38.9	6.7	21.9	41.7	20.6
4 " 5.....	19.5	11.1	5.6	23.3	21.9	16.7	17.5
5 " 6.....	....	7.4	11.1	3.3	6.3	8.3	5.0
6 " 7.....	2.4	....	....	....	....	8.3	1.3
7 " 8.....	2.4	....	....	....	3.1	....	1.3
8 " 9.....	....	....	....	....	3.1	....	.6
9 " 10.....	....	....	....	6.7	3.1	....	1.9
Total...	100.0	100.0	100.0	100.0	100.0	100.0	100.0
Number of cases	41	27	18	30	32	12	160

TABLE 116

WEEKLY WAGE IN FIRST JOB

Per Cent Distribution by Institutional Groups of Women Employed at Occupations other than Domestic Service

Weekly Wage in First Job	Institutional Groups						Total
	Bedford	Auburn	Magdalen	Penitentiary	Workhouse	Probation	
$0 to $1	....	8.0	....	2.0	5.9	2.3	2.5
1 " 2	2.0	....	....	....	5.9	....	1.3
2 " 3	....	16.0	5.4	....	5.9	....	3.3
3 " 4	11.8	8.0	21.6	8.0	11.8	11.6	12.1
4 " 5	17.7	8.0	8.1	6.0	11.8	18.6	12.1
5 " 6	23.5	24.0	21.6	10.0	11.8	11.6	16.7
6 " 7	17.7	16.0	18.9	16.0	14.7	14.0	16.3
7 " 8	5.9	8.0	5.4	14.0	2.9	20.9	10.0
8 " 9	11.8	....	10.8	6.0	8.8	4.7	7.5
9 " 10	3.9	4.0	....	8.0	2.9	2.3	3.8
10 " 11	2.0	....	2.7	4.0	2.9	2.3	2.5
11 " 12	2.0	4.0	....	4.0	....	....	1.7
12 " 13	....	4.0	2.7	8.0	5.9	2.3	3.8
13 " 14	....	....	2.7	....	2.9	2.3	1.3
15 " 16	....	....	....	2.0	....	4.7	1.3
20 " 21	....	....	....	2.0	....	....	.4
22 " 23	....	....	....	2.0	....	....	.4
24 " 25	....	....	....	....	2.9	....	.4
25 " 26	2.0	....	....	2.0	....	2.3	1.3
27 " 28	....	....	....	2.0	....	....	.4
35 " 36	....	....	....	2.0	2.9	....	.8
45 " 46	....	....	....	2.0	....	....	.4
Total	100.0	100.0	100.0	100.0	100.0	100.0	100.0
Number of cases	51	25	37	50	34	43	240

total group the range is from living only to $10 a week plus living. The range varies, however, between the groups, with Auburn and the Magdalen having the shortest range, the Penitentiary and the Workhouse the longest.[16]

The first wages in the occupations other than domestic service, it will be seen from Table 116, have a much longer range than domestic service wages, running up to $45 in the Penitentiary. In this group of wages as well, the Penitentiary and the Workhouse have the long-

[16] The Workhouse figures for wage are probably slightly higher in proportion to the other groups because of the fact that it was practically impossible to verify the most of this information, making it necessary to accept the subject's statement, which invariably tends to be higher.

TABLE 117

Correlation between Grade Finished in School and Weekly Wage in First Job

Includes only Women of Total Group whose First Job was in Domestic Service or Allied Occupations where Living is in Addition to Wage

First Wage (+living)	Grade Finished												Totals	Means (Grade Finished)
	0*	1		3	4	5	6	7	8	1st Yr. H. S.	2nd Yr. H. S.	4th Yr. H. S.		
$9 –10	1						1	1					3	
8 – 9			1										1	
7 – 8			1										1	4.9
6 – 7			1					1					2	
5 – 6			1	1		1	2		1			1	7	
4 – 5	3	2	2	3	2	2	2	2	3	1			22	4.2
3 – 4	2	1	1	5	4	5		1	2	2			23	4.3
2 – 3	2		7	2	7	5	3	2	4			1	33	4.5
1 – 2	3		1	3	2	1	1	1	2				14	3.8
0 – 1	6	2	1	3	4	3		1	1				21	2.8
Totals	17	5	16	17	19	17	9	9	13	3	0	2	127	4.10
Means [First Wage (+living)]	$2.5	$3.5		$2.8	$2.4	$2.8	$4.1		$3.3				$3.06	

Grade finished: Mean = 4.10 σ = 2.72
First wage (+living): Mean = $3.06 σ = $1.93
Coefficient of correlation: r = .14 ± .087
Correlation ratios: First wage (+living) on grade finished, η = .29 ± .081 Blakeman's Criterion = 2.2
Grade finished on first wage (+living), η = .23 ± .083 Blakeman's Criterion = 1.6

* Includes those who have never been in school and those who have attended but never finished first grade.

est range. The mean wages for the total groups will be considered later.

It is commonly thought that the child who leaves school early and goes directly to work, gets into unskilled work and therefore earns less than the child who goes to school until he has reached a higher grade and so stands a better chance of getting into more skilled employment. To determine whether there is such a relationship in our group of women between the grade finished and the weekly wage in the first job, the following tables are presented.

Table 117 shows that for those who first found work in domestic service, the mean grade finished, 4.10, has a relatively large standard deviation of 2.72. The average first wage for those whose first employment was in domestic service is $3.06±1.93. The coefficient of correlation is .14±.087 and the correlation ratios are .23±.08 and .29±.08. The amount of relationship, as we might expect, is small since there is more or less of a standard wage for women in domestic service which tends to change little even with the worker's increase of experience and years. The more striking fact about the relationship is the tendency for the women with the least education to earn the smaller amounts. Women who earn less than two dollars a week at domestic service show a slightly earlier average grade at leaving school than those who earn more than that amount.

If we turn to the relationship between grade finished and wage in the first job where this work was other than housework, we find that the coefficient of correlation is .17±.067. The regression of first wage on grade, showing the average change in wage for changes in grade moves in a slightly irregular but fairly consistent progression. The ratio of .29±.063 indicates that there is a small relationship here. The regression of grade on first wage, however, shows a much more irregular line of the means for grade finished. The ratio of grade on first wage, .19±.067, indicates a small degree of relationship between first wage and grade finished in school. Unlike the situation for domestic workers the relationship between grade finished and wage is more apparent for those who receive the higher wages. There seems to be little difference in the amount of schooling for women receiving less than nine dollars per week, but women receiving more than nine dollars per week show an appreciably higher average grade attainment.

This low relationship between extent of education and first wage is not surprising. On the whole, the factor of education would seem logically to have less relationship to the first wage than to the later

TABLE 118

Correlation between Grade Finished in School and Weekly Wage in First Job

Includes only Women of Total Group whose First Job was in an Occupation other than Domestic Service

First Wage	Grade Finished: 0*	1	2	3	4	5	6	7	8	1st Yr. H. S.	2nd Yr. H. S.	4th Yr. H. S.	Totals	Means (Grade Finished)
$33 –$36								1					1	
30 – 33													0	
27 – 30							1						1	
24 – 27					1			1	1				3	6.0
21 – 24							1						1	
18 – 21				1									1	
15 – 18				1			1				1		3	
12 – 15	1	1		1	1		2	4	1				11	5.1
9 – 12	2		1	3		2	1	2	3	1		2	17	5.8
6 – 9	8	2	5	8	8	7	12	5	11	1			67	4.6
3 – 6	5	3	6	11	18	21	15	8	5	1			93	4.5
0 – 3	2		1		2	2	2	1	1				11	4.3
Totals	18	6	13	25	30	32	35	22	22	3	1	2	209	4.73
Means (First Wage)	$6.3	$7.0	$6.0	$7.5	$6.1	$5.2	$7.6	$9.5	$8.2				$7.07	

Grade finished: Mean = 4.73 σ = 2.46
First wage: Mean = $7.07 σ = $4.58
Coefficient of correlation r = .17 ± .067
Correlation ratios: Grade finished on first wage: η = .19 ± .067 Blakeman's Criterion = .8
First wage on grade finished, η = .29 ± .063 Blakeman's Criterion = 2.5

* Includes those who have never been in school and those who have attended but never finished first grade.

earnings, since without *special* training the majority of people start work with a low wage.

(2) *Wage in Latest Job.* The following tables on wage in latest job for the two occupational groups are presented merely to show the range of wages within the institutional groups and for reference. The range does not go above that for wage in first job in any group except Auburn, where one woman was earning from fifteen dollars to sixteen dollars a week plus living in her latest job. This woman, however, was a midwife and might be expected to have a slightly higher wage than regular domestic service workers. The 21.4 per cent in the Probation group who received living only is made up of only three cases, so that the importance of this percentage is lessened by observing the total number of cases.

TABLE 119

WEEKLY WAGE IN LATEST JOB

Per Cent Distribution by Institutional Groups of Women Employed at Domestic Service and Allied Occupations Where Living Was in Addition to Wage

Weekly Wage in Last Job	Institutional Groups						Total
	Bedford	Auburn	Magdalen	Peni-tentiary	Work-house	Probation	
Living only....	16.7	....	8.3	4.2	....	21.4	8.1
$1 to 2......	6.7	....	....	4.2	3.6	....	3.3
2 " 3......	....	20.0	25.0	4.2	17.9	14.3	11.4
3 " 4......	20.0	6.7	33.3	25.0	21.4	14.3	20.3
4 " 5......	33.3	20.0	....	20.8	17.9	14.3	20.3
5 " 6......	6.7	20.0	8.3	20.8	21.4	21.4	16.3
6 " 7......	....	13.3	16.7	8.3	10.7	7.1	8.1
7 " 8......	16.7	13.3	8.3	8.3	....	7.1	8.9
8 " 9......	....	....	....	....	3.6	....	.8
9 " 10......	....	....	....	4.2	3.6	....	1.6
15 " 16......	....	6.7	....	....	....	....	.8
Total...	100.0	100.0	100.0	100.0	100.0	100.0	100.0
Number of cases	30	15	12	24	28	14	123

For the occupations other than domestic service, the latest wage in all of the groups except the Penitentiary has a wider range than the first wage, with less massing around the lower wages. We should expect to find this tendency for the beginning and end of a work record to vary in wage-earning ability.

TABLE 120

WEEKLY WAGE IN LATEST JOB

Per Cent Distribution by Institutional Groups of Women Employed at Occupations other than Domestic Service

Weekly Wage in Last Job	Institutional Groups						Total
	Bedford	Auburn	Magdalen	Penitentiary	Workhouse	Probation	
$0 to $1	....	....	....	....	....	....	.0
1 " 2	....	....	....	2.1	2.3	....	.8
2 " 3	2.0	....	....	....	2.3	....	.8
3 " 4	7.8	3.7	....	2.1	2.3	....	2.8
4 " 5	5.9	14.8	2.8	6.3	4.7	....	5.2
5 " 6	17.7	14.8	16.7	6.3	4.7	6.4	10.3
6 " 7	19.6	14.8	22.2	16.7	23.3	12.8	18.3
7 " 8	9.8	7.4	11.1	8.3	9.3	19.2	11.1
8 " 9	9.8	....	11.1	10.4	4.7	12.8	8.7
9 " 10	11.8	14.8	2.8	16.7	18.6	10.6	12.7
10 " 11	3.9	14.8	5.6	8.3	14.0	8.5	8.7
11 " 12	....	....	11.1	....	2.3	4.3	2.8
12 " 13	2.0	3.7	....	10.4	4.7	4.3	4.4
13 " 14	....	....	....	2.1	....	4.3	1.2
14 " 15	2.0	....	....	....	....	....	.4
15 " 16	....	....	2.8	....	2.3	6.4	2.0
16 " 17	....	....	2.8	2.1	....	....	.8
17 " 18	....	....	2.8	....	....	....	.4
18 " 19	....	....	....	2.1	....	4.3	1.2
19 " 20	....	....	....	....	....	2.1	.4
20 " 21	2.0	....	....	....	....	2.1	.8
23 " 24	2.0	....	....	....	....	....	.4
25 " 26	2.0	7.4	5.6	2.1	2.3	....	2.8
27 " 28	....	....	....	2.1	....	....	.4
28 " 29	....	....	....	2.1	....	....	.4
30 " 31	....	3.7	2.8	....	....	....	.8
31 " 32	....	....	....	....	....	2.1	.4
32 " 33	....	....	....	....	2.3	....	.4
65 " 66	2.0	....	....	....	....	....	.4
Total	100.0	100.0	100.0	100.0	100.0	100.0	100.0
Number of cases	51	27	36	48	43	47	252

(3) *Wage at First Conviction.*—The wage at first conviction for those engaged in domestic service is based on 44 cases, with only two cases in the Probation group. It is obviously absurd to draw even the most general conclusions from so few cases in the institutional groups. The table shows a shorter range of wage than the other domestic service groups in first and latest jobs.

TABLE 121

WEEKLY WAGE AT TIME OF FIRST CONVICTION

Per Cent Distribution by Institutional Groups of Women Employed at Domestic Service and Allied Occupations Where Living Was in Addition to Wage

Weekly Wage at Time of First Conviction	Institutional Groups						Total
	Bedford	Auburn	Magdalen	Penitentiary	Workhouse	Probation	
Living only....	5.0	....	25.0	....	25.0	....	6.8
$1 to $2......	15.0	....	....	20.0	....	....	9.1
2 " 3......	....	33.3	50.0	20.0	50.0	50.0	20.5
3 " 4......	20.0	11.1	25.0	....	....	....	13.6
4 " 5......	25.0	11.1	....	20.0	....	....	15.9
5 " 6......	20.0	22.2	....	40.0	....	50.0	20.5
6 " 7......	....	11.1	....	....	25.0	....	4.6
7 " 8......	15.0	....	....	....	....	....	6.8
8 " 9......	....	....	....	....	....	....	.0
9 " 10......	....	....	....	....	....	....	.0
15 " 16......	....	11.1	....	....	....	....	2.3
Total...	100.0	100.0	100.0	100.0	100.0	100.0	100.0
Number of cases	20	9	4	5	4	2	44

The wage table showing earnings of those in occupations other than domestic service at the time of first conviction is based on only 52 cases, with so few numbers in the institutional groups that again no more comment is justifiable than that there were no women earning under three dollars a week and that the range of wages is shorter in most of the institutional groups than for the previous considerations of non-housework jobs.

TABLE 122

WEEKLY WAGE AT TIME OF FIRST CONVICTION

Per Cent Distribution by Institutional Groups of Women Employed at Occupations other than Domestic Service

Weekly Wage at Time of First Conviction	Institutional Groups						Total
	Bedford	Auburn	Magdalen	Penitentiary	Work-house	Probation	
$0 to $1	....	....	....	....	....	....	.0
1 " 2	....	....	....	....	....	....	.0
2 " 3	....	....	....	....	....	....	.0
3 " 4	....	12.5	....	....	....	....	1.9
4 " 5	25.0	12.5	....	12.5	....	11.1	13.5
5 " 6	25.0	12.5	25.0	....	33.3	....	15.4
6 " 7	25.0	12.5	25.0	25.0	....	11.1	19.2
7 " 8	6.3	12.5	12.5	12.5	33.3	22.2	13.5
8 " 9	....	....	....	25.0	....	....	3.9
9 " 10	....	25.0	12.5	12.5	33.3	11.1	11.5
10 " 11	6.3	....	....	....	....	22.2	5.8
14 " 15	6.3	....	....	....	....	....	1.9
15 " 16	....	....	....	....	....	11.1	1.9
17 " 18	....	....	12.5	....	....	....	1.9
20 " 21	6.3	....	....	....	....	11.1	3.9
22 " 23	....	....	....	12.5	....	....	1.9
25 " 26	....	....	12.5	....	....	....	1.9
30 " 31	....	12.5	....	....	....	....	1.9
Total	100.0	100.0	100.0	100.0	100.0	100.0	100.0
Number of cases	16	8	8	8	3	9	52

(4) *Wage at Latest Conviction.*—If we turn to the wage at latest conviction for the domestic service workers, we see in Table 123 that the numbers working in domestic service at this time are about the same as at first conviction, and that the distribution of wages among the institutional groups are not radically different.

TABLE 123

WEEKLY WAGE AT TIME OF PRESENT CONVICTION

Per Cent Distribution by Institutional Groups of Women Employed at Domestic Service and Allied Occupations Where Living Was in Addition to Wage

Weekly Wage at Time of Last Conviction	Institutional Groups						Total
	Bedford	Auburn	Magdalen	Peni-tentiary	Work-house	Probation	
Living only	15.4	....	25.0	....	....	....	6.7
$1 to $2	15.4	....	....	9.1	....	....	6.7
2 " 3	....	25.0	....	....	42.9	50.0	13.3
3 " 4	15.4	....	50.0	9.1	14.3	....	13.3
4 " 5	30.8	12.5	....	9.1	....	....	13.3
5 " 6	....	25.0	....	36.4	....	50.0	15.6
6 " 7	....	12.5	25.0	18.2	28.6	....	13.3
7 " 8	23.1	12.5	....	18.2	....	....	13.3
8 " 9	....	....	....	....	14.3	....	2.2
9 " 10	....	....	....	....	....	....	.0
15 " 16	....	12.5	....	....	....	....	2.2
Total	100.0	100.0	100.0	100.0	100.0	100.0	100.0
Number of cases	13	8	4	11	7	2	45

Table 124 shows the distribution of wages at time of latest conviction for the 57 workers in occupations other than domestic service. The wages run higher than at the time of first conviction though the cases at the upper limit are scattering.

TABLE 124

WEEKLY WAGE AT TIME OF PRESENT CONVICTION

Per Cent Distribution by Institutional Groups of Women Employed at Occupations other than Domestic Service

Weekly Wage at Time of Last Conviction	Institutional Groups						Total
	Bedford	Auburn	Magdalen	Penitentiary	Workhouse	Probation	
$0 to $1	....	....	....	....	....	....	.0
1 " 2	....	....	....	9.1	....	....	1.8
2 " 3	7.7	....	....	....	....	....	1.8
3 " 4	....	12.5	....	....	....	....	1.8
4 " 5	7.7	12.5	....	....	....	....	3.5
5 " 6	15.4	12.5	28.6	....	....	....	8.8
6 " 7	46.2	12.5	28.6	18.2	18.2	....	22.8
7 " 8	7.7	12.5	14.3	18.2	27.3	14.3	15.8
8 " 9	....	....	14.3	....	....	14.3	3.5
9 " 10	....	25.0	....	18.2	9.1	14.3	10.5
10 " 11	....	....	....	....	9.1	28.6	5.3
11 " 12	....	....	....	....	9.1	....	1.8
12 " 13	....	....	....	18.2	9.1	....	5.3
13 " 14	....	....	....	9.1	....	....	1.8
14 " 15	7.7	....	....	....	....	....	1.8
15 " 16	....	....	....	....	....	14.3	1.8
17 " 18	....	....	14.3	....	....	....	1.8
20 " 21	....	....	....	....	....	14.3	1.8
22 " 23	....	....	....	9.1	....	....	1.8
25 " 26	....	....	....	....	9.1	....	1.8
30 " 31	....	12.5	....	....	....	....	1.8
32 " 33	....	....	....	....	9.1	....	1.8
65 " 66	7.7	....	....	....	....	....	1.8
Total	100.0	100.0	100.0	100.0	100.0	100.0	100.0
Number of cases	13	8	7	11	11	7	57

(5) *Average Wage for Prevailing Work.* If, instead of taking the wage of these women at any specified time, we consider the average wage for the prevailing work, we have an index of their general earning capacity. The average wage is obtained by allowing for the time element—that is, making a simple weighted average with the length of time in each of the jobs in the prevailing work the weight. The following table shows that the average weekly wage for domestic service workers begins at living only in all groups except the Magdalen and runs to no more than nine dollars in three of the groups and not over seven dollars a week in the other two. Living, of course, is in addition to these wages.

TABLE 125

Average Weekly Wage for Prevailing Work of Women Employed at Domestic Service and Allied Occupations where Living was in Addition to Wage

Per Cent Distribution by Institutional Groups

Average Weekly Wage plus Living	Institutional Groups						Total
	Bedford	Auburn	Magdalen	Peni-tentiary	Work-house	Probation	
Living only	8.7	11.1	....	3.1	5.7	9.5	6.7
$1 to $2	15.2	3.7	....	6.3	2.9	....	6.2
2 " 3	34.8	18.5	33.3	25.0	14.3	14.3	24.2
3 " 4	8.7	29.6	33.3	18.8	20.0	9.5	18.4
4 " 5	19.6	22.2	....	25.0	34.3	38.1	24.2
5 " 6	4.4	14.8	27.8	9.4	14.3	4.8	11.2
6 " 7	8.7	....	5.6	....	5.7	19.1	6.2
7 " 8	....	....	....	3.1	....	....	.6
8 " 9	....	....	....	9.4	2.9	4.8	2.8
Total	100.0	100.0	100.0	100.0	100.0	100.0	100.0
Number of cases	46	27	18	32	35	21	179

The following table (Table 126), on the other hand, has a much longer range, from $1 to $46, with the Penitentiary and the Workhouse having the longest range. The Probation group has the fewest cases in the lowest wage groups, and has none who have earned less than $4 a week for their average wage where their prevailing work was in an occupation other than domestic service.

TABLE 126

Average Weekly Wage for Prevailing Work of Women Employed at Occupations other than Domestic Service

Per Cent Distribution by Institutional Groups

Average Weekly Wage	Institutional Groups						Total
	Bedford	Auburn	Magdalen	Penitentiary	Workhouse	Probation	
$1 to $2	2.1	....	....	....	....	....	.5
2 " 3	....	....	2.8	....	....	....	.5
3 " 4	2.1	9.1	5.6	4.4	7.1	....	4.0
4 " 5	18.8	4.6	11.1	4.4	10.7	4.6	9.4
5 " 6	18.8	27.3	19.4	6.5	10.7	11.4	14.7
6 " 7	20.8	18.2	13.9	10.9	14.3	11.4	14.7
7 " 8	14.6	9.1	16.7	15.2	7.1	25.0	15.6
8 " 9	6.3	9.1	8.3	8.7	17.9	13.6	10.3
9 " 10	2.1	4.6	8.3	13.0	3.6	9.1	7.1
10 " 11	4.2	....	2.8	6.5	7.1	4.6	4.5
11 " 12	2.1	....	....	4.4	....	2.3	1.8
12 " 13	2.1	4.6	2.8	4.4	3.6	2.3	3.1
13 " 14	2.1	....	....	....	....	2.3	.9
14 " 15	....	....	....	2.2	....	....	.5
15 " 16	....	....	2.8	....	3.6	2.3	1.3
16 " 17	....	....	....	2.2	....	....	.5
17 " 18	....	....	2.8	....	....	....	.5
19 " 20	....	....	....	2.2	....	4.6	1.3
20 " 21	2.1	....	....	....	....	2.3	.9
22 " 23	....	....	....	4.4	....	....	.9
24 " 25	....	....	....	....	3.6	....	.5
25 " 26	2.1	9.1	2.8	2.2	3.6	4.6	3.6
27 " 28	....	....	....	2.2	....	....	.5
28 " 29	....	....	....	2.2	....	....	.5
30 " 31	....	4.6	....	....	....	....	.5
32 " 33	....	....	....	....	3.6	....	.5
35 " 36	....	....	....	2.2	3.6	....	.9
45 " 46	....	....	....	2.2	....	....	.5
Total	100.0	100.0	100.0	100.0	100.0	100.0	100.0
Number of cases	48	22	36	46	28	44	224

Charts XIXa and XIXb show graphically how the average wage for prevailing work varies between the domestic service workers and those in other occupations. The charts are based on the figures for the total group, and indicate that while the range of wage for the domestic service workers is short, that for the workers in other occupations is very long, broken and irregular.

The preceding tables on wage, which have been included largely for reference to determine how the total group is made up, will be

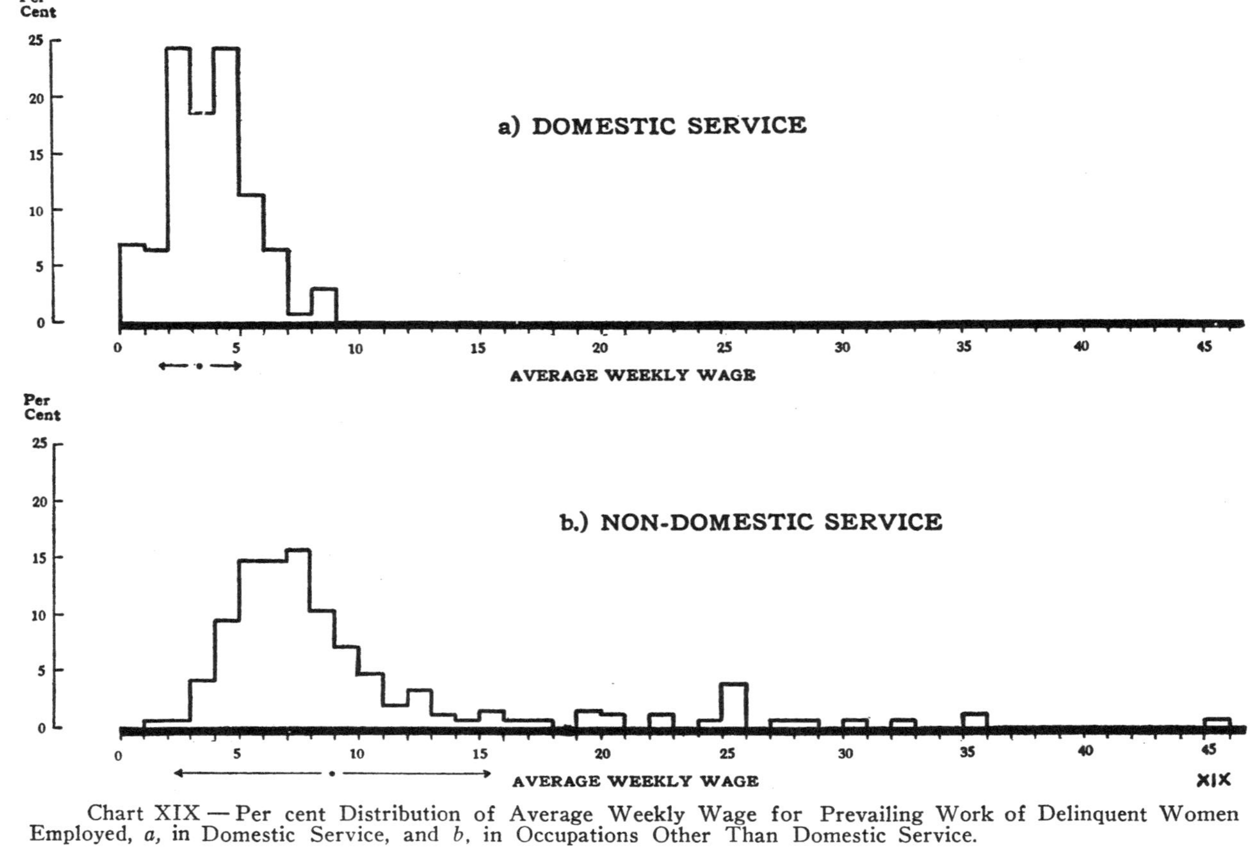

Chart XIX — Per cent Distribution of Average Weekly Wage for Prevailing Work of Delinquent Women Employed, *a,* in Domestic Service, and *b*, in Occupations Other Than Domestic Service.

TABLE 127

WEEKLY WAGE EARNED BY DELINQUENT WOMEN AT SPECIFIED TIMES DURING THEIR WORK HISTORIES

Per Cent Distribution of Women Employed at Domestic Service and Allied Occupations Where Living Was in Addition to Wage

Weekly Wage	Specified Times				
	In First Job	In Latest Job	At Time of First Conviction	At Time of Present Conviction	Prevailing Work
Living only	15.6	8.1	6.8	6.7	6.7
$1 to $2	11.3	3.3	9.1	6.7	6.2
2 " 3	25.0	11.4	20.5	13.3	24.2
3 " 4	20.6	20.3	13.6	13.3	18.4
4 " 5	17.5	20.3	15.9	13.3	24.2
5 " 6	5.0	16.3	20.5	15.6	11.2
6 " 7	1.3	8.1	4.6	13.3	6.2
7 " 8	1.3	8.9	6.8	13.3	.6
8 " 9	.6	.8	....	2.2	2.8
9 " 10	1.9	1.6	....	....	....
15 " 16	....	.8	2.3	2.2	....
Total	100.0	100.0	100.0	100.0	100.0
Number of cases	160	123	44	45	179
Mean	2.56	3.94	3.66	4.29	3.25
σ_m	±.147	±.203	±.384	±.400	±.131
σ	1.85	2.25	2.55	2.68	1.75
σ_σ	±.104	±.143	±.272	±.283	±.109

of much more interest if these totals are combined, showing what wages the women engaged in domestic service and those in other occupations were earning at specified times during their work histories, and for their prevailing work. Table 127 presents the wages for women in domestic service and gives in addition to the actual percentages of women earning given wages the mean wage and standard deviation for each group. The mean wage in the first job, $2.56±1.85 is, it will be seen, considerably less than the mean wage in the latest job, $3.94±2.25. This trend is in the direction we should expect, that one should earn larger wages with increase of experience. The comparison of the mean wage earned at first conviction and in the first job indicates that these women were earning more at the time of first conviction, though there was a wider dispersion of wages.

TABLE 128

WEEKLY WAGE EARNED BY DELINQUENT WOMEN AT SPECIFIED TIMES DURING THEIR WORK HISTORIES

Per Cent Distribution of Women Employed at Occupations other than Domestic Service

Weekly Wage	Specified Times				
	In First Job	In Latest Job	At Time of First Conviction	At Time of Present Conviction	Prevailing Work
$0 to $1	2.5	....	....	....	.0
1 " 2	1.3	.8	....	1.8	.5
2 " 3	3.3	.8	....	1.8	.5
3 " 4	12.1	2.8	1.9	1.8	4.0
4 " 5	12.1	5.2	13.5	3.5	9.4
5 " 6	16.7	10.3	15.4	8.8	14.7
6 " 7	16.3	18.3	19.2	22.8	14.7
7 " 8	10.0	11.1	13.5	15.8	15.6
8 " 9	7.5	8.7	3.9	3.5	10.3
9 " 10	3.8	12.7	11.5	10.5	7.1
10 " 11	2.5	8.7	5.8	5.3	4.5
11 " 12	1.7	2.8	....	1.8	1.8
12 " 13	3.8	4.4	....	5.3	3.1
13 " 14	1.3	1.2	....	1.8	.9
14 " 15	....	.4	1.9	1.8	.5
15 " 16	1.3	2.0	1.9	1.8	1.3
16 " 17	....	.8	....	....	.5
17 " 18	....	.4	1.9	1.8	.5
18 " 19	....	1.2	....	....	.0
19 " 20	....	.4	....	....	1.3
20 " 21	.4	.8	3.9	1.8	.9
22 " 23	.4	....	1.9	1.8	.9
23 " 24	....	.4	....	....	.0
24 " 25	.4	....	....	....	.5
25 " 26	1.3	2.8	1.9	1.8	3.6
27 " 28	.4	.4	....	....	.5
28 " 29	....	.4	....	....	.5
30 " 31	....	.8	1.9	1.8	.5
31 " 32	....	.4	....	....	.0
32 " 33	....	.4	....	1.8	.5
35 " 36	.8	....	....	....	.9
45 " 46	.4	....	....	....	.5
65 " 66	....	.4	....	1.8	.0
Total	100.0	100.0	100.0	100.0	100.0
Number of cases	240	252	52	57	224
Mean	6.78	9.17	8.52	10.2	8.90
σ_m	±.356	±.409	±.789	±1.26	±.441
σ	5.51	6.495	5.69	9.54	6.60
σ_σ	±.251	±.0837	±.558	±.893	±.312

It must be remembered, however, that a very large percentage of women who were included in the wage table for the first job were not working at the time of the first conviction and were, therefore, not included in the table under discussion. A comparison of the mean wages at first and latest convictions also shows that the women were earning more at latest conviction than at the first, and more than at any of the other times which we have specified. The average wage for prevailing work which applies to 179 women is $3.25±1.75. That is, the average wage for the prevailing work, while higher than the average wage in the first job, is lower than the average wage in the latest job, or the wage at the time of first or present conviction. Throughout, the average wage for women employed at domestic service is low, with a maximum of a mean weekly wage of $4.29±2.68. There is also little variation between the lowest wage of $2.56 and the highest wage of $4.29.

Table 128 presents the wages earned by women in occupations other than domestic service, and the average wages for each of the specified times. The trend is in the same direction as that in Table 127, with the lowest mean wage of $6.78 in the first job, in contrast to the higher wage of $9.17 in the latest job. The standard deviation, however, is relatively large in both of these cases. The wage at first conviction, $8.52, is based on 52 cases only and though the mean is smaller than the average wage of $10.20, earned at present conviction, the standard deviation of the latter is so large, proportionately, as to lessen markedly the importance of the larger mean. The mean of the average wage for prevailing work is $8.90±6.60. The average wage for prevailing work, therefore, would seem to be larger than either the wage in the first job or the wage at first conviction. On the whole, the wages are low, and the frequency tables show a wide scattering with only a few cases at the upper wage limit. As shown in Table 113, the prevailing work of 40.4 per cent of the delinquent women was housework, while 56.1 per cent of the women were engaged in other work. This 40 per cent of women were earning an average of $3.25 a week plus living at domestic service, while over 50 per cent of the women were earning an average of $8.90 a week.

Since the numbers of women in institutional groups are too few for comparison of the means when divided into occupations, a correlation ratio has been worked between the institutional groups and the average weekly wage for prevailing work. The ratio of .25±.070 as given in Table 129 shows that between institutional groups and the

TABLE 129

Correlation between Institutional Groups and Average Weekly Wage for Prevailing Work of Women Employed at Domestic Service and Allied Occupations where Living Was in Addition to Wage

Total Group

Institutional Groups	Average Weekly Wage for Prevailing Work									Totals	Means (Average Weekly Wage for Prevailing Work)
	\$0–\$1	1– 2	2– 3	3– 4	4– 5	5– 6	6– 7	7– 8	8– 9		
Bedford	4	7	16	4	9	2	4			46	\$3.13
Auburn	3	1	5	8	6	4				27	3.42
Magdalen			6	6		5	1			18	3.88
Penitentiary	1	2	8	6	8	3		1	3	32	4.06
Workhouse	2	1	5	7	12	5	2		1	35	4.07
Probation	2		3	2	8	1	4		1	21	4.35
Totals	12	11	43	33	43	20	11	1	5	179	\$3.74

Average weekly wage for prevailing work: Mean = \$3.74 $\sigma = 1.75$

Correlation ratio: Average weekly wage for prevailing work on institutional groups, $\eta = .25 \pm .070$

average weekly wage for women whose prevailing work was domestic service, there is a small but probably significant relationship. Reference to the average wages earned by the women in the several institutional groups shows that the order of arrangement of the institutional groups in accordance with increasing average weekly wage for prevailing work where that work is housework is as follows: (1) Bedford, (2) Auburn, (3) Magdalen, (4) Penitentiary, (5) Workhouse, (6) Probation.

In a correlation ratio between the institutional groups and average weekly wage for prevailing work of women employed at occupations other than domestic service, we find that $\eta = .25 \pm .063$. This ratio also would indicate that the relationship between the two factors is small but probably significant. The order of arrangement of the institutional groups in accordance with the increasing average weekly wages varies from the order of arrangement in Table 129, and is as follows: (1) Bedford, (2) Magdalen, (3) Auburn, (4) Probation, (5) Workhouse, (6) Penitentiary.

From the two tables discussed above (Tables 129 and 130), it seems evident that there is a tendency for the Bedford women to receive a lower average wage than the women of the other groups. There are variations between the wages at various times in all of the other groups except the Workhouse, which comes near the highest wage limit in both domestic service and occupations other than domestic service.

(*b*) *Relationship Between Average Wage and Social Factors*

(1) *Relationship Between Average Wage and Grade Finished.*—In Tables 117 and 118 we discussed the relationship between the grade finished and the first wage received, showing that the grade finished has a very slight relationship to the wage one is first able to earn in either domestic service or in occupations other than domestic service. If we consider the relationship between the grade finished and the average wage for prevailing work of those employed in domestic service and in occupations other than domestic service, we find evidence of somewhat higher relationships. Table 131 shows a coefficient of correlation of $.29 \pm .077$. This indicates a tendency for those who reach the higher grades to earn a higher average wage for prevailing work, where the prevailing work is domestic service.

TABLE 130

Correlation between Institutional Groups and Average Weekly Wage for Prevailing Work of Women Employed at Occupations other than Domestic Service

Total Group

Institutional Groups	Average Weekly Wage for Prevailing Work																							Totals	Means (Average Weekly Wage for Prevailing Work)
	$1–$3	3–5	5–7	7–9	9–11	11–13	13–15	15–17	17–19	19–21	21–23	23–25	25–27	27–29	29–31	31–33	33–35	35–37	37–39	39–41	41–43	43–45	45–47		
Bedford	1	10	19	10	3	2	1			1			1											48	$7.33
Auburn		3	10	4	1	1							2		1									22	9.36
Magdalen	1	6	12	9	4	1		1	1				1											36	7.75
Penitentiary		4	8	11	9	4	1	1		1	2		1	2				1					1	46	11.87
Workhouse		5	7	7	3	1		1				1	1			1		1						28	10.60
Probation		2	10	17	6	2	1	1		3			2											44	9.65
Totals	2	30	66	58	26	11	3	4	1	5	2	1	8	2	1	1		2					1	224	$9.39

Average weekly wage for prevailing work: Mean = $9.39 $\sigma = 6.60$

Correlation ratio: Average wage for prevailing work on institutional groups, $\eta = .25 \pm .063$

TABLE 131

Correlation between Grade Finished in School and Average Weekly Wage for Prevailing Work of Women Employed at Domestic Service and Allied Occupations where Living Was in Addition to Wage

Total Group

Average Weekly Wage for Prevailing Work	Grade Finished 0*	1	2	3	4	5	6	7	8	First Year High School	Second Year High School	Fourth Year High School	Totals	Means (Grade Finished)
$8 to $9							1	1	1	1			4 }	
7 " 8	1												1 }	5.5
6 " 7			2	2			2	1		2			9 }	
5 " 6	1	1	1	1		3		1	1	2		1	12	5.5
4 " 5	2	2	2	8	2	8	5	3	2				34	4.3
3 " 4	1	1	5	3	7	2	2	2	1	1			25	4.0
2 " 3	4		7	5	6	7	1	2	3				35	3.8
1 " 2	2	1	1	3	2	1			1				11	3.0
0 " 1	1	1	2	2	2	1	1	1					11	3.4
Totals	12	6	20	24	19	22	12	11	9	6	0	1	142	4.16
Means (Average Weekly Wage for Prevailing Work)	$3.2	$3.3	$3.2	$3.5	$2.8	$3.6	$4.5	$4.2	$4.8 (8 through Fourth Year High School)				$3.63	

Grade finished: Mean = 4.16 σ = 2.48
Average weekly wage for prevailing work: Mean = $3.63 σ = $1.79
Coefficient of correlation: r = .29 ± .077
Correlation ratios: Grade finished on average weekly wage for prevailing work: η = .29 ± .077 Blakeman's Criterion = .56
Average weekly wage for prevailing work on grade finished, η = .35 ± .074 Blakeman's Criterion = 1.8

* Includes those who have never been in school and those who have attended but never finished first grade.

In Table 132 a similar relationship is shown between the grade finished and the average wage for prevailing work of women in occupations other than domestic service. The coefficient of correlation (.25±.066) gives evidence of a small, significant relationship in this case also. It may be noted that there is a distinct rise in weekly earnings for the women who have had more schooling than the average amount for the group. On the whole, we may state that there is a tendency among all of the working women in our group for those with more education to earn a higher wage in their prevailing work than those with less education.

(2) *Relationship Between Average Wage and Number of Convictions.*—In trying to determine whether there is any relationship between the extent of delinquency measured by number of convictions and economic efficiency as measured by average wage for prevailing work, the partial correlation coefficient of number of previous convictions and average weekly wage for prevailing work, for constant age, has been used. Before considering this coefficient, it may be of interest to present Tables 133 and 134, showing the relationship between age and average wage for the two occupational groups.

Table 133 shows this relationship for women employed at domestic service, giving a correlation coefficient of zero. The regression of wage for prevailing work on age is, however, non-linear; the correlation ratio for this is .27±.069. The tendency here is toward a slight increase in wage from the earliest ages and a decrease in wage in the highest ages. The tendency between ages 26 and 44 is not clear except in so far as the wage is, in general, higher than for either the very young or the very old. The regression of age on wage for prevailing work with a correlation ratio of .11±.07 shows no trend of significance.

If we turn to the correlation of age with average weekly wage of women in occupations other than domestic service, we find more relation between age and wage for prevailing work than in the previous comparison. The regression of age on wage for prevailing work shows that the women receiving less than $7 a week are below the average in age. The correlation ratio is .37±.058. There is a clearly marked tendency for these women as they grow older to increase in wage-earning capacity. From these two tables it would seem that domestic service is like a blind alley for the women who do that work mainly for a living, while the workers in other occupations tend to increase their wages as they grow older.

TABLE 132

Correlation between Grade Finished in School and Average Weekly Wage for Prevailing Work of Women Employed at Occupations other than Domestic Service

Total Group

Average Weekly Wage for Prevailing Work	Grade Finished												Totals	Means (Grade finished)
	0*	1	2	3	4	5	6	7	8	First Year High School	Second Year High School	Fourth Year High School		
$35 to $37								1					1	7.0
33 " 35													0	
31 " 33													0	4th Year H. S.
29 " 31												1	1	
27 " 29							1					1	2	6.3
25 " 27	1			1	1			2	3				8	
23 " 25													0	7.0
21 " 23							1		1				2	
19 " 21				1		1		1			1		4	5.8
17 " 19					1								1	
15 " 17				1				1	1		1		4	5.1
13 " 15	1			1		1							3	
11 " 13				1	1	1	3	1	3				10	5.6
9 " 11	3		1	3	1	5	3	3	4			2	25	
7 " 9	4	2	3	3	7	10	9	5	9				52	4.7
5 " 7	6	1	4	6	7	12	9	4	8				57	
3 " 5	1	1	1	4	10	2	7	2	1	1			30	4.7
1 " 3	1					1							2	
Totals	17	4	9	21	28	33	33	20	30	1	2	4	202	5.03
Means (Average Weekly Wage for Prevailing Work)	$8.1		$8.6		$7.5		$9.5		$11.7				$9.02	

Grade finished: Mean = 5.03 σ = 2.56
Average weekly wage for prevailing work: Mean = $9.01 σ = $5.79

Coefficient of correlation: r = .25 ± .066

Correlation ratios: Grade finished on average weekly wage for prevailing work, η = .29 ± .065 Blakeman's Criterion = 1.5
Average weekly wage for prevailing work on grade finished. η = .25 ± .066 Balkeman's Criterion = .6

* Includes those who have never been in school and those who have attended but never finished first grade.

TABLE 133

Correlation between Age and Average Weekly Wage for Prevailing Work of Women Employed at Domestic Service and Allied Occupations where Living Was in Addition to Wage

Total Group

Average Weekly Wage for Prevailing Work	Age (Years) 14 to 17	17 to 20	20 to 23	23 to 26	26 to 29	29 to 32	32 to 35	35 to 38	38 to 41	41 to 44	44 to 47	47 to 50	50 to 53	53 to 56	56 to 59	Totals	Means (Age)
$9 to $10																0 }	
8 " 9				1		2		1	1							5 }	31.8
7 " 8			1													1 }	
6 " 7	1	1	1	1	3	2	2									11 }	25.6
5 " 6		1	3	3	4	4	1		1	2		1				20 }	
4 " 5	1	8	6	7	3	5	3	3	3	4						43 }	27.9
3 " 4		2	6	9	2	6			3	2	2				1	33 }	
2 " 3	3	10	6	3	4	3	4	3		3	1	1	1		1	43 }	28.1
1 " 2		2	5	1		1		2								11 }	
0 " 1	1	2		2	1		3	1	1		1					12 }	26.7
Totals	6	26	28	27	17	23	13	10	9	11	4	2	1	0	2	179	27.82
Means (Average Weekly Wage for Prevailing Work)	$3.2		$3.7		$4.4		$3.3		$4.1		$2.9					$3.74	

Age: Mean = 27.82 σ = 8.72
Average weekly wage for prevailing work: Mean = $3.74 σ = $1.75

Coefficient of correlation: r = .000 ± .075
Correlation ratios: Age on average weekly wage for prevailing work, η = .11 ± .074 Blakeman's Criterion = 1.1
Average weekly wage for prevailing work on age, η = .27 ± .069 Blakeman's Criterion = 2.7

TABLE 134

Correlation between Age and Average Weekly Wage for Prevailing Work of Women Employed at Occupations other than Domestic Service

Total Group

Average Weekly Wage for Prevailing Work	Age (Years) 14 to 17	17 to 20	20 to 23	23 to 26	26 to 29	29 to 32	32 to 35	35 to 38	38 to 41	41 to 44	44 to 47	47 to 50	50 to 53	53 to 56	56 to 59	59 to 62	62 to 65	65 to 68	Totals	Means (Age)
$47 to $49																			0	
45 " 47				1															1	
43 " 45																			0	
41 " 43																			0	
39 " 41																			0	
37 " 39																			0	
35 " 37			1													1			2	32.3
33 " 35																			0	
31 " 33											1								1	
29 " 31											1								1	
27 " 29				1			1												2	
25 " 27			1	1		4	1	1											8	
23 " 25													1						1	
21 " 23											1		1						2	
19 " 21		1	2	1			1												5	29.2
17 " 19				1															1	
15 " 17			1		2		1												4	
13 " 15			1	1	1														3	
11 " 13		1		4		1	1	1	2				1						11	31.5
9 " 11		3	6	2	3	2	3			1		4			1		1		26	
7 " 9		10	11	15	6	6	1	4		1		2	2						58	24.9
5 " 7	7	15	10	11	10	6	3	3	1										66	
3 " 5		12	4	6	4	1	1		1	1									30	22.8
1 " 3		1		1															2	
Totals	7	43	37	45	26	20	13	9	4	3	3	6	5	0	1	1	1	0	224	26.46
Means (Average Weekly Wage for Prevailing Work)	$6.4		$9.5		$9.2		$11.4		$12.4				$16.2						$9.39	

Age: Mean = 26.46 σ = 8.73
Average weekly wage for prevailing work: Mean = $9.39 σ = $6.60

Coefficient of correlation: r = .26 ± .062

Correlation ratios: Age on average weekly wage for prevailing work, η = .37 ± .058 Blakeman's Criterion = 2.9
Average weekly wage for prevailing work on age, η = .33 ± .060 Blakeman's Criterion = 2.2

Of special importance for estimating the relationship between economic efficiency and criminal record is the correlation between average weekly wage for prevailing work and number of previous convictions. Table 135 gives the correlation between number of previous convictions and average weekly wage for women employed in domestic service and allied occupations. The coefficient of correlation here is $.046 \pm .075$. Obviously this is insufficient to indicate the presence of any relationship. Because of the probability of a non-linear relationship the correlation ratios were computed. Both ratios are sufficiently small in relation to their standard deviations so that they are of little importance as further evidences of relationship. We have gone a step further and attempted to discover whether any significant relationship would appear if allowance were made for the age factor. Computing the partial correlation we find: r (average weekly wage with number of previous convictions, age constant) $= .047 \pm .075$.[17] The upshot of our analysis of these data is, therefore, the indication that there is no relation between average wage and number of convictions if we consider those women whose prevailing work has been of the nature of domestic service.

Table 136 figures the relationship between weekly wage and number of previous convictions for women in occupations other than housework. The correlation coefficient of $-.067 \pm .067$ is insufficient to indicate a relationship of any significance. Moreover, as in the case of the women employed at domestic service, the correlation ratios need not be taken into consideration because of the small values of these ratios and the lack of regular trend in the lines of means. Computing the partial correlation coefficient, with age constant, we get the following result: r (average weekly wage with number of previous convictions, age constant) $= -.169 \pm .065$.[18] From this we might conclude that, if allowance be made for age, there is evidence of a very slight negative correlation between average wage, at occupations other than domestic work, and number of convictions. This does not show whether this slight relationship is due to the fact that women with

[17] The data used in computing this coefficient are as follows:
r (wages with convictions) = .046
r (wage with age) = .000
r (convictions with age) = .175

[18] The data used in computing this coefficient are as follows:
r (wage with convictions) = — .067
r (wage with age) = .264
r (convictions with age) = .331

TABLE 135

Correlation between Number of Previous Convictions and Average Weekly Wage for Prevailing Work of Women Employed at Domestic Service and Allied Occupations where Living Was in Addition to Wage.

Total Group

Average Weekly Wage for Prevailing Work	Number of Previous Convictions: 0	1	2	3	4	5	6	7	8	9	10	11	12	13	14	15	16	17	18	Totals	Means (Number of Previous Convictions)
$9 to $10..																				0	3.6
8 " 9..	4																		1	5	
7 " 8..					1															1	1.4
6 " 7..	7	1		1	1	1														11	
5 " 6..	10	4	3	2		1														20	1.4
4 " 5..	18	12	3	5	1		1	2				1								43	
3 " 4..	11	6	8	1	1	1	2		2	1										33	1.9
2 " 3..	20	10	8		1		1				1		1		1					43	
1 " 2..	5	6																		11	1.1
0 " 1..	5	2	2	1		1	1													12	
Totals...	80	41	24	10	5	4	5	2	2	1	1	1	1	0	1	0	0	0	1	179	1.64
Means..... (Average Weekly Wage for Prevailing Work)	$3.9	$3.4	$3.3	$4.4	$3.9			$4.0												$3.74	

Number of previous convictions: Mean = 1.64 $\sigma = 2.69$

Average weekly wage for prevailing work: Mean = $3.74 σ = $1.75

Coefficient of correlation: r = .046 ± .075

Correlation ratios: Number of previous convictions on average weekly wage for prevailing work, $\eta = .16 \pm .073$

Blakeman's Criterion = 1.5

Average weekly wage for prevailing work on number of previous convictions, $\eta = .18 \pm .072$

Blakeman's Criterion = 1.8

TABLE 136

Correlation between Number of Previous Convictions and Average Weekly Wage for Prevailing Work of Women Employed at Occupations other than Domestic Service

Total Group

Average Weekly Wage for Prevailing Work	Number of Previous Convictions: 0	1	2	3	4	5	6	7	8	9	10	11	12	13	14	Totals	Means (Number of Previous Convictions)
$47 to $49																0	
45 " 47	1															1	
43 " 45																0	
41 " 43																0	
39 " 41																0	
37 " 39																0	
35 " 37	1		1													2	0.9
33 " 35																0	
31 " 33							1									1	
29 " 31	1															1	
27 " 29	1		1													2	
25 " 27	5	3														8	
23 " 25	1															1	
21 " 23	1			1												2	
19 " 21	4	1														5	
17 " 19		1														1	0.8
15 " 17		3	1													4	
13 " 15	2			1												3	
11 " 13	4	2		3				1			1					11	
9 " 11	11	7	2	1	1			2		1		1				26	2.2
7 " 9	30	13	7	3	3	1								1		58	
5 " 7	26	19	6	3	5	4		1			1				1	66	1.4
3 " 5	9	12	4	1	2	1		1								30	
1 " 3		2														2	1.4
Totals	97	63	22	13	11	6	1	5	0	1	2	1	0	1	1	224	1.46
Means (Average Weekly Wage for Prevailing Work)	$10.4	$8.4	$9.3	$9.8	$6.6		$ 10.6									$9.39	

Number of previous convictions: Mean = 1.46 σ = 2.28
Average weekly wage for prevailing work: Mean = $9.39 σ = $6.60

Coefficient of correlation: r = —.067 ± .067

Correlation ratios: Number of previous convictions on average weekly wage for prevailing work, η = .16 ± .065 Blakeman's Criterion = 1.6
Average weekly wage for prevailing work on number of previous convictions, η = .18 ± .065 Blakeman's Criterion = 1.9

better earning capacity get into trouble slightly less often because of their better financial status, or to the fact that a woman who gets into trouble frequently thereby interrupts her working career and lowers her rate of earning.

(c) *Brief Comparison of Average Wage with Wage of Certain Groups in General Population*

The number of our women in any one occupation is too small for significant comparison with the wage studies in given occupations which have been made within recent years. If we compare the totals of our domestic service and occupations other than domestic service, the basis of comparison is changed, because we can not get wage statistics in New York State for each of the occupations included in this total. In spite of the discrepancies in the basis of comparison, we shall present a few of the wage figures for certain occupations in New York State and neighboring states, to see if the trend of wages among our delinquents differs from them to any marked degree. Unfortunately, there are no reliable figures on wages for women in domestic service so that a comparison of the wages of this group will not be possible. Domestic service is still an occupation where the individual barters with the individual for the sale and purchase of labor. In certain sections of urban communities there is what approaches a standard wage, but these standards may vary radically within the different parts of the same city.

In making any comparisons, the average wage for prevailing work of the delinquent women will be used, since this wage is probably the least affected by the time element which must be considered in dealing with individuals of varying ages. The wage at time of present conviction, of course, applies to work done within the years 1915-1916, but since so many of the women (over 50 per cent) were not working, it seems more advisable to use a wage which will include a larger number of women. We are citing various isolated studies for specified occupations in order to estimate roughly how the earning capacity of our women stands in comparison with that of any groups of the general population. (See table, p. 359.)

This crude method of estimating comparative wages indicates that our group of women has a smaller percentage earning under $8 a week in their prevailing work than the box-makers, those in candy factories and in small neighborhood or department stores. Those in the large department stores in New York and those in the dress and

	Percentage Earning Weekly Wages:			
	Under $4	Under $6	Under $8	Under $10
Delinquent Women Average wage for prevailing work (not domestic service) . .	5.0	29.1	59.4	76.8
Box Industry, N. Y. State, 1914 [19a]	8.8	38.1	64.2	85.4
Confectionery Industry, N. Y. State, 1914 [19a]	12.3	54.6	80.5	90.6
Stores: [19a]				
Large department store	. . . .	. . . .	53.0	. . . .
Small neighborhood store	. . . .	. . . .	68.0	. . . .
5 and 10 cent store	. . . .	. . . .	99.0	. . . .
Dress and Waist Industry, N. Y. City, 1913 [19b]				
Week-workers	0.2	5.3	21.1	39.3
Clothing Factories, New Jersey, 1913-1914 [19c]	4.2	23.6	55.9	91.7
Clothing Factories, Massachusetts, 1913 [19d]				
Men's Clothing	1.9	13.5	42.8	74.0
Women's Clothing	1.1	13.6	39.6	66.8

waist industry in New York have a smaller percentage earning under $8 a week than has our group of delinquent women. The two industries cited in neighboring states, New Jersey and Massachusetts, show that there is a smaller percentage than in our delinquent group, earning the small wage of less than $8 or less than $10 a week in the clothing industry. From this we may see that the wages in the different industries noted vary considerably, but that aside from the workers in the dress and waist industry, our group of women shows no appreciably higher percentage earning under $8 a week, and in several instances the percentage of delinquent women earning over $8 a week is larger than the percentage of workers earning this amount in the occupations cited. In the same report from which the above figures were taken [19] the statement is made: "There is ample ground for the conclusion that from two-thirds to three-fourths of women workers in factories, stores, laundries, and in industrial wage-earning occupations generally, work at wages under $8 a week. Since practically all findings of

[19] Most of the above figures were taken from "Conditions of Labor in American Industries" by W. Jett Lauck and Edgar Sydenstricker. Funk and Wagnalls Co., N. Y. C., 1917, pp. 53-57. The reports cited are:

a. Fourth Report of the New York Factory Investigating Commission, Feb. 15, 1915. Vol. 2. Albany, J. B. Lyon Co.
b. U. S. Bureau of Labor Statistics: Wages, etc., in the dress and waist industry in New York City, 1913 (Women).
c. New Jersey, Bureau of Statistics: Annual report on the statistics of manufactures for the year ending Oct. 31, 1913 (16 years and over).
d. Massachusetts, Bureau of Statistics: Annual report on the statistics of manufactures for the year 1913 (18 years and over).

minimum wage commissions and boards in the United States and the estimates of investigators agree that the independent woman worker can not live decently and without detriment to her health on less than $8 a week, this fact has been given a great deal of emphasis during recent years."[20]

We might also compare with the wages of our group the wages of workers in silk mills and in department stores in 1908. These figures are given in a study of these industries in the report on the Condition of Woman and Child Wage-earners in the United States.[21] The first study gives in detail the percentage of women over fifteen earning specified wages in the silk mills in New Jersey and Pennsylvania. The second study gives the percentages of women employees earning specified wages in department and retail stores in New York City, Chicago and Philadelphia. The total workers in stores include cash girls, messengers, inspectors, bundle wrappers, packers, saleswomen, office employees and buyers.

	Percentage Earning Weekly Wages: Under $8	Under $10
Delinquent Women (not in domestic service).....	59.4	76.8
Workers in silk mills in New Jersey	55.4	69.8
Workers in silk mills in Pennsylvania	87.5	96.4
Employees in department and retail stores in New York City, Chicago and Philadelphia	57.5	76.1

From these investigations made several years ago it seems evident that, except for the workers in silk mills in Pennsylvania who were earning very low wages, the delinquent group is like the workers in silk mills in New Jersey and the employees in stores in the percentage of women earning under $8 a week, though there are slightly more of the delinquents than of the other two groups earning the lower wages. The delinquents have a somewhat larger percentage than the workers in silk mills earning under $10 a week, and only a very slightly larger percentage than the workers in department stores. The report under consideration gives the average weekly wage of the total group of workers in department stores as $7.93. In the delinquent group the average weekly wage for prevailing work is $8.90 with the large standard deviation of $6.60. The longer range of wages of the delinquent group would indicate that its standard deviation is larger than that for the group of women in stores. The average wage for

[20] *Op. cit.*, p. 43.

[21] U. S. Department of Labor, Bureau of Labor Statistics: "Summary of the Report on Condition of Woman and Child Wage-earners in the United States." pp. 196 and 216.

the saleswomen alone is $8.84 a week, but these wages also have a short range, so that the standard deviation is probably small. From this scattering material we have gathered on wage, it would seem that our delinquent group has earned an average wage as high as and in a few cases higher than the weekly wage earned by women in specified occupations in New York State and certain neighboring states. The following discussion will show the estimate of regularity of work of the delinquent women, and will indicate that a very high percentage have worked less than one half of the time, so that their actual average income has been much less than a statement of wage would indicate.

Before proceeding to discuss the regularity of work, it may be of interest to note Miss Conyngton's findings regarding low wages as a cause of delinquency. She writes:[22] "Not one worker assigned poverty or low wages as a direct and immediate cause of immorality. It was agreed that indirectly their influence is great, but in the whole inquiry only five cases were found in which the workers reporting them believed that the women had been driven into wrong-doing by want."

ESTIMATE OF REGULARITY OF WORK

We have attempted to "size up" the work records of the women whom we have studied intensively, both by an estimate of the regularity of employment and by a total estimate of the work record. Unfortunately, it is not possible to present similar figures for either of these for the general population. We have tried to get figures from employment agencies which would have a record of individual applicants for a period of years so that we might determine how much of the time the rank and file who applied for work were employed. These figures could not be obtained, however, and so we present our data as merely descriptive of our total group. In considering the regularity of work we have aimed to show how much of the time in a woman's work history she was actually working when she had no other legitimate means of support. We have grouped the women who have done any work into five classes showing the amount of time working. In order to determine this, we have observed the range of the expected work period,—that is, from the date of the first job to present conviction, or to the time to which she would be expected to work, and have based the regularity on the length of time working during this

[22] *Op. cit.*, p. 82.

period. Neither the time when married and keeping house, nor the time in institutions has been counted as idle. The five classes are as follows:

1. *Those who have worked practically none, but may have held one or two jobs for short times.*
   a. A typical case in this class is the colored girl in Bedford, 23 years old, who began work at 16 years as nursegirl for a family on Long Island. She worked for 2 months in 1909 and then ran away from her employer. Since that time she has prostituted practically all of the time and has done no legitimate work.
   b. Another girl in the Workhouse, 20 years of age, began to work at 16 and held 3 short jobs in quick succession,—2 weeks in a factory for manufacturing pennants, 1 week as attendant in an orphan asylum, and a few days coloring films. Her entire work period covered less than a month while the expected work period was 4 years.
2. *Those who have worked about one-quarter of the time.*
   a. Here we might cite the girl of 17 years who started work at 16 years and during the year of her expected work period held 5 jobs as follows:
      1. Seamstress in waist factory, 3 weeks.
      2. Removing foil from scrap candy, 1 month.
      3. Spinner in yarn factory, 7 days.
      4. Housework, 2 weeks.
      5. Seamstress in factory, 1 week.

      That is, she worked about 11 weeks or approximately one-fourth of the time she was supposed to be working.
3. *Those who have worked about one-half of the time.*
4. *Those who have worked about three-quarters of the time.*
5. *Those who have worked practically all of the time.* The number of women in this class is very few and nearly all are those who have had excellent work records. The individual records will not be enumerated here, since in nearly every case they are a repetition of one job after another with very short or no intervals between the jobs.

If we turn to Table 137, we may see how the institutional groups vary in the estimate of regularity of work. It is obvious, first of all, that the percentages are very much alike in the various institutional groups. Probation, it is true, has a smaller percentage who did very little work, and it also has a larger percentage in the two upper classes.

The Workhouse has the smallest percentage of women in the two upper classes, and this serves to justify the impression one gets by reading over the work records of the Workhouse women. Their own statements of number of jobs held and length of time in them is so indefinite, particularly with the older women, that many of the jobs were verified only with great difficulty and were then found to have been held for only a few days. For the women in the Workhouse, which has the largest number of recidivists, the work history is a story of many repetitions,—coming out of the Workhouse, finding a position for a few days, committing an offense against the law again, being recommitted to the Workhouse, and so on. For the total group of women there are in the first three classes, 60.9 per cent who worked approximately less than half the time, and who could not have earned enough in the time working to tide them over the rest of the time. Only about 3.5 per cent were surely able to support themselves, while 35.6 per cent by working about three-quarters of the time may have had sufficient money by careful saving to tide them over the time of idleness.[23]

TABLE 137

REGULARITY OF EMPLOYMENT

Per Cent Distribution of Delinquent Women in Institutional Groups

Regularity	Institutional Groups						Total
	Bedford	Auburn	Magdalen	Penitentiary	Workhouse	Probation	
Worked almost none	11.2	10.1	6.9	10.0	8.8	3.9	8.6
Worked about one-fourth of time	23.5	17.4	27.8	22.2	35.0	16.7	23.9
Worked about one-half of time	26.5	29.0	31.9	27.8	25.0	31.2	28.4
Worked about three-quarters of time	36.7	42.0	30.6	32.2	30.0	42.9	35.6
Worked nearly all of time	2.0	1.5	2.8	7.8	1.3	5.2	3.5
Total	100.0	100.0	100.0	100.0	100.0	100.0	100.0
Number of cases	98	69	72	90	80	77	486

[23] It should be remembered that the time in idleness does not include the time keeping house for one's family or parents, or the time in institutions, so that idleness without money means no legitimate means of support.

It may be of interest here to add Table 138 showing the distribution of estimate of regularity of work among the nativity groups. From this table it seems that the foreign born have worked much more of the time than either the native white or native colored. That is, 44.8 per cent of the foreign born were employed less than half of the time while 66.5 per cent of the native white and 70.5 per cent of the native colored fall in this group. The native colored have the poorest showing in the regularity of work.

TABLE 138

REGULARITY OF EMPLOYMENT

Per Cent Distribution of Delinquent Women Classified by Nativity and Color

Regularity	Nativity and Color				Total
	Total Foreign Born	Total Native Born	Native White	Native Colored	
Worked almost none	4.2	10.5	10.6	10.2	8.7
Worked about one-fourth of time	15.4	27.2	25.2	33.0	23.7
Worked about one-half of time	25.2	29.8	30.7	27.3	28.5
Worked about three-quarters of time	48.3	30.4	31.5	27.3	35.5
Worked nearly all of time	7.0	2.1	2.0	2.3	3.5
Total	100.0	100.0	100.0	100.0	100.0
Number of cases	143	342	254	88	485

TOTAL ESTIMATE OF WORK RECORD

The total estimate of the efficiency of the work history, considering all phases of the work record, is based on the following factors:

1. Prevailing wage.
2. Regularity of work.
3. Ability as reported by employers, etc.
4. Increase or decrease in wage, regularity of work and ability as shown by a survey of the entire work record.

The estimate we have used is divided into five classes which have been made up on the following basis. The points suggested under each class are not arbitrary and there are innumerable combinations of good and poor qualities in certain individual work histories which might arise to place the estimate in one or another class. The following scheme was used only as a means of showing the trend of the most of the records.[24]

1. *Very poor.* May include cases with
   a. Very low prevailing wage (not enough to live on independently).
   b. Very irregular work record (class 1 or 2).
   c. Ability very poor as reported by employers.
   d. No increase to higher wages, etc., and cases with actual decrease.
2. *Poor.*
   a. Low prevailing wage.
   b. Irregular work record (class 2 or 3).
   c. Ability poor.
   d. Very little or no increase or development in work record.
3. *Mediocre.* Includes women who are probably self-supporting, but barely so.
   a. Wage large enough to live on but with no possibility of saving.
   b. Fairly regular work record (about class 4). Includes cases of seasonal unemployment where women are out of work through no fault of their own.
   c. Mediocre ability. Able to keep job requiring no skill.
   d. Possibly slight increase in wage.
4. *Good.* Women who are thoroughly self-supporting and good workers.
   a. Good prevailing wage.
   b. Regular work (class 5 or occasionally 4).
   c. Well spoken of by employers.
   d. Record shows fairly consistent development in wage, regularity and ability.
5. *Very good.* Exceptionally good work record.
   a. Consistently high wage.
   b. Regular work (class 5 or occasionally 4).
   c. Very well recommended by employer.
   d. Consistent development.

[24] These estimates were made separately on each institutional group by two persons and checked by a third person so that the method of treating each case was uniform.

We shall cite a few examples of work records which have been estimated to belong in one or another of these five classes and which are typical of many cases in each of the institutional groups.

Class 1. A girl 16 years, 2 months old at time of conviction for vagrancy (prostitution), is very low grade mentally and comes from most abominable home surroundings. She began to work when 14, has an expected work period of 2 years and worked 7 months. Her jobs are as follows:

a. General housework for Mrs. M., M——, New York, 2 months, 1915, earning $6 a week. (Her own statement which could not be verified and which is probably untrue.)
b. Helped with housework, Mrs. M——, S——, New York, 1 week, 1915, earning $1 a week. Was discharged because she was so unsatisfactory. Could not learn how to do anything, was very careless and dirty.
c. General housework, Mrs. S——, M——, New York, 2 months, 1916, earning $1 a week. Says she left because there were too many boarders. Employer does not remember her.
d. Winder in silk mill, M——, New York, 3 days, Dec. 20-23, 1916, at rate of $4.50 a week. Was very unsatisfactory.
e. Piece worker on fireworks, 19 days. May 29—June 16, 1917, at $6 a week. Was very unsatisfactory, flirted with men and could not do the work. Was arrested while working here.

This girl earned not more than $75 during two years. She worked about one-fourth of the time, her employers report her as unable to do the work, and her record shows no consistent increase in wage, or ability to do work.

Class 2. A girl, 16 years, 9 months of age, was committed to Bedford for vagrancy (prostitution). She is also of low grade mentality. She started work at 15 and has an expected work period of 21 months, during which she worked about 16 to 17 months. Her work was as follows:

a. General housework, 4 months, 1915, earning $3 a week. Said she left because work was too far from home. (Could not be verified.)
b. General housework, 4 weeks, 1916, at $2 a week. Said she left because she could not eat Jewish food. (Could not be verified.)
c. General housework, 7 months, 1916, earning from $1.50 to $2 a week. Was discharged for dishonesty and employer said she grew so careless in her work she could not keep her.

d. Helper in hotel dining room, 7 weeks in spring of 1916 and 4 weeks in the summer, earning $2.50 to $3 a week. Her work was reported as unsatisfactory. She was absent-minded and inefficient.
e. General housework, 2 weeks, 1916, earning $3 a week. Was discharged as "unsatisfactory and very dirty."
f. Cigar-making in factory, in July, 1916 at $3 a week. Was discharged as unsatisfactory.
g. Cleaning house, 4 days, November, 1916, at $.35 for half a day's work. Was very dirty and unreliable and thoroughly unsatisfactory.

This girl earned a low prevailing wage of about $2.33 weekly plus maintenance, she worked about three-quarters of the time, but her ability was nil and she was discharged from four places. Her work shows no consistent development. Because of her fairly regular work record she was placed in class 2, instead of class 1 where her ability alone would place her.

Class 3. A girl, 18 years, 5 months of age, was convicted of vagrancy (prostitution). She is very bright, quick and learns easily. She began work when 15, and in an expected work period of 38 months worked about half of that time.

a. Nursegirl, 2 weeks in September, 1913, at $2 a week. Was discharged because she was unreliable and unsatisfactory.
b. Sorting paper in paper mill 1 year, from May, 1914, to May, 1915, earning $5 a week. Employer says she was "equal to average."
c. Banding cigars in factory, 3 months at $6 a week. Left because work made her ill. Employer says she was "O.K. but not steady."
d. Feeder on forming machine in hat factory for 3 months, earning $10 a week. Was very good at first but finally had to be discharged on account of her character.
e. Banding cigars for 1 week previous to arrest at $6 a week.

This girl averaged $5 a week in her prevailing work, she worked about half of the time, had good ability if she would use it, and showed possibilities of increase in earning capacity and length of time in jobs. Her whole work record, though unsatisfactory because of the two discharges, might be called mediocre.

Class 4. A woman of 29 years, 10 months, was convicted of possessing opium. She started work at 15 and worked for 11 years, singing and dancing in vaudeville performances. Though there was only a slight increase in her wage up to $25 a week and traveling expenses, she made a name for herself in many of the small places near New York and was very successful as a dancer. She was placed in class four, because she had a fairly high average wage, because she had ability, and because she worked steadily up until the last 4 years before her conviction when she acquired a drug habit.

Class 5. A woman, 25 years, 7 months of age, was convicted of violating the Tenement House Law. She began work at 14 and held 13 jobs, covering 9 years, during her work period of 11 years. The work record is rather too long and too much the same to give all of the details but the main trends are as follows: ten of the thirteen jobs were in general housework, the other three being waitress, usher in theater for two weeks, and laundry work in a laundry for six weeks. The wage begins at $2 a week in the first jobs and runs progressively through $4 a week, $5 a week, $6 a week and $7 a week and living, which she had been earning in her two latest jobs. Several of the records we were not able to verify because the employers had moved, but those from whom we heard, speak of her as "very satisfactory," "excellent," "the best worker we ever had," and "A, No. 1." Though this girl was out of work practically two years out of the 11, she was placed in the highest class because of her steadily increasing wage, and her unusually good ability which was spoken of by every employer.

(a) *Distribution for Institutional Groups*

If we apply this estimate to the institutional groups, we find in Table 139 that there is considerable variation between the groups though there is the same trend running through each. As with the estimate of regularity of work, the Probation group has the smallest percentage, only 6.5 per cent, in the very poor class, while the Workhouse runs up to 17.5 per cent for the same class. It is also of interest to note that the Workhouse and Bedford, those whose records were known least and those which were known most thoroughly, have no representative in the very good class. Only 1.7 per cent of the total group have exceptionally good work records and only 12.3 per cent a record that might be called good. Roughly, by the method of our estimate, the women in classes 1 and 2 could not possibly be self-supporting if they lived on what they earned from their legitimate employment. Those in class 3 might, with great care and with no occasion for large additional expenditures, get along on their earnings, while those in the two upper classes ought to be able to live on their wages.

By this standard, we find that for the total group of women, 49.7 per cent, almost half of the women, have poor or very poor work records and could not possibly be self-supporting on the amount they have earned, 36.4 per cent of the total group have mediocre records and could with great care have lived on their earnings, while 14.0 per cent have good work records and could probably be called entirely self-supporting. It is a striking commentary on the economic competence of this group of delinquent women that as a group they have worked so irregularly and that half of them at least have done so little and such poor work that they could not have lived on their earnings.

TABLE 139

ESTIMATE OF WORK RECORD

Per Cent Distribution of Delinquent Women in Institutional Groups

Estimate of Work Record	Institutional Groups						Total
	Bedford	Auburn	Magdalen	Penitentiary	Workhouse	Probation	
Very poor.....	14.3	13.2	11.8	12.2	17.5	6.5	12.7
Poor..........	50.0	33.8	39.7	32.2	36.3	27.3	37.0
Fair..........	31.6	36.8	36.8	27.8	35.0	53.2	36.4
Good.........	4.1	11.8	8.8	26.7	11.3	10.4	12.3
Very good.....	....	4.4	2.9	1.1	....	2.6	1.7
Total....	100.0	100.0	100.0	100.0	100.0	100.0	100.0
Number of cases	98	68	68	90	80	77	481

(b) *Distribution for Nativity Groups*

If we turn to Table 140, showing the distribution of women in nativity groups by the estimate of the work record, we note first of all the very small percentage of the foreign born who fall in the poorest class, the larger percentage of the native white in this class and the very much higher percentage, almost five times as many women, among the native colored. The native colored have no representatives in the exceptionally good work records, while the native white have only .8 of a per cent and the foreign born 4.3 per cent. If we use the larger groupings by combining classes 1 and 2, and 4 and 5, we find that the foreign born have 32.2 per cent in the class which could not possibly be self-supporting from the amount earned in legitimate work, while the native white have 44.8 per cent in this class and the colored 62.5 per cent. In the mediocre class, it will be seen, the foreign born have 43.6 per cent, the native white 34.5 per cent and the native colored 30.7 per cent. In the upper class of those probably self-supporting, we find 25.0 per cent among the foreign born, 10.3 per cent among the native white and 6.8 per cent among the native colored. From this it would seem that the foreign group are more efficient and regular workers, if we view their work records as a whole, than either the native white or the native colored, and that the native colored have the most unsatisfactory work records. In order to explain this, we might turn back to Table 138 which shows that the foreign born have worked much more of the time than have the native born. Table 112 also shows us that the prevailing work of the foreign born differs quite markedly from the prevailing work of either the native white or native colored, with slight differences in certain of the occupations but very striking differences in occupations such as domestic service or factory work.[25]

(c) *Relationship to Factors Within Work Record*

In this connection we shall try to determine whether there is any relationship between the nature of prevailing work and the estimate of the work record. The relationship of these two factors is tabulated in Table 141. From this it is seen that there is no striking relationship. Perhaps the most noteworthy thing about the table is the fact that both domestic service and factory work are represented by individuals of all degrees of efficiency as indicated by the total work history. The failure of the clerical workers to show any individuals with very good or very poor records is striking, as is the fact that of the three professional women of the group none show a record better than fair.

[25] In answer to the objection which may be raised that the foreign born seem to have a better work record because we have been able to verify less of their work record and they tend to exaggerate their ability in their own statement of work, we give the following figures showing whether the data on which the estimates are based are largely verified or largely unverified. This shows that about the same percentage of records are verified among the foreign born and the native colored, while the native white have a larger percentage verified.

	Largely Verified	Largely Unverified
Foreign Born	55.0	45.0
Total Native Born	64.7	35.3
Native White	67.9	32.1
Native Colored	55.7	44.3
Total Group	61.9	38.1

TABLE 140

ESTIMATE OF WORK RECORD

Per Cent Distribution of Delinquent Women Classified by Nativity and Color

Estimate of Work Record	Nativity and Color				Total
	Total Foreign Born	Total Native Born	Native White	Native Colored	
Very poor	4.3	16.2	14.3	21.6	12.7
Poor	27.9	40.6	40.5	40.9	37.1
Fair	43.6	33.5	34.5	30.7	36.5
Good	20.7	8.8	9.5	6.8	12.3
Very good	4.3	.6	.8	....	1.7
Total	100.0	100.0	100.0	100.0	100.0
Number of cases	140	340	252	88	480

TABLE 141

Nature of Prevailing Work in Relation to Estimate of Work Record

Nature of Prevailing Work	Estimate of Work Record					Total
	Very Poor	Poor	Fair	Good	Very Good	
Domestic service	26	81	63	21	2	193
Factory work	12	43	49	14	2	120
Home work	1	4	11	3	....	19
Restaurant and hotel work	5	10	11	4	....	30
Work in stores	6	13	16	3	2	40
Vaudeville performers	1	3	7	8	....	19
Clerical work	....	8	4	1	....	13
Professional service	1	....	2	....	....	3
Personal service	1	4	3	3	2	13
Charwomen	2	....	1	....	....	3
Miscellaneous	2	1	2	....	....	5
Total	57	167	169	57	8	458

It is of interest here to see if there is a relationship between the kind of work one does when she first starts working and the estimate of the work record which follows. Table 142 shows this relationship. As in the preceding table there is little indication of any striking relation. One starting in almost any occupation has a fair chance of making either a good or a poor work record, although the chances are overweighted toward the latter probability except in case of two of the very small groups.

TABLE 142

Estimate of Work Record in Relation to Kind of Work in First Job

Kind of Work in First Job	Estimate of Work Record: Very Poor	Poor	Fair	Good	Very Good	Total
Domestic service	23	75	70	21	2	191
Factory work	19	45	57	13	2	136
Home work	2	5	6	1	..	14
Restaurant and hotel work	5	15	7	2	..	29
Work in stores	4	19	14	5	3	45
Vaudeville performers	2	1	5	5	..	13
Clerical work	..	10	4	5	..	19
Professional service	1	..	2	2	..	5
Personal service	1	4	3	2	1	11
Charwomen	1	..	1	..	..	2
Miscellaneous	2	3	3	1	..	9
Total	60	177	172	57	8	474

(d) *Relationship to Other Social Factors*

A reason often advanced by child labor propagandists for much of the economic inefficiency is that those who start work earliest have no opportunity for training, that they start work in an unskilled occupation, get into a rut, and are never able to progress. As they grow older they become slower and are gradually pushed out to more and more casual work, while younger persons fill their places. In order to see whether in our group of delinquent women there is any tendency for those who start work earliest to have any less satisfactory work records, the following correlation table is presented (Table 143). By calculating the correlation ratio we find that $\eta = .14$ with a standard deviation of .047. From this it would seem that there is a significant but a small relationship between the age at starting work and the estimate of the work record. The means of the age at starting work show that for the three lowest classes of the estimate of the work record, the average ages at starting work are about the same, though there is a very slight increase in age from class 1 to class 3. The age at starting work is appreciably higher, 20 years, in both classes 4 and 5, showing that those who have been most competent industrially have started work at a later age than those who have had very poor work records. As stated before, the relationship is low and would seem to indicate that the factor of starting work early, though it has a slight effect on the later efficiency of the work record, is not one of the important factors operating in the determination of a very good or very poor record.

Another factor which is often considered as influencing the efficiency of a work record is the amount of schooling, and as a measure of this we shall use grade finished. Table 144 shows the relationship between the grade finished and the estimate of the work record. The correlation ratio of $.13 \pm .049$ indicates that there is a genuine but a small relationship. The means show only a small increase in the changes in grade for the changes in efficiency of record, but the trend of the average grade increases in regular order from the lowest to the highest class of the estimate. The factor of amount of schooling, therefore, like the factor of age at starting work, probably has had only slight influence in determining the character of the work record in the case of the women under consideration.

There is still another factor which may have a significant relationship to the estimate of the work record, and that is the estimate of conditions in the home during childhood and adolescence. A girl brought up in the lowest kind of home surroundings may be made relatively much more incompetent for good work later on by these conditions than she would be fitted for good work by a long period of schooling, for example. Table 145 presents the coefficient of contingency of the estimate of the work record with the estimate of home conditions, and shows by the coefficient of $C = .24$ that there is a small relationship between the two factors, with a tendency for those with

TABLE 143

Correlation between Age at Starting Work and Estimate of Work Record

Total Group

Estimate of Work Record	Age at Starting Work (Years)														Totals	Means (Age at Starting Work)
	6–10	10–14	14–18	18–22	22–26	26–30	30–34	34–38	38–42	42–46	46–50	50–54	54–58	58–62		
Very good		1	5				1	1							8	20.0
Good		4	29	7	4	5	3	1	1		2				56	20.0
Fair	6	22	81	27	13	8	3		1	2				1	164	17.5
Poor	2	24	88	23	8	6	3	1	3	1					159	17.3
Very poor		9	32	12			1	1			1				56	17.1
Totals	8	60	235	69	25	19	11	4	5	3	3	0	0	1	443	17.72

Age at Starting Work: Mean = 17.72 $\sigma = 6.61$
Correlation Ratio: Age at starting work on estimate of work record, $\eta = .14 \pm .047$

TABLE 144

Correlation between Grade Finished in School and Estimate of Work Record

Total Group

Estimate of Work Record	Grade Finished: 0*	1	2	3	4	5	6	7	8	First Year High School	Second Year High School	Third Year High School	Fourth Year High School	Totals	Means (Grade Finished)
Very good		1			1	1	1			2			1	7	6.6
Good	5	1	4	5	8	4	4	6	9				2	48	5.0
Fair	22	2	10	13	13	19	24	14	17	3	2		2	141	4.7
Poor	11	2	13	26	26	28	15	11	13	2	1		2	150	4.5
Very poor	5	4	5	5	12	4	8	6	3	1				53	4.2
Totals	43	10	32	49	60	56	52	37	42	8	3	0	7	399	4.60

Grade Finished: Mean = 4.60 $\sigma = 2.667$
Correlation Ratio: Grade finished on estimate of work record, $\eta = .13 \pm .049$

* Includes those who have never been in school and those who have attended but never finished first grade.

good home conditions to have a better work record than those with poor home conditions.

TABLE 145

Contingency of Estimate of Work Record with Estimate of Home Conditions

		Estimate of Work Record					Total
		Very Poor	Poor	Fair	Good	Very Good	
Estimate of Home Conditions	Very poor.....	7	15	5	5	....	32
	Poor..........	24	67	54	13	1	159
	Fair..........	27	77	90	30	6	230
	Good.........	2	7	9	9	1	28
	Very good.....	....	1	1	....	....	2
	Total....	60	167	159	57	8	451

Coefficient of contingency of estimate of work record with estimate of home conditions, C = .24

If we summarize the factors we have considered which might have a possible causal influence in determining the kind of work record, we find that there are no very high relationships demonstrable but that each factor has a slight and probably significant relationship in the determination of the efficiency of the work record. These low relationships will be noted again briefly.

1. There is a small relationship between the estimate of the work record and the nature of prevailing work, indicating that there is a tendency for those who do certain kinds of work to have a more satisfactory work history than those doing other kinds of work.

2. There is a still smaller relationship between the estimate of the work record and the kind of work in the first job indicating that there is a slight tendency for those who first go into certain kinds of work to have more efficient work records than those who start in with other work.

3. There is only a small relationship between the age at starting work and the estimate of the work record with a tendency for those who start work earliest to do the least satisfactory work after that.

4. The element of grade finished in school has a small relationship

to the estimate of the work record, and indicates that there is a slight tendency for those who have finished more grades in school to do better work than those who have had less schooling.

5. The relationship between estimate of work record and estimate of home conditions is small and indicates that the factor of good or poor home conditions, though they may effect to some extent the efficiency of the work record, do not do so to any marked degree.

SUMMARY

From the data which have been presented in this chapter and which have aimed to show the development of the occupational histories of 587 delinquent women, from the age at starting work to the estimate which summarizes the most important factors of the entire work record, we can not draw as definite conclusions as we should like because of the difficulty of obtaining comparative data for the general female population of New York State. We may note, however, the main factors we have observed in the work records of this group of delinquent women.

First of all, we find that our group of women has 14.8 per cent starting work before they were fourteen, while the general female population has only 0.1 of a per cent working between ten and fourteen years of age. This indicates a trend for these delinquent women to go to work earlier than the general female population in New York State. The age at starting work, however, allowing for the factor of present age, seems to have no significant relationship to the age at first conviction.

Data offered on the kind of work done show that the domestic service workers have much more than their expected percentage, if compared with the women over fifteen in New York State. The vaudeville performers, also, have a larger percentage among the delinquents, while the more skilled workers, such as those in clerical work and professional service, have a much smaller representation among the delinquent group than among the general population. The same trend has been found in other studies, particularly that of Miss Mary Conyngton, in the series of "Woman and Child Wage-earners in the United States." [27] A correlation between grade finished and nature of work shows that there is a significant relationship in the tendency of the occupational groups to differ in respect to school attainment. The domestic service workers have reached a lower average grade than the women in any other occupations except charwomen and the miscel-

[27] *Op. cit.*, p. 30.

laneous group, both of which have too small numbers to be significant.

One of the most striking facts in observing the nature of work is to find how large a part of the women were idle at the time they committed the offenses which led to both their first and present convictions. This tendency has also been noted by Miss Conyngton[28] and by Dr. Glueck in a study of male felons in Sing Sing.[29]

The study of wage in our groups is difficult because the women are of varying ages and their work records cover different periods of time. Recognizing this unavoidable difficulty, we have, however, computed the average wage for the prevailing work of those in occupations other than housework, and find by comparing this with certain scattering wage studies in specified employments that the women in our group probably earned no less than the women in the occupations noted. From the figures given in the reports used no exact comparison is possible, but in general we may note that the average wage of the delinquents is probably not so low as to be directly accountable for their getting into difficulties with the law.

In a correlation between grade finished and average weekly wage for prevailing work there seems to be a significant relationship, with a tendency for both the domestic service workers and those in occupations other than domestic service to receive a higher average wage if they have finished the higher grades. No significant difference was demonstrable in a correlation between grade finished and first wage.

Referring to the correlation between average weekly wage and number of convictions, we find no evidence of a significant relationship in the case of women in domestic service, and evidence of only a slight degree of association, in the direction of negative correlation, for women in other occupations. The striking relationship which might be anticipated between proved earning capacity and degree of recidivism is notably lacking.

In summarizing the regularity of work we have used an estimate which shows that 60.9 per cent of the women have worked half of the time or less, while only 3.5 per cent have worked nearly all of the time. Upon applying this estimate to the color and nativity groups we find that the foreign born have worked with much more regularity, while the native colored have the poorest showing in this respect.

A summary of all of the factors in the work record is made in the estimate of the work record, which indicates that on the whole the

[28] *Op. cit.*, pp. 46-47.
[29] *Op. cit.*, p. 138.

work records are poor, only 14.0 per cent of the total group falling in the class above mediocre, while 49.7 per cent fall in the two groups of very poor and poor work records. Here, also, the foreign born show better work records than either the native white or native colored.

In an attempt to find what factors in the personal histories of these women have a significant relationship to the efficiency of the work records, we have computed the correlation between estimate of work record and age at starting work, grade finished in school and estimate of early home conditions. In each of these correlations a very small but probably significant relationship is demonstrable. The relationship is so small, however, that it would be difficult to say any real causal influence existed.

On the whole, the records show, for the most part, poor ability, great irregularity, and a low wage, though probably no lower wage than the bulk of unskilled workers in the same occupations outside are earning. It would seem that the delinquents in this study are drawn almost entirely from this large class of the unskilled workers, but that this fact is not, as might be argued by the Socialist School, the fundamental cause of the delinquency. We have noted elsewhere the low grade attained in school as compared with the majority of children who have been in public school the same length of time, the low mentality as measured by intellectual tests, the poor home conditions and lack of training. It would, therefore, be impossible for us to state that the economic relations of these women are in any sense exclusively the causative factors of delinquency. In many cases there is, undoubtedly, a close association between the limited, poorly paid, industrial opportunities and the continuance of illegal acts. In many cases, the economic possibilities for the father or mother in the family have been so poor that the women in this study did not have proper educational advantages as children and were forced into work with no future and a small wage. For the most part, however, we believe that the elements of occupational influences and low wages are not the direct and immediate causes of the delinquency, though indirectly their influence is great.

CHAPTER XII

HISTORY OF SEX IRREGULARITIES

THE study of delinquent women in several institutions, some of which take the petty offender and some the criminal who has committed the more serious offenses, shows that the history of these women with reference to sexual irregularity divides itself into three general classes. First there is the professional prostitute who earns her entire living by this method. Secondly, there is the woman who prostitutes herself either regularly or irregularly, but who earns money in addition to this by stealing or by other illegal methods. And, thirdly, there is the woman who may have been sexually promiscuous, but not for money; or the woman who may have lived with one or more consorts for any length of time. In this discussion, we shall attempt to show the status of degree of sexual irregularity among the total group of women, and by institutional groups, giving whatever data we have been able to gather about the first contacts with sex life. Since the prostitutes constitute the most important part of the sex problem, they will be separately considered and the main factors in their social histories compared with similar factors in the lives of prostitutes studied elsewhere.

FIRST SEX EXPERIENCE

(a) *Age at First Sex Offense*

The age at first sex offense refers to the time that the first illicit sexual intercourse occurred, whether the woman consented at that time or was raped. The distribution by four year age groups given in Table 146 is for the age at first sex offense of the women in institutional groups. The range of years runs from 6 to 51 years and the age group from 14 to 18 years has the largest number of cases. In the lowest age group Bedford has four cases, one who was raped at six, and one at eight years, and two who consented to have sexual intercourse when they were nine years old. The one Auburn case which falls in this group was nine years of age when she was raped by her cousin in whose home she was visiting. Only one case of the

Probation women falls in this lowest age group, and she was raped at nine years. The higher age groups have representatives, of course, only in the institutions which have women of the older age.

The comparison of the means and standard deviations for the age at first sex offense shows that Bedford has the youngest mean age at first sex offense with the smallest standard deviation and that, in order of increasing average ages, follow the Magdalen, Probation, the Penitentiary, Workhouse and Auburn. The range of average ages is from 16.2 years in Bedford to 21.4 years in Auburn. The average age at first sex offense for the total group is 18.72±.312 years with a standard deviation of 5.82±.221 years.

TABLE 146

AGE AT FIRST SEX OFFENSE

Per Cent Distribution of Delinquent Women in Institutional Groups

Age at First Sex Offense	Institutional Groups						Total
	Bedford	Auburn	Magdalen	Penitentiary	Workhouse	Probation	
6 to 10 years	4.4	2.4	....	....	....	1.9	1.7
10 " 14 "	13.0	2.4	5.1	4.0	7.8	....	6.3
14 " 18 "	54.4	38.0	55.9	42.0	39.2	35.2	45.7
18 " 22 "	22.8	19.1	27.1	24.0	25.5	37.0	25.9
22 " 26 "	3.3	9.5	8.5	16.0	7.8	11.1	8.6
26 " 30 "	1.1	9.5	1.7	6.0	3.9	13.0	5.2
30 " 34 "	1.1	11.9	1.7	4.0	3.9	1.9	3.5
34 " 38 "	....	2.4	....	....	5.9	....	1.2
38 " 42 "	....	2.4	....	4.0	5.9	....	1.7
50 " 54 "	....	2.4	....	....	....	....	.3
Total...	100.0	100.0	100.0	100.0	100.0	100.0	100.0
Number of cases	92	42	59	50	51	54	348
Mean.........	16.19	21.4	17.34	19.76	20.7	19.67	18.72
σ_m	±.380	±1.27	±.416	±.864	±1.07	±.581	±.312
σ............	3.65	8.25	3.20	6.11	7.63	4.27	5.82
σ_σ..........	±.269	±.900	±.294	±.611	±.756	±.411	±.221

(b) *Rape or Consent*

Table 147 shows the percentages of women who were forced and those who consented to have first sexual intercourse. In this table the percentages of women who were raped vary markedly between institutional groups. The Workhouse has the smallest percentage who were forced to have sexual intercourse and the percentages increase progressively through Auburn, the Penitentiary, Probation, Magdalen and Bedford. In the total group, 22.6 per cent of the women were raped while 77.4 per cent willingly consented to have sexual intercourse. A large part of the 22.6 per cent is made up of the women falling in the youngest age groups shown in Table 146.

TABLE 147

RAPE OR CONSENT AT FIRST SEX OFFENSE

Per Cent Distribution of Delinquent Women in Institutional Groups

Rape or Consent	Institutional Groups						Total
	Bedford	Auburn	Magdalen	Peni-tentiary	Work-house	Probation	
Rape.........	35.9	9.3	34.5	16.3	8.5	18.9	22.6
Consent.......	64.1	90.7	65.5	83.7	91.5	81.1	77.4
Total....	100.0	100.0	100.0	100.0	100.0	100.0	100.0
Number of cases	92	43	58	49	59	53	354

Classified by nativity and color, the distribution of age at first sex offense shows that the range of years for the foreign born is from 12 to 51 years, for the native white from 8 to 39 years, and for the native colored from 6 to 39 years. There is a concentration of cases in the lower age groups of the native colored, with only 7.3 per cent who committed their first sex offense when they were thirty or over. The native white have their concentration of cases in the age groups slightly above those noted for the native colored, but have 4.0 per cent who were first sexually immoral when they were 30 or over. The foreign born, on the other hand, show few cases in the earlier age groups, and have 13.3 per cent who were 30 or over at time of their first sex offense. It would seem from this that there is a tendency for the native colored to get into sexual difficulties at the younger ages, and for the foreign born to commit their first sex offenses much later in life.

TABLE 148

AGE AT FIRST SEX OFFENSE

Per Cent Distribution of Delinquent Women Classified by Nativity and Color

Age at First Sex Offense	Nativity and Color				Total
	Total Foreign Born	Total Native Born	Native White	Native Colored	
6 to 10 years.......	....	2.2	2.0	2.9	1.7
10 " 14 "	2.7	7.4	5.9	11.6	6.3
14 " 18 "	33.3	49.3	47.8	53.6	45.8
18 " 22 "	33.3	23.5	26.1	15.9	25.7
22 " 26 "	12.0	7.7	8.4	5.8	8.7
26 " 30 "	5.3	5.2	5.9	2.9	5.2
30 " 34 "	6.7	2.6	2.0	4.4	3.5
34 " 38 "	1.3	1.1	1.5	....	1.2
38 " 42 "	4.0	1.1	.5	2.9	1.7
50 " 54 "	1.3	....	....	....	.3
Total..........	100.0	100.0	100.0	100.0	100.0
Number of cases......	75	272	203	69	347

(c) *Sex Instruction*

Since the question of giving proper sex instruction to children is being stressed at present throughout the country, it is of interest to see how many of the women in this study were instructed by persons who were competent to give children the information they ought to have about sex matters. Sex instruction, as we have used it, refers to the minimum of even the simplest and most general statements concerning reproduction and sex matters. In many cases the instruction given by the mother, for instance, was nothing more than a warning to "keep away from the fellows now" with a few admonitions about the consequences. We have included as sex instruction, however, even these crudest and most unintelligent attempts to tell the girl what things she must be careful about. The number who have received intelligent instruction on sex matters from those who are in a proper position to tell them is much smaller, therefore, than the number we have included.

However, it is interesting to note in Table 149 the large percentage of these women who received no adequate sex knowledge except from girl friends, by reading or by observation. In the total group, 52.7 per cent of the women received a certain amount of sex knowledge

TABLE 149

SOURCE OF SEX INSTRUCTION

Per Cent Distribution of Delinquent Women in Institutional Groups

Source of Sex Instruction	Institutional Groups						Total
	Bed-ford	Auburn	Mag-dalen	Peni-tentiary	Work-house	Proba-tion	
Members of Family	45.5	58.2	57.6	45.6	60.5	51.7	52.7
Mother	29.3	37.3	45.5	31.3	41.9	27.6	35.3
Father	1.0	....	....	....	....	....	.2
Husband	5.1	4.5	1.5	1.2	....	13.8	3.9
Other relatives	10.1	16.4	10.6	13.1	18.6	10.3	13.3
Friends	46.7	37.4	28.7	9.6	3.5	32.7	26.2
Consort	5.1	....	....	....	....	5.2	1.8
"Friends"	16.2	19.4	24.2	9.6	3.5	24.1	15.3
Girl friends in school	15.2	9.0	1.5	....	....	1.7	5.0
Girl friends at work	5.1	6.0	1.5	....	....	1.7	2.4
Girl friends in institutions	5.1	3.0	1.5	....	....	....	1.7
Teacher or matron in institution	4.0	....	1.5	....	1.2	1.7	1.5
Physician	1.0	....	....	....	....	....	.2
Employer	2.0	....	....	1.2	....	....	.7
Reading or observation	1.0	3.0	10.6	42.2	34.9	10.3	17.7
Self or "none"	....	1.5	1.5	1.2	....	3.5	1.1
Total	100.0	100.0	100.0	100.0	100.0	100.0	100.0
Number of cases	99	67	66	83	86	58	459

from members of their families. The number receiving no such training until they were told by their husbands should be thrown out of any consideration of sex instruction that was of value to the child. Instruction by friends includes that of friends met on the street, friends in school, at work, in institutions. A teacher or matron in an institution or a physician are legitimate sources of information, and the three cases noted who were instructed by an employer were young nurse-girls, who were very intelligently told of sex matters at the time menstruation was established. As a whole, we may divide the total group into (1) those who were given sex instructions, even very inadequate instructions, by persons who were in a position to give this information intelligently, and (2) those who were improperly instructed by girls of their own age, or by reading and observation which was unsuitable. Redistributed in this way for the total group the percentages fall as follows:

(1) Sex instructions given by proper source, including mother, father and other relatives; teacher or matron in institution; physician and employer=51.2 per cent.

(2) Sex instructions given by improper source or too late, and those who had no instructions except the things they observed=48.9 per cent.

By this division it appears that almost half of the cases "picked up" whatever knowledge they have of sex matters, through sources which could not present the matter in the right way. This is, we realize, a very liberal estimate for those who have had sex instructions, since many we have included in the first group as instructed by "members of family" were told very little that would be of benefit to them.

EXTENT OF SEXUAL IRREGULARITY

(a) *Distribution by Institutional Groups*

If we proceed to a discussion of the extent of sexual irregularity which followed these first sex offenses, we may note in Table 150 that the first class, the prostitutes, have the bulk of the cases in each group except Auburn and the Penitentiary, both of which have the largest percentage of felons. By "prostitute" we mean one who has practised indiscriminate sexual intercourse for money. We have included here not only the professional prostitutes who made their entire living in this manner, but also the irregular prostitutes who supplemented other earnings by prostitution. The second class which we have called "sexually irregular" includes women who may have been sexually promiscuous at times, but not for money; or women who may have lived with one or more consorts for any length of time. "Occasional sex offenders" includes those who may have had illicit sexual intercourse a few times, but who are only occasional and random offenders. "Never a sex offender" includes those who have never had illicit sexual intercourse.

Table 150 followed by Chart XX shows that the percentages of women in these various classes vary considerably. The Workhouse has the highest number, 93.0 per cent of its total, who were prostitutes. The Probation group which follows has, as would be expected, a high percentage of prostitutes, since the court from which we selected the Probation cases was designed particularly for women of the prostitute class. Bedford has the third highest percentage of prostitutes and the Magdalen the fourth. As previously noted, the Penitentiary and Auburn have an appreciably smaller prostitute class than any of the other groups, but the percentages of women in these two institutions who fall in the sexually irregular class is larger than in any of the other institutional groups. The occasional sex offenders have a small percentage in each group except the Workhouse, which has none. Those who have never had illicit sexual intercourse constitute 35.5 per cent of the Penitentiary group, 23.4 per cent of the women in Auburn, 9.2 per cent in the Magdalen, 7.0 per cent in the Workhouse, 5.6 per cent in the Probation group and 2.0 per cent in Bedford. In the total group we find that 66.2 per cent of the women are prostitutes, 17.8 per cent sexually irregular, 2.0 per cent occasional sex offenders, and 14.0 per cent who have never been sex offenders.

If we divide our institutional groups into a more general classification of (1) those who have been prostitutes and sexually irregular, and (2) those who have been random sex offenders only or never sex offenders, we find that while Auburn and the Penitentiary still keep the lowest places in the first group, their percentages are, nevertheless, very high. That is, in the first class defined above, Auburn has 72.8 per cent and the Penitentiary 63.5 per cent, in contrast to

TABLE 150

EXTENT OF SEXUAL IRREGULARITY

Per Cent Distribution of Delinquent Women in Institutional Groups

Extent of Sexual Irregularity	Institutional Groups						Total
	Bedford	Auburn	Magdalen	Penitentiary	Workhouse	Probation	
Prostitutes	77.3	32.5	68.5	35.5	93.0	87.8	66.2
Sexually Irregular (not for money)	17.8	40.3	21.1	28.0	....	3.3	17.8
Occasional Sex Offenders	3.0	3.9	1.3	.9	....	3.3	2.0
Never a Sex Offender	2.0	23.4	9.2	35.5	7.0	5.6	14.0
Total	100.0	100.0	100.0	100.0	100.0	100.0	100.0
Number of cases	101	77	76	107	100	90	551

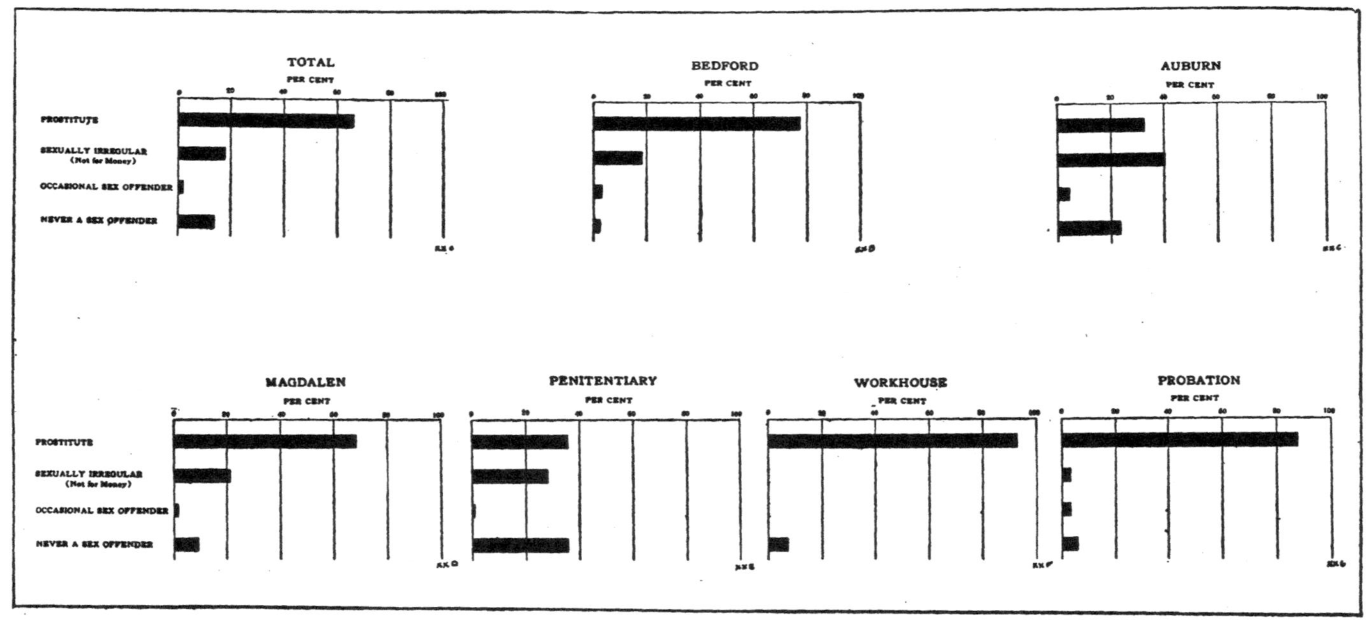

Chart XX

Extent of Sexual Irregularity

Per cent distribution by institutional groups.

95.1 per cent in Bedford, 93.0 per cent in the Workhouse, 91.1 per cent in the Probation group and 89.6 per cent in the Magdalen. The fact that in our total group only 16.0 per cent of the cases have never been sex offenders, or only occasionally so, is sufficient evidence that the sex problem is one of the most prevalent ones in a study of delinquent women, and that even the more serious offenders are a large part of the problem, though to a lesser extent than the petty offenders.

A similar comparison of extent of sexual irregularity for color and nativity groups shows that the foreign born have the smallest percentage of prostitutes, the native white the next larger percentage and the native colored the largest percentage. The percentage of sexually irregular women, on the other hand, is largest in the foreign born group, next smaller among the native whites and smallest among the native colored. The foreign born have a very much larger percentage of women who have never been sex offenders than either of the other groups, and the native colored have the smallest percentage. If we divide the classes of sexual irregularity into two groups as we did with the institutional groups, we find that among those who have been either prostitutes or sexually irregular, though not for money, the foreign born have 66.6 per cent, the native white 90.5 per cent

TABLE 151

EXTENT OF SEXUAL IRREGULARITY

Per Cent Distribution of Delinquent Women Classified by Nativity and Color

Extent of Sexual Irregularity	Nativity and Color				Total
	Total Foreign Born	Total Native Born	Native White	Native Colored	
Prostitutes	46.1	75.1	71.8	84.7	66.2
Sexually Irregular (not for money)	19.5	17.0	18.7	12.2	17.8
Occasional Sex Offenders	3.0	1.6	1.8	1.0	2.0
Never a Sex Offender	31.4	6.3	7.8	2.0	14.0
Total	100.0	100.0	100.0	100.0	100.0
Number of cases	169	382	284	98	551

and the colored 96.9 per cent. From any combination of classes of sexual irregularity, it would seem that the foreign born have a much smaller percentage of women who are professional prostitutes, and a much larger percentage of those who are not sex offenders. An indication of this was found in Chapter VI, in considering the nature of present offense for the women classified by nativity and color. There, also, it was evident that the foreign born had a much smaller percentage of women convicted of offenses against chastity than had the native white or native colored.

(b) *Length of Time in Prostitution*

In order to show the range of time during which the women we are studying have been prostitutes, or sexually irregular, we present Tables 152 and 153. Table 152, showing the length of time that certain of the women prostituted themselves, covers a range of from a few days to 26 years. The first group—under two years—includes all who have just started the life of a prostitute, as well as those who have been

TABLE 152

TOTAL LENGTH OF TIME IN PROSTITUTION

Per Cent Distribution of Professional and Irregular Prostitutes in Institutional Groups

Length of Time	Institutional Groups						Total
	Bedford	Auburn	Magdalen	Penitentiary	Workhouse	Probation	
Less than 2 years	35.2	....	54.6	15.4	16.7	75.5	36.6
2 to 4 years	29.6	30.4	20.5	23.1	20.0	14.3	22.7
4 " 6 "	21.1	17.4	6.8	7.7	16.7	6.1	13.6
6 " 8 "	5.6	17.4	11.4	7.7	13.3	4.1	9.2
8 " 10 "	7.1	4.4	2.3	3.9	10.0	....	5.1
10 " 12 "	....	8.7	....	15.4	13.3	....	5.1
12 " 14 "	1.4	8.7	....	7.7	1.7	....	2.2
14 " 16 "	....	8.7	2.3	7.7	1.7	....	2.2
16 " 18 "	....	....	2.3	3.9	1.7	....	1.1
18 " 20 "	....	....	....	....	3.3	....	.7
20 " 22 "	....	4.4	....	3.9	1.7	....	1.1
22 " 24 "	....	....	....	....	....	....	.....
24 " 26 "	....	....	....	3.9	....	....	.4
Total	100.0	100.0	100.0	100.0	100.0	100.0	100.0
Number of cases	71	23	44	26	60	49	273

in it any time up to two years. The number of years in prostitution has the longest range in the Penitentiary, Workhouse and Auburn, and the shortest in Bedford, the Magdalen and Probation where the average age is youngest and where the women have not had a chance to be in this life for a long period of time. The very much shorter range in the Probation group is explained by the fact that the women in this group are supposed, for the most part, to be first offenders, in the sense of this being their first conviction, and are chosen from the most promising women who go through the court. This process of selection naturally eliminates the older women who have been prostitutes for many years and who would be entirely hopeless on probation. In the total group, the concentration of number of years in prostitution is among the smaller groups of years,—up to six years.

(c) *Length of Time Sexually Irregular*

The total length of time these women have been sexually irregular, including in addition to the time in prostitution the years sexually promiscuous, though not for money, shows that the range of years by

TABLE 153

TOTAL LENGTH OF TIME SEXUALLY IRREGULAR

Per Cent Distribution by Institutional Groups of Professional and Irregular Prostitutes and Those Sexually Irregular

Length of Time	Institutional Groups						Total
	Bedford	Auburn	Magdalen	Penitentiary	Workhouse	Probation	
Less than 2 years	39.1	6.5	51.7	26.1	16.7	76.5	36.9
2 to 4 years	27.6	45.7	26.7	34.8	20.0	13.7	27.4
4 " 6 "	20.7	13.0	6.7	6.5	16.7	5.9	12.6
6 " 8 "	4.6	10.9	8.3	4.4	13.3	3.9	7.4
8 " 10 "	5.8	2.2	3.3	2.2	10.0	....	4.3
10 " 12 "	1.2	4.4	....	8.7	13.3	....	4.3
12 " 14 "	1.2	8.7	....	4.4	1.7	....	2.3
14 " 16 "	....	4.4	1.7	4.4	1.7	....	1.7
16 " 18 "	....	2.2	1.7	4.4	1.7	....	1.4
18 " 20 "	....	....	....	....	3.3	....	.6
20 " 22 "	....	2.2	....	2.2	1.7	....	.9
22 " 24 "	....	....	....	....	....	....	....
24 " 26 "	....	....	....	2.2	....	....	.3
Total	100.0	100.0	100.0	100.0	100.0	100.0	100.0
Number of cases	87	46	60	46	60	51	350

two-year groups is the same as in Table 152, but that there is slightly more of a concentration in the lower groups. The three institutions made up of women of older average age have a longer range of years in which they have been either sexually promiscuous (not for money) or prostitutes.

SPECIAL STUDY OF PROSTITUTES

(a) *Age at Entering Prostitution*

The part of the sex problem in which we are particularly interested is that of the prostitute, the woman, who, for the most part, gives up other means of earning money for this easier and more lucrative way. The most of the data we present for this will be for the total group of prostitutes, since, if divided by institutional groups, the numbers are too small for significant use. Bearing in mind that 66.2 per cent of our total group are prostitutes, we shall proceed to the consideration of age of these women at the time they began to prostitute. Table 154 gives by three-year age groups the distribution for in-

TABLE 154

AGE AT ENTERING PROSTITUTION

Per Cent Distribution of Prostitutes in Institutional Groups

Age at Entering Prostitution	Institutional Groups						Total
	Bedford	Auburn	Magdalen	Penitentiary	Workhouse	Probation	
10 to 13 years	....	5.3	....	4.4	....	....	.8
13 " 16 "	25.0	21.1	2.3	13.0	5.5	....	11.7
16 " 19 "	30.6	31.6	40.9	13.0	16.4	27.8	27.3
19 " 22 "	27.8	21.1	31.8	21.7	25.5	22.2	26.1
22 " 25 "	6.9	5.3	18.2	30.4	12.7	19.4	14.1
25 " 28 "	5.6	5.3	2.3	....	12.7	22.2	8.4
28 " 31 "	2.8	5.3	4.6	17.4	5.5	5.6	5.6
31 " 34 "	1.4	....	....	....	9.1	....	2.4
34 " 37 "	....	5.3	....	....	7.3	....	2.0
37 " 40 "	....	....	....	....	1.8	2.8	.8
40 " 43 "	....	....	....	....	1.8	....	.4
49 " 52 "	....	....	....	....	1.8	....	.4
Total...	100.0	100.0	100.0	100.0	100.0	100.0	100.0
Number of cases	72	19	44	23	55	36	249

Mean age at entering prostitution. (Total group)..... $20.68 \pm .350$

σ .... $5.53 \pm .249$

stitutional groups of the age at entering prostitution. The youngest age, ten years, applies to a woman in Auburn who has had a long record not only of prostitution but of other illegal acts. The one Penitentiary case in this lowest age group was only twelve years when she began to prostitute. The one woman in the oldest age group was 49 when she began to prostitute. Her husband had just died and she knew of no easier way to earn her living. The numbers in the institutional groups, as seen in Table 154, are too small for significant use of the mean and standard deviation, so these are presented only for the total. The average age at entering prostitution for the total group is 20.68±5.53. (See also Chart XXI.)

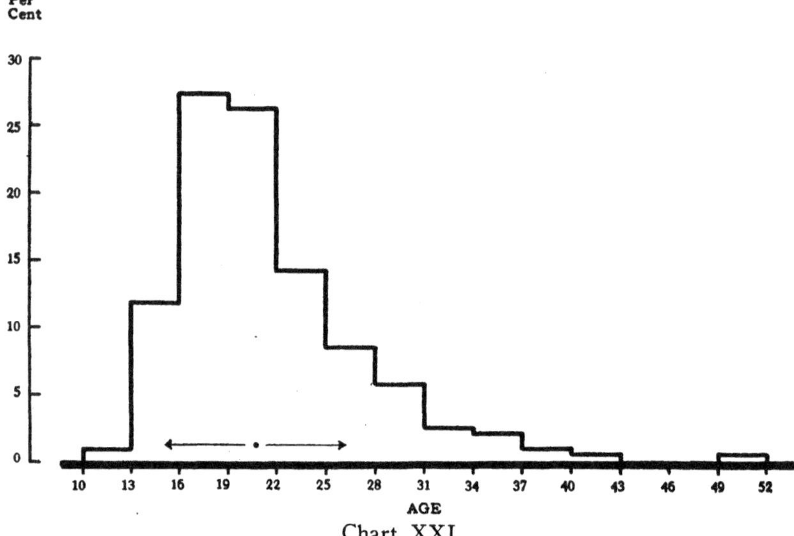

Chart XXI
Age at Entering Prostitution
Per cent distribution for total group (249 cases).

This average age at entering prostitution is somewhat higher than the age found by Dr. Davis[1] both in her study of Bedford prostitutes and of street cases. The comparison of the means for age at entering prostitution are as follows:

269 Bedford prostitutes	18.7 years.
1106 street cases	19.44 years.
249 prostitutes in this study	20.68 years.

The higher age at entering prostitution for our group is probably due to the fact that we have women of many ages from institutions

[1] *Op. cit.*, pp. 216 and 245.

which have varying percentages of prostitutes. Likewise our group contains many of the more serious offenders who did not become prostitutes until later in life when that became incidental to the other illegal acts which they were committing.

(1) *Age at Entering Prostitution for Nativity Groups.* If we observe the age at entering prostitution in the nativity and color groups, as shown in Table 155, we see that the range of years for the foreign born is longer than for the native white and native colored, and that there is, therefore, less concentration about the younger age groups. The means and standard deviations show that the average age at entering prostitution is lowest among the native colored, 19.87±5.13. The native white have the next larger average age at entering prostitution, 20.31±4.63, while the foreign born have the oldest average age, 23.0±7.87 years.

TABLE 155

AGE AT ENTERING PROSTITUTION

Per Cent Distribution of Prostitutes for Total Group Classified by Nativity and Color

Age at Entering Prostitution	Nativity and Color				Total
	Total Foreign Born	Total Native Born	Native White	Native Colored	
10 to 13 years	....	1.0	.7	1.8	.8
13 " 16 "	11.6	11.7	10.0	16.4	11.7
16 " 19 "	18.6	29.3	30.0	27.3	27.4
19 " 22 "	25.6	25.9	26.0	25.5	25.8
22 " 25 "	18.6	13.8	12.7	14.6	14.1
25 " 28 "	2.3	9.8	12.0	3.6	8.5
28 " 31 "	4 7	5.9	6.0	5.5	5.7
31 " 34 "	2.3	2.0	2.0	3.6	2.4
34 " 37 "	7.0	1.0	.7	1.8	2.0
37 " 40 "	4.7	....	....	....	.8
40 " 43 "	2 3	....	....	....	.4
49 " 52 "	2 3	....	....	....	.4
Total	100.0	100.0	100.0	100.0	100.0
Number of cases	43	205	150	55	248
Mean	23.0	20.20	20.31	19.87	20.68
σ_m	±1.20	±.333	±.378	±.692	±.352
σ	7.87	4.77	4.63	5.13	5 54
σ_σ	±.849	±.236	±.267	±.489	±.249

Chart 22 shows graphically the ages at which the foreign born and native born entered prostitution. The dots indicating the means and the arrows indicating the standard deviations illustrate how much older, on the average, the foreign born were when they began to prostitute.

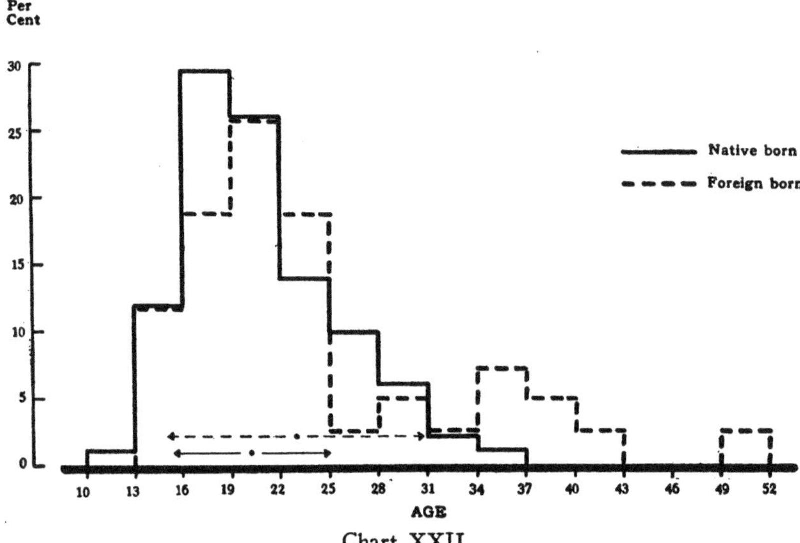

Chart XXII
Age at Entering Prostitution
Percentage comparison between native and foreign born.

The differences we have just noted are crude, however, and are not of great significance unless we can demonstrate whether or not they might have occurred by chance. Accordingly in Table 156 the means and standard deviations of the age at entering prostitution have been computed for the native white and native colored groups. The difference of the means is .44 and the difference of the standard deviations, —.51. From Table 156 we see that the former difference is only .56 times the standard deviation of the difference and therefore not demonstrably valid.

Since we have shown that there is no valid difference between the central tendencies of the native white and native colored with reference to their ages at entering prostitution, it will not be necessary for us to compare either of these groups separately with the foreign born if we use the total native born for comparison. Table 157 gives us this comparison and shows that there is a large crude difference both

TABLE 156

NATIVE WHITE AND NATIVE COLORED

Comparison of the Means and Standard Deviations of Age at Entering Prostitution for the Native White and the Native Colored

	Native White	Native Colored	Difference	$\frac{d}{\sigma_d}$	Chances that real difference does not exist are 1 in:
Mean.............	20.31	19.87	.44	.56	3
σ_m...............	±.378	±.692			
σ................	4.63	5.13	−.50	.91	6
σ_σ...............	±.267	±.489			
Cases.............	150	55			

of the means and standard deviations. The ratios that have been computed show these differences to be genuine, with a tendency for the foreign born to go into prostitution at a later age, and to have a wider scattering than the native born. The differences which we find to be valid between the foreign and native in respect to this part of their sex life is of particular interest since it was shown in an earlier discussion that the foreign born have a much smaller percentage of prostitutes than the other groups have, and also because they show a smaller percentage of women whose present conviction was for an offense against chastity.

TABLE 157

TOTAL NATIVE BORN AND TOTAL FOREIGN BORN

Comparison of the Means and Standard Deviations of Age at Entering Prostitution for the Total Native Born and Total Foreign Born

	Total Native Born	Total Foreign Born	Difference	$\frac{d}{\sigma_d}$	Chances that real difference does not exist are 1 in:
Mean.............	20.20	23.0	−2.80	2.25	82
σ_m...............	±.333	±1.20			
σ................	4.77	7.87	−3.10	3.52	5000
σ_σ...............	±.236	±.849			
Cases.............	205	43			

TABLE 158

Correlation between Age at Entering Prostitution and Number of Previous Convictions

Total Group

Number of Previous Convictions	Age at Entering Prostitution (Years)														Totals	Means (Age at entering Prostitution)
	10 to 13	13 to 16	16 to 19	19 to 22	22 to 25	25 to 28	28 to 31	31 to 34	34 to 37	37 to 40	40 to 43	43 to 46	46 to 49	49 to 52		
18				1											1	
17															0	
16															0	
15															0	
14		1		1											2	
13															0	18.8
12		1													1	
11															0	
10			1				1								2	
9				2	1										3	
8		1	1	2											4	
7			2	3	1		1	1							8	21.2
6		1		2	1	1									5	
5		1	2	3	3		1		2						12	22.8
4	2	1	4	5	1	3				1					17	20.1
3		2	6	6	3	1	3	3	1						25	22.7
2		4	11	6	9	3			1		1				35	20.6
1		10	17	15	6	5	5	1	1						60	20.2
0		7	24	19	10	8	3	1		1				1	74	20.4
Totals	2	29	68	65	35	21	14	6	5	2	1	0	0	1	249	20.67
Means (Number of Previous Convictions)	2.6		1.7	2.8	2.1	1.5	2.6	2.6							2.23	

Age at entering prostitution: Mean = 20.67 σ = 5.53
Number of previous convictions: Mean = 2.23 σ = 2.75

Coefficient of correlation: r = .001 ± .063

Correlation ratios: Age at entering prostitution on number of previous convictions, η = .18 ± .061 Blakeman's Criterion = 2 1
Number of previous convictions on age at entering prostitution, η = .17 ± .061 Blakeman's Criterion = 2.0

(2) *Age at Entering Prostitution, and Number of Convictions.* It may be of value to know whether there is any relationship between the age at entering prostitution and other social factors. It is of especial importance to know whether there is any tendency for those who enter prostitution when very young to have more convictions than those who became prostitutes later in life. To see whether there is any association between these two, Table 158 is presented, and gives the coefficient of correlation between age at entering prostitution and number of previous convictions. The coefficient of correlation .001± .063 indicates that there is no genuine relationship here. Referring to the correlation ratios we note that both of these are high enough so that they would indicate a very slight degree of relationship were it not that the lines of the means are so irregular that it is impossible to locate any significant trend of relation. It seems probable, therefore, that any relationship between the age at entering prostitution and number of convictions is so small that it is of little significance. The very slight trend which may be observed is for those who started to prostitute at a very early age to have the largest number of convictions.

(3) *Age at Entering Prostitution, and Grade Finished.* Of considerable importance, also, is the association between the age at entering prostitution and the grade finished in school. Table 159 shows a correlation coefficient of .20±.066 indicating a significant relationship, with a slight tendency for those who began to prostitute themselves at the youngest ages to have completed the lower grades only and vice versa. The line of the means of age at entering prostitution on grade finished is so irregular that it is difficult to find any definite progression of change in age at entering prostitution for change in grade finished. The regression line of the other ratio, however, grade finished on age at entering prostitution, shows a small but consistent trend of changes in grade finished for changes in age at entering prostitution.

(4) *Age at Entering Prostitution, and Estimate of Home Conditions.*—We might very well expect that there would be a relationship between the age at entering prostitution and the estimate of the early home conditions. This we find to be the case in Table 160. The correlation ratio of .29±.067 indicates that there is a significant relationship. Reference to the mean ages at entering prostitution, also, shows that the average age at entering prostitution for those who come from the poorest homes is 16.5 years. These average ages at entering prostitution become progressively older as we go to the next

TABLE 159

Correlation between Age at Entering Prostitution and Grade Finished in School

Total Group

Grade Finished	Age at Entering Prostitution (Years)																													Totals	Means (Age at entering Prostitution)
	12	13	14	15	16	17	18	19	20	21	22	23	24	25	26	27	28	29	30	31	32	33	34	35	36	37	38	39	40		
4th Year H.S.																	1													1	
3rd Year H.S.																														0	
2nd Year H.S.									2		1																			3	22.9
1st Year H.S.								1			1																			2	
8						5	1	5	1	2		4		3		2		1	1	1	1	1			1					29	
7				2	4	1	2	3	1	1	1			2	2		1	1												21	20.3
6		3	3		2	3	2	1	3	3	2	1		3		1		1	1		1									30	20.1
5			1		5	4	4	2	2	1	3	1	2	1			1						1							28	19.9
4			1	4	5		6	5	2	2	3	3	1	1	1								1	1						36	19.9
3		1	2	2	5	4	1	4		1	1	1	1																	23	17.5
2		1		1	1	2	1	1	5		1	2					1		1											17	19.5
1				1	1	1			1																					4	
0*	1		2	4		1			2	2	2	1	2				1												1	19	20.1
Totals	1	5	9	14	23	21	17	22	19	12	15	13	6	10	3	3	5	3	3	1	2	1	2	1	1	0	0	0	1	213	20.19
Means (Grade Finished)		3.7			4.2			4.9			4.7			5.3			6.3							5.6						4.74	

Age at entering prostitution: Mean = 20.19 σ = 4.91
Grade finished in school: Mean = 4.74 σ = 2.51

Coefficient of correlation: r = .20 ± .066

Correlation ratios: Age at entering prostitution on grade finished, η = .29 ± .063 Blakeman's Criterion = 2.4
Grade finished on age at entering prostitution, η = .23 ± .068 Blakeman's Criterion = 1.3

* Includes those who have never been in school and those who have attended but never finished first grade.

TABLE 160

Correlation between Age at Entering Prostitution and Estimate of Home Conditions

Total Group. Workhouse Omitted

Estimate of Home Conditions	Age at Entering Prostitution																												Totals	Means (Age at entering Prostitution)
	10	11	12	13	14	15	16	17	18	19	20	21	22	23	24	25	26	27	28	29	30	31	32	33	34	35	36	37		
Very good																													0	
Good								3		2	2	1				1					1			1					11	21.6
Fair				2	1	4	4	7	4	7	7	7	9	5	1	4	1		3		1				1			1	69	20.6
Poor	1		1	3	5	6	14	8	9	7	9	3	4	3	2	3	1	3	2	1	2								87	19.0
Very poor				1	2	2	4	3	2	2		1																	17	16.5
Totals	1	0	1	6	8	12	22	21	15	18	18	12	13	8	3	8	2	3	5	1	4	0	0	1	1	0	0	1	184	19.53

Age at entering prostitution: Mean = 19.53 σ = 4.47
Correlation ratios: η = .29 ± .067

higher classes of home conditions, indicating a definite trend for the average age at entering prostitution to increase in years with changes for the better in early home conditions.

(b) *Other Social Factors in Lives of Prostitutes*

Although the age at first sex offense is not so important as the age at entering prostitution because it may be a random or unintentional affair, while the other has intent and is, in most cases, a deliberate choice, we shall consider it here because of its importance in relation to the age at entering prostitution. The age at first sex offense has a range of from eight to forty years for the prostitute group with, however, only one case in each of these extreme groups. The average age at first sex offense for the prostitutes is 18.46±.30 with a standard deviation of 5.36. This average age is younger than the average age at entering prostitution, 20.68 years, and might indicate that the first offense is in many ways only casual, but that often it undoubtedly serves to break down the barriers of restraint sufficiently to make the more serious offenses come easily later.

If we proceed to other social factors in the lives of the prostitute group, we may note first the average age of this class at the time of the present conviction. This age we find to be 27.13±.443 years, with a standard deviation of 8.46±.313. In comparison with the total group which, however, is heavily weighted with the prostitutes[2] we find that the average age of the prostitutes is younger, that of the total group being 28.79 years with a standard deviation of 10.13 years. Dr. Davis' study, previously noted,[3] shows the following comparison for average age at time of present conviction:

647 Bedford prostitutes	20.09 years.
598 street cases	22.66 years.
365 prostitutes in this study	27.13 years.

This, again, shows we are dealing with an older group than that studied by Dr. Davis and that the age factor undoubtedly enters in to make significant differences in the most of the comparisons.

The birthplace of the prostitute group shows the following:

Total foreign born	21.4 per cent
Total native born	78.6 per cent
Native white	66.8 per cent
Native colored	22.8 per cent

[2] A comparison of our total group with the prostitutes in the total group is obviously of little significance since the prostitutes make up 66.2 per cent of the total.

[3] *Op. cit.*, pp. 216 and 232.

In comparison with our total group, the percentage of foreign born has decreased to a large extent. This results in the foreign born prostitutes having, in a more marked degree than the total group, a smaller representation than we should expect from their percentages in the general population. Dr. Davis found among the Bedford prostitutes 24.11 per cent foreign born, 62.75 per cent native white and 13.14 per cent native colored.[4] These figures are not at great variance with ours, except as they show a higher percentage of native white and a somewhat smaller percentage of native colored.

The data on schooling for the prostitute group show that the average number of years they have been in school is 6.82 with a standard deviation of 2.71 years. This mean is slightly larger than that for the total group in which the average number of years is 6.50 with a standard deviation of 3.05. For the prostitute group there are 4.5 per cent who never attended school and the range of years in school is from no schooling to thirteen years. If we observe the grade finished in school, we find that the average grade finished by the prostitutes is 4.74 with a standard deviation of 2.44. The frequency distribution shows a range of cases from those who never finished the first grade to two women who finished high school. One of these women who went through high school was sentenced to the Magdalen on a prostitution charge; the other is in the Probation group, for the same offense. Both are bright, fond of pretty things, and went into prostitution that they might be able to get what they wanted with less effort than they would have needed to expend by working eight hours a day and earning an honest living.

The work record of the prostitute group is a large subject in itself, and affords an interesting field for detailed case studies. Since this is not practicable at this point, we shall give the same type of treatment to this group that was used in discussing the work histories of the total group. The age at starting work has a range of from 8 to 58 years for the prostitute group and the average age at starting work is $17.40 \pm .351$ years, with a standard deviation of 6.23. The percentage starting work under fourteen years is 16.6 per cent, almost exactly the same percentage as for the total group.

Table 161 gives the kind of work done by prostitutes at various times during their work careers. The kind of work in the first job indicates that the largest percentage of the prostitutes first went into domestic service and the next largest percentage into factory work.

[4] *Loc. cit.*, p. 198.

TABLE 161

KIND OF WORK DONE BY PROSTITUTES AT SPECIFIED TIMES DURING THEIR WORK HISTORIES

Per Cent Distribution for Total Group

Kind of Work	Specified Times				
	In First Job	In Latest Job*	At Time of First Conviction	At Time of Present Conviction	Prevailing Work
Domestic service	40.8	32.1	9.0	9.2	40.8
Factory work	23.7	27.0	5.5	5.3	23.1
Home work	2.8	4.5	1.0	1.4	3.9
Restaurant and hotel work	6.8	12.6	1.9	2.2	6.9
Work in stores	10.7	7.5	1.3	.6	9.6
Vaudeville performers	3.4	5.4	1.0	.6	4.8
Clerical work	4.5	3.3	.3	.3	3.6
Professional service	.6	.3	....	....	.3
Personal service	2.3	2.1	.3	.8	2.7
Charwomen	.3	1.5	....	....	.6
Miscellaneous	1.7	1.2	.3	.6	1.5
Own housework	....	....	6.8	12.3	....
Idle	....	....	69.0	64.1	....
Never worked	2.5	2.7	3.5	2.5	2.7
Total	100.0	100.0	100.0	100.0	100.0
Number of cases	355	334	310	357	335

*Includes only those who have had more than one job.

In comparing this with the latest work done we find a decrease in domestic service workers and an increase in those who did factory work. The kind of work done at the time of the first conviction is of particular interest in showing the number of women who were idle. The per cent of prostitutes (69.0) who were idle at this time is larger than the per cent of the total group (59.9) who were idle at the time of first conviction. The high percentage of domestic service workers, with factory workers having second place, still obtains at time of the first conviction. If we turn to the kind of work done at the time of the present conviction, we may still observe the very large percentage of idle women, though not quite so many as at the time of the first conviction. The percentage of women who were doing their own housework shows a fairly large increase between the time of first and present conviction and would indicate that a certain number of the women had married in this interim. On the whole, there seems to be little change in the kind of work done during the time between these two convictions. The prevailing work shows, again, the high percentage of domestic service and factory workers in the prostitute group, and for the other kinds of work a striking similarity to the percentages in the same occupations at the time of the first job.

In general, the discussion of the kind of work done shows principally that there were more women in domestic service than in any other occupation, and that the factory workers have the next highest percentage. The number of idle women at the time of the first and present convictions is of particular importance, especially in connection with the estimate of regularity of work which will be considered later. In the prostitute group, as with the total group, we find a very small percentage of skilled workers, such as women in professional service and clerical work.

The wages which were earned by these women at the specified times are given in Tables 162 and 163. Table 162 shows the range of wages for women employed at domestic service in the first job, the latest job, work at time of first and present conviction, and the

TABLE 162

WEEKLY WAGE EARNED BY PROSTITUTES AT SPECIFIED TIMES DURING THEIR WORK HISTORIES

Per Cent Distribution of Women Employed at Domestic Service and Allied Occupations Where Living Was in Addition to Wage

Weekly Wage	Specified Times				
	In First Job	In Latest Job	At Time of First Conviction	At Time of Present Conviction	Prevailing Work
Living only	15.8	10.0	10.7	7.7	7.3
$1 to $2	8.8	3.3	10.7	7.7	6.5
2 " 3	24.6	10.0	14.3	11.5	21.0
3 " 4	21.9	20.0	14.3	11.5	21.8
4 " 5	18.4	22.2	17.9	19.2	25.0
5 " 6	4.5	17.8	21.4	11.5	8.0
6 " 7	1.8	7.8	3.6	15.4	7.3
7 " 8	1.8	6.7	7.1	11.5	.8
8 " 9	.9	1.1	....	3.8	2.4
9 " 10	1.8	1.1	....	....	....
Total	100.0	100.0	100.0	100.0	100.0
Number of cases	114	90	28	26	124

TABLE 163

WEEKLY WAGE EARNED BY PROSTITUTES AT SPECIFIED TIMES DURING THEIR WORK HISTORIES

Per Cent Distribution of Women Employed at Occupations other than Domestic Service

Weekly Wage	Specified Times				
	In First Job	In Latest Job	At Time of First Conviction	At Time of Present Conviction	Prevailing Work
$0 to $1	1.9	....	....	....	....
1 " 2	1.3	.6	....	....	....
2 " 3	2.5	.6	....	....	.7
3 " 4	14.6	2.3	....	....	5.3
4 " 5	14.6	6.8	16.7	6.4	12.5
5 " 6	12.1	8.6	16.7	6.4	11.9
6 " 7	15.3	18.8	10.0	25.8	13.9
7 " 8	8.9	11.4	13.3	16.1	13.2
8 " 9	8.9	8.6	3.3	3.2	10.6
9 " 10	2.5	12.0	13.3	9.7	6.6
10 " 11	3.2	9.7	10.0	9.7	5.3
11 " 12	1.3	3.4	....	3.2	2.0
12 " 13	5.1	4.6	....	3.2	4.6
13 " 14	1.9	1.1	....	....	1.3
14 " 15	....	.6	3.3	3.2	.7
15 " 16	1.9	2.9	3.3	3.2	2.0
16 " 17	....	.6	....	....	....
17 " 18	....	.6	3.3	3.2	.7
18 " 19	....	1.1	....	....	....
19 " 20	....	.6	....	....	1.3
20 " 21	....	.6	3.3	....	.7
23 " 24	....	.6	....	....	....
24 " 25	.6	....	....	....	.7
25 " 26	1.3	2.9	3.3	3.2	4.0
27 " 28	.6	....	....	....	.7
31 " 32	....	.6	....	....	....
35 " 36	1.3	....	....	....	1.3
65 " 66	....	.6	....	3.2	....
Total	100.0	100.0	100.0	100.0	100.0
Number of cases	157	175	30	31	151

average wage for prevailing work. The numbers were too few to justify computing the means and standard deviations for certain of the wage groups. The wages show a wider range, however, for the first and latest jobs than for the job at first and present conviction or for the prevailing work. The one woman who raised the range to $16 for the total group (Chapter XI, Table 127) is not a prostitute and therefore does not fall in this group.

The wages earned by prostitutes who were employed at occupations other than domestic service at specified times show a range similar to that for the total group (Chapter XI, Table 128). The one prostitute who was earning $65 at the time she was sentenced to Bedford was a dancing instructor in New York City. She also "picked up" private pupils on the roof gardens and made a great deal of money by teaching them how to dance. The absence of any cases earning the lowest wages at the time of first and present conviction would indicate that the women who have the lowest wage-earning capacity drop out of work at those times.

As we should expect, from the percentages of women who were idle at the time of first and present convictions, the work records show great irregularity. The percentages of prostitutes in the five classes of the estimate are as follows:

Worked almost none,	11.4 per cent
" about one-quarter of time	27.6 " "
" about one-half of time	27.6 " "
" about three-quarters of time	31.6 " "
" nearly all of time	1.8 " "

By this method of estimation, it appears that 66.6 per cent of the women worked half of the time or less. For the total group, the percentage who worked half of the time or less was 60.9, even with the prostitutes included in this total. It would seem that the prostitutes do not combine with the kind of life they are living any serious attempt to work. This is, of course, obvious after talking with many of them and after working over their histories for any length of time. Sometimes a prostitute has a nominal trade which she pretends to follow, in order to protect herself in case of arrest. There are rare cases, also, of girls who work during the day at legitimate work and go out for purposes of prostitution occasionally at night in order to supplement their earnings. There is in the Bedford group a girl of eighteen who worked during the day in a department store for $7 a week. She found she could not buy the clothes she wanted for that money and so she began to go out with a "friend" and then with another for two or three nights a week. By this method, she was able to have what she wanted, and she was able to make her mother think she was earning the extra money in the store.

The estimate of the work record shows a predominance of poor work. The prostitutes distribute themselves in these five classes as follows:

Very poor	15.8 per cent
Poor	40.3 " "
Mediocre	35.3 " "
Good	8.1 " "
Very good	.6 " "

This estimate shows that 56.1 per cent of the women were entirely unable to live on their earnings because of the irregularity, inefficiency and low wages involved in the work record. There were only two cases in the estimate of very good,—one in the Magdalen and one in the Probation group. The latter one had just gone into prostitution and was arrested the second or third time she solicited a man on the street. As a whole, the work records are poor and show great instability.

In considering the criminal record of the prostitute class, we shall first observe the age at first conviction. The range is from eight years to 61 years, with eighteen cases or 4.2 per cent of the total who were convicted as juvenile delinquents under sixteen years of age. The mean age at first conviction for the total group is $24.69 \pm .427$, and there is a standard deviation of 8.12 years.

The offenses which caused the first conviction fall in the prostitute group as follows:

Offenses against the Person	.8 per cent
Offenses against Chastity	61.6 " "
Offenses against Family and Children	.8 " "
Offenses against Regulations for Public Health, etc.	6.2 " "
Offenses against Administration of Government	...
Offenses against Property Rights	5.4 " "
General Criminality	25.0 " "

The offenders against chastity have the largest percentage, with relatively small percentages in each other group except the general criminality group containing the semi-juvenile offenders. It is interesting to compare the nature of the first offenses of this special group with the first offenses of the total group of which, we must remember, the prostitutes form a large part. In the total group the offenders against chastity at time of the first conviction were only 44.3 per cent. The offenders against property rights, on the other hand, had 18.8 per cent of the cases, while among the prostitutes this class has only 5.4 per cent. One is reminded here of the remark so often made by many of the prostitutes who take men to a furnished room or a hotel but never to creep houses where they are to be robbed: "Well," they will say in trying to justify their own deeds, "I may be a prostitute, but I'm not a thief. What I get money for, I earn, and a thief,—she just steals and don't give nothing in return."

The number of convictions for this group shows that the range is from those who have never had any previous conviction (39.8 per cent of the cases) to one woman in the Penitentiary who has had eighteen previous convictions. The average number of previous convictions is 1.83±.135 with a standard deviation of 2.62. The women in the total group who have the larger number of convictions, 20 and 31, have their history of deliquency complicated by excessive alcoholism. As noted in Chapter VII the Intoxication Group in the Workhouse, though its mean number of convictions is about four times as large as that for the total group, has only four instances of convictions for offenses against chastity out of the 212 convictions for the total group.

If we turn to the early home conditions of this group, we find that in the total estimate the homes of the prostitutes seem to be poorer than for the total group. The distribution is as follows:

	Very Poor	Poor	Mediocre	Good	Very Good
Economic Status in Early Home ..	5.5	39.8	42.1	12.2	.4
Moral Standards in Early Home ...	11.4	29.1	44.1	15.4	...
Parental Supervision in Early Home	16.9	50.8	29.9	2.4	...
Estimate of Early Home	8.3	44.1	42.9	4.7	...

As with the total group the lack of parental supervision seems to be one of the most striking things. The economic standards, again, approximate the total estimate more than any other factor entering into the estimate, which would seem to indicate that the economic factor is very important in the consideration of what makes up a good or a poor home. The methods of making up the estimates and illustrative cases for each class have been given in Chapter IX.

A somewhat isolated item, but one which is of importance because of the common belief that excessive drug and alcohol using are common among prostitutes, is the consideration of habits. The following distribution, if compared with Tables 32, 34 and 35, Chapter VII, shows that there is among the prostitute group a larger percentage of women who use alcohol, drugs and tobacco than there is in the total group. The distribution for the prostitute group is as follows:

	Alcohol	Drugs	Tobacco
Non-users	49.6	77.2	67.1
Moderate	28.3	...	7.5
Excessive	22.1	22.8	25.4

There is, of course, much overlapping present here, many of the same women being addicted to more than one habit.

VENEREAL DISEASE

The subject of venereal disease among the women in our institutional groups has been included in this chapter dealing with the sex history, because, in most cases, there is a close connection between irregularities in sex life and the diseases usually resulting from this life. There are, however, several exceptions in our group of women who, so far as we know, have not been sexually promiscuous, but who have contracted syphilis from their husbands. Unfortunately, we have been unable to obtain adequate data for comparison on all of the institutional groups regarding the amount of syphilis and gonorrhea. The Probation women were given no blood tests and we have data on only the few cases in this group where the clinical manifestations of venereal disease were so evident that the girl had to be sent to a hospital for treatment during her probation period. These cases, however, are too few in number to use. The 22 Penitentiary women who had blood tests given have been used for comparison with the other groups, though this is, perhaps, unfair since only the women were tested who were suspected of being syphilitic or women who were in need of other treatment and to whom the blood test was given as an incidental thing. Each of the cases we have used in making up Table 164 has had specimens of blood taken and a series of complement fixation tests performed to determine by the Wassermann test whether the reaction was positive, that is, whether there was evidence of syphilis, and by the complement fixation test for gonorrhea whether gonorrhea was present as shown by a positive reaction. We have considered as a positive reaction all reactions of 4+, 3+ or 2+. A doubtful reaction includes 1+ or±, and negative includes only those cases in which there was no reaction.

Table 164 shows the percentages of women in institutional groups who had positive, negative or doubtful reactions to the complement fixation tests for syphilis and gonorrhea. The Magdalen has the smallest percentage of women who had a positive reaction to the Wassermann test for syphilis. This is probably determined by the fact of the Magdalen being a private institution which has the right to refuse any cases so that an elimination of the most diseased girls takes place. Auburn has the next larger percentage of women with a positive reaction, and this we might expect because of the fact that Auburn has a small percentage of prostitutes. Bedford and the Workhouse follow with the next largest percentages of women with

TABLE 164

VENEREAL DISEASE

Per Cent Distribution of Delinquent Women in Institutional Groups by Results of Wassermann and Complement Fixation Tests for Syphilis and Gonorrhea*

Institutional Groups	Wassermann Test				Complement Fixation Test			
	Positive	Negative	Doubtful	Number of Cases	Positive	Negative	Doubtful	Number of Cases
Bedford	36.0	48.0	16.0	100	2.0	67.7	30.3	99
Auburn	31.0	62.1	6.9	58	....	68.6	31.4	35
Magdalen	24.3	64.3	11.3	70	....	82.4	17.7	68
Penitentiary	40.9	59.1	....	22	....	....	....	....
Workhouse	39.3	47.2	13.5	89	3.6	68.7	27.7	83
Total	33.9	54.3	11.8	339	1.8	71.6	26.7	285

*Positive includes reactions to the Wassermann or Complement Fixation Tests of 4+, 3+, or 2+. Doubtful includes reactions of 1+ and ±. Negative includes only −.

positive reactions and the Penitentiary has the largest percentage. This high percentage in the Penitentiary, as has been stated before, is probably due to the fact that only the cases which were suspected of being syphilitic were given the blood tests. In the total group of delinquent women studied, we find that 33.9 per cent have a positive reaction to the Wassermann test for syphilis,—that 54.3 per cent show no reaction and that 11.8 per cent give a doubtful reaction.

If we turn to the percentage of women in institutional groups who show positive, doubtful or negative reactions to the complement fixation tests for gonorrhea, we see that the results are quite different. To explain the obviously misleading percentages, we might state that the lack of positive reactions in the Magdalen group is due to the fact that a girl who is suffering from gonorrhea is not allowed to be kept in the institution and is transferred to the City Hospital for cure. We were able to obtain no records of this test for the Penitentiary group and found records on only 35 of the Auburn women. This part of the data is, therefore, unsatisfactory and probably quite unreliable, except for the Bedford and Workhouse groups where returns of this test were made on approximately as many cases as for the Wassermann test. By examining the vaginal smears it is also true that many cases of gonorrhea are found which might not show in the blood, particularly if the girl had been recently infected. As the figures stand, 1.8 per cent of the total group examined gave a positive reaction to the complement fixation test for gonorrhea, 71.6 per cent gave a negative reaction, and 26.4 per cent a doubtful reaction.

The percentage of women among the prostitute group infected with venereal disease is, as we might expect, higher than for the total group. The figures for the prostitutes are as follows:

	Wassermann and Complement Fixation Tests for: Syphilis	Gonorrhea
Positive	42.5 per cent	1.9 per cent
Negative	41.6 " "	68.7 " "
Doubtful	15.9 " "	29.4 " "

These figures show a large percentage, 42.5 per cent, who gave a positive reaction to the Wassermann test for syphilis. In comparison with 466 prostitutes studied by Dr. Davis,[5] all of whom were given Wassermann tests, it appears that in the prostitute group we are studying there is a larger percentage who have positive reactions for syphilis alone. The figures for the Bedford women in Dr. Davis' study are as follows for the Wassermann reaction:

	Syphilis	Gonorrhea
Positive	37.7 per cent	29.0 per cent
Negative	58.6 " "	50.0 " "
Doubtful	3.6 " "	21.0 " "

In this connection it is important to note that the discrepancies occurring between our group and other studies, in the matter of venereal disease, are due largely to the changes in laboratory technique for the various studies. We have observed in one institution, such as Bedford for instance, that the reported percentages of infected cases varied markedly as the blood examinations were made by one or another laboratory, or subjected to modifications of the examination. This undoubtedly explains the much higher percentage of cases of gonorrhea found in Dr. Davis' study than among our cases.

In any event, the percentage of women in institutions, infected with syphilis, is large. It is appalling to contemplate the chance for infection by many of these women who are promiscuous in their sexual relations and who have no moral scruples about spreading the disease they have contracted. An example of the harm which may be done by one person infected with syphilis is found in the history of a woman known as the "Leopard" because of the spots on her skin. She was a prostitute in Chinatown, New York City, for years

[5] *Loc. cit.*, pp. 189 and 190.

and contracted syphilis. She allowed herself to get into a frightful state, until the Chinamen who had been supporting her took up a collection of money and offered to send her to a hospital for treatment. She refused to go and continued to have sexual relations with young boys who did not know about the disease and who were attracted by her attentions to them. She undoubtedly infected a great many persons, many of them boys whom she deliberately chose, knowing her condition, in order that she might show the Chinamen she was still able to "get" some one.

SUMMARY

In summarizing the data that have to do with the history of sex irregularities, we have seen that the prostitutes constitute 66.2 per cent of our total group and that those who have been sexually irregular, though not for money, make up 17.8 per cent more. Only 16.0 per cent of the women were not serious sex offenders. These percentages vary between institutional groups, the two institutions consisting of the largest percentage of felons having the smallest percentage of prostitutes but the largest percentage of those sexually irregular.

In a comparison between the nativity and color groups it appears that the foreign born have the smallest percentage of prostitutes and the largest percentage of non-sex-offenders, while the native colored have the most prostitutes and the fewest,—only two cases,—who were never sex offenders.

In considering the age at entering prostitution, it also appears that the foreign born do not begin prostitution until a later age, and that there is a valid difference between the foreign born and the total native born with respect to the age at entering prostitution. There seems to be no similar significant difference between the native white and native colored.

A rough attempt, because such information is hard to obtain, to find how many of these women had sex instructions from any one who was competent to give them such training, shows that 48.9 per cent, at a very liberal estimate, were given no sex instructions except what they "picked up" from girl friends, from reading or their own observation.

In attempting to show the relationship between age at entering prostitution and other social factors we find that:

(1) There is a very small and possibly not significant relationship between the age at entering prostitution and the number of previous

convictions, with, however, a tendency for those who enter prostitution when youngest to have the largest number of convictions.

(2) There is a small but significant relationship between the age at entering prostitution and the grade finished in school, with a tendency for those who entered prostitution at the earliest ages to have finished the lower grades in school, and vice versa.

(3) There is a significant relationship demonstrated in the correlation ratio between age at entering prostitution and estimate of home conditions. The mean ages at entering prostitution show a progressive increase from the lowest class of the home conditions through the highest class.

In the data which have been presented on the prostitute class, we have shown that, for the most part, these women came from poor homes, that their work was irregular and poor, that they are in fairly large numbers addicted to drugs, alcohol and tobacco, and that they have a large percentage of women infected with venereal disease. Detailed comparisons with the total group, regarding schooling and criminal record, particularly, are difficult to make since the total group is so heavily weighted with the prostitutes who constitute 66.2 per cent of its number.

The venereal disease in the group studied, based on returns from the Wassermann and the complement fixation tests for syphilis and gonorrhea, shows that there are varying percentages within the groups, giving positive reactions, and that the total group has 33.9 per cent with a positive reaction to the Wassermann test for syphilis, 54.3 per cent with no reaction, and 11.8 per cent in which the reaction was doubtful. The percentages, stating the various reactions to the complement fixation test for gonorrhea show 1.8 per cent with a positive reaction, 71.6 per cent with a negative reaction, and 26.7 per cent with a doubtful reaction.

CHAPTER XIII

MENTAL CAPACITY: COMPARISON WITH THE GENERAL POPULATION

THE question of the relation between criminality and mental capacity, or, as it is generally conceived, between criminality and mental inefficiency, is one of primary importance. Goring's judgment concerning the importance of this relationship is well indicated in the following statement, summarizing the results of his investigations:

"Our final conclusion is that English criminals are selected by a physical condition and a mental constitution which are independent of each other—that the one significant physical association with criminality is a generally defective physique; and that the one vital mental constitutional factor in the etiology of crime is defective intelligence." [1]

Other equally positive statements might be cited from many sources, both in the literature of criminology and in that of feeble-mindedness.[2] In most of these discussions, however, the tendency has been to make general statements based entirely on descriptive data concerning the group studied, or, and this is more unfortunate, to make comparisons with the general population based on a rather vague hypothesis of the mental ability of the "average" non-delinquent individual. Where the information sought is concerned with the inter-relations inherent in the group,—such, for example, as the relationship between an individual's mental capacity and his criminal record, it is of course necessary to restrict comparisons to the group studied, but where the object is to determine whether the delinquent group as such is to be distinguished from the general population with respect to mental

[1] *Op. cit.*, p. 263.
[2] See, for example, the following:
Ellis, Havelock. "The Criminal." 1895. pp. 133-139.
Aschaffenburg, G. "Crime and Its Repression." Trans. by Albrecht, A. 1913. pp. 178-180.
Tredgold, A. F. "Mental Deficiency." 2nd Ed. 1914. pp. 319-324.
Goddard, H. H. "Feeble-mindedness. Its Causes and Consequences." 1914. pp. 8-15.

capacity, it is essential that we have reliable information concerning reasonably representative samples of the whole population. The dearth of such information affords the ready explanation for its almost complete omission from the literature. Nevertheless it must be evident that without the possibility of some such comparison between offenders against the law and the rest of the population we can not progress far in our evaluation of the significance of mental inferiority as a contributory factor in criminality.

The most serious effort at comparison of the two groups from this point of view is that of Goring, who finds his common ground in the figures giving percentages of "weak-minded" individuals among criminals and in the general population. On the basis of the most careful estimates available he offers, as a minimum figure for the percentage of prisoners who are weak-minded, 10 per cent, and, as a maximum, 20 per cent. For comparison with these he cites the enumeration of mental defectives made in 1908 by the British Royal Commission for the Care and Control of the Feeble-Minded, in which they estimated that .46 per cent of the general population were mentally defective. By these figures the preponderance of mental defect among the prisoners is strikingly suggested.

In Chapter IV we have discussed Goring's use of the method of estimates and the limitations on the objectivity of this method. This point applies with special force to an investigation covering as many different types of groups as are included under the general population. A further factor enters in to lessen the certainty of the comparison. In spite of the fact that the Royal Commission performed its work with the utmost care it necessarily lacked the sort of opportunity for the direct observation of each individual which the prison situation makes possible. This would tend to produce an under-estimation of the number of weak-minded in the general population. It remains for later investigations to discover whether the degree of difference, which Goring maintains exists between the two groups, represents any serious degree of over-statement.

The psychometric methods, on which we have based our study, do not entirely escape the limitations discussed above. While free from the subjective variations incident to the method of estimates, they meet the same obstacle of inadequate information concerning the population at large. The extreme difficulty of securing such representative data is readily apparent. Through the mechanism of the common schools it is reasonably possible to assemble data concerning relatively unselected groups of children. But in adult life individuals tend to separate along very definite lines of cleavage, so that when we attempt to secure unselected adult groups we find ourselves obtaining groups of business men, or of college students, or of factory operatives, or of some other specialized segment of the population. The measurement of intelligence is obviously not a form of record taking which can ever be included in a general census enumeration, which would afford the only complete data.

At last, however, mass data of importance, if not of conclusive finality, concerning the adult male population are available as a result of the examination of army recruits in this country during 1917 and 1918. This constitutes our most satisfactory standard of reference, in spite of certain limitations affecting the interpretation of these data, to be discussed later. Next in importance to these are the data obtained by Dr. Woolley on girls of sixteen to eighteen years of age who came under the supervision of the Cincinnati Bureau of Vocational Guidance. The make-up of this group will be discussed in connection with its use. Other minor groups are also noted for comparison, but are far more restricted in their significance than the two just mentioned.

In the following section we offer such data regarding non-delinquent adults as have been presented by other investigators in such form that comparison with our material is possible. With the data which we have obtained on Test Aggregate as a measure of mental capacity (see p. 58) we have, as we have said, no possibility of comparison with other groups. Its use is, therefore, restricted to that of making comparisons within the delinquent group. Similarly, we are unable to utilize the most comprehensive material available from the army testing, because it is based on the special group tests—alpha and beta—designed for the use of the United States army and restricted to such use during the period of the war. The three measures which furnish common ground for comparison with other groups are the Stanford-Binet Scale, the Yerkes-Bridges Point Scale, and the tests of the Woolley series.[3]

In our comparison with outside groups, both criminal and non-criminal, we have restricted ourselves entirely to consideration of

[3] We shall not discuss the results of this series, since an extensive comparison of results obtained from a group of Bedford women with data obtained by Dr. Woolley from working girls of fourteen and fifteen years of age has already been published from this laboratory. See Weidensall, Jean: "The Mentality of the Criminal Woman." 1916.

other adult groups, that is, to those made up of individuals of 16 years or over. We have, therefore, omitted all reference to the excellent studies made by Healy, Williams, Haines, Grace Fernald, Kelly, and others.

COMPARISON BASED ON STANFORD-BINET

Because of the special importance of the army data as affording standards of reference we shall consider first the relationship between the results obtained with delinquent women and the data available from the army testing.[4] Common ground for this comparison is found in the Stanford-Binet, which was used with both groups. The army data were obtained from nine camps in different sections of the country. The groups were taken at random as they came for examination.[5] When the results were in, records of individuals born in non-English-speaking countries were rejected, in order that it might be certain that the scores were not affected by marked language handicap in any case. Only white recruits were included in these groups. A total of 653 Stanford-Binet records of white individuals born in English-speaking countries was thus obtained.

Before proceeding to our comparison the limitations affecting this material should be noted. The group under consideration is at least two steps removed from being a random sample of the total white population born in English-speaking countries, of which we wish to consider it typical. In the first place there is the uncertainty as to whether the group of 653 is itself representative of the enlisted personnel of the army. Some information on this point was available, since the other tests which were used so extensively with the army were also used with this group. On the basis of this evidence it was felt that data from this group were reasonably representative of the army as a whole, at least in so far as this was expressed in terms of the central tendency.

In the second place there is uncertainty as to how far the enlisted personnel of the army represents the general population. The fact that the personnel of the army under consideration was assembled under the operation of the Selective Service Act tends to make it

[4] For an account of the results of the psychological examinations given in the army see "Psychological Examining in the United States Army," Memoir of the American Academy of Science.

[5] This is important as distinguishing these data from the much larger body of Stanford-Binet records amassed in the routine of the army examining but obtained from men who were conspicuously low in the group tests. The latter material is obviously valueless for our present purposes.

more representative than would have been the personnel of the army recruited during times of peace. Even so there were selective processes at work, the effect of which it is impossible adequately to evaluate. Only males were included, and these fell mainly within a certain range of ages. Moreover, selection took place which presumably did not occur evenly over the intelligence scale. From the upper levels men had been removed by selection as officers, by admission to officers' training camps or to special forms of service requiring superior ability, and in numerous other ways. From the lower levels men had been rejected through the discarding of the obviously defective and incompetent by the local draft boards and by the medical examining boards at the various cantonments. These and other limiting factors prevent the army data from serving as an exact picture of the general population. Even if we might assume that elimination had been equal from the two extremes of the scale—an assumption which we have no justification for making—the general form of the distribution curve would still be influenced to some degree by these selective processes.

Even in view of the limitations noted above, however, we recur to our earlier assertion that the army data afford our best indications at present as to the mental caliber of the general population. It is very probable, in fact, that they will continue to be our best source of information concerning adults for some time to come.

With reference to the delinquent group, the most important limitation to bear in mind is the fact that we are dealing with the delinquent women who have been caught, and not with all who are delinquent. Presumably, those who have succeeded in escaping conviction are somewhat superior in intelligence. How much superior they are, we have no means of knowing. None of the conclusions reached in this chapter should be given wider application than to the group of convicted women delinquents of New York State.

Table 165 gives the percentage distribution and constants for the army group examined by the Stanford-Binet. The mean mental age is here shown to be 13.4 years, a surprisingly low figure in view of Terman's initial assumption that the average adult has a mental age of 16 years.[6] It requires, however, no argument to show that the group of adults available for his use at the time when this assumption was made, constituted as it was of 32 high school students over

[6] Terman, L. M., etc. "The Stanford Revision and Extension of the Binet-Simon Scale for Measuring Intelligence." pp. 49ff.

TABLE 165

MENTAL CAPACITY AS MEASURED BY STANFORD-BINET

Per Cent Distribution of Delinquent Women and of Army Group, with Constants

White, English-speaking Cases Only

Mental Age	Delinquent Women	Army Group
19.0 to 20.0	.2	.8
18.0 to 19.0	.4	5.2
17.0 to 18.0	1.0	7.2
16.0 to 17.0	2.2	8.3
15.0 to 16.0	6.0	9.6
14.0 to 15.0	6.7	11.8
13.0 to 14.0	10.5	10.6
12.0 to 13.0	13.9	12.4
11.0 to 12.0	17.0	10.6
10.0 to 11.0	19.9	10.1
9.0 to 10.0	13.4	9.5
8.0 to 9.0	6.7	3.4
7.0 to 8.0	1.3	.2
6.0 to 7.0	.7	.3
5.0 to 6.0		.2
Total	100.0	100.0
Number of cases	447	653
Mean	11.8	13.4
σ_m	±.106	±.111
σ	2.24	2.85
σ_σ	±.075	±.079

sixteen years of age and 30 business men of moderate success and very limited educational advantages, is very much further removed from being a random sample of the population than is the army group under consideration. This point is readily admitted by Terman, who has re-formulated his views, in the light of the more recent data, in the following statement written under date of August 20, 1918, which he authorizes us to quote:

"It has become evident, from the results of psychological work in the army, that 'Average Adult' intelligence is considerably lower than the score of 16 on the Stanford revision.

"Because of the numerous factors of selection operative, I hesitate to venture an estimate as to what the real average adult score is. I do not think it is below 14, but I doubt whether it is much above this figure.

"Even if the true 'Average Adult' score were known, this, of course, would not tell us exactly at what point mental growth ceases, because there is still the question of determining the true average score for unselected children just below the age of maturity.

"I believe that the peculiar and unsatisfactory conditions under which the army tests have been made tend to make the average score of the recruit lower than it would be under normal testing conditions."

The above statement shows that Terman judged the army data which we are using, and which constituted a part of the data before

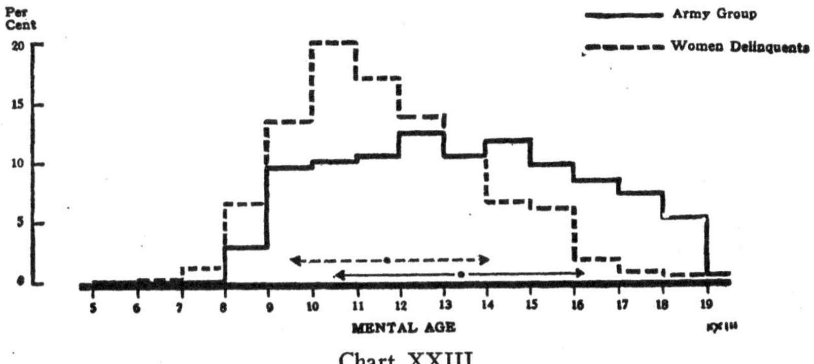

Chart XXIII

Mental Capacity as Measured by Stanford-Binet

Percentage comparison between delinquent women and army recruits. White, English-speaking cases only.

him at this time, to err in the direction of under-estimation of the mentality of adults in general, though not to the same degree that the previous figures erred in the opposite direction.

For comparison with army data we offer, in Table 165, the data on the white, English-speaking women from all six delinquent groups.[7] It is evident from consideration both of the distribution and of the means that the delinquent group is inferior mentally to the army group.

Comparison of the distributions is facilitated by Chart XXIII. While the range of the delinquent group is practically coextensive with

[7] The various groups contribute to this total in the following proportions:

Bedford	Auburn	Magdalen	Penitentiary	Workhouse	Probation
217	29	52	56	38	55

It is evident that elimination of both the colored and the non-English-speaking reduces the numbers to very small figures except in the case of Bedford. The large numbers in the latter group are due to the fact that figures on the larger Bedford group (see p. 17) were available.

that of the army group, it is apparent that the delinquent group is more heavily weighted at the lower end of the scale and less heavily at the upper end. If we take, for example, two arbitrary dividing lines and consider the percentages of each group falling (1) below 10 years mental age and (2) above 15 years, we obtain the following figures:

	Below 10 years mental age	Above 15 years mental age
Delinquent Women	22.1%	3.8%
Army group	13.6%	21.5%

The difference is quite striking in favor of the army group, especially for the comparison of percentages of individuals who rank high on the intelligence scale. If we consider the proportions falling in the lower portion of the scale, in comparison with Goring's figures (see p. 414), it is at once apparent that our figures, while quite convincing as to the fact of difference, indicate a far less extreme degree of divergence between the delinquent and the non-delinquent group than do his. Even if allowance be made for the possible slight inferiority of the present army group in comparison with the general population, no such extreme variation as Goring reports would appear.

Superiority of the army group to the delinquent women appears also when we compare the means of the two groups. (See Table 166.) The difference in mental age of 1.6 years may be accepted as valid, beyond any reasonable question, since it amounts to more than ten times the standard deviation of the difference.

TABLE 166

MENTAL CAPACITY AS MEASURED BY STANFORD-BINET

Comparison of Means and Standard Deviations of Delinquent Women and of Army Group

White, English-speaking Cases Only

	Delinquent Women	Army Group	Difference	$\frac{d}{\sigma_d}$	Chances that real difference does not exist are 1 in:
Mean Mental Age	11.8	13.4	−1.6	10.4	∞
σ_m	±.106	±.111			
σ	2.24	2.85	− .61	5.6	∞
σ_σ	±.075	±.079			
Cases	447	653			

TABLE 167

MENTAL CAPACITY AS MEASURED BY STANFORD-BINET

Per Cent Distribution of Delinquent Women by Institutional Groups, with Constants

English-speaking Cases Only

Mental Age*	Institutional Groups						Total
	Bedford	Auburn	Magdalen	Penitentiary	Workhouse	Probation	
19	.4	....	....	....	....	....	.2
18	....	....	....	1.3	1.4	....	.4
17	.8	....	....	1.3	....	1.7	.8
16	1.2	....	3.8	3.9	....	3.4	1.8
15	4.6	4.7	3.8	7.8	4.1	6.7	5.1
14	2.7	4.7	15.4	11.7	2.7	6.7	5.6
13	9.6	14.0	15.4	7.8	9.6	11.7	10.4
12	11.5	18.6	17.3	11.7	12.3	13.3	12.9
11	16.2	18.6	13.4	15.6	15.1	16.6	16.0
10	21.2	23.3	15.4	19.5	20.5	18.3	20.2
9	17.3	9.4	9.6	9.1	19.2	18.3	15.2
8	9.6	7.0	5.7	6.5	11.0	1.7	8.0
7	3.5	....	....	3.9	2.7	1.7	2.6
6	1.5	....	....	....	1.4	....	.9
5	....	....	....	....	....	....	....
Total	100.0	100.0	100.0	100.0	100.0	100.0	100.0
Cases	260	43	52	77	73	60	565
Mean	11.2	11.7	12.3	12.1	11.1	11.9	11.5
σ_m	±.136	±.270	±.287	±.283	±.253	±.285	±.094
σ	2.19	1.77	2.07	2.48	2.16	2.21	2.24
σ_σ	±.086	±.191	±.203	±.200	±.179	±.201	±.067

*A mental age of 5 here signifies from 5.0 to 6.0, etc. The mid-value of the intervals are, therefore, 5.5, 6.5, etc.

We note also, by reference to Table 166, that the variability of the army group is wider than that of the delinquent group and that we are justified in accepting this difference as valid. This is especially important in view of the fact that all the other comparisons which we are able to present between delinquent and non-delinquent groups show the opposite tendency with regard to variability (see Tables 170 to 174), that is, the delinquent group shows consistently the wider dispersion. The reduced variability of the other non-delinquent groups would arise naturally from the fact that they are picked, as we have noted previously, from a more or less restricted portion of the general population.

In Table 167 the percentage distribution and constants for the various institutional groups are offered. These figures apply to the actual groups as examined, except for the necessary elimination of cases handicapped by language difficulty. In general, throughout this study we have presented the institutional groups as units, without elimination of the colored, because the latter constitute an integral part of the institutional population. It seems desirable, therefore, to offer the data on mentality on the same basis. It should be remembered, however, in considering the figures of Table 167 that all groups except the Magdalen include colored women. The final column gives data on the total English-speaking group, which differs from our preceding total group by the presence of the colored. Reference to the figures show that the difference between the two groups is small. The explanation lies in the fact that the colored portion of the group, though appreciably lower mentally than the white (see pp. 480-4), constitutes a relatively small proportion of the total.

Among the institutional groups two are of particular interest; the Bedford and the Magdalen. The former deserves special attention because the figures offered may be accepted as peculiarly representative of the institution (see pp. 39-40). Not only do they cover larger actual numbers, but they represent a longer period of study, and were obtained under the most satisfactory conditions of any of our groups. Since the mean for the Bedford group (11.2 years) is one of the lowest two, among the institutional groups, it is obvious that the Bedford women would appear even more convincingly inferior to the army group than did the delinquent group previously considered. Table 168 shows that such is the case. (The elimination of the colored women from the Bedford group would not affect the comparison to any important degree, owing to the small numbers of colored cases. The mean mental age for the Bedford white is 11.4 years, differing from the army mean by two years.) The distribution of the Bedford group is shown graphically in Chart XXVII for purposes of another comparison.

The special interest in the Magdalen Home is based on the fact that it ranks highest in mentality among the institutional groups on the present basis of measurement. Comparison with the army group is, therefore, important in order to discover whether any of the groups of delinquent women reach the mental level of the group

TABLE 168

MENTAL CAPACITY AS MEASURED BY STANFORD-BINET

Comparison of Means and Standard Deviations of Army Group and Bedford Women

English-speaking Cases Only

	Bedford Women	Army Group	Difference	$\frac{d}{\sigma_d}$	Chances that real difference does not exist are 1 in:
Mean Mental Age.. σ_m..............	11.2 ±.136	13.4 ±.111	−2.2	12.6	∞
σ................ σ_σ................	2.19 ±.096	2.85 ±.079	− .66	5.3	∞
Cases............	260	653			

which we are accepting tentatively as representative of adults in general. Table 169 presents the data for this comparison. The difference is still in favor of the "general" group, and, although the amount of difference is reduced to 1.1 years, this is sufficient to justify the assertion of a genuine distinction between the two groups. Since there are no negroes in the Magdalen group no qualification of the results from this point of view is needed. Again the army group is more variable by a significant degree.

TABLE 169

MENTAL CAPACITY AS MEASURED BY STANFORD-BINET

Comparison of Means and Standard Deviations of Army Group and Magdalen Home Group

White, English-speaking Cases Only

	Magdalen Women	Army Group	Difference	$\frac{d}{\sigma_d}$	Chances that real difference does not exist are 1 in:
Mean Mental Age.. σ_m..............	12.3 ±.287	13.4 ±.111	−1.1	3.6	5500
σ................ σ_σ................	2.07 ±.203	2.85 .079	− .78	3.6	5500
Cases............	52	653			

The evidence at hand, therefore, shows all the delinquent groups to be appreciably inferior mentally to the army group and to have a narrower range of variability. If we grant the probable truth of the contention that the army figures fail to do full justice to the general population with respect to mentality, it is apparent that we have understated by at least a slight degree the amount of this difference. Of its existence there can, we think, be no reasonable question.

We have previously cited the figures on the mental ages of adults offered by Terman (see pp. 417-8). Without lingering over these data we may consider briefly the relationship of our delinquent women to his 62 adults. In view of the evident superiority of his group to adults in general, it is not surprising to find a considerable difference between the means of the two groups in favor of Terman's adults, as well as a decided difference in the degree of variability in favor of the delinquent group (see reference to latter point, pp. 421-2). The constants for Terman's 62 adults are as follows:

$$\text{Mean Mental Age} = 16.1 \pm .146$$
$$\sigma = 1.15 \pm .103$$

In view of the recognition by Terman that these figures are not adequately representative of the general population further elaboration of the comparison is unnecessary.

COMPARISON BASED ON YERKES-BRIDGES POINT SCALE

Turning to the figures based on the data from the Yerkes-Bridges Point Scale we discover four groups of non-delinquent adults available for comparison as follows: (1) 25 male students in the Boston Y. M. C. A., (2) 25 mill operatives, (3) 109 Cincinnati working girls, (4) a combination of the above working girls with 78 girls who had continued in school. The first two groups mentioned can lay no claims to being representative and will, therefore, be considered only in passing. The first of these, the Y. M. C. A. student group, obviously consists of superior individuals as Yerkes himself points out.[8] He states that "each of these individuals had had a partial or complete high school education, and several of them are college graduates." The mean for this group (94.66 ± .926) naturally falls entirely outside the range of means for the delinquent groups, among which the Magdalen shows the highest mean value (76.58 ±

[8] Yerkes, R. M., Bridges, J. W. and Hardwick, R. S. "A Point Scale for Measuring Mental Ability," 1915, pp. 91-92.

1.65). The standard deviation on the other hand is conspicuously low, 4.63±.685, as compared, for example, with that for Magdalen of 12.03±1.166. This narrow variability emphasizes again the restricted range of selection of the student group in question.

The mill operative group cited by Yerkes [9] shows no such obvious reason for being considered a superior group. We know only that they were mill operatives (male), that their ages fall between 17 and 27 and that no one of them had had better than grammar school education and few had completed the work in grammar school. The group is too small to have significance for our purposes, in view especially of its lack of definition. The constants are, however, presented herewith. They show the same direction of difference from the delinquent groups as do the figures for the student group just discussed.

YERKES' MILL OPERATIVES

Mean Score in Points = 88.42 ± 1.64
σ = 8.19 ± 1.83
Number of Cases = 25

The data from the Cincinnati groups of girls constitute our only useful source of comparison based on the Yerkes-Bridges Point Scale. We have obtained, through the courtesy of Dr. Woolley, the records of the testing by this scale of 187 white girls, sixteen, seventeen and eighteen years of age, made at the Cincinnati Bureau of Vocational Guidance. This is composed of two groups. One group of 109 was taken from the working girls, *i.e.,* those that had left school at sixteen to go to work, and one of 78 from the school group, *i.e.,* those that had continued in school beyond the time when they were legally permitted to leave. This fact in itself, Dr. Woolley believes, indicates that the latter is a superior group, and since the members of the working girl group were picked out as being somewhat inferior, she considers that the combined group "should make a fairly good average for the whole community." Whether or not such a statement is entirely justified, we are interested to see how our data compare, first, with the combination of her groups, and second, with the group of working girls recognized as inferior. All cases in the Cincinnati groups had completed at least the 6th grade. This of itself would tend to eliminate the very inferior.

Table 170 presents the data on these two groups, and also, for comparison, the figures for the white, English-speaking portion of

[9] *Op. cit.,* pp. 90-91.

TABLE 170

MENTAL CAPACITY AS MEASURED BY YERKES-BRIDGES POINT SCALE

Per Cent Distribution of Delinquent Women and of Two Groups of Cincinnati Girls—Working Girls and Combination of Working and School Girls — with Constants

White, English-speaking Cases Only

Score in Points	Delinquent Women	Cincinnati Groups	
		Working Girls	Working and School Girls
96–100	.8	2.8	13.9
90–96	6.1	11.9	27.8
84–90	13.4	21.1	18.7
78–84	18.4	24.8	16.6
72–78	15.5	16.5	9.6
66–72	16.7	9.2	5.4
60–66	11.1	8.3	4.8
54–60	7.7	3.7	2.1
48–54	5.2	....	....
42–48	3.1	1.8	1.1
36–42	1.1	....	....
30–36	.6	....	....
24–30	.2	....	....
Total	100.0	100.0	100.0
Cases	478	109	187
Mean	71.80	78.83	84.62
σ_m	±.608	±1.07	±.830
σ	13.29	11.18	11.36
σ_σ	±.416	±.832	±.707

the total delinquent group. The distributions of these groups are also shown graphically in Chart XXIV. Inspection of the chart shows a marked difference between the delinquent group and each of the Cincinnati groups. We are at once impressed by the greater flatness of the delinquent curve, as well as by the location of the massing. We note that the dot indicating location of the mean falls lower in case of the delinquents, and that the span of the arrows, showing the range of the standard deviation above and below the mean, is wider. It is noteworthy also that the range of the delinquent group runs lower than that of either Cincinnati group. So marked a difference

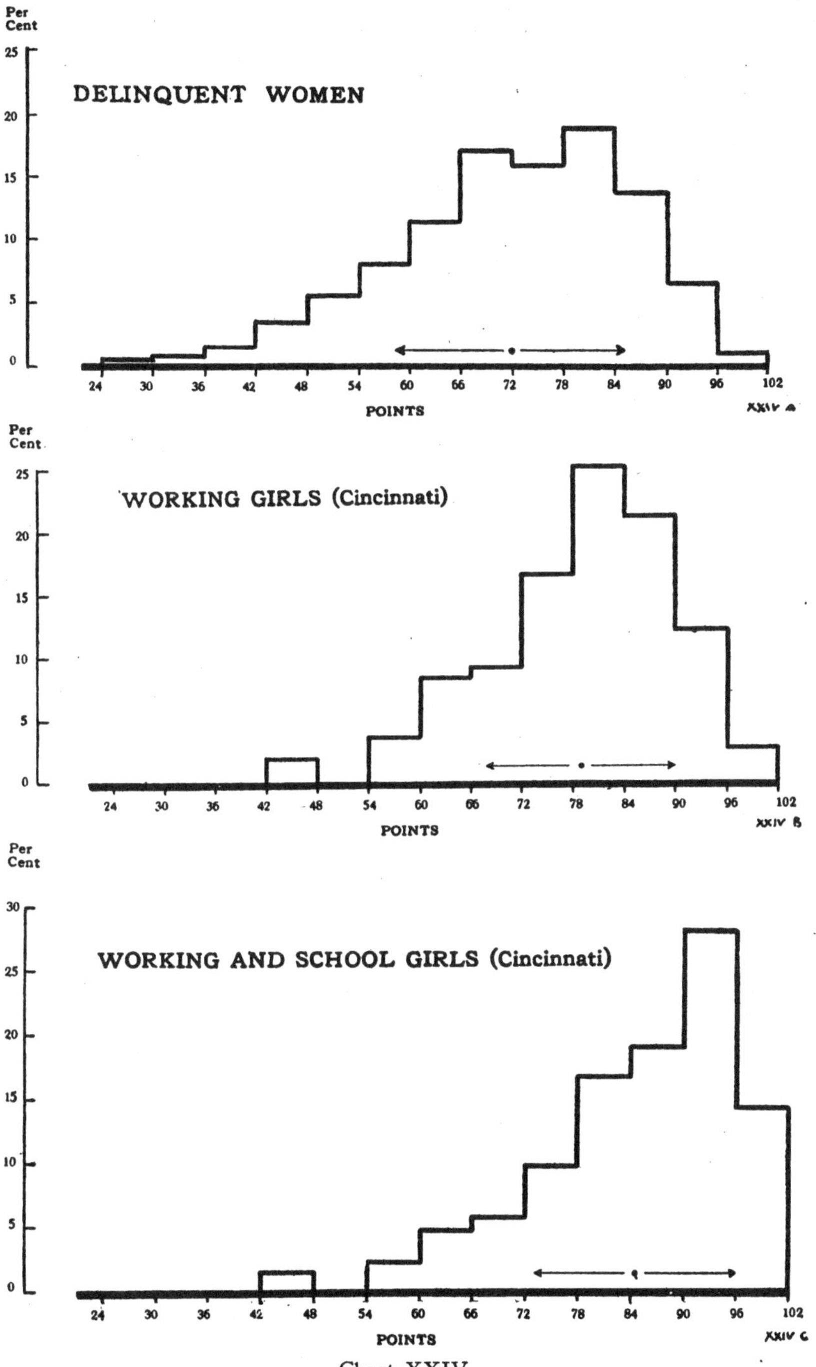

Chart XXIV

Mental Capacity as Measured by Yerkes-Bridges Point Scale

Per cent distribution of delinquent women and of two groups of Cincinnati girls: (1) working girls, and (2) working and school girls. White, English-speaking cases only.

in this respect undoubtedly reflects the eliminations from the lower portion of the Cincinnati group involved in the requirement of 6th grade completion. Turning to statistical comparison to determine how far we are justified in accepting the evidence of inspection, we learn from Table 171 that the inferiority of the delinquent group to both of the Cincinnati groups is established beyond any reasonable question. The difference in variability of the two groups, in favor of the greater spread of the delinquent group, appears also to be almost certainly valid.

TABLE 171

MENTAL CAPACITY AS MEASURED BY YERKES-BRIDGES POINT SCALE

Comparison of Means and Standard Deviations of Delinquent Women with those of (1) Cincinnati Working Girls and (2) Working and School Girls (Cincinnati)

White, English-speaking Cases Only

	Delinquent Women	Working Girls	Difference	$\frac{d}{\sigma_d}$	Chances that real difference does not exist are 1 in:
Mean σ_m	71.80 ±.608	78.83 ±1.071	−7.03	5.7	∞
σ σ_σ	13.29 ±.416	11.18 ±.832	2.11	2.3	86
Cases	478	109			
	Delinquent Women	**Working and School Girls**			
Mean σ_m	71.80 ±.608	84.62 ±.830	−12.82	12.4	∞
σ σ_σ	13.29 ±.416	11.36 ±.707	1.93	2.4	107
Cases	478	187			

For further comparison with the Cincinnati groups we offer the data for the several units of the total delinquent group (Table 172). As in the case of the Stanford-Binet comparison the Bedford and the Magdalen groups are of special interest to us, and for the reasons previously given. The distributions of these two groups are shown graphically in Chart XXV.

Since Bedford ranks mentally as one of the lowest of the delinquent groups it is to be expected that it should be even more clearly distinguished from the Cincinnati groups than is the total white delinquent group. Reference to Table 173 shows that even when compared with the poorer of the Cincinnati groups the Bedford group is inferior mentally by a significant difference.

TABLE 172

MENTAL CAPACITY AS MEASURED BY YERKES-BRIDGES POINT SCALE

Per Cent Distribution of Institutional Groups, with Constants

English-speaking Cases Only

Score in Points	Institutional Groups						Total
	Bedford	Auburn	Magdalen	Penitentiary	Workhouse	Probation	
96–100	.4	....	1.9	....	2.7	....	.7
90–96	3.2	2.3	5.7	16.5	....	8.5	5.3
84–90	11.6	20.5	26.4	14.0	9.3	8.5	13.2
78–84	13.3	25.0	24.5	14.0	18.7	22.5	17.0
72–78	15.1	13.6	13.2	15.0	13.3	18.3	15.0
66–72	19.6	9.1	9.4	12.7	10.7	12.7	15.2
60–66	11.9	13.6	7.5	7.6	9.3	15.5	11.2
54–60	9.1	9.1	5.7	10.1	13.3	8.5	9.4
48–54	7.4	2.3	3.8	6.3	8.0	2.8	6.1
42–48	5.3	2.3	1.9	2.5	12.0	1.4	4.8
36–42	1.4	2.3	....	1.3	1.3	1.4	1.3
30–36	1.4	....	....	....	....	....	.7
24–30	.4	....	....	....	1.3	....	.3
Total	100.0	100.0	100.0	100.0	100.0	100.0	100.0
Cases	285	44	53	79	75	71	607
Mean	68.53	72.73	76.58	73.64	66.61	72.61	70.44
σ_m	±.811	±1.877	±1.650	±1.629	±1.706	±1.441	±.563
σ	13.69	13.45	12.03	14.48	14.78	12.14	13.88
σ_σ	±.535	±1.280	±1.166	±.908	±.972	±.928	±.360

A very different situation exists, however, in case of the Magdalen group. The appearance of the distribution curve (Chart XXV) is markedly different from that of the other delinquent groups, with the sudden piling up of cases toward the upper portion of the scale. The range of the Magdalen cases extends no lower than that of the Cincinnati groups. The mean falls lower in the Magdalen group than the mean for either of the other two but the difference is not

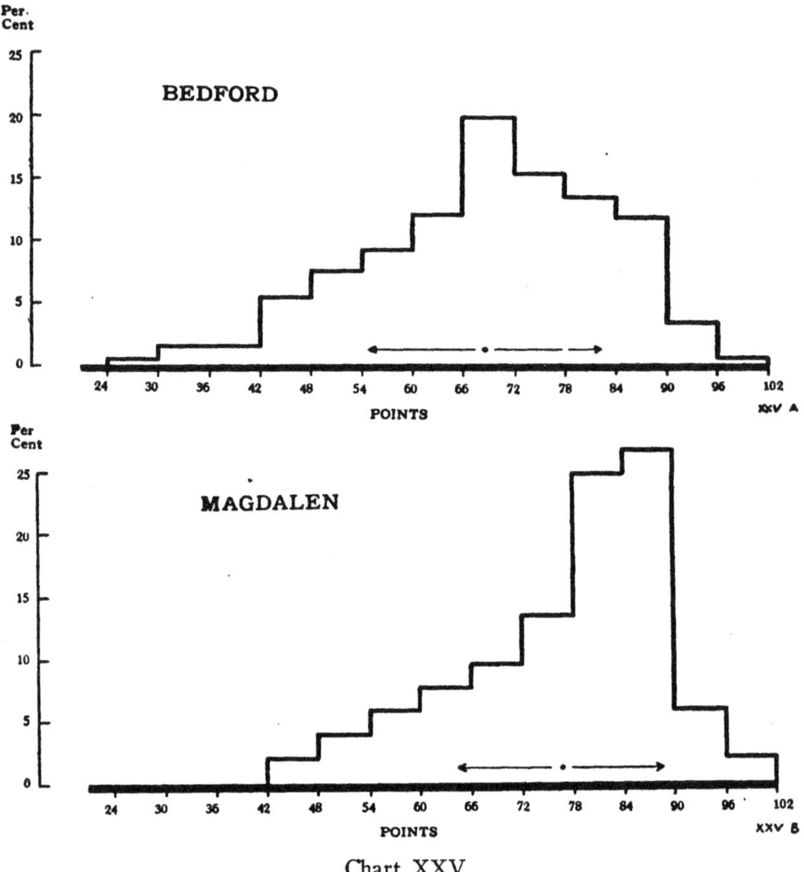

Chart XXV

Mental Capacity as Measured by Yerkes-Bridges Point Scale

Per cent distribution of Bedford and Magdalen institutional groups—English-speaking cases only.

great enough so that we can determine by inspection whether or not it might have occurred by chance. From Table 174 we learn that we need not question the validity of the difference between the means of the Magdalen and the combined group of school and working girls. In comparison with the Cincinnati working girl group

TABLE 173

MENTAL CAPACITY AS MEASURED BY YERKES-BRIDGES POINT SCALE

Comparison of the Means and Standard Deviations of Bedford Women with those of (1) Cincinnati Working Girls and (2) Working and School Girls (Cincinnati)

English-speaking Cases Only

	Bedford	Working Girls (Cincinnati)	Difference	$\frac{d}{\sigma_d}$	Chances that real difference does not exist are 1 in:
Mean	68.53	78.83	−10.30	7.67	∞
σ_m	±.811	±1.071			
σ	13.69	11.18	2.51	2.54	182
σ_σ	±.535	±.832			
Cases	285	109			
	Bedford	**Working and School Girls**			
Mean	68.53	84.62	−16.090	13.86	∞
σ_m	±.811	±.830			
σ	13.69	11.36	2.34	2.64	244
σ_σ	±.535	±.707			
Cases	285	187			

however, the slight difference between the means can not be stressed as significant, since as great a difference as this might occur, by chance, as often as 1 in 8 times. No demonstrable difference in mentality appears, therefore, between the best of the delinquent groups and the poorest of the non-delinquent. This is not at variance with our other findings, since the extensive overlapping of range of delinquent and non-delinquent groups has been apparent in all our comparisons. We should anticipate that, if we increased the number and variety of our samples of non-delinquents, we should find groups appreciably lower than certain of the delinquent groups.

Table 174 shows also that there is no demonstrable difference in variability between the Magdalen and either of the Cincinnati groups.

COMPARISON BY MEANS OF WOOLLEY SERIES

As we stated earlier in this chapter, we shall not attempt to make any comparison of the results obtained by us, through application of the Woolley series of tests to delinquent groups, with Dr. Woolley's results from working girls, since an extended study along these lines has already appeared from this laboratory. As indicative of the general results of this comparison, we quote the following paragraph:

"Thus when the mentality of the criminal women is measured by the number of tests in which their ability is at or above that of the median working girl of fifteen, again about a third of them (35 per cent) fall within the range of the better fifty per cent of the working girls of

TABLE 174

MENTAL CAPACITY AS MEASURED BY YERKES-BRIDGES POINT SCALE

Comparison of Means and Standard Deviations of Magdalen Home Women with Those of (1) Cincinnati Working Girls and (2) Working and School Girls (Cincinnati)

White, English-speaking Cases Only

	Magdalen	Working Girls	Difference	$\frac{d}{\sigma_d}$	Chances that real difference does not exist are 1 in:
Mean.............	76.58	78.83	−2.25	1.13	8
σ_m...............	±1.650	±1.071			
σ................	12.03	11.18			
σ_σ................	±1.166	±.832	.85	.59	4
Cases.............	53	109			
	Magdalen	**Working and School Girls**			
Mean.............	76.58	84.62	−8.04	4.4	147,000
σ_m...............	±1.650	±.830			
σ................	12.03	11.36	.67	.49	3
σ_σ................	±1.166	±.707			
Cases.............	53	187			

fifteen, about two-thirds below the median, 54 per cent poorer than all but the poorest 25 per cent of the standard, 30.7 per cent as poor as the poorest 5.7 per cent and 17 per cent poorer than any of the working girls."[10]

It is evident that the data from this source are likewise confirmatory of the trend toward a relatively low average mentality in the delinquent group.

SUMMARY

Summarizing, then, the results of such comparisons as we have been able to make of the mental capacity of delinquent women with that of non-delinquents, it appears:

(1) That the average mental capacity of the delinquent women whom we have examined is lower than that of any groups of non-delinquent adults with regard to whom we have data.[11]

(2) That, however, the above statement does not imply a selection of individuals entirely from the lower end of the scale of intelligence for the delinquent group. There is, in fact, an extensive amount of overlapping of the delinquent with the non-delinquent groups. The range of the delinquent group was found to be practically coextensive with that of the army group, our most representative sampling of the general population. Further, the difference between the means of the delinquent and the non-delinquent groups, while affording adequate indication of a distinction between the two groups, is not extreme in amount. In other words, this is definitely not a case of an "all or none" relationship.

(3) The data are somewhat ambiguous regarding the relative variability of the two groups. From consideration of our most representative material, the army data, we conclude that the variability of the delinquent group is less than that of the adult population in general. Reference to the other non-delinquent groups, however, shows that the variability is in all these cases lower than that of the delinquent group. The evidence at hand, therefore, indicates that a group of non-delinquent adults, picked at random from any specialized segment of the population, is likely to show a narrower dispersion than a group of adult delinquents. Our data are, however,

[10] *Op. cit.*, p. 274.

[11] It should be remembered that the statements of this summary refer to the white, English-speaking portions of the delinquent and the non-delinquent groups.

far too slight to justify us in maintaining that this rule will always hold. Fundamentally, of course, it would depend upon the breadth of the category which determined the basis of selection of the non-delinquent group.

It is evident from the foregoing statement that our findings are in accord with Goring's as regards the fact of a difference and its direction. They indicate, however, a slighter degree of difference than he implies. They fail absolutely to justify the view expressed recently by certain propagandists that delinquency and defective intelligence are practically synonymous, and that, accordingly, solving the problem of mental deficiency will solve the problem of delinquency.

CHAPTER XIV

MENTAL CAPACITY: INTER-COMPARISON OF DELINQUENT GROUPS

IN the preceding chapter we have endeavored to discover the relationship between our group of delinquent women and the general population, with respect to intelligence. In the present chapter we shall be concerned with a comparison of different delinquent groups with one another, a problem of importance from several points of view. If differences, significant in amount, are found to exist in the case of delinquent groups now available for consideration, a knowledge of the amounts of such differences may suggest the nature of the limitations to be imposed upon the universality of conclusions based on a study of any particular group or combination of groups. Further, it is important to know whether differences of any considerable size are found between the different *types* of groups under consideration, and also to know whether the institutions which we have chosen to represent particular types of institutions bear a close resemblance to others of these types. It is also desirable, wherever possible, to compare groups of women delinquents with corresponding groups of men delinquents, with a view to discovering to what extent any particular findings must be qualified as valid for offenders of one sex but not for those of the other sex.

The various comparisons suggested above will be carried out, so far as the available data permit, in the present chapter. Scantiness of data for comparison, however, is such as greatly to limit the thoroughness of our treatment.

COMPARISON OF GROUPS CONSIDERED IN PRESENT INVESTIGATION

The first step in the comparison of different delinquent groups with respect to general intelligence is the inter-comparison of the six groups which constitute the units from which our total is made up. As the simplest method of indicating whether intelligence had been a dominating factor in determining the disposition of cases, we

TABLE 175

Correlation between Mental Capacity Measured by Test Aggregate and Institutional Groups

English-speaking Cases Only

Institutional Groups	Test Aggregate: 47 to 49	49 to 51	51 to 53	53 to 55	55 to 57	57 to 59	59 to 61	61 to 63	63 to 65	65 to 67	67 to 69	69 to 71	71 to 73	73 to 75	75 to 77	77 to 79	79 to 81	81 to 83	83 to 85	85 to 87	87 to 89	89 to 91	91 to 93	93 to 95	95 to 97	Totals	Means (Test Aggregate)
Bedford			2	1	3	7	6	6	6	10	13	14	22	15	24	19	14	23	14	13	7	11	4	1	1	236	75.1
Auburn	1		1					1	1		3	4	4	2	4	4	6		5	4		2				42	75.4
Magdalen							1		1	1	3	1	3	4	1	5	6	8	4	4	4	2	1		1	50	79.1
Penitentiary		1			2		3	1	4	2	3	5	7	2	8	5	2	3	6	2	6	6	2	2	2	74	76.7
Workhouse					1	2	3	3	5	3	5	6	4	5	4	5	6	7	2	4	2			1	1	69	73.3
Probation					1			1	1		3	6	3	4	5	3	3	2	7	2	2	4	1	1		49	77.5
Totals	1	1	3	1	7	9	13	12	18	16	30	36	43	32	46	41	37	43	38	29	21	25	8	5	5	520	75.70

Test aggregate: Mean = 75.70 $\sigma = 9.27$
Correlation ratio: Test aggregate on institutional groups $\eta = .17 \pm .043$

computed a correlation ratio with Test Aggregate as the quantitative variable and the six groups of delinquent women as a series of qualitative arrays. The relationship between intelligence and type of sentence is shown in Table 175, from which a correlation ratio of .17 ±.043 was obtained. This would indicate that the degree of relationship is extremely slight, but significant. With a view to further analysis of these differences we have made more detailed inter-comparisons among the groups.

(a) *Comparison of Total English-Speaking Portions of Groups*

The seven figures of Chart XXVI show the percentage distribution of scores on Test Aggregate for each of the six groups and for the combined total. (These distributions appear in numerical form in Table 175.) An inspection of these shows the most noticeable items to be the wide distribution of the Penitentiary and, to a lesser extent, of the Bedford group; the relatively low, flat curves of these two groups and of the Workhouse as compared with the marked concentration about the mode shown by the Magdalen; the lack of representation at the poor end for the Magdalen group; the small percentage found in the high end of the Workhouse group; and differences in the location of the mean, indicated by the position of the dot on each curve. (Table 176 gives the numerical values of the means and standard deviations for these groups.) We see

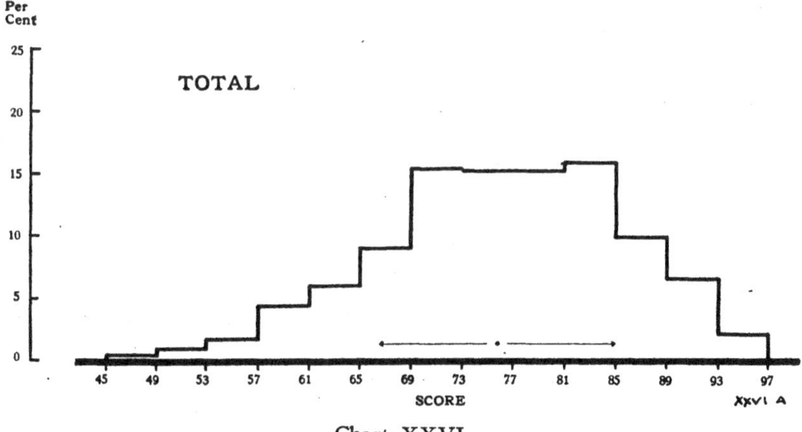

Chart XXVI
Mental Capacity as Measured by Test Aggregate
Per cent distribution by institutional groups.

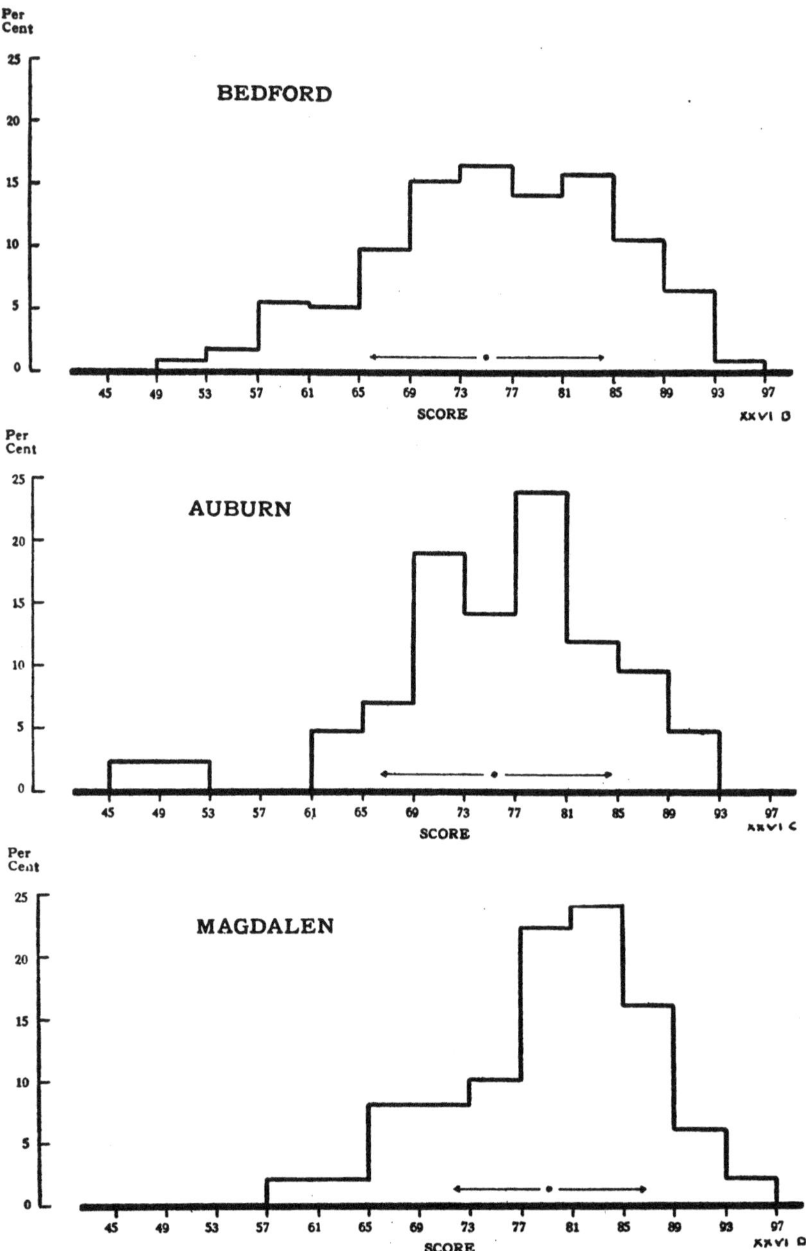

Chart XXVI (Continued)
Mental Capacity as Measured by Test Aggregate
Per cent distribution by institutional groups.

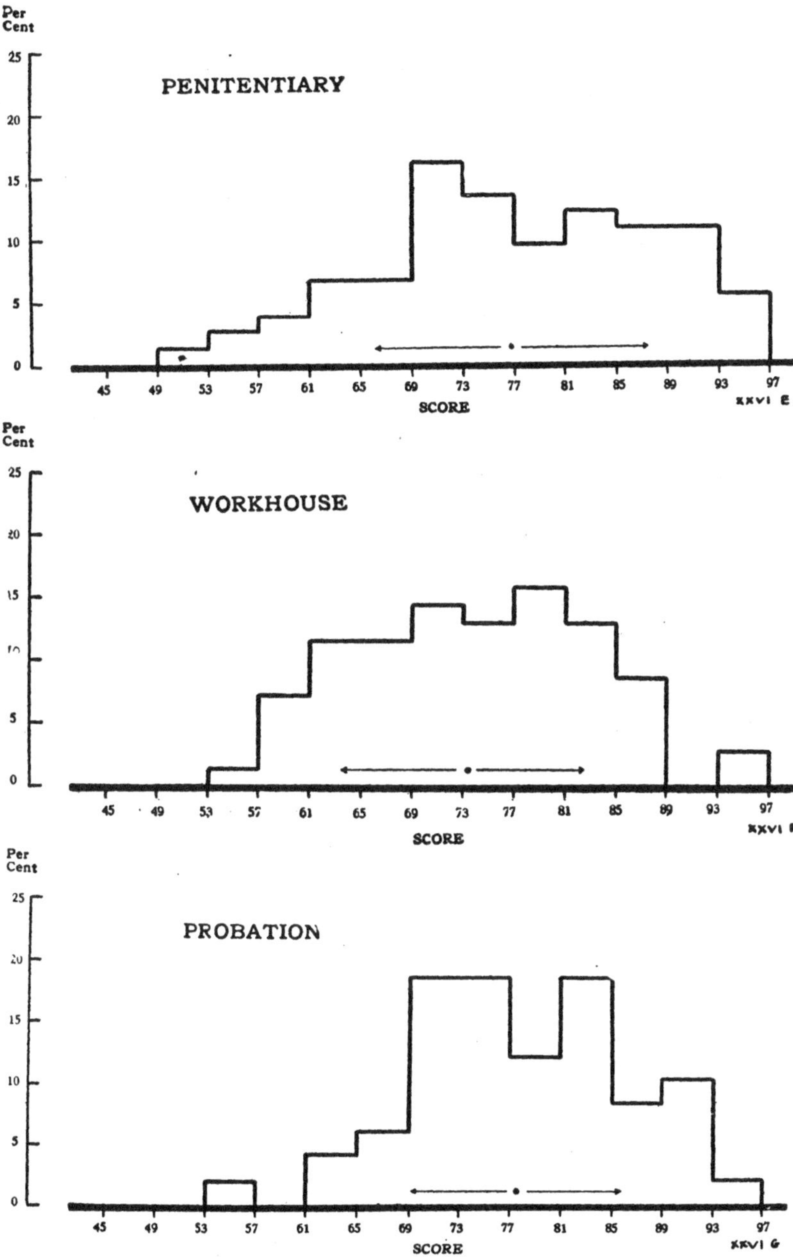

Chart XXVI (Continued)
Mental Capacity as Measured by Test Aggregate
Per cent distribution by institutional groups.

TABLE 176

MENTAL CAPACITY MEASURED BY TEST AGGREGATE

Comparison of Constants by Institutional Groups

English-speaking Cases Only

	Bedford	Auburn	Magdalen	Peni-tentiary	Work-house	Probation	Total
Mean.........	75.05	75.38	79.10	76.72	73.31	77.49	75.65
σ_m............	±.594	±1.39	±1.06	±1.24	±1.09	±1.19	±.406
σ.............	9.12	9.01	7.52	10.67	9.08	8.30	9.27
σ_σ............	±.376	±1.30	±.720	±.738	±.650	±.763	±.266
Cases.........	236	42	50	74	69	49	520

that the averages for mental capacity run in order of excellence, Magdalen, Probation, Penitentiary, Auburn, Bedford and the Workhouse, with the widest steps coming between the Magdalen and Probation and between Bedford and the Workhouse. The Magdalen and the Workhouse seem then to be indicated as clearly superior and clearly inferior groups respectively. As we have suggested, the Magdalen group would seem to owe its excellence not so much to a piling up of the most superior cases, *i.e.*, those in the highest two intervals, for example, but rather to the lopping off of the inferior end and a high concentration of cases which are well above the average. The Workhouse in its turn would seem to have derived its inferiority from its small percentage of superior women and its uniform distribution above and below the average rather than from any unusual representation in the lowest group. The Penitentiary and Bedford groups include a wide range of cases from those very low to those very superior. They differ from each other in that while Bedford is sparsely represented in the most superior region, the Penitentiary has a greater percentage of cases here than is found even in the Magdalen group. Auburn and the Probation group are alike in that they both show some evidences of bimodality, but the numbers are too few to attempt to draw conclusions.

In order to find out whether these differences are valid or whether they are only such variations as might occur from sampling, we have made inter-comparisons of the means and standard deviations of these prison groups. We print below a table (Table 177) showing the inter-relations expressed in terms of the ratio of the difference of the means to the standard deviation of this difference. (As earlier stated [see p. 35] we are considering as indicative of a valid difference a ratio of two or more times the standard deviation.)

From this table we see that a difference sufficient to be regarded as almost certainly valid occurs in only five of the comparisons, namely: between the Magdalen and Bedford, the Magdalen and the Workhouse, the Magdalen and Auburn, the Workhouse and Probation, and the Workhouse and the Penitentiary. From this we would infer that intellectual capacity, either primarily or secondarily, may have been a factor in determining the disposition of a case where there was a choice between these institutions. On the whole we note that the institutional groups are mutually overlapping and that no one group is demonstrably superior or inferior to all the others. As a possible reason to account for the relative superiority of the Magdalen and inferiority of the Workhouse groups, we may say that the Magdalen is the only one of the institutions studied which may itself exercise any choice in the matter of the inmates it receives. The Magdalen, being a private institution, has the privilege of refusing to receive, or of returning as undesirable, cases which seem unpromising. It seems possible, therefore, that this might function as a selective factor in that it would tend to

TABLE 177

MENTAL CAPACITY MEASURED BY TEST AGGREGATE

Inter-comparison of Means of Institutional Groups in Terms of the Ratio of the Difference between the Means to the Standard Deviation of the Difference

	Auburn	Magdalen	Penitentiary	Workhouse	Probation
Bedford	−.22	−3.33	−1.21	1.40	−1.84
Auburn		−2.07	− .18	1.17	− .12
Magdalen			1.46	3.93	.10
Penitentiary				2.07	− .45
Workhouse					−2.60

Explanation of table: The number in each space gives the value for $\frac{d}{\sigma_d}$ for the two institutional groups designated at the head of the column and to the left of the row, respectively. A minus sign indicates that the mean of the institutional group at the left is smaller than the mean of the group heading the column.

raise the standard mentally as well as otherwise of the girls committed there.

There is another factor also which may conceivably act as a selective agent to account both for the superiority of the Magdalen and the inferiority of the Workhouse. This is the matter of color. There are no colored women committed to the Magdalen, while the Workhouse contains a larger percentage than any of the other groups, 36 per cent, as against 20 per cent at the Penitentiary, 20 per cent at Bedford, 17 per cent at Auburn, and 9 per cent on Probation. As we shall later show (Table 201), there is a large and unquestionably significant difference between the means of the colored and the white women.

There is the further fact, which might well carry weight with judges familiar with conditions in the various institutions, that the Workhouse offers least, in the way of opportunities for training, of any of the institutions, with the possible exception of the Penitentiary.

Considering now the amount of variability in each group as shown by their respective standard deviations, we find that while the evident order runs Penitentiary, Bedford, Workhouse, Auburn, Probation, Magdalen, Table 178 shows that there exists a demonstrably valid difference only between the Penitentiary and Probation and between the Penitentiary and the Magdalen.

TABLE 178

MENTAL CAPACITY MEASURED BY TEST AGGREGATE

Inter-comparison of Standard Deviations of Institutional Groups in Terms of the Ratio of the Difference between the Means to the Standard Deviation of the Difference

	Auburn	Magdalen	Penitentiary	Workhouse	Probation
Bedford	.08	1.97	−1.85	.02	.97
Auburn		1.00	−1.11	− .05	.75
Magdalen			−3.05	−1.62	− .74
Penitentiary				1.62	2.23
Workhouse					.78

Explanation of table: The number in each space gives the value for $\frac{d}{\sigma_d}$ for the two institutional groups designated at the head of the column and to the left of the row, respectively. A minus sign indicates that the standard deviation of the institutional group at the left is smaller than that of the group heading the column.

It seems possible that here again the factor of the elimination of the colored from the Magdalen and their practical elimination from the Probation group may explain the facts.

(b) *Comparison of Institutional Groups: White Women Only*

In order to be certain whether or not the question of color was a significant factor in determining the degree of difference in mental capacity of these groups, we have calculated new frequency tables, using only the white women of each group. This has unfortunately made our numbers very small in some groups.

Table 179 shows the means and standard deviations of each group. The most noticeable change is, as we should expect, the raising of the means of the Workhouse and Penitentiary.

TABLE 179

MENTAL CAPACITY MEASURED BY TEST AGGREGATE

Comparison of Constants by Institutional Groups

English-speaking White Women Only

	Bedford	Auburn	Magdalen	Penitentiary	Workhouse	Probation	Total
Mean	76.00	75.64	79.10	79.07	76.58	77.98	77.03
σ_m	±.647	±1.682	±1.06	±1.323	±1.497	±1.214	±.442
	8.96	8.90	7.52	9.72	8.98	8.23	8.91
σ_σ	±.457	±1.190	±.720	±.935	±1.058	±.859	±.305
Cases	192	28	50	54	36	46	406

Table 180 shows the significance of the difference between the means of the various white groups in the same way that Table 177 showed the validity of the difference between the totals, *i.e.*, combined colored and white, of each group.

From this it appears that, when we eliminate the colored women from the comparison, we are no longer able to demonstrate the existence of a difference between the Magdalen and Auburn, the Magdalen and the Workhouse, or the Workhouse and the Probation group. Reference to Table 179, in relation to Table 176, makes it clear, however, that the differences referred to have not been eradicated by elimination of the colored but merely reduced in amount.

TABLE 180

MENTAL CAPACITY MEASURED BY TEST AGGREGATE

Inter-comparison of Means of White Women of Institutional Groups in Terms of the Ratio of the Difference between the Means to the Standard Deviation of the Difference

	Auburn	Magdalen	Penitentiary	Workhouse	Probation
Bedford	.20	−2.50	−2.09	−.36	−1.44
Auburn		−1.74	−1.60	−.42	−1.13
Magdalen			.02	1.37	.70
Penitentiary				1.25	.61
Workhouse					− .72

Explanation of table: The number in each space gives the value for $\frac{d}{\sigma_d}$ for the two institutional groups designated at the head of the column and to the left of the row, respectively. A minus sign indicates that the value of the constant for the institutional group at the left is smaller than that of the group heading the column.

The *validity* of the distinction has been affected by the reduction in numbers involved in dropping the colored as well as by the reduction in amount of difference.

There still remains, however, a difference which is almost certainly valid between the mental capacity of the Magdalen women and that of the white women sent to Bedford. Apparently it is not the presence of the 16 per cent of colored women in the Bedford group which makes it inferior to the Magdalen group.

There appears also a valid difference, which the presence of the colored women obscured in the previous comparison, between the Penitentiary and the Bedford groups. Elimination of the figures for the colored women from the total for the Penitentiary group raises the mean from 76.72 to 79.07, while the mean for the Bedford group is raised from 75.05 only to 76.00 by the corresponding change. In possible explanation of the superiority, with regard to intelligence, of the white women of the Penitentiary over the white women at Bedford the following points may be noted.

Table 4 in Chapter VI shows that of the women at Bedford there are 62.7 per cent convicted for offenses against chastity and 16.7 per cent for offenses against property, while at the Penitentiary there are only 6.4 per cent convicted for offenses against chastity and 56.4 per cent for offenses against property. In the following chapter it is shown that there is a difference in the mental capacity of the chastity and property offenders which is in favor of the latter. It would seem, then, that the difference in mentality between Bedford and the Penitentiary may simply reflect this difference in proportions of the two types of offenders mentioned above.

On the matter of the variability of the group, when we are considering only the white women of each group, we see from Table 181 that we lose the distinctions which were seen to be present in the other table (Table 178), between the Penitentiary and the Magdalen, and the Penitentiary and the Probation group. When we consider, then, just the white women of these groups, we can see no difference in the degree of variability displayed by each. Reduction in number of cases affects this comparison as well as that of the means.

TABLE 181

MENTAL CAPACITY MEASURED BY TEST AGGREGATE

Inter-comparison of Standard Deviations of White Women in Institutional Groups in Terms of the Ratio of the Difference between the Means to the Standard Deviation of the Difference

	Auburn	Magdalen	Penitentiary	Workhouse	Probation
Bedford	.05	1.69	− .73	− .02	.75
Auburn		.99	− .54	− .05	.45
Magdalen			−1.87	−1.14	−.64
Penitentiary				.52	1.17
Workhouse					.55

Explanation of table: The number in each space gives the value for $\frac{d}{\sigma_d}$ for the two institutional groups designated at the head of the column and to the left of the row, respectively. A minus sign indicates that the value of the constant for the institutional group at the left is smaller than that of the group heading the column.

SUMMARY

We have found only a small relationship between mental capacity and the institution to which the women were committed. Intercomparison of the groups shows that the means run in order of excellence: Magdalen, Probation, Penitentiary, Auburn, Bedford and Workhouse. An effort to prove the validity of these differences shows that they are significant in only four instances, *i.e.,* between Magdalen and Auburn, Magdalen and Bedford, Magdalen and Workhouse, and Workhouse and Probation. Eliminating the colored women, whose mental capacity is markedly inferior to the white, we found that a demonstrably valid distinction no longer appeared between the mental capacity of the Magdalen group and that of the white women at Auburn and at the Workhouse; and between the white women at the Workhouse and those on Probation. The difference remains as almost certainly valid, however, between the Magdalen group and the white women at Bedford, and a difference previously obscured appeared between the white women at Bedford and those at the Penitentiary in favor of the latter. We suggest for this latter distinction the fact that the Bedford group is made up largely of chastity offenders, and the Penitentiary of property offenders, between whom a difference in mental capacity is found to exist. The difference between the mental capacity of the Magdalen and the white women at Bedford, both of which institutions contain a large percentage of chastity offenders (Bedford 62.7 per cent and Magdalen 77.6 per cent), we attribute possibly to the selection privileges possessed by the Magdalen Home. The difference in the amount of variability displayed in the different groups was seen to be significant only between the Penitentiary and the Magdalen, and the Penitentiary and Probation groups. When the colored women are eliminated from the groups there are no distinctions which approach the limits of certain validity.

It must not be forgotten that, while the presence of the colored women explains many of these distinctions between groups, they are themselves intrinsic parts of the groups in which they are present and must not be thought of as extraneous when the comparison is between institutional groups *per se*.

The main outcome of our comparison of institutional groups is the indication that the similarity of the various groups, as regards both mental level and variability, is more striking than their differences. This similarity of the groups has an important bearing on the general significance of the figures on the mentality of the total group. We have noted, in Chapter II, that our total group does not contain representatives of the women of the different types of institutions in the proportions in which they actually occur in the total delinquent population. Certain groups within our total accordingly exercise an undue weight on the general result. This can not, however, appreciably distort the results as to mentality, when the inter-institutional differences are no greater than we find them.

COMPARISON OF OUR DELINQUENT GROUPS WITH OTHERS

Turning now to a comparison of our delinquent women with other groups of delinquent adults, we shall consider such groups as we have been able to discover of either men or women, which are comparable in type with the delinquent groups which we have studied and which have been examined by the same test methods.

(a) *Bedford and Albion Reformatories*

In one of the publications of the Bureau of Analysis and Investigations[11] there is contained a brief report by J. L. Herrick on the testing of 194 inmates at the Western House of Refuge at Albion, New York. These women range in age from sixteen to forty years and are directly comparable with our Bedford women, as the Western House of Refuge handles the same types of cases from the western part of New York State that Bedford does for the eastern. The Stanford-Binet was given among other tests and Dr. Herrick prints a table of frequencies by mental ages in years. (For corrsponding data on Bedford group, see Table 167.) Chart XXVII presents graphically the distributions of 343 Bedford cases and 194 cases from the Albion Reformatory.

It will be seen that the groups suggest each other in general outline, the spread of the distribution being very similar, with a standard

[11] Herrick, J. L. "Mental Examinations." P. 7, Eugenics and Social Welfare Bulletin, No. XI. Publication of the Bureau of Analysis and Investigation. 1917.

TABLE 182

Comparison of the Means and Standard Deviations of the Mental Capacity Measured by Stanford-Binet Mental Age between Bedford Women and Women from the Western House of Refuge at Albion

	Bedford Women	Albion Women	Difference	$\frac{d}{\sigma_d}$	Chances that real difference does not exist are 1 in:
Mean σ_m	11.11 ±.136	11.60 ±.155	−.49	2.39	119
σ σ_σ	2.2 ±.10	2.16 ±.110	.04	.260	3
Cases	261	194			

deviation of 2.20±.096 for one as against 2.16±.110 for the other. There is a difference of almost half a year in the central tendency, 11.60±.155 as against 11.11±.136, and this difference is in favor of the Albion women. Table 182 shows the degree of validity that may

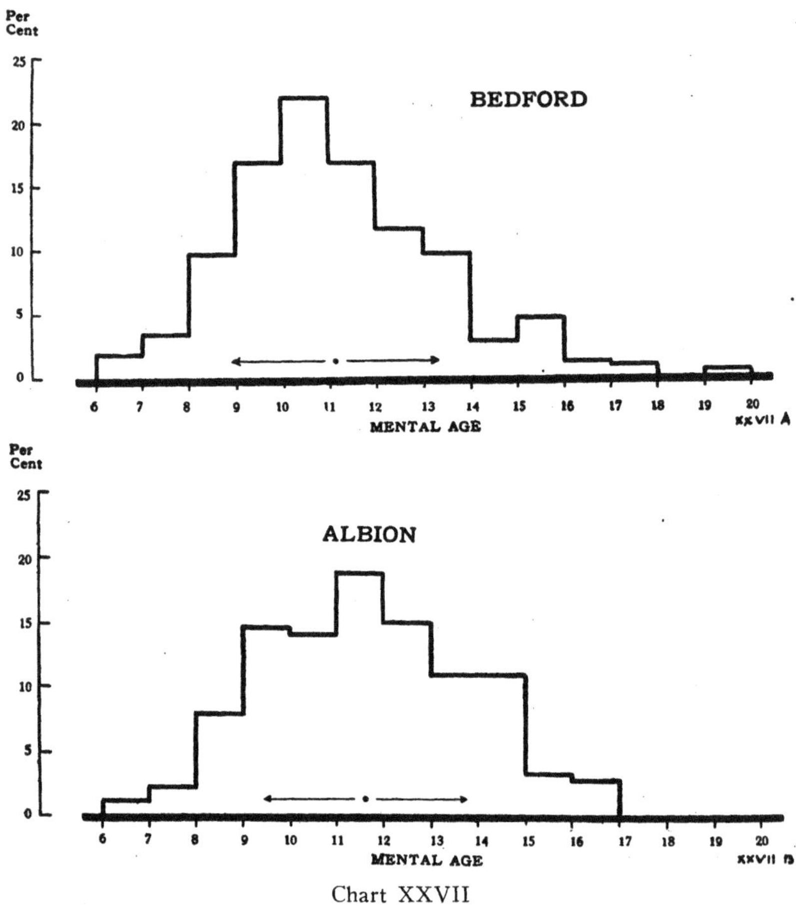

Chart XXVII

Mental Capacity as Measured by Stanford-Binet

Percentage comparison between Bedford Reformatory women and Albion Reformatory women—English-speaking cases only.

be attached to these differences. It is evident that the slight amount of difference between the two standard deviations can be accounted for in terms of chance, but that the half year's difference between the means is almost certainly of valid significance. We can say, therefore, that while these groups of women at Bedford and Albion cover about the same range of variability in their mental capacity as shown by this scale, the Albion women are on the average slightly superior. It is of interest to note, however, that Bedford has a slight representation higher on the scale than the Albion group extends.

(b) *Bedford Reformatory and Chicago House of Correction*

The work by Dr. Kohs[12] at the Chicago House of Correction may also be compared with the Bedford group. The study was made of 335 boys from 17 to 21 years of age, the testing being done with the Goddard modification of the Binet-Simon scale. We had earlier

TABLE 183

MENTAL CAPACITY AS MEASURED BY BINET-SIMON (GODDARD REVISION)

Per Cent Distribution of Bedford Women and of Men at the Chicago House of Correction (Chicago), with Constants

	Mental Age							Number of cases	Mean	σ
	6—	7—	8—	9—	10—	11—	12—			
Bedford Women.....	..	1.0	5.0	28.0	38.0	28.0	..	100	10.32 ±.091	.91 ±.065
House of Correction Men (Chicago)......	.6	.6	5.4	20.0	31.6	35.2	6.6	335	10.58 ±.059	1.08 ±.042

in our work at the Laboratory used this scale on a group of 100 Bedford cases whose results we can, therefore, compare with those of Dr. Kohs' group. Table 183 presents the data on these two groups for comparison. A point of difference in method enters in, in that Dr. Kohs had added to the Goddard scale tests XV[2] and XV[4] from the original Binet scale to compensate for any accidental variations, while our figures represent the Goddard scale unmodified. This gives the Chicago group a slight advantage over ours. From a comparison of the constants it is seen that there is a small but, as Table 184 shows, an almost certainly significant difference be-

[12] Kohs, Samuel C. "The Practicability of the Binet Scale and the Question of the Borderline Case." Bulletin No. 3, Psychopathic Department Series No. 2. Publications of the Research Department, Chicago House of Correction, 1915.

TABLE 184

Comparison of the Means and Standard Deviations of Mental Capacity Measured by Binet Mental Ages (Goddard) between Bedford Women and Men at Chicago House of Correction

	Bedford Women	Chicago House of Correction Men	Difference	$\frac{d}{\sigma_d}$	Chances that real difference does not exist are 1 in:
Mean	10.32	10.58	−.26	2.43	133
σ_m	±.091	±.059			
σ	.91	1.08	−.17	2.15	63
σ_σ	±.065	±.042			
Cases	100	335			

tween the means and standards deviations of these two groups. Considering the slight advantage which accrues to the Chicago group as a result of the difference in procedure of testing, we should not feel justified, however, in stressing so slight a difference. We should, therefore, feel safe in saying that, measured by the Goddard modification of the Binet-Simon scale, our Bedford group appears no better and probably not appreciably worse than the men tested by Dr. Kohs at the Chicago House of Correction.

(c) *Auburn Women and Auburn Men*

For purposes of comparison with the group of Auburn women, we are relying mainly on data obtained by Dr. Frank L. Heacox on a group of men at Auburn Prison. We are indebted to him for the advance use of data on 473 men tested by the Yerkes-Bridges Point Scale and 100 men tested by the Stanford-Binet. Chart XXVIII shows the distribution, in terms of points on the Yerkes-Bridges Point Scale, of our 44 English-speaking Auburn women in comparison with that of 473 consecutive admissions (with minor exceptions), of English-speaking men in the men's prison at Auburn. The marked irregularity of the curve for the Auburn women is explicable on the ground of the small number of cases. Aside from this difference between the curves there is no important difference in general outline. The crude mode falls in the same interval, and the direction of skewness is the same, although the range of the men's scores is slightly greater in both directions. The means are practically identical,

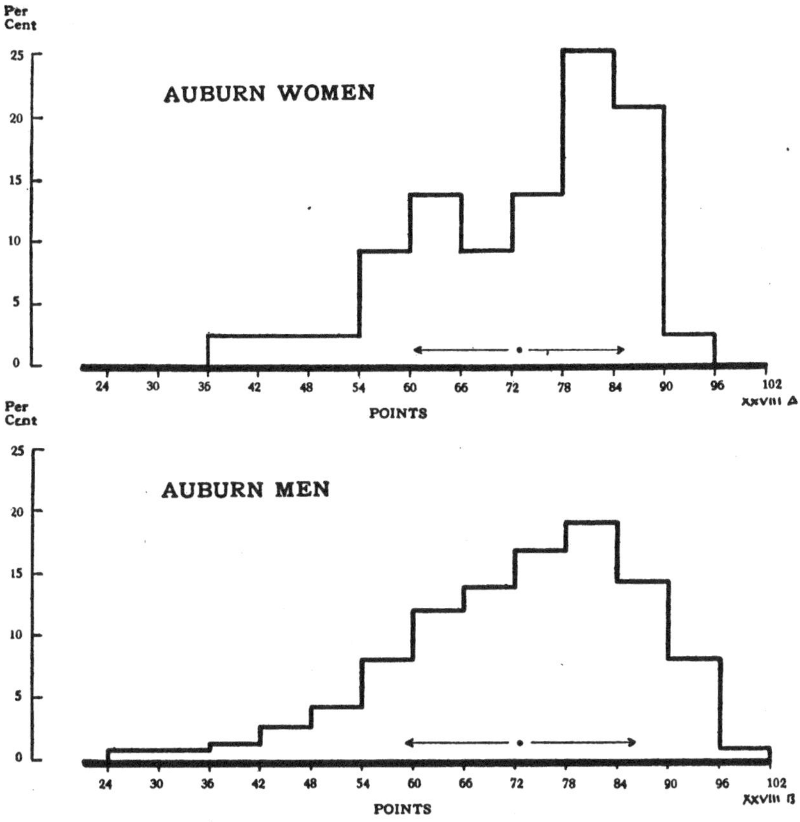

Chart XXVIII

Mental Capacity as Measured by Yerkes-Bridges Point Scale

Percentage comparison between Auburn women and Auburn men—English-speaking cases only.

TABLE 185

Comparison of the Means and Standard Deviations of Mental Capacity Measured by Yerkes-Bridges Point Scale between Women at Auburn Prison and Men at Auburn Prison

	Auburn Women	Auburn Men	Difference	$\frac{d}{\sigma_d}$	Chances that real difference does not exist are 1 in :
Mean (Points).....	72.73	72.66	.07	.03	2
σ_m...............	±1.88	±.622			
σ..................	12.45	13.53	−1.08	.80	4
σ_σ.................	±1.28	±.440			
Cases.............	44	473			

72.73±1.87 as against 72.66±.622. Table 185 shows that this infinitesimal difference is insignificant, the chances being 1 in 2 that as much difference could occure by pure chance. The divergence

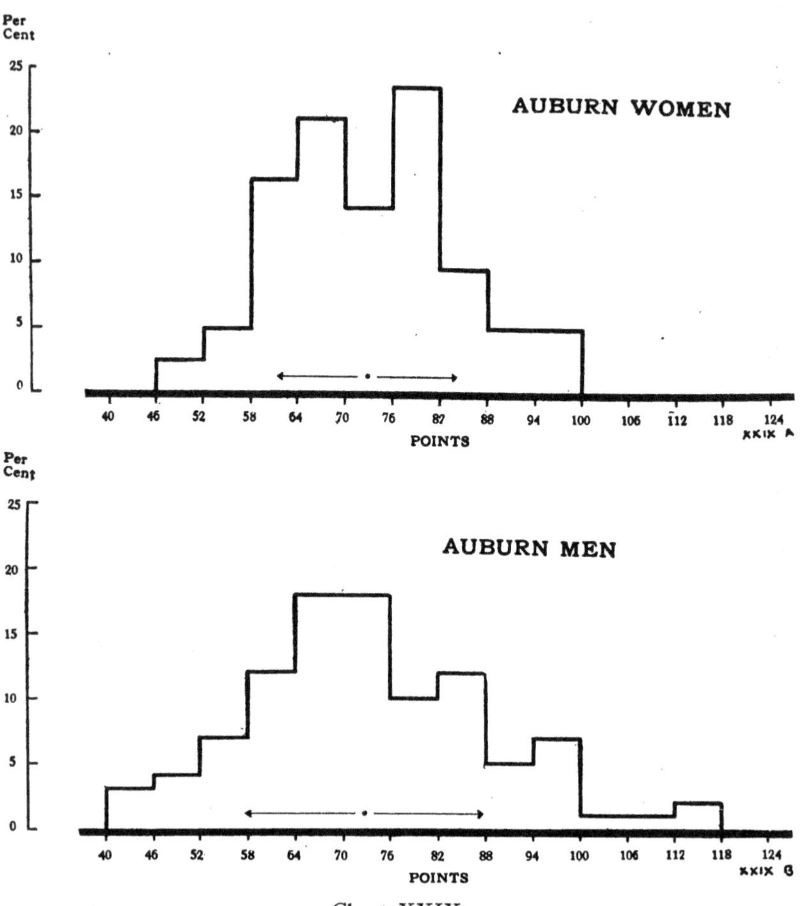

Chart XXIX

Mental Capacity as Measured by Stanford-Binet

Percentage comparison between Auburn women and Auburn men—English-speaking cases only.

between the standard deviations, *i.e.,* between 13.53±.440 and 12.45±1.280, might be expected to occur through sampling 1 time in 4.

Comparison of the same group of Auburn women with a group of 100 Auburn men, both measured by the Stanford-Binet intelligence quotient, is presented graphically in Chart XXIX. Intelligence quotient rather than mental age has been used, since we have given the former measure the preference, except where it has been necessary to use mental age for comparison with other data. Referring to Chart XXIX we note that the greater range of variability in the group of Auburn men is more evident here than in the comparison on the Yerkes-Bridges Scale.

Especially is this noticeable at the superior end, which extends for three intervals beyond anything which we obtained in our group. It is only fair to recall here that three of the apparently brightest and best educated women in our Auburn group refused to be examined and that this perhaps helps to explain our lack of representation at this end. Whatever the explanation, it is evident that our group, as it stands, forms a more compact unit than that of the men. Table 186 shows that while there is no difference demonstrable between the means, there is an almost certain difference between the respective degrees of variability shown in the two groups

TABLE 186

Comparison of the Means and Standard Deviations of Mental Capacity Measured by Stanford-Binet I. Q. between Women at Auburn Prison and Men at Auburn Prison

	Auburn Women	Auburn Men	Difference	$\frac{d}{\sigma_d}$	Chances that real difference does not exist are 1 in:
Mean σ_m	72.73 ±1.709	72.70 ±1.506	.03	.02	2
σ σ_σ	11.21 ±.736	15.06 ±1.076	−3.85	2.95	625
Cases	43	100			

We had hoped to make some comparison of our data on this group with the results obtained by Dr. Glueck in his work at Sing Sing,[13] but, although he states that he has employed both the Yerkes-Bridges and the Stanford-Binet scales, he gives no figures showing distributions. He diagnoses as defective 98 of his native-born cases and says that while he bases this diagnosis on their previous history and present reactions as well as on the laboratory findings, none of them possessed a degree of intelligence beyond that of the average

[13] *Op. cit.*

twelve-year-old American child. We regret also that we can not make a comparison between our results on this group and the testing of 330 inmates of the Massachusetts State Prison which was made by Rossy [14] in 1917. He has used the Yerkes-Bridges Point Scale as a

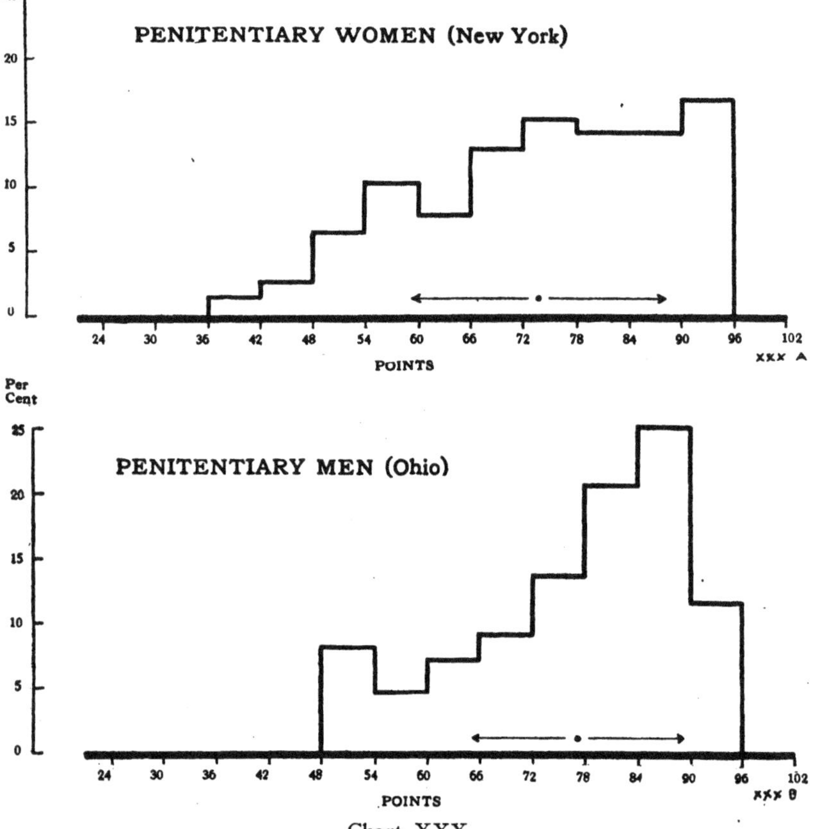

Chart XXX

Mental Capacity as Measured by Yerkes-Bridges Point Scale

Percentage comparison between New York Penitentiary women and Ohio State Penitentiary men—English-speaking cases only.

measure and prints his frequencies so that comparison would have been simple were it not for the fact that he has used the mental age

[14] Rossy, C. S. "Report of the First Three Hundred Cases Examined at the Massachusetts State Prison." Bulletin No. 17 of the Mass. State Board of Insanity. Jan., 1916.

TABLE 187

Comparison of the Means and Standard Deviations of Mental Capacity Measured by Yerkes-Bridges Point Scale between New York Penitentiary Women and Ohio State Penitentiary Men

	New York Penitentiary Women	Ohio Penitentiary Men	Difference	$\frac{d}{\sigma_d}$	Chances that real difference does not exist are 1 in:
Mean (Points).....	73.64	77.10	−3.46	1.67	21
σ_m...............	±1.63	±1.29			
σ..........	14.48	12.01	2.47	2.08	53
σ_σ................	±.908	±.761			
Cases.............	79	87			

as a measure without stating from which one of Yerkes' curves he has derived these ages.

(d) *New York Penitentiary Women and Ohio Penitentiary Men*

For purposes of comparison with our Penitentiary group, we have relied mainly on the study by Dr. Haines, who tested 100 consecutive admissions to the Ohio State Penitentiary by the Yerkes-Bridges Point Scale.[15] Of these only 87 are included in the data given, as 13 were too foreign to make such examination reliable. Chart XXX shows the curve for this group in comparison with that for our group of Penitentiary women. The most striking difference between the two curves is in respect to the degree of concentration of cases about any given point. Our Penitentiary group shows an approximate evenness of distribution over quite a wide range, whereas Haines' group shows a sharp concentration about a mode in the upper portion of the scale. The range of our group is wider than that of the other, by virtue of the fact that it extends lower in the intelligence scale. Although there appears to be a slight difference between the means in favor of Haines' group, reference to Table 187 shows that this difference is probably to be accounted for by sampling. As regards the amount of variability, however, there is an almost certain degree of difference in the direction of the greater variability of our group.

[15] Haines, Thomas H. "Feeble-mindedness Among Adult Delinquents." *Jour. of Criminal Law and Criminology.* 1917. Vol. 7, No. 5.

TABLE 188

Comparison of the Means and Standard Deviations of Mental Capacity Measured by Yerkes-Bridges Point Scale between New York Workhouse Women and Columbus (Ohio) Workhouse Men

	New York Workhouse Women	Columbus Workhouse Men	Difference	$\frac{d}{\sigma_d}$	Chances that real difference does not exist are 1 in:
Mean (Points)	66.61	71.88	−5.27	2.35	106
σ_m	±1.71	±1.46			
σ	14.78	14.57	.21	.155	2
σ_σ	±.972	±.901			
Cases	75	100			

The work done at the Joliet Penitentiary by Louise E. Ordahl and George Ordahl[16] would seem to furnish data on a similar group, but their method of combining two scales, the Stanford and Kuhlman revisions, make their results impossible of comparison.

(e) *Workhouse Women (New York) and Workhouse Men (Ohio)*

The figures which are available for comparison with our Workhouse group are the results of a study made by R. A. Gilliland on 100 men at the Workhouse at Columbus, Ohio.[17] Their ages varied from 18 to 53; 28 were colored and 72 were white. The cases were chosen by the crimes committed in proportion to their representation in the entire group, the only exception being that more than the correct percentage of vagrancy cases were chosen. Chart XXXI shows the distribution of the scores on the Yerkes-Bridges Point Scale, by which they were tested, and, for comparison, the distribution of scores made on this scale by our group of Workhouse women.

Inspection of the curves shows a certain similarity as regards the spread of the curves, but a greater concentration of cases in the upper end of the Ohio group. From Table 188 we see that there exists an almost certainly valid difference between the central tenden-

[16] Ordahl, Louise E. and Ordahl, George. "A Study of 49 Female Convicts." *Journal of Delinquency.* 1917. Vol. II, No. 6, pp. 331-351.

[17] Gilliland, R. A. "The Mental Ability of 100 Inmates of the Columbus (O.) Workhouse." *Journal of Criminal Law and Criminology.* Vol. 7, No. 6, March, 1917.

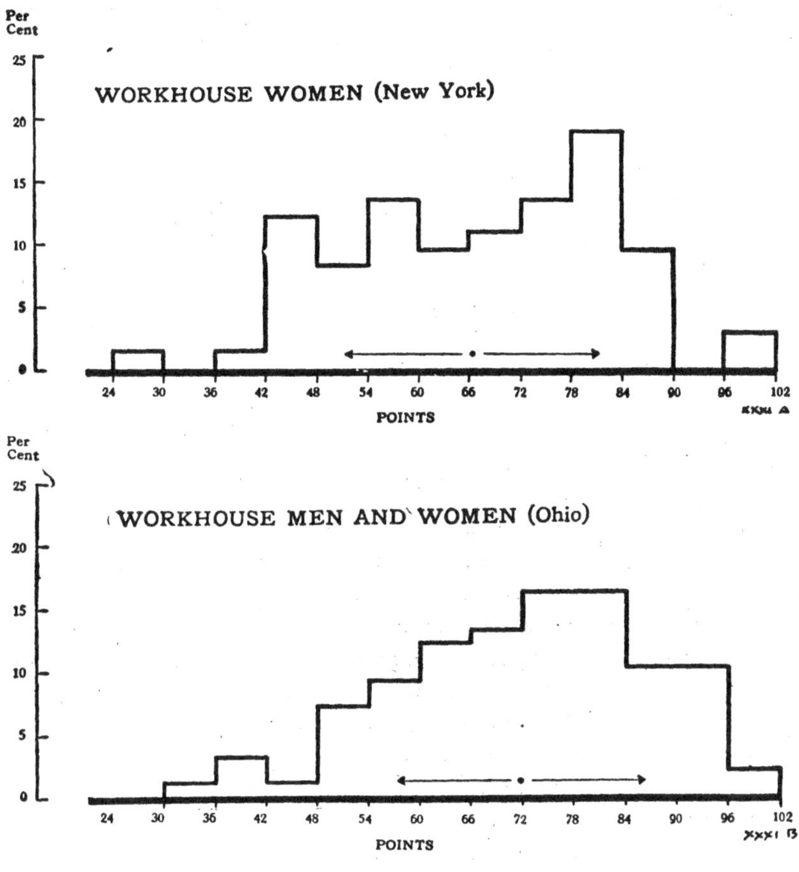

Chart XXXI

Mental Capacity as Measured by Yerkes-Bridges Point Scale

Percentage comparison between New York Workhouse women and Ohio Workhouse group composed of men and women—English-speaking cases only.

cies of the two curves, with the New York group inferior to the other, but that, as regards the degree of variability shown, no difference can be demonstrated which is not explicable by sampling.

Summary

Summarizing these results, we can see, then, that if we assume as adequate measures of intellectual capacity the various scales that have been used, we can make the following statements:

The Bedford women, as compared with those in a similar institution at Albion, differ by a small but almost certainly valid amount as to their averages, but no difference between the amount of variability around the average can be demonstrated for the two groups. Both groups approach symmetry in their distribution.

In comparison of the Bedford women with the group of young men studied by Kohs at the Chicago House of Correction, both the mean and the degree of scatter about the mean are found to be slightly greater for the latter group. This difference appears to be significant though perhaps to be accounted for as a result of the somewhat greater leniency in examination in the case of Kohs group. It seems, therefore, that in comparison with these two other groups of offenders of the reformatory type, our women are not markedly inferior.

When we compare the group of women committed to Auburn Prison with Heacox's study of male inmates of the same place, we see that no difference can be demonstrated in the average of their mental capacity by either of the two measures employed, but that by one of these scales a difference in variability is indicated. It would seem, therefore, that the average mental capacity of the male and female convicts in this institution is not demonstrably different but that the men convicts would appear to exhibit a slightly greater variability than the women, at least as measured by the Stanford Revision.

Regarding the two Penitentiary groups, it appears that Haines' group is less spread out than the New York Penitentiary women and somewhat better on the average, though the validity of the latter distinction is open to question.

The New York Workhouse women seem to be clearly inferior to the men studied by Gilliland in a similar institution. Their average on the Yerkes-Bridges Point Scale is more than five points lower and this difference has been shown to be almost certainly valid. (We may say, moreover, that our mean would undoubtedly have been lower if the women committed to the Workhouse for intoxication had been included in our group. Our sample of 19 such cases shows a mean of 64.52.) The variation in the amount of scatter between these groups is insignificant and easily accounted for by sampling.

Owing to the small amount of material available on delinquent groups other than ours, the scanty information regarding the selective processes operative in determining the make-up of these groups, and the uncertainty as to whether the technique of administration of the tests was in every case comparable with ours, we offer no general interpretation of the above comparisons. One negative inference suggested by the material at hand might, however, be noted. In view of the slightness and statistical uncertainty of the majority of the differences observed between our groups and others from similar types of institutions, it would appear that ours are not eccentric to any marked degree.

CHAPTER XV

MENTAL CAPACITY: RELATED TO VARIOUS FACTORS WHICH AFFECT THE DELINQUENT GROUP

IN the following discussion we shall limit ourselves to comparisons made possible by our own data on the women of the six delinquent groups studied. We shall consider especially the relationship of mental capacity, as measured by the showing in certain tests, to the main social factors in the records of these women.

MENTAL CAPACITY IN RELATION TO CRIMINAL CAREER

(a) *Mental Capacity and Nature of Offense*

The contention is frequently heard that certain types of offenders are mentally superior to those guilty of other kinds of delinquencies. It is possible to obtain some information with regard to the accuracy of this contention, at least as it applies to women delinquents, through the mechanism of correlation. In Table 189 we have used as a quantitative variable the mental capacity measured by Test Aggregate and as a qualitative classification that employed by the New York City Police Department (see Chapter VI, p. 85). The correlation ratio which this table yields is .23±.049, which would seem to indicate that there probably exists a small but significant degree of association between the intellectual capacity of a woman and the kind of crime, classified in this way, that she commits. The means run, in order of excellence,—Offenses against Property Rights, against Regulations for Public Health, against Chastity, against the Family, General Criminality, Offenses against the Person, and Offenses against Administration of Government. The numbers in some of the groups are, of course, too few to make the means significant.

If we consider, however, the two classes of offenses for which we have a reasonable number of cases, those against property and those against chastity, we obtain the curves figured in Chart XXXII. The central tendency of the property offenders is noticeably higher than that of the chastity offenders, 78.48±.993 as over against 75.52±.619, but

TABLE 189

Correlation between Mental Capacity Measured by Test Aggregate and Nature of Present Offense Classified by New York City Police Department Classification

English-speaking Cases Only

	Test Aggregate																									Totals	Means (Test Aggregate)
	47–49	49–51	51–53	53–55	55–57	57–59	59–61	61–63	63–65	65–67	67–69	69–71	71–73	73–75	75–77	77–79	79–81	81–83	83–85	85–87	87–89	89–91	91–93	93–95	95–97		
Offenses against the Person........			1		1			1	1		3			1	2		1		1	1						13	69.4
Offenses against Chastity..........	1				5	3	5	6	7	2	13	16	17	17	16	13	20	21	14	13	6	8	3	1	2	209	75.5
Offenses against the Family........							1	1		2			1		1		2					1				9	71.6
Offenses against Regulations for Public Health................		1			1		1	1	3	3	2	1	5	2	3	5	3	1	3		4	3		2		44	75.3
Offenses against Administration of Government.................											1	1														2	67.9
Offenses against Property Rights...						1	3	1	2		4	8	7	2	7	9	4	5	7	6	5	8	2	1	3	85	78.5
General Criminality...............						1				3	1	2	3		1		1				1					13	70.6
Totals..................	1	1	1	0	7	5	10	10	13	10	24	28	33	22	30	27	31	27	25	20	16	20	5	4	5	375	75.66

Test Aggregate: Mean = 75.66 σ = 9.39
Correlation ratio: η = .23 ± .049

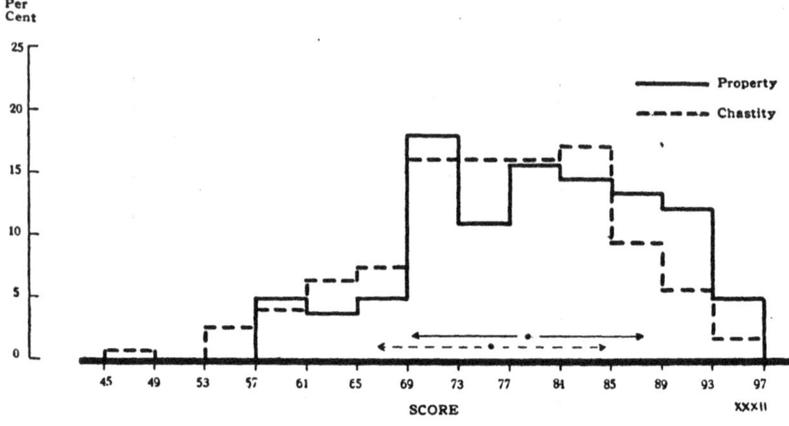

Chart XXXII

Mental Capacity as Measured by Test Aggregate

Percentage comparison between offenders against property and offenders against chastity. English-speaking cases only.

the amount of variability displayed is not greatly different for the two groups, 9.15±.584 for the property offenders and 8.95±.442 for the chastity offenders. It might seem to be of interest to note that the scores of the offenders against chastity follow more closely the lines of the normal curve while the curve of property offenders tends to be

TABLE 190

OFFENDERS AGAINST PROPERTY AND OFFENDERS AGAINST CHASTITY

Comparison of the Means and Standard Deviations of Mental Capacity, as Measured by Test Aggregate, of Offenders against Property and Offenders against Chastity

Total Group. English-speaking Cases Only

	Offenders against Property	Offenders against Chastity	Difference	$\frac{d}{\sigma_d}$	Chances that real difference does not exist are 1 in:
Mean............ σ_m...............	78.48 ±.993	75.52 ±.619	2.96	2.53	175
σ............... σ_σ...............	9.15 ±.584	8.95 ±.422	.20	.28	3
Cases............	85	209			

bimodal, but the cases of the latter are probably too few to make this significant. From Table 190, it appears that this observed superiority of the offenders against property may be regarded as almost certainly significant. For the slight difference which exists in the standard deviations, however, no valid significance can be demonstrated.

We have next taken the entire group and instead of using this six-fold division have classified their offenses simply as misdemeanors and felonies. The two groups thus obtained are distributed, as to mental capacity, as shown in Chart XXXIII. Although there is a noticeable

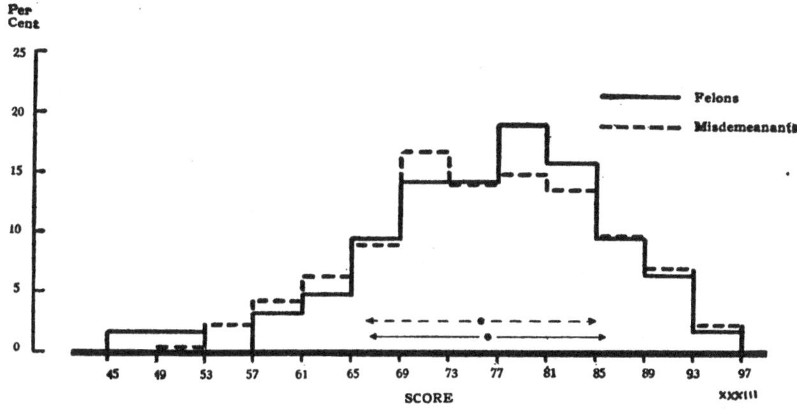

Chart XXXIII

Mental Capacity as Measured by Test Aggregate

Percentage comparison between felons and misdemeanants. English-speaking cases only.

difference between the crude modes of these two groups, in favor of the felons, the actual difference in the means is slight. We see by Table 191 that this difference of .46 in favor of the felons, taken in connection with its standard deviation is too small to be demonstrated as valid and that the slight difference in the degree of variability can also be accounted for by sampling. There would seem to be, then, no demonstrable difference between the means and the standard deviations of those women guilty of felonies and those convicted of misdemeanors.

An effort to compare our results with Goring's with reference to nature of offense was quite abortive, due to the extreme difference in classification.

(b) *Mental Capacity and Extent of Criminal Record*

As described in Chapter VI, we have used as a measure of an individual's criminal record; first, the number of previous convictions and, second, the number of months incarcerated. The relationship between mental capacity and the former measure is shown in Table 192. The correlation coefficient is negligible in size (—.05±.052) and would indicate absence of any correlation between these two factors. The correlation ratios (.18±.05C and .14±.050) suggest the existence of at most a small degree of relationship between the mental capacity of a woman and the number of times she has been convicted. Examining the scatter table and noticing the lack of a regular trend in the line of means, however, we become dubious of the existence of even the small relationship suggested, although there is a faint indication of a tendency toward lower mentality with increase in number of convictions.

It is evident at once that the ages of the women in question would have to be taken account of here. A partial correlation with age constant, however, gave a coefficient practically identical with the former coefficient, –.053 as against –.054. We might, therefore, assume that the matter of age is not a contributing factor in this relationship.

If we next consider the relation of intellectual capacity as shown by Test Aggregate to the period of time spent in penal institutions,

TABLE 191

FELONS AND MISDEMEANANTS ON PRESENT CONVICTION

Comparison of the Means and Standard Deviations of Mental Capacity, as Measured by Test Aggregate, of those Classified as Felons and Misdemeanants on Present Conviction

English-speaking Cases Only

	Felons	Misdemeanants	Difference	$\frac{d}{\sigma_d}$	Chances that real difference does not exist are 1 in:
Mean	76.1	75.57	.53	.40	3
σ_m	±1.20	±.531			
σ	9.57	9.36	.21	.20	2
σ_σ	±.958	±.323			
Cases	64	311			

TABLE 192

Correlation between Mental Capacity Measured by Test Aggregate and Number of Previous Convictions

English-speaking Cases Only

Number of Previous Convictions	Test Aggregate: 47 to 49	49 to 51	51 to 53	53 to 55	55 to 57	57 to 59	59 to 61	61 to 63	63 to 65	65 to 67	67 to 69	69 to 71	71 to 73	73 to 75	75 to 77	77 to 79	79 to 81	81 to 83	83 to 85	85 to 87	87 to 89	89 to 91	91 to 93	93 to 95	95 to 97	Totals	Means (Test Aggregate)
20																					1					1	
19																										0	
18										1		1														2	
17																										0	
16																										0	
15																										0	
14									1																	1	75.1
13																										0	
12																	1									1	
11														1		1										2	
10													1			2										3	
9												1				1				1						3	
8											1	1		1												3	
7											1		1				2			1		1				6	73.9
6							1			1		2	1		1						1					7	
5			1		2			1	1	1		2		1		1	1	1			1					13	68.5
4	1	1					1				2		1	1	2	1	1	5		1	1	1	2			21	75.8
3							1	2		2	2		4	1		3	4	2	4	2		3	2	2		34	78.3
2						1		3	5	2	1	3	3	5	3	2	4	2	2	2	1	3			1	43	74.5
1					1	2	3	1	2	1	7	7	10	7	9	6	5	8	6	7	5	7		1	2	97	76.6
0					4	2	4	3	4	2	10	11	11	5	15	10	13	9	13	6	6	5	1	1	2	137	75.6
Totals	1	1	1	0	7	5	10	10	13	10	24	28	32	22	30	27	31	27	25	20	16	20	5	4	5	374	75.67
Means (Number previous convictions)	1.9						1.7		3.1		2.1		1.9		1.7		1.8		1.3		2.1		1.8			1.88	

Test aggregate · Mean = 75.67 $\sigma = 9.41$
Number of previous convictions Mean = 1.88 $\sigma = 2.75$
Coefficient of correlation. $r = -.05 \pm .052$
Correlation ratios: Test aggregate on number of previous convictions, $\eta = .18 \pm .050$ Blakeman's Criterion = 2.5
Number of previous convictions on test aggregate, $\eta = .14 \pm .050$ Blakeman's Criterion = 1.8

we see by Table 193 that here again the coefficient is small and, in consideration of its standard deviation, probably unreliable, .09±.051. Here, as before, we feared that the factor of age might be complicating the relationship, but a partial correlation making age constant brought about no change in the coefficient. The correlation ratios (.16±.050 for Test Aggregate on time served, and .10±.051 for time served on Test Aggregate) can indicate at most only a slight association. Reference to the means (Table 193) shows that whatever correlation exists is positive, that is, that the tendency is toward an association of longer periods of imprisonment with higher levels of mentality.

Regarding this matter of the relation of intelligence to the criminal record, as shown in these two ways, we quote from Goring. It will be remembered that his intelligence scale is a five-fold judgmental one and that his measure of criminal record differs from ours in that he has used as a measure the number of convictions per year of freedom and the number of months imprisoned per year of freedom. (For further explanation see page 104 of this work.)

"With increasing frequency of conviction, the proportion of convicts who are mentally defective progressively increases from 19 per cent to .36 per cent, and their mean intelligence decreases from +.39 to —.27; on the other hand, with increasing periods of imprisonment, the average intelligence of convicts increases from —.08 to +.32—the proportion of the mentally defective correspondingly diminishing from 33.6 per cent to 23.6 per cent. Evidently, the characteristic of the penal records of relatively weak-minded offenders is frequency of conviction to short periods of imprisonment, for trivial offenses; and the distinguishing features of the penal records of the more intelligent recidivists are fewer convictions, but longer sentences, for serious offences." . . .

"Correlation of intelligence with frequency of conviction:

Coefficient r . . .	—.16±.03
Ratio (intelligence upon convictions)	.20

"Correlation of intelligence with time of imprisonment:

Coefficient r . . .	.10±03
Ratio η (intelligence upon imprisonment)	.12

"It will be seen that the correlation coefficient of intelligence with convictions is —.16, which measures the extent to which defective intelligence is associated with frequency of conviction; and that the coefficient of imprisonment with intelligence is +.10, which measures the strength of bond uniting length of imprisonment, or sentence, with good intelligence."[1]

[1] *Op. cit.*, p. 271.

TABLE 193

Correlation between Mental Capacity Measured by Test Aggregate and Number of Months Served in Penal Institutions

English-speaking Cases Only

Number of Months Served	Test Aggregate: 47 to 49	49 to 51	51 to 53	53 to 55	55 to 57	57 to 59	59 to 61	61 to 63	63 to 65	65 to 67	67 to 69	69 to 71	71 to 73	73 to 75	75 to 77	77 to 79	79 to 81	81 to 83	83 to 85	85 to 87	87 to 89	89 to 91	91 to 93	93 to 95	95 to 97	Totals	Means (Test Aggregate)
90 to 96																							1			1	
84 " 90																1			1							2	
78 " 84																					1					1	
72 " 78																										0	
66 " 72																	1									1	
60 " 66																										0	76.4
54 " 60																										0	
48 " 54															1	1										2	
42 " 48													1							1						2	
36 " 42									1	1	1		1	1	1		1									7	
30 " 36											1	1	1			2		1	3		1	1				11	79.2
24 " 30											2	1	1	3	1	1		1	1	1	1	1	1			15	77.9
18 " 24												1	1	2	1	3	2				2			1		13	78.8
12 " 18					1			1	1	1	1	3	3		2	1	2	1	2	1		2				22	74.4
6 " 12	1	1	1		1	2	4	3	2	3	2	5	2	2	1	1	4	5	1	5	1	4	1		1	53	72.8
0 " 6					5	3	6	6	9	5	17	17	22	14	22	17	21	19	17	12	10	12	2	3	4	243	75.9
Totals	1	1	1	0	7	5	10	10	13	10	24	28	32	22	29	27	31	27	25	20	16	20	5	4	5	373	75.67
Means (Number Months Served)	5.0					4.7					6.9					8.1					9.6					7.34	

Test aggregate: Mean = 75.67 $\sigma = 9.42$

Number of months served in penal institutions: Mean = 7.34 $\sigma = 13.69$

Coefficient of correlation: $r = .09 \pm .051$

Correlation ratios: Test aggregate on number of months served in penal institutions, $\eta = .16 \pm .050$ Blakeman's Criterion = 1.9

Number of months served in penal institutions on test aggregate, $\eta = .10 \pm .051$ Blakeman's Criterion = .8

It will be seen that such relationships as we discovered in our groups tended in the same directions as did Goring's—that is, to a negative association between intelligence and frequency of conviction and a positive correlation between intelligence and total length of imprisonment. In view of the slightness of the relationships indicated by our figures, however, we should not feel justified in making so definite a statement on this point as does Goring. We are inclined to feel, in fact, that his verbal formulation leaves the reader with a sense of a more impressive relationship than is justified by the size of his correlation coefficients.

In this connection it should also be noted that our situation is somewhat different from his, in that a long sentence which is the result of a serious offense in the cases studied by Goring may either have the same significance for our group or may result from relatively trivial causes. This is brought about by the fact, first, that we have included, as Goring evidently has not, the time spent in juvenile institutions where the sentence is generally for the period of the subject's minority; second, that at least three of the institutions studied receive cases on indeterminate sentence, which means that, of two women brought in for the same offense, one might get 20 days in the Workhouse, and the other three years at Bedford, dependent on whether or not she was considered a "reformatory type." In view of the attendant ambiguity in this measurement, we have not regarded the number of months served as a very satisfactory measure of a woman's criminal record.

If we next consider the mental capacity of the women who were first offenders and those who may be classed as recidivists, we obtain the curve shown in Chart XXXIV. It is evident that in general form the two present a similar distribution. The means are almost identical, $75.64 \pm .765$ as against $75.68 \pm .627$. Table 194 shows that from these figures we can not demonstrate the existence of a difference, the chances being even that such difference could occur by chance. On the matter of variability, it can be seen that the standard deviation of the recidivists is slightly greater than that of the first offenders but this difference is not large, and according to Table 194 its validity is not established. We are, then, unable to demonstrate that there exists any difference, other than might be accounted for by sampling, in either average mental capacity or variability between those women delinquents who are now convicted for the first time and those who have received two or more convictions. It would seem, therefore, that the two classes represent relatively similar groups.

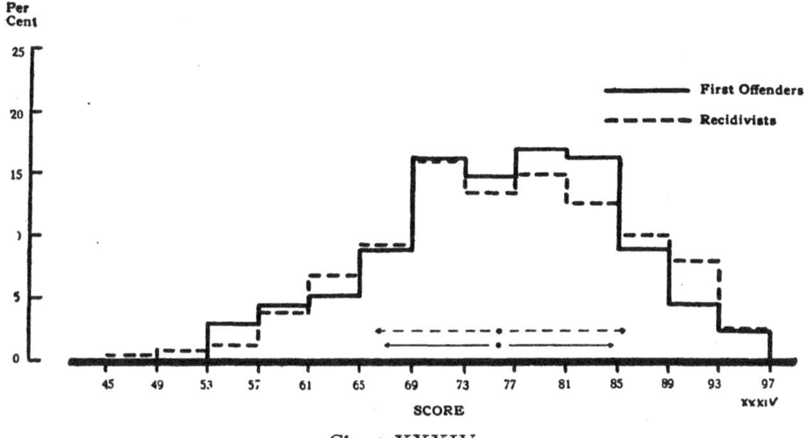

Chart XXXIV

Mental Capacity as Measured by Test Aggregate

Percentage comparison between first offenders and recidivists. English-speaking cases only.

There is nothing in our data to support the assertion of Anderson's[2] that "there is a high correlation between the frequency of offense and the mental condition of these individuals; 39.3 per cent of first offenders, 47.2 per cent of second offenders and 84.2 per cent of recidivists were suffering from severe mental handicaps." Our definition of

TABLE 194

FIRST OFFENDERS AND RECIDIVISTS

Comparison of the Means and Standard Deviations of Mental Capacity, as Measured by Test Aggregate, of First Offenders and Recidivists

English-speaking Cases Only

	First Offenders	Recidivists	Difference	$\frac{d}{\sigma_d}$	Chances that real difference does not exist are 1 in:
Mean	75.64	75.68	−.04	.042	2
σ_m	±.765	±.627			
σ	8.96	9.66	−.70	1.10	7
σ_σ	±.493	±.402			
Cases	137	237			

[2] Anderson, V. V. "The Immoral Woman." *Journal of Criminal Law and Criminology,* Vol. 8, No. 6. March, 1918. p. 910.

recidivist differs from his, since he defines a recidivist as one who has had at least two previous convictions. Moreover, he apparently includes in this percentage of those having serious mental handicaps a small number of psychopathic cases in addition to those mentally inferior. Even making all such allowances, our results would, however, appear to be quite at variance with his.

(*c*) *Mental Capacity and Factors Connected with Beginnings of Criminal Career*

The relationship between the mental capacity of these women and the ages at which they were first convicted is of interest since the common view is to the effect that individuals with inferior mentality are more likely to be led into delinquency at an early age, and, further, are less skilful in evading detection than are their more intelligent associates. Reference to Table 195, which presents these factors in relationship to each other, reveals at once the absence of any readily discernible trend of association between the two variables for the women delinquents whom we have studied. The scatter over all parts of the table is marked, which is reflected in the negligible correlation coefficient of $-.07 \pm .052$. Even a closer analysis of the table fails to discover any significant trends of relationship. The correlation ratio of test aggregate on age at first conviction ($.08 \pm .052$) shows no appreciable increase over the correlation coefficient, making it apparent that our data afford no grounds for inferring the level of mentality of a woman offender from a knowledge of her age when first convicted. Can we nevertheless discover any consistent variations in age at first conviction with varying levels of mentality? At first consideration of the value of the ratio ($.21 \pm .050$) we might hope to find a relationship of some significance even though small, but reference to the irregularity of the line of means indicated by the values on the lowest row of the table shows that it is impossible even to state the direction of the association—*i.e.*, whether the more intelligent women tend to be convicted at an earlier or at a later age than do the less intelligent.

It is doubtless unnecessary to point out that failure to discover evidence of an association between these factors from our data does not prove absence of any such relationship. It may well be obscured by the presence of other factors, such, for example, as difference in social and economic backgrounds, local differences in closeness of police supervision, and other equally important conditions. Unfortunately our

TABLE 195

Correlation between Mental Capacity Measured by Test Aggregate and Age at First Conviction

English-speaking Cases Only

Age at First Conviction	Test Aggregate 47–49	49–51	51–53	53–55	55–57	57–59	59–61	61–63	63–65	65–67	67–69	69–71	71–73	73–75	75–77	77–79	79–81	81–83	83–85	85–87	87–89	89–91	91–93	93–95	95–97	Totals	Means (Test Aggregate)
61–63 Years								1																		1	
59–61 "																										0	
57–59 "											1			1												2	
55–57 "																										0	
53–55 "																										0	
51–53 "													1													1	76.0
49–51 "															2						1				1	4	
47–49 "								1				1														2	
45–47 "																		1			1					2	
43–45 "																	1						1			2	
41–43 "	1						2						3		1				1	1						9	75.1
39–41 "											1	1				1	2				1				1	7	
37–39 "								1	1				1			1			1					1		6	
35–37 "									1		1	3	3		1		1									10	73.8
33–35 "					1		1	1		1	1		2	2	1	1			2	1		2		1		17	
31–33 "						1	1		1			1	1		1	1	1	3	1			1				13	
29–31 "												1	1	2		2	1		1	1	1	3				13	76.1
27–29 "						1	1	1	3	1	2	1	1	2	1	1	2	3	2			1	1	1		25	
25–27 "					2						4	2		1	2	1	3	1	2	3		3		1	1	26	
23–25 "					1		2	1	2	2	4	4			6	3	3	1	4	3	2	4			1	43	76.1
21–23 "					2	1	1		2	1	2	2	7	1	3	4	3	3	2	3	2	2	1			42	
19–21 "						2		1	2	1	1	6	5	8	1	2	2	5	4	1	2	3				46	
17–19 "		1					2	2		2	3	4	4	3	4	4	4	5	4	4	3		1		1	51	75.5
15–17 "			1		1				1		4	2	1	2	3	1	5	4	1	3	2					31	
13–15 "										1	1		2		1	2	1	1				1				10	
11–13 "															1	1	1									3	
9–11 "																1										1	77.0
7– 9 "																							1			1	
Totals	1	1	1	0	7	5	10	9	13	9	25	28	32	22	28	26	30	27	25	20	15	20	5	4	5	368	75.668
Means (Age at first conviction)	24.1					26.7		28.0		23.6		25.4		24.0		22.8		23.2		23.7		24.7		31.2		24.46	

Test aggregate: Mean = 75.67 σ = 9.43
Age at first conviction: Mean = 24.46 σ = 8.30
Coefficient of correlation: r = —.07 ± .052
Correlation ratios: Age at first conviction on test aggregate, η = .21 ± .050 Blakeman's Criterion = 2.8
Test aggregate on age at first conviction, η = .08 ± .052 Blakeman's Criterion = .18

numbers are not large enough to make possible any control of these external factors by selecting for consideration only the more homogeneous portions of our group. The most that we can state, therefore, is the fact that the relationship within our group is, at least, not a sufficiently dominant influence to stand out as appreciable in amount in face of the other factors operative.

The situation is evidently different in the group of men convicts studied by Goring.[3] He states that he finds a coefficient of .34 for the correlation between mental grade and age at first conviction, which he speaks of as "a relatively high degree of association between defective intelligence and conviction at an early age." Later he says, "We conclude that undoubtedly the principal factor conducing to the early first conviction of convicts is defective intelligence."

The relationship between the mental capacity of an individual and the nature of the first offense is shown in Table 196. In comparing this table with Table 189, which shows a similar correlation of mental capacity with the nature of the present offense, it should be remembered that many individuals fall inevitably into identical groups in the two tables, since the first offense is actually the present offense in over a third of the group. We note, however, that there is a consistent cutting down of the numbers occurring in each of the first six divisions and an increase in the numbers given in the group of general criminality. This, as was explained on page 94, is easily comprehensible when it is understood that under this heading are included all the semi-juvenile offenses such as Disobedient Child, Associating with Vicious and Disorderly Persons, etc.,—the type of offense upon which many of the women who are convicted young are first sentenced. In spite of the variation in this arrangement, we find here no great change in the amount of association which can be shown to exist between the variables. The correlation ratio between mental capacity and the nature of the first offense is .20 ± .050.

The only group conspicuous as having mentality above the average is that made up of individuals whose first offense was against property. The three groups which fall appreciably below the general average—offenders against the person, against the family, and against the administration of government—are too small to carry any weight.

If we compare the means of each subdivision in the two tables (Table 189 and Table 196) we see that the only change of any size in

[3] Op. cit., p. 282.

TABLE 196

Correlation between Mental Capacity Measured by Test Aggregate and Nature of First Offense, Classified by New York City Police Department Classification

English-speaking Cases Only

	Test Aggregate																									Totals	Means (Test Aggregate)
	47–49	49–51	51–53	53–55	55–57	57–59	59–61	61–63	63–65	65–67	67–69	69–71	71–73	73–75	75–77	77–79	79–81	81–83	83–85	85–87	87–89	89–91	91–93	93–95	95–97		
Offenses against the Person					2			1	1				1	1					1	1						8	68.4
Offenses against Chastity			1		4	4	4	4	4	5	13	11	15	10	13	10	13	17	11	10	4	8	2		2	165	75.2
Offenses against the Family							1			1			1		1		1					1				6	73.0
Offenses against Regulations for Public Health	1				1		1	1		1	2	2	3	1	3	1	3	2	1	1	3	2		2		31	75.9
Offenses against Administration of Government											1															1	67.0
Offenses against Property Rights							1	1	2	1	4	5	3	1	6	6	2	2	6	3	4	7	1	1	3	59	79.2
General Criminlaity		1				1	3	3	6	2	4	10	9	9	7	10	11	6	6	5	4	2	2	1		102	74.9
Totals	1	1	1	0	7	5	10	10	13	10	24	28	32	22	30	27	30	27	25	20	15	20	5	4	5	372	75.62

Test aggregate: Mean = 75.62 $\sigma = 9.41$
Correlation of ratio: $\eta = .20 \pm .050$

the mentality of given groups is in this last division of general criminality.

	Mean Mental Capacity (Test Aggregate): At First Offense	At Present Offense
Offenses against the Person	68.4	69.4
Offenses against Chastity	75.2	75.5
Offenses against Family	73.0	71.6
Offenses against Public Health	75.9	75.3
Offenses against Administration of Government	67.0	67.9
Offenses against Property Rights	79.2	78.5
General Criminality	74.9	70.6

When we consider the group under the more general classification of misdemeanants and felons on first conviction, we find that the difference is slight in amount and not demonstrably certain (see Table 197). Neither is there a demonstrable difference in the variability of the two groups. It will be noted that there is an appreciably smaller proportion of individuals guilty of felonies on first convictions than on later conviction.

TABLE 197

FELONS AND MISDEMEANANTS ON FIRST CONVICTION

Comparison of the Means and Standard Deviations of Mental Capacity, as Measured by Test Aggregate, of Those Classified as Felons and Misdemeanants on First Conviction

English-speaking Cases Only

	Felons	Misde-meanants	Difference	$\frac{d}{\sigma_d}$	Chances that real difference does not exist are 1 in:
Mean............	77.8 ±1.39	75 35 ± 519	2 45	1.63	19
σ......	9.00 ±.868	9 42 ± 334	−.42	.46	3
Cases............	42	330			

If we consider the relation of mental capacity to the question of the disposition of the cases on first conviction, we find a correlation ratio of .20±.050 (Table 198). This would seem to indicate that the relationship, though small, is probably valid. The means run in decreasing order: State Prison, 77.6; Fines, 77.3; Probation, etc., 77.2; Reformatory, 76.9; Juvenile Institutions, 76.8; Penitentiary and Workhouse, 73.1. It will be noticed that the only mean which would seem

TABLE 198

Correlation between Mental Capacity Measured by Test Aggregate and First Sentence

English-speaking Cases Only

First Sentence	Test Aggregate 47–49	49–51	51–53	53–55	55–57	57–59	59–61	61–63	63–65	65–67	67–69	69–71	71–73	73–75	75–77	77–79	79–81	81–83	83–85	85–87	87–89	89–91	91–93	93–95	95–97	Totals	Means (Test Aggregate)
Probation or suspended sentence					2	1	1	3	3	2	8	8	8	8	7	4	6	6	10	6	4	14	1	1	1	104	77.2
Fine	1								1			2	1	1	1			2		1	1	2			1	14	77.3
Juvenile institution											1		1	1	1	3	2						1			10	76.8
Reformatory institution					1	2	3	1		1	7	6	8	6	9	5	11	11	7	6	5	4	1		1	95	76.9
Penitentiary, Workhouse, etc.		1	1		4	2	6	5	9	7	8	11	12	5	10	12	10	8	4	6	5		2	3	2	133	73.1
State's Prison								1				1	2	1	2	3	2		4	1	1					18	77.6
Totals	1	1	1	0	7	5	10	10	13	10	24	28	32	22	30	27	31	27	25	20	16	20	5	4	5	374	75.67

Test aggregate: Mean = 75.67 $\sigma = 9.41$
Correlation ratio: Test aggregate on first sentence, $\eta = .20 \pm .050$

to differ materially from the others is that for the women committed to the Penitentiary and Workhouse. We feel confident that a part, at least, of the explanation for this lies in the tendency of the judges to send to the Workhouse on their first offense colored women who "had they been white" might have been put on probation or otherwise disposed of. It has been shown in Chapter VIII that a much larger percentage of the colored than of the white had been sent to institutions of the Penitentiary and the Workhouse type on their first convictions. Table 201 shows that the mean score which the colored women as a whole are able to make on Test Aggregate is decidedly lower than that of the white, so that it seems logical that an undue percentage of colored in the Workhouse and Penitentiary group might be the reason for the decided drop in this mean as compared with the others.

It is evident that our figures do not agree with those which Goring offers as showing that with progressively more and more severe sentences the mean intelligence of his subjects increases. We print an abbreviation of his table[4] and quote him as follows:

Nature of First Sentence	Intelligence: Means
Less than 3 months	.59
3 months	1.47
6 months	2.35
1 year	...
5 years and over	3.63
Birched	.58
Reformatory school	.64
Birched and school	.30
Fined	.10
Nil	.25
Total	1.38

"It will be observed that the mean intelligence of convicts increases progressively as the sentence, resulting from thir first conviction, for crime becomes progressively more and more severe. Now, in the case of first offenders, a slight sentence presupposes a trivial offense: from which it follows that the more mentally defective a convict may be, the more trivial will his first offense have been. . . . It is evident that the condition most closely related to petty crime, the most fruitful source of nearly all that is meant by the term crime in this country, must be mental defectiveness."

It will be remembered, however, that his supposition that a slight sentence presupposes a proportionately slight offense does not strictly

[4] *Op. cit.*, p. 283.

apply in our case, since with our women the same offense, *e.g.*, soliciting, may result in fines, probation, reformatory, or Workhouse sentence, depending upon the judgment of the court. The only indication of a tendency of our results to support the theory advanced by Goring is that the means for those women sent to state prison on their first offense is slightly higher than any other.

As was shown in Chapter VI, the number of those who have juvenile convictions is very small, only 40 cases out of 587. When these numbers have been pruned still further by the elimination of those

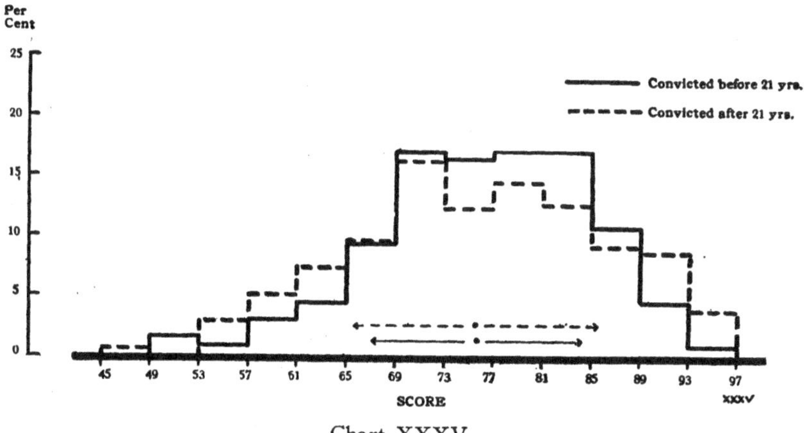

Chart XXXV

Mental Capacity as Measured by Test Aggregate

Percentage comparison between women convicted first before 21 years of age and women convicted first after 21 years of age. English-speaking cases only.

who failed to be represented in all parts of Test Aggregate, the numbers become too small to be suitable for statistical treatment. As a substitute for this we have attempted to group together those cases who were first convicted before 21 years and those whose first conviction came after they were 21. Chart XXXV shows the distribution for the two. It will be seen that the means are practically identical but the scores of those convicted after 21 years tend to scatter more about the mean than those earlier convicted. Table 199 proves that there is in fact no demonstrable difference between the means but that the amount of difference in the standard deviations is almost certainly valid. We may say, therefore, that, if there is a difference in the average mental capacity of those whose first conviction came at an

TABLE 199

FIRST CONVICTED BEFORE 21 YEARS AND FIRST CONVICTED AFTER 21 YEARS OF AGE

Comparison of the Means and Standard Deviations of Mental Capacity, as Measured by Test Aggregate, of those First Convicted before 21 Years and those First Convicted after 21 Years of Age

English-speaking Cases Only

	Convicted before 21	Convicted after 21	Difference	$\frac{d}{\sigma_d}$	Chances that real difference does not exist are 1 in:
Mean	75.70	75.65	.050	.0517	2
σ_m	±.714	±.664			
σ	8.53	9.96	−1.422	2.178	68
σ_σ	±.518	±.397			
Cases	143	225			

early age as compared with those whose first conviction came later in life, 21 years is not the boundary which makes the separation, but that those first convicted late have a greater degree of variability with respect to intelligence.

Summary

Summarizing our findings concerning the relationship between the mental capacity of our group and the main aspects of their criminal records, we note:

(1) That we find a small but probably significant degree of association when the mental capacity of these women as measured by Test Aggregate is related to the nature of the crimes which they commit, classified according to the form employed by the New York City Police Department. The mean of the property offenders is sensibly better than that of offenders against chastity and this difference is demonstrated as almost certainly valid. We can say, then, that the women of this group who have been convicted for offenses against property form a group mentally superior to those convicted for offenses against chastity.

(2) Dividing the total group into misdemeanants and felons we find no demonstrable distinction in mental capacity. If the distinction between felons and misdemeanants can be thought of as roughly representing the seriousness of offenses the indications are that the men-

tal capacity of women offenders varies with the nature of the offense rather than with the degree of the offense. We hesitate to emphasize the point, however, in view of the unsatisfactory nature of the distinction between felonies and misdemeanors. (See Chapter VI.)

(3) Between the mental capacity of these women as measured by Test Aggregate and the extent of their criminal record as measured by the number of previous convictions, we have found only very slight and more or less ambiguous indications of a negative correlation.

Using as a measure of criminal tendency the length of time a woman has been imprisoned, we have again found a small relationship which, as before, is not free from considerable ambiguity. In this case the tendency is toward positive correlation.

In considering both these relationships, we have allowed for the factor of present age and found that it made no appreciable difference in the correlation.

(4) We have found no demonstrable difference between the mental capacity of recidivists and that of those who are first offenders.

(5) No evidence is available from our data to show the existence of an appreciable correlation between mental capacity and age at first conviction.

(6) We found a correlation ratio between intellectual capacity and nature of first offense, arranged according to the New York City Police Department classification, very similar to that found between intellectual capacity and the present offense so classified.

(7) Classifying the first offense as misdemeanors or felonies, we found a slight difference between the two groups in favor of the felons, but a difference not convincingly valid.

(8) A small relationship was found to exist between the mental capacity of the women and the disposition of their case on first offense. We note that the group of women who, on first conviction, were sentenced to the Penitentiary or the Workhouse, is separated from the others by a greater interval than occurs elsewhere. We are inclined to think this may be explained by the large percentage of colored women committed to these institutions, whose mental capacity is found to be inferior to that of the white women.

(9) We have found no demonstrable difference in the average mental capacity of those first convicted before 21 and those first convicted at a later age, but have found that those who were convicted later show a greater variability around their mean than do those whose first conviction was earlier.

MENTAL CAPACITY IN RELATION TO GENERAL FACTORS

There are certain general factors whose relation to mental capacity one feels called upon to consider and which, although not properly associated have, for convenience of handling, been grouped together in Chapter VII and will be so treated here.

(*a*) *Mental Capacity and Age*

We have considered first the matter of age as it relates to intellectual capacity. Table 200 shows the correlation which exists between the two. The coefficient obtained is practically zero, —.01±.052. Calculating the ratios shows one to be negligible, .08±.051 and the other to be slight, .18±.050, but considering the irregularity of its line of means, not very significant. We feel safe in saying, then, that our results tend to confirm the belief that, among adults, there is little if any variation in mental capacity with age.

This fact is especially important since the factor of age is one which seemingly should be allowed for in many correlations, but which, by reason of the small size of its correlation with intelligence, has, as we have seen in the partial obtained between mental capacity and number of convictions with age constant, made only an insignificant change in the size of the coefficient, thereby relieving us of the necessity of making this allowance in many cases.

(*b*) *Mental Capacity and Classification by Color and Nativity*

In order to consider next the question of color in its relation to mental capacity as measured by Test Aggregate, we have plotted the distribution curves as shown in Chart XXXVI. It requires only the most casual inspection of this chart to prove the decided superiority of the white women. The white women are represented at the extreme lower end of the scale, it is true, but the curve of the colored women rises to its summit and falls away again at an earlier point than that of the white and is moreover unrepresented in the last interval. The means are 77.13±.442 for the white as against 70.91±.839 for the colored. Table 201 shows that this difference is unquestionably significant. We have no hesitation in saying, then, that there exists a decided difference in mental capacity between the colored and the white women as measured by this standard. As regards the amount of variability displayed by the two groups, it is interesting to note that they are nearly identical.

TABLE 200

Correlation between Mental Capacity Measured by Test Aggregate and Age

English-speaking Cases Only

Age	45–47	47–49	49–51	51–53	53–55	55–57	57–59	59–61	61–63	63–65	65–67	67–69	69–71	71–73	73–75	75–77	77–79	79–81	81–83	83–85	85–87	87–89	89–91	91–93	93–95	95–97	Totals	Means (Test Aggregate)
	Test Aggregate																											
65 to 68																											0	
62 " 65									1																		1	
59 " 62															1							1					2	74.3
56 " 59												1					1										2	
53 " 56																											0	
50 " 53									1					1		1			1		1						5	
47 " 50		1											1	1		1					1	1		1		1	8	78.5
44 " 47										1				2				1				2			1		7	
41 " 44								3					1	1		1	1	2		1		1			1	1	13	75.4
38 " 41									1		1	1	2	2	1	2		1		2		1	1				15	
35 " 38						1				1	1	2	1	4	1		3	1			1			1			17	74.5
32 " 35							1		1	2	1	1	2	1	2	1	1	1	5	1		1	3				24	
29 " 32								3	2	2	1	1	3	3	4	1	4	1	3	4	1		5		1		39	76.3
26 " 29						2	1			1	1	5	2	1	1	2		7	3	4	2	1	3		1	1	38	
23 " 26						1	1	2	1	3	2	5	6	2	1	10	5	4	2	6	4	1	2	1		1	60	75.4
20 " 23			1			2	2		1	2		3	4	6	6	4	1	5	4	3	7	2	4			1	58	
17 " 20				1				2	2	1	3	4	6	7	5	4	7	6	8	4	2	3	2	2			69	75.8
14 " 17						1						1		1		2	3	2	1		1	2					14	
Totals	0	1	1	1	0	7	5	10	10	13	10	24	28	32	22	29	26	31	27	25	20	16	20	5	4	5	372	75.67
Means (Age)	26.5						28.5		30.1		26.7		27.8		26.5		25.7		25.7		27.9		27.1		34.1		27.15	

Test aggregate: Mean = 75.67 σ = 9.43
Age : Mean = 27.15 σ = 9.24

Coefficient of correlation: r = —.01 ± .052

Correlation ratios: Test aggregate on age, η = .08 ± .051 Blakeman's Criterion = 1.2
Age on test aggregate, η = .18 ± .050 Blakeman's Criterion = 2.5

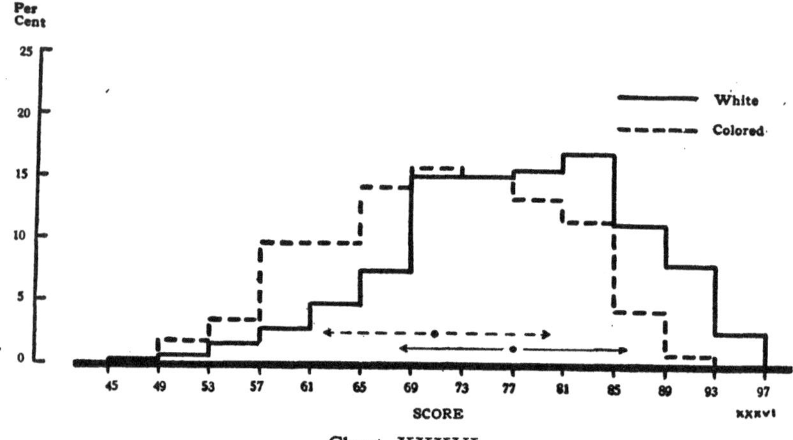

Chart XXXVI

Mental Capacity as Measured by Test Aggregate

Percentage comparison between white (407) and colored (113). English-speaking cases only.

For further interest we have figured here also the percentage distribution curves for the colored and white women on the Yerkes-Bridges Point Scale, the Stanford-Binet, and our group of Performance Tests. Charts XXXVII, XXXVIII, and XXXIX show these. An inspection of these makes it clear that they agree in showing the white to be clearly a superior group. It is significant that the tests

TABLE 201

COLORED AND WHITE

Comparison of the Means and Standard Deviations of Mental Capacity, as Measured by Test Aggregate, of Colored and White Women

English-speaking Cases Only

	White	Colored	Difference	$\frac{d}{\sigma_d}$	Chances that real difference does not exist are 1 in:
Mean............. σ_m...............	77.03 ±.442	70.91 ±.839	6.12	6.45	∞
σ................ σ_σ................	8.91 ±.305	8.92 ±.654	−.01	.083	2
Cases.............	407	113			

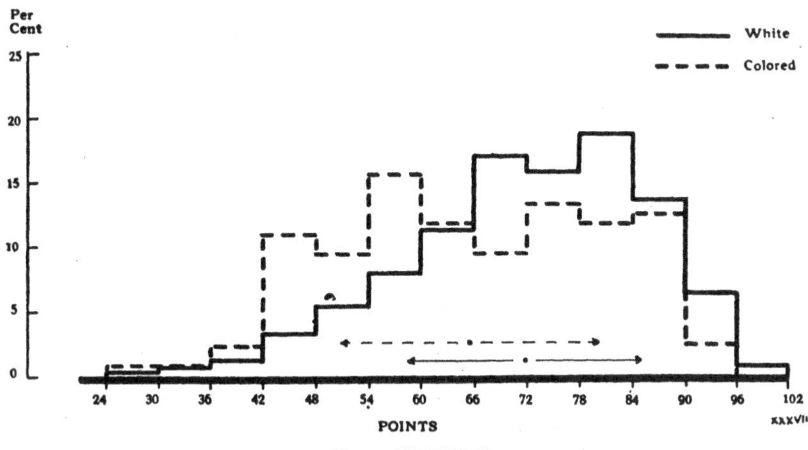

Chart XXXVII

Mental Capacity as Measured by Yerkes-Bridges Point Scale

Percentage comparison between white (478) and colored (129). English-speaking cases only.

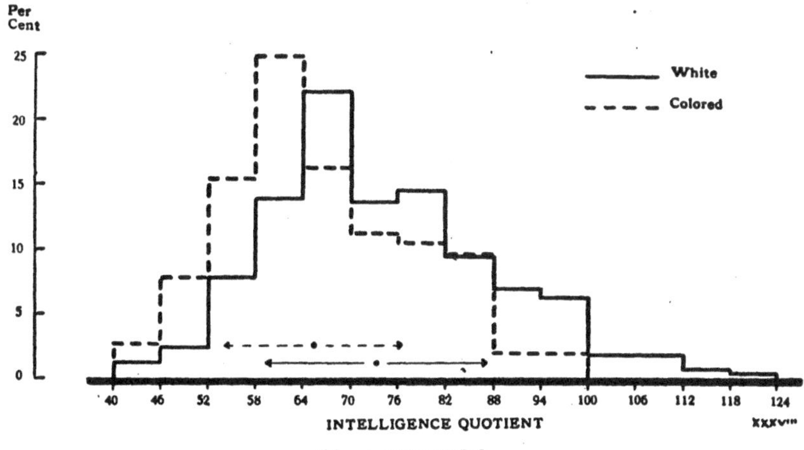

Chart XXXVIII

Mental Capacity as Measured by Stanford-Binet

Percentage comparison between white (447) and colored (118). English-speaking cases only.

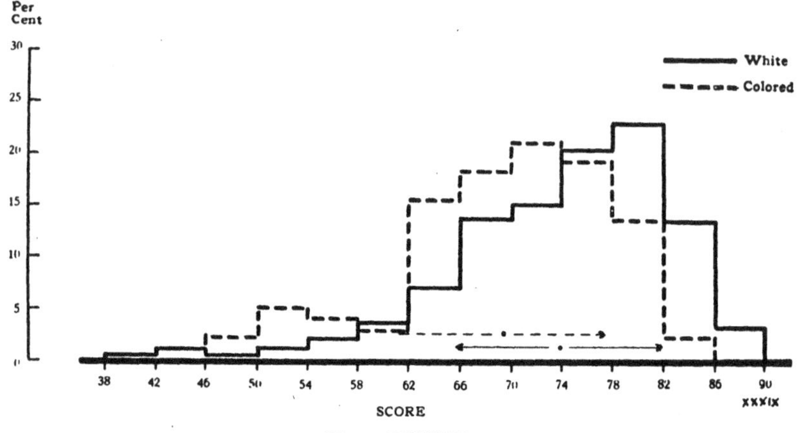

Chart XXXIX
Mental Capacity as Measured by Performance Tests
Percentage comparison between white (453) and colored (107).

in which language is not involved agree with the other types of tests in these findings. The constants for each are shown below.

	Mean			
	White	Colored	White	Colored
Test Aggregate......	77.03 ±.442	70.91 ±.839	8.91 ±.305	8.92 ±.654
Yerkes-Bridges Scale.	71.80 ±.608	65.4 ±1.30	13.29 ±.416	14.82 ±.687
Stanford-Binet......	73.25 ±.661	65.4 ±1.10	14.01 ±.713	11.90 ±.461
Performance Tests...	73.78 ±.379	69.26 ±.777	8.08 ±.367	8.04 ±.596

Our only possible basis of comparing native with foreign groups with respect to mentality is the group of Performance Tests, since these can be given to all individuals. In the present comparison we have distinguished the groups in accordance with our classification of English-speaking versus non-English-speaking (see page 59) rather than on an exact basis of nativity. Chart XL shows the relationship between these two groups. The superiority of the English-speaking group, by this measure, is readily apparent. Its mean is sufficiently higher than that of the non-English-speaking group so that there is no question of the validity of the difference (73.67±.363 as against

67.95±.957) and the higher location of the mode may be seen by inspection. Whether the superiority indicated in favor of the English-speaking delinquent women over the non-English-speaking can be considered wholly established remains, however, something of a question, since it is probable that at least a slight handicap persists for the very foreign and frequently wholly uneducated women of the non-

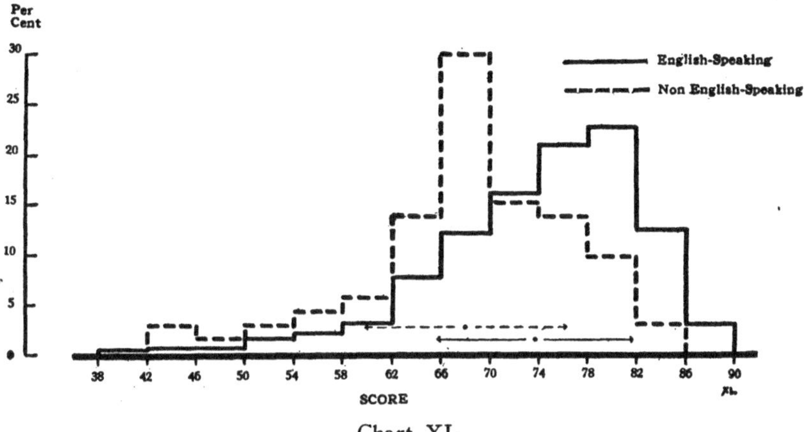

Chart XL

Mental Capacity as Measured by Performance Tests

Percentage comparison between English-speaking cases (486) and non-English-speaking cases (74).

English-speaking group. Accordingly, we would not emphasize this distinction overmuch, but merely offer the comparison as the best which our data make possible.

(c) *Mental Capacity and Use of Drugs and Alcohol*

We have attempted to see if the using of drugs or alcohol has had any effect on the mental capacity of these women as measured by Test Aggregate. Chart XLI shows the distribution of those women who have used drugs in comparison with those that have not. As will be seen the curves resemble each other closely. The means are almost identical and Table 202 shows that the slight difference can not be demonstrated as significant. The difference in the variability shown by the two groups is likewise very small and not demonstrably significant. We feel safe in concluding, therefore, that delinquent women who have been addicted to drugs do not differ appreciably in mental capacity from those who have not.

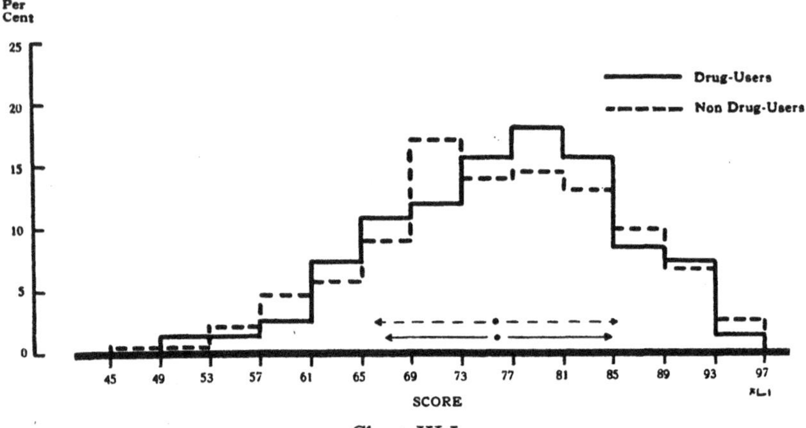

Chart XLI

Mental Capacity as Measured by Test Aggregate

Percentage comparison between drug-users and non-drug-users. English-speaking cases only.

In order to measure the possible relation between mental capacity and the use of alcohol we have calculated a correlation ratio with mental capacity as the quantitative variable and the use of alcohol, classified as excessive, moderate, and non-alcoholic, as the qualitative. We have added to the first group those cases from the special "Intoxication Group" at the Workhouse that were tested by Test Aggregate. Table 203 shows the correlation of the two factors. The correlation

TABLE 202

DRUG-USERS AND NON DRUG-USERS

Comparison of the Means and Standard Deviations of Mental Capacity, as Measured by Test Aggregate, of Drug-users and Non-Drug-users

English-speaking Cases Only

	Drug-users	Non-Drug-users	Difference	$\frac{d}{\sigma_d}$	Chances that real difference does not exist are 1 in:
Mean	75.71	75.63	.08	.076	2
σ_m	±.986	±.570			
σ	9.03	9.57	−.54	.703	4
σ_σ	±.668	±.361			
Cases	84	282			

TABLE 203

Correlation between Mental Capacity Measured by Test Aggregate and Degree of Alcoholism

English-speaking Cases of Total Group and of Special Intoxication Group from Workhouse

Degree of Alcoholism	Test Aggregate																										Totals	Means (Test Aggregate)
	45–47	47–49	49–51	51–53	53–55	55–57	57–59	59–61	61–63	63–65	65–67	67–69	69–71	71–73	73–75	75–77	77–79	79–81	81–83	83–85	85–87	87–89	89–91	91–93	93–95	95–97		
Excessive		1				1	1	3	4	5	3	5	8	7	6	6	10	7	6	4	5	5	3		3	1	94	74.9
Moderate			1	1		2		3	2	2	6	9	9	8	6	9	4	8	5	8	6	5	6	3		1	104	75.3
Non-Alcoholic						4	4	4	5	7	2	11	12	17	10	17	12	16	16	13	9	7	11	2	1	3	183	75.9
Totals	0	1	1	1	0	7	5	10	11	14	11	25	29	32	22	32	26	31	27	25	20	17	20	5	4	5	381	75.51

Test aggregate: Mean = 75.51 σ = 9.36

Correlation ratio: Test aggregate on degree of alcoholism, η = .044 ± .051

ratio obtained is practically zero, .044±.051. On the chance that this distinction was too fine and the possible difference might be between those who have used alcohol to excess and those who have not, we have grouped together the moderate users and the non-alcoholics and compared them with those who have used alcohol to excess. Chart XLII shows the relative distributions. The difference in both the central tendency and the amount of variability is negligible (see Table 204).

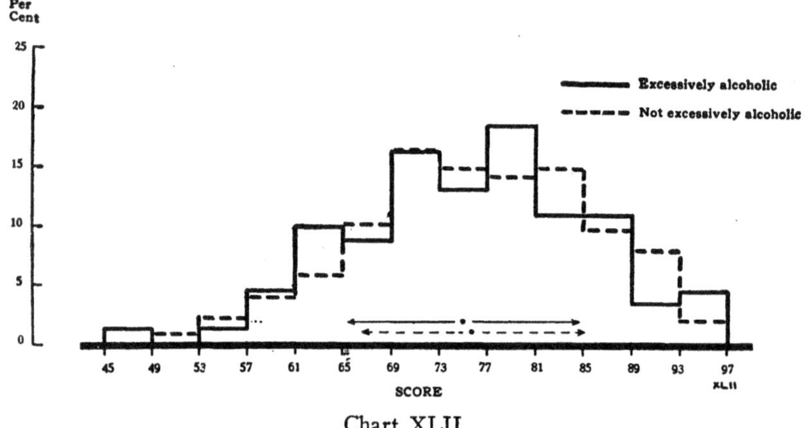

Chart XLII

Mental Capacity as Measured by Test Aggregate

Percentage comparison between women who have been excessively alcoholic and women who have not been excessively alcoholic. English-speaking cases only.

We feel, therefore, justified in stating that those of our group who have been alcoholic, however this term may be interpreted, do not differ significantly with respect to mental capacity from those that have not.

Summary

Summarizing this section, then, we can say:

(1) Our data confirm the accepted theory that for a group of adults there is no demonstrable correlation between mental capacity and age.

(2) Our results show also that white women of our delinquent groups are superior in intellectual capacity to colored women. We have found little difference in the degree of variability shown between the white and colored groups. The evidence at hand indicates, further, that the women delinquents, born in English-speaking countries, are somewhat superior to those born in non-English-speaking countries.

TABLE 204

EXCESSIVELY ALCOHOLIC AND NOT EXCESSIVELY ALCOHOLIC

Comparison of the Means and Standard Deviations of Mental Capacity, as Measured by Test Aggregate, for those Excessively Alcoholic and those not Excessively Alcoholic. Total Group Including Special Intoxication Group from Workhouse

English-speaking Cases Only

	Excessively Alcoholic	Not Excessively Alcoholic	Difference	$\frac{d}{\sigma_d}$	Chances that real difference does not exist are 1 in:
Mean	74.95	75.69	−.74	.655	4
σ_m	±.995	±.546			
σ	9.64	9.25	.39	.499	3
σ_σ	±.703	±.353			
Cases	94	287			

(3) We have found no demonstrable difference between the mental capacity of those women who have used drugs and those who have not, and no demonstrable difference in the mental capacity of the women who have used alcohol and those who have not.

MENTAL CAPACITY IN RELATION TO HOME CONDITIONS

We will consider next the relationship between the mental capacity of these women and (1) the home conditions which surrounded them in childhood and adolescence, and (2) the possible hereditary factors which might have affected their mentality.

(*a*) *Mental Capacity and Estimate of Home Conditions*

In order to examine the first of these relationships we have plotted the correlation between mental capacity as measured by Test Aggregate and the estimate of home conditions (Table 205). This estimate of home conditions, as was earlier stated, has been based upon a combination of the several factors of economic condition, moral standards and parental supervision. This has then been divided into five grades, grade 1 being the lowest in order of excellence. The correlation ratio obtained is .31±.053, which indicates that there is a clear degree of relationship existent between the mental capacity of these women and

TABLE 205

Correlation between Mental Capacity Measured by Test Aggregate and Estimate of Home Conditions

Total Group, Workhouse Omitted. English-speaking Cases Only

Home Conditions	Test Aggregate 47–49	49–51	51–53	53–55	55–57	57–59	59–61	61–63	63–65	65–67	67–69	69–71	71–73	73–75	75–77	77–79	79–81	81–83	83–85	85–87	87–89	89–91	91–93	93–95	95–97	Totals	Means (Test Aggregate)
Very good																									1	1	96.0
Good								1			1	1	1		2			4	1		2	4			1	18	81.2
Fair					2	2	3		2	2	3	10	9	5	7	7	12	7	12	11	7	11	3	3	2	120	78.8
Poor	1	1	1		2		3	3	4	4	7	9	16	8	13	9	8	8	7	4	5	4				117	74.0
Very poor					1	1		2	1		5	1	2	3	2	4	4	1	3	1			1			32	73.7
Totals	1	1	1	0	5	3	6	6	7	6	16	21	28	16	24	20	24	20	23	16	14	19	4	3	4	288	76.47

Test aggregate: Mean = 76.47 $\sigma = 9.31$
Correlation ratio: Test aggregate on estimate of home conditions, $\eta = .31 \pm .053$

the excellence of their home conditions in early life. As has been noted earlier (cf. Chapter IX), it has been necessary to omit the Workhouse group from the comparison because of the impossibility of verifying such data on many of this group and the evident tendency to exaggeration in their own statements on this particular matter.

We have plotted also (Table 206) the relation between mental capacity and economic status alone,—one of the factors which go to make up the estimate of the home conditions—and find that the correlation ratio obtained is identical with the preceding ratio, .31±.053. Measured either by the economic status alone or by the estimate of home conditions, there is a clear tendency for those women whose early home condions have been good to make a better showing on Test Aggregate than do those who come from poorer homes.

(*b*) *Mental Capacity and Hereditary Factors*

We have next considered the possible effect of heredity on the mental capacity of these women. Data have been collected by social investigation on many factors, such as alcoholism, insanity, venereal disease, etc., in the family which have been recognized, more or less universally, as possible causes of defective intelligence in the offspring. When, however, we have attempted to compute these separately our numbers were found to be too small to be reliable, and if we try to subdivide these again into the presence of any one factor in one parent alone we still further reduce our figures. Recognizing the impossibility of making any reliable comparisons in this exact way, we have, therefore, considered the presence of any one of these factors in either parent, or in the siblings where the defect was present from early childhood, and have called it possible evidence of a defective strain in the heredity. We have disregarded cases beyond the immediate family. The factors which we have taken account of are alcoholism, amentia, epilepsy, insanity, neurotic constitution, gonorrhea and syphilis. These may not all be factors universally recognized as either symptomatic of or productive of hereditary defect and there are probably others of importance of which we have taken no account. The varying amounts of each of these factors in our group are given in Table 79, Chapter IX. Cases where the field workers had been unable to obtain any data whatever on this point were omitted altogether. There were 129 cases where defective strain was present in father, mother or siblings, and 231 where there was no indication of such. The mean for the former is 75.26±.816 and that for the latter 75.79

TABLE 206

Correlation between Mental Capacity Measured by Test Aggregate and Estimate of Economic Conditions in Home during Childhood

Total Group, Workhouse Omitted. English-speaking Cases Only

Economic Conditions	Test Aggregate 45–47	47–49	49–51	51–53	53–55	55–57	57–59	59–61	61–63	63–65	65–67	67–69	69–71	71–73	73–75	75–77	77–79	79–81	81–83	83–85	85–87	87–89	89–91	91–93	93–95	95–97	Totals	Means (Test Aggregate)
Very good																							1			1	2	92.5
Good									1	1	1	1		4	1	2	1		4	3	4	4	4	1	1	2	35	81.4
Fair		1	1			1	2	4	1	1	1	5	12	7	3	11	5	15	7	10	7	7	12	2	2	1	118	77.6
Poor				1		3	1	2	4	5	3	6	8	14	11	11	12	7	7	9	5	3	2				114	73.9
Very poor						1					1	4	1	3	1		2	2	2	1				1			19	73.9
Totals	0	1	1	1	0	5	3	6	6	7	6	16	21	28	16	24	20	24	20	23	16	14	19	4	3	4	288	76.47

Test aggregate: Mean = 76.47 $\sigma = 9.31$
Correlation ratio: Test aggregate on economic home conditions, $\eta = .31 \pm .053$

$\pm$.621. The standard deviations were respectively 9.26$\pm$.577 and 9.44$\pm$.439. The differences are insignificant and, as Table 207 shows, can not be demonstrated as conditioned by anything other than chance.

TABLE 207

DEFECTIVE STRAIN AND NOT DEFECTIVE STRAIN

Comparison of the Means and Standard Deviations of Mental Capacity, as Measured by Test Aggregate, of those whose Immediate Family Show Defective Strain and those whose Immediate Family Show No Defective Strain

English-speaking Cases Only

	Defective Strain	No Defective Strain	Difference	$\frac{d}{\sigma_d}$	Chances that real difference does not exist are 1 in:
Mean σ_m	75.26 $\pm$.816	75.79 $\pm$.621	−.53	.515	3
σ σ_σ	9.26 $\pm$.577	9.44 $\pm$.439	−.18	.248	2
Cases	129	231			

As far as our data are significant, therefore, we have nothing to prove that the mental capacity of these women, as measured by Test Aggregate, is in any way affected by the presence of what we have termed defective strain in the immediate family.

Summary

We can say in summary, then:

(1) That there is a small but significant degree of association between mental capacity and the kind of home conditions by which these individuals were surrounded in early life.

(2) We have been unable to demonstrate any relationship between mental capacity and the presence in the immediate family of a defective strain represented by any cases of alcoholism, amentia, epilepsy, insanity, neurotic constitution or venereal disease.

MENTAL CAPACITY IN RELATION TO EDUCATIONAL BACKGROUND

A twofold interest attaches to the question of the relation between mental capacity as measured by any of our tests and the educational background of the women under consideration. We are interested to know, first, whether our data cast any light on the assumption, frequently made in Chapter X, to the effect that the grade finished is of itself something of an index of the intelligence of the individual and that this is true of the measures of educational *opportunity* to much slighter degree. On the other hand, we are concerned to know whether the relationship between schooling and education is so close as to suggest that in our tests we are measuring the influence of education rather than native ability.

We have attempted to answer these questions by the use of several different combinations of data. First, using the total English-speaking portion of our delinquent group, on whom we had both the test results and the necessary information on schooling, we obtained the following correlations:

Correlation of Mental Capacity as Measured by Test Aggregate with		
Age at Leaving School	Number of Years in School	Grade Finished
r = .27 ± .049 (352 cases)	.29 ± .046 (383 cases)	.60 ± .032 (383 cases)

(The correlation array for the first of the above relationships is given in Table 208. The others are not shown.)

From these figures it is apparent that there is a much higher relationship of mental capacity, thus measured, with grade finished than with either age at leaving school or number of years in school. Obtaining the partial correlation coefficient of mental capacity with grade, for years in school constant, we find that r = 54. It is very little affected by controlling the factor of school opportunity in the sense of the number of years spent in school. On the other hand the partial correlation coefficient of mental capacity with years in school for constant grade drops to zero (.003). It appears therefore that length of time spent in school is symptomatic of intelligence only to a very slight degree and only when it shows results in appropriate grade accomplishment: but that the grade attained has a much higher diagnostic value and that this value is not greatly affected by differences in school opportunity.

To determine how these relationships were affected by more accurate information the same correlations were computed, using only those cases on whom we had verified record of both years in school and grade, with the following results: The correlation of mental capacity, measured by Test Aggregate, with years in school was found to be .32 (159 cases): that of mental capacity with grade finished .75

TABLE 208

Correlation between Mental Capacity Measured by Test Aggregate and Age at Leaving School

English-speaking Cases Only

Age at Leaving School	Test Aggregate 45–47	47–49	49–51	51–53	53–55	55–57	57–59	59–61	61–63	63–65	65–67	67–69	69–71	71–73	73–75	75–77	77–79	79–81	81–83	83–85	85–87	87–89	89–91	91–93	93–95	95–97	Totals	Means (Test Aggregate)
19																	1				2					2	5	88.2
18							1								2	1			1								5	71.8
17									1	1						4		2		1	1		1		2		13	79.4
16								1		1		2	5	7	1	1	3	3	4	2	3	3	6	1	1		44	78.6
15						3	1	2	1	3	2	5	3	4	4	11	9	9	9	9	5	7	5				92	76.8
14						1	1	2	2	1	2	8	11	6	7	7	6	8	7	7	4	3	5	2	1	1	92	76.2
13								1	2	3	1	4	5	4	3	1	3	4	5	4	2	1	3	1		1	48	75.9
12						1	1	2	1	1	3	3	3	2	3	2	1	2	1	1	1						28	70.3
11						1		1			1	2		4		2	1	1			1						14	71.0
10	1								2	1			1			1		1									7	65.6
9								1						1	1												3	67.7
8																											0	....
7																	1										1	77.0
Totals	1	0	0	0	0	6	4	10	9	11	9	24	28	28	21	30	25	30	27	24	19	14	20	4	4	4	352	75.88
Means (Age at Leaving School)	10.0				13.7		13.6		13.6		13.5		13.8		14.3		14.2		14.5		14.9		14.8		16.1		14.193	

Test aggregate: Mean = 75.88 σ = 9.09
Age at leaving school: Mean = 14.193 σ = 1.767
Coefficient of correlation: r = .27 ± .049
Correlation ratios: Test aggregate on age at leaving school, η = .35 ± .047 Blakeman's Criterion = 3.1
Age at leaving school on test aggregate, η = .32 ± .048 Blakeman's Criterion = 2.3

(164 cases). (The latter correlation is figured in Table 209.) It is evident that these results confirm the evidence of the foregoing correlations, showing an even more striking relationship between intelligence and grade.

To test still further the significance of this relationship we computed the correlations of mental capacity both as measured by Stanford-Binet and as measured by the Performance Tests, with the measures of schooling—years in school and grade. These correlations were based on completely verified data for 80 Bedford cases. The interrelations of the various factors for this particular group are shown below:

	Stanford-Binet	Years in School	Grade
Years in School	.23		
Grade	.74	.39	
Performance Tests	.60	.36	.70

The partial correlation of Stanford-Binet with grade, for constant number of years in school, is .721: that of Stanford-Binet with years in school, for constant grade, is —.095. The partial coefficient of the Performance Tests with grade, for constant years in school, is .644: that of the Performance Tests with years in school, for constant grade, is .133. These figures, therefore, are entirely in accord with our previous findings. The Performance Tests, it may be noted, show the contrasts less strikingly than do either Stanford-Binet or Test Aggregate.

Summary

(1) Whatever measure of intelligence we have used—Test Aggregate, Stanford-Binet, or Performance Tests—a high relationship with school grade has appeared, but only a slight relationship with number of years in school.

(2) This confirms our impression that grade attainment, in itself, affords some index of one's mentality.

(3) The fact that the correlation of the results of the various intelligence tests with grade is so high, while that of test results with years in school is so low, and that, moreover, the partial correlation of test results with grade, for constant number of years in school, is high, while that of test results with years in school, for constant grade, is zero or nearly zero, is sufficient to allay any fears that the test results measure effect of schooling rather than mentality. Were this the case there is every reason to expect that we should find approximately

TABLE 209

Correlation between Mental Capacity Measured by Test Aggregate and Grade Finished in School

English-speaking Cases Only. Verified Data

Grade Finished	Test Aggregate: 51–53	53–55	55–57	57–59	59–61	61–63	63–65	65–67	67–69	69–71	71–73	73–75	75–77	77–79	79–81	81–83	83–85	85–87	87–89	89–91	91–93	93–95	Totals
10*....																				1			1
9*....																					2		2
8....																2			4	4	1		11
7....													1	1		2	1	1	1	2	1		10
6....											2	2	3	1	6	2	5	6		1		1	29
5....							1			4		4	3	6	4	6	1	3					32
4....	1							1	4	4	7	1	6	2	1	2	1	1		1			32
3....		1	1	1	1	1	1	3	3	1	5		3	2	1	1	2						27
2....	1			1	4	2	2		3	1			2										16
1....								1				1											2
0....			2																				2
Totals	2	1	3	2	5	3	4	5	10	10	14	8	18	12	12	15	10	11	5	9	4	1	164

Test aggregate: Mean = 75.60 $\sigma = 9.21$
Grade finished: Mean = 4.65 $\sigma = 1.87$
Coefficient of correlation: $r = .75 \pm .034$

* Grades 9 and 10 refer to 1st and 2nd years of high school, respectively.

as high a correlation with the time spent in school as with the grade achieved, or possibly even a higher correlation.

MENTAL CAPACITY IN RELATION TO WORK RECORD

We will next consider the relation between mental capacity as measured by Test Aggregate and the various phases of the work record of these women. It would seem a justifiable assumption that, all other considerations being eliminated, the better the mentality of an individual the better would be the work that she could do and, consequently, the greater would be her earning capacity.

(*a*) *Mental Capacity and Age at Starting Work*

Following the order adopted in Chapter XI, we have first considered the age at starting work in its relation to mental capacity, in order to attempt to find out whether there is any tendency for the brighter women to start work at an earlier age than those less bright, or whether this condition is just reversed and it is the stupider women who seek employment younger, or whether neither fact can be demonstrated, and the factor of mentality is in no way concerned with the age at which they begin working. We have, accordingly, plotted the correlation which is figured in Table 210. The correlation coefficient is found to be .19±.053. The correlation ratios are only slightly larger: .26±.051 for the ratio of age at first employment on Score in Test Aggregate and .24±.052 for score in Test Aggregate on age at first employment.

The widest divergence of the means in adjacent groups lies between those starting work from 10 to 14 years and those starting work from 14 to 18. If we take the percentage of cases in these two age groups which lie above and below the approximate mean of the group in Test Aggregate, we find that, of those who start work between 10 and 14 years of age, 38 per cent are above the average in mental capacity as measured by Test Aggregate and 62 per cent are below, while for those starting work between 14 and 18, 58.7 per cent are above average intellectually and 41.3 per cent are below. This fact undoubtedly links up with the correlation between intellectual capacity and age at leaving school, which gives a coefficient of .32±.049, indicating a distinct tendency for the less intelligent women to leave school at an earlier age (see Chapter X). This in turn would probably be a factor in determining the age at starting work. The significance, in this connection,

TABLE 210

Correlation between Mental Capacity Measured by Test Aggregate and Age at Starting Work

English-speaking Cases only

Age at Starting Work	Test Aggregate 47–49	49–51	51–53	53–55	55–57	57–59	59–61	61–63	63–65	65–67	67–69	69–71	71–73	73–75	75–77	77–79	79–81	81–83	83–85	85–87	87–89	89–91	91–93	93–95	95–97	Totals	Means (Test Aggregate)
58–62														1												1	
54–58																										0	
50–54																										0	
46–50													1													1	
42–46																		1					1			2	80.8
38–42												1			1	1										3	
34–38														1							1				1	3	
30–34																				1	1					2	
26–30							1	1					1	1	1	1	1		1		1	1		1	1	12	79.0
22–26								1			1			1	1	2	1	1	3					1	1	13	79.3
18–22					2	2	1	1	4		5	1	3	4	7	3		4	4	4	1	7	1		1	55	76.0
14–18					3	2	4	3	7	6	10	17	16	8	11	16	20	17	14	7	7	11	3	1	1	184	76.1
10–14	1	1			1		3	3	1	2	7	4	6	3	5	1	2	2	2	3	2	1				50	71.4
6–10												1	2													3	
Totals	1	1	0	0	6	4	9	9	12	8	23	24	29	19	26	24	24	25	24	15	13	20	5	3	5	329	75.74
Means (Age at Starting Work)	15.5							16.6		15.0		16.1		18.2		16.7		17.4		17.6		18.6		24.3		17.07	

Test aggregate: Mean = 75.74 $\sigma = 9.41$
Age at starting work: Mean = 17.07 $\sigma = 5.93$
Coefficient of correlation: $r = .19 \pm .053$
Correlation ratios: Age at starting work on test aggregate, $\eta = .26 \pm .051$ Blakeman's Criterion = 2.4
Test aggregate on age at starting work, $\eta = .24 \pm .052$ Blakeman's Criterion = 1.9

of the age of fourteen as the common upper age limit in compulsory education laws need hardly be emphasized.

(*b*) *Mental Capacity and Kind of Work*

We considered next the relation of intellectual capacity to the nature of the work, in order to see if women of one grade of intelligence tend to find employment in one line of work while those of another grade gravitate toward another occupation. To this end we have made a correlation table (Table 211) with Test Aggregate as the quantitative variable and the occupations of domestic service, factory work, home work, restaurant and hotel work, work in stores, vaudeville performance, clerical work, professional service, personal service, work of charwoman, and miscellaneous, at which these women were mainly employed, as a series of qualitative arrays. From such a table we have obtained a correlation ratio of .46±.043. This would seem to be clear indication that there is a decided degree of relationship between the mental capacity so measured and the kind of work at which a woman has been predominantly employed.

If we compare Table 211 with Table 212, which shows the relation between mental capacity and the nature of the *first* work in which the women were engaged, we find that the respective means are on the whole very similar. The means for mental capacity (Test Aggregate) run in order of excellence:

First Work			Prevailing Work
Professional service (4)	86.0	87.5	Professional service (2)
Clerical work (15)	83.6	86.6	Personal service (7)
Vaudeville performers (11)	83.0	82.5	Vaudeville performers (16)
Personal service (5)	81.6	82.3	Work in stores (37)
Work in stores (40)	80.7	81.3	Clerical work (9)
Restaurant and hotel work (24)	76.9	79.6	Restaurant and hotel work (21)
Home work (7)	76.9	75.4	Home work (12)
Factory work (102)	75.7	75.1	Factory work 88)
Miscellaneous (7)	74.3	72.3	Miscellaneous (3)
Domestic service (141)	72.1	71.8	Domestic service (142)
Charwomen (1)	59.0	67.0	Charwomen (2)

The correlation ratio obtained for mental capacity on the nature of first work is .41±.044. It will be seen that the arrangement of the means is in general similar for the nature of work in the first job and in the prevailing job, and it seems clearly evident that the mental capacity of these women is a factor in determining both the kind of work which they first enter and that which, subsequently, they continue to

TABLE 211

Correlation between Mental Capacity Measured by Test Aggregate and Nature of Prevailing Work

English-speaking Cases Only

Prevailing Work	Test Aggregate																									Totals	Means (Test Aggregate)
	47–49	49–51	51–53	53–55	55–57	57–59	59–61	61–63	63–65	65–67	67–69	69–71	71–73	73–75	75–77	77–79	79–81	81–83	83–85	85–87	87–89	89–91	91–93	93–95	95–97		
Domestic Service	1	1	1		5	4	4	7	9	8	13	11	14	8	11	11	7	4	9	4	4	2	3	1		142	71.8
Factory Work					2	1	2		2	1	6	9	10	7	7	12	9	8	4	2	3	3				88	75.1
Home Work							2	1					1		1		1	3	2	1						12	75.4
Restaurant and Hotel Work									1		2	1	1	1	2		1	2	3	2	2	3				21	79.6
Work in Stores							1				1	2	1	1	2	2	2	5	3	3	4	7	1		2	37	82.3
Vaudeville Performers											1	1		1	2		1	2	1	2	1	2			2	16	82.5
Clerical Work													1	1	1	1			1	2	1			1		9	81.3
Professional Service																	1								1	2	87.5
Personal Service																	1	1		2		1	1	1		7	86.6
Charwomen							1								1											2	67.0
Miscellaneous											1			1	1											3	72.3
Totals	1	1	1	0	7	5	10	8	12	9	24	24	28	20	28	26	23	25	23	18	15	18	5	3	5	339	75.560

Test aggregate: Mean = 75.56 σ = 9.55
Correlation ratio: η = .46 ± .043

TABLE 212

Correlation between Mental Capacity Measured by Test Aggregate and Nature of Work in First Job

English-speaking Cases Only

Nature of First Job	Test Aggregate 47–49	49–51	51–53	53–55	55–57	57–59	59–61	61–63	63–65	65–67	67–69	69–71	71–73	73–75	75–77	77–79	79–81	81–83	83–85	85–87	87–89	89–91	91–93	93–95	95–97	Total	Mean (Test Aggregate)
Domestic Service	1	1			6	3	3	7	8	8	15	11	15	8	8	9	11	5	7	5	4	2	2	2		141	72.1
Factory Work			1		1	2	2	2	3	1	5	7	11	7	11	11	9	9	7	2	4	6	1			102	75.7
Home Work							1						1			1		3	1							7	76.9
Restaurant and Hotel Work							1		2		1	2		3	1	2	2	3	3	2	1	1				2[illegible]	76.9
Work in Stores							1	1			1	4			3	3	4	4	5	4	2	6			2	40	80.7
Vaudeville Performers										1	1			1	1					2	1	2			2	11	83.0
Clerical Work												1	2		1			1	1	2	2	2	2	1		15	83.6
Professional Service																	1	1			1				1	4	86.0
Personal Service															1		1	1		2						5	81.6
Charwomen							1																			1	59.0
Miscellaneous							1						1	1	3							1				7	74.3
Totals	1	1	1	0	7	5	10	10	13	10	23	25	30	20	29	26	28	27	24	19	15	20	5	3	5	357	75.62

Test aggregate: Mean = 75.62 $\sigma = 9.45$
Correlation ratio: Test aggregate on kind of first job, $\eta = .41 \pm .044$

do. The small number of cases in many of the above groups has deterred us from making detailed inter-comparisons.

Since, however, the domestic service group contains over 40 per cent of the cases we have made a comparison between the mental capacity of this group and that of women employed at occupations other than domestic service. The mean for domestic service is 71.83± .802 and for all other occupations 78.25±.613. Table 213 indicates

TABLE 213

DOMESTIC SERVICE AND NOT DOMESTIC SERVICE

Comparison of the Means and Standard Deviations of Mental Capacity, as Measured by Test Aggregate, of those whose Prevailing Work is Domestic Service and those whose Prevailing Work is other than Domestic Service

English-speaking Cases Only

	Domestic Service	Not Domestic Service	Difference	$\frac{d}{\sigma_d}$	Chances that real difference does not exist are 1 in:
Mean	71.83	78.25	−6.42	6.36	∞
σ_m	±.802	±.613			
σ	9.56	8.60	.96	1.34	11
σ_σ	±.567	±.433			
Cases	142	197			

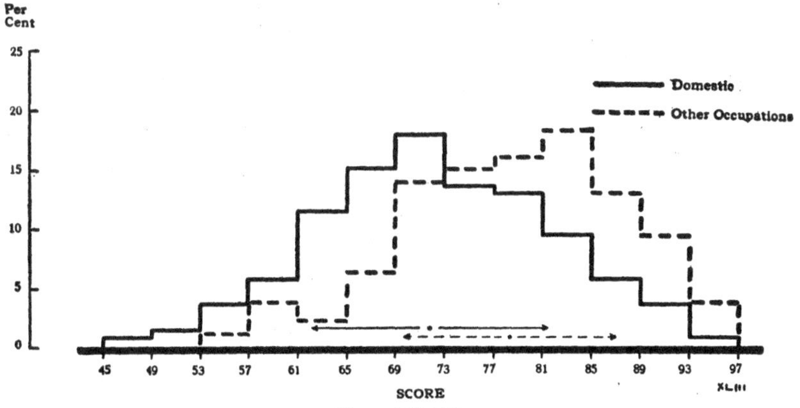

Chart XLIII

Mental Capacity as Measured by Test Aggregate

Percentage comparison between those whose prevailing work has been domestic service and those whose prevailing work has been other than domestic service. English-speaking cases only.

the validity of the distinction in favor of those employed at occupations other than domestic work. Chart XLIII shows the marked difference in distribution for the two groups, making evident that the higher standing shown by the mean is based on no eccentric massing but is due both to higher percentages of cases with superior mental ratings and lower percentages with inferior ratings. We are, therefore, justified in stating that the women whose prevailing work is domestic service are less mentally capable on the average than those who are employed at other occupations.

(*c*) *Mental Capacity and Wage*

We have next considered the possible relationship which one would expect to find between mental capacity and the economic status of these women as represented by the average weekly wage which they have received at their prevailing work. The method of assembling these data on the work record has already been explained in Chapter XI. There has been explained also the necessity of dividing the material on wage earned into two groups, domestic service and allied occupations where board and lodging are in addition to the wage, and occupations other than domestic service which provide no maintenance. If we plot the figures on the former of these, *i.e.*, average wage of women whose prevailing work has been domestic service in relation to their mental capacity as measured by Test Aggregate, we obtain Table 214. The correlation coefficient obtained is very low, $-.03 \pm .089$. The correlation ratios are $.14 \pm .087$ for the regression of wage on Test Aggregate and $.09 \pm .088$ for the regression of Test Aggregate on wage, both negligible. Our results, therefore, fail to show any relationship between the mental capacity of women whose prevailing work was domestic service and their average wage.

When we come next to compare the scores obtained on this test with the wage obtained at occupations other than domestic service, we find the situation easier of interpretation. Table 215 shows the relation of these factors to each other. The correlation coefficient obtained is $.31 \pm .070$, which would seem to indicate a clear and, in the light of its standard deviation, significant, correlation between the two. We may say in general that, as the mental capacity of these women increases, there is a progressive increase in the amount of money they earn at occupations other than domestic service. This is of interest in view of our inability to establish any such relationship between mental capacity and the amount earned at domestic service.

TABLE 214

Correlation between Mental Capacity Measured by Test Aggregate and Average Weekly Wage for Prevailing Work of Women Employed at Domestic Service, etc.*

English-speaking Cases Only

Weekly Wage	Test Aggregate 49–51	51–53	53–55	55–57	57–59	59–61	61–63	63–65	65–67	67–69	69–71	71–73	73–75	75–77	77–79	79–81	81–83	83–85	85–87	87–89	89–91	91–93	93–95	Totals	Means (Test Aggregate)
$8.00 to $9.00									1											1				2	
7.00 " 8.00	1																							1	70.9
6.00 " 7.00				1		1			1				1			1							2	7	
5.00 " 6.00					1	1		1			3							2		•				8	
4.00 " 5.00					2	1	1	1	3	3	1	2	1	3	4	3	1	2	1		2			31	73.3
3.00 " 4.00							2	2		3	3	4		3	2	1		3	2					25	73.2
2.00 " 3.00				2		2	4	2	2	2	2	2	2	3	3	1	2	3	1	1	1	2		37	72.9
1.00 " 2.00				1			1			1		4	1						1					9	71.9
.00 " 1.00											1	1	1		2		1							6	
Totals	1	0	0	4	3	5	8	6	7	9	10	13	6	9	11	6	4	10	5	2	3	2	2	126	72.65
Means (Wage)	$4.1				$3.7				$3.5				$3.4				$3.5				$4.2			$3.56	

Test Aggregate: Mean = 72.65 σ = 9.48
Wage: Mean = $3.57 σ = $1.59
Coefficient of correlation: r = —.03 ± .089
Correlation ratios: Wage on test aggregate, η = .14 ± .087 Blakeman's Criterion = 1.10
Test aggregate on wage, η = .09 ± .088 Blakeman's Criterion = 0.67

* Living is in addition to wage.

TABLE 215

Correlation between Mental Capacity Measured by Test Aggregate and Average Weekly Wage for Prevailing Work of Women Employed at Occupations other than Domestic Service

English-speaking Cases Only

Weekly Wage	Test Aggregate: 55–57	57–59	59–61	61–63	63–65	65–67	67–69	69–71	71–73	73–75	75–77	77–79	79–81	81–83	83–85	85–87	87–89	89–91	91–93	93–95	95–97	Totals	Means (Test Aggregate)
$45.00–47.00																					1	1	
43.00–45.00																						0	
41.00–43.00																						0	
39.00–41.00																						0	
37.00–39.00																						0	
35.00–37.00										1								1				2	85.2
33.00–35.00																						0	
31.00–33.00																	1					1	
29.00–31.00																						0	
27.00–29.00											1							1				2	
25.00–27.00														1	1	1		1				4	
23.00–25.00																						0	
21.00–23.00																				1		1	
19.00–21.00							1				1			1		1						4	
17.00–19.00																1						1	83.1
15.00–17.00																1	1				1	3	
13.00–15.00								1							1							2	
11.00–13.00							1		1			1	3	2				1				9	
9.00–11.00							1	2	1	1	2	3		3		2		3			1	19	79.4
7.00– 9.00		1			1		1	3	5	3	4	3	3	1	3	3	1	4	1		1	38	
5.00– 7.00			2	1	2	1	3	2	4	3	3	7	4	7	4	2	4	3				52	77.4
3.00– 5.00	1		2				4	4	2	2	4		3	1	1	1	2	1				28	
1.00– 3.00								1														1	73.7
Totals	1	1	4	1	3	1	11	13	13	10	15	14	13	16	10	12	9	15	1	1	4	168	77.93
Means (Wage)	$5.9					$7.7		$7.0		$9.3		$7.5		$9.4		$10.7		$13.8				$9.09	

Test Aggregate: Mean = 77.93 σ = 8.47
Wage: Mean = $9.09 σ = $6.64
Coefficient of correlation: r = .31 ± .070
Correlation ratios: Wage on test aggregate, η = .33 ± .069 Blakeman's Criterion = 1.2
Test aggregate on wage, η = .34 ± .068 Blakeman's Criterion = 1.5

Although there is no appreciable correlation between mental capacity and age, there is a correlation of .264 between age and wage earned at these occupations. We have, therefore, felt called upon to compute a partial correlation between mental capacity and wage with age constant. The result obtained is .323±.068, a coefficient not appreciably different from the preceding. Since there is practically no correlation between age and wage at domestic service we have not felt it necessary to make this correction there.

The correlation between mental capacity measured by Test Aggregate and the wage earned at *first* job for the women in domestic service and allied occupations is .03±.094. For those in occupations other than domestic service this correlation is .29±.069. Since these appear to resemble quite closely the corresponding correlations of mental capacity with prevailing wage, we have not presented the scatter tables for these relationships.

(*d*) *Mental Capacity and Estimates of Work Record*

We have next attempted to find out whether there is any relation between the mental capacity of these women and the *regularity* with which they have held employment. Table 216 shows such a correlation where regularity of employment is divided into five grades (see Chapter XI). The correlation ratio (.13 ± .053) indicates that there is at most only a very slight association between mental capacity and regularity of employment. There are undoubtedly some whose irregular work record is the result of their mental incompetence, which prevents their holding a job for any length of time, but there are others mentally well equipped whose failure in this respect must be explained by some wholly different factor.

If we consider last the relation of mental capacity to the estimate of the *efficiency* of the work record, we obtain Table 217. (The explanation of the method of arriving at this estimate is given in Chapter XI.) The correlation ratio obtained is .20±.052, which would seem to indicate that there exists a small but significant degree of relationship between mental capacity and excellence of work record, as based on this estimate.

Summary

Summing up our results on this section we can see, then, that the mental capacity of these women plays some part in the various phases of their work records in that:

TABLE 216

Correlation between Mental Capacity Measured by Test Aggregate and Estimate of Regularity of Work

English-speaking Cases Only

Regularity of Work	Test Aggregate 45–47	47–49	49–51	51–53	53–55	55–57	57–59	59–61	61–63	63–65	65–67	67–69	69–71	71–73	73–75	75–77	77–79	79–81	81–83	83–85	85–87	87–89	89–91	91–93	93–95	95–97	Totals	Means (Test Aggregate)
Very good						1							1						1		2		1		1		7	79.9
Good						2	2	6	4	3	1	12	6	6	3	9	9	7	8	8	6	4	8	1	1	2	108	75.6
Fair		1				1	1	1	2	4	3	5	7	8	9	9	5	10	10	8	4	5	6	1	1	1	102	76.4
Poor			1			3		1	3	3	3	6	10	10	5	6	10	6	4	4	6	3	4	1			89	74.4
Very poor				1			1	2	1	3	1	1	2	5	3	3	1	2	3	2		2	1			1	35	73.3
Totals		1	1	1		7	4	10	10	13	8	24	26	29	20	27	25	25	26	22	18	14	20	3	3	4	341	75.39

Test Aggregate: Mean = 75.39 $\sigma = 9.46$
Correlation ratio: Test aggregate on regularity of work, $\eta = .13 = .053$

TABLE 217

Correlation between Mental Capacity Measured by Test Aggregate and Estimate of Efficiency of Work

English-speaking Cases Only

Work Record	Test Aggregate: 47–49	49–51	51–53	53–55	55–57	57–59	59–61	61–63	63–65	65–67	67–69	69–71	71–73	73–75	75–77	77–79	79–81	81–83	83–85	85–87	87–89	89–91	91–93	93–95	95–97	Totals	Means (Test Aggregate)
Very good																	1			1				1		3	86.0
Good					1	1	2				1	3	1	1	4	1	2	3		4	2	4	1	1	1	33	78.6
Fair					3	1	3	2	3	3	12	6	8	4	10	9	5	11	10	4	5	10	1		2	112	76.3
Poor	1	1			2	2	3	6	7	3	6	14	14	10	9	12	11	10	10	9	5	5	1	1	1	143	74.8
Very poor			1		1		2	2	3	2	4	3	6	5	4	3	5	2	2		2	1				48	72.4
Totals	1	1	1	0	7	4	10	10	13	8	23	26	29	20	27	25	24	26	22	18	14	20	3	3	4	339	75.40

Test Aggregate: Mean = 75.40 $\sigma = 9.47$
Correlation ratio: Test aggregate on estimate of work record, $\eta = .20 \pm .052$

(1) There is a tendency for the less bright women to begin working at an earlier age than those more capable. This is especially to be noticed for those who begin work before they have completed the compulsory school period, *i.e.*, before fourteen years, as contrasted with those starting work after fourteen.

(2) There is a decided correlation between mental capacity and the kind of work which these women have done, both in their first job and in the prevailing occupation they have followed. Nearly half of these women have been employed at domestic service and we have shown that they are, on the average, unquestionably of lower grade intellectually as measured by our standard than are the women who have been employed in occupations other than housework.

(3) As regards the average wage which they have earned, we can not demonstrate any unambiguous relationship between this and mental capacity, where the occupation has been domestic service, but we can show a clear correlation between mental capacity and the wage earned for occupations other than domestic service. It would seem, therefore, that, not only are the women of this group who have been employed at domestic service less mentally capable than those otherwise employed, but their varying grades of mental capacity have not been met by a similarly varying earning capacity as have those whose work has been other than domestic service.

(4) Finally, there exists a small but significant relationship between mental capacity and the degree of excellence indicated by the estimate of the work record, but the degree of regularity of work, which is one of the factors on which the estimate of the work record was based, can not be shown to have played an important part in this relationship.

MENTAL CAPACITY IN RELATION TO SEX HISTORY

The relation between the sex history of these women and their mental capacity is of considerable importance in a group such as ours. Table 150, page 386, shows that, out of our total of 551 cases on which we have information, only 78, or 14 per cent, have not at some period of their lives been sexually irregular.

(*a*) *Mental Capacity and Age at First Sex Offense*

Following the order adopted in Chapter XII, we have first considered the relation between the mental capacity of these women and the age at which they committed their first sex offense. (See Table 218.)

TABLE 218

Correlation between Mental Capacity Measured by Test Aggregate and Age at First Sex Offense

English-speaking Cases Only

Age at First Sex Offense	Test Aggregate 49–51	51–53	53–55	55–57	57–59	59–61	61–63	63–65	65–67	67–69	69–71	71–73	73–75	75–77	77–79	79–81	81–83	83–85	85–87	87–89	89–91	91–93	93–95	95–97	Totals	Means (Test Aggregate)
37 to 40 years												1								1			1	1	4	79.4
34 " 37 "												1	1			1									3	
31 " 34 "				1																	1				2	
28 " 31 "														1	2	2		2			2				9	
25 " 28 "								1					2	1		1	1		1						7	
22 " 25 "				3		1				1	2	1	1	3	2		1	1	1	1	2				20	74.0
19 " 22 "				1	1	1	2	2			2	3		5	3	1	3		4	1	4	2	1		36	76.9
16 " 19 "				1	2	2	3	2	4	4	7	10	7	6	7	8	12	11	9	4	5	1			105	76.5
13 " 16 "		1				4	2	4	3	8	3	6	5	5	4	10	4	2	4	4		1			70	73.9
10 " 13 "	1						1					1	1		1	1					1				7	72.4
7 " 10 "											1		1		1	1									4	
4 " 7 "											1														1	
Totals	1	1	0	6	3	8	8	9	7	13	16	23	18	21	20	25	21	16	19	11	15	4	2	1	268	75.77
Means (Age First Sex Offense)	18.6						16.8		15.8		17.3		18.4		17.7		18.0		17.8		21.6				17.98	

Test aggregate: Mean = 75.77 $\sigma = 9.25$
Age at first sex offense: Mean = 17.98 $\sigma = 5.17$
Coefficient of correlation: r = .14 ± .060
Correlation ratios: Test aggregate on age at first sex offense, $\eta = .20 \pm .059$ Blakeman's Criterion = 1.5
Age at first sex offense on test aggregate, $\eta = .25 \pm .057$ Blakeman's Criterion = 2.5

The coefficient of correlation (.14 ± .060) is so small as to indicate the presence of at most a very slight degree of relationship. The correlation ratio of mental capacity on age at first offense is .20 ± .059, with a sufficient degree of regularity in the line of means of test aggregate to indicate that this ratio probably measures fairly the extent of the relationship. On the other hand, the ratio of age at first sex offense on test aggregate (.25 ± .057) is rendered ambiguous in significance because of the great irregularity of the lines of means.

(b) *Mental Capacity and Classification as Sex Offenders*

Chart XLIV shows the distribution of those who have been sex offenders and those who have not been sex offenders, that is, who have not been sexually promiscuous. It is evident that the sex offenders are a slightly inferior group. Table 219 shows that so great a difference as this could occur by chance only once in 313 times. We are convinced, therefore, that the average mental capacity is a trifle higher for those who have not been sexually promiscuous than for those that have. As far as the variability of the two groups is concerned, the sex offenders would seem to have a slightly greater range, but this difference can not be considered established.

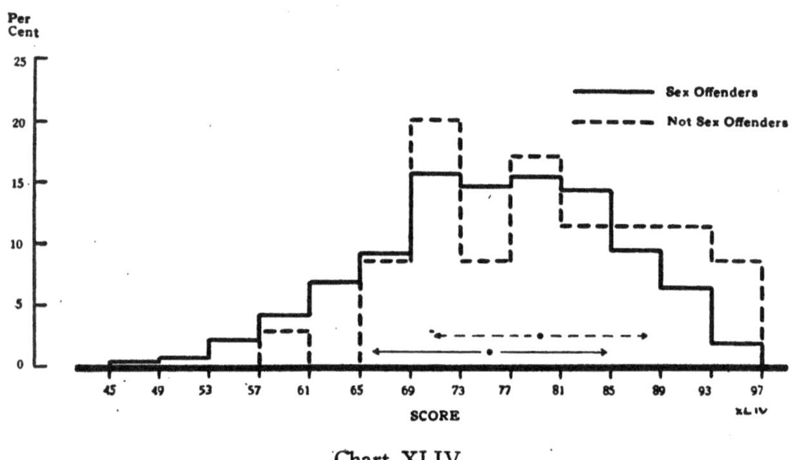

Chart XLIV

Mental Capacity as Measured by Test Aggregate

Percentage comparison between those who have been sex offenders—sexually promiscuous—and those who have not. English-speaking cases only.

TABLE 219

SEX OFFENDERS AND NOT SEX OFFENDERS

Comparison of the Means and Standard Deviations of Mental Capacity, as Measured by Test Aggregate, of Sex Offenders and Those Not Sex Offenders*

English-speaking Cases Only

	Sex Offenders	Not Sex Offenders	Difference	$\frac{d}{\sigma_d}$	Chances that real difference does not exist are 1 in:
Mean	75.28	79.4	−4.12	2.73	313
σ_m	±.507	±1.43			
σ	9.34	8.49	.85	.87	5
σ_σ	±.326	±.926			
Cases	339	35			

*The distinction here is between those who have been sexually promiscuous and those who have not.

Out of a total of 551 cases there were 365 who were prostitutes at the time of conviction or had been so at some period in their history. They comprise, then, 66.2 per cent of our total group. In Chart XLV we have compared the distribution of the scores on Test Aggregate of those women who have been prostitutes with that of those

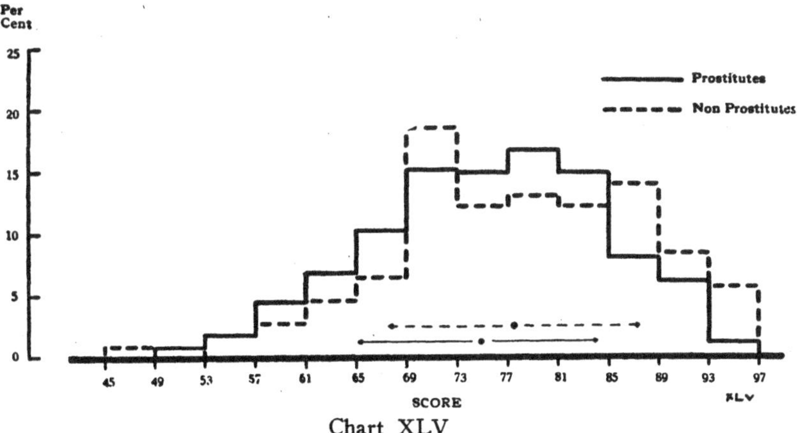

Chart XLV

Mental Capacity as Measured by Test Aggregate

Percentage comparison between those who have been prostitutes and those who have not. English-speaking cases only.

who have not. The mean of the non-prostitute group is sensibly higher, 77.40 ± .960 as against 74.97 ± .556, and Table 220 shows this difference to be almost certainly valid.

The degree of variability is slightly smaller for the prostitute class, 9.07 ± .350 as against 9.97 ± .641, but Table 220 shows this difference to be only possibly demonstrable, the chance being one in nine that as great a difference would occur from sampling.

TABLE 220

PROSTITUTES AND NON-PROSTITUTES

Comparison of the Means and Standard Deviations of Mental Capacity, as Measured by Test Aggregate, of Prostitutes and Non-Prostitutes

English-speaking Cases Only

	Prostitutes	Non Prostitutes	Difference	$\frac{d}{\sigma_d}$	Chances that real difference does not exist are 1 in:
Mean............	74.97	77.40	−2.43	2.19	70
σ_m...............	±.556	±.960			
σ................	9.07	9.97	− .90	1.23	9
σ_σ................	±.350	±.641			
Cases............	266	108			

In Table 221 we have attempted to make a finer distinction in the matter of sex irregularity and have divided the group into (1) prostitutes, which includes those who have been either regularly or semi-regularly receiving money in return for sex relations, (2) those sexually irregular, which here includes those who have been indiscriminate in their relations but have not made a practice of taking money for it, and (3) those who have never been sexually immoral and those whose delinquency has been restricted to a single offense. With this threefold distinction we have plotted the correlation between mental capacity shown by Test Aggregate and the degree of sex irregularity.

The correlation ratio obtained is only .14 ± .051, a figure too low to be very significant. The means are seen to run respectively: prostitutes 75, sexually irregular 76.4, and those not sexually irregular 79.4. It seems clear, then, from this in connection with Tables 219 and 220 that the real distinction in mental capacity comes between those

TABLE 221

Correlation between Mental Capacity Measured by Test Aggregate and Degree of Sexual Irregularity

English-speaking Cases Only

	Test Aggregate																										Totals	Means (Test Aggregate)
	45 to 47	47 to 49	49 to 51	51 to 53	53 to 55	55 to 57	57 to 59	59 to 61	61 to 63	63 to 65	65 to 67	67 to 69	69 to 71	71 to 73	73 to 75	75 to 77	77 to 79	79 to 81	81 to 83	83 to 85	85 to 87	87 to 89	89 to 91	91 to 93	93 to 95	95 to 97		
Prostitutes			1	1		5	4	8	9	9	8	19	18	22	20	19	18	26	23	16	14	7	14	2	1	2	266	75.0
Sexually irregular		1				2		2	1	4	2	2	6	7	2	8	6	2	3	6	6	5	3	2	2	1	73	76.4
Not sexually irregular							1					3	4	3		3	3	3	1	3		4	3	1	1	2	35	79.4
Total		1	1	1		7	5	10	10	13	10	24	28	32	22	30	27	31	27	25	20	16	20	5	4	5	374	75.67

Test aggregate: Mean = 75.67 $\sigma = 9.40$
Correlation ratio: Test aggregate on degree on sexual irregularity, $\eta = .142 \pm .051$

who have not been sexually irregular and those who have, and that, in the further distinction between professional prostitutes and those who have been promiscuous without being prostitutes, the factor of mentality does not play a part.

In order to determine whether or not the matter of mental capacity had any relation to the length of time these women have been sexually irregular, we have plotted Table 222 which shows the correlation between mental capacity measured by Test Aggregate and the number of years they have been sexually irregular. This includes both the years they have been prostitutes and the time they have been simply promiscuous. The correlation coefficient obtained is —.13 ± .061, which would indicate a negative relationship between the two which is, however, questionable in the light of its relatively large standard deviation. The correlation ratios of .16 ± .060 and .20 ± .059 further indicate a relationship which is at most slight. Consideration of the means shows that whatever relationship exists is negative. Our data on this point are, as has been explained in Chapter XII, quite unsatisfactory in view of the fact that there are a goodly number of women who are known to have been prostitutes or sexually irregular for a long time but from whom we have been unable to obtain any statement as to the exact number of years. Nearly 50 per cent of these are Workhouse cases, "old rounders" who are quite uniformly characterized by low intelligence, and whose records, if they were obtainable, would have undoubtedly increased the negative correlation. We feel inclined to believe, therefore, that there is probably a valid, though small association, and that there exists a significant negative correlation between mental capacity as shown in this way and the number of years sexually irregular.

(*c*) *Mental Capacity and Venereal Disease*

If, in considering next the relation between mental capacity of those who are infected with venereal disease, as indicated by the Wassermann and Complement Fixation tests, and those who are free from the same, we plot the distributions graphically, we obtain the curves shown in Chart XLVI. It is at once evident that those free from venereal disease form a superior group. There is a clear difference in the means 77.34 ± .879 as against 73.96 ± .969, and Table 223 shows this difference to be almost certainly valid. The difference is very slight as regards the degree of concentration with which the cases

TABLE 222

Correlation between Mental Capacity Measured by Test Aggregate and Sum of Years Sexually Irregular

English-speaking Cases Only

Sum of Years Sexually Irregular	Test Aggregate: 49 to 51	51 to 53	53 to 55	55 to 57	57 to 59	59 to 61	61 to 63	63 to 65	65 to 67	67 to 69	69 to 71	71 to 73	73 to 75	75 to 77	77 to 79	79 to 81	81 to 83	83 to 85	85 to 87	87 to 89	89 to 91	91 to 93	93 to 95	Totals	Means (Test Aggregate)
25–26 Years												1												1	
24–25 "																								0	
23–24 "																								0	
22–23 "																								0	
21–22 "															1									1	
20–21 "											1				1									2	76.6
19–20 "																1								1	
18–19 "																	1		1					2	
17–18 "													1											1	
16–17 "												1		1								1		3	
15–16 "									1					1	1									3	
14–15 "		1											1											2	
13–14 "										2	1					1			1					5	70.6
12–13 "							1	1												1				3	
11–12 "											1	1				1	1							4	
10–11 "	1					1								1		3					1			7	72.9
9–10 "						1							1											2	
8– 9 "					1		1	1	2	1	1	2		1	1									11	
7– 8 "						1					1	1	1	2			1	1	2		1			11	72.5
6– 7 "				1			1	1		1	1	1				1	2	1	1					11	
5– 6 "				1		1	1		1		1	1		1		4	1	1	1	1	1			16	
4– 5 "					1		1			4	2	2		2	1	4	1		2			1		21	74.5
3– 4 "				2	1	2		1	1		2		3		4	3	5	1	1	1	1			28	
2– 3 "				2			2			1	3	3	3	4	3		2		3		1			27	
1– 2 "								3	1	3	4	4	3	1	3	1	1	4	2	4	1	1	2	38	76.7
½– 1 "						2		2	1	4	1	4	4	8	6	5	7	4	4	3	5	1		61	
Totals	1	1	0	6	3	8	7	9	7	16	19	21	17	22	21	24	22	12	18	10	11	4	2	261	75.23
Means (Sum of Years Sexually Irregular)	5.6						4.9		.9		5.5		4.3		5.3		3.5		4.0		3.5			4.65	

Test aggregate: Mean = 75.23 σ = 9.05
Sum of years sexually irregular: Mean = 4.65 σ = 4.75

Coefficient of correlation: r = −.13 ± .061

Correlation ratios: Sum of years sexually irregular on test aggregate, η = .16 ± .060 Blakeman's Criterion = 1.1
Test aggregate on sum of years sexually irregular, η = .20 ± .059 Blakeman's Criterion = 1.9

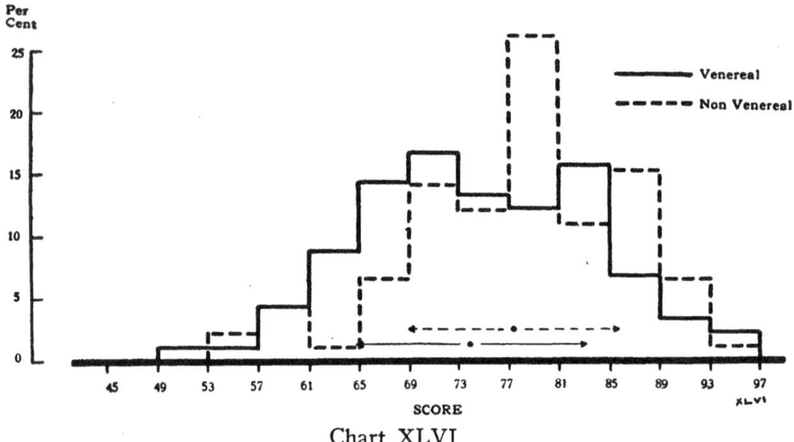

Chart XLVI

Mental Capacity as Measured by Test Aggregate

Percentage comparison between those having venereal disease and those free from venereal disease. English-speaking cases only.

are grouped around the mean, however, as shown by comparison of the standard deviations. Table 223 shows that so slight a difference is only possibly significant.

TABLE 223

PRESENCE OR ABSENCE OF VENEREAL DISEASE

Comparison of the Means and Standard Deviations of Mental Capacity, as Measured by Test Aggregate, of those Having Venereal Disease and those Free from Venereal Disease*

English-speaking cases only

	Venereal Disease	Free from Venereal Disease	Difference	$\frac{d}{\sigma_d}$	Chances that real difference does not exist are 1 in:
Mean	73.96	77.34	−3.38	2.59	208
σ_m	±.969	±.879			
σ	9.19	8.43	.76	.87	5
σ_σ	±.602	±.630			
Cases	90	92			

*Reactions of 4+, 3+ and 2+ to either the Wassermann or Complement Fixation test taken as positive indications and reactions of — or ± as negative indications.

As earlier stated in Chapter XII, data for the diagnosis of venereal disease are based upon the findings in the Wassermann and Complement Fixation tests. For purposes of the present comparison 4+, 3+ and 2+ were regarded as positive indications of the presence of disease and — and ± as negative. The reports of 1 + were omitted as not being either clearly positive or negative. It will, of course, be objected that we have not selected an infallible means of detecting venereal disease. We do not, however, claim to be doing anything other than comparing the intellectual capacity of those who, by the indications of the blood tests cited, are diagnosed as having, or being free from, syphilis or gonorrhea.

(*d*) *Mental Capacity and Age of Entering Prostitution*

Table 224 shows the relationship existing between mental capacity measured by Test Aggregate and the age at which these women entered prostitution. The correlation coefficient is .20 ± .069 and the ratios slightly higher but affected by irregularities of the means. There would, therefore, seem to be a sensible and significant, though slight, correlation between the mental capacity of prostitutes and the age at which they begin prostituting.

From an examination of the scatter table one notes the interesting fact that, if lines are drawn through the table at the approximate means of mental capacity and age at entering prostitution, thus dividing the table into four quadrants, while the lower quadrants contain almost identical numbers, in the upper quadrants two-thirds as many cases fall in the right hand quadrant as in the left. This would seem to indicate that there are as many bright women as dull women who enter prostitution early but there are a greater percentage of bright than dull women who enter prostitution late. (The terms "bright" and "dull," as used here, are purely relative, designating those above and below the average of this group, respectively.)

If we compare next the number of years that the women have been in prostitution with mental capacity as measured by Test Aggregate, we obtain the distribution figured in Table 225. This shows a relationship wholly comparable with that of the preceding table, as indicated both by correlation coefficient and by ratios, although the coefficient is necessarily negative in this case to show the same type of relationship. Separating this sheet into quadrants at the line of the means as in the previous table, we see that here the two upper quadrants have more nearly equal percentages but that there is a greater percentage in the right hand lower quadrant than in the left.

TABLE 224

Correlation between Mental Capacity Measured by Test Aggregate and Age at Entering Prostitution

English-speaking Cases Only

Age at Entering Prostitution	Test Aggregate: 49–51	51–53	53–55	55–57	57–59	59–61	61–63	63–65	65–67	67–69	69–71	71–73	73–75	75–77	77–79	79–81	81–83	83–85	85–87	87–89	89–91	91–93	93–95	Totals	Means (Test Aggregate)
36 Years																1								1	
35 "																								0	
34 "															1									1	
33 "																					1			1	
32 "																	1	1						2	80.3
31 "																			1					1	
30 "														1	1	2					1			5	
29 "												1			2									3	
28 "									1														1	2	
27 "										1			1			1			1		1			5	
26 "																	2							2	
25 "								2						2	1	1	1		1			1		9	78.4
24 "						2	1					1									1			5	
23 "				1			1	1		1	1	1			1		1		2		1			11	73.7
22 "				1							2				3	1	2	1			1			11	
21 "								1	1	1	1			1		2		1			3			11	
20 "						1	1		1	1	1			4	1	1	1		2	2				16	75.0
19 "				1	1					1	4	4	1	1	1		5				1			20	
18 "					1	1				1		2	4				1	3	1		1			15	
17 "								1		2	2		4			3	3	2	2	1		1		21	75.7
16 "					1	1	1	1		1	1	2	1	1	2	4	2	1		1				20	
15 "		1				2			1	4			1	1		1			1	1				13	
14 "				1					1			1	1	1	1	1	2							9	
13 "							1					1				3								5	
12 "	1																							5	71.3
11 "																								1	
10 "																1								0	
Totals	1	1	0	4	3	7	5	6	5	13	12	13	13	12	14	22	21	9	11	5	11	2	1	191	75.19
Means (Age at Entering Prostitution)	18.1						20.3		18.7		19.2		19.0		20.7		20.0		20.3		23.5			19.92	

Test Aggregate: Mean = 75.19 $\sigma = 9.18$
Age at entering prostitution: Mean = 19.92 $\sigma = 4.76$
Coefficient of correlation: r = .20 ± .069
Correlation ratios: Age on test aggregate, η = .27 ± .067 Blakeman's Criterion = 1.8
Test aggregate on age, η = .26 ± .068 Blakeman's Criterion = 1.7

TABLE 225

Correlation between Mental Capacity Measured by Test Aggregate and Number of Years in Prostitution

English-speaking Cases Only

Number of Years in Prostitution	Test Aggregate 49–51	51–53	53–55	55–57	57–59	59–61	61–63	63–65	65–67	67–69	69–71	71–73	73–75	75–77	77–79	79–81	81–83	83–85	85–87	87–89	89–91	91–93	93–95	Totals	Means (Test Aggregate)
25–26 Years												1												1	
24–25 "																								0	
23–24 "																								0	
22–23 "																								0	
21–22 "															1									1	
20–21 "											1				1									2	75.3
19–20 "																								0	
18–19 "																			1					1	
17–18 "													1											1	
16–17 "																								0	
15–16 "									1					1			1							3	
14–15 "		1											1			1								3	
13–14 "										2	1					1								4	70.9
12–13 "								1												1				2	
11–12 "											1	1				1								3	
10–11 "	1					1								1		3					1			7	73.5
9–10 "													1											1	
8– 9 "					1		1	1	1	1	1	2		1	1									10	
7– 8 "						1					1			1			1	1	2					7	71.3
6– 7 "				1			1	1		1	1	1					2	1						9	
5– 6 "				1		1	1		1		1					4	1	1	1	1	1			14	
4– 5 "					1		1			3	1	1		2	1	3	1		1					15	74.8
3– 4 "					1			1	1		2		2		1	2	5	1	1					17	
2– 3 "				2			1			1	1	3	2		3		2		1		1			17	
1– 2 "								1	1	3	1	2	2		2	1	1	4	2	1	1	1	1	24	77.6
½– 1 "						2				3		1	4	6	6	6	7	2	3	1	6	1		48	
Totals	1	1	0	4	3	5	5	5	5	14	12	12	13	12	16	22	21	10	12	4	10	2	1	190	75.41
Means (Number of Years in Prostitution)	5.9						6.0		5.2		6.9		4.5		5.0		3.3		4.6		2.0			4.81	

Test Aggregate: Mean = 75.41 $\sigma = 8.99$
Number of years in prostitution: Mean = 4.81 $\sigma = 4.85$
Coefficient of correlation: r = − .21 ± .069
Correlation ratios: Years in prostitution on test aggregate, η = .26 ± .067 Blakeman's Criterion = 1.7
Test aggregate on years in prostitution, η = .27 ± .067 Blakeman's Criterion = 1.8

This would seem to indicate that while there are as many bright as dull women who have been for long periods in prostitution, there are more bright than dull women who have been in it only a short time.

Summary

To summarize this section, we feel that we can say regarding the relations which have been found to exist between the mental capacity of these women as measured by Test Aggregate and the phases of their sex history considered:

(1) That there is a slight positive relationship between mental capacity measured by Test Aggregate and the age at which these women committed their first sex offense.

(2) We have found a small, and perhaps questionable, negative correlation of —.13 ± .061 between mental capacity and number of years sexually irregular. We are inclined to believe that this would be increased if we could include the hundred-odd cases whom we know had been sexually irregular for a long time, but on whom we have been unable to get a record of the exact length of time.

(3) Comparing the means of the mental capacity of those women who are infected with venereal diseases, as evidenced by the reactions to the Wassermann and Complement Fixation Tests, with those whose reactions to these tests were negative, we found an appreciable difference in favor of the latter. The difference in the amount of variability shown by the two groups was small and only possibly significant.

(4) When we compare the mental capacity of the women who have been either prostitutes or sexually irregular with those who have not been sexually promiscuous, we find that there is a difference in the central tendency of the two groups in favor of those who have not been sexually irregular. The amount of scatter about the mean which the distributions show is not noticeably or significantly different.

Making the division, however, between prostitutes and non-prostitutes, *i.e.*, by combining those who have been sexually irregular and those who have not been sexually irregular, and comparing them with the prostitutes, we obtain a sensible difference in the means which is almost certainly significant. This difference is, it will be noted, not as great as that between the combination of prostitutes and those sexually irregular compared with those not sexually irregular. It would seem, therefore, that, as far as mental capacity is concerned the difference between those who have prostituted and those who have simply been sexually irregular is insignificant and that it is the presence of those not sexually irregular in the comparison between prostitutes and non-prostitutes which gives it its significance.

A classification of the group into three divisions—prostitutes, those sexually irregular who have not prostituted, and those not sexually irregular—shows that the above assumption is correct.

(5) There is a sensible though small correlation between the mental capacity and the age at entering prostitution, and an inspection of the scatter table would indicate that this seems to be brought about by a lack of representation of the stupider women among those who enter prostitution late rather than a concentration of the brighter women there.

(6) A negative correlation of —.21 ± .069 was found between mental capacity and the number of years in prostitution. Here an inspection of the scatter table would seem to indicate that the women who stay for a long time in prostitution are about equally divided into those above and below the average mentally but that there is a greater concentration of the brighter women among those who remain in it less time.

CHAPTER XVI

SUMMARY AND CONCLUSIONS

THE purpose of this study has been to achieve a more adequate understanding of women delinquents. To some extent such an understanding is furthered by the mere assembling of facts about the group. Such information may at least help to remove and to prevent certain misconceptions regarding their characteristics. For a more basic understanding, however, these facts must be brought into relation with other facts. That is, comparisons must be made of one portion of the delinquent group with others, and of the group of delinquent women both with groups of men delinquents and with the general population. These comparisons we have attempted to carry through, wherever the necessary data were available. We have had occasion constantly throughout this study to comment on the dearth of such information with reference to the general population. This lack is responsible, more than any other one thing, for a general want of conclusiveness about our findings.

In the present brief statement it is not our intention to indicate the results of our study in any detail. Such material has been given in summarized form, in the various chapters concerned. Here, we are interested only in showing major trends and the more general indications of our findings. Any discussion of the more detailed relationships and distinctions between different portions of the delinquent group would involve unnecessary duplication. For such information the reader is, therefore, referred to the earlier statements.

It should be remembered that the women delinquents regarding whom we offer information are those convicted of legal offenses, through due process of law: and that they do not include those closely related cases who offend in essentially the same ways but escape arrest and conviction.

It may be desirable, also, to remind the reader that we make no claim to comprehensiveness in our survey of the factors of importance in connection with delinquency. Certain very obvious ones have been omitted,—some because we did not find it practicable to include them in this investigation, others because of difficulty in reducing our observations to definite objective form, and still others because they appeared so general as to elude exact observation, requiring perhaps the perspective of time or of the knowledge of many localities for even an attempt at precise formulation. Noteworthy omissions to be accounted for from these various points of view are the following: information regarding the physical condition of the women of our group; data regarding their emotional organization and the more general characteristics of the personality as a whole; data regarding the general environmental background, including especially the quality and the number of the recreational opportunities; facts about the public opinion of the community with reference to moral standards, particularly as these concern sex matters; these and other factors perhaps equal in importance. We shall not be drawn aside into a discussion of the significance of these factors, important though we believe them to be, since we lack the factual material to support any views which we might offer.

Turning to the positive aspects of our investigation, we note two lines of influence which seem to have a bearing on the problem of delinquency among women, namely: (1) poor economic background with few advantages or opportunities, including such conditions as poor homes, very limited school opportunity, early age at starting work and meager industrial training; and (2) a somewhat inferior mentality.

A survey of the early home conditions in which these women grew up shows that a large percentage came from the poorest homes included in our estimate of home conditions, and that less than ten per cent came from homes considered better than mediocre in respect to economic status, moral standards and parental supervision. Though there is no possibility of determining what percentage of the homes of non-delinquents would fall in the lower grouping, we are able to show within the delinquent group that there is a tendency for those brought up in the poorer homes to enter prostitution when younger, and to be convicted at an earlier age, than those who were brought up in better homes.

With reference to educational background we find, again, that, without reliable standards for the general population, we have no way of knowing how far the delinquent group lags behind the general population in this respect. We have found, however, that the delinquent group falls decidedly behind the requirements of present opinion regarding the minimum amount of schooling which should be accepted as furnishing the rudiments of preparation for meeting the demands of adult life. This is especially true as regards school *attainment*. The record for the total group, with regard to school grade completed, shows that on the average they have finished less than the fifth grade. We saw reason for believing that this was to some extent a secondary effect of the somewhat inferior intelligence of the group. We were not able to discover more than very slight relationships between the educational factors and the various aspects of the criminal career.

Referring to the work records of the delinquent group, we note many indications of general industrial inefficiency. Not only is the average prevailing wage low, but the records show much irregularity of work, and a massing in the occupations which demand least in the way of general educational background or special industrial training. That the situation in these respects is any worse than among women wage earners as a whole it is impossible to say. It is necessary to remember that the community has been very slow to apply the same standards of industrial efficiency and remuneration to women that it has applied to men, and that inability to earn a decent living for herself and family is not considered an indication of incompetency in a woman to the same degree as in a man. Further, the occupations which demand least in the way of background and special training—domestic service and factory work—are the occupations which include the largest numbers of women wage-earners in general. The available data tended to show, however, that the proportions in these occupations were somewhat overweighted for the delinquent group as compared with the whole body of working women.

It seems worthy of note that the women of this group, taken as a whole, have evidently had demands upon them, during at least certain periods in their lives, to be financially productive. Only about 3 per cent of the total group have never been gainfully employed. It appears, further, that over half of the group were idle, that is, not engaged in a legitimate occupation, at the time of the present conviction. It does not follow, however, that they were not earning at this time, for it must be remembered that in general the offenses committed by this group bring in remuneration, often on a scale decidedly above that which the same individuals can reach in legitimate occupations. If, then, we urge the importance of economic factors in relation to delinquency among women, it is not because we contend either that the delinquent women, as a whole, could not earn a living wage in some occupation, or that the wages which they do earn are conspicuously lower than those of working women who have not become delinquent. It is rather, in the first place, because some degree of economic necessity is operative in the case of this group, and, in the second place, because the offenses of most frequent occurrence offer financial attractions sufficiently great so that they may at least compete with the legitimate occupations as a source of income. If inhibitions of one sort or another are not sufficient to deter a woman, it may well be that the greater probable lucrativeness of prostitution, shop-lifting, or other forms of delinquency may prove the adequate explanation for her entrance upon this career in at least a fair proportion of the cases.

In our reference to inferior mentality we have in mind especially the *general intelligence* of the group. Had we adequate data, in sufficiently exact form, we should make this category more comprehensive and include certain characteristics of temperament and emotional organization, which we believe to be quite as important as the factor of intelligence but which are far more difficult of measurement. With regard to intelligence, all indications are that the group of delinquent women is somewhat inferior to the general population, though the difference is slight and the overlapping large. This statement holds, though in varying degrees, whether we consider the separate sub-groups or the composite group. It should be noted, however, that our data have indicated a less extreme distinction, with respect to intelligence, between the delinquent and the non-delinquent groups than that urged by many recent investigators, notably Goring. The most that we are prepared to say is that, other things being equal, there is apparently a greater presumption in favor of delinquency in a group of women who are below the average in intelligence than in a group above the average. In view of this apparent overweighting of the delinquent group in the direction of mental inferiority it is somewhat surprising to find how slight are the indications of relationship between intelligence and the various aspects of the criminal career, such as degree of recidivism, age at first conviction, nature of offense, etc. Apparently low intelligence has more weight in swinging the balance so that the woman will appear within the delinquent group than in determining what type of delinquent she will be or how serious an offender.

The factors mentioned above have impressed themselves upon us as important general influences associated with delinquency. Nevertheless, when we turn to any specific comparison, involving these factors in relation to some aspect of delinquency, we are even more impressed by the smallness of the relationships than by the fact of their existence. Even when we compare the delinquent group with the general population we find relatively slight distinctions and much overlapping. This fact may be exaggerated, to some degree, by the inadequacy of our information regarding the general population, as well as by the small numbers in the delinquent group. The evidence available indicates very strongly, however, that even with fuller data we should still be dealing with small differences. This suggests, further, that any search for a well-defined type of individual, appearing as *the delinquent woman,* will probably be fruitless. Apparently the concept of such a type can not be saved even by expanding it beyond Lombroso's anthropological criminal type and pruning off certain of the absurdities incorporated in his idea. Within all groups and all classes there are doubtless individuals whose adjustment to the demands of society is more or less precarious. Whether or not they become delinquent will depend, not so much upon the appearance of a single decisive factor, as upon the massing of factors in such a way as to disturb a more or less unstable initial adjustment. That certain factors, notably poor economic conditions, variously operative, and inferior intelligence, are particularly likely so to disturb the balance is the main point which we should urge in emphasizing these conditions.

In further support of this point of view we would call attention to our findings regarding inter-comparisons within the group of delinquents. Reference to the detailed discussions of the foregoing chapters makes it clear that even those factors which we consider most important in their bearing on delinquency have, apparently, not been very effective in determining the place of an individual within the delinquent group with respect to the seriousness or the frequency of offenses or other similar categories. It is interesting to note, for example, with reference to intelligence, that there is more difference between the colored and the white of our group, or between those who have been in domestic service and those who have not, than between recidivists and first offenders, or between felons and misdemeanants, or between offenders against chastity and offenders against property. Instances could be multiplied to show that a dichotomy of the delinquent group, based on factors not intrinsic to the problem of delinquency, frequently yields more striking distinctions than does one based on differences which are fundamental from point of view of delinquency.

On the basis of our findings we can not agree with Goring in the importance that he attaches to the constitutional factors in contrast with the environmental factors, as determinants of crime. He states, for example:[1] "While with many of the former, high degrees of association have been revealed, with practically none of the latter do we discover any definite degree of relationship." And again: "Crime is only to a trifling extent (if to any) the product of social inequalities, of adverse environment, or of other manifestations of what may comprehensively be termed the force of circumstances." To the extent of insisting upon the slightness of observable relationships we are in agreement with Goring. We disagree, however, in the preëminence attached to such a constitutional factor as defective intelligence in contrast with economic factors. The relationships which we have observed have been, if anything, more slight in case of the measures of intelligence than in that of the indices of social and economic factors. Fundamental differences between Goring's group and ours may be offered in partial explanation of the disagreement. We would suggest, as further possible explanations of his findings, on the one hand, the fact that he dealt only with *estimates* of intelligence, which are markedly subject to the influence of the personal equation, and on the other hand, the fact that his data regarding environmental factors are less complete and well controlled than are his other data. It is at least possible that more thoroughgoing investigation into the social and economic factors would have disclosed quite as much reason for ascribing significance to the environmental factors as to the constitutional, with no one factor of either sort appearing as extreme in importance. Our own findings would suggest such an outcome.

[1] *Op. cit.*, p. 371.

BIBLIOGRAPHY

ABBOTT, GRACE: "Immigration and Crime." *Journal of the American Institute of Criminal Law and Criminology;* November, 1915.

ANNUAL REPORT of the Commissioner General of Immigration, 1914.

ANNUAL REPORT of the State Commission of Prisons, 1916.

ANNUAL REPORT, Police Department, City of New York, 1916.

ASCHAFFENBURG, G.: "Crime and Its Repression." Translated by A. Albrecht; 1913.

AYRES, L. P.: "A Scale for Measuring the Quality of Handwriting of School Children." *Russell Sage Foundation;* 1912.

—— "Child Accounting in the Public Schools." *Cleveland Education Survey;* 1915.

—— "Laggards in Our Schools," 1909.

BINET, A., and TH. SIMON: "Method of Measuring the Development of the Intelligence of Young Children." Translated by C. H. Town.

BOGARDUS, E. S.: "The Relation of Fatigue to Industrial Accidents." *American Journal of Sociology;* 1911-1912.

BONSER, F. G.: "The Reasoning Ability of Children of the Fourth, Fifth and Sixth School Grades." *Teachers College, Columbia University, Contributions to Education;* No. 37, 1910.

BRECKINRIDGE, SOPHONISBA P., and EDITH ABBOTT: "The Delinquent Child and the Home." *Russell Sage Foundation;* 1912.

BUCKINGHAM, B. R.: "Spelling Ability, Its Measurement and Distribution." *Teachers College, Columbia University, Contributions to Education;* No. 59, 1913.

CODE OF CRIMINAL PROCEDURE, State of New York, Title VI.

CONYNGTON, MARY: "Relation Between Occupation and Criminality of Women." *Report on Condition of Woman and Child Wage-Earners in the United States,* Vol. XV: Government Printing Office, Washington, 1911.

COURTIS, S. A.: "Manual of Instruction for Giving and Scoring the Courtis Standard Tests."

DAVENPORT, CHARLES B.: "The Family History Book." *Bulletin No. 7,* Eugenics Record Office: Cold Spring Harbor, N. Y., September, 1912.

DAVIS, KATHARINE BEMENT: "The Rational Treatment of Women Convicted of Crime in the Courts of New York City."

—— "A Study of Prostitutes Committed to the State Reformatory for Women at Bedford Hills," Chapter VIII of "Commercialized Prostitution in New York City," by George J. Kneeland; 1913.

ELLIS, HAVELOCK: "The Criminal"; 1895.

FRANZ, S. I.: "Mental Examination Methods"; 1912.

GILLILAND, A. R.: "The Mental Ability of 100 Inmates of the Columbus (O.) Workhouse." *Journal of the American Institute of Criminal Law and Criminology;* Vol. 7, No. 6; 1917.

GLUECK, BERNARD: "A Study of 608 Admissions to Sing Sing Prison." *Mental Hygiene,* Vol. 2, No. 1; 1918.

GODDARD, H. H.: The Standard Method for Giving the Binet Test." *Training School,* Vol. X, No. 2; 1913.

—— "The Binet-Simon Measuring Scale for Intelligence." *Training School,* Vol. VIII, No. 4; 1911.

—— "The Form Board as a Measure of Intellectual Development in Children." *Training School,* Vol. IX; 1912.

—— "Feeble-mindedness. Its Causes and Consequences"; 1914.

GORING, CHARLES: "The English Convict. A Statistical Study." T. Fisher Unwin: London, W. C., 1913.

GUIBORD, ALBERTA S. B.: "Physical States of Criminal Women." *Journal of the American Institute of Criminal Law and Criminology,* Vol. VIII, No. 1; 1917.

HAINES, THOMAS H.: "Feeble-mindedness Among Adult Delinquents." *Journal of the American Institute of Criminal Law and Criminology,* Vol. VII, No. 5; 1917.

HEALY, W.: "A Pictorial Completion Test." *Psychological Review,* Vol. 21; 1914.

—— "The Individual Delinquent." Boston: Little, Brown & Co.; 1915.

—— and G. M. FERNALD: "Tests for Practical Mental Classification." *Psychol. Monog.,* Vol. 13, No. 54; 1911.

KENT, G. H., and A. J. ROSANOFF: "A Study of Association in Insanity." *American Journal of Insanity,* Vol. 47; 1910.

KNEELAND, GEORGE J.: "Commercialized Prostitution in New York City." The Century Co.; 1913.

KNOX, H. A.: "A Scale Based on the Work at Ellis Island for Estimating

Mental Defect." *Journal of the American Medical Association,* Vol. 62; 1914.

Kohs, Samuel C.: "The Practicability of the Binet Scale and the Question of the Borderline Case." Bulletin No. 3, Psychopathic Department, Series No. 2. Publications of the Research Department, Chicago House of Correction; 1915.

Lauck, W. Jett and Sydenstricker, Edgar: "Condition of Labor in American Industries." Funk & Wagnalls Co., New York; 1917.

Lombroso, Cæsare: "Crime: Its Causes and Remedies." Translated by Henry P. Horton. Boston: Little, Brown & Co.; 1911.

Marx, Karl: "A Contribution to the Critique of Political Economy." Translated from the Second German Edition by N. I. Stone. New York: The International Library Publishing Co.; 1904.

Norsworthy, N.: "The Psychology of the Mentally Deficient."

Ordahl, Louise E., and George Ordahl: "A Study of 49 Female Convicts." *Journal of Delinquency,* Vol. II, No. 6; 1917.

Osborne, Thomas Mott: "Society and Prisons." Yale University Press; 1916.

Pearson, Karl: "On the Relationship of Intelligence to the Size and Shape of the Head, and to Other Physical and Mental Characters." *Biometrika,* Vol. 5.

Pintner, R., and M. M. Anderson: "The Picture Completion Test." *Educ. Psychol. Monog.,* No. 20.

—— and D. G. Paterson: "A Scale of Performance Tests"; 1917.

Report of the City Council Committee on Crime of the City of Chicago, March 22, 1915.

Report of the Superintendent of State Prisons. New York, 1917.

Richmond, Mary E.: "Social Diagnosis." *Russell Sage Foundation;* New York, 1917.

Rossolimo, G.: "Die psychologische Profile zur Methodik der quantitativen Untersuchung der psychische Vorgänge in normale und pathologische Fällen." *Klinik d. psych. und nerv. Krankh.* Vol. 6; 1911.

Rossy, C. S.: "Report of the First Three Hundred Cases Examined at the Massachusetts State Prison." Bulletin No. 17 of the Mass. State Board of Insanity; January, 1916.

[illegible]l, Beardsley: "The Reliability of Mental Tests in the Division of an Academic Group." *Psychol. Monog.,* Vol. 24, No. 4; 1917.

Stenquist, J. L., E. L. Thorndike, and M. R. Trabue: "The Intellectual Status of Children Who Are Public Charges." *Arch. of Psychol.*, Vol. 5, No. 33; 1915.

Sylvester, R. H.: "The Form Board Test." *Psychol. Monog.*, Vol. 15, No. 65; 1913.

Terman, L. M.: "The Measurement of Intelligence"; 1916.

—— and others: "The Stanford Revision and Extension of the Binet-Simon Scale for Measuring Intelligence." *Educ. Psychol. Monog.*, No. 18; 1917.

Thompson, H. B.: "Psychological Norms in Men and Women"; 1903.

Thorndike, E. L.: "Handwriting." *Teachers College Record*, Vol. 11, No. 2; 1910.

—— "Reading Scale and Visual Vocabulary, Scale A," and "Administration Scale A for Visual Vocabulary." *Teachers College Record*, September, 1914.

—— "The Elimination of Pupils from School." *Bulletin No.* 379, Department of the Interior, Bureau of Education; 1907.

Trabue, M. R.: "Completion-Test Language Scales." *Teachers College, Columbia University, Contributions to Education*, No. 77; 1916.

Tredgold, A. F.: "Mental Deficiency." Second Edition, 1914.

United States Census: Abstract "Thirteenth United States Census Report," 1910.

—— "Occupational Statistics," 1910.

—— "Prisoners and Juvenile Delinquents," 1910.

—— "Special Report of the Census Office: Prisoners and Juvenile Delinquents in Institutions," 1904.

—— "Thirteenth Census of the United States," Vol. III, 1910.

Weidensall, Jean: "The Mentality of the Criminal Woman"; 1916.

Whipple, G. M.: "Manual of Mental and Physical Tests"; 1915.

Woodworth, R. S., and F. L. Wells: "Association Tests." *Psychol. Monog.*, Vol. 13, No. 57; 1911.

Woody, C.: "Measurements of Some Achievements in Arithmetic." *Teachers College, Columbia University, Contributions to Education*, No. 80; 1916.

Woolley, Helen Thompson, and Charlotte R. Fischer: "Mental and Physical Measurements of Working Children." *Psychol. Monog.*, Vol. 18, No. 1; 1914.

Yerkes, R. M., J. W. Bridges, and R. Hardwick: "A Point Scale for Measuring Mental Ability"; 1915.

INDEX

D

E

F

G

H

I

www.ingramcontent.com/pod-product-compliance
Lightning Source LLC
LaVergne TN
LVHW021238110826
845150LV00002B/347

* 9 7 8 1 4 2 5 5 6 2 3 6 6 *